# Psychological complexity and preference: a hedgehog theory of behavior

Edward L. Walker has devoted his life to the study
of the processes involved in human motivation and
learning. He attended several universities—Indiana,
Iowa, and Stanford—before joining the staff of the
Department of Psychology at the University of
Michigan. He has been a Career Investigator for
the National Institute of Mental Health and is a
Fellow of the Center for Advanced Study in the
Behavioral Sciences. He is the author of numerous
journal articles and several books.

# Psychological complexity and preference: a hedgehog theory of behavior

Edward L. Walker
*The University of Michigan*

Brooks/Cole Publishing Company
Monterey, California
*A Division of Wadsworth, Inc.*

Printed in the United States of America

10 9 8 7 6 5 4 3 2 1

Library of Congress Cataloging in Publication Data:

Walker, Edward L
    Psychological complexity and preference.
    Includes bibliographical references and index.
    1. Psychology—Philosophy.  2. Psychological
research.  I. Title.
BF38.W33     150'.1     79-20291
ISBN 0-8185-0379-3

Acquisition Editor: *William Hicks*
Production Editor: *John Bergez*
Interior and Cover Design: *Ruth Scott*
Illustrations: *Lori Heckelman*
Typesetting: *Linda Andrews, Ashland, Oregon*

This work is dedicated
to three people who can
no longer know or care,

*Alice, Bruce, and Frank,*

and to three people who
can still know and who
might care,

*Kathryn, Robert, and William.*

# preface

I began to develop psychological complexity and preference theory in the late 1950s, largely in response to the stimulating ideas being developed by William Dember and Robert Earl while they were graduate students at the University of Michigan. I think the future course of my work was clearly set when I read Daniel Berlyne's book, *Conflict, Arousal and Curiosity*, which appeared in 1960. To me it seemed that this scholarly and enormously productive man had begun a revolution in behavior theory, a revolution I was more than ready to join.

Two features of Berlyne's efforts bothered me. He chose to optimize the energy variable, arousal. I felt at the outset that organisms would choose to optimize a structural variable, and, after considerable thought and self-debate, I chose psychological complexity as an appropriate variable for the basic theoretical structure. My first attempt to formulate the theory was presented at the Nebraska Symposium (1964).

Much of the research generated by the theory has been published in appropriate journals. Publication of the results of other research was withheld for inclusion in this book for two reasons. First, the interpretation of the results of a single study have occasionally had to be modified in the light of subsequent studies. Second, in many cases the major implications of a single study would be unclear without the context of the theory and the sequence of studies of which it was a part.

This book has been exceptionally difficult to organize because of two inherent problems. Because psychological complexity and preference theory is a simple theory that becomes complex in its implications, it is necessary for the reader to have a grasp of all of the theory in order to understand the character of any one part. Writing about the theory in sequential fashion is analogous to attempting to reduce a sphere to a single straight line without losing the spherical quality. The second difficulty has arisen from the multiple objectives associated with presenting the theory in a single volume. Among my aims are an explication of the theory, a demonstration that the theory offers a different perspective on classical studies and concepts in experimental psychology, the report of supportive research that has not been published elsewhere, the development of the heuristic value of the theory through the suggestion of potential but undeveloped avenues of research, and the demonstration that a simple psychological theory based on laboratory research can have profound and practical applications to important human problems. To resolve these problems, it was necessary to make some very serious compromises. The book is approximately one-third of the maximum length once projected for it. The present organization is the last of a long series of patterns, none of which is wholly satisfactory.

The book begins with a ten-word version of psychological complexity and preference theory and an explanation of the conceit of the Hedgehog. A more complete picture of the nature of psychological complexity and preference theory is presented in Chapter 2. This version is sufficiently elaborate to provide a context for the more detailed elaborations in subsequent chapters.

There follows a disquisition on language (Chapter 3). Even though it is a diversion from the substantive development of the theory, it is placed in this position because it provides potential precision in the understanding of the theoretical language used in the remainder of the text and summarizes the results of a series of investigations into the ways in which experimental subjects use the language. These studies are reported in greater detail in the Appendix.

The next eight chapters (4–11) contain elaborations of the theory, efforts to show how the theory can be integrated with concepts and concerns of experimental psychology, and reports of research directed to fostering that integration.

Aesthetics is an area in which the Hedgehog has particular potential for stimulating illuminating research. Chapters 12 and 13 report research on visual and auditory materials in the tradition of experimental aesthetics. The studies described in these chapters were generated from the theory and were designed to test and to document aspects of it.

Chapter 14 is a condensed version of several potential chapters on aspects of human development and education. It constitutes a small sample of the many implications and radically different perspectives the Hedgehog, for all of its apparent simplicity, suggests in regard to critical human problems.

*Edward L. Walker*

## ACKNOWLEDGMENTS

It is not possible to acknowledge all of the debts one accepts in the process of developing a theory such as this and in doing the research stimulated by it. At the risk of omitting many who contributed, I should like to mention a few whose names do not appear elsewhere in the text. Much of the research on visual aesthetics that appears in Chapter 12 was contributed by Rivka Fine, Howard Gadlin, Daneen Hart, and Kathy Nagy. Barbara Stoddard helped with the research on skin resistance in the rat. Nathaniel Ehrlich carried out a number of studies of verbal behavior. Camille Buda collected much of the data for Chapter 3 while serving as both secretary and research assistant.

Particular acknowledgment should go to a long list of teachers disguised as students whom I have enjoyed over the years. Nothing much happens without the stimulation of students. Therefore, whatever is of merit in this volume should be credited to them.

Special acknowledgment should go to three young men whose influence on this work was profound, all of whom died before their enormous potentials could be realized. Steven Sales died when the aluminum mast of his sailboat came in contact with power lines. John Paul Scott, Jr. was murdered by a hitchhiker he was attempting to befriend. My son, Bruce, died of melanoma before he reached 30. Their influence reaches far beyond the citations that appear in the text.

Thanks are also due the National Institute of Mental Health for providing the opportunity to develop this work faster than would have been possible otherwise through a "life-time" research career award (K6-MH-21, 868) granted in 1964, as well as through generous research grants (HD 00904). The Center for Advanced Study in the Behavior Sciences also provided a year of accommodation that made progress in this endeavor possible while I was completing Dr. Bert E. Boothe's book (Boothe, Rosenfeld, & Walker, 1974).

Kind permission has been granted by Academic Press to use any part of a chapter I wrote for presentation at a NATO-supported conference in Korsør, Denmark, that appeared in a book entitled *Pleasure, Reward, Preference* (Berlyne & Madsen, 1973). The chapter bears the same title as this volume and consists of an early and much condensed version (Walker, 1973c).

The following figures have been published in "Stimulus-Produced Changes in the Discharge Rate of an Electric Fish and Their Relation to Arousal," by D. A. Dewsbury, *The Psychological Record*, 1966, *16*, 495–504, and have been reprinted by permission: Figures 10-4, 10-5, 10-10, 10-13, 10-21, 10-26, 10-33, and 10-34.

I should like to extend my thanks and gratitude to A. Wade Boykin, Russell Dewey, Charlotte Doyle, and Matthew Olson, who read part or all of the manuscript without compensation.

Special recognition must be accorded manuscript editor John Bergez, who was required to master the content of this volume in order to edit it.

# contents

**one**    *The Hedgehog*   1

The Hedgehog Introduced   1

**two**    *Psychological Complexity and Preference Theory*   4

The Stream of Psychological Events   4
The Psychological Event   5
Thoughts, Behavior, and Neurophysiology   5
Psychological Complexity   6
Optimal Complexity Level   7
Arousal   8
Effects of the Occurrence of
   Psychological Events   8
Developmental and Individual Differences   9
Hedgehog Anatomy   9
Hedgehog Behavior   10

**three**    *A Hodgepodge of Hedgehog Dogma Wherein One May Learn to Read the Book*   14

Language Problems   14
Some Problems of Experimentation and
   Data Analysis   24
Summary   33

**four**    *The Stream of Psychological Events*   34

Creative Accounts of the Stream
   of Psychological Events   35
Objective Descriptions of the Stream
   of Psychological Events   36
Dynamic Accounts of the Stream
   of Psychological Events   46
Summary   54

**five**    *Characteristics of Individual Psychological Events*   55

A Reminder Concerning Elementary
Characteristics of the Theory   56

The Initiation, Development, Decline,
and Termination of a Single
Psychological Event    57
A Quantitative Model for the Intensity and
Temporal Characteristics
of Psychological Events    65
Summary    68

**six**    *Temporary Effects of Occurrence
of Psychological Events    70*

Habituation and Sensitization as Distinguished
from Learning    70
Direction of Effects of Repeated Occurrence
of Psychological Events    71
The Groves and Thompson Theory
of Habituation and Sensitization    75
The Hedgehog Account of the Temporary Effects
of Repeated Activation
of Psychological Events    77
Temporary Effects of Occurrence
of Psychological Events in Free Choice Situations
(Alternation Phenomena)    108
Some Generalities    126

**seven**    *Enduring Effects of Occurrence
of Psychological Events    129*

Learning and Psychological Complexity    130
The Effect of Experience on Psychological
Complexity and Preference in Animals    133
The Effect of Experience on Psychological
Complexity of, and Preference for, Musical
Compositions and Visual Art    140
The Hedgehog and Verbal Learning    143
Summary    195

**eight**    *Voluntary and Involuntary Psychological
Events and Their Enduring Effects    197*

The Central Processor    198
Automatic Functions    203
Voluntary Functioning    222
Structure and Structural Changes
in Psychological Events    263

**nine** Motivation, Preference,
and All of That   265

Traditional Motivational Concepts   265
Varieties of Preference Functions   269
Summary   284

**ten** Arousal   285

The Concept of Arousal in the Hedgehog   285
Empirical Studies of Arousal   292
Basic Studies   299
Arousal and Biological Drives   326
Arousal and Incentives   337
The Concept of Arousal and Data on Skin
Resistance in the Rat and on Discharge
Frequency in Fishes   347

**eleven** Arousal and Learning   350

Empirical Studies of Arousal, Learning,
and Performance   351
Arousal and Verbal Learning   388

**twelve** The Hedgehog as Aesthetic Mediator:
Visual Stimuli   400

The Hedgehog and Issues in Aesthetics   400
Experimental Studies of Stimulus
Complexity and Preference   410
Aesthetics in Cognitive Tasks   434
Visual Aesthetics in Animals   435
Summary   438

**thirteen** The Hedgehog as Aesthetic Mediator:
Auditory Stimuli   439

The Hedgehog and Problems in the Experimental
Aesthetics of Music   439
Complexity and Preference for Melodies   439
Consonance and Dissonance   445
The Hedgehog and Aesthetics   471

**fourteen** The Hedgehog and Problems
of Lifelong Learning   473

Hedgehog Concepts and
Academic Achievement   474

The Hedgehog in an Educational Context  486
The Hedgehog and Issues of Educational Policy,
 Practice, and Outcome  496
Précis  513

*fifteen*  *A Matter of Faith*  515

*appendix*  *Studies in the Semantic Space
 of Experimental Subjects*  516

Introduction  516
Free Association Data  516
Similarity Association Data  519
Judged Semantic Distance Data  530
Summary  543

*References*  545
*Index*  559

# Psychological complexity and preference: a hedgehog theory of behavior

# chapter one

# The hedgehog

"A theory is the more impressive the greater is the simplicity of its premises, the more different are the kinds of things it relates and the more extended the range of its applicability."

*Albert Einstein*

### THE HEDGEHOG INTRODUCED

Psychological complexity and preference theory, which I refer to as the Hedgehog, is a very simple theory of motivation and learning. It is simple in the sense that it can be stated in very few words: *Psychological events nearest optimum complexity are preferred. Occurrence produces simplification.* This book is an elaboration of those ten words. In application the Hedgehog can become nearly as complicated as human behavior itself.

I have chosen to refer to psychological complexity and preference theory as a hedgehog theory of behavior because of an endearing and highly functional characteristic of this little animal. Hedgehogs, as you probably know, are Old World insectivorous mammals with spines pointing in every direction. They are similar in some respects to New World porcupines, although hedgehogs and porcupines are not closely related biologically. Superficially, hedgehogs appear to be relatively uncomplicated, to have very simple brains, and to be rather stupid. The most remarkable thing about hedge-

1

hogs is that, while they don't do very much, what they do, they do exceedingly well, and that is to roll up in a ball. Hedgehogs roll up

Awake                    Asleep and Otherwise

FIGURE 1-1. *Hypothetical Hedgehog*

in a ball when they are tired, excited, or frightened. In fact it doesn't seem to matter much *what* happens; they roll up in a ball. This limited talent has earned hedgehogs a place in literature and possibly a degree of grudging admiration. In the seventh century B.C., Archilocus said something that Erasmus later paraphrased as:

> The fox has many tricks.
> The hedgehog has but one,
> But that is the best of all.

Foxes, of course, are very clever animals. They have a very large repertoire of tricks. I suppose it is this characteristic that makes foxes interesting animals to hunt. They aren't likely to take the same path twice, and they will resort to innumerable strategems to throw dogs or humans off the scent. One might say that foxes are the kind of animal who have more solutions than they have problems.

In the world of ideas, the distinction between hedgehogs and foxes has been made by others. There is a book by Isaiah Berlin (1966), for example, in which he describes intellectual hedgehogs as having one central idea around which everything is organized. Their intellectual worlds are centripetal and deductive. They are generalists who have difficulty seeing the trees for the woods. Foxes, by contrast, live in centrifugal worlds. They have disparate ideas, and they operate inductively. They are specialists who are unable to see the woods for the trees. Berlin applied these figures to Tolstoy and his views of history, which Berlin summarized by saying that Tolstoy was a fox who aspired to be a hedgehog.

Psychological theories can be grouped into hedgehog theories and fox theories. Because of the imputed holy power of the reinforcement principle, Skinner might be categorized as a hedgehog theorist. Freud was a fox, because he could predict the same thing in several very different ways. Psychological complexity and preference theory is a hedgehog theory of behavior because it has only one trick and attempts to meet successfully a large variety of situations and problems without additional tools or weapons.

# $\mathcal{P}$sychological complexity and preference theory

Psychological complexity and preference theory is a simple theory involving a very small number of concepts. As it has evolved (Walker, 1964, 1969b, 1970, 1973a) my strategy has been to keep it tightly integrated and uncomplicated—a true hedgehog. However, this tight integration has the consequence of making it difficult to discuss any one concept of the theory without reference to the other concepts of the theory. I have tried to solve the resulting problem of how to explicate the theory in the following way. Chapter 1 contained a complete statement of the theory in ten words. In this chapter, I spell out a somewhat more elaborate and semiformal version and give a preliminary account of the key concepts. It should therefore be possible in later chapters to discuss isolated elements and areas of application with the context of the whole theory available to the reader. Chapters subsequent to this one can thus be considered to be a third and still more elaborate restatement of the theory.

## THE STREAM OF PSYCHOLOGICAL EVENTS

The seminal problem in psychology is to account for the content and the course of the stream of psychological events, including subjective experience, overt behavior, and neural activity. William James wrote several versions of a chapter on the stream of consciousness (see, for example, James, 1893). In these he undertook to give an account of the moment-to-moment character of the stream of thought and to speculate on what determined the content of the successive items in the stream. Whereas James addressed himself to the stream of thought or consciousness, Roger Barker (1963) has given the title *The Stream of Behavior* to a book that describes a number of studies undertaken to record the moment-to-moment items of overt and observable behavior displayed by selected citizens of Kansas. In the Hedgehog, the *stream of psychological events* is a theoretical concept. If well understood, it should offer an explanatory account of both the stream of thought and the stream of behavior, and perhaps the stream of neural events as well.

### THE PSYCHOLOGICAL EVENT

Although the experience of one's own thought or the observed behavior of someone else appears to be continuous, on closer examination the stream of psychological events proves to be discontinuous and discrete. In the Hedgehog, a psychological event is conceived as a basic unit of activity. It is a theoretical concept relevant to thought, behavior, and neural activity. The duration of a psychological event can range from a few milliseconds to a second or more. For most molar behavior, a practical minimum is probably about one-half second (500 milliseconds, or $500\sigma$), although events of shorter duration can be induced in restricted situations. The maximum duration is probably not much greater than the magic $500\sigma$.

The concept of a psychological event has much in common with what has been called a psychological *moment*. Much of psychology can be interpreted as an effort to account for the choice of the next psychological event in the stream or to account for changes in the frequency of choices of a class of psychological events. For example, to say that an organism is hungry is equivalent to saying that the frequency of psychological events associated with obtaining food is temporarily elevated.

It is an inherent property of psychological events as conceived in the Hedgehog that, once initiated, the individual event is terminated abruptly and automatically. Behaviors or thoughts that appear to occupy a time span significantly greater than $500\sigma$ are actually composed of strings or sequences of individual psychological events.

### THOUGHTS, BEHAVIOR, AND NEUROPHYSIOLOGY

One role of theory is to simplify the complex. The Hedgehog assumes that the behaviorist, the cognitive psychologist, and the neurophysiologist all have something cogent to say about human behavior. Theoretical terms in the Hedgehog serve as a device to permit the coordination or correlation of data from all three realms of discourse. It is assumed that data are data whatever their nominal sources and that the question of whether they are related to one another is an empirical one. Thus the stream of behavior, the stream of thought, and the stream of activity in the nervous system can all be reflections of the stream of psychological events. It follows then, that *psychological event* is a theoretical term that can be reflected in a behavioral event, a cognitive event, or a neural event.

## PSYCHOLOGICAL COMPLEXITY

I use the term *psychological complexity* to refer to the complexity of psychological events. As such it denotes a characteristic of a psychological process. It is a theoretical variable.

*Psychological complexity* should not be confused with similar sounding terms. *Stimulus complexity* refers to a fixed characteristic of an external stimulus. *A priori complexity* applies to some assumed complexity value of a stimulus where the values are unmeasured but are assumed to have face validity. *Subjective complexity* is used to refer to quantitative judgments of the complexity of a stimulus made by human individuals. Such judgments constitute measurements or data. *Consensual complexity* is some group evaluation of the complexity of a stimulus or psychological event. It can be a mean of subjective complexity values. Stimulus and a priori complexity remain unchanged. Subjective complexity can differ between individuals—and within an individual, depending on the circumstances—even though the stimulus complexity value remains fixed. *Psychological complexity* is never measured directly. As we will see, its value or values can be estimated from each of the other evaluations of complexity.

Psychological complexity is a property of an individual psychological event. Thus, the psychological events arising from the perceptions of individual letters of the alphabet can vary greatly in complexity. Psychological complexity can also be a property of a string of psychological events. For example, in the perception of a picture, a series of fixations—and thus a series of individual psychological events—may be required to develop a percept of the entire picture. An individual's judgment of the complexity of a picture is based on both the number of psychological events and the relative complexities of the individual psychological events. One can therefore refer to the psychological complexity of a single psychological event or to the psychological complexity of a group of events constituting an integrated experience.

### OPTIMAL COMPLEXITY LEVEL

Psychological events can be ordered relative to one another on a dimension of psychological complexity. There is a point on the psychological complexity dimension that is the *optimal complexity level* (OCL) for an individual at a given time. In a situation in which there are a number of events that *could* occur, the Hedgehog contends that the event nearest optimal complexity is the one that *will* occur. Potential events that are either more or less complex than the optimum will occur only when no event nearer to optimum is available.

The basic preference function of the Hedgehog is pictured in Figure 2-1. The dimension of preference, running from positive through neutral to negative preferences, is on the ordinate. The curve relating preference to psychological complexity is an inverted-U-shaped function that is often described as the Wundtian hedonic curve. Optimal complexity level is indicated by the vertical broken line and is projected from that point on the complexity dimension that is determined by the maximum of the preference function.

According to the Hedgehog, all preference functions are to be derived from optimal complexity level, and preference is perfectly correlated with the probability of occurrence of an event. In a completely free-responding situation, whichever event is closest to optimal complexity will occur. When there are constraints, so that the organism may choose only between two or more alternatives that are somewhat removed from the optimum, the organism will choose the event closest to the optimum, regardless of whether it is more or less complex than the optimum.

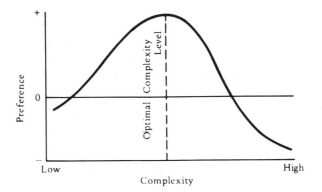

FIGURE 2-1. Basic Preference Function

There are two kinds of constraints on the choices of an organism, environmental and programmatic. *Environmental constraints* are the physical circumstances that limit the set of potential psychological events that can occur at a given moment. One cannot choose to speak while gagged or to see while blindfolded. *Programmatic constraints* may either be biological in origin, such as the periodic increase in the frequency of behaviors associated with the hunger state, or they may be cognitive in origin, such as the following of a plan or the observance of the rules of grammar.

## AROUSAL

*Arousal* is a state of an organism that can serve to modulate both the organism's optimal complexity level and the psychological complexity of the events that occur in a given state. There are diurnal variations in arousal. During sleep, arousal is low, and optimal complexity is correspondingly low. When the organism is in a highly aroused state, an event will be more complex than a similar event occurring when the organism is in a low arousal state. Thus, arousal level may affect both the complexity of a psychological event and the optimal level that determines the attractiveness of that event. This dual function may account for the apparent anomaly of the failure to perceive pain from a wound received in the heat of battle.

## EFFECTS OF THE OCCURRENCE
## OF PSYCHOLOGICAL EVENTS

After the automatic and inevitable termination of a psychological event, there are aftereffects of its occurrence of considerable importance. The most consistent aftereffect is a negative bias against repetition of that particular event. This antirepetition bias lasts for a considerable period of time. The effect is related to the very similar physiological concept of habituation and has considerable biological significance. It helps to release the organism from environmental control and to produce variability in the organism's choices. Variability in choice behavior has great survival value, for without it there could be no learning.

When a psychological event occurs, the fact of occurrence almost always produces a change in the character of the event. There is almost always a reduction in the psychological complexity of the event; with repeated occurrence the event undergoes a progressive simplification. This gradual reduction in the complexity of psychological events is the essence of all learning, and the course of simplification will usually produce the typical exponential learning or growth curve. Events of different inherent complexities will simplify to different asymptotes; for example, with equal experiences of the concepts of a point and of the world, the concept of the world is likely to remain more complex than the concept of a point.

There can be perturbations in the learning curve, however. Aspects of concept formation, sudden insight, ordinary problem solving, and thinking can lead to sudden decreases in psychological complexity as a complex situation is seen in a simpler light. Further, certain kinds of experiences lead to an *increase* in complexity. There are many games that appear to be simple and can be perceived in their true complexities only after considerable experience.

## DEVELOPMENTAL AND INDIVIDUAL DIFFERENCES

For nearly a century psychologists have concerned themselves with differences between individuals and the sources of those differences. Of special importance are differences in rates of academic achievement. As a theory of learning and motivation, the Hedgehog suggests two sources of differences in achievement. One is associated with the rates at which individuals process information and the other with characteristic differences in level of arousal.

Individuals can differ in information processing rate. The difference is probably related, at least in part, to the rate of habituation of a single psychological event and the rate of recovery from habituation. A person with a low rate of information processing will learn less in a fixed period of time than a person with a high rate of information processing. One effect of this difference is that the individual with the high rate of information processing will be able to deal with more complex information sooner than the individual with the lower rate, even though they are the same age. A small difference in information processing rate will thus have a cumulative effect that will eventually result in substantial differences in achievement as well as in scores on tests presumed to measure intelligence. An individual with a slow rate of information processing may overcome this deficit either by spending more time in the learning situation or by working more efficiently.

There are developmental patterns that are probably related to aspects of arousal. Newborn infants may seem to process information at a low rate only because they spend a disproportionate amount of time in a sleep state, with its low optimal complexity level. Many aspects of the behavioral differences between adolescents and the elderly may be simple correlates of arousal rather than differences in "ability" in the constitutional sense.

## HEDGEHOG ANATOMY

Psychological complexity and preference theory is a very simple machine—a true hedgehog. There is one concept, the *psychological event;* there is one dimension, *psychological complexity;* there is one nodal point, *optimal complexity level;* and there is one dynamic principle, an *exponential simplification of psychological events with experience.*

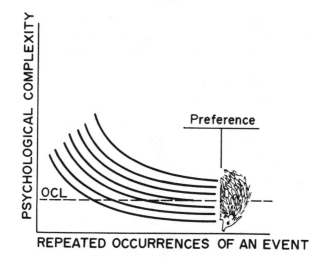

FIGURE 2-2. Hedgehog Anatomy

Figure 2-2 is a display of this anatomy, with an emphasis on the manner in which preference and learning interact. For example, if one follows the lowest of the seven curves in the figure, an event is portrayed that is sufficiently above the organism's optimal complexity level that it would not occur in the absence of substantial constraints. If induced to occur repeatedly, it becomes progressively simpler and progressively more attractive until it reaches optimal complexity level. Further experience leads to further simplification and a progressive decrease in preference to the point where that event becomes boring. Here again, it will not recur without the employment of constraints. Other events can become asymptotic (subject to little further change) at or near optimal complexity level, while still other events are inherently so complex that they can never become preferred.

## HEDGEHOG BEHAVIOR

All the essential pieces of the Hedgehog are now in place. The hedgehog is a compact little animal. Psychological complexity and preference theory is a compact little theory. Human behavior within the framework of the theory shares this quality of compactness. No matter how complex and various the details of human existence, the processes required to account for it are both simple in nature and compact in organization. Thus, we can think of human behavior in its course and dynamics as analogous to that of the theoretical Hedgehog. If we think of human behavior as a Hedgehog in this sense, the principles enumerated thus far are all we need to set the little beast off and running. Within the limits of environmental and programmatic constraints, it will continue to run autonomously as long as the organism lives.

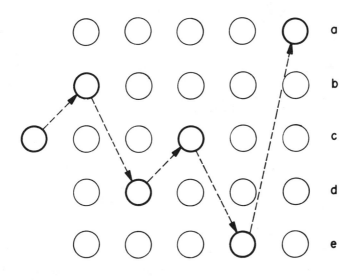

FIGURE 2-3. *The Stream of Psychological Events*

Figure 2-3 depicts a short segment of the stream of psychological events. It shows event *c* occurring at the left. At the termination of *c*, the complexity of which has been reduced by its occurrence, *b* is chosen as the event nearest optimum. As *b* is automatically terminated, *d* becomes the event nearest to optimum and is therefore chosen. By this time, *c* has recovered sufficiently from habituation that it is once again nearest optimal complexity level and occurs again. It is followed by events *e* and then *a*, each in its turn closest of available events to optimal complexity level at the moment of occurrence. Figure 2-3 shows at each point a set of events available to the organism. Only the events that actually occur can be observed by someone else. Thus, the sequence of events of Figure 2-3 will appear as they are in Figure 2-4 (next page) to an external observer.

Many of the important characteristics of Hedgehog behavior should now be apparent. A Hedgehog is fully autonomous. An event occurs. No matter how pleasurable the event, it will promptly, inevitably, and automatically come to a halt. There is no way for an event to be sustained. At best it can be repeated a few times. Probably the most predictable characteristic of organismic behavior is

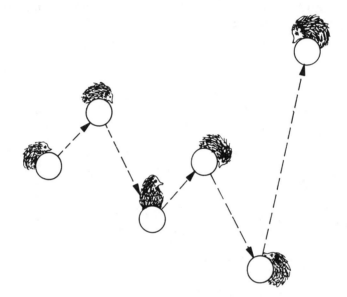

FIGURE 2-4. Hedgehog Choosing

the fact that events do not survive the psychological moment. The automatic termination mechanism is the basic dynamic principle of boredom, and organisms are first of all creatures of boredom.

During the occurrence of one event, the Hedgehog is sampling available events—sniffing them, if you will. From among those available, it chooses to activate the one nearest to its optimum. Its sniffing and its choice, however, can be fully automatic responses, and a machine could be built or a computer programmed to behave in a similar manner. Most of the time organisms are free to choose among a large variety of events; they exercise free will. In such periods their states alternate between boredom at the end of an event and the satisfaction of the occurrence of a new event. If nonoptimal events are imposed on the Hedgehog through the operation of environmental and programmatic constraints, then it reacts to their complexity levels with signs of low preference, feelings of unpleasantness, and possibly avoidance behavior.

The second most predictable characteristic of organismic behavior is that, when organisms are free to choose events without constraints, the events that occur will all be at about the same level of psychological complexity. The stream of psychological events is somewhat like a string of beads in which the beads are all about the same size but differ from one another in shape and color.

This account of the events in the streams of thought or behavior could be likened to the story of Sisyphus, where the choice of an event is to push the rock up the hill, and where the habituation phase is the sliding back down to the starting point. The imagery would be fine if Sisyphus had had a variety of hills to try in succession, but he didn't. We shall have to settle for a perky little Hedgehog meandering its vagulous, protean way through the streams of consciousness and behavior—sometimes through both at once.

Finally, a Hedgehog has a voracious appetite for information. It is rare that a psychological event occurs without the character of the event being changed in the process. Thus a Hedgehog learns continuously. It is never a question of whether a Hedgehog is learning but what it learns. That is determined by the course of the stream of psychological events.

_____chapter three_

# A hodgepodge of hedgehog dogma wherein one may learn to read the book

The Hedgehog was developed with guidance from a strongly held set of principles governing the use of language, the logic of experimentation, and issues concerning the analysis of data. In this chapter, I discuss a few of these principles to aid the reader in his or her efforts to judge the merits of developments in subsequent chapters.

## LANGUAGE PROBLEMS

### Theoretical Language

In any theoretical discussion, the precise meanings of key terms become crucial. In a very lengthy seminar on this subject, the late, great Edward Tolman identified an awkward and thorny choice. The theorist can choose to use common language, which usually connotes more than it denotes. In this case, the theorist is constrained to make common terms denotive by providing very precise definitions of the intended meanings, together with instructions to ignore all connotations not included in the definitions. More often than not, the reader soon loses the precision of the definitions provided and substitutes familiar connotations not intended by the theorist. The other alternative, the one Tolman chose, is to choose unusual terms or invent new ones—for example, Tolman's _sign Gestalt expectations_. The hazard of this procedure is that no one will remember to use the unusual word. In fact, Tolman confessed that Ernest R. Hilgard succeeded in mercifully reducing Tolman's jaw-breaker to the simple word *expectations.*

Since the hedgehog is a very common beast, I have chosen to use common words in the theory. In Chapter 2, psychological complexity and preference theory was stated in terms of five concepts— *psychological event, psychological complexity, arousal, preference,* and *optimal complexity level.* This list of five comprise a complete set of concepts in the Hedgehog. They are theoretical variables.

One characteristic of the theoretical variables is that they mean precisely what I say they mean, no more and no less. For example, I have defined the concept of preference in terms of the probability of the occurrence of psychological events. Within the theory, none of the many other possible definitions of preference has relevance.

A second common characteristic of the theoretical variables is that they are never subject to direct measurement. The value of a theoretical variable is always inferred from empirical information. The isolation of the theory from the data has the advantage of permitting the statement of the theory in absolute and inflexible terms. At the same time, it permits the theorist the necessary freedom to rationalize variable empirical results without having to generate a plethora of ad hoc special theories—thus remaining a hedgehog rather than a fox.

### Problems in Relating Theoretical Language to Empirical Language

There are a number of issues related to the task of coordinating empirical measurements and constructs to theoretical variables that are sufficiently general and sufficiently subject to confusion to justify brief treatment in general terms. Many of them are illustrative of the need to distinguish between theoretical and empirical variables.

*Varieties of Scales of Complexity.* I pointed out earlier that it is important to distinguish *psychological complexity,* a theoretical variable in the Hedgehog, from a number of empirical terms commonly employed in complexity and preference research. Here I want to elaborate on these distinctions.

The term *stimulus complexity* almost always refers to some fixed characteristic of the stimulus, usually described as a physical property. The most commonly employed stimuli in complexity and preference research are dot patterns, checkerboard patterns, and random polygons. The most common dimensions are the number of dots, the number or proportion of black and white squares, and the number of sides of random polygons. These stimuli are easy to generate and have considerable face validity as variations of complexity.

Stimulus complexity values can be assigned on the basis of the rules of generation of the stimuli or on the basis of the character of each stimulus after it has been generated. The two procedures can yield quite different values for the same set of stimuli. This point has been made clearly by Chaitin (1975), who discusses two meanings of the word *randomness* in any formal system. To illustrate, suppose a coin is flipped 20 times to produce a random sequence of heads and tails. The procedure can be repeated many times to produce many such sequences. We tend to think of such sequences as being random because of the randomness of the generation procedure. However, Chaitin argues that there are $2^{20}$ possible sequences of 20 heads and tails, including one composed exclusively of heads and one composed exclusively of tails. These two series, along with many others, do not present the appearance of being random, despite the random operation that generated them. Chaitin therefore suggests the concept of *degrees* of randomness, the degrees to be determined by some measurement operation applied to the products of the random-generation procedure.

Chaitin's particular proposal is to calculate the length of the computer program required to generate a given series. Sequences of 20 heads or 20 tails would be assigned the lowest degree of randomness, because they would require a minimum program to regenerate them. A high degree of randomness would be assigned to a series so unpredictable that the program required to regenerate the series would be as long as the series. Program length would therefore constitute a physical scale of randomness and in turn could be used to represent the complexity of the stimulus. Thus, stimuli that would be regarded as equally complex on the basis of identical rules of generation would constitute a large range of complexities on the basis of the lengths of the programs required to reproduce them exactly.

However, there are other problems with physical scales of stimulus complexity, whether they are based on rules of generation or on assessments of the products of the generation procedure. First, even though the number of dots in a dot pattern remains fixed, the psychological process induced by exposure to the pattern can be expected to change with experience. Second, the usual procedure is to present a limited range of stimulus complexity values, which creates the illusion of a monotonically increasing or even linear scale. However, if the number of dots is increased indefinitely, the stimulus display will very soon become homogeneous and therefore very simple psychologically.

The illusion of a linear scale of stimulus complexity can also occur in the middle of the scale under certain circumstances. Suppose one generates sequences of random polygons by some automatic procedure for adding and moving dots to be connected. Some such sequences will remain single random polygons through a large range of manipulations, while others will become multiple, but connected, polygons as randomly moving dots cross the borders of the original figure. In such cases all semblance of a linear reaction to a linear scale of number of sides or number of transformations will quickly disappear.

Some stimulus manipulations employed in complexity and preference research produce what might be called *a priori complexity*. One example is a pair of drawings of human figures. One drawing depicts a "normal" figure, while the second shows the head displaced to some unusual position. The second drawing, because of its incongruity, is assumed to be more complex on a priori grounds. Although procedures like this one can be experimentally useful, it is often overlooked that the scale on which the stimuli are assumed to be arrayed is a subjective scale.

I shall use the term *subjective complexity* to refer to the judgment of a single human subject. It will be assumed to be the best estimate of psychological complexity usually available. This use of subjective complexity has several advantages. It can reflect individual differences in reaction to the same stimulus; it can reflect progressive changes that occur with experience; and it can be used to assess the psychological complexity of many stimuli, including social situations, in which no physical measure of complexity is available.

So far I have suggested that physical dimensions of complexity can be misleading and in some circumstances unavailable, that a priori scales have limited usefulness, and that subjective complexity is applicable only to individuals and is subject to considerable variation for a number of reasons. Consequently, there is still a need for a universally obtainable and stable measure of the complexity of stimuli. One such scale that I find useful is *consensual complexity*. The fundamental operation for obtaining this measure is to establish a reference population, such as the standard college sophomore, have a significant number of the members of this population rate a set of stimuli for complexity under standard conditions, and then determine the mean values. The resulting scale values are the consensual values assigned by the reference population. This measure avoids most of the difficulties associated with other scales, including the irrationalities involved in stimulus complexity and the instability associated with subjective complexity.

*Overestimates of Complexity from the Stimulus and Underestimates from the Response.* It is generally true that there is a relatively large amount of information in the stimulus situation, much less information in the psychological event induced by that stimulus, and very much less information in the response that might be made to index that psychological event. Selective attention alone can account for a large reduction in information as one goes from the stimulus to the psychological event, and there is probably further filtering as the stimulus is processed into a percept representing a psychological event. A complex psychological event or sequence of psychological events is often reflected in a simple response such as a yes-or-no answer or a minor physical movement.

Most studies of complexity and preference involve the presentation to experimental subjects of stimuli that cover a range of complexity values (in some terms). Each subject makes some discriminative response indicating relative complexity, relative preference, relative arousal, or some combination. If one undertakes to estimate the complexity of the psychological event from the stimulus, one is most likely to err in the direction of overestimation because of the likelihood that the stimulus contains far more information than is processed by the subject. If one estimates the psychological complexity of the event from the response, then one is likely to err on the low side because of the smaller amount of information in the response than in the psychological event the response reflects.

### Behavioral, Verbal, and
### Neurophysiological Language and Data Realms

The Hedgehog chooses to regard the languages of behavior, cognition, and neurophysiology as differences in convenience rather than differences in metaphysical status or psychological school. Whether, and in what ways, the three data realms are related is a question for empirical test rather than sophist argument and debate.

One of the major benefits of a theory in which the major variables are unmeasured is that it offers the potential for the simultaneous coordination of behavioral, verbal, and neurophysiological data. A theory that creates expectations in all three realms is obviously a more general theory than one that is confined to only one realm.

Of the three realms, that of verbal expression or verbal rating of stimuli or reactions is by far the richest, because the verbal report of a human subject may contain far more potential information than a behavioral index or a neurophysiological measure. For this reason, most studies of complexity and preference employ verbal measures. Behavioral and neurophysiological measures' are most frequently used with nonverbal subjects. Although there may be no alternative in these instances, inherent problems arise from the small amount of information there is in a behavioral or neurophysiological measure compared to the rather large amount of information there is in the psychological event of which they are indices.

One example of such problems is the dilemma imposed by the need to determine both complexity information and preference information from the same behavior. It is easy to ask human subjects to evaluate complexity and preference independently on verbal scales. It is more difficult to make this discrimination in an overt behavioral index.

The use of overt behavioral data as a direct index of complexity is relatively rare. Much more commonly, complexity is presumed to vary along some physical dimension, and an overt behavioral measure, such as looking time, is taken as an index of preference or interest. However, there are a few instances in which differences in the complexity of overt behavior can be taken as an index of the complexity of the stimulus.

Wohlwill (1971) employed one such measure in the context of a developmental study. He constructed sets of shapes out of plywood to study tactile (haptic) exploration in children. The stimuli had three, six, ten, 20, or 40 sides. The children each handled ten stimuli (two at each level of complexity) with one hand extended through a hole in a screen. They were each asked to imagine that they were like a blind child who might "like to feel things just like another child might like to look at pictures." They were then instructed to feel each shape with one hand for as long as they wanted to and to say "Next" when they wanted to go on to the next shape.

Exploration time did vary with the number of sides in a steady progression, from about 22 seconds for the three-sided figure to almost 40 seconds for the 40-sided figure. Exploration time also varied with age. Kindergarten children explored the shapes for an average of about 26 seconds, whereas sixth-grade children explored the shapes for an average of about 37 seconds.

This difference in exploration time suggested to Wohlwill that the younger children generally were not exploring the figures as completely as the older children were. In order to investigate this possibility, he developed a rating scale for the quality (complexity) of the exploratory behavior itself. He assigned points to each exploratory performance in the following manner:

| *Points* | *Behavior* |
|---|---|
| 1 | Passive holding |
| 2 | Unsystematic exploration with three or more fingers being used simultaneously |
| 3 | Similar to 2, but with only one or two fingers |
| 4 | Systematic tracing with one or two fingers once around the outline |
| 5 | Similar to 4, but either twice around the outline or with repeated back and forth movements |

Using this rating system, Wohlwill found that the complexity of the overt behavior did increase with the maturity of the subjects. Kindergarten children scored at about the 2 level, third-grade children at about the 3 level, and sixth-grade children at about the 4 level on the scale.

Wohlwill did not report mean exploration scores for the five stimuli, and it is not at all certain that such differences should be expected, given the nature of the point system. It does seem likely that with slight modifications to include the counting of the number of movements or something similar, Wohlwill's behavioral index could be converted to a system that would reflect differences in the complexities of the stimuli.

Eye movement records such as those produced by use of the Mackworth camera also offer the potential for providing a behavioral index of complexity. For example, Mackworth and Morandi (1967) have reported a correlation between the amount of information in the segments of a two-dimensional visual display and the proportion of time spent attending to the various segments. His thesis is that the more information in a particular location, the greater the amount of time spent attending to that location. Whether his thesis is justified or not, the eye movement records clearly vary in complexity among segments, and indices of complexity could be extracted from them.

Assuming that we have available a behavioral index of complexity, we are still left with the problem of determining when the complexity of the behavior reflects the complexity of the psychological event and when it reflects some form of preference. If Wohlwill's subjects had been directed in a manner that emphasized exploration of the complexity of the stimuli, the behavioral index might have offered a close approximation to psychological complexity. In most studies in which nonverbal performance measures are employed, it is not clear whether the complexity of the overt behavior reflects the complexity of the psychological event or whether it reflects preference.

Neurophysiological indices offer more difficult problems than do behavioral indices in discriminating among complexity, arousal, and preference. EEG recordings can be correlated with the arousal dimension from deep sleep (slow waves) to the awake state (desynchronization). Basal resistance level (BRL) of the skin or sustained heart rate can be interpreted as measures of gross arousal level, and galvanic skin response (GSR) and shifts in heart rate can be interpreted as indices of arousal change.

Eventually, we may hope to find neurophysiological correlates for complexity and preference as well as for arousal. However, it is by no means apparent what they would be. The basic problem is similar for any attempt to relate behavior to neurophysiological data. Do we look for general characteristics of neurophysiological activity, or do we look for specific locations within the nervous system representing particular aspects of behavior, in this instance complexity and preference?

### Theoretical Language, Empirical Language, and the Language of Experimental Subjects

Confusion arises in studies in which the empirical language associated with a theory, as well as other language assumed to be closely related to the empirical language, is used in instructions to experimental subjects. The presumption of this procedure is that the semantic relationships assumed by the experimenter are very similar, if not identical, to the relationships that obtain in the semantic space of experimental subjects. This presumption may or may not be well founded. It is very easy for me, as a researcher, to mull over a word such as *interestingness* for a number of years until it comes to have a precise and special meaning for me. That meaning may or may not be shared by my experimental subjects, with the result that I may be misled when I attempt to interpret the results of a study in which I have asked experimental subjects to rate a set of stimuli for "interestingness."

Although such considerations are applicable to nearly all research in the areas of complexity and preference, let me expand the point with reference to my own theoretical approach to the problem. The theory I am using has in common with a number of others the fact that it includes three classes of variables. The three classes are structural, energetic, and evaluative. The structural variable is the concept of psychological complexity, the energy variable is the concept of arousal, and the evaluative variable is preference. These are theoretical constructs with postulated relationships to one another. They are subject to my own definition and interpretation. Within the theory, they mean exactly what I say they mean—no more, no less, no different.

Each of these theoretical variables is then coordinated to empirical constructs, which may or may not have identical or similar names. Thus, the theoretical term *arousal* is coordinated to the empirical term *arousal,* so that there can be identity between the terms on the theoretical and empirical levels. There can be other empirical coordinates of the theoretical concept of arousal, including different sounding terms such as EEG and GSR. Psychological complexity can be coordinated to stimulus complexity or subjective complexity, with the result that the confusion might be only slightly less than is the case with the arousal concept. Preference can be coordinated to a preference judgment but can also be coordinated to a scale of relative liking. In each of these cases, the nature of the relationship is to be postulated by the theorist or hypothesized and tested. Whatever the relationship, it is determined by the theorist, with or without empirical data.

Suppose I now do an experiment in which I present an array of visual stimuli and ask subjects to rate each stimulus for complexity and then to indicate which they prefer. The subjects may or may not interpret the terms *complexity* and *preference* as I do, and they may not agree with one another in their interpretations. The situation is further complicated if I ask the subjects to tell me how "interesting" each stimulus is. I cannot be certain whether their answers are evaluative (in which case the results should be parallel to those obtained when I ask how well they "like" the stimulus), or whether I should classify their responses as structural under the assumption that they are responding to the information processing demands of the stimulus. In the former instance, I might expect an inverted-U-shaped relationship to complexity. In the latter instance, I might expect a monotonically increasing relationship to complexity.

The situation can be complicated even further. I can ask for verbal appraisals of variables that should properly be measured in terms of overt behavior or neurophysiological activity. Rather than observe approach and avoidance behavior directly, I can ask subjects for verbal appraisals of the stimuli along a dimension of going toward or going away from. Rather than take some physiological measure of arousal, such as GSR, I can simply ask subjects how arousing each stimulus is.

This set of semantic problems is portrayed in Table 3-1. What is obviously needed is a set of empirical investigations of the ways in which experimental subjects use the words relevant to complexity and preference theory. The basic questions for which answers should be sought are: (1) How much uniformity is there in the manner in which experimental subjects use the words relevant to the experiments conducted in this area? (2) How much agreement is there between the ways in which subjects use the words and the ways in which they are used in the empirical and theoretical language of complexity and preference theory? (3) To what extent can the relationships within the theory be tested within the semantic space of experimental subjects?

In the Appendix of this book, I discuss a small beginning on this series of issues. The Appendix contains reports of studies that have been carried out in my own laboratory and that have not been reported elsewhere. The purpose of these studies was to determine something of the character of the relevant semantic space of individuals who are typically used as experimental subjects in studies of complexity and preference. The subjects in these experiments were therefore graduate and undergraduate university students. They represent the universe of typical experimental subjects rather than the universe of all possible English-speaking subjects.

A clear and persistent conclusion from these studies is that there are very large individual differences in the ways in which experimental subjects see the relevant words of the theory in relation

*TABLE 3-1.* Theoretical Language, Empirical Language, and the Language of Experimental Subjects

| Variable Class | Theoretical Language | Empirical Language | Subjects' Language |
|---|---|---|---|
| Structural | Psychological complexity | Stimulus complexity<br>Subjective complexity | Complex/Simple<br>Difficult/Easy |
| Energetic | Arousal | Arousal<br>GSR<br>EEG | Aroused/Unaroused<br>Active/Passive |
| Evaluative | Preference | Preference<br>Liking<br>Pleasantness<br>Interestingness | Approach/Avoidance<br>Go toward/Go away from<br>Interesting/Boring<br>Pleasant/Unpleasant<br>Like/Dislike<br>Prefer/Prefer not<br>Beautiful/Ugly<br>Good/Bad<br>Bright/Dull<br>Love/Hate<br>Desirable/Undesirable<br>Reward/Punishment |

to one another. Thus, the employment of any general conclusion concerning the semantic space of experimental subjects must be weighted in terms of how representative such a conclusion really is.

Even if one accepts the general findings of these studies, and thus ignores the individual differences, there is little evidence that psychological complexity and preference theory exists only within the semantic space of experimental subjects and in the absence of relevant experimental stimuli. The energetic dimension appears to have no special or complex relation to the other two, while the structural dimension and the evaluative dimension have a linear relationship for some people and something resembling an inverted-U-shaped relationship for others.

The results of the semantic studies offer considerable guidance in the conduct of experiments. Some relevant findings are these. In the absence of experimental stimuli, the dimensions of complexity and difficulty seem nearly equivalent. Among evaluative dimensions, those of pleasantness, interestingness, and liking are seen as being almost linearly related to each other, thus suggesting that they are nearly interchangeable. Words that are semantically opposite, such as *black* and *white,* differ in their associates, a finding which suggests care in the labeling of the ends of dimensions in experimental studies.

## SOME PROBLEMS OF
## EXPERIMENTATION AND DATA ANALYSIS

There are a number of matters related to procedures for carrying out experiments and analyzing the data that should be discussed briefly before substantial empirical material is presented. They relate to the manner in which some of these experiments were carried out, to possible flaws in the design and analysis of some of them, and to persistent flaws in the relevant research that has appeared in the literature.

### The Occultation Effect

Most of us have the intuitive feeling that distal stimuli remain fixed and unchanging over time. Yet we are all aware that our reactions to a single stimulus can undergo considerable change from one time to another. For example, ambiguous figures are of psychological interest precisely because the perception of the same physical stimulus can change dramatically from a beautiful young lady at one moment to an ugly old lady the next moment, even though the physical stimulus has remained unchanged.

The fact that the psychological reaction to a fixed physical stimulus can change from time to time brings us to a frequently ignored problem associated with the measurement of psychological complexity. Most theories of complexity and preference suggest that experience with a stimulus produces a semipermanent change in the reaction to that stimulus. In the Hedgehog, any occurrence of an event inevitably leads to temporary changes in both complexity and preference and usually leads to semipermanent changes. Consequently, in any measurement technique that requires repeated measurements from the same subject, each answer the subject provides represents an evaluation of a different psychological event, even though the stimulus remains fixed. Thus, if one uses the paired-comparisons technique with eight stimuli, each stimulus will be exposed a minimum of seven times by being paired at least once with every other stimulus. The values that are usually reported in journal articles are averages of seven values that differ in complex ways from one another, depending on the extent of recovery from habituation and the amount of semipermanent change that occurs. Moreover, these values can be expected to be quite discrepant from the values of the stimulus in either a subsequent experiment with the same subjects or an experiment with new, unexposed subjects. I call this phenomenon the *occultation effect*, for the act of assessing the value of the event obscures or hides its true value.

Dealing with the occultation effect in the conduct of experiments requires an awareness of the problem that is relatively uncommon among experimenters, as well as an ingenuity in either solving the problem or minimizing its effects. For example, it might be possible to use one group of subjects as a reference population from which one obtains measurements of the complexity and preference values for a set of stimuli, and a different but comparable population of subjects in the conduct of the experiment proper.

The occultation problem has been recognized by Thomas (1966), who minimized the effect in the following manner. He avoided multiple experiences of the same stimulus in the paired-comparisons technique by preparing multiple stimuli to represent each value of the stimulus. To scale five values of complexity for random polygons having five, ten, 15, 20, and 25 sides using Thomas' technique, one would need four polygons with each number of sides. Each time a five-sided polygon was paired with one of the other values of random polygons, a different example of a five-sided polygon would be used. In this manner, all ten possible pairs of different stimuli could be presented without the same physical stimulus being presented twice. Although this procedure minimizes the occultation effect, it does not eliminate it if there is any generalization between stimuli. It can usually be presumed that there is some degree of generalization. There is no easy solution to the occultation problem, but it cannot be ignored.

### The Number of Experimental Stimuli

There are many studies in the literature that have reported ambiguous results because they have used too small a number of experimental stimuli. The number of stimuli used in complexity and preference research is critical. To simplify the problem, suppose the theoretical expectation is that the optimal complexity level of an individual may be above all of the stimuli in the set, below all of the stimuli, or somewhere between the simplest and the most complex. Assume further that the data are nonmetric and consist of preferential orders given by subjects. If we use three experimental stimuli, labeled *C, M,* and *S,* for complex, medium, and simple, then there are only six possible preferential orders. Of these, four (C > M > S, S > M > C, M > C > S and M > S > C) represent monotonically increasing, monotonically decreasing, and inverted-U-shaped functions and are thus acceptable preference order relationships within the theory. Only two of the six possible orders are unacceptable. These are C > S > M and S > C > M, which yield U-shaped functions that violate the theory. If the results were truly random, two-thirds of the results would agree with the theory and one-third would not. Thus, it would be exceedingly difficult to test the theory with only three stimuli. The literature contains reports of many studies employing only two values of the stimulus dimension. In these cases the theory cannot be tested at all.

Table 3-2 shows the number of possible combinations of stimuli, N!, that arise from various numbers of stimuli, N. It is obvious that three stimuli are infinitely better than two, four better than three, five better than four, and so on.

The techniques for analysis of ordinal data of the kind usually obtained in complexity and preference research come largely from the work of Coombs (1964), where it is largely unintelligible to me. A version I find somewhat easier to understand appears in Coombs, Dawes, and Tversky (1970). Basically, Coombs refers to a preference order, such as 34215, as an *I-scale*. If each number represented a political candidate, the I-scale would indicate the most preferred candidate, 3, followed by the others to the least preferred candidate, 5. An I-scale can be *unfolded* to determine whether there is an underlying *J-scale*—a unidimensional scale on which each of the stimuli, as well as the ideal position of the subject, can be arrayed. The political candidates might differ on a dimension ranging from very liberal, 1, to very conservative, 5. This could be an underlying J-scale. The preferential order given by the subject indicates that he occupies a position on the scale nearest to candidate 3, closer to 4 than to 2, and so forth. He is therefore neither an extreme conservative nor an extreme liberal. The preference order 31542 is not an acceptable preference order relationship, because it cannot be un-

TABLE 3-2. Effects of Numbers of Experimental Stimuli

| Number of Stimuli (N) | N! | Number of Acceptable Preference Order Relationships | Percentage of Possible Preference Order Relationships That Are Acceptable |
|---|---|---|---|
| 1 | 1 | 1 | 100.00 |
| 2 | 2 | 2 | 100.00 |
| 3 | 6 | 4 | 66.67 |
| 4 | 24 | 8 | 33.33 |
| 5 | 120 | 16 | 13.33 |
| 6 | 720 | 32 | 4.44 |
| 7 | 5,040 | 64 | 1.33 |
| 8 | 40,320 | 128 | .32 |
| 9 | 362,880 | 256 | .07 |
| 10 | 3,628,800 | 512 | .01 |

folded into a unidimensional J-scale that preserves the numerical sequence 12345. If the numbers refer to liberalism and conservatism, one would conclude that this dimension was not the basis of the subject's choice of candidates.

In the Hedgehog, if the underlying J-scale of 12345 represents psychological complexity, then the preference order 34215 is acceptable to the theory. On the other hand, the preference order 31542 is not acceptable preference order relationship, because it cannot be unfolded into a unidimensional J-scale. When a subject gives such preference judgments, one can appeal to errors of measurement, conclude that the subject is not responding exclusively to the experimental dimension (in this case complexity), or conclude that the theory is wrong or inapplicable in the situation.

A much more elegant and detailed exposition of some of the problems of testing theories of complexity and preference using Coomb's scaling procedures is given by Thomas (1971), who is somewhat pessimistic concerning the testing of bimodal curves from ordinal data. Biomodal curves are expected from Adaptation Level Theory (Helson, 1959) and discrepancy theories of motivation such as those of McClelland and Clark (1953) and Hebb (1949). Thomas shows that any result involving three stimuli can fit a bimodal discrepancy prediction. Thus, a much larger number of stimuli would be required to verify a bimodal distribution than is required for the inverted-U shape.

### Measurements of Single and Multiple Psychological Events

Psychological complexity and preference theory is based on data in which most measures are taken with respect to a momentary reaction to a presented stimulus. The measurement is presumed to refer to a single psychological event. On the other hand, there are many instances in which the unit of behavior under study occupies a longer period of time—a period long enough to suggest that what has been measured refers to a sequence or string of psychological events. There is a problem in determining whether the theory is equally applicable, without modification, to units of analysis larger than the single psychological event.

In some cases there is reasonable certainty that one is dealing with a single psychological event. For example, two-dimensional displays of dot patterns can be presented by means of a tachistoscope and the exposure interval controlled so that only a single visual fixation is possible. An immediately rendered judgment by the subject in this case would certainly refer to a single psychological event.

If a longer exposure time is permitted, it seems certain that the result will be a series of visual fixations and thus a series of psychological events. If the subject is asked to make a judgment about the stimulus (How complex is it? How many dots are there?), the judgment will be made with reference to the subject's total experience with this particular stimulus—that is, to a series of psychological events.

If the stimulus is a more complicated visual stimulus (Mackworth), or if it is an auditory stimulus for which variation in time is the essence, or if it is an object to be explored tactilely (Wohlwill), then the judgment is certainly made with respect to a sequence of psychological events.

In simple memory experiments, subjects are often presented with a series of items and asked to report them back. Here one is clearly dealing with two sequences of psychological events—one when the items are presented and the second when the subject is asked to report them back.

Several fundamental issues are posed by the set of situations just described. The series began with a perception that involved a single visual fixation, proceeded through sequential experiences in three modalities that can probably be appropriately regarded as unitary experiences with single stimuli, and ended with a learning operation. In the light of the fact that visual stimuli are presumed to be subject to special principles of perceptual organization, some of which are applicable to a single fixation and some only to sequences, can complexity and preference theory be applied to *both* single events *and* sequences? If complexity and preference theory *is* applicable to both single events and sequences in cases of visual perception, is it equally applicable to perception in *any* sensory modality? If it is applicable to perceptual sequences, is it also applicable to the kinds of information processing sequences involved in short-term memory operations?

Because the theory is a hedgehog theory, my strategy will be to assume that it is applicable both to single events and to larger units that have sequential aspects. This position will be maintained until data force the recognition of a fundamental distinction between *complexity*, which seems intuitively applicable to a single psychological event, and *difficulty*, which seems applicable to the length of the chain in a memory experiment. In effect, I will consider both judgments of complexity and judgments of difficulty as estimates of psychological complexity.

### The Problem of Multidimensionality

The Hedgehog is based on only two dimensions, psychological complexity and preference, which are plotted orthogonally to each other. Empirical measures related to either can prove to be multidimensional. The Hedgehog strategy is to relate multiple empirical dimensions of either complexity or preference back to the simple structure of the Hedgehog. The alternative procedure is to invent new theoretical dimensions to represent each new empirical dimension. This is fox-like procedure.

Thomas has attempted to differentiate the concept of stimulus complexity into more than one dimension in at least two studies. In one of them (Thomas, 1968), he obtained similarity judgments for pairs of random polygons and then analyzed the results using Kruskal's scaling procedure. This procedure permits the detection of multiple dimensions if they exist in the data. Thomas reports quantitative evidence that there might be as many as two or three meaningful dimensions underlying the similarity judgments. However, I question whether there really is more than one dimension. In reporting the results of his research, Thomas presents the results of two-dimensional Euclidean solutions for eighth-grade children and for college adults. I find no difficulty in interpreting the first dimension in each case as representing something appropriately called "complexity." However, I have difficulty seeing a meaningful second dimension. Thomas gives a tentative interpretation of the second dimension as representing "symmetry." Whether or not one chooses to go this far with Thomas, there is little question that nearly all of the variance in the similarity judgments are extracted by the "complexity" dimension.

I have had similar experiences with the Shepard-Kruskal multidimensional analysis of complexity judgments of abstract paintings, tartan patterns, and representational graphic art materials (Walker, 1970). In no case could my colleagues and I find a clear and meaningful second dimension in judgments of complexity.

Thomas has reported another study (1969) illustrating a second general technique for differentiating the concept of complexity. In this one, he manipulated characteristics of the stimulus display in order to find the effects of variability and numerosity on preference judgments. Numerosity was manipulated by varying the number of dots in the display; variability was manipulated independently by controlling the relative redundancy, or patternedness, of the display. He concluded that preference was determined primarily by numerosity for both younger and older subjects, while older subjects responded to pattern variability under some conditions.

One can almost conclude from these studies, and others like them, that in paradigms in which the experimenter attempts to analyze verbal judgments of complexity made in reference to stimulus materials, a single, relatively unambiguous dimension of complexity emerges. This is a somewhat gratifying conclusion from a theoretical standpoint, if one is a Hedgehog.

Unfortunately, the same lack of ambiguity does not obtain in paradigms in which there is semantic manipulation of the affective words in relation to visual stimulus materials. For example, Berlyne and Peckham (1966) employed Osgood's semantic differential scales to evaluate characteristics of a set of stimulus materials that have been employed many times by Berlyne and his students and colleagues. They utilized the evaluative dimension (ugly/beautiful), the potency dimension (weak/strong), and the activity dimension (slow/fast) (Osgood, 1952; Osgood, Suci, & Tannenbaum, 1957). Including data from previous studies, Berlyne and Peckham had available data showing the relation of seven different variables to the same set of stimulus materials ordered in terms of increasing complexity. The seven variables were the three Osgood dimensions; judgments of complexity, interestingness, and pleasantness; and EEG desynchronization.

Although judgments of complexity confirmed the a priori ordering of the stimuli, the other six variables did not conform to any simple pattern in their relations to complexity. Ratings of pleasantness/unpleasantness, beauty/ugliness and weak/strong all showed about the same relation to complexity. A different pattern emerged for two variables, ratings of interestingness and the Osgood dimension of slow/fast, and these two showed patterns similar to each other. The EEG desynchronization data showed still a different relation to complexity that was nearly the inverse of that shown by the pleasantness ratings.

These results are somewhat disappointing. Since the three Osgood dimensions are uncorrelated with one another, they might have been expected to fall into three different clusters. They did not, and thus did not provide the hoped-for theoretical structure needed to organize the results. Nor did they offer a solution to the question of whether the evaluative dimension is unidimensional, as expected in psychological complexity and preference theory, or is a multidimensional variable. Pleasantness and interestingness showed relations to complexity that are different from each other. Thus this elaborate set of results failed to provide definitive solutions to the problem of the multidimensionality of the evaluative dimension.

Two studies by Day illustrate further frustration in trying to determine the composition of the evaluative dimension. In the first of these (Day, 1965, reported in Berlyne & Peckham, 1966), Day obtained ratings of complexity, pleasingness, and interestingness. The results for the ratings of pleasingness and those for interestingness were grossly different. In a later study, Day and Crawford (1971) used random polygons and obtained ratings of simpleness, interestingness, pleasingness, and liking. In this study, the three affective ratings—interestingness, pleasingness, and liking —yielded curves that had very similar pattern relationships to complexity but that differed somewhat in mean value.

From these and similar results, Berlyne has been led to distinguish two kinds of exploration—*specific* and *diversive*—that are related to judgments of interestingness and pleasantness. *Specific exploration* expresses a need to familiarize oneself with the environment; the amount of time spent exploring each element is likely to increase monotonically with the complexity of the element. *Diversive exploration,* according to Berlyne, expresses true preference and is likely to be an inverted-U-shaped function of the complexity of the stimuli.

To invent two theoretical variables to account for exploratory behavior is fox-like. In the Hedgehog, both kinds of exploration are the product of the same mechanism operating with respect to two different sets of stimuli. What Berlyne calls specific exploration may be expected to occur when the character of the response is determined by stimuli extrinsic to the properties of the immediate stimulus. Diversive exploration should occur when the behavior is determined by the intrinsic properties of the stimulus. Psychological complexity and preference theory is to be applied in an identical manner to the organism's predictable responses to two different aspects of the situation.

To cite a concrete example, some evidence of a shift in attention from one set of stimuli to another in the same situation appeared in the behavior of rats exposed to four levels of a priori stimulus complexity (E. L. Walker & Walker, 1964). Either the walls of a four-compartment maze were lined with materials of four different levels of visual complexity, or the compartments contained differing numbers of baffles to operationalize four levels of complexity. We described the behavior of the rats in these situations in the following manner.

When the animal is first introduced to the maze, the most common pattern of behavior begins with a tentative, VTE-like, and largely visual exploration of the four compartments. This behavior is typically followed by a more complete, locomotor exploration of several, if not all four, of the compartments. This phase might be described as the "information gaining" type of exploratory behavior. This behavior usually merges into a subsequent phase that appears to be more nearly a choice of a compartment on the basis of preference. . . . The duration of the "information gaining" type of exploration tended to decrease throughout the five day period. However, there was a wide range of individual differences between animals in this respect. A few explored in this way for only a few minutes on the first day and little, if any, after that. Others engaged in lengthy exploration on the first day and were still engaged in some such activity on the last day.

The exploratory behavior that we referred to as the "information gaining" type appears to correspond to Berlyne's "specific exploration," while the subsequent expression of preference appears to correspond to Berlyne's "diversive exploration." In my terms, the initial reaction to the maze situation reflects the fact that stimuli other than the experimental elements are initially optimal. After a sufficient period of experience with the extrinsic stimuli in the situation, the psychological events associated with them will simplify until they are farther from optimal complexity level than the experimental stimuli. It is only subsequently to this general reduction in uncertainty that the animal begins to respond to the specific stimuli of the four compartments and to express discriminative preferences among them. The reactions to both extrinsic and intrinsic stimuli are governed by the same set of principles of Hedgehog theory.

A serious question remains, however, whether one is justified in identifying two kinds of exploration with verbal ratings of interestingness and pleasantness. There are two reasons why the wisdom of this identification seems doubtful. First, one of the two studies by Day seemed to support such a difference between ratings of interestingness and pleasantness, but the other did not. Second, experimental subjects may not always agree with theorists on the meanings of such words.

The materials I have reviewed are a sample of findings that have led others, chiefly Berlyne, to develop a proliferation of theoretical concepts. Although some of these findings appear to defy any simple ordering, by either hedgehogs or foxes, none appears to require departure from the simple structure of the Hedgehog.

## The Fallacy of the Group Mean

Because there are large individual differences in complexity and preference, there is a possibility of misrepresentation when individual results are combined into means and plotted in curves representing group results. Let me give you an example in which each of the individual results verify the theory, while the means, representing the group performance, appear to refute the theory.

Suppose that we have five stimuli that vary in complexity. We ask five subjects to rank them for preference. If the five stimuli are ordered in complexity from 1 to 5, the five subjects might give the following orders of preference: 12345, 21345, 32145, 43215, and 54321. Each of these individual results would be predictable from complexity and preference theory. The first subject prefers the simplest stimulus and shows less preference for stimuli as they become more complex. The next three subjects show optimal complexity levels near 2, 3, and 4 and show decreasing preference in an orderly fashion for stimuli that are either more or less complex than the preferred stimulus. The last subject prefers the most complex stimulus and shows decreasing preference for simpler stimuli.

We can obtain a group result by averaging the preference rankings of each of the five stimuli. For example, the simplest stimulus, 1, was ranked first, second, third, fourth, and fifth by the five subjects. The mean of these ranks is 3.0. The five mean ranks in order of complexity from the simplest to the most complex are: 3.0, 2.4, 2.4, 3.0, and 4.2. If these group means are plotted against complexity, the resulting curve is U-shaped, since it is high at either end and low in the middle. Such a curve would appear to refute the theory, even though each individual subject gave results that were in accordance with the theory.

Many of the results of experiments relevant to complexity and preference theory that appear in the literature may be regarded with considerable skepticism because they do not report individual results. Group results that cannot be matched with individual results must be examined closely to determine whether they might in fact misrepresent the true nature of the functional relationship.

### SUMMARY

In this chapter I have undertaken to provide a context for psychological complexity and preference theory to permit the reader to see the theory as I see it and to provide a general background for the ways in which some of the research has been designed and the data analyzed. Language was discussed because of the large difference in status between theoretical and empirical constructs. Problems of experimentation and of data analysis were discussed because of their general importance and because the principles that have been chosen for discussion have been particularly important in shaping the nature of the Hedgehog.

# chapter four

## The stream of psychological events

Human life can be described as a stream of psychological events beginning early in the organism's prenatal history and continuing without interruption until the organism dies. It is the task of behavioral science in general and psychology in particular to give scientific accounts of the character of individual psychological events and of patterns in their sequences. For example, the fields of sensation and perception are devoted primarily to the analysis of the character of individual psychological events or short sequences of psychological events. The fields of learning and memory concern the effects of past experience on present psychological events. Concepts such as motivation, attitude, and trait reflect efforts to understand certain consistencies in the pattern of psychological events. Psychopathology is concerned with anomalies in the stream. Thus, the analysis of the stream of psychological events offers the potential for a common framework for all of psychology as well as other aspects of behavioral science.

In this chapter I consider a variety of approaches to the description of the stream of psychological events, as well as accounts of the determinants of the choice of items in the stream. I then suggest that the Hedgehog offers a suitable set of principles to account for the stream of psychological events.

## CREATIVE ACCOUNTS OF
## THE STREAM OF PSYCHOLOGICAL EVENTS

### Living, Creating, and Recreating Streams

Each of us lives a stream of psychological events. Second to living them, observing and analyzing streams must be the most pervasive of human enterprises. We can control our own behavior on the basis of plans and expectations based on our observations of our own streams, of the environment, and of the streams of others with whom we interact. The quality of execution of a plan depends on the accuracy with which we observe the interacting streams of our own and others, whether the plan is something as simple as leaving work and driving home at the end of the day or something as complex as the plan of a 16-year-old to become President of the United States.

Roger Barker (1963) has appropriately pointed out that a professional concern for the stream of psychological events is widespread. The novelist, the poet, the playwright, and the choreographer all create streams, while a range of professionals from the historian to the psychoanalyst undertake to recreate them. The different observers, analysts, creators, and recreators of the stream of psychological events differ widely in the taxonomies they use in describing the stream, the size and character of the units of interest to them, and probably most of all in terms of the purposes of their intellectual efforts.

### Streams of Thought

The observation of the stream of thought may be the most difficult of all scientific enterprises. Not only are we limited to the observation of our own private experience of the stream, but the very act of trying to observe the untrammelled stream of thought influences its course and character. Looking inward in an attempt at self-observation must of necessity produce occultation of the natural flow, distorting it from the path it might have followed if the act of observation had not intruded as a part of the stream itself. The stream of thought is therefore certain to be highly processed before it can be made available for an examination of its character.

William James' chapters on the stream of thought or consciousness (see, for example, James, 1893) contain a number of psychological insights and above all have great literary merit, but he failed to stimulate an enduring intellectual tradition, partly because of the introspective character of his efforts.

Something approximating the stream of thought can be attained when a human being can be induced to talk about his own stream. The free association method in psychoanalytic therapy falls into this class. However, the correspondence between the actual stream of thought and the stream of words is nearly indeterminate. In therapy, verification of the accuracy or representativeness of the stream of words is indirect, tortuous, and difficult in the extreme. It basically depends on estimates of the success of the therapy, and success in therapy is notoriously difficult to evaluate.

If one undertakes to dictate a stream of words that reflects one's own stream of thought, one cannot help but be impressed with the relative sterility of the spoken words in comparison with the variety and richness of the stream of thought they represent. To close the gap between the richness of the stream of thought and the poverty of the correlated stream of words requires enormous literary talent most of us do not possess. Few of us could do as well as William James or as well as James Joyce, who wrote a lengthy reconstruction of a stream of thought in the soliloquy of Molly Bloom in *Ulysses* (1961). Almost any sample from that section of the book would suffice to make the point. This one is drawn almost at random.

> ... with a bit of toast so long as I didn't do it on the knife for bad luck or if the woman was going the rounds with the watercress and something nice and tasty there as a few olives in the kitchen he might like I never could bear the look of them in Abrines I could do the criada the room looks all right since I changed it the other way you see something was telling me all the time Id have to introduce myself not knowing me from Adam very funny wouldnt it Im his wife or pretend we were in Spain with him half awake without a Gods notion where he is dos huevor estrellados señor Lord the cracked things come into my head sometimes itd be great fun supposing he stayed with us . . .

Regardless of the literary quality of the stream of words, the stream of thought is a private experience. It is the stream of words that constitutes data that can be analyzed objectively. Thus, the stream of thought must become the stream of behavior—verbal behavior—before it can become an integral part of the account of the stream of psychological events.

## OBJECTIVE DESCRIPTIONS
## OF THE STREAM OF PSYCHOLOGICAL EVENTS

### Casual Observation

The stream of behavior is much easier to deal with objectively, because it is available to the immediate experience of a number of individuals. However, something more systematic than casual observation is required. A feeling for some of the problems can be gained from the following anecdote and observational record.

At a symposium held in Korsør, Denmark, in June of 1972, I undertook to stress the point that very few items in the stream of behavior could be related to established biological and social needs. In a playful but derisive *ad hominem* response, Professor Hans Eysenck rejected my thesis by recounting his self-observations of the stream of his own behavior over the past day or so. He felt that he could account for all of his overt behavior in terms of need/ goal relationships.

At the lunch table that day, I concocted a scheme to provide a response to his criticism of the position I had taken. Four of us who happened to be sitting together agreed to observe Professor Eysenck for a period of five minutes from precisely 14:30 to 14:35 that afternoon, during the talk of another speaker. In addition, I took a five-minute sample as a single observer in the period 14:21 through 14:25, immediately prior to the joint observation period we had agreed upon.

The sample of Professor Eysenck's behavior that I took alone is in Table 4-1. The simultaneously obtained records produced by the four observers are contained in Table 4-2. Although these records served well enough to pose the question of whether the units in the stream of behavior fall naturally into the need/goal pattern, some rather obvious deficiencies are apparent. The first record, for the single observer, looks complete enough, but it is quite apparent that much structure has been imposed on the record by the observer. The units are sentences, even though one would not expect the behavior

*TABLE 4-1.* Time Sample of Overt Behavior of Professor Eysenck during Lecture, Collected by a Single Observer

| | |
|---|---|
| 14:21 | Reaches in pocket |
| | Removes handful of change from pocket |
| | Sorts coins and organizes by size of coins |
| | Laces fingers together with thumbs opposed |
| 14:22 | Moves thumbs |
| | Changes position of hands |
| | Looks up from knees to look at speaker |
| | Looks down at desk |
| 14:23 | Reaches in pocket |
| | Removes medium sized coin |
| | Inserts coin under sheet of paper |
| | Removes pen from coat pocket |
| | Uses pen to produce a "rubbing" of coin on sheet of paper |
| 14:24 | Removes coin from position under paper |
| | Returns coin to pocket |
| | Puts pen in coat pocket |
| | Turns paper over so that rubbing is not visible |
| 14:25 | Leans forehead on hand |
| | Touches nose |
| | Leans back in chair |
| | Examines knuckles |

TABLE 4-2. Time Sample of Behavior of Professor Eysenck during Lecture—Four Observers, Simultaneous Observation

| Time | Observer #1 | Observer #2 | Observer #3 | Observer #4 |
|---|---|---|---|---|
| 14:30 | Hands clasped | Appears drowsy, eyes closed | | Appears drowsy |
| | Looks up at speaker | Eyes up | | |
| | Drops eyes to low level | Eyes close | | |
| | Looks to right | Eyes up | | Jerks to attention |
| | Looks up at speaker | Looks left at speaker | Moves body | |
| | Rubs thumb on lip | Left hand to mouth, rubs | Blinks eyes | Looks at hands |
| | Looks back at speaker | | | |
| 14:31 | Wiggles thumbs | From left, slight movement | | |
| | Looks down at desk | | Moves head | |
| | Looks up at speaker | Looks up | Blinks eyes | |
| | Looks down at desk | | Moves head | |
| | Puts hand on forehead | Left hand on head | Hands on forehead | Hand to left temple |
| | Pulls lip | Rubs nose | Hand to nose | |
| 14:32 | Uncross, recross legs | Changes legs, crossed again | | Shifts position |
| | Fingers lip | Rubs nose, chin, and (xxx) | | Rubbing mouth with fingers |
| | Fingers nose | Scratches nose | Hand to face touching nose | Rubbing nose with index finger and left thumb |
| | Spreads fingers to forehead | Head in hand | Hand to head | Left hand to temple—drowsy |
| | Looks down | | | |
| | Closes eyes | | | |
| | Fingers nose | Rubs chin, upper lip | Hand to face, nose | Rubbing corner of mouth |
| | Rubs chin | | | |
| | Turns hand over | | | |
| | Rubs hand | | | |
| 14:33 | Looks down | Looks up slowly | | |
| | Puts hand in lap | Pushes spectacles | | |
| | Straightens body in chair | Sits up and folds arms | Sitting up in chair | Shifts position—arms folded |
| | Crosses arms | Sighs | | |
| | Slumps down extending legs | Stretches legs | Looks at speaker | |
| | Looks far left | Looks at me (Observer) | | |
| 14:34 | Looks back at speaker | | Turns head, blinking | Turns head to left |
| | Raises knees | Upper body up | Turning head | |
| | Lowers knees | Upper body down | Sitting up in chair | Shifting sitting position |
| | Raises head | | | Purses lips |
| | Looks at speaker | | Turning head | Moves head to left |
| | | | Moves head | |

38

to have the same grammatical structure that language has. Duration information is missing, and it cannot be determined from the record whether there are periods in which no codable behavior was occurring. Examination of the records obtained by the four different observers reveals further difficulty. It is true that the four observers were sitting in different positions in the room and thus had different angles of observation, but the lack of agreement among the four records cannot be accounted for exhaustively by this factor. Even though all four observers indicated the passage of time by recording the moment at which each minute began, the correlation of the four records in time was a creative enterprise on my part, and it involved considerable uncertainty. To be scientifically useful, such an observational enterprise requires thoughtful development of a behavioral coding scheme and training of observers to produce reliable and valid records. Let us examine several more respectable efforts.

## Statistical Accounts of Group Behavior

There is a degree of uniformity in the streams of many humans if they are in similar or like circumstances, beyond the normal life cycle of birth, parenthood, and death. For example, there is a diurnal pattern so pronounced that it can even show up in a highly regular fashion in grouped data. Aspects of this uniformity can be seen in data collected by a large team of investigators and reported in a volume edited by Szalai (1972). The manner in which a great many individuals spend their time was classified into 96 categories. These categories were then grouped into eight or nine larger categories. Graphs of the frequencies of these behaviors show the distribution of these classes of activity over a 24-hour day, Monday through Friday. Despite what must be considerable individual variation, the curves attest to an impressive degree of similarity in what most people are actually doing at any given moment during the day. Some of this uniformity is imposed largely by custom—the eight-to-five workday, some of it is biologically induced—the patterns of sleeping and eating at certain times of the day.

However interesting these grouped data might be, they offer the psychologist less useful material than would the raw elements of individual streams of psychological events. Of the multitude of codable human behaviors, only a few are sufficiently correlated with time to permit such a statistical account. Furthermore, there is no assurance that dynamic principles that account for group behavior would be applicable to the behavior of the individual. Accounts of individual streams are therefore required.

### Analysis in Terms of Assumptions
### Concerning the Need/Goal Account of Behavior

A scientifically objective account of the stream of behavior has been achieved by Barker and Wright and their colleagues over the past quarter of a century or more. A five-minute sample of behavior as recorded by Barker and Wright appears in Table 4-3. Barker (1963, pp. 8–9) provides considerable information concerning the subject, the physical and social setting, and the date and time of day. This five-minute sample of the behavior of a young Yorkshire schoolboy looks very like the casual observations we recorded of the behavior of Professor Eysenck, except that Barker and his observers have had a great deal of practice and can demonstrate very high reliability coefficients between the codings of different observers, thus eliminating many of the problems apparent in our records of Professor Eysenck's behavior.

Barker offered this sample of the behavioral stream in order to illustrate the manner in which he and Wright code the stream of behavior. The smallest units of behavior are referred to as behavior tesserae; they correspond roughly to the single sentences used in my account of Eysenck's behavior. The term *tesserae* was chosen by analogy with the bits of stone or glass (tesserae) used in the construction of a mosaic. This leads Barker to describe them as fragments of behavior that are created or selected by the investigator in accordance with his scientific aims. They are arbitrary behavioral fragments containing no complete behavior unit.

Behavioral units, for Barker, are identified and unitized in terms of structural-dynamic properties based on their content. Units have the common feature that each is directed throughout its course toward a single end state or goal, and the structural-dynamic characteristics reflect the fact that the behavioral content can vary quite widely within the unit. As shown in Table 4-3, behavioral units may overlap each other, or one unit may be entirely enclosed within another. Whereas in some places there may be a single current of behavioral units, in other places there may be dual, parallel channels.

The particular scientific interests of Barker and Wright account for the designation of behavior tesserae as fragments of behavior that are of little or no intrinsic interest. These interests also lead them to make the basic assumption that behavior is, in fact, organized dynamically in terms of need/goal relationships and to code the behavioral units in these terms. If one has other scientific interests, the Barker and Wright methods of recording and coding data may not be suitable or appropriate. For example, suppose one had an interest in the appearance, persistence, and disappearance of the tesserae themselves and perhaps in the period of time before the reappearance of a particular tessera. In this case, recording of these

*TABLE 4-3.* Five Minutes in the Life of Brett Butley, Yoredale County School

10:39  Miss Graves (Brett's teacher) came through the yard leading a loudly crying little girl, and turned her over to Miss Rutherford (the teacher of the Lower Infants) who was near the canteen building.

Brett glanced at this.

*Noting Hurt Child*

He stood watching the cricket game.

*Watching Cricket*

He stuffed the last piece of orange into his mouth.

*Eating Orange*

Miss Rutherford came by with the girl who now had a large discolored bump on her forehead.

Brett glanced at the girl with mild interest.

*Noting Hurt Child*

10:40  Brett walked over to the boy who had been batting.

He took the bat which was handed to him as though this was expected by both of them.

The cricket bat was full-sized and as tall as Brett.

He stood quietly with the end of the bat resting on the ground as he waited for the bowl.

Orin bowled.

Brett struck at the ball rather awkwardly and failed to hit it.

It was difficult for Brett to swing the bat.

The ball was thrown back to Orin and he bowled again.

This time Brett succeeded in hitting the ball.

*Playing Cricket*

It went a short distance and was thrown back to Orin.

Six of the boys playing chain tag came rushing arm in arm through the edges of the cricket game and disrupted it momentarily.

The cricket players including Brett waited patiently, watching the tag game.

*Waiting for Boys to Move Away*

Orin bowled.

Brett made a hit. He seemed mildly pleased.

The ball was returned to Orin and he bowled to Brett.

Brett tried but failed to hit.

A group of bigger boys, 12-year-olds, came out for their break.

10:43  Orin bowled to Brett.

Brett hit the ball energetically.

One of the big boys reached out and caught the ball as it was thrown to Orin. The big boy then bowled rather gently to Brett.

Brett tried but missed.

The big boy evidently intended to bowl, and Orin moved to the batter's position. Orin took the bat from Brett.

*Playing Cricket*

Brett appeared to make no objection.

10:44  Brett stood passively with his fingers in his mouth watching as the game continued.

*Watching Cricket*

From *The Stream of Behavior*, by R. G. Barker. Copyright 1963 by Appleton-Century-Crofts. Reprinted by permission.

fragments without an account of their temporal duration would be inadequate. Furthermore, Barker and Wright's scientific interests and corresponding method of coding would lead to a predisposition to omit many tesserae from the record on the assumption, conscious or unconscious, that their presence or absence in the record would not have any determinative effect on subsequent use of the record. It is likewise true that, if one wanted to investigate the question of whether or not behavior was dynamically organized in terms of need/goal relationships, coding it in those terms preempts the question. Thus, the nature of the dynamic process cannot be investigated easily in Barker and Wright data on behavioral units, because the coding already contains an assumed answer to the question.

### Analysis in Terms of
### Arbitrary Time Units of Behavior

Norton (1968) has reported a technique for recording behavior in such a manner that the character of the tesserae themselves is susceptible to analysis, while the raw data permit one to analyze the stream in terms of a variety of possible dynamic organizations. Rather than unitize behavior at the data level, she slices behavior at fixed points in time. In her work with rats, for example, she might confine an animal to some space within the focal distance of a movie camera lens and record a picture of the animal every second, every two seconds, or some other time period that is suitable to the speed with which the stream of behavior is running. This photographic record can then be analyzed repeatedly, if necessary, with several varieties of coding categories and repeated coding with the same categories to establish reliability of coding. The basic virtue of this procedure is that future analyses are not bound absolutely by irrevocable coding decisions made at the data level. Using this technique, Norton has been able to employ more than 30 categories of behavior of a rat in a rather sterile environment.

Some of the virtues of this technique were sacrificed by Timberlake (1969), largely to gain efficiency in data handling and analysis. He observed the animals directly, coded the behavior that was occurring in ten mutually exclusive and exhaustive categories, made a judgment concerning what was occurring every second by punching one of ten keys that registered the elements of the stream in computer-compatible form, and thus bypassed the bulky data record and laborious data transfer problems associated with Norton's procedures.

The magnitude of these problems can be perceived, perhaps, from these figures. Timberlake observed a total of eight rats. Each rat was observed for a ten-minute period each day for 60 days. The stream of behavior for one rat in one session consisted of 600 judgments, which became 36,000 successive items in the stream of behavior over the 60-day period. Since he had eight animals, the resulting 288,000 items of data would have represented a formidible problem for hand manipulation.

Using this procedure required considerable pretraining of the observer and by its very nature made estimates of reliability difficult to obtain. Timberlake was able, however, to train another observer and establish high inter-observer reliabilities in coding the same stream of behavior.

Timberlake's procedure sets limits on the number of categories of behavior. Where Norton could code more than 30 categories from film, Timberlake could code no more than ten categories in direct observation, probably because of the limitations of human information-processing channel capacity and the fact that he had only ten fingers to use in identifying ten categories of behavior. This number of categories may well have been sufficient for Timberlake's purposes, especially since he observed his animals in isolation from other animals and under conditions in which they were relatively free from basic biological needs and the means of their satisfaction. However, examination of the descriptions Timberlake employed indicates that the ten categories, while very close to the actual behavior, do require considerable preprocessing by the observer. Furthermore, although the categories were constructed to be mutually exclusive and exhaustive in the sense that whatever the animal was doing in any one-second time bin was classified into one of the ten categories, the criterion that the categories be mutually exclusive was difficult to realize. The animal may engage in pointing behavior, for example, while rearing, but the pointing behavior will not be so coded if it occurs during "Rearing." Finally, although the descriptions appear to be essentially free of interpretation, the labels applied to the ten categories appear to be less free. For example, Timberlake was able to show systematic changes in the frequencies of categories of exploratory and grooming behavior over time and to demonstrate predictable changes in those frequencies when various stimuli were introduced or withdrawn in the situation. However, to a certain extent, the labeling of the ten categories shows a predisposition on Timberlake's part to find the associations within the four grooming categories and the five exploratory categories that were revealed in later analysis.

The procedures used by Norton and Timberlake represent a paradigm of observation of the stream of behavior that comes very close to matching ideal requirements. Although the animals are observed in fairly sterile environments, occultation of the stream by the behavior of the observer is minimized by the mechanical impersonality of the camera set-up for Norton and the great care taken to isolate the animal from any variation in stimuli associated with the observational procedure. Furthermore, in both procedures, such an effect, if it were occurring, could very well show up in the analyses. Both sets of coding categories permit highly reliable coding and, at least at the descriptive level, appear to involve very little prior bias. In the case of Norton's film record, even that bias could be eliminated by recoding the stream revealed in the film. The records of both Norton and Timberlake contain all the basic information—frequency, duration, inter-event time, and sequential relations. The records obtained by these two scientists make clear the limitations of Joyce's record of Molly Bloom's stream of thought, my records of Professor Eysenck's lecture-listening behavior, and even the highly sophisticated records of Barker and Wright and their colleagues.

Nevertheless, an ideal, and thus exhaustive, *analysis* of the ideal record is a state that can be approached but not easily attained. There are two formidible problems. One is a classic problem of how to integrate a treatment of frequency data and time or duration data, and the second concerns the nearly limitless possibilities involved in sequential analysis.

The first is a complicated and persistent problem that is resident in the question of whether two occurrences of the same event (for instance, "Pointing" from Timberlake's categories), each of which lasts two seconds, are the same as or different from one instance that lasts four seconds. In other situations, this is the problem of whether there is a trade-off between speed and accuracy in performance, and, if there is, what its nature is. The procedures employed by Norton and Timberlake offer a potentially creative solution to this problem. If the stream of psychological events is arbitrarily sliced into equal time units or time bins, duration information is converted to frequency information; the duration of an event is measured by the frequency with which that event occurs in successive time bins. Whether this procedure represents the beginning of a solution to the frequency/duration problem, or whether it only amounts to hiding it under the rug, remains for further analysis and consideration.

Some of the difficulties involved in producing an exhaustive analysis of sequential possibilities can be seen by contemplating this fact. If, for some idiotic reason, one asked a computer to print out all the possible sequences of Timberlake's ten categories that could occur in a ten-second period in one rat, the task does not seem particularly difficult on the surface. However, the actual number of total possible patterns is $10^{10}$, or ten billion, and the computer time required would be very expensive and would fill a large room with the paper required to print out the results. Truly exhaustive analyses of sequential information is for all practical purposes impossible.

The analysis of what items of behaviors follow what other classes of items of behavior is perhaps the essence of psychology, but the magnitude of the problem of analysis is very great, and much of the potential of sequential analysis is unrealized. Something of the magnitude of the problem of analysis can be appreciated by an examination of one of the primary analyses Timberlake carried out in terms of sequential probabilities (or frequencies). The basic statistic is an instance in which any one of the ten classes of behavior is followed in the next moment in time (time bin) by any of the ten categories of behavior. Given the procedure of slicing time into arbitrary bins of one-second duration, a given class of behavior will be followed by itself through as many time bins as are required to mark off its duration. It will then be followed by an instance of a transition to another of the ten categories. A count of these transitions can then be arranged into a transitional frequency table.

Although the raw frequencies reported by Timberlake are revealing of many aspects of transitional contingencies, one can ask whether a part of the transition from one behavior to another is a chance phenomenon based on the fact that the ten classes of behavior appear in very different absolute frequencies in the stream and would thus of necessity follow each of the other nine a large number of times without there being any necessarily meaningful connection between the two. For example, in one sample of the stream, Pausing is followed by Locomotor Exploration 561 times. A calculation of the expected frequency of this association (627) reveals essentially chance association. Thus the calculation of expected frequencies and the subsequent calculation of $X^2$ values for the transitional frequencies seem to be required. With this calculation it can be determined that the high frequency with which Pausing is followed by Locomotor Exploration must actually be interpreted as a negative tendency for this sequence to occur.

An interesting use of $X^2$ to produce a visual display of the magnitude and character of an experimental effect is provided by Norton (1968). She observed 16 rats for a fixed period using her recording technique and then analyzed the first-order transitional frequencies in a manner similar to that employed by Timberlake. Then she dosed her animals with amphetamine and made a second observation. She arranged the control $X^2$ values in numerical order from high to low, and they formed a reasonably orderly line. She then plotted the new values obtained after the administration of amphetamine for each of the 97 pairs. The effect of amphetamine on the disorganization or reorganization of the sequential aspects of behavior is highly apparent visually.

As useful and interesting as the analysis of first-order transitional frequencies might be found to be, this level of analysis represents only a first step. In addition to extracting first-order frequency transitions, Timberlake moved on to second-order transition matrices, which will not be reproduced here. Such a matrix takes each possible sequential pair—for example, Pausing followed by Exploration—and tabulates the frequency with which this pair is followed by either Pausing or Grooming. Without going into details, these three item sequences were far from random. When the second-order transitional matrices for the ten categories of behavior analyzed independently were examined, more than 80 possible three-item sequences were found to occur together with greater than chance probability, and a similar number were found to occur with significantly less than chance probability.

It should be obvious that the analysis of sequential aspects of the stream of behavior when one begins with an observational record of the raw stream (a) is rich in meaningful relationships and (b) very quickly expands into a very complicated set of alternate contingent patterns that are exceedingly difficult to interpret exhaustively. Furthermore, this happens with first-order transitional frequencies when the number of categories is very large, and it happens with second-order transitional frequencies even when it is small. Since many of the psychologically interesting constraints in the contents of the stream of behavior have to do with associations that are very much more remote than could be found with second-order transitional frequencies, further advances are clearly needed in analysis techniques if one is to deal with the full richness of the stream of behavior. For example, the execution of most human plans would involve relationships between bits and short sequences that are separated from each other by many irrelevant actions, or at least actions that are irrelevant to the execution of the plan. How could one discover my plan to go to work in the morning from the stream in which relevant elements of getting in the car, backing out of the garage, and driving out of the driveway are followed by irrelevant acts such as turning on the radio, lighting a cigarette, watching for the radar patrol car that sometimes operates a speed trap on the route, observing an unusual amount of trash here, an obvious effort to beautify the environment there, stopping to drop letters in the mailbox stationed along the route, and so on, intertwined with other acts that are necessary to the execution of the plan of getting to work? Something more than an analytic approach to the raw stream of behavior in an environment rich in potential actions is needed.

## DYNAMIC ACCOUNTS OF THE
## STREAM OF PSYCHOLOGICAL EVENTS

The discussion so far has centered on techniques of recording the stream of psychological events and on techniques of analysis that amount to inductive determinations of patterns in the stream. An alternative approach is essentially deductive in character. I will discuss three such efforts, one developed by Newell and Simon (1972), one developed by Atkinson and Birch (1970) in *The Dynamics of Action*, and the Hedgehog.

## Human Problem Solving

The Newell and Simon (1972) work on human problem solving illustrates the shift from an inductive to a deductive approach to a particular kind of stream of psychological events. In the inductive phase, they induced individuals to articulate what they were thinking during the process of solving mathematical problems. In the deductive phase, they programmed a computer to deal with mathematical problems in the manner indicated by the stream of verbal behavior of the human subjects. The computer was then given similar mathematical problems to solve, and it did so with a success rate comparable to that of the human problem solvers. The presence of the deductive phase suggests strongly that the stream of words emitted by the subjects during the problem solving process corresponded closely to the associated stream of thought.

Although the technique of computer simulation of human behavior is general and the Newell and Simon accomplishments are prodigious, the technique as it has been employed has limitations. The computer program generated in this manner is relevant only to the solving of a particular class of mathematical problems and is therefore highly specific. The focus on similarities in the problem solving techniques among the subjects studied results in a deemphasis on the need to account for the vagaries of individual behavior. Finally, even though the computer has been demonstrated to produce overt behavior similar to that of the human problem solver, it is dangerous to assume that the underlying processes are the same or even similar.

## The Dynamics of Action

The Atkinson and Birch book (1970) is purely deductive and is intended to be a model for all kinds of behavior. They have developed a mathematical model that can be used to generate a simulated stream of behavior that has some of the general characteristics of the actual stream. To the extent to which the model can reflect the actual stream, it can be assumed that the processes used to generate the simulated stream are close to those that actually generate human behavior.

The units of the stream have quantitative and qualitative properties. The formal, quantitative properties include the requirement that the observable actions be discrete—that is, with an identifiable beginning, integrity throughout occurrence, and an identifiable termination. The stream is continuous in the sense that one action is always followed by another action, so that there are no moments in the stream in which nothing is occurring. Actions may be compatible, with the result that more than one action can be occurring at a given moment in time. Actions may be incompatible and thus be required to compete for expression in the stream. Different acts may theoretically bear family relationships to each other (for example, eating behavior); thus, both displacement and substitution can occur involving common or related instigation (hunger) on the one hand and common or related consummation (eating) on the other.

The dynamics of action model is addressed to the problem of change from one action to another. Actions have measurable durations, and over a significant time period the frequency of occurrence becomes a primary measurement. An important additional measurement that is derived from frequency and duration is the time between occurrences of a particular category of action.

Atkinson and Birch intend their dynamics of action system to be highly flexible with respect to the taxonomy of the content of the stream. Although it is usually easier or even necessary to deal with the stream of overt behavioral acts, the approach is assumed to be equally applicable to the stream of thought or conscious experience. In fact, they have a primary interest in situations in which the stream of thought might serve to instigate overt action.

The system appears to have no inherent property or characteristic that limits it to actions of one particular size unit or range of sizes, although Atkinson and Birch choose to be concerned primarily

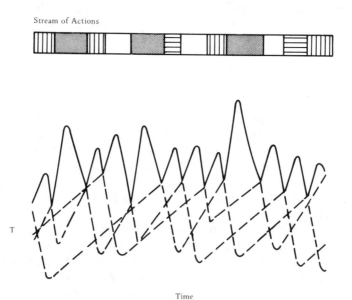

FIGURE 4-1. *Synthesis of the Stream of Action*

with action units ranging from a few seconds to episodes of the size coded by Barker and Wright. Rather, the dynamics of action model appears to be applicable over the whole range of psychologically interesting actions.

Something of the manner in which the model operates can be visualized as drawn in Figure 4-1. This is a schematic diagram that portrays the appearance and disappearance of five discrete actions that might occur in the stream (black, white, horizontal, vertical, and stippled) and the changing levels of five *resultant action tendencies*, $\bar{T}$, which constitute the theoretical account of the existence and the strengths of the five tendencies both during periods when the relevant action is observed to be occurring and during periods in which it is not. In the figure, the value of $\bar{T}$ is drawn as a solid line when the act is occurring and as a broken line when the tendency exists in some value but is not resulting in action. Since a change in activity occurs whenever the value of $\bar{T}$ for the ongoing act is exceeded by the value of $\bar{T}$ for an alternate act, it is clear that the occurrence and duration of an act is not only dependent on its own resultant action tendency, $\bar{T}$, but also on the characteristics of the act that preceded it and the act that follows it. Thus, the primary focus of the Atkinson and Birch theory is on the determinants of a shift from one category of action to another. The fluctuating values of the resultant action tendency, $\bar{T}$, are determined by positive forces (instigating forces), by gradual reduction as the act occurs (consummatory forces), and by forces operating to prevent the act from occurring ("negaction" tendencies). All of these are parameters that determine the rate or direction of change of $\bar{T}$ over the time during which the particular value is operating and thus subject to change.

Family relationships can be demonstrated by either a positive or a negative correlation over time of two or more activities. However, it should be noted that it is exceptionally difficult to determine familial patterns without experimental manipulation of a definitive nature. Familial relations between actions could result in their occurring together in abundance over a short period of time. The family relations of eating actions could result in bursts of eating appetizers, actions of eating the several elements of the main course, and actions of eating dessert. On the other hand, family relations could result in the members of the family never occurring together if one action is an effective substitute for another member of the same family. The logical difficulty of the analysis of family relationships without experimental manipulation is apparent from the fact that, since there are no empty time units in the stream of action, it is a logical necessity that the nonrandom occurrence of one act in increased frequency necessitates the nonrandom, nonfamilial nonoccurrence of other acts.

### The Hedgehog in the Stream of Psychological Events

The Hedgehog is a device to provide a dynamic and useful account of all of the various streams of thought and behavior discussed in this chapter. It is an alternative approach and alternative dynamic mechanism to those offered by Newell and Simon on the one hand and Atkinson and Birch on the other. In contrast to the tightly constructed mathematical account of the Atkinson and Birch model, the Hedgehog is loosely and simply constructed. Within the Hedgehog, the universe of possible psychological events is conceived as a very large set that can be ordered in terms of the position each event occupies on a scale of psychological complexity. There are a number of constraints, however, that limit the set of events from which the organism may choose at any given moment. Constraints have their origin in the environment or in the nature and state of the organism and may be referred to as environmental constraints or programmatic constraints.

*Environmental Constraints.* It is possible to conceive of circumstances in which the environment is so insistent and demanding that the particular events and the sequence of events are completely determined externally. An example might be the stream immediately following the accidental touching of one's finger to a hot stove. However, such circumstances are assiduously avoided by Hedgehogs and with sufficient success that complete environmental determination of psychological events is rare.

Roger Barker has asserted that, if one wants to make predictions concerning what a person is doing at any given time, the best prediction is to be made from knowledge of where the person is at that time. Even though this statement is probably correct, environmental determination of behavior is not to be deduced from it. Although to a certain extent the environment may select behavior, most of the accuracy of Roger Barker's prediction arises from the circumstance that the person made a prior choice that placed him or her in that particular environment. Thus, the environment is usually passive, and its major role in the selection of psychological events consists of the extent to which it limits the organism's choices. Environmental constraints are chiefly constraints of availability.

*Program Constraints.* Much of the behavior of the organism occurs in the service of programs of internal origin. It is sometimes convenient to distinguish biological and psychological programs, even though the distinction has limited usefulness. It is sometimes argued that biology and psychology constitute two different levels of analysis, and that to deal with both simultaneously constitutes an effort to reduce psychology from a higher level to biology at a lower level.

No such problem exists for the Hedgehog. It is an empirical matter whether two sets of data stand in a functional relation, and it matters not that one is presumed to have a biological and the other a psychological origin.

Programs vary significantly in terms of their flexibility and their universality. Breathing is a program that is highly inflexible and universal in humans. Other biological programs, such as those associated with hunger, thirst, sex, and pain are nearly universal in the species but exhibit considerable flexibility and variation in their expressions in the stream of psychological events. Some programs of psychological origin, such as the use of language, show near universality and significant constraint even though variation in choice of word and expression is evident within those constraints.

Some programs are of interest precisely because they are not universal. Traits, attitudes, and such social motives as need for achievement are studied because they permit differential predictions concerning the content of streams of psychological events in different individuals in the same situation.

Finally, there are programs that are essentially unique to the individual. Because no two individuals have identical past histories, no two individuals will bring to a situation identical repertoires of potential events. Just as any given environment sets limits of availability on the universe of events that can occur, the general character and idiosyncratic past history of the particular organism also sets limits of availability.

I believe that a complete moment to moment record of the stream of psychological events would reveal two general characteristics of programs. First, a number of programs are likely to be occurring simultaneously, and rarely, if ever, does a single program have a monopoly over more than a small number of events in sequence. Second, programs are typically manifested by a temporary increase in frequency of events that can be seen as related to one another, even though they are embedded in a great variety of other events that are related to other programs.

*The Limits of Choice.* Within the constraints imposed by the environment and those imposed by programs within the organism, the essence of human existence is choice behavior. The Hedgehog is a creature of choice. As a psychologist, I am motivated to determine the nature of the environmental and programmatic constraints that make behavior predictable. Aspects of my efforts can be seen in the diagram in Figure 4-2. The larger, darker circle in the center that is labeled $E_0$ represents the psychological event occurring at any given moment in time, $M_0$. The circles to the left represent psychological events that have occurred in the immediate past. The dashed curved lines leading to the lower circles represent the fact that events in the very immediate past are in short-term memory storage, while events in the more remote past are in long-term memory storage.

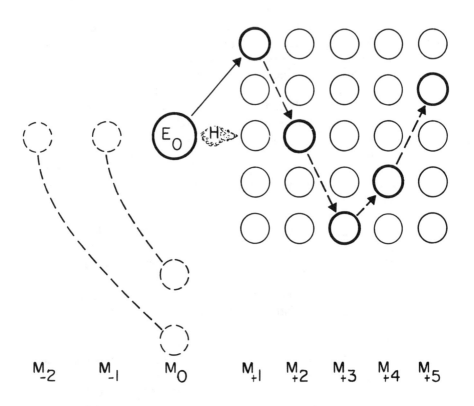

$M_{-2}$    $M_{-1}$    $M_0$    $M_{+1}$    $M_{+2}$    $M_{+3}$    $M_{+4}$    $M_{+5}$

FIGURE 4-2. *Sequence of Psychological Event Selection*

To move from event $E_0$ to the right requires principles governing the termination of $E_0$ so that we can progress to $H$, which is the focal point on which all psychological principles affecting choice come to bear. The symbol $H$ was chosen to stand for the Hedgehog and can also stand for uncertainty in information theory or even for "hesitancy" when appropriate. In the treatment to follow, the Hedgehog will always be relevant, while the $H$ of information theory and hesitancy will not be so universally applicable.

The rows and columns of circles to the right of $E_0$ represent the set of alternative next events that might occur. Each alternative that actually does occur then becomes $E_0$, and the previous $E_0$ passes into short-term memory and finally into the long-term memory store. Each choice of an available alternative almost certainly changes the set of available subsequent alternatives, a condition not represented in the diagram.

The diagram is intended to be a very general one. It should be applicable to James' stream of consciousness, Barker's stream of behavior, or to any other set of serial data representing successive events in the life of an organism. Such descriptive accounts, however, only follow the path indicated by the arrows in the diagram and thus reveal something about those events that actually do occur. The alternative events that were in some sense potential events but that were not in fact chosen and therefore did not occur are not apparent in most descriptive accounts of the stream of psychological events. They must be revealed by experiment.

Thus, human behavior is to be accounted for in terms of three sets of factors. The environment is a partial determinant, both in terms of the physical constraints imposed and in terms of the sensations and perceptions it induces. The second set of factors might be referred to as the grammar of behavior. By this I mean to encompass consistencies in the sequential patterns in the stream of psychological events, whether they are attributable to genetic or experiential determinants of current behavior. I mean to include in the grammar of behavior such patterns as those attributed to personality, biological and social motives, execution of planned sequences, traits, attitudes, motor skills, and other acquired patterns, as well as the language behavior from which the label was borrowed by analogy. The third set of factors is the Hedgehog, an integrated set of principles governing the selection, persistence, and termination of psychological events.

Given these three sets of constraints, where in the system is there room for choice behavior? It can be argued that the principle that optimal complexity is the state constantly sought by a Hedgehog produces conditions in which the beast is almost always faced with a free choice among a number of alternative next events, such as the five portrayed in the diagram. Although it is actuarily true that the environment tends to select the behavior, it must also be remembered that a Hedgehog actively avoids nonoptimal environments and actively seeks environments of appropriate complexity level. Since its own internal programs help define what is and what is not an optimal environment, suitability for execution of an internal program is a part of the definition of what is an optimal environment.

Perhaps the nature of the freedom of choice can be made more explicit by one more examination of the Hedgehog in Figure 4-2. It will usually be the case that the animal has already been able to avoid nonoptimal environments that are either too complex or too simple, and thus unsuitable for the execution of whatever plan is in progress. Thus the organism is faced with five alternatives, all of which are approximately equal in complexity. A major determinant of the complexity of each of the events is that it contains within it whatever anticipations of future consequences the organism can generate. Thus, as it sniffs at each of the alternatives, all aspects of its past and foreseeable future are brought to bear on the decision. It feels as if it has free choice. It says it has free choice. Since these are the data, it clearly has free choice.

## SUMMARY

In this chapter I argued that an analysis of the stream of psychological events is the proper concern of psychology. I pointed out a variety of approaches to the description, analysis, and generation of such streams. I then indicated that, since the stream of thought can be dealt with objectively only when it is converted to a stream of verbal behavior, the task of psychology is reduced to the analysis of the behavioral data, whether the data represent the stream of thought or the stream of overt behavior. I have not mentioned neurophysiological data in this context only because of the paucity of relevant data in this area.

Finally, I have suggested the Hedgehog model as a mechanism that provides a suitable dynamic account of the operation of the stream. While properly mechanical in character, a Hedgehog exercises free choice within the limits set by memory of the past, anticipation of the future, the constraints imposed by the environment chosen, and the plans chosen for execution.

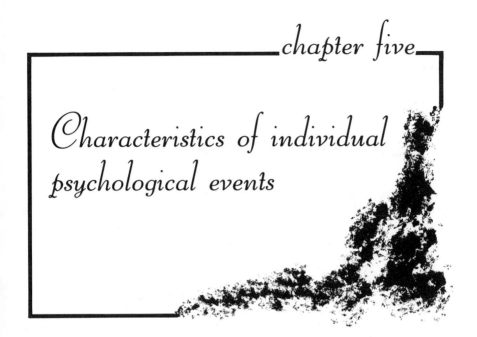

# chapter five

# Characteristics of individual psychological events

The stream of psychological events has the appearance of a smooth, flowing, unbroken river. The feeling of continuity is pervasive but is, in fact, an illusion. The stream of psychological events is discontinuous in nature. An illustration is the illusion of continuity and the fact of discontinuity in the motion picture. Still pictures succeed each other on the screen at rates such as or 16 or 24 images per second, and the screen is actually dark about one-half the time. The underlying process is discontinuous, and the illusory experience is continuous.

The most predictable characteristic of human (or organismic) behavior is that whatever event is occurring at any given time will be terminated quickly and replaced by another event. An event occurs either because it is initiated by a demanding stimulus or because it is chosen as the preferred event among freely available alternatives. It endures briefly, terminates quickly, automatically, and inevitably, and is succeeded by a different event.

The occurrence of an event has aftereffects. The responsiveness of the organism to a demanding stimulus may change, the character of the event may change, or the probability of recurrence of a freely chosen alternative may change. It is useful to distinguish between temporary aftereffects, which are expected to dissipate with the passage of time, and semipermanent effects. The first type are usually referred to as habituation and the second as learning. However, there is no clear-cut temporal point of distinction between habituation and learning, and any such distinction is somewhat arbitrary.

In this chapter, I characterize the occurrence of individual psychological events. Temporary aftereffects are the subject of Chapter 6, and in Chapter 7 I consider more permanent changes associated with the occurrence of psychological events.

## A REMINDER CONCERNING ELEMENTARY CHARACTERISTICS OF THE THEORY

Since I am undertaking to account for as many as possible of the known characteristics and aftereffects of the occurrence of events with an extremely simple theory, it would be well for the reader to keep in mind some elemental facts concerning psychological complexity and preference theory.

Since psychological complexity is the only structural dimension in the theory, all phenomena associated with the occurrence and recurrence of events are to be accounted for in terms of this variable. Only two kinds of changes can occur: the event may undergo *simplification*, or it may undergo *complication.*

When neural aspects of a psychological event are under consideration, complexity could be represented by the size of the set of elements involved at any one time, or it could be represented by the frequency with which individual elements are fired during the occurrence of the event. Since this distinction is rarely made on a data level, and since both the number of elements and the frequency of firing are represented in most measures of intensity, I will assume that the *intensity of activity* and the *complexity of the activity* are to all intents and purposes perfectly correlated. Thus, a rise in intensity is to be interpreted as an increase in complexity, and a drop in intensity as a decrease in complexity.

At the most fundamental level of psychological complexity and preference theory, the phenomena of habituation and of learning are highly integrated. It is convenient, however, to distinguish between temporary and semipermanent effects of experience. The occurrence of an event can result in the simplification of the event (the most usual effect) or in the complication of the event. Either of these results can dissipate with the passage of a relatively brief period of time and thus be regarded as a temporary effect. On the other hand, changes in the relative complexity of events may endure for substantial periods of time and thus represent semipermanent changes. Most of what is usually studied under the label of habituation represents temporary effects, while most of what is studied under the labels of learning, problem solving, or the occurrence of insight are semipermanent effects.

Although it is assumed that the determinants of elicited responses and freely chosen responses are much the same, there is one fundamental difference between them. The *elicitation* of a psychological event involves the application of a stimulus with high demand properties. That is, stimulus-induced processes with significant specific components result in the reliable appearance of a particular response when the stimulus is applied. Preference is not a factor when a psychological event is elicited by a stimulus with high demand characteristics. Preference *is* a factor when the organism chooses freely among two or more alternatives, and, according to the theory, it will choose to activate the event that is nearest to its optimal complexity level.

## THE INITIATION, DEVELOPMENT, DECLINE, AND TERMINATION OF A SINGLE PSYCHOLOGICAL EVENT

This section could have been given the label "The Magic Number $500\sigma$ x/÷ 2–10." A single psychological event, representing a psychological moment, appears to occupy a relatively fixed and small amount of time—essentially $500\sigma$. However, there are variations. Kristofferson (1967), for example, has developed a strong argument for the fundamental character of $50\sigma$ in studies of the discrimination of minimal temporal intervals. It is not particularly important whether the basic interval is $50\sigma$, $500\sigma$, or $5000\sigma$. It *is* important that any pattern of behavior occupying a substantial period of time, such as several minutes, is composed of a *sequence* of psychological events.

Events initiated by stimuli with high demand characteristics appear to vary in duration to some extent with variation in the intensities of the stimuli that initiated them. When an event occurs through free choice of the organism from among readily available alternatives, the duration may be controlled largely by the complexity of the event. Moreover, since choice behavior is postulated to be based on the relative complexity of events, and since complexity increases with intensity, choice behavior is also assumed to be a function of the relative intensity of events. For this reason both temporal patterns and the intensity of events should be examined in as much detail as possible. In what follows, I will consider first the characteristics of events initiated by stimuli with high demand characteristics and then proceed to more internally induced events.

### Characteristics of Stimulus-Induced Visual Images

Certain of the characteristics of stimulus-induced psychological events are revealed in studies conceived as representing an information processing approach to visual perception. From work of individuals such as Sperling (1960), Averback and Coriell (1961), Neisser (1967), Hochberg (1968), and Haber (1970a, 1970b, 1971) emerges a four-phase conception of the visual image. The first stage is referred to as the feature detection or extraction phase, in which only the features of contour, line, angle, orientation, motion, retinal disparity, and color are detected by specialized cells in the cortical visual field. The feature extraction phase is followed by the development of an icon. The term *icon* was employed by Neisser to distinguish it from a visual image, since the icon, even when fully formed, is assumed not to involve any effects of set, expectation, or any other product of past experience. Although the arguments for this native, inborn-only characteristic of the icon are strong, the existence or generality of this freedom from past experience will require reexamination in the light of the sampling-of-alternatives requirement of choice behavior. This issue will be discussed later. The third stage in the information processing approach to visual perception appears to involve some sort of cognitive structure and memorial effects of prior experience to permit the beginnings of interpretation of the icon. The fourth stage involves stored memory.

I would like to examine some of the available data in the light of an hypothesis that the time required for the first two stages is approximately $250\sigma$ and that the time required for the last two stages is also approximately $250\sigma$. If these are reasonable estimates, then all four stages might require the magic number of $500\sigma$. I will also note what evidence there is for parallel processing of information in visual perception and discuss the question of whether phases of successive percepts can overlap within this $500\sigma$ processing time.

In the experimental procedure developed by Sperling (1960), two rows of perhaps eight letters each are exposed briefly. Some time after the beginning of the exposure, but after the stimulus has been removed, a marker appears to indicate which of the 16 letters the subject is to report. If the marker appears about $250\sigma$ after the stimulus begins, accuracy in reporting the letter in the position indicated by the marker is nearly perfect. As the appearance of the marker is delayed beyond $250\sigma$, the accuracy of the report declines rapidly. Investigators have taken this as evidence that approximately $250\sigma$ is required for the full development of the icon, which fades rapidly thereafter. A variation of this procedure also yields a value of $250\sigma$ for the development of the icon. In this latter procedure, the stimulus is exposed, and some time afterwards, a second stimulus described as visual noise is exposed. If the visual noise is exposed any time during the $250\sigma$ required for the development of the icon, the accuracy of report is reduced, but if it is delayed $250\sigma$ or longer, subjects are able to report accurately what they have seen.

Studies of the persistence of the icon in visual memory also yield a similar figure. If the stimulus is quite brief (perhaps of the order of 10$\sigma$), the icon persists for about 250$\sigma$. If the stimulus endures for 500$\sigma$, persistence of the image after the disappearance of the stimulus is of the order of 50$\sigma$. If the stimulus endures for a full second, then the icon persists for less than 30$\sigma$. Thus, the mechanism accounting for the formation of the icon appears to guarantee that under normal circumstances it will persist for a minimum of 250$\sigma$. With stimuli of that duration or longer, persistence becomes negligible. These considerations appear to set a minimum of 250$\sigma$ for the development of the icon (Haber, 1970a, 1970b, 1971).

In studies of reading behavior it is found that a single fixation endures for about 250$\sigma$ and that the transition time between fixations is from 30 to 50$\sigma$. According to Haber, these temporal characteristics of reading behavior are not influenced by whether readers are slow or fast or by whether they are reading letters, words, phrases, or whole lines and passages at a single fixation. Furthermore, in studies of icon formation, the durations of the first two stages are unaffected by the amount of information in the stimuli (Haber, 1971). If the icon of one fixation is erased by the icon of the next, then in ordinary reading the beginnings of successive fixations allow about 300$\sigma$ for each icon to be relatively undisturbed before it is erased by the next. The times involved would seem to require that stages three and four associated with one fixation must be occurring in parallel with the development of stages one and two of the subsequent fixation.

The question of the time required for the accomplishment of stages three and four and the "erasing" of the immediately prior icon is complicated by the apparent necessity for the interaction of the effects of at least two successive fixations for the construction of such elementary perceptual properties as figure-ground organization of the visual percept (see Neisser, 1967; Hochberg, 1968). Even though motion is a property detected in the feature extraction stage, it is also likely that the perception of motion is highly dependent upon the interaction of successive fixations.

It would appear that whether the icon of one fixation is erased by a subsequent fixation depends on the pattern relationships between the two images as well as on their timing. Smooth, continuous motion is perceived in moving pictures over a range of exposure rates. If the rate is 25 still pictures per second, then the stimulus might be present for 20$\sigma$, the screen dark for the next 20$\sigma$, with 40$\sigma$ separating the initiation of two successive images. The icon of one exposure is not erased by the icon of the next. Rather, the successive icons interact to produce the perception of meaningful motion, a smooth stream built from successive discrete icons initiated 40$\sigma$ apart. At some stage during the 250$\sigma$ required for full development of the icon, an interaction, rather than disruption, occurs, and the result is in part the perception of motion. When the eye moves rapidly over a fixed visual environment, a similar blending must occur to permit the construction of a stable percept. It is possible, of course, that each icon develops relatively unaffected by others and that the integrations of motion and of complex visual images are produced in stages three and four of successive psychological events.

There is a distinct possibility that the native character of stages one and two of visual perception is a special property of that modality. Thus, it might not characterize the initial stages of psychological events that are initiated by external stimuli in other modalities or that are centrally initiated. For example, Haber (1970a, 1970b) believes that there may be a difference between the perceptual processing of pictorial and verbal material. Partly on the basis of a study conducted with Standing (Haber & Standing, 1970), and probably on the basis of his own earlier work on eidetic memory, Haber suggests that pictorial material is received and stored permanently without significant loss of detail. In the 1970 study, Haber and Standing exposed experimental subjects to 2560 pictures with a 10-second inter-exposure interval over either two or four days time. They then tested for recognition of the picutres by presenting pairs in which only one of the pictures had been seen before. Their subjects were able to choose correctly with 85–95% accuracy, depending on the subject. Haber suggests that the results would have been essentially the same if there had been 25,000 pictures rather than 2500. Semantic memory, however, is ordinarily not processed exclusively as a visual image. Words are at least transduced into meanings and ideas before storage.

The studies of stabilized images, such as those of Pritchard, Heron, and Hebb (1960), yield a slightly different value for the duration of a visual image. Since the eye is subject to tremor with periods as low as $1$–$2\sigma$, the icon that develops from a stimulus exposed as long as $10\sigma$ does not develop from a fixed image but rather from multiple placements of the image on the retina. In the stabilized image studies, a tiny projector is fastened to the cornea so that, whenever the eye moves, the image moves accordingly, and the optical image on the retina is truly fixed. Under these conditions, the percept undergoes fluctuations in character after a brief period in which it is a faithful representation of the stimulus. The undistorted percept can be sustained for only a few seconds at most.

Thus, the data on stimulus-induced visual perception establish a development time of approximately $250\sigma$ for the icon. It can be sustained only for a few seconds at most if undisturbed, but under ordinary circumstances it is disturbed by a new fixation and by the development of a subsequent icon. The typical or normal rate of progression has a period of about $300\sigma$, which means that, if a psychological event has four stages occupying a minimum of about

500σ, then there is ordinarily some degree of parallel or simultaneous processing of successive psychological events. If the first two stages of the development of a visual image do in fact constitute the development of an icon in which past experience is not a factor, then these considerations pose a problem for the mechanism of choice between alternative psychological events.

## Time Factors in
## Conditioning and Reaction Time Studies

The classical studies of the optimal CS-UCS interval in human eyeblink conditioning are those of Reynolds (1945) and Kimble (1947). In these studies, the optimal interval for conditioning is reported to be approximately 450σ. These data were employed by Hull (1952) as the basis for his second postulate concerning the rise in intensity of the stimulus process. There are, of course, several reasons why Hull's estimate might not be a good estimate of the rise of the stimulus process alone. The conditioning paridigm involves two stimuli and thus the rise of two stimulus processes rather than one. If we use the data from the development of the icon in visual perception as an analogy, the icons for the two stimuli might each develop in 250σ, and the optimal interstimulus interval could be controlled by the optimum time interval for the interaction of stages three and four for each stimulus. Furthermore, at least one of the stimuli, if not both, produces an overt response with a massive afferent feedback into the system.

In studies of reaction time with two different stimuli and two different responses, the two reaction times appear to be independent if the two stimuli are applied 500σ or more apart. At intervals less than 500σ, the reaction to the second stimulus is delayed; this effect is at a maximum when the interstimulus interval is as short as 50σ. For example, Posner and Boies (1971) found optimum intervals of 500σ both for an alertness condition and in a selectivity situation. In one situation the procedure consisted of a warning signal followed by the exposure of a letter. A second letter was then exposed some time later. The task of the subject was to judge whether the two letters were the same or different. The reaction time was minimal when the interval between the exposure of the two letters was 500σ and was longer when the interval was either shorter or longer than the 500σ optimum. Thus, although the development of the afferent effects of a stimulus might require only 250σ, the development of a complete psychological event with a response component appears to require at least 500σ.

Although the logic of this discussion may seem reasonable enough and the magic number 500σ reasonably magic, there is little question that it is possible to obtain other numbers. For example, even though 450σ does appear to be a stable value for human eyelid conditioning, the optimal CS-UCS interval is subject to considerable modification in response to variation in the stimulus parameters. Snyder and Papsdorf (1968), for example, were able to manipulate the optimal interstimulus interval in rabbit nictitating membrane over a considerable range, both longer and shorter than 450σ.

### Time Factors in Internally Induced Psychological Events

Not all psychological events are the results of external stimuli. In the stream of thought, one event follows another without the necessary intervention of an external stimulus. Whether or not one chooses to regard one event in the stream as the "stimulus" for the next, it seems certain that such "stimuli" do not have the demand characteristics of the flashed optical stimuli of an information processing study or the insistent quality of a puff of air in eyeblink conditioning studies. The essence of the stream of thought is its autonomous character and the freedom of choice exercised among alternative cognitive events.

While one may be free to choose which event to activate in the stream of thought, one has little choice, apparently, in how long to sustain an event in the stream. Pillsbury (1913) summed up data on the span of attention when subjects were asked to voluntarily maintain attention to one thing as long as possible. A duration of approximately 500σ corresponds to the middle of the range identified by Pillsbury, which extended from .1 to 1.0 second. One can attend to the same thing repeatedly but can attend continuously for only about 500σ.

There is some evidence that, in a free choice situation, the duration of a psychological event is maximal at optimal complexity level and is less if the event is either more or less complex than the optimum. Sales (1968) tested this possibility. He devised a box that consisted of a compartment measuring about a foot in each dimension. The box was totally dark when the lid was in place. On one side of the box was a small hole through which a rat was able to stick its head far enough to see what was in the adjacent compartment, in the process breaking a photoelectric cell beam. The photoelectric cell was used to record the behavior of the rat.

The adjacent compartment was arranged with a translucent panel positioned about five inches from the hole at floor level and slanted slightly toward the animal at the top. This panel was back lighted and was replaceable. Stimulus complexity was varied by the use of nine such panels, consisting of checkered patterns and differing in number of elements—two, four, nine, 16, 25, 64, 100, 196, and 256.

Nine groups of 15 rats each (total 135, 108 male and 27 female) were handled extensively and then introduced individually to the box. Ten seconds after introduction, the light was turned on in the adjacent compartment. Each animal was left in the box for a total of eight minutes. Each was tested only once and with a single stimulus. The photocell recorded the frequency of response through the counter and the total duration of responding through a clock that accumulated the amount of time the animal's head was in a position to break the photobeam.

Rats will stick their heads through almost any available hole. In this situation, since they could not see the stimulus without sticking their heads through the hole, the *frequency* of this behavior was unrelated to the stimulus on the other side. As can be seen in Figure 5-1, on the average, each group of 15 rats tended to poke a head through the hole very slightly over once a minute during eight minutes spent in the box.

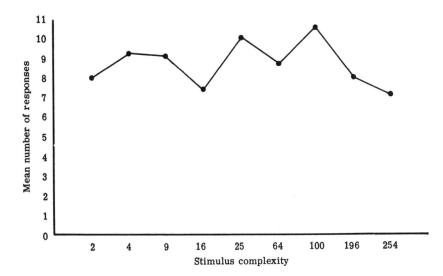

FIGURE 5-1. *Frequency of Response as a Function of Stimulus Complexity. Mean responses in eight-minute periods for nine groups of animals exposed to nine levels of stimulus complexity. (Redrawn from "Stimulus Complexity as a Determinant of Approach Behavior and Inspection Time in the Hooded Rat," by S. M. Sales,* Canadian Journal of Psychology/Review of Canadian Psychology, *1968, 22, 11–17. Reprinted by permission.)*

On the other hand, Figure 5-2 indicates that the *length of time* they kept their heads in the hole and in a position to be exposed to the stimuli did vary with the complexity of the stimuli. On the average, the durations of self-exposure to the stimuli ranged from about 850σ to 1750σ. The animals exposed to the 16-element stimulus looked the longest, and the animals exposed to the two-element stimulus looked for the shortest period of time.

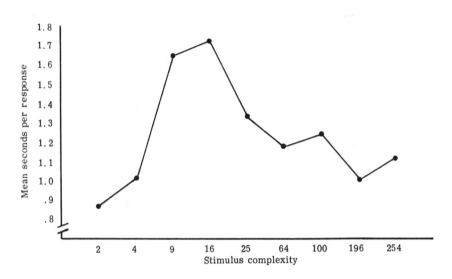

FIGURE 5-2. *Duration of Response as a Function of Stimulus Complexity. Mean response durations for nine groups of animals exposed to nine levels of stimulus complexity. (Redrawn from "Stimulus Complexity as a Determinant of Approach Behavior and Inspection Time in the Hooded Rat," by S. M. Sales,* Canadian Journal of Psychology/Review of Canadian Psychology, *1968, 22, 11-17. Reprinted by permission.)*

In these data, the duration of individual psychological events and the number of fixations (and thus separate psychological events) are confounded. If it were possible to separate the two, either of the two possible outcomes would be of interest for psychological complexity and preference theory. If the durations of fixation are essentially the same in all instances, roughly $450–500\sigma$, then the optimal stimulus requires twice as many fixations to produce a change of stimulation from the lighted to the black compartment as does the simple, two-element stimulus. On the other hand, it is possible that the longer self-exposure to the optimum stimulus is attributable to fixations with sufficiently prolonged durations that the number of fixations is relatively constant regardless of the complexity of the stimulus. Whichever it proves to be, there is no evidence in these data of a monotonically increasing self-exposure as a function of the complexity of the stimulus.

### Time Factors in Neurophysiological Data Relevant to the Psychological Event

Something approximating the magic number $500\sigma$ can show up in neurophysiological data. There is a study by Groves, Lee, and Thompson (1969, reported and interpreted in Thompson, Groves,

Teyler, & Roemer, 1973) that seems to mark off the effects of an interstimulus interval of 500σ or less from one of greater duration. They were studying habituation phenomena utilizing the hindlimb flexion response to weak cutaneous stimuli in the acute spinal cat. They varied the interstimulus interval in a train of 200 stimuli. The intervals were 130, 250, 500, 1000, and 2000σ. The results are plotted in terms of the percent reduction from the initial amplitude of the response with subsequent stimulations of the reflex. They conclude: "There appears to be a discontinuity in the function re-lating habituation to stimulus frequency for stimulus rates faster than about 1 per sec., at least in certain systems." Each of the five habituation curves appears to be approaching an asymptote. From visual examination of the curves, it appears that the curves for inter-stimulus intervals of 500, 1000, and 2000σ do not vary significantly from an expected asymptote of 50% of the control (initial) values, although the curve for 1000σ could be coming to a slightly higher asymptote. The curve for an interstimulus interval of 250σ appears to be asymptotic at about 45% of the control value, and the curve for an interstimulus interval of 130σ is clearly becoming asymptotic at a value near to 25% of the initial value of the response. It is difficult to determine from these data at precisely what interval the discontinuity begins. However, it is clear that, when the same stim-ulus is applied repeatedly at intervals as short as 250σ, there is a cumulative effect beyond that which occurs at the longer intervals. That the critical interval is somewhere in the range of 450–500σ does not seem unreasonable.

## A QUANTITATIVE MODEL FOR
## THE INTENSITY AND TEMPORAL
## CHARACTERISTICS OF PSYCHOLOGICAL EVENTS

There is sufficient agreement among this set of descriptions of the time and intensity characteristics of the occurrence of a single psychological event that a model time and intensity function can be drawn. Figure 5-3 represents such an attempt. The drawing is modeled after one in Hull (1952) mentioned previously and is based on the eyelid conditioning data of Reynolds (1945) and Kimble (1947). If the particular psychological event is induced by an external stimulus, it could rise to any level of intensity with respect to the optimal complexity level, but I have arbitrarily pic-tured the state of affairs one would expect if the event in question was one selected by the organism and one that rose precisely to optimal complexity level.

The neural substrate for the event has a resting level that serves as an intensity base. The initiation of the event consists of a rather rapid rise in intensity to a maximum, followed by an abrupt, in-

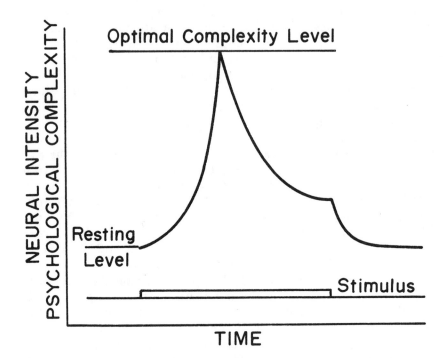

FIGURE 5-3. *Time Course of a Single Psychological Event—A Quantitative Model for the Intensity and Temporal Characteristics of a Psychological Event*

evitable, and automatic fall to a very low level. These two temporal characteristics are indicated in the figure. If the stimulus is continued, the level to which the activity will drop will be above the resting level. When the stimulus is terminated, there will be a return to the resting level under most circumstances.

The figure shows a rising phase and two decay phases. They have sufficient regularity and consistency in time and form to induce attempts to specify their mathematical form. For example, in Hull's second postulate on the molar stimulus trace (1952, p. 11), he arrives at a power function that has the following general form:

*Molar stimulus trace equation:*

$C\psi = m \times t^c$, where
$C\psi$ = psychological complexity (by our definition),
$m,c$ = c̄onstants, and
$t$    = time.

Hull's empirical equation reaches a "maximum and termination" at approximately $450\sigma$. Hull also describes the decay function in the continued presence of the stimulus as a power function of the following general form:

*Stimulus trace decay equation:*

$C\psi$ = $m (t' + j)^{-b}$, where
$C\psi$ = psychological complexity,
$m, j, b$ = constants, and
$t'$ = $t - 450\sigma$ ($t$ from the previous equation).

The power function describing the decay in neural intensity and psychological complexity, even when the stimulus that induced it continues to be present, is probably very similar to the decay function that obtains when the stimulus is removed.

Although these equations are essentially arbitrary, being neither theoretical nor precisely empirical, they do provide something more structured than the verbal descriptions employed so far. As such, they suggest a large number of testable propositions, some of which will be noted here and elsewhere.

For example, the Hullian version used as a base for these equations specifies the maximum of intensity at $450\sigma$. If I have interpreted the data on the development of the visual icon correctly, the maximum in that case is reached in $250\sigma$ in the light-adapted eye. However, when the persistence of the icon is examined in the dark-adapted eye, the duration extends to $400\sigma$ or as much as $450\sigma$ (Haber, 1971). By examining the curve or the equation, it is not difficult to see how the time to maximum intensity might be extended or reduced. If the resting level is lowered, then the time to rise to a maximum could be extended markedly. On the other hand, with no change in resting level, but with the application of a stimulus inducing a reaction much above optimal level, it would seem likely that the time to reach maximum would not be increased appreciably even with very intense stimuli.

On the other hand, since the intensity of the event would determine the asymptote of the decay curve while the stimulus continues to be present, the intensity of the event could play a role in the resistance of one event against supplantation by another, as in the reaction time studies. That is, if there are some central elements common to the two reactions, it might be possible that the more intense the first, the longer the delay in the second reaction time.

The shape of the hypothetical curve in Figure 5-3 invites speculation concerning the nature of the neural mechanism underlying the rise and decline in intensity of the event. The rapid rise to a maximum would appear to reflect excitatory recruitment. The time involved, of the order of 250 to $450\sigma$, would suggest a variety of pathways varying in the degree of directness and the number of synapses involved, and thus in the amount of time involved in bringing their effects to bear at the effector end of the system or at the recording site. As I will discuss in more detail later, Thompson and Groves (see Thompson, Groves, Teyler, & Roemer, 1973; Groves & Thompson, 1973) distinguish between direct S-R pathways and state pathways, which are assumed to have the essential characteristics to accomplish the recruitment necessary to produce the rising phase of the curve. It seems reasonable to assume that the mechanisms required to account for the curve would be the same or very similar to the mechanisms required to account for habituation phenomena, which will be discussed in Chapter 6.

The decline in intensity of the psychological event, even while the stimulus continues to be applied, could be accounted for, as might habituation phenomena, on the basis of either or both of two possible synaptic control mechanisms. The decline in intensity could be the result of the depletion of the excitatory transmitter substance in the synapse or of the involvement of inhibitory effects from specialized inhibitory fibers extrinsic to the synapse.

Without careful experimental analysis, one would have to expect the answer to be that both mechanisms would be involved in determining the shape of the function in the figure. The abrupt damping effect as the curve reaches a maximum and begins its precipitous decline would seem to require a massive inhibitory effect with a precisely timed arrival that could only be accomplished by specific inhibitory fibers or endings, the effects of which are delayed by extensive neural and synaptic transmission delays. There seems little question that depletion of the excitatory transmitter substance is also involved. For example, since the persistence of the visual icon appears to grow progressively shorter as the duration of the stimulus is increased from 250 to $1000\sigma$, representing a shortening of the period of the second decline phase after the stimulus is removed in Figure 5-3, the effect has the appearance of exhausted transmitter substance.

### SUMMARY

The stream of psychological events appears to be continuous, but the underlying processes are discontinuous. Even when triggered by a very brief stimulus, an event appears to have a rise time of about $250\sigma$ and a declining phase of similar length, giving rise to the magic number $500\sigma$. Although other values are possible within limits, the magic number appears to hold with remarkable consistency in stimulus-induced events such as the development of the visual image, in conditioning and reaction time studies, and in voluntary events such as the span of attention in humans and looking time in rats. The magic number appears to hold as well in neurophysiological data in which there is a reasonable assumption that the rapid rise in intensity of the event is a product of an increasing number of units becoming involved as additional time permits the involvement of more and more indirect pathways. The precipitous decline of the event appears to require inhibitory units inherent in the neural system underlying the event and with a substantial delay of influence. The most predictable characteristic of organismic behavior is that psychological events develop quickly, endure briefly, terminate quickly, automatically, and inevitably, and are succeeded by different psychological events.

# chapter six

# Temporary effects of occurrence of psychological events

In the Hedgehog there is an intimate and integrated relation between the characteristics of the psychological event during its occurrence and the aftereffects of its occurrence, both temporary and semipermanent. Perhaps the most consistent pattern in the stream of psychological events is a negative bias against repetition of a freely chosen event. The pattern has many names. In overt choice behavior it can be referred to under the name of alternation phenomena; in the games of chance it is sometimes called the gambler's fallacy. The phenomenon is so pervasive that it must reflect a basic organismic mechanism. The major effect of the operation of this mechanism is to produce behavior that is much more varied than would otherwise be the case. However, there are also circumstances in which the occurrence of a psychological event has the opposite effect—namely, an increase in the tendency for that event to occur. Both of these effects may be temporary or relatively permanent. In this chapter, I attempt to analyze the temporary effects of the occurrence of psychological events.

## HABITUATION AND SENSITIZATION AS DISTINGUISHED FROM LEARNING

Many of the effects to be discussed in this chapter are usually called *habituation effects*. The term *habituation* refers to a decrement in one or more response characteristics when the same stimulus is used to elicit the same response repeatedly over a short period of time. The number of phenomena that have been studied under this rubric is large, and the problems they raise are complicated. A great many such effects have been reviewed by Jane Mackworth (1969) in a short book; an even broader review that only partly overlaps Mackworth's book has been published in two large volumes edited by Peeke and Herz (1973). Let me undertake to explore some of the phenomena associated with the term *habituation* as translated into the terms of psychological complexity and preference theory.

As indicated earlier, only two kinds of change can occur within the theory. A psychological event may undergo *simplification,* or it may undergo *complication.* Such changes may be essentially *temporary,* or they may be *semipermanent.* If a change under repeated occurrence is in the direction of simplification and is temporary in character, I will refer to the process involved as *habituation.* If the change with repeated occurrence is in the direction of complication and is temporary in character, I will refer to the process as *sensitization.* If a change in either direction, simplification or complication, proves to be semipermanent in character, I will refer to the process involved as *learning.* Thus:

| *Direction of Effect of Repeated Elicitations* | *Duration* | *Process* |
|---|---|---|
| Simplification | Temporary | Habituation |
| Complication | Temporary | Sensitization |
| Simplification | Semipermanent | Learning |
| Complication | Semipermanent | Learning |

It should be noted that the distinction between habituation and sensitization is very similar but not identical to a distinction made in Groves and Thompson (1970, 1973) and in Thompson, Groves, Teyler, and Roemer (1973). Although their concept of habituation is essentially identical to the one I will employ, I have chosen a slightly different meaning for the term *sensitization.* I will use the term to describe the process of an *increase* in the intensity, and thus the complexity, of a psychological event. As I will discuss in more detail later, they use the term to describe a process that may first increase and then undergo a decrease.

## DIRECTION OF EFFECTS OF REPEATED OCCURRENCE OF PSYCHOLOGICAL EVENTS

The need to distinguish between the conditions that produce the processes of habituation and sensitization is self-evident in that the operations for the two effects are the same even though the effects are different and opposite in direction. In fact, repeated occurrence of the same psychological event may have three different effects. There are circumstances in which there appears to be no significant change in the character of the response, circumstances in which the amplitude of the response may increase, and circumstances in which the amplitude of the response may decrease.

## No Change in Response with Repeated Occurrence

Some organismic responses do not appear to undergo changes—either habituation or sensitization—with repeated elicitations. Sparrows are reported not to habituate to an owl or to a model of an owl, even in hand-reared specimens (Nice & Pelkwyk, 1941). Dewsbury (1966, reported in more detail in Walker, 1969b) made extraordinary efforts to induce a decrease in the frequency of the electrical response of the weak electric knife fish *gymnotus carapo* to several stimuli, including the introduction of a metallic object into the water. Intense massing of the stimulus failed to produce any decrement in the response and thus any evidence of habituation. Nor was there an increase in the response, reflecting sensitization.

From a biological standpoint, it seems reasonable that responses to certain kinds of stimuli in some organisms might not show either the more usual decrement, reflecting habituation, or the increment, reflecting sensitization. In the sparrow, habituation to the stimulus of an owl would leave the organism vulnerable to the "cry wolf" tactic. An owl would only have to flush the same sparrow repeatedly until the sparrow's flight response habituated, at which point the owl could strike with assurance that the reduced response of the sparrow would be too sluggish to effect escape. Although not all the functional uses of the electrical output of the weak electric knife fish have been explored, the fish is nocturnal and frequently lives in muddy water. Its output frequency drops during an apparent resting phase and increases markedly in response to external stimuli. Since it not only has the capacity to transmit electrical pulses of variable frequency but has receivers in the lateral line organs for detecting such stimuli, it seems likely that this sensory system is the primary source of information concerning the environment. Under such conditions, each stimulus application might require treatment as a "new" stimulus to ensure survival.

On a neurophysiological level, there is considerable evidence that some areas of the brain do not exhibit significant changes in output under continued stimulation. It is a common finding that self-stimulation in so-called "reward" centers frequently shows an absence of habituation. In a study by Wester (1971, reported in Thompson, Groves, Teyler, & Roemer, 1973), the head turning response elicited by stimulation in certain intralaminar nuclei in the cat proved highly resistant to habituation. Furthermore, in their studies of the flexion reflex in the acute spinal cat, Groves and Thompson (1973) found individual cells (Type N neurons) that do not undergo any change in output with repeated stimulation.

## Response Increment with Repeated Stimulation

The intensities of some responses increase or potentiate, at least through a number of repetitions. In most instances the incremental phase is followed by a decremental phase. Perhaps one of the most obvious examples is the primary sexual response, which appears to increase or to undergo potentiation through a number of stimulus-induced events until orgasm is reached, after which there is a decrement in the intensity that results from further stimulation.

On the gross behavioral level, a number of experimental examples might be cited. Among those mentioned by Thompson, Groves, Teyler, and Roemer (1973) is a rise and fall in human GSR to repeated application of intense tones (Raskin, Kotses, & Bever, 1969; see Figure 6-4). There is also a study by Peeke (1969) of the aggressive striking behavior of the three-spined stickleback to conspecifics and models of conspecifics. Testing of the stickleback was at one-minute intervals, with 15 tests per day on four different days. Although aggressive behavior was much more frequently displayed toward live conspecifics than it was to the models, the pattern of responding to each within and between days was essentially the same. On the first day, the frequency of aggressive striking behavior increased markedly in response to the first few stimulations and then showed a decline over the last few. An initial increase was also observed on the second day but was less marked. On the third and fourth days, only a decrement in response was observed.

A response increment from repeated stimulation can accumulate over much longer periods of time. For example, there is a study by Franzisket (1963) of the wiping response made by spinal frogs when their nostrils are stroked every ten seconds. The data are reported in terms of the frequency of the response during daily sessions of perhaps 100 stimulations per day over 12 days. The frequency of responding increased markedly from 8 and 12 responses on the first two days to a range from 70 to 81 on days 9 through 12. Very similar results were obtained by Kimble and Ray (1965) in the intact frog. However, Kimble and Ray found an increment only when they stimulated slightly different areas around the nostrils and found a progressive decrement when they stimulated the same place repeatedly.

Examples with less intact organisms can also be cited. In the previously cited study of the head turning response in cats, Wester (1971) also found intralaminar sites that exhibited potentiation to repeated stimulation. Thompson, Groves, Teyler, and Roemer (1973) report potentiation of the hindlimb flexion response in the acute spinal cat.

It might also be noted that, in studies of self-stimulation for intracranial reward, it is usually necessary to "prime" the animal to initiate self-stimulation. Thus, the experimenter appears to "sensitize" the stimulation before it can achieve a self-maintenance level.

At the single cell level, Groves and Thompson (1973) report finding a number of what they refer to as Type S (sensitization) neurons in the spinal cord of the cat. Of the 77 such neurons from which they obtained records, 23 showed an initial increase that was then maintained or that did not return to the initial level. The remaining 54 showed the initial increase followed by a progressive decrease below the initial level. Type S neurons are described as having relatively long latencies with a range from 6 to 180$\sigma$, and they had firing patterns of either one or a few discharges or a long train of discharges.

Thus, increases in the intensity or frequency of responses have been observed under certain circumstances in the intact organism, in neurophysiological preparations, and at the single cell level. Although such a response pattern is not typical, neither is it rare.

### Response Decrement with Repeated Stimulation

The typical effect of repeated activations of psychological events is a decrement in some manifestation of the intensity or complexity of the event. Jane Mackworth (1969) has compiled almost a catalogue of responses that show an orderly reduction with repeated activations. She lists evidence of habituation in such diverse tasks as attentional deployment, psychomotor tracking tasks, mental tracking tasks, motion aftereffects, reaction time, and a rather large group of sensory thresholds, including those for auditory pitch and loudness and varieties of visual acuity and brightness. Nearly every dependent variable one can think of has been shown to undergo response decrement with repeated activation. Mackworth's catalogue is thorough with respect to human performance variables.

Eisenstein and Peretz (1973) catalogue a variety of studies showing habituation in intact or neurophysiological preparations ranging from the mammal to protozoa. They detail nine different parameters of response decrement and whether or not they have been demonstrated in each preparation. The whole two-volume set by Peeke and Herz (1973) is replete with instances of response decrement in subsystems of the central nervous system, especially in the chapter by Graham (1973).

At the single cell level, Groves and Thompson report finding 79 cells in the spinal cord of the cat that show decremental characteristics to repeated stimulation. These cells have comparatively short onset latencies (5 to 12.5$\sigma$) to cutaneous shock. The firing pattern of these cells is reported to be invariably a high frequency burst of discharges. Groves and Thompson refer to these as Type H (habituation) cells.

They also report finding two cells they label "unclassified." An alternate label for these cells might be H-S cells. The description given by Groves and Thompson is as follows:

> It exhibited an early discharge, which according to latency and firing pattern criteria could be classified as a type H pattern. It also, however, exhibited a late discharge that appeared only when the stimulus rate was increased from the control rate (1 per 15 seconds) to the normal experimental rate (2 per second). This late discharge, unlike the early burst of discharges, showed only sensitization.

Thus, sensitization had the form of rising rapidly and then slowly returning to baseline.

### THE GROVES AND THOMPSON THEORY OF HABITUATION AND SENSITIZATION

Theory sometimes serves to produce simplicity in the face of complexity. (The formulation of theory is thus a manifestation of psychological complexity and preference theory itself.) Groves and Thompson (1970) have proposed a simple theory to account for the complex effects of occurrences of psychological events. It is a truly elegant theory in attempting to account for essentially all the phenomena related to the temporary aftereffects of repeated occurrences of psychological events on the basis of three simple dichotomies: between *habituation* and *sensitization* processes, between *S-R* and *state* pathways, and between *Type H* and *Type S* neurons.

#### Habituation and Sensitization

Figure 6-1 is an idealized account of how Groves and Thompson would undertake to account for one possible result of repeated activation of a psychological event. What is pictured is a solid line curve representing an event that first increases and then decreases in amplitude. *Habituation* is defined as a process that decreases in output under continued activation with a reasonably short interstimulus interval. *Sensitization* is defined as a process that may rise to an asymptote, may rise and fall back to the initial level (as drawn in the figure), or may rise and fall below the initial level. The amplitude of the response is the result of the interaction of the two processes.

Since the operation that can produce a decrease in response characteristics can also produce an increase in the same response characteristics, the independence of the two processes requires the demonstration that, when sensitization does occur, the two processes behave differently in response to significant experimental variables. Some of the differences between the two processes are the

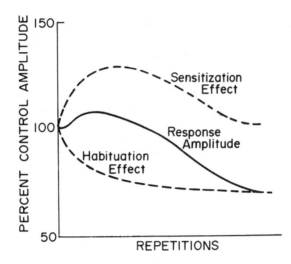

FIGURE 6-1. Interaction of Sensitization and Habituation. Idealized curves illustrate the interaction between the processes of habituation and sensitization in producing changes in response amplitude during repeated, closely spaced elicitations of a psychological event.

following. There are many circumstances in which only habituation appears to be operating. In these circumstances there is general agreement that the shape of the curve relating response characteristics to the number of elicitations is a decreasing negative exponential or a very similar logarithmic or power function. Sensitization, on the other hand, has an effect opposite in direction from that of habituation; the most frequent pattern is a rise and then fall in amount. The two processes respond differently to variation in interstimulus interval. At very long intervals, neither process appears to be involved. At shorter intervals, habituation will occur; the shorter the interval, the faster the rate of change and the greater the amount of decrease. On the other hand, at high stimulus intensities, sensitization may occur, but probably only at interstimulus intervals shorter than those necessary for habituation. Furthermore, as the interstimulus interval is shortened still further, the rate of increase grows progressively faster, and the amount of the increase becomes greater. Finally, if sessions are repeated with a significant time interval between sessions, habituation tends to occur faster and in greater amount in successive sessions, while sensitization tends to decrease in rate and amount, and its effects may tend to disappear altogether. There seems little doubt that, on the basis of these and other differences, Groves and Thompson are justified in distinguishing two processes, habituation and sensitization.

## S-R versus State Pathways

Groves and Thompson argue that every stimulus that evokes a behavioral response has two properties: (1) it elicits a response, and (2) it influences the state of the organism. However circuitous, redundant, and variable the S-R pathway may be, it is the most direct route through the central nervous system from stimulus to discrete motor response, regardless of whether the response is learned or unlearned. The state of the organism is its general level of excitation, arousal, activation, tendency to respond, and so on. It is mediated by a collection of pathways, systems, and regions that determine the general level of responsiveness of the organism.

In the Groves and Thompson model, the S-R pathway contains only N (nonplastic) and H (habituating) neurons, while the state system contains S (sensitizing) neurons and probably N and H types of neurons as well.

## THE HEDGEHOG ACCOUNT OF THE TEMPORARY EFFECTS OF REPEATED ACTIVATION OF PSYCHOLOGICAL EVENTS

I have detailed the Groves and Thompson account of the effects of repeated activation of psychological events because the Hedgehog version is very similar and is based, in part, on the developing Groves and Thompson theory. The essential ways in which the two accounts differ are these. First, the Hedgehog account is somewhat more general in that an effort is made to rely on continuous processes rather than dichotomies. Second, an effort will be made to tie the processes underlying a single occurrence of a psychological event to the effects of repeated activations. Third, in the Hedgehog, when "sensitization" is invoked to explain an effect, the process is one that can only *increase* the intensity and thus the complexity of the event; the event cannot, as in Groves and Thompson, show first a rise and then a fall in intensity.

### Simplification (Habituation)

In the Hedgehog, *habituation* is the term applied to the progressive simplification of a psychological event that occurs during repeated and closely spaced activation. Furthermore, for the effect to be purely one of habituation, it must dissipate with time. If there is any residual effect of repeated activations, then, by definition, learning has also occurred.

One of the many possible diagrams that could be drawn to detail some of the parameters of habituation is shown in Figure 6-2. In this particular diagram, an effort has been made to portray a possible course of events if the psychological event in Figure 5-3 (p. 66) were

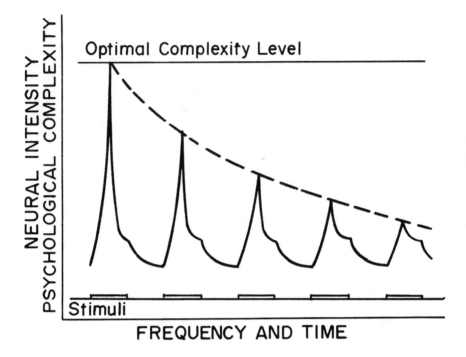

*FIGURE 6-2. Habituation of a Psychological Event*

activated five times with stimulus durations and interstimulus intervals each of 500σ. Although preference will not be considered in detail until later on, it should be noted that, if the event is of optimal intensity/complexity level when first activated, the effect of habituation will be to produce events that recede rapidly from optimal complexity level.

There is general agreement that both behavioral and neurophysiological habituation data become approximately linear when plotted on log paper, or when plotted against the square root of time, and are easily fit with a simple exponential equation. The following is exponential equation that can be used to fit a pure habituation curve (the broken line in Figure 6-2).

*Simplification equation:*

$C\psi = kC_u (10^{-aN}) + C_u$, where
$C\psi$ = psychological complexity (intensity),
$k$   = constant,
$C_u$ = ultimate complexity (unreducible complexity),
$a$   = constant of complexity reduction (rate), and
$N$   = number of elicitations of the event.

This equation will also be used in Chapter 7 to describe the common semipermanent effects of repeated activations of psychological events, or learning. For the moment, however, let us confine our consideration to the relation of certain parameters of habituation to parameters of the equation.

Figure 6-2 is drawn to reflect a situation in which the neural activity associated with individual events has ceased (returned to baseline) before the subsequent event is activated. The habituation process portrayed by the broken line is therefore one that is not dependent on the interaction of active neural processes. Rather, the habituation process portrayed should reflect changes in the synapse itself, probably a depletion of the excitatory transmitter substance. Groves and Thompson (1973) make a careful, extensive, and convincing argument that "pure" habituation cannot be attributed exclusively to extrinsic inhibition, on either side of the synapse. They cite evidence that, at least in certain preparations, habituation is specifically related to presynaptic depression. Their argument does not deny a functional role for extrinsic inhibition in the total complex of processes diagrammed in Figure 6-2, but they do make a strong case for enduring synaptic depression.

It will be recalled that H neurons are assumed to lie in the most direct S-R pathway and that these neurons have a very short onset latency, of the order of 5 to $12.5\sigma$. Consequently, along with one or more N-type neurons, neurons that show habituation would be the first involved and would therefore have a primary influence on the parameters of the rising phase of the developing psychological event. Since habituation is one form of the effects of experience, the short latency of these plastic neurons means that the effects of experience (whether habituation or learning) can become operative in the first few milliseconds of a potential psychological event. It is important that this be true if one is to be able to develop a neural mechanism for choice behavior that does not involve full development of all alternative events before a choice can be made between them.

It is also important to note that, in the studies of visual information processing cited in Chapter 5, it was asserted that the first two stages—the feature detection and the icon formation stages—did not involve any effect of past experience. It follows from this claim that psychological events initiated by an optical pattern on the retina cannot be subject to a choice decision prior to full initiation, a condition that does not seem entirely unreasonable. On the other hand, it also follows that the development of an icon under repeated, closely spaced activations is not subject to habituation, a condition that does not seem so reasonable.

The fact that the short-latency, plastic, H-type neurons are among the first neurons involved in the initiation of a psychological event further implies that the excitatory capacity of these early elements in the chain of neurons involved in a psychological event is the major determinant of the value of $m$ in the molar stimulus trace equation, $m \times t^C$, given in Chapter 5. Suppression in these synapses would produce smaller values of $m$ and would therefore control the height to which the curve would rise on any given elicitation of the event.

Habituation phenomena are, by definition, time-bound phenomena. Learning phenomena, to all intents and purposes, are not. The habituation equation was written without involving $t$, for time, to show its identity with the learning equation to be discussed in Chapter 7. Let us make the assumption that the value of $m$ in the molar stimulus trace equation reflects the initial intensity value for a reaction, and the ultimate asymptote. Further, let us assume that the rate of change with repeated activations is essentially independent of intensity. In that case, the appropriate value of $t$ can be involved in the habituation equation by substituting $m \times t^C$ for $C_u$, the asymptotic value of psychological complexity (and thus intensity).

### Complication (Sensitization)

The broken-line curve in Figure 6-2 shows only a simplification (habituation) effect, and its regularity depends upon a fixed value for the asymptote ($C_u$). Thus, the "habituation" portion of the Groves and Thompson theory portrayed in Figure 6-1 involves a fixed asymptotic value. Within the Hedgehog, any operation resulting in a departure from the exponential simplification curve must involve a change in the asymptote of the curve and thus the value of $C_u$. Therefore, "sensitization" must involve a basic change in the complexity of the psychological event being manipulated. The many ways in which the value of $C_u$ can be modified defies simple mathematical representation. However, most experimental parameters yield fairly clear expectations of both the direction and the amount of change to be expected in the asymptotic value.

### Spontaneous Recovery

It is generally agreed that psychological events that have undergone a decrement under repeated activations show spontaneous recovery with the passage of a significant period of time. Ratner (1970) reviews a number of studies showing that the durations of decremental effects vary quite widely. He cites some reports in which the decremental effects appear to have dissipated in six to 24 hours, but he also cites a number in which decremental effects have persisted for at least a week in such varied responses as rotational nystagmus in cats and dogs (Collins & Updegraff, 1966), a rat's approach response in a maze (Denny & Leckart, 1965), and the orientation components of a bird's reaction to predators (Hinde, 1960). There is some difficulty associated with the interpretation of such nonparametric data. If the response does show eventual full recovery, then the effect is a temporary one. If full recovery does not occur, then it is a learning effect possibly governed by variables other than those controlling temporary effects. The long period during which some responses show persistence of temporary effects (if that is the interpretation) suggests that such persistence is a process somewhat more complicated than that of a simple restoration of depleted excitatory substance at the relevant synapses. Such a metabolic restoration function might well be expected to show a simple exponential decay.

Ratner (1970) reports a study carried out by one of his graduate students (VanDeventer, 1967) in which four retention intervals were tested. Figure 6-3 shows VanDeventer's data on the percent recovery of the original contractile response to tactile stimulation in planaria over a period of 96 hours. It is clear from the figure that full recovery had not occurred in 96 hours. From the apparent shape of the curve, it also seems likely that (a) full recovery might be expected after the passage of a sufficient additional interval, and (b) the shape of the curve is not a simple exponential decay function. Rather,

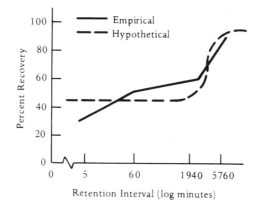

FIGURE 6-3. *Spontaneous Recovery. The empirical data (solid line) are taken from VanDeventer (1967) as reported in Ratner (1970). The four retention intervals are repositioned from Ratner to indicate appropriate spacing on a scale of log-time. The hypothetical curve (broken line) is almost entirely fictitious, but it has some function in an account of certain time and intensity factors in the effects of repeated activations of psychological events. (Redrawn from "Habituation: Research and Theory," by S. C. Ratner. In J. H. Reynierse (Ed.),* Current Issues in Animal Learning. *Copyright 1970 by the University of Nebraska Press. Reprinted by permission.)*

this recovery function appears to show a possible flat effect in the middle retention intervals that is not entirely eliminated by plotting the recovery function on a log-time scale, as I have done here.

Although it is not entirely justified on the basis of the data presented here, let us make a simplifying assumption. Let us assume that the usual course of spontaneous recovery from the temporary effects of repeated activations of psychological events is sustained without major change in value over a variable length of time, after which recovery begins to occur and then proceeds at a reasonably rapid pace. Direct evidence for such a pattern in the recovery from temporary effects of elicitation is minimal. However, indirect evidence will be indicated subsequently (see Figure 6-20).

### Simplification and Complication in Temporary Effects of Occurrence of Psychological Events

Let us examine a number of the experimental parameters of repeated activations of the same (and slightly different) psychological events in the light of the Hedgehog theory that (a) simplification (habituation) is a temporary decremental effect of activation and (b) complication is the only variable necessary to account for any other result (barring sudden reorganization of the event, as when insight occurs during problem solving).

*Stimulus Number and Interstimulus Interval.* At least three ranges of interstimulus interval can be identified in which the effects of repeated elicitations of the psychological event can be expected to differ. The first is the period of continued neural activity in the ongoing event, the second is the period after neural activity has ceased in the system but during which the synaptic suppression persists, and the third is the period after recovery from the temporary suppression produced by the prior activations.

The period of continued neural activity comprising the occurrence of a single psychological event is portrayed in Figures 5-3 and 6-2. Although the duration of this active phase might be expected to vary over a wide range of time periods, an argument was made earlier that under many circumstances the event endured for a period of $500\sigma$. This estimate was made primarily on the basis of a variety of behavioral data.

Groves and Thompson (1973) provide two general ways of classifying types of neurons. The first classification is described as follows:

> Interneurons that respond to the cutaneous stimulus can be classified into three broad categories of firing pattern in agreement with those reported by Frank and Fuortes (1956) and by Wall (1959): (1) those responding to the cutaneous stimulus with a short latency, high frequency

burst; (2) those responding with one or several discharges at a longer latency; and (3) those exhibiting a prolonged train of discharges usually with a longer latency [p. 178].

The second classification was in terms of neuron types N, H, S, and one that might be labeled H-S. Aside from whether these neurons show habituation, sensitization, both, or neither, they vary widely in the temporal and frequency characteristics of their firing patterns. They vary in latency from 5 to $180\sigma$, and they also vary widely in burst duration from as short as 20 to as long as $500\sigma$, judging from the oscilloscope tracings provided by Groves and Thompson. It is not necessary to deny the existence of types of neurons to imagine combinations of neurons with differing firing characteristics that could produce the pattern depicted in Figures 5-3 and 6-2.

Interstimulus interval might therefore be expected to have a different effect when it occurs between 0 and $250\sigma$, and thus on the rising phase of the development of the psychological event, from that which it has when it occurs between 250 and $500\sigma$, in the declining phase of the psychological event.

From the data on the development of the visual icon, we know that stimulus duration during the first $250\sigma$ appears to have little effect on the development of the icon. Rather, the stimulus appears to act as a trigger at onset. If a different stimulus is applied during this period, it appears to act as an eraser. If the same stimulus is applied repeatedly during the $250\sigma$ development period, it is quite possible that the character as well as the intensity of the psychological event will be modified. It will be recalled that the neurons Groves and Thompson identify as H-type (habituation) have a very short firing latency, of the order of 5 to $12.5\sigma$. Thus, if a minimum of one additional stimulus is applied during the first $250\sigma$ after the application of the first stimulus, the activation of H-type neurons could very well affect the development phase of the event and actually prevent the full development of the event that might have occurred without the intervening stimulus. With an interstimulus interval of $130\sigma$, for example, H-type neurons could function to prevent the full development of the event in addition to producing longer-term habituation effects. In Figures 5-3 and 6-2, such an immediate, short-term effect could cut off the rising phase approximately halfway through its course. The data previously cited from Groves, Lee, and Thompson (1969), on the habituation of the hind-limb flexion reflex in the acute spinal cat with various interstimulus intervals, can be interpreted to show precisely this effect. In interpreting their results, they suggest that there is a discontinuity in rate and amount of habituation for interstimulus intervals of one second and above in comparison with shorter interstimulus intervals. A case can be made from their data for a discontinuity at an interstimulus interval below 250$\sigma$. They present five curves representing the results with interstimulus intervals of two seconds, one second, 500$\sigma$, 250$\sigma$, and 130$\sigma$. Each curve is plotted as a percentage of the control amplitude. I have undertaken a crude estimation of the asymptotes to which each of these curves appears to be progressing. Beginning with the longest interstimulus interval, these estimates are 50%, 57%, 49%, and 45% through 250$\sigma$. The apparent asymptote for the 130$\sigma$ interval appears to be no greater than 25%, or approximately half the level of the other four intervals. Although this analysis does not establish a dual effect of habituating neurons at intervals shorter than 250$\sigma$, such an interpretation appears quite reasonable.

To the extent that this speculation is reasonable, it gives rise to some fairly powerful theoretical predictions concerning the relation between effects of interstimulus intervals between 0 and 250$\sigma$. Given the shape of the stimulus trace function ($m \times t^c$), and given the condition that the value of $m$ determines the height of intensity/ complexity to which the psychological event rises, the precise proportion of the decrement to be expected from this second effect of habituation should be predictable. For example, an increase from 10 to 20$\sigma$ in interstimulus interval should have a smaller effect on the asymptote of the habituation curve than an increase from 200 to 210$\sigma$. The interval between 1 and 12.5$\sigma$ should be highly ambiguous in effect because of the question of whether the second effect of habituation would be brought to bear or not. If the rate of change in the simplification curve is controlled by the exponent in the equation and is the same for all simplification curves, then the discontinuity involved in interstimulus intervals shorter than 250$\sigma$ should be located between the control point on the habituation curve and all others resulting from repeated activations. Specifically, the control level point should be above a habituation curve projected back to this point, since the second effect of habituation should be completely apparent on the first experimental point involving this interstimulus interval.

If one undertakes a judgment concerning the effects of an interstimulus interval between 250 and 500$\sigma$ from these same data, one would have to conclude that no profound effects occurred at these intervals that did not also occur at longer intervals. This conclusion would coincide with the finding that visual noise does not "erase" the visual icon if it is applied as much as 250$\sigma$ after the application of the initiating stimulus.

Once the active phase of a psychological event is terminated, the relation of the number of activations and the interstimulus interval to the course of habituation would depend on the nature of the spontaneous recovery function. In Figure 6-3, the hypothetical recovery function does not change over a period of 12 or more hours. It then begins a recovery period that appears rapid when plotted on a log scale but would appear quite gradual if plotted on a linear scale. If this hypothetical function accurately describes the course of the recovery function, intertrial intervals between $250\sigma$ and some very long period, such as 12 hours, should not show differences in the asymptotes of relevant habituation or simplification curves. There should be no differences in the amount of recovery during the interstimulus intervals. On the other hand, if different interstimulus intervals result in different asymptotic values for habituation curves, the recovery function must have some other form.

The data presented by Thompson, Groves, Teyler, and Roemer (1973) are contradictory in this respect. I have already cited the study by Groves, Lee, and Thompson (1969), which I interpreted as not showing significantly different asymptotes for interstimulus intervals of $250\sigma$, $500\sigma$, $1000\sigma$, and $2000\sigma$. Thompson and colleagues also cite a study by Thompson and Spencer (1966) in which interstimulus intervals of $1000\sigma$ and $3200\sigma$ appear very similar when plotted against N. This study involved the hindlimb flexor reflex in an acute spinal cat. They also report a study by Farel (1973) of habituation in the flexion reflex of a spinal frog in which no differences are apparent with interstimulus intervals from 30 seconds to 10 minutes. These data all tend to support the rather unlikely flat hypothetical function plotted in Figure 6-3.

The same article, however, cites a study by Farel and Thompson (1973) in which very clear effects of interstimulus intervals, within the same range I have been discussing, appear in the asymptotes of the habituation curves. The preparation in this instance involved the ventral root response to dorsal root stimulation in the isolated frog spinal cord. With an interstimulus interval of two seconds, the asymptote appears to be no more than 55% of the control response level. When the interstimulus interval is five seconds, the asymptote appears to be of the order of 75%; with an interstimulus interval of ten seconds, the asymptote appears to be about 85% of the control value. Because of normal variability in the plotted results, these estimates of the asymptotic level are quite uncertain, and they cannot be distinguished from a straight line when plotted against log-time. If the plot is truly a straight line, then in this instance no "holding pattern" such as that drawn in Figure 6-3 appears to be operating, and spontaneous recovery from habituation appears to be proceeding in a negative exponential course.

For the moment, at least, the possibility must be admitted that there are at least two spontaneous recovery functions: one that recovers exponentially and for which the interstimulus interval does function to control the asymptotic value of the habituation function, and a quite different "holding pattern" of spontaneous recovery in which the interstimulus interval can be varied over a wide range without influencing the amount of interstimulus spontaneous recovery and thus the asymptote of the habituation function. In the data I have presented here, there is no simple, obvious way to distinguish between the conditions under which one or the other of the two functions might be expected to appear.

The picture is further complicated by the existence of data on interstimulus interval in which there are intervals resulting in a response increment rather than a response decrement. One of the clearest examples is seen in the study by Farel (1973) of the habituation of hindlimb flexor reflex in the chronic spinal frog. In that study, an interstimulus interval of 30 minutes resulted in pronounced potentiation of the response, which had reached as much as 140% of the control level after 20 stimuli, and the curve shows no signs of becoming asymptotic. In this study, intervals of ten minutes and shorter produced decrements.

Response increment with repeated activations has also been reported where within-day interstimulus intervals of short duration are confounded with very long interstimulus intervals between days. I noted earlier that Franzisket (1963) and Kimble and Ray (1965) had obtained this result in the wiping response in the frog to cutaneous stimulation of the nostrils. The frequency of the response increased over days in blocks of 100 stimulations.

It should be apparent that no simple summary of the effect of interstimulus interval can be made without taking other factors into account. What appears to be the most certain effect occurs during the first $250\sigma$. During this period, a second stimulus, either the same or different from the first, probably has a disruptive effect and can thus be expected to produce a response decrement with repeated activations. Interstimulus interval has been reported to have had no effect on the amount of decrement with intervals from $250\sigma$ to $2000\sigma$ in one study, from one second to 3.2 seconds in another, and from 30 seconds to ten minutes in a third. A lessening of the amount of decrement with increasing interstimulus interval has been reported between intervals of two to ten seconds in one study and between five minutes and 96 hours in another. An increment in response strength with successive elicitations has been reported for intervals as short as one per minute to intervals of 24 hours.

At all but the shortest intervals ($250\sigma$ or less), such temporary decremental or incremental effects must most likely be attributed to enduring hypopolarization or hyperpolarization of crucial synapses involved in the activation of the event. The effect of hypopolarization of synapses early in the net of neural units involved in the activation of the event would have the effect of reducing the number of units involved, whereas hyperpolarization of units almost anywhere in the sequence would have the effect of increasing the number of units involved and therefore increasing the intensity and complexity of the psychological event.

*Stimulus Intensity.* The relationship of stimulus intensity to the temporary effects of occurrence of psychological events involves a number of interesting problems. In dealing with the effect of the number of occurrences and the effects of interstimulus interval, it has been possible to deal almost exclusively with the quantitative effects of response increment or decrement. The most profound effects in the quantitative aspects of the response with different stimulus intensities are shown in Figure 6-4, which has been taken from Thompson, Groves, Teyler, and Roemer (1973). However, in dealing with the effects of stimulus intensity, it becomes necessary to recognize qualitative differences as well.

For example, Sokolov (1963) has demonstrated that very strong stimuli may elicit an immediate defensive reaction, while stimuli that are less strong may elicit first an orientation reaction and then a defensive reaction. It is certain that still weaker stimuli may elicit only an orientation reaction, while still weaker stimuli may elicit only momentary attention with no overt component. Furthermore, the qualitative characteristics of the response to the same stimulus may change with repeated elicitations. Sokolov observed that moderately high electrocutaneous stimuli that evoke first an orientation reaction and then a defensive reaction on first presentation may come to elicit only the defensive reaction with repeated presentations. Fewer trials are required to accomplish this transition as the original stimulus becomes more intense.

Ratner (1970) has also noted that different parts of the response sequence undergo habituation at different rates, with resulting changes in what he refers to as the "topography" of the response. Ratner cites a study by Gardner (1966) in which two components of the earthworm response to vibratory stimulation habituated at different rates. A withdrawal response essentially disappeared by the ninth trial, while a hooking response did not disappear until the 19th. Furthermore, it will be recalled that Groves and Thompson (1970) report individual units with early and late components in which the early component shows habituation with repeated stimulation, while the late component shows sensitization. At all levels, repeated stimulation leads to qualitative as well as quantitative changes.

Both sets of curves in Figure 6-4 are plotted in terms of percentage change from the initial or control levels of response to stimuli of each intensity. In absolute terms it is true that, the more intense the stimulus, the larger the initial response and the higher the ultimate or asymptotic level of response. Even on relative bases (as plotted), it is obvious that each of the three curves in each set has not only a different asymptote but a different rate of approach to its asymptote. Most of the curves in the figure show a rising phase followed by a declining phase. On a neural level, the curves imply

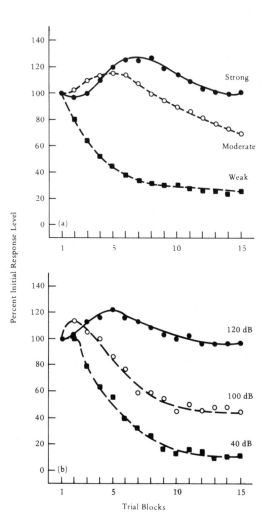

FIGURE 6-4. Intensity and Habituation. The upper graph shows the course of response amplitude changes in the hindlimb spinal flexion reflex in the acute spinal cat to three intensities of stimulation, as reported in Groves and Thompson (1970). The lower graph shows similar changes in skin potential level in the intact human to three sound intensities, as reported by Raskin, Kotses, and Bever (1969). Both curves are taken from Thompson, Groves, Teyler, and Roemer (1973). (Redrawn from "A Dual-Process Theory of Habituation: Theory and Behavior," by R. F. Thompson, P. M. Groves, T. J. Teyler, and R. A. Roemer. In H. V. S. Peeke and M. J. Herz (Eds.), Habituation, Vol. 1. Copyright 1973 by Academic Press. Reprinted by permission.)

that, over a series of trials, more and more units are recruited to the response and that, the more intense the stimulus, the greater the number of trials required to accomplish that recruitment. The fact that the recruitment process appears to be steeper with moderate stimulus intensities may be an artifact of the expression in relative values and the longer endurance of the recruitment process with the more intense stimuli.

It takes little imagination to expand on the possibilities implicit in Figure 6-4 to account for the observations made by Sokolov. If the responses of defensive reaction, orientation reaction, attention without overt orientation, and no reaction are ordered in terms of decreasing intensities of stimuli required to elicit them, then the following possibilities are suggested. With a very strong stimulus, no recruitment is necessary to produce a defensive reaction. With a slightly weaker stimulus, orientation is induced by the initial value, while the recruitment process will soon bring the response to the defensive reaction level. As the intensity of the stimulus is decreased still further, orientation may occur initially, while recruitment may be insufficient to produce a defensive reaction and yet sufficient to maintain the orientation reaction over a large number of trials. With further reduction in stimulus intensity, the initial orientation reaction may disappear as the intensity of the reaction is reduced through habituation.

There is no question that the effect of stimulus intensity is to increase the intensity of the initial reaction, as well as the asymptote, or minimal level to which response intensity may be reduced through repeated elicitations. The effect of stimulus intensity on the rate of reduction is not so obvious. With very weak stimuli, the absolute amount of change in response is so small that the rate of change is hidden in the variability of the response measure. At very high intensities, the rate of habituation (simplification) is masked by the process of recruitment (complication) occurring simultaneously. Thompson, Groves, Teyler, and Roemer (1973) suggest that the relative amount of habituation is the same regardless of stimulus intensity. Thus, they argue that, in the simplification equation given earlier in this chapter, the exponent, $a$, should be the same regardless of the initial and asymptotic values. It is possible, however, that the rate of reduction in response amplitude with repeated activations is a variable rather than a constant.

For example, in a study by Askew (1969, covered in Ratner, 1970), the number of head shakes in response to air puffs of varying intensities was observed in the rat. A puff of .5mm did not produce head shakes above the operant level. A puff of 1mm produced head shakes several times the operant level on the first trial, and the curve appears to have reached asymptote by the second trial. Puffs of 2mm produced more than twice as many head shakes on the first trial, and the curve appears to have reached asymptote by the fifth trial. Puffs of 10 and 100mm produced curves similar to each other. They start at a higher level than that for 2mm, and it is not clear that they have reached asymptote by the tenth trial. In these data, it appears that, the more intense the initiating stimulus, the more intense the initial response, the higher the eventual asymptote (within limits), and the *slower* the approach to asymptote.

If one examines the rates of habituation of responses initiated by stimuli that vary in structural complexity, rather than intensity, the exponent and the asymptote seem to be correlated. Caron and Caron (1969) measured the fixation time of infants exposed to checkerboard patterns that varied in complexity (2 x 2, 12 x 12, and 24 x 24). On initial exposure, fixation times were approximately 17, 18, and 19 seconds for the three stimuli. By the fifth successive exposure, fixation times were approximately 8.5, 15, and 17 seconds. In this case, it appears that, the higher the ultimate asymptote, the slower the approach and thus the smaller the exponent. On the other hand, in studies of human verbal learning to be discussed in Chapter 8, it will be found convenient, if not necessary, to fit curves describing the semipermanent changes in complexity with exponents that increase in size as the asymptote of complexity increases.

When one considers the possible biological utility of a slow or rapid rate of habituation, it seems reasonable that there might be differences depending on the survival value of particular reactions to different classes of stimuli. It is biologically useful to habituate very quickly to many stimuli that offer no threat to the organism, regardless of their intensity and complexity. It is also biologically useful to habituate very slowly, if at all, to certain classes of stimuli that have actual or potential meaning to the organism. Earlier I described Dewsbury's failure to find any evidence of habituation in the electrical response of the knife fish to the insertion of a metal object in the water. In effect, the response has a high asymptote, and the exponent is effectively zero. I suggested that it would not be biologically useful for this fish to habituate to such a stimulus, no matter how often the stimulus is applied. Thompson, Groves, Teyler, and Roemer (1973) may therefore be correct in concluding that the exponent controlling the rate of habituation is constant over different intensity values of the stimulus as long as the data come from very similar reflex systems. However, the generalization does not appear to hold across widely different systems with different biological functions.

*Intensity Generalization.* The phenomena of habituation (simplification) and recruitment (complication) that I have discussed so far presumably involve the repeated application of precisely the same stimulus. When a stimulus that differs either quantitatively or qualitatively from the stimulus that has been presented repeatedly is now presented, one can observe the effects of generalization on the temporary effects of repeated activation. Figure 6-5 displays the results of a study of intensity generalization of habituated stimuli done by James and Hughes (1969). They measured human GSR to tones of two different intensities, 67 dB and 76 dB. They then ran generalization tests at two stimulus intensities above the lower training stimulus for the group trained at the lower intensity and below the higher training stimulus of the second group. In the figure, I have added a straight line connecting the two training points to represent an estimate of the simple effect of intensity, and I have projected test points above and below those actually employed by James and Hughes. I have done this to emphasize visually the dis-

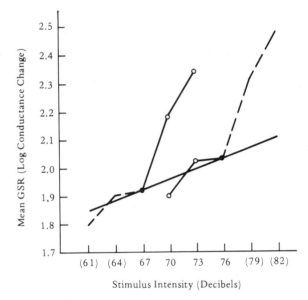

*FIGURE 6-5. Stimulus Intensity Generalization. The two solid circles represent the mean GSR levels after repeated presentation of tones of 67 dB and 76 dB to different groups of human subjects. The group habituated to 67 dB was tested at 70 dB or 73 dB, while the group habituated at 76 dB was tested also at 73 dB or 70 dB. The empirical test points are represented by open circles and are connected by solid lines. I have drawn a straight line through the two habituation values to represent the effects of stimulus intensity on the asymptotic values of GSR to these stimuli. I have also added projections of what the response might have been had there been test points higher than 76 dB and lower than 67 dB. (The data are taken from "Generalization of Habituation of the GSR to White Noise of Varying Intensities," by J. P. James and G. R. Hughes, Psychonomic Science, 1969, 14, 463–464. Reprinted by permission.)*

crepancy between what James and Hughes actually found and what one might expect from the simple interaction of ordinary generalization gradients and the effects of intensity on the asymptote.

If the pitch of the tones had been varied, rather than their intensity, one would have expected the amount of relief from habituation to be equal increases or decreases in the pitch of the test stimulus. It would be reasonable to account for such a symmetrical generalization gradient in terms of sets of neural units common to the training and test stimuli. The farther the test stimulus from the training stimulus in either direction, the less the proportion of common neural units, and therefore the less the effect of habituation shown by the response to the test stimulus.

Since the study was a test of intensity generalization, it would be assumed that the size of the set of neural units activated by the more intense stimulus would be larger than the set activated by the less intense stimulus. This difference in set size would be indicated in the figure by the straight line drawn between the two training values. Given only these two factors, differences attributable to intensity and differences attributable to distance between the training and test stimuli, one would have expected results in which the difference between a test upward from a training stimulus and one downward from a training stimulus would have reflected a simple algebraic sum of the effects of the two factors. It is obvious in the figure that the response to a test stimulus lower than the training stimulus is severely depressed on a relative basis, while the response to a test stimulus higher than the training stimulus is just as markedly elevated.

Thompson, Groves, Teyler, and Roemer (1973) give an ingenious account of these results. They do so while adhering to the general concept of the results being attributable to the proportion of common elements activated by each of the stimuli involved. It is assumed that the two stimuli activate sets of neurons of quite different sizes, with the more intense stimulus activating the larger set. Some of the neurons are common to the two sets. The common neurons form a larger portion of the set activated by the weaker stimulus than of the set activated by the stronger stimulus. In a limiting case, all the neurons activated by the weaker stimulus would be included in the set activated by the stronger stimulus. In that case, the generalization gradient down the intensity dimension would lie precisely on the straight line drawn in the figure, but, by this logic, no point could fall significantly *below* the presumed asymptotic value for direct habituation of the test stimulus. In the figure, the empirical point obtained with a stimulus of 70 dB after habituation to a stimulus of 76 dB does lie significantly below the point on the straight line that indicates the asymptotic value of the response if habituation training had been carried out at 70 dB.

Thompson, Groves, Teyler, and Roemer (1973) suggest two deviations from the limiting case just analyzed. In the first place, they suggest that the stronger stimulus will activate most, but not all, of the elements activated by the weaker stimulus. In the second place, they suggest that the set of elements affected by either stimulus is larger than the set of elements in which spikes are observed to occur. Some elements will be activated below spike threshold, the so-called "subliminal fringe." The effect of both additional sets, those not subjected to habituation by the more intense stimulus and those activated below spike level by either stimulus, would lead to an expectation that the generalization curve for a weaker test stimulus would be above the theoretical asymptote line in the figure.

To account for the "below asymptote" point in Figure 6-5, it is necessary to invoke some mechanism that could operate in generalization but that does not operate effectively in direct habituation. One such mechanism can be constructed from hypothetical effects of inhibition. Although Thompson, Groves, Teyler, and Roemer argue effectively that habituation occurs because of intrinsic changes at the synapse and does not involve extrinsic inhibition, it is possible that inhibitory fibers are involved in the suppression of alternate responses. Thus, stimulation of a flexor response may actively inhibit extensor pathways. It is also possible that the discrimination of the intensity of one sound from the intensity of another may involve the active inhibition of elements that would be involved in the alternate and discriminated tone. If so, then generalization downward to a less intense tone could simultaneously be depressed by common elements that had been intrinsically habituated by intrinsic mechanisms, and extrinsically by inhibitory mechanisms involved in discrimination. Generalization to a more intense tone would have such inhibitory effects masked by the large increase in the number of elements activated to spike level by the more intense stimulus.

Such a hypothetical involvement of extrinsic inhibition of a stimulus process other than the training process could be invoked to account for another instance of "below asymptote habituation." Davis and Wagner, in a study (1968) discussed both by Ratner (1970) and by Thompson, Groves, Teyler, and Roemer (1973), observed the probability of a startle response in rats to tones of various intensities. In addition to finding the expected increase in probability of response with increased stimulus intensity, they compared one group subjected to a large number of trials with an intense stimulus (120 dB) with a second group for which the stimulus initially had a lower value but was increased during training until it was also 120 dB in the final block of trials. The final performance level for the group for which the stimulus was "faded into" the high intensity was significantly less than that of the group subjected to the intense stimulus repeatedly. If reaction to one stimulus involves inhibition to some extent of alternative stimulus processes, then such inhibition would suppress certain units that would have been activated by the more intense stimulus if the inhibitory units had not been activated first by the stimulus of lower intensity. The accumulation of such suppression as the intensity of the stimulus is gradually increased would account for the lower response level to the intensity of stimulation gradually approached in comparison with one not so approached and therefore not directly involved in the effects of inhibition.

This account of generalization below asymptotic habituation levels does not require that such a result will always occur. The result will depend on the mix of units that have undergone habituation, the units that have been inhibited extrinsically, the units that have been activated below spike threshold, and the new excitatory units activated by the new stimulus. Variation in the proportions of the four sets could very well produce a generalized response well above the asymptotic habituation level.

*Dishabituation.* The phenomenon referred to as *dishabituation* is very similar to the phenomenon of intensity generalization, except that the restoration of a habituated response occurs when an extraneous stimulus is applied. An extraneous stimulus that differs in character and possibly in intensity from the habituated stimulus might be expected to activate different portions of the same sets of neural units. However, a qualitatively different stimulus might be expected to activate a greater portion of new elements not activated by the original stimulus. To the extent that these elements can contribute to the intensity of the dishabituated response, dishabituation from an extraneous stimulus should have a greater effect than intensity generalization. To the extent that the extraneous stimulus activates an incompatible response, however, the intensity of the dishabituated response should be reduced.

*Some Other Variables That Affect Habituation.* Any variable that increases the complexity of a psychological event should affect the parameters of habituation in the same way that an increase in intensity does. Any variable that decreases the complexity of a psychological event should have an effect similar to that of a less intense stimulus.

Mackworth (1969) offers several generalizations that corroborate this expectation, including one concerning task complexity in studies of vigilance. According to Mackworth, "Tasks which require active head movements for scanning or involved difficult and complex decisions may show less decrement during the session than tasks which offer single sources and require simple decisions" (pp. 196–197).

Mackworth also states that any change in the pattern of the regularly repetitive stimulation produces dishabituation. Any irregularity in timing, intensity, or quality of the stimulus should produce dishabituation and thus evidence of an increase in the complexity of the response.

The effects of drugs on habituation should also be predictable in terms of whether they could be expected to produce excitatory effects, and thus increase the number of neural units activated by a stimulus, or produce inhibitory effects, and thus decrease the number of neural units activated. Mackworth says that stimulant drugs, such as amphetamine, prevent the decrement in performance or detection that occur in monotonous tasks, whereas depressant drugs increase the rate of habituation.

*Individual, Age, and Sex Differences.* That there are individual differences in rate and amount of habituation should come as no surprise. Eysenck has long held that differences in the amount and rate of habituation are highly correlated with personality characteristics, especially the introversion/extraversion scales. Inhibitory processes occur more rapidly in extraverts than in introverts, leading Eysenck to suggest that the optimal level of stimulation was much lower in introverts for this reason (see Mackworth, Jane, 1969, p. 99). Mackworth cites a dramatic example of individual differences from Koepke and Pribram (1966), who classified individuals into labiles and stabiles on the basis of observed rates of spontaneous GSRs. The habituation curve for the stabiles across trial blocks in response to pure tones presented at random intervals falls to a much lower level than does the curve for the labiles.

Certain developmental differences will be discussed in more detail later. It is worthy of note here that age differences are not apparent in some tasks. For example, in a study by N. H. Mackworth and Otto (1970), there were no consistent differences in habituation of looking time in three groups of children, aged 2–3, 4–5, and 6–7 years. The stimulus was the appearance of a novel red circle in an otherwise uniform matrix of stimuli. Yet developmental differences are frequently found in the amount and rate of habituation in other tasks.

A more surprising finding is that, occasionally, there are clear sex differences in amount and rate of habituation and in spontaneous recovery. In the previously cited study by Caron and Caron (1969), habituation in fixation time to checkerboard stimuli was observed over five trials of the same stimulus in 48 boys and 48 girls at 3.5 months of age. The girls showed greater habituation (reduced fixation time) than the boys, and the habituation appeared to generalize more extensively to the varied stimuli that were presented after the habituation trials. In the Mackworth and Otto study just cited, boys showed a rapid recovery from habituation after a rest interval, but girls did not.

*Habituation and Learning.* There are frequent efforts in the literature to relate habituation phenomena to learning and extinction (see, for example, Thompson & Spencer, 1966; various comments by Mackworth, 1969; Petrinovich, 1973). Although the Hedgehog's treatment of the problem was stated earlier in the chapter, and although learning phenomena are to be discussed later, it may be useful to restate the Hedgehog position within the context of a chapter on the temporary effects of occurrence of psychological events.

I have so far reviewed temporary effects of repeated occurrences of psychological events. In Chapter 7, I consider aspects of semipermanent effects. The only difference between the two in the Hedgehog is their relative permanence. The most common effect of repeated occurrences of the same response is progressive simplification, as described in the simplification equation presented earlier in this chapter. If the effect is temporary, then the equation describes the temporary reduction in complexity of the event. If the effect is semipermanent, the equation can also be used to describe the progress of this semipermanent change.

Given this definition of learning, it is obvious that curves produced under conditions described as experimental extinction are *learning* curves, even though they appear to be the reverse of an improvement in performance. Learning curves measured in terms of a number of variables such as latency of response or number of errors also decline and would therefore seem to offer little conceptual problem.

I will argue that rising curves—the more typical learning curves—occur only when (a) an operation is performed that complicates a psychological event and (b) the full development of that complication requires repeated trials. In this chapter, we have seen one instance of such an operation in the effects of repeated application of a very intense stimulus. Recruitment may require only a few trials, yielding a curve that rises slightly and then declines to a low asymptote. With more intense stimuli, the curve may rise and fall more slowly and become asymptotic at the initial value. Still more intense stimuli may result in curves that rise to a high asymptote without ever exhibiting a declining phase. Many rising learning curves result when two events arising from two stimuli are paired to make possible a more complex event than either one alone would be. Examples include the effort to associate two words in paired associates learning, a CS and a US in conditioning, and a lever press with the consumption of a pellet of food. The rising phase will be treated in each case as a gradual complication of an otherwise simple event. Thus, the simple psychological event initiated by the stimulus

"BOY" must be complicated so that the stimulus now elicits the more complex event "BOY–KJX." The simple event normally elicited by the CS alone must now, in addition, elicit some part of the event originally elicited only by the US, a much more complex event. The simple event of an animal turning left in a T-maze must now become a much more complex event that includes the anticipation of the pellet. All such events tend to have a recruitment or rising phase, and a remarkable number of them will be found to have a subsequent declining phase as well, without a change in the stimulus conditions.

*Habituation and Preference.* Little has been said so far in this chapter concerning the problem of preference, largely because most of the studies in which temporary effects have been observed have involved either the employment of stimuli with high demand characteristics or other situations in which the organism's choice was constrained. Preference is most evident in free choice behavior. However, one result that seems relevant was noted in the treatment of stimulus intensity. Extremely intense stimuli, it was observed, tended to elicit immediate defensive or avoidance behavior, which appears to be a clear indication of negative preference for such intense stimuli. Further, stimuli of somewhat lesser intensity first elicited an orientation reaction (possibly a sign of positive preference) and then a defensive reaction (a sign of negative preference) after several presentations. The shift in preference appeared to correspond to the recruitment of elements into the reaction to increase the intensity and complexity of the reaction, with the result that the stimulus elicited a defensive reaction because of the acquired complexity/intensity level. However, this account of the relation between complexity and preference in a habituation situation may not be correct.

The effect of habituation on preference constitutes a somewhat difficult theoretical problem. There are two possible ways in which preference could be related to the temporary effects of occurrence of psychological events. (1) The elegant and parsimonious solution to the problem is to assume that simplification and complication from repeated activations are no more than modifications in the psychological complexity of the event, and that preference is to be derived from the relation of the momentary psychological complexity value to distance in either direction from optimal complexity level. If so, complex events undergoing complication (recruitment or sensitization) would become progressively less preferred, while complex events undergoing simplification would become more preferred as they came closer and closer to optimal complexity level. Simple events undergoing further temporary simplification would grow less and less preferred. (2) A less elegant possibility is that habituation (simplification) leads to reduced preference whatever the relation between the psychological complexity of the event and the optimum.

I am unaware of a definitive study that would resolve this issue. A relevant finding is shown in Figure 6-6. In one of the studies of aspects of verbal learning to be discussed in Chapter 7, a large number of experimental subjects rated 350 three-letter words for complexity and for affectively (interestingness, pleasantness, and approachability combined into a single rating). Most of the subjects actually rated the full set of words twice and thus made 700 successive ratings. It was an extremely boring task—so boring, in fact, that a large number of subjects refused to complete it. As seen in the figure, there was a tendency for the complexity ratings to decline through the session and a tendency for the affectivity ratings to decline even more. The data seem to establish a correlation between complexity and affective ratings, but they do little to resolve the issue of whether preference for a complex stimulus would rise and fall or merely fall with repetition.

A study involving less familiar stimuli was carried out by Heyduk (1972). I will discuss this study in detail because of the interpretative potential it has, even though it does not offer a completely convincing solution to the problem.

Heyduk began by constructing four musical compositions with several common properties. Each lasted 30 seconds. Each had three parts: an original statement consisting of seven chord changes played with both hands and lasting four bars (ten seconds), an interlude of six bars with five chord changes and some melody in the right hand (15 seconds), and a resolution of two bars with three chord changes played with both hands (five seconds). An attempt was made to vary the complexity levels of the four compositions in two ways: by varying the chord structure and by varying the amount and kind of syncopation. The four compositions can be labeled *A, B, C,* and *D,* with *A* intended to be the least complex and *D* the most complex. Composition *A* had only two chords, both of which were major chords (100%). *B* had four different chords, three of which (75%) were major chords. *C* had eight different chords, four of which (50%) were major chords. *D* had 12 different chords, four of which (33%) were major chords. In addition, *A* was played with no syncopation, *B* was played with left-right coordinated syncopation, *C* had syncopation in the right hand and no coordination, and *D* had different syncopations in the two hands. Played on the piano, the four compositions are reasonably musical, and they cover a perceptible span of the complexity dimension, even to the unmusical ear.

The basic experimental plan was as follows: Tapes of the four compositions were played twice each for a subject or a group of subjects. The subjects were then asked to rate each composition the second time it was heard for how much they liked it. The rating

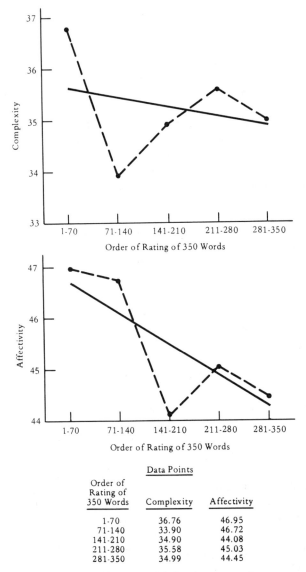

FIGURE 6-6. Generalized Habituation of Complexity and Affectivity Ratings. *The curves represent complexity and affectivity ratings of 350 three-letter words as a function of the order of rating. One group of 146 subjects gave both ratings sequentially (thus rating 700 words). Half of these rated complexity first and then affectivity. Complexity only was rated by 25 additional subjects, while affectivity was rated by 27 additional subjects. The data are from a study to be discussed in Chapter 7.*

scale ranged from "dislike very much" (1) to "like very much" (13). Then each selection was rated for how complex it sounded on another 1-13 scale, ranging this time from "extremely simple" to "extremely complex."

Following the initial ratings for all four compositions, each subject heard one of the compositions 16 times in succession, rating it for liking and complexity after each exposure. Finally, each of the four compositions was played again and given a final rating for liking and complexity.

The effects of experience can be examined in a number of ways within these data. An assessment of the long-term effects of experience, unconfounded by short-term effects, can be made by examining differences between the ratings of subjects who differ in the amount of musical involvement in their past histories. Heyduk asked all the subjects how involved they were in music. He then chose the 20 subjects who indicated the greatest involvement and the 20 who indicated the least involvement.

The complexity and preference ratings for these two groups of subjects are plotted in Figure 6-7. The most and least experienced do not differ appreciably in their ratings of complexity, but they do differ significantly in their ratings of liking. These results are predictable from the theory. Those with the least experience should like the simpler compositions more, while those with more experience should show an added preference for the complex stimuli. The data, plotted here in terms of the more conservative assumptions involved in mean ranks rather than mean ratings, agree with this expectation.

Earlier I gave the name *occultation effect* to what occurs when the act of measuring some property of an event changes the value of what is measured.[1] Primary occultation is evidenced in systematic changes in the value of an event when the same event is measured repeatedly. Something that might be called secondary or generalized occultation occurs when the measurement of one psychological event affects the value of some other event. In Heyduk's study, the order in which the subjects rated the four compositions was controlled so that the effect of the order of rating could be determined. Each composition was equally represented in each order position. Figure 6-8 is a plot of the effect of the order of rating. Through the sequence of four ratings, ratings of complexity increase, and ratings of liking decrease. The effects are small (note that Figure 6-8 is plotted on an expanded ordinate scale) but appear to be

---

[1] C. S. Peirce (1932) refers to experimental science as "occult" science. He cites Petrus Peregrinus, who described an experiment as a procedure for making available to immediate experience what had been occult, or unavailable to immediate experience before the experiment was performed. Thus, experimental procedures reveal what would otherwise be hidden, but they may also hide what would otherwise be there.

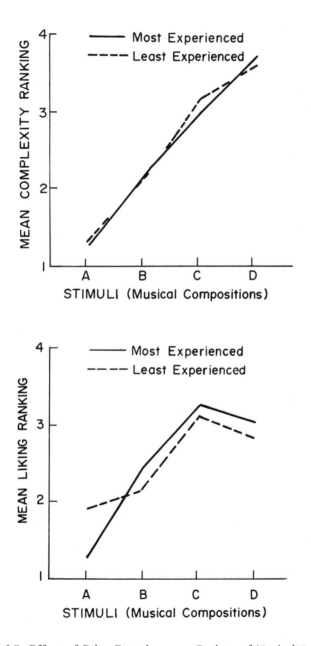

FIGURE 6-7. *Effect of Prior Experience on Ratings of Musical Compositions for Liking and Complexity. (Adapted from* Static and Dynamic Aspects of Rated and Exploratory Preference for Musical Compositions, *by R. G. Heyduk. Unpublished doctoral dissertation, University of Michigan, 1972. Reprinted by permission.)*

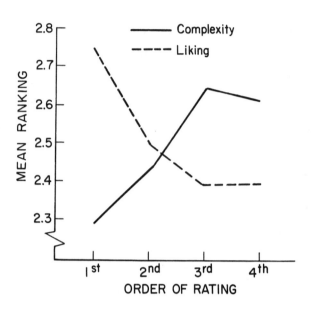

FIGURE 6-8. *Effect of Order of Rating on the Ratings of Musical Composi-*
*tions for Complexity and Liking. (Adapted from* Static and Dynamic Aspects
of Rated and Exploratory Preference for Musical Compositions, *by R. G. Hey-*
*duk. Unpublished doctoral dissertation, University of Michigan, 1972. Reprinted*
*by permission.)*

systematic. Figure 6-8 thus provides a clear example of generalized
occultation.

The major effect of experience is to be seen in the ratings of
the same musical composition heard a total of 19 times in close
succession. Figure 6-9 shows that the general effect of experience
on rated complexity was a gradual decrease in the rating. Liking
ratings appear to rise over the first few repetitions and then fall.
When viewed as an instance of primary occultation, the changes in
value are both dramatic and complex. When they are viewed as a
demonstration of the long-term effects of experience on complexity
and preference, problems arise because of the close spacing of the
experiences and the possibility that the result is a mixture of long-
term (learning) and short-term (habituation) effects.

Since little or nothing is known concerning the time course of
recovery from habituation, there is no external basis for deciding
whether the observed effects are attributable to habituation or to
long-term changes in the psychological complexity of, and preference for, the musical compositions. One is left, then, with a somewhat tortuous and inconclusive logical analysis.

As previously noted, Groves and Thompson (1970) showed

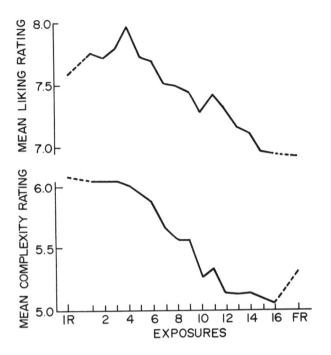

*FIGURE 6-9. Effect of Repeated Experience on Ratings of Musical Compositions for Complexity and Liking. (Adapted from* Static and Dynamic Aspects of Rated and Exploratory Preference for Musical Compositions, *by R. G. Heyduk. Unpublished doctoral dissertation, University of Michigan, 1972. Reprinted by permission.)*

that habituation can consist of either an exponential decrease in responsiveness or an initial rise in responsiveness followed by a fall. They say that every stimulus that evokes a response has two properties: it elicits a response, and it influences the state of the organism. The decrement is a property of the response system, and the increment is a product of the state of the organism.

If this logic is applicable to the cognitive response of the subject to a musical composition, then the expected effect would be a rise in rating followed by a fall in both variables and for all compositions. The liking ratings follow this pattern, but the complexity ratings show no rise and thus no sensitization. On the other hand, the picture in Figure 6-8, representing means over all four compositions, does represent all four in the sense that they all follow the same general pattern. Thus, the fact that the two curves differ in shape would argue *against* a habituation interpretation, and the fact that the curves for all four compositions follow essentially the same pattern would argue *for* a habituation interpretation.

Another way to look at the changes in complexity and preference with this concentrated experience is to tabulate the amount of change that occurs over the course of the experiment. Since each subject rated all four compositions, then heard one repeatedly 16 times, and then rated all four again, each subject rated three stimuli that were heard only twice, at the beginning and at the end of the experiment. These two ratings provided estimates of the amount of change that can occur without intervening experience of the stimuli. Two estimates of the effect of experience can be obtained. One is the difference between the initial and final ratings of the experienced stimuli, and the other is the difference between the ratings on the first and the 16th trials of the experience condition. Heyduk ran six groups of 20 subjects each. Two groups experienced Composition *A,* and two experienced Composition *D.* Each group yielded two estimates of the effect of experience and three estimates of the generalized effects of that experience, if any. The 30 algebraic means are displayed in Figure 6-10 in a manner that permits visual analysis.

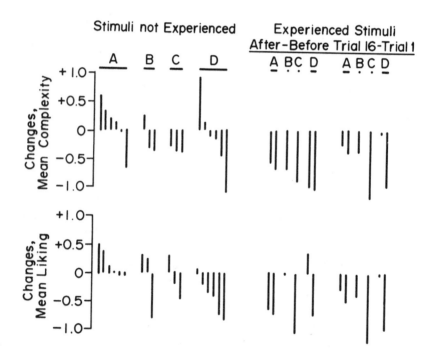

FIGURE 6-10. *Shifts in Ratings of Musical Compositions with Experience.* (*Adapted from* Static and Dynamic Aspects of Rated and Exploratory Preference for Musical Compositions, *by R. G. Heyduk. Unpublished doctoral dissertation, University of Michigan, 1972. Reprinted by permission.)*

The left side of the figure shows the amount and direction of shift in rating when there is no intervening experience, while the right side shows the direction and amount of shift in rating when there is intervening experience between the two ratings, initial and final.

The effects of experience on rated complexity and on rated liking do not appear to differ greatly from one musical composition to the next. The effect on rated complexity is universally downward, the effect on liking nearly so. The generalized effects on the compositions that were heard and rated only twice do appear to differ between compositions. Composition *A*, the simplest, shows most of the increases in both complexity and liking. This finding suggests the predicted elaboration and complication of a simple stimulus that can only be elaborated and complicated in order to be made tolerable. This hint led to the possiblity that trial to trial rises in complexity rating for Composition *A* might be accompanied by a similar rise in liking. A similar correlation with Composition *D*, the most complex, should be zero. The latter correlation in the data is, in fact, zero, but the correlation for Composition *A*, while positive, does not differ significantly from zero.

Another approach to the problem of whether the observed effects are to be attributed to habituation or to long-term changes in psychological complexity stems from a differential expectation if the changes are of the long-term variety. If the long-term effect is assumed, all complexity ratings should decrease (except Composition *A*, as noted above) and liking ratings should rise or fall, depending on whether the original complexity value is above optimum (thus an increase in liking) or below optimum (thus a decrease in liking). A piece of indirect evidence appears to suggest that the long-term effect predominates in this experiment.

Heyduk performed a revealing analysis on the individual protocols of the change-with-experience data to reveal the degree of agreement with three theories of expected change. What Heyduk calls "satiation theory" predicts that all ratings will be downward, regardless of the original preference rating. "Mere exposure theory" (Zajonc, 1968) predicts that any increase in familiarity will lead to an increase in liking. Psychological complexity and preference theory makes different predictions depending on the location of the optimal complexity level of each individual. Optimal complexity level can be determined for different individuals from their original preference ratings of the four stimuli. If a subject originally prefers *D*, then his optimal complexity level must be nearer to *D* than to *C*. If he originally prefers *C*, then his optimal complexity level must be nearer to *C* than to either *B* or *D*, and so on. Once individuals' optimal complexity levels are determined, knowledge of these levels can be used to predict the direction of long-term changes in liking.

TABLE 6-1. Effects of Repeated Experience on Ratings of Liking of Musical Compositions

| | Individual Protocol Analysis | | | | |
|---|---|---|---|---|---|
| Theory of Effect of Repeated Exposure | Observed Number of Supporting Protocols | Expected Number of Supporting Protocols | Expected Proportion of Supporting Protocols | $X^2$ | $p$ |
| Psychological Complexity Theory | 71 | 50.2 | .418 | 14.1 | $< .001$ |
| Satiation Theory | 51 | 39.6 | .330 | 4.5 | $< .05$ |
| Mere Exposure Theory | 21 | 39.6 | .330 | | n.s. |

Adapted from *Static and Dynamic Aspects of Rated and Exploratory Preference for Musical Compositions*, by R. G. Heyduk. Unpublished doctoral dissertation, University of Michigan, 1972. Reprinted by permission.

Table 6-1 contains the results of Heyduk's analysis. Psychological complexity theory succeeds in predicting the direction of change in 71 of 120 instances, a success rate that is significantly better than chance. Satiation theory (which does not differ in its prediction from the expected effects of habituation, making the reasonable assumption that sensitization, if any, has disappeared by the 16th trial) is successful in 51 instances, significant beyond the .05 level. Mere exposure theory is correct in only 21 instances, less than the number expected by chance. The fact that psychological complexity theory predicts better than satiation (or habituation) theory appears to indicate that the long-term effects of experience are predominant in these data.

There is some possibility of discrimination between the effects of repeated experience on preference in an early study by Verveer, Barry, and Bousfield (1933). They had subjects rate the pleasantness/unpleasantness of either one of a pair of jazz recordings played on a victrola. One of the recordings was described as familiar to the subjects, while the other was unfamiliar. Subjects listened to one recording 16 times, each time rating it for pleasantness. The first four listenings were separated only by the time required to make the ratings. Then each subject heard the other record once, followed by the experimental record four more times in that experimental session. This procedure was repeated exactly a week later. Mean pleasantness ratings for the two experimental records are shown in Figure 6-11.

The most obvious effect of repeated listenings is the decline in pleasantness ratings within sessions. The most general effect of habituation is to produce a rather sharp decline in preference. When a week intervenes between experimental sessions, ratings of both recordings show considerable spontaneous recovery. In the case of the familiar recording, recovery appears to be approximately to the original value. Ratings of the unfamiliar recording, however, appear to recover to a point substantially higher than the original value. We might infer that no more learning, in the sense of a permanent change in complexity, occurred with the familiar recording, and that such a change in subjective complexity had occurred in at least some of the subjects who listened to the unfamiliar one. If so, then the

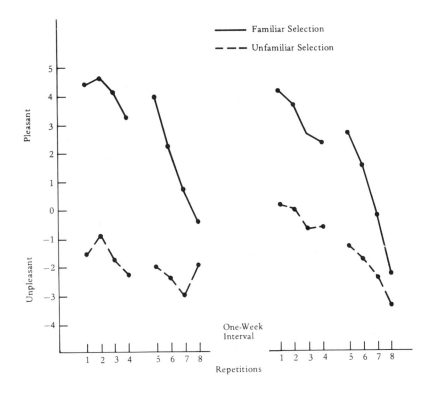

*FIGURE 6-11. Pleasantness Ratings of Jazz Compositions Heard Repeatedly. One composition (solid line) was familiar to all the subjects, while the other (broken line) was unfamiliar. Each group heard one of the compositions four times with time between trials sufficient to permit pleasantness ratings. After hearing the alternate composition once, they heard and rated the original four more times. The procedure was repeated exactly for each group one week later. (Adapted from "Change in Affectivity with Repetition," by E. M. Verveer, H. Barry, Jr., and W. A. Bousfield,* American Journal of Psychology, *1933, 45, 130-134. Reprinted by permission of the University of Illinois Press.)*

direction of change must have been one of semipermanent simplification. An increase in the pleasantness rating would then reflect a
change from a more complex to a less complex psychological event,
where both were more complex than optimum.

It would then follow that the effect of habituation was always
a decrease in preference, regardless of the original complexity and
preference value of the stimulus. Such an interpretation ignores the
rise in pleasantness between the first and second presentations in
the ratings of both recordings. Such a rise also appears in the data
from Heyduk (1972) in Figure 6-9. One can only conclude that the
question of whether simplification by habituation and simplification
by learning have the same or different effects on preference cannot
yet be resolved.

### TEMPORARY EFFECTS OF OCCURRENCE OF PSYCHOLOGICAL EVENTS IN FREE CHOICE SITUATIONS (ALTERNATION PHENOMENA)

So far in this chapter, I have considered the effects of repeated
occurrences of psychological events that have been induced primarily by stimuli with high demand characteristics. Most of the
events that occur in the stream of psychological events are freely
chosen, and many are not the product of any external or obvious
internal stimulus, if "stimulus" means afferent neural activity. Yet
these freely chosen events also show aftereffects of occurrence. If
the aftereffects are decremental, and they usually are, then the
occurrence of a particular psychological event in the stream should
produce a decrease in the probability of its recurrence. Since freely
chosen psychological events are all close to optimal complexity
level (at least much closer than an event initiated by a very strong or
a very weak stimulus), changes in the probability of recurrence can
be very sensitive indicators of the effects of some of the variables
already discussed as well as significant variables not yet treated.

Perhaps some of the issues can be clarified by a diagram such
as that in Figure 6-12. The upper part of the diagram is patterned
after Figure 4-2 (p. 52) and shows a sequence of psychological
event selection from a set of five alternatives. The bottom portion
represents the course of occurrence of each of five events, with each
of the five a representation of the diagram in Figure 5-3. Figure
6-12 is drawn to represent a condition in which each of the five
approaches optimal complexity level at its maximum. If one con-
trived to induce any one of them to occur five times in a row, then
the usual effect would be the declining (habituated, simplified) value
shown in Figure 6-2.

There are two common paradigms to be explored for habituation effects in this section, operant responding and alternation

phenomenon. In the operant situation, the usual procedure is to place an organism in an extremely dull environment, one in which very few of the activities available to the organism are close to optimal complexity level. One activity (the one to be manipulated) should occur in this environment with sufficient frequency that its normal frequency (its operant level) can be established. The frequency of its occurrence will be controlled under these circumstances by the time it takes for the response to recover from the

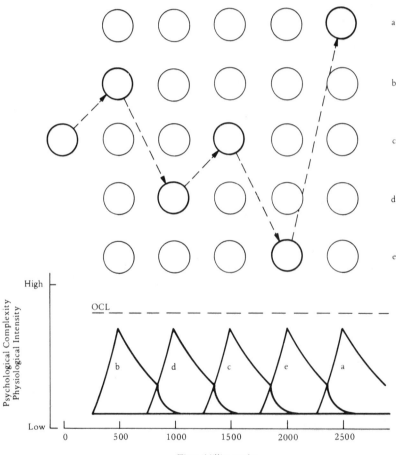

FIGURE 6-12. Sequence of Psychological Event Selection

habituation effects of a single occurrence and the relative attractiveness of other available activities. In the alternation paradigm, the available alternatives are reduced effectively to a fixed number (usually two), which are designed to be equally complex and equally attractive. Under these circumstances, the habituation effects of one occurrence of one alternative can be traced in the duration of the aftereffect in increasing the probability of the occurrence of the second alternative.

It is especially important to examine the effects of habituation in these two paradigms, because the effects of habituation (simplification) are precisely the opposite of the usual meaning of the word *learning* within these paradigms. In the operant paradigm, *learning* is defined as an increase in the probability of the response over operant level, and *extinction* is said to have occurred when the probability of the response decreases with the omission of contingent reward. In the alternation paradigm, learning is frequently studied by inducing one of the available events to change from a probability of occurrence of close to .5 to a probability of 1.0. Thus, in the ordinary sense of the term *learning*, the effects of habituation must be overcome if learning is to be demonstrated. The two phenomena are therefore intimately associated. It is, of course, one of the theses of this book that the same mechanisms underlie the phenomena usually referred to as *habituation, learning,* and *extinction.*

### The Involuntary Character of Human Nonrandomness

One of the most fundamental and important characteristics of human (or organismic) behavior is that it is nonrandom. Human behavior is predictably nonrandom even when a person is trying his or her best to generate a random sequence. A significant aspect of nonrandomness is the general tendency to avoid repetition—in other words, a negative bias against doing again whatever it was that one has just done.

Some years ago, Dr. Thomas Sawyer, Jr. and I made an effort to determine whether human subjects could, through instruction, be induced to produce random sequences of behavior. The apparatus we used was a computer keypunch machine. We masked the keyboard with a flat board into which two, three, or four holes had been drilled. Then we made extensions for the two, three, or four keys that projected through the masking board so that the subject had easy access to the limited set of keys. The subject's responses could then be punched directly into precoded cards for subsequent computer analysis.

The participants in this experiment were then treated to a 30-minute lecture on the nature of randomness, during which they were instructed in the character of random distributions and were shown tables of random numbers, normal distributions, and distributions of run lengths (that is, how many times a coin would be expected to come up heads in a sequence before coming up tails, and so on). The subjects then sat down in front of the machine and made 18,000 responses per subject in groups of 1000. All responses were made under the instruction to do the very best they could to produce random series of responses.

There were three variables in the experiment. There could be either two, three, or four alternatives. The rate of responding was paced at either 100, 200, or 300 responses per minute. There was also an effort to produce two levels of arousal or involvement through the establishment of "reward" and "no reward" conditions. In the "reward" condition, the subjects were instructed that a random pattern had been predetermined and built into the machine. If their responses happened to correspond with the random responses, a bell would ring. They were told that there was no possibility of learning any pattern, since it was random, but that they would thereby know that their responses had been the same as the random pattern. In these conditions, the bell rang on 50%, 33%, or 25% of the alternatives, depending on the number available in that condition. Compared to the "no reward" condition, this operation served visibly to increase subjects' interest and involvement in the task. With three numbers of alternatives, three rates of responding, and two arousal conditions, there were 18 conditions, and each subject experienced all 18 in a controlled order.

Four of the nine sets of results produced by these subjects are shown in Figures 6-13, 6-14, 6-15, and 6-16. The five additional figures are not reproduced here, because they added no information. In each of the four figures, a comparison of the theoretical and empirical curves demonstrates that the subjects were unable to produce random sequences. The subjects switched from one key to the other and back again more often than a truly random machine would have. This finding appears in all four panels, as well as in the five that are not shown. Thus, whether there were two, three, or four alternatives, and whether the pace of responses was 100, 200, or 300 per minute, the subjects varied their responses more than a random machine would have.

It should be noted that the paces set for the subjects in this experiment produced responses every 600, 300, or 200$\sigma$. It was expected that the fastest pace might have produced results that were different from those produced by the slower paces. There is a suggestion of a greater tendency to vary responses at the fastest pace, but the variance was not significantly different from what it was at the slower paces. Likewise, the "reward" and "nonreward" conditions might have been expected to differ, if the reward condition

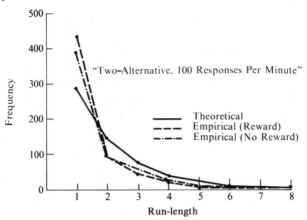

FIGURE 6-13. Human "Random" Response Sequences (Two Alternatives, 100 Responses per Minute)

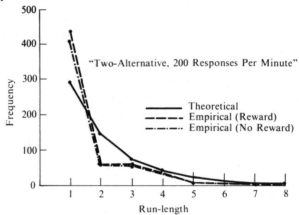

FIGURE 6-14. Human "Random" Response Sequences (Two Alternatives, 200 Responses per Minute)

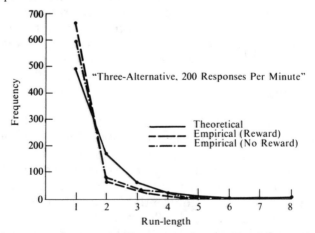

FIGURE 6-15. Human "Random" Response Sequences (Three Alternatives, 100 Responses per Minute)

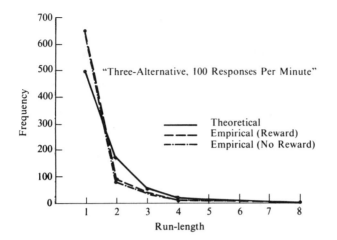

*FIGURE 6-16. Human "Random" Response Sequences (Three Alternatives, 200 Responses per Minute)*

produced a more intense psychological event. Again, the difference was in the direction one might expect, but it was not statistically significant.

The response of punching one key is very like the response of punching another. Consequently, the two, three, or four psychological events involved in the experiment were very much alike, both in terms of their overt characteristics as observed by another person and probably in terms of their afferent feedback. Jay Caldwell therefore decided to vary the complexity of the event associated with two alternatives to see whether this variable would have an effect on the nonrandomness of human choices.

Caldwell built an apparatus with a single switch that could be toggled to the left or to the right. The subject faced a panel of 24 lights in a 4 x 6 matrix. Caldwell devised three conditions of variation in the pattern of lights that would be turned on when the switch was thrown. In an "Identical" condition, a random pattern of eight lights was turned on when the switch was thrown; the pattern was the same regardless of the response made by the subject. In a "Different" condition, a pattern of eight lights came on whichever way the switch was thrown, but the two patterns were completely different in the sense that they each involved a different set of lights. In the "Overlapping" condition, four of the lights were common to the sets of eight that lighted when the switch was thrown in the two directions.

Caldwell used ten subjects in each of the groups, and each subject made 300 responses at a comfortable pace. The results are shown in Figure 6-17. There were many more runs of length 1 when the light patterns were different for the response of pushing the switch right or left. The "Identical" and the "Overlapping" conditions did not differ. Interestingly, when one serves as a subject in this condition, it is the common set of four that stands out, so that the perceptual effect is very similar to the condition in which all eight lights are the same. Thus, within the limits of the manipulations in these studies, the tendency toward nonrandomness in human behavior increases as the difference between the alternatives, and thus the complexity of the alternatives, increases.

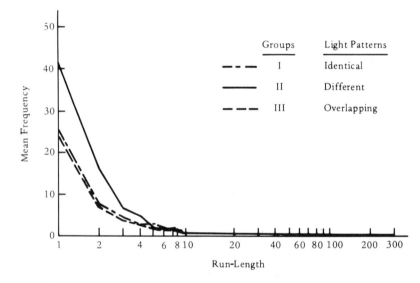

| Groups | Light Patterns |
| --- | --- |
| I | Identical |
| II | Different |
| III | Overlapping |

*FIGURE 6-17. Stimulus Variation Effects on Human "Random" Response Sequences. Frequency plot of average number of run lengths for three groups that differed in the stimulus consequences of their responses. Each of ten subjects made 300 responses. (Study designed and executed by Jay Caldwell.)*

### Nonrandom Behavior in Animals

In a multiple choice situation, the effects of a given choice can be shown to endure through a sequence of choices. A. W. Boykin, placed animals in the central compartment of a hexagonally shaped maze. From there the animal could choose to enter any one of five pie-shaped compartments. The study was designed to test for preference among five levels of complexity of wall pattern. Since an animal was free to choose the most preferred alternative at

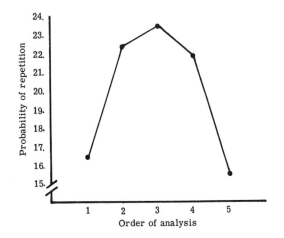

FIGURE 6-18. *Temporary Effects of a Choice in a Five-Choice Situation. The probability of repetition of a given choice through the next five opportunities to choose by rats in a hexagonal maze. (A. W. Boykin, Jr., in Walker, 1969b.)*

any given time, the relative probabilities, uncomplicated by temporary aftereffects of previous choices, are unknown, and the chance probability of .20 is meaningless. Nevertheless, an analysis procedure can be devised to show the endurance of the aftereffects of a choice of any one alternative.

To analyze for the endurance of the aftereffects of a choice, the central compartment was taken as a base. The first choice the animal made from the central compartment was noted. The next time the animal paused in the central compartment and chose one of the five alternatives, it was noted whether this choice was the same or different from the first. This comparison was labeled a first-order tendency to repeat the first choice. The next time the animal paused in the central compartment, its choice was again recorded and labeled as a repetition or nonrepetition in reference to the first choice after the first pause in the central compartment. This comparison was a second-order repetition probability. This process was continued through the fifth order. The analysis was then moved to the next pause in the central compartment and begun again.

With 18 animals observed for ten-minute trials on 12 consecutive days, a very large number of sequences were observed, yielding very stable results. If every animal had chosen the same alternative on every occasion, the curve in Figure 6-18 would have been a straight horizontal line, with a repetition probability of 1.0. If the choice behavior of the animals had been purely random, the curve would have been a straight line, horizontal at a probability value of .2. In fact, the probability of repetition is quite low for the first-order opportunity to repeat and rises and then falls again by the fifth order. It should be obvious that the processes involved in the figure are extremely complex, since the five alternatives available vary in their preference values, and since the actual frequency of occurrence of the zero-order or reference choice increases cumulatively from left to right in the figure. Nonetheless, there is clear evidence of the endurance of the aftereffect of one choice through a series of subsequent choices.

### The Effect of Rewards on Temporary Aftereffects of Occurrence of Psychological Events

The effect of "rewards," such as water for a thirsty animal, on habituation and the temporary aftereffects of occurrence of a psychological event involves something of an intellectual paradox. A response that is made to a contingent reward tends to undergo a rapid *increase* in the probability of its recurrence. Yet a response closely associated with a reward should undergo greater habituation and should therefore show a temporary *decrease* in the probability of its recurrence. Let me consider the second of these two propositions, since it will seem to be the puzzling one to most readers. I will consider it at two levels, first a theoretical level and then an empirical level.

Consider a two-alternative situation in which two responses, turning right (R) or turning left (L), are equally complex, thus equally attractive, and thus equally probable. Let us arrange a situation in which a large number of animals are presented this choice after they have been made thirsty. Let us further arrange that one of the choices leads immediately to water, while the other does not. What should be the effect of the water reward on the habituation of the choice that led to it? To the extent that the two psychological events—choosing one of the alternatives and taking a drink of water—interact, the access to water should make the choice that led to it more complex and its neural base more intense than would have been the case if the choice had not led to water.

As we saw earlier in this chapter, the effect of stimulus-induced increase in intensity is to produce a more intense reaction, which in turn is followed by a much larger habituation effect. In most of the data presented, these effects were masked by the presentation of the results in terms of proportions, either of a control response intensity or of the intensity of the first response. In absolute terms, the more intense the stimulus the greater the absolute amount of habituation. Therefore, the effect of the water reward should be to produce a stronger temporary habituation decrement than is created for the response that does not lead to reward. If the animal is returned to the choice point within a reasonable period of time, the temporary habituation effect should lead the animal to choose the unchosen alternative. Furthermore, since the effect of reward should be to increase the temporary habituation effect, those animals for which the first choice led to water should show a greater tendency to subsequently select the unchosen alternative than those animals for which the first choice did not lead to reward.

The empirical demonstration of this theoretical expectation has been documented in an extensive study (Walker, 1956). In this study, comparisons were made between the alternation behavior of animals who found water on either side with animals who found water on neither side. The effect in this case was slight in amount but statistically significant in "purified" data—data from which those trials were eliminated in which the rewarded animals did not drink or in which animals took a long time (ten seconds or more) to make a choice.

A much clearer demonstration of the role of rewards in alternation behavior was reported in Walker and Motoyoshi (1962). In this study, hungry animals found food reward on either side, but the amount differed between two groups. In one group the reward was eight small pellets, and in the other group it was only one small pellet. In the eight-pellet group, 87.5% of the animals alternated between the first and second trials, while in the one-pellet group, only 68.75% of the animals alternated. Thus, the larger reward produced a more intense and complex reaction, a greater amount of habituation, and a greater tendency to alternate.

There are several ways in which this negative effect of reward on repetition can be reversed. An obvious way is to make the reward contingent on the performance of only one of the two responses and to provide enough time and trials for permanent effects to accumulate. This was done in the Walker and Motoyoshi study, and the animals with the eight-pellet reward learned faster than the animals with the one-pellet reward. The spacing of the trials was also manipulated. One group had a trial every 12 hours (so that temporary habituation effects could be assumed to dissipate between trials). This group learned faster than a second group with the same two trials per day, but 30 seconds apart so that the second trial reflected habituation from the first and thus reflected alternation phenomena.

A second, less obvious way to eliminate the effect of reward on alternation is to use very intense stimuli. In Figure 6-4 it is shown that, with very large increases in intensity, the direction of the habituation effects can be reversed. With very intense stimuli, sensitization, or complication, replaces habituation, or simplification, as a temporary effect of activation. In a study by DeValois (1954), when shock was used to motivate animals to run through a multiple-choice point maze in which there was no contingency resulting from any choice, increasing the shock level led to a decrease in the variability of the responses within and between trials. This would be the result from a stimulus strong enough to produce recruitment over time or trials or both.

Still another way to reduce the effect of reward on alternation is to run a large number of trials under conditions in which the noncontingent relation between the response and the reward can become differentiated and discriminated by the organism. Under this condition, the reward should lose its capacity to complicate a given response and thus increase the tendency to alternate. Scott (1972) constructed an automated maze that had the functional pattern of a figure eight on its side. The animal, in this case a rat, could run down the center alley and then choose to turn either left or right to return to the point from which it started. A series of gates prevented it from retracing its steps. Under food privation, a number of animals were permitted to run this maze for one night as rapidly and frequently as they chose to do so. During this period, an animal would make on the order of 100 choices. There then followed a series of daily three-hour sessions under several different schedules of rewards, which were never contingent on what the animal did. Each animal was trained on a schedule that provided a reward on every return to the choice and goal point, and then 13 of the 15 animals were shifted to one of five reward schedules that remained unchanged through the seven days of performance. Since an animal was free to run at its own pace, the number of daily responses varied from about 300 to 700 or more. Through the period of the experiment, an individual animal might thus generate a stream of L and R responses as short as 3000 and as long as 6000. Besides CRF, VR-2, VR-4, and FR-3, the schedules of reward included two somewhat more complex schedules, $VR_3$-4 and $VR_3$-6. On the first of these, the animal was rewarded on every third trial with a probability of .75; on the latter, the animal was rewarded on every third trial with a probability of .5. Thus, the average number of trials to reward were 4 and 6 in the two schedules.

These maneuvers produced 15 streams of psychological events. Each stream consisted of several thousand choices between only two alternatives, and the environment of the stream had in it only one source of variation, the noncontingent presence or absence of reward in any one of six patterns.

If one does not have a theory to determine the character of the expected pattern of responses in this apparently simple situation, the task of exhaustive pattern analysis is to all intents and purposes impossible. Markovian chains involve assumptions that are not met by the data. Contingent probabilities offer a basic approach but become unwieldy as one progresses through higher order contingencies.

Scott approached the analysis problem by developing a series of algorithms that consisted of instructions to the computer on how to go about looking for consistencies in the behavior of the animals under these conditions. After a series of trial algorithms, the final analysis was made by using a program called $SCOT_3$. Scott described this particular algorithm as attempting to "develop a set of predictors such that any choice can be predicted from the pattern of choice and reinforcement on previous trials (e.g., an unreinforced R followed by a reinforced L is always followed by a R choice). As many preceding trials as necessary are utilized. Limits can be placed on the maximum number of preceding trials utilized, and the latencies of trials can also be used for the prediction."

A number of interesting patterns emerged from Scott's techniques of analysis of these raw but highly constrained streams of behavior. Only those who expect the effects of reward to be some kind of magic will be surprised to learn that, in general, the appearance of reward was not followed by any general tendency to repeat the choice that had led to the reward. Over many long segments of the streams of choices of all the rats, there was a general tendency to alternate choices to some degree and to depart from chance distributions of choices in the direction of greater than chance variability.

Scott found two somewhat more complicated patterns of behavior that characterized major segments of the streams of a few of the rats. He labeled one pattern *restart alternation.* In this pattern, a tendency to alternate choices following nonreward occurred with a probability of about .97. However, when a reward appeared in the sequence, the first choice following the reward was not predictable from the previous choices, including the last rewarded choice in the sequence. It is almost as if the animal tried first one turn then the other in a regular pattern until it achieved a pellet of food, and then started again with a coin flip. This pattern was found in one of the animals on an FR-3 schedule and in all four of the animals who were on $VR_3$-4 or $VR_3$-6 schedules of reward.

Scott called the second complicated pattern revealed by his algorithms *spontaneous counting.* In this pattern, found in two of the animals on FR-3 schedules, the choice on the trial to be rewarded was predictable from the behavior on the previous rewarded trial but was not predictable from the two intervening trials. One of these two animals tended to repeat trials leading to reward, and the other tended to alternate them. It is also worthy of note that eight of Scott's animals never showed lengthy periods of consistency in their patterns of choice. These included two animals on a CRF schedule, two on VR-2, 3 on VR-4, and one on FR-3.

Scott's study shows that, when reward is not made contingent on a particular response, no tendency to repeat a response because it is followed by reward is evident. It shows as well that, when there is a clear discrimination between the psychological event that constitutes the response and the event that constitutes the receiving of a reward, no integration of the two events occurs, and reward does not have the effect of decreasing the probability of occurrence of the rewarded response. Finally, Scott's study demonstrates an obvious need for further development of techniques for analyzing the raw stream of psychological events. The paucity of available techniques, together with the complexities involved in interpreting the results of their application, justify the highly creative effort of Atkinson and Birch (1970) to synthesize the stream and produce the quantified, computerized simulation mentioned in Chapter 4.

### Duration of Temporary Aftereffects of Occurrence of Psychological Events

It is a common assumption that the temporary aftereffects of occurrence of psychological events dissipate as a simple exponential function of time. Yet, in an earlier section of this chapter on spontaneous recovery from habituation effects, it was observed that such effects sometimes endured unchanged for a considerable period of time. A dramatic illustration of that endurance in an alternation situation is shown in Figure 6-19. The figure is taken from Walker,

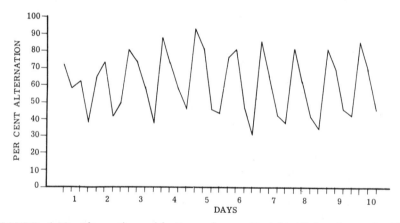

FIGURE 6-19. Alternation with Reward over Variable Delay Intervals. The figure shows alternation behavior between trials of a T-maze study. Animals were thirsty and received water reward on all trials. There were four trials per day for both days. Plot is percent alternation between the first two trials of the day, between the second and third, the third and fourth, and between the last trial of one day and the first trial of the next. The interval between trials varied over a wide range. The within-day interval could be more than an hour on the first day and as little as 15 minutes on the tenth. The between-day interval ranged from 20 to 23 hours. (From "Drive Specificity and Learning: The Acquisition of a Spatial Response to Food under Conditions of Water Deprivation and Food Satiation," by E. L. Walker, M. C. Knotter, and R. L. DeValois, Journal of Experimental Psychology, 1950, 40, 161–168.)

Knotter, and DeValois (1950) but was not analyzed in this form in that article.

The data in the figure came from a study of latent learning. Rats were given four trials per day while thirsty in a two-alternative maze and were rewarded with water regardless of which choice they made. The procedure was to give each of a sizable group of animals one trial, then give each a second trial, then a third, and then a fourth within a daily session. Since this procedure required more than four hours the first day and slightly more than one hour on the tenth day, the intertrial interval varied from about an hour on the first day to approximately 15 minutes on the tenth day. Although there is variation in the curve, the most remarkable characteristic is the consistency across the ten days despite variation in the intertrial interval. It seems obvious that recovery from temporary aftereffects endured for a considerable period of time, over which the value did not appear to change markedly. This result inspired an effort to trace the recovery process through time, and the result of that study is shown in Figure 6-20.

In this experiment, thirsty animals were placed twice a day for seven days in a two-alternative maze. A given animal either always received a water reward or never received one. Time between choices was controlled experimentally from 15 seconds to four hours. Added to this controlled delay in every case were (a) a fixed 60-second period during which the animal was left in the goal box after the first choice and (b) a variable amount of time taken by the animal to make a second choice after it was placed in the starting box. The intervals plotted in Figure 6-20 are mean values of the sums of these fixed and variable intervals. It is obvious from the figure that the habituation-produced bias against repetition endures for a considerable period of time. The lower, theoretical, curve is an effort to reflect a period during which the recovery function might endure essentially unmodified. It is also an effort to reflect expectations from a theoretical neural model of the effects of reward on habituation and learning. That model (Walker, 1956) led to the following summary statement:

> Any psychological action is followed by an action decrement—a lowered capacity for rearousal of the same event. The action decrement is a direct manifestation of the process of perseverative consolidation which is necessary for retention and subsequent performance. The action decrement persists for a limited time and then dissipates. Under many circumstances the dissipation of the action decrement is followed by an action increment which is learning or habit strength.

It follows from the model that any factor, such as a reward, should produce a more profound temporary decrement, faster recovery, and greater action increment, or learning.

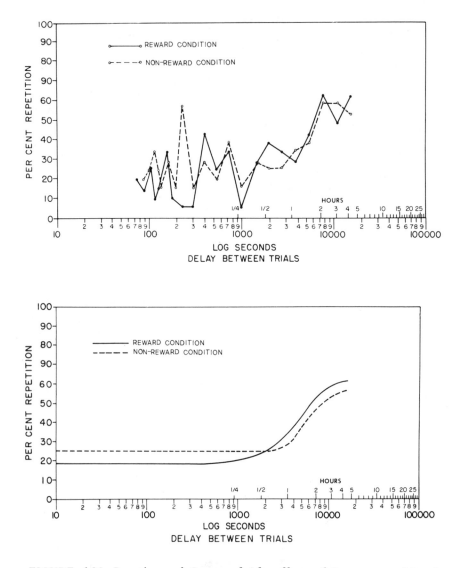

FIGURE 6-20. *Duration and Course of Aftereffects of Occurrence of Psychological Events with and without Reward. The upper curve shows the empirical results. The delay intervals ranged from a minimum of about 80 seconds to approximately four hours. All animals were thirsty. The rewarded group received water in either goal box, while the nonrewarded group received water in neither. The lower (theoretical) curve is an arbitrarily smoothed function fitted to the data in the empirical curve. (Adapted from* "Action Decrement and Its Relation to Learning," *by E. L. Walker,* Psychological Review, *1958, 65, 129-142. Copyright 1958 by the American Psychological Association. Reprinted by permission.)*

## Psychological Event Intensity and Alternation

If reward associated with a psychological event has the effect of intensifying (and thus complicating) the event, then the effect of reward on habituation should be the same as the effect of intensity. In an alternation situation, the second choice is made between an alternative just habituated from the previous choice and one not so habituated. If reward has increased the decrement, then the choice should be made more quickly when reward is involved than when it is not. In the study I have just reported (Walker, 1956), the animals who received reward took 12.5 seconds, on the average, to make the second choice, with a range of 8.0 to 18.3 seconds. The animals who never received reward required an average of 21.1 seconds, with a range of 10.4 to 44.9 seconds. Thus, the prediction concerning choice latency is confirmed.

In an operant situation in which the effect of one response is measured in terms of its effect on the next occurrence of the same response, the effect of event intensity on response latency should be exactly the reverse. The more intense the event, the greater should be the decrement, the longer should be its duration, and therefore the longer the next free operant response should be delayed.

One way to vary the intensity of an operant response is to vary the force necessary to depress a lever to obtain a reward. Appley (1949) trained rats to press a lever to obtain food when hungry and varied the pressure required in 10-gram steps from 10 to 50 grams. A rat has little difficulty in depressing a 10-gram lever, but depressing a 50-gram lever requires considerable effort for a rat weighing something like 300 grams. Appley managed to train 20 rats in each of the five weight groups but in the process found that, although only one animal failed to learn at 10 grams, 17 failed to learn to criterion at 50 grams.

Among the animals that did manage to make 50 rewarded responses in two days of training (after three days of shaping), the time between presses did vary markedly with the amount of effort required to depress the lever. Figure 6-21 shows that, in terms of average interresponse time for the first 25 responses, the range is from about 38 seconds for the 20-gram group to nearly 124 seconds for the 50-gram group. The differences in the figure should be attributable to differences in the duration of habituation produced by the differences in the amount of effort required.

Learning—in the sense of the simplification of, and change in, the character of the psychological event with repeated experience— is shown, in part, by the large drop in interresponse time in the second set of responses shown in the lower line in the figure. Several kinds of changes are occurring simultaneously as the animal executes the lever-pressing response more precisely and with less average effort, but the duration of the habituation effect, as revealed in the

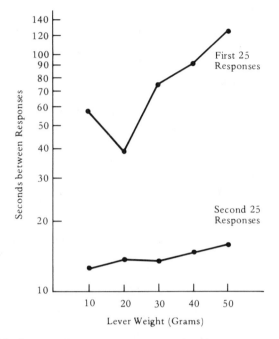

FIGURE 6-21. Operant Response Latency and Effort. The figure shows mean seconds between responses in an operant lever-pressing situation when the pressure required to activate the magazine varied from 10 to 50 grams. The upper curve shows mean latency for the first 25 responses, the lower curve for the second 25 responses. (Adapted from The Role of Effort in Learning and Extinction, by M. H. Appley. Unpublished doctoral dissertation, University of Michigan, 1949. Reprinted by permission.)

lower line in the figure, has become much reduced during the learning process. Yet it still appears to reflect differences in effort and therefore differences in length of time before the next response is initiated.

### Other Correlations between Amount of Habituation Decrement and Amount of Learning

It seems clear that quantitative variations in intensity are equivalent to qualitative differences and that both ultimately function in keeping with the relative complexities of the events they reflect. It might still be worthwhile to make clear that qualitative differences in stimuli that relate to ease of learning also relate to habituation and thus to alternation. The general proposition, again, is that any factor capable of producing increased decrements should also be capable of producing increased semipermanent increments, and thus learning.

ingenious manipulation developed independently by Glanzer (1953) and by Montgomery (1952). Both reasoned that, when an animal alternated in a T-maze, one could not tell whether it was turning right because it had previously turned left, or whether it went to a white side because it had tried the black side the last time. Both built + shaped mazes they could use as T-mazes from either the top or the bottom by closing off one starting alley. If an animal is given a trial from one end and turns left to the black, and if its second trial is from the other starting alley, it can alternate responses and turn right to the black, or repeat the left turn and alternate stimuli to go to the white. However, it cannot alternate with respect to both stimulus and response simultaneously. It was found that animals tended to alternate stimuli, S, and thus repeat responses, R.

Subsequently, several colleagues and I (Walker, Dember, Earl, & Karoly, 1955) went a step further, placing the + maze on wheels. With a somewhat more complex design, we were able to offer animals a choice of alternation with respect to all three—stimulus, place, and response—or any one against the other two. In this setting, we found that stimulus was most important, place was next important, and response was last. Following that experiment, it was reasoned that the response could be made a significant factor in alternation if the feedback to the two responses was made qualitatively very different. To accomplish this, a slightly modified + maze was built. The animal was required to twist in three dimensions to enter the goal alley, and the responses to the two sides required very different movement patterns. We referred to this maze as the sidewinder or contortion maze. The previous design was now repeated (Walker, Dember, Earl, Fawl, & Karoly, 1955), and it was found that the response was now a considerable factor in alternation. It is now my belief that the animal alternates in these situations with respect to whatever aspect of the situation it attends to while making the two responses.

What is important in this context is that these two studies yielded eight conditions in which the proportional tendency to alternate, and thus what facet of the situation underwent habituation during a choice event, was known. It remained then for Walker and Paradise to run learning studies in which each of the eight factors was made the relevant contingency that was followed by reward. We predicted that the factor that produced the greatest tendency to alternate would prove to be the cue that produced the fastest learning. This proved to be the case, as is shown by the rankings in Table 6-2. Alternation scores ranged from about 94% for the situation in which the animal could alternate with respect to stimulus, place, and response simultaneously in the vertical maze (SPR-V) to only 25% (ranked eighth) for place alone in the vertical maze when, to alter-

TABLE 6-2. Correlation of Alternation and Learning

| | | Rank Orders | |
| --- | --- | --- | --- |
| Cue[a] | Alternation | Days to Learning Criterion | Total Errors |
| SPR-V | 1 | 1 | 1 |
| SPR-H | 2 | 2 | 2 |
| S-H | 3 | 3 | 3 |
| S-V | 4.5 | 4.5 | 4.5 |
| R-V | 4.5 | 4.5 | 4.5 |
| P-H | 6 | 7 | 7 |
| R-H | 7 | 6 | 6 |
| P-V | 8 | 8 | 8 |

[a]SPR indicates that all three potential cues—stimulus, place, and response—were relevant. A letter alone, such as S, indicates that the stimulus was relevant, while the other two, place and response, were irrelevant. H designates the horizontal maze, while V designates the vertical, sidewinder, or contortion maze. (From Walker & Paradise, 1958.)

nate with respect to place, the animal had to repeat both the stimuli and the responses of the two choices. Days to a learning criterion ranged from about three days for SPR-V to about 9.2 days for P-V. The total number of errors ranged from about seven to about 31.5. The predicted correlation between alternation and learning scores showed one reversal at the sixth and seventh ranks but still yielded a statistically significant Tau value of .89. Thus, the unlikely correlation was clearly demonstrated. Whatever operated to produce a large temporary response decrement through habituation also operated to produce a very large semipermanent response increment, or learning.

## SOME GENERALITIES

In Chapters 5 and 6, I have undertaken to review three classes of phenomena ordinarily treated separately, as if they were not related to one another. The three classes of phenomena are: (a) aspects of the occurrence of a single psychological event, (b) temporary effects of occurrence of psychological events elicited repeatedly by stimuli with high demand characteristics and usually referred to as habituation phenomena, and (c) the temporary effects of the occurrence of one choice on a second subsequent choice between two alternatives, usually referred to as alternation phenomena. I have tried to demonstrate that the three are intimately interrelated. This interrelation encompasses both the expected behavioral effects of the manipulation of the same variables, such as the intensity of the event or the frequency of occurrence of the event, and the character of the probable underlying neural mechanisms. I have also tried to show how these variables, behavioral effects, and mechanisms also underlie learning phenomena, which will be discussed in the next chapter. Some of these relationships appear self-evident, such as the fact that strong stimuli lead to large habituation effects and rapid learning. Some are apparently paradoxical, such as the tendency of rewards to produce greater habituation and thus bias against repetition of a rewarded response, which is opposite in direction from the effect of repeated contingent reward.

There is little need to adumbrate the biological significance of the priority of stimuli with high demand characteristics. I have argued for a normal duration for most psychological events of approximately one-half second. Such a limited and nearly fixed duration of psychological events permits the organism to terminate the processing of one event and commence the process of a second event, without interference between the two, at a rate of about two events per second. Longer durations would produce significant reductions in the processing capacity of the organism. Furthermore, during the processing of one event, the organism is vulnerable in the sense that it cannot change events in midstream. Thus, the course of the stream of psychological events can be changed at half-second intervals but not at shorter intervals. Half-second flexibility is apparently sufficient for high probability of survival for humans and most other mammals. The interval may very well be significantly longer for some reptiles and significantly shorter for some birds and insects. Within a species, it may well be short for some systems and long for others. However, since the duration of psychological events controls the flexibility of the stream and the latency of its capacity to change, there seems little question that the duration of psychological events could be subject to selective pressure in the evolutionary sense.

We have seen that some responses in some organisms do not show habituation; in these instances, the organism stands ready to respond to such stimuli at all times. Habituation is rapid to some stimuli, primarily weak ones. On the other hand, some intense stimuli actually reverse the decremental process and show increments when applied repeatedly. It is easy to imagine evolutionary selection of organisms that do not adapt to stimuli with informational significance for them, that adapt to others that do not in themselves signify threats, and that show increased responsiveness to others intense enough to produce damage if applied repeatedly.

A limited bias against repeating what one has just done also has great biological value. It produces exploration and thus knowledge of a much larger environment than would be the case without it. That a reward produces a greater bias against immediately repeating the rewarded response also has biological utility. An organism that would stop to consume a large reward immediately would be much more endangered than one that responded to such a finding by an intensive exploration of the surrounds before settling down to eat.

Finally, habituation and its manifestation in alternation phenomena produce the basic variability upon which instrumental learning is built. If there is no variability in behavior, it cannot be modified through instrumental learning operations. The greater the range of responses that can occur in a situation, the greater the potential for learned uniformity in the situation. Thus, variability in behavior is the basis for invariability in learning.

# chapter seven

# Enduring effects of occurrence of psychological events

The character of psychological events, and changes in their character as a product of their occurrence, are the concerns of a great many psychologists who study only one aspect of the problem. Thus, studies of sensation, perception, motivation, learning, decision process, problem solving, and thinking, among others, involve aspects of the character of psychological events. A focus for these disparate concerns is a concept such as that of a *central processor,* an inadequate name for the core of being, the channel through which the stream of psychological events flows. It is the point at which events are affected by conscious awareness as well as unconscious factors and is the locus of choice behavior and the exercise of free will.

In this chapter, I emphasize the enduring effects of one aspect of learning—the frequency of occurrence of psychological events. I have chosen this emphasis because of the importance that frequency plays in all theories of learning and because the discussion of the effects of frequency will provide useful concepts and values in developing a theoretical account of more complex processes such as chunking and decision making. The role of psychological complexity and preference theory in dealing with complex processes is the subject of Chapter 8.

## LEARNING AND PSYCHOLOGICAL COMPLEXITY

Enduring effects of the occurrence of psychological events are generally considered to be learning. Within the Hedgehog, learning consists of a reduction in the complexity of an event and can be the product of the simple occurrence of the event. Since this definition is slightly different from others commonly employed in psychology, especially in that neither reward nor multiple occurrence of events is necessary, let me indicate some of the ways in which I see traditional learning and cognitive paradigms to be subsumed under complexity reduction.

Learning can occur in a single trial. A single occurrence of a psychological event can produce a sudden reorganization of the event such that it is reasonable to say that insight has occurred or that a problem has been solved. In both cases, the complexity of the event has undergone sudden reduction and seems simpler, and would probably be reported as simpler, than it was before. Learning has taken place without multiple occurrences of the event.

In serial learning or paired associates learning, even though the individual items are familiar and not grossly removed from optimal complexity level, the task of reproducing the list in serial order or of associating a strange pair is usually far above optimal complexity level. Repetition is necessary to simplify the event to a level that permits reproduction by the subject. The strength of association between a pair of words is a measure of the extent to which this decrease in complexity has occurred because of prior experience with the items. The usual measures of learning in these tasks— number correct or, sometimes, the latency of response—are indirect measures from which the complexity of the associated event can be inferred. It is an easy prediction that more direct measures of the complexity of the events during the acquisition process would show a steady decline as the subject progresses toward the learning criterion. Such measures are rarely obtained.

Within the Hedgehog, rewards generally operate to make one event more complicated and nearer to optimal level than alternative events. For rewards of a nonbiological variety to function in the control of behavior, it is necessary to arrange a situation in which all available events, including the desired event, are suboptimal. In one such situation, for example, a rat will come to choose a maze arm that leads to a novel stimulus because any maze arm that leads to a novel stimulus represents an event that is nearer to optimal complexity level than that represented by any of the other maze arms.

When a biological motive such as hunger is involved, and the reward is food, the choice of the maze arm that leads to food can be doubly determined. I suggest that hunger is a state in which there is a large afferent input into the central nervous system. This input creates internally insistent psychological events that are superoptimal. They can be brought nearer to optimal level or made to disappear only through eating. Thus, a hungry rat will come to choose a maze arm leading to food, especially if the food is somewhat novel, both because the food reduces the superoptimal complexity level and because the arm with novel food is nearer to optimum than any of the empty arms.

This analysis leads to a prediction about performance that may be surprising to some readers. If an organism comes to choose one of a set of available alternatives because it is closer to optimal complexity level than the others, the frequency of its choice of that alternative will increase, and the frequency of choice of the alternatives farther from optimum will decrease. Since repeated occurrence of a particular event produces progressive simplification, under repeated occurrences the event should gradually simplify until it approaches or reaches the complexity levels of the alternative events. When that occurs, the organism should no longer show a preference for the "learned" alternative. Thus, "learning" curves induced in this manner should show a rise, reach asymptote, and then begin a decline. As I have indicated elsewhere (Walker, 1964, 1969a), some "acquisition" curves do rise and fall even though acquisition conditions (continued presence of reward or continued application of the unconditioned stimulus) are continued. Many acquisition curves that do not show the decline fail to do so only because the experimenter discontinued the acquisition conditions at or near asymptote performance and did not continue that phase of the experiment long enough to reveal the entire process. An empirical example will be cited later.

In the Hedgehog, all learning is to be accounted for by changes in the complexity levels of psychological events, and all performance is to be accounted for in terms of the distances between the complexity levels of events and optimal complexity level. The hedgehog character of the theory is nowhere more apparent than in its intended simplicity and universality in the complex field of learning and performance.

When a psychological event occurs repeatedly at intervals of sufficient length that habituation effects are not a significant factor, the complexity of the event usually undergoes a progressive reduction in level as an exponential function of the frequency of occurrence. The following is a reasonable mathematical description of this change in complexity:

$$C_\psi = kC_u (10^{-aN}) + C_u, \text{ where}$$
$$C_\psi = \text{psychological complexity,}$$
$$C_u = \text{ultimate or irreducible psychological complexity,}$$

$k$    = constant,
$a$    = constant controlling rate of reduction in complexity, and
$N$   = frequency of occurrence of the event.

The suggested equation is an empirically derived equation that fits many learning curves. However, the choice of this equation has several interesting theoretical consequences. Figure 7-1 is an idealized plot of changes in the psychological complexity levels of seven events that differ primarily in the value of $C_u$, the ultimate or asymptotic complexity level. They are arranged in quite reasonable relations to optimal complexity level and thus to the associated preference function drawn in a superimposed position on the right side of the figure.

Some of the interesting implications are these. If I know the psychological complexity values of a range of stimuli, I can choose a set composed only of stimuli above optimum. I can then have the stimuli rated for complexity and preference and obtain a monotonic curve in which the least complex are the most preferred. I can as easily choose a set in which stimuli in the middle of the complexity range will be preferred, yielding the inverted-U-shaped function. If I select only very simple stimuli, I can obtain a monotonic curve in which the most complex stimuli are the most preferred. Thus, the question of curve shape is not critical without independent assessment of psychological complexity and optimal complexity level.

The effects of repeated experience on preference are equally varied. I can choose a complex stimulus as might be represented by the four upper curves and obtain a preference function with experience that verifies Zajonc's (1968) variant of an old saw, "Familiarity

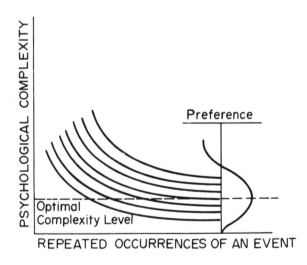

FIGURE 7-1. *Basic Psychological Complexity and Preference Theory*

breeds content." I can as well choose a stimulus slightly above optimal complexity level and obtain a preference curve with experience that confirms an inverted-U-shaped pattern. I can also choose a stimulus that is so simple that repeated experience produces a progressive decrease in preference. Again, meaningful predictions require independent assessment of psychological complexity and optimal complexity level.

What follows is an account of a number of experimental studies designed to demonstrate the functional relationships between psychological complexity and a variety of traditional measures of learning as they are affected by frequency and duration of experience.

## THE EFFECT OF EXPERIENCE ON PSYCHOLOGICAL COMPLEXITY AND PREFERENCE IN ANIMALS

There is a difficult logical problem involved in animal research on stimulus complexity and preference. It is easy to ask human subjects how complex they think a given stimulus is and then ask them to rate their preference for it. It is more difficult to ask an animal to distinguish between these two questions. If one presents an array of stimuli to an animal, and if the animal approaches one element of that array, it is reasonable to assume that it prefers that stimulus to the others. If the array is composed of stimuli that have a dimension of complexity that is obvious to the experimenter (a priori complexity), one can infer that the animal has expressed a preference for the chosen stimulus on the basis of its relative complexity. However, the inference is not a strong one. If the pattern of successive choices is orderly along this complexity dimension, the inference that the animal is responding to the complexity of the stimuli seems strengthened.

The lack of independent evidence for complexity and preference is the major disadvantage in working with animals on this problem. The advantages lie in the assumed relative simplicity of the animal and the degree of control that the experimenter can exercise.

Several of the studies I will describe involve the use of a four-foot square box that was divided into four compartments by walls projecting from the centers of the four sides. These walls stopped short of the center, leaving a central area from which a rat could have free access to any of the four compartments. Stimuli varying in a priori complexity could be arranged in the four compartments. An animal could then be introduced to the center of the box for a period of time on several days. A record could then be made of how long the animal spent in the presence of each of the four stimuli, as well as of the order in which the animal chose to visit each.

One study (E. L. Walker & Walker, 1964) involved simple wall patterns. One compartment had walls of a uniform gray, a second had a set of horizontal stripes, a third had vertical stripes, and a fourth had a checkered pattern. The assumption is that these stimuli represent four levels of two-dimensional stimulus complexity for the rat. Animals were placed in the central area and observed for 30 minutes on each of five successive days. A simple complexity index was calculated by assigning the values 1 through 4 to the four sets of stimuli. Time spent in the presence of each stimulus multiplied by the complexity value and divided by the total time yields a simple value ranging from 1.00 for an animal who spent the entire time in the presence of the simple stimulus to a value of 4.00 for an animal who spent the entire time in the presence of the most complex stimulus. The learning postulate of psychological complexity and preference theory yields the prediction that the complexity index should increase in value with extended exposure to the alternatives.

In Figure 7-2 there is a general tendency for the complexity index to increase in value with the passage of time, both within and between days. Thus, the expected gradual shift in preference from simpler stimuli to more complex stimuli was confirmed. However, neither curve is monotonic, and the low complexity indices reflect a marked preference for the simplest (gray) compartment.

A similar study was done in which the stimuli varied in three dimensions (E. L. Walker & Walker, 1964). One of the compartments was identical with the gray compartment of the first study. A second had a baffle extending from one of the exterior walls. A third had two such baffles, and a fourth had more short baffles in a complex pattern. Again, there was a clear tendency for the animals to shift preference over time toward the more complex stimuli. This was especially true between days, as shown in Figure 7-3.

Although the results seem clear enough within each of the two studies, the very different complexity indices in the two raise a question of whether the seven stimuli used could be ordered from these data. In the first study, the gray compartment was preferred to any of the others until the last day; in the second study, the most complex baffle compartment was preferred by most of the animals after the first day, and the gray compartment was virtually ignored throughout. Although the seven stimuli could be ordered in terms of preference, the results are not sufficiently robust to make one confident in that ordering.

The ordering could be tested, however by combining some of the stimuli from the two studies in a single set. The plain gray compartment was selected as the least complex, a one-baffle pattern as more complex, the horizontal stripes as slightly more complex, and a very complex compartment with three baffles and vertical stripes on the walls as the most complex. Exposure duration was increased from the previous 150 minutes to 600 minutes, 100 minutes per day for six days.

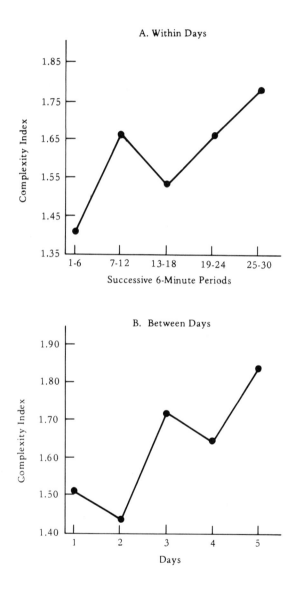

FIGURE 7-2. *Shifting Preference for Two-Dimensional Stimuli. Changing preference for wall patterns in rats. The gray pattern is assigned a value of 1, horizontal stripes a value of 2, vertical stripes a value of 3, and a checkered pattern a value of 4. Each index shows preference calculated from time spent in the presence of the four stimuli. (Redrawn from "Response to Stimulus Complexity in the Rat," by E. L. Walker and B. E. Walker,* Psychological Record, *1964, 14, 489–497. Reprinted by permission.)*

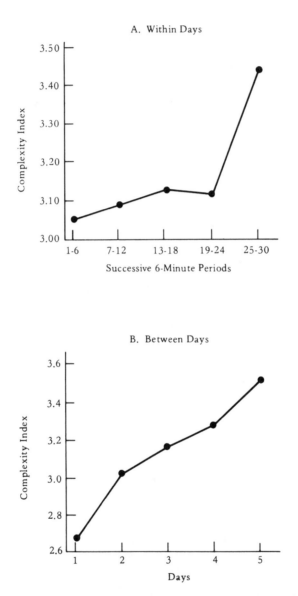

FIGURE 7-3. *Shifting Preference for Three-Dimensional Stimuli. The empty compartment is assigned a value of 1, a compartment with one baffle a value of 2, a compartment with two baffles a value of 3, and a compartment with a complex set of baffles a value of 4. (Redrawn from "Response to Stimulus Complexity in the Rat," by E. L. Walker and B. E. Walker,* Psychological Record, *1964,* 14, *489–497. Reprinted by permission.)*

With the longer exposure, very orderly results are apparent in Figure 7-4 both within and between days, even though only three animals were tested with this set of stimuli. The slight elevation of the complexity index in the first 20-minute block of the graph for within days is attributable to the tendency, noted in Chapter 3, for animals to explore all four compartments in an information-gaining phase, a tendency that tends to disappear between days.

The behavior of the animals can be analyzed in a slightly different manner that does not involve the rather arbitrary complexity index. The exposure periods can be divided into ten-minute blocks. Each block for each animal can be assigned to one of the four compartments on the basis of which compartment was the preferred one (in terms of time spent in the compartment) during that time block. Tabulations can then be made both within and between days, as shown in Table 7-1. The gradual and very orderly shifts in preference from the simple to the complex is quite apparent.

In each of the preceding animal studies, the animals were permitted free choice from among an array of stimuli that differed in

*TABLE 7-1.* Preferred Stimuli. Three animals were exposed for 100 minutes per day for 6 days. The preferred stimulus is identified as the place where the animal spent the most time in each ten-minute time block.

| Within Days<br>Minutes | Gray | One Baffle | Horizontal Stripes | Vertical Stripes and Three Baffles |
|---|---|---|---|---|
| 1–10 | 2 | 14 | 0 | 2 |
| 11–20 | 1 | 11 | 4 | 2 |
| 21–30 | 4 | 9 | 3 | 2 |
| 31–40 | 3 | 9 | 4 | 2 |
| 41–50 | 5 | 6 | 5 | 2 |
| 51–60 | 4 | 6 | 6 | 2 |
| 61–70 | 2 | 6 | 7 | 3 |
| 71–80 | 4 | 3 | 6 | 5 |
| 81–90 | 3 | 5 | 5 | 5 |
| 91–100 | 3 | 5 | 5 | 5 |
| *Between Days*<br>*Day* | | | | |
| 1 | 20 | 9 | 0 | 1 |
| 2 | 6 | 17 | 7 | 0 |
| 3 | 1 | 15 | 14 | 0 |
| 4 | 2 | 12 | 12 | 4 |
| 5 | 2 | 13 | 5 | 10 |
| 6 | 0 | 8 | 7 | 15 |

Study by B. E. Walker, reported in E. L. Walker, 1969b.

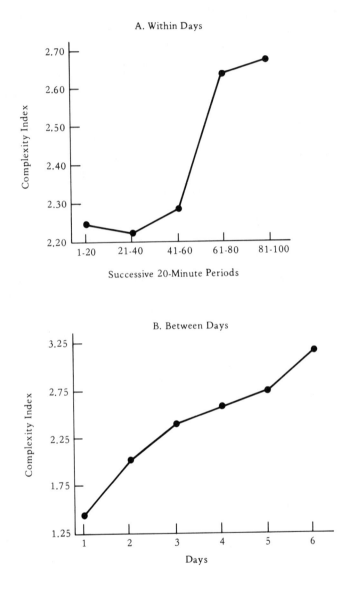

FIGURE 7-4. Shifting Preference for Mixed Two- and Three-Dimensional Stimuli. The gray compartment is assigned a value of 1, a one-baffle compartment a value of 2, a compartment with horizontal stripes a value of 3, and a multiple-baffle compartment lined with vertical stripes a value of 4. (Redrawn from "Learning, Extinction, and Relearning of Running and BRL in a Segmented Straight Alley," by B. E. Walker and E. L. Walker, Psychological Record, 1964, 14, 507–513. Reprinted by permission.)

a priori complexity. Changes in the psychological complexities of the events elicited by these stimuli are indexed by shifting preference for more complex stimuli. If only one level of stimulus complexity is available, changes in psychological complexity and shifts in preference can be indexed by increases and decreases in learned performance. For example, at the beginning of training in an avoidance conditioning situation, the event or events represented by the presentation of a conditioned stimulus, the presentation of an unconditioned stimulus, and the occurrence of resulting response are far above optimal complexity level. When the response first anticipates the aversive stimulus, the sequence undergoes a rather sudden simplification because of the omission of the aversive unconditioned stimulus. The organism now has two options—to respond quickly and avoid the unconditioned stimulus, or to delay responding and receive the unconditioned stimulus. If the unconditioned stimulus is severe enough, the avoidance response will continue to appear over a great number of trials even though the event of CS-R (avoidance) undergoes progressive simplification and may fall far below optimum. However, if the US-UCR is not too aversive, the psychological complexity of the avoidance response may reach a level of simplification that may carry it a greater distance from optimum on the simple end than the US-UCR is from optimum on the complex end. When this occurs, the avoidance response will disappear. The result of this sequence of events will be a learning curve that rises to a maximum and then declines again to zero or to a low level.

A number of learning curves that rise and fall without a change in the conditions leading to acquisition have been reported in the literature; I have cited a variety involving each of the major learning paradigms (Walker, 1964, 1973a). An example will be sufficient here.

Figure 7-5 shows the results of an avoidance conditioning study in rats. Robert Earl conditioned a head lifting response in three rats to avoid a dazzlingly bright light in the eyes (Walker, 1964). The proportion of avoidance responses rose to a maximum and then fell during 25 days of avoidance training. The interpretation of this result in terms of complexity and preference theory is as follows. In the early phases of training, the event represented by successful avoidance was nearer optimum than the event representing failure to avoid. As both events became progressively simpler, the avoidance response progressed sufficiently below optimum, and the nonavoidance response involving exposure to the dazzling light came sufficiently close to optimum, that preference was reversed, and the animals chose not to avoid the light.

### Summary of Results of Animal Studies

In each of the studies reviewed, there is evidence that continued or repeated exposure to stimuli leads to a gradual shift in preference

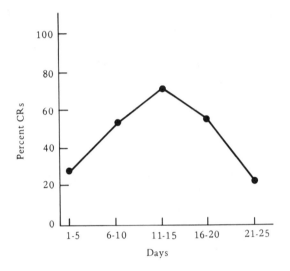

FIGURE 7-5. *Light-Avoidance Conditioning. The figure displays the course of appearance and disappearance of a head-lifting avoidance response in rats with continued pairing of a conditioned stimulus and a dazzling bright light. (Redrawn from "Psychological Complexity as a Basis for a Theory of Motivation and Choice," by E. L. Walker. In D. Levine (Ed.),* Nebraska Symposium on Motivation. *Copyright 1964 by the University of Nebraska Press. Reprinted by permission.)*

toward more complex stimuli, or to an increasing and then decreasing preference for the same stimulus. Although such results serve to confirm the expectations of psychological complexity and preference theory, their relevance depends on two factors: the assumption that stimuli selected on a priori grounds do, in fact, differ in complexity for the animal and the simultaneous inferences concerning psychological complexity and preference from a single performance. More convincing evidence can be obtained from human subjects, who offer the possibility of independent assessment of complexity and preference.

### THE EFFECT OF EXPERIENCE ON PSYCHOLOGICAL COMPLEXITY OF, AND PREFERENCE FOR, MUSICAL COMPOSITIONS AND VISUAL ART

The effects of experience on psychological complexity and preference can be examined either by manipulating the experience a subject has with a given set of stimuli or by making use of some aspect of well known differences in past experience with sets of stimuli. In Chapter 6 I discussed a study by Heyduk (1972) and one by Verveer, Barry, and Bousfield (1933) in which the effects of manipulated experience with musical compositions showed changes in complexity and preference that were in the directions predicted. In both studies, large changes in complexity and preference were evident as a result of massed experience, indicating a substantial temporary effect of habituation. In both studies, there was some evidence of a more enduring learning effect, and in both there was some evidence of predicted differences attributable to differences in past experience. However, the learning effects were relatively small compared to the habituation effects.

An example of a fairly substantial and expected effect of prior experience can be seen in a study by Kay Sinclair (Walker, 1969b) that will be reported in detail later. Sinclair had subjects rate a number of well known black-and-white graphics for complexity and preference. One group of her subjects were students working toward doctoral degrees in art. They were able to identify most of the pictures by name and by artist, and thus they can be assumed to have had considerable experience with these and similar materials. A middle-experience group was drawn from students of the history of art. A low-experience group was drawn from law students, whose lack of experience was evident in that none of them could name any of the pictures or artists. Mean complexity and preference ratings for these stimulus materials, shown in Figure 7-6, demonstrate the expected effects.

The less experienced law students produced a curve that is relatively flat, and they tended to use most of the range of complexity. However, the flatness of the curve indicates that they did not show very consistent preferences. If there is an optimum preference, it is in the middle of the scale of complexity. Both of the more experienced groups used a more constricted range on the complexity scale and showed more definite preferences. There was a general tendency for the art history students to prefer more complex pictures than did the law students and for the most advanced art students to prefer more complex pictures than did the history of art students.

Presumed differences in prior experience with the stimulus materials has been a variable in a number of the studies of visual and auditory materials reported in this volume. The differences are always in the direction predicted by the learning postulate of complexity and preference theory, but they are rarely robust and rarely reach acceptable levels of statistical significance. When all such results are contemplated together, two closely related factors stand out as possible sources of an account of the problems involved. First, some means of determining amount of prior experience appear to guarantee greater differences than others. For example, the classification of students in the Sinclair study has great face validity as

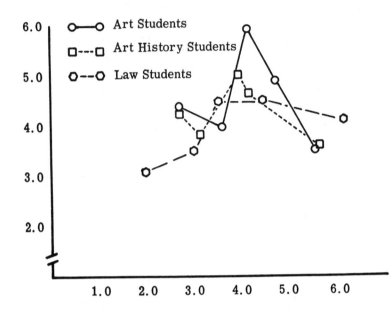

FIGURE 7-6. *Effects of Prior Experience on Ratings of Complexity and Prefer-ence for Black-and-White Graphics. The figure shows mean complexity and preference ratings of well known black-and-white graphics by three groups with different amounts of prior experience with works of visual art. (Study by Kay Sinclair, reported in Walker, 1969b.)*

representing large differences in experience, and significant dif-ferences were obtained. In contrast, several studies in which sub-jects were simply questioned about the amount of prior musical experience they had yielded less convincing differences. The second variable is also related to the validity of the "experience" designa-tion. Many of the stimuli are clearly within the range of common experience. Sinclair's graphic prints, Heyduk's miniature musical compositions, and the jazz records of Verveer, Barry, and Bous-field fall in this class and show clear effects of amount of prior experience. Many other stimuli employed in relevant studies may be sufficiently outside the range of ordinary experience that the prior experience variable may be relatively meaningless. In the interest of having a quantitative scale of stimulus complexity that is independent of the reactions of the subjects involved, stimuli are frequently generated by some fixed rule. In the case of visual stimuli, the rule may govern the number of sides of a polygon or the num-ber and degree of changes in direction of a scribble; in the case of auditory stimuli, the use of laboratory sound generators, unmusical combinations of sounds, or unmusical temporal patterns may pro-duce stimuli that look or sound strange to most subjects. It should be obvious that, if the stimuli look or sound strange to all subjects, then relevant differences in prior experience with such stimuli do not exist. Thus, it is generally true in these studies that the more "normal" the stimuli and the more meaningful the classification of relevant prior experience, the greater the observed differences attributable to prior experience. This observation suggests that it might be useful to study the psychological complexities and preferences for words, since there would be no question about the "normality" of the stimuli, and since much is known about the relative frequency of occurrence of words in the language.

## THE HEDGEHOG AND VERBAL LEARNING

Verbal learning offers a critical universe in which to test the usefulness of the Hedgehog. Elements of the English language vary in frequency of occurrence, creating a strong presumption that adults have had a long period of differential exposure to, and use of, these elements. Furthermore, data are available with respect to the frequency of occurrence of individual letters, pairs of letters, triplets, and words of various lengths. These quantitative properties of language make it a particularly useful field for trying to establish the utility of psychological complexity and preference theory. In addition, much is known about the ease with which different verbal materials are learned and about the variables that influence such learning.

The increased precision involved in the use of verbal learning materials may justify the employment of the empirically derived exponential equation for describing the learning process.

$$C_\psi = kC_u \,(10^{-aN}) + C_u$$

$C_\psi$ can represent the psychological complexity of an event involving a word. $N$ can represent the frequency of occurrence of the word. Available knowledge concerning the relative frequencies of occurrence of words in the English language offers the potential for numerical values to be inserted in the equation. $C_u$ is assumed to be the ultimate complexity level of an event with an infinite number of occurrences and thus represents the asymptote of the exponential curve. Events should differ in $C_u$ to the extent that they vary in inherent structure, which sets limits on how simple they may become. Since words differ in length, and since length should set a lower limit on how simple an item may become with repeated experience, $C_u$ should increase with word length in an orderly sequence. An argument can also be made that the value of $a$, which controls the rate of approach to the asymptote with experience, might also vary systematically with the length of the word. The argument could be based on the assumption that the exponent should be smallest for single letters, since letters must be learned before one progresses to words. Furthermore, long words tend to be composed of components that are identical or similar to shorter words. The result would be that the learning of shorter words would generalize to the learning of longer words and thus produce faster learning. If so, the value of *a*, indicating the rate of simplification with experience, would be increased.

Since the Hedgehog is assumed to be a complete theory of motivation as well as of learning, applying the Hedgehog to verbal learning material offers the potential of supplying this field with motivational principles. This achievement might be a useful one, inasmuch as the field of human verbal learning has traditionally eschewed any appeal to motivation in its formulations. In the studies of the psychological complexity of verbal materials to be reported in this chapter, preference ratings were systematically collected. These results and the role of motivation will be discussed in this context; a systematic discussion of problems of motivation and preference occurs in Chapter 9.

The following series of experiments is based almost exclusively on data published by Underwood and Schulz (1960), with an assist from Thorndike and Lorge (1944). In *Meaningfulness and Verbal Learning*, Underwood and Schulz present a long series of experiments devoted to an analysis of the bases on which language elements are differentially easy or difficult to learn. Their work is so elegant and precise, and the data are presented in such complete detail, that it is possible to use the data and materials they present and to build new studies directly on their findings.

The experiments I will report tend to follow a single pattern. Stimulus materials are taken from Underwood and Schulz, along with the data they have gathered and presented. These stimuli are presented to new groups of subjects, who are asked to evaluate the stimuli for relative complexity or relative preference. It is then possible to relate these new variables to all the variables presented by Underwood and Schulz. The advantage of this procedure is that it permits the building of a very substantial edifice of integrated data. It has the disadvantage of requiring rather patient plodding through the details of a series of experiments before the larger picture becomes apparent.

### Empirical Questions

As an aid in separating the most important issues from the details of experimentation, I will focus on three questions throughout the presentation of the experiments, present a summary of answers to these three questions, and finally present a summary of information related to a fourth question.

*Psychological Complexity and Frequency.* The first question on which I would like to focus is: *do measures of subjective complexity correlate with data on natural frequency?* For example, letters of the alphabet occur with very different frequencies in English. It can be presumed that English-speaking adults have experienced the letter *e* many more times than they have experienced the letter *q*. In the Hedgehog, the psychological event induced by the presentation of the letter *e* should be psychologically simpler than the event induced by the letter *q*. This theoretical difference in the relative psychological complexities of the two events should be reflected in differences in both subjective complexity (ratings of complexity supplied by a single experimental subject) and consensual complexity (mean ratings). The same logical expectation can be explored with bigrams (naturally occurring two-letter sequences), trigrams (naturally occurring three-letter sequences), nonsense syllables, and words.

*Various Estimates of Psychological Complexity.* The second question on which I will focus is: *To what extent are different estimates of psychological complexity correlated?* Subjective complexity and consensual complexity are very good estimates of psychological complexity under most circumstances. In other contexts it has been established that subjects are quite consistent in making ratings of the relative complexities of a wide range of stimuli. This consistency holds both within and between subjects. However, subjective complexity is only one of many possible estimates of psychological complexity that could prove useful. For example, ratings of pronounceability could very well turn out to be excellent estimates of psychological complexity with an emphasis on the motor elements of a psychological event. The different sets of stimulus materials used in these studies offer several such alternate estimates of psychological complexity. I will therefore focus on the interrelationships among estimates where alternates are available.

*Psychological Complexity and Learning.* Perhaps the most interesting of the three focus questions is: *Do measures of subjective complexity predict differences in the rate at which verbal materials are learned?* The goal of much research in verbal learning is the determination of the parameters of stimuli that lead to differences in the ease or difficulty with which various verbal materials are learned as response items. This is the major goal of the Underwood and Schulz volume. The question is not whether subjective complexity is a better predictor of ease of learning than meaningfulness, frequency, or other traditional variables. The question is rather whether psychological complexity, as estimated by scaling subjective complexity, is a sufficiently powerful variable that it can serve as a bridge between the field of verbal learning and the many other areas in which the Hedgehog is clearly applicable.

*Psychological Complexity and Preference.* The fourth question concerns *the functional relationship between psychological complexity and the other variables of verbal learning, on the one hand, and measures of preference, or evaluative variables, on the other.* The primary data on this question will be presented in the exposition of each of the experiments in turn, but consideration of the major implications of these data will be delayed until a number of the relationships can be considered at once.

### Complexity and Preference in Language Materials

*Alphabetic Frequency.* The letters of the alphabet occur with somewhat varying frequencies in any language. A number of efforts have been made to estimate the relative frequencies of occurrence of letters through the counting of various samples of written material. Underwood counted letter frequencies in 150 pages of 100 words each selected from a wide variety of sources. These are presented in Underwood and Schulz (1960, Table 6, p. 69) as the U Count. The frequencies and frequency ranks for this count are listed in Table 7-2.

Underwood and Schulz also report comparative learning data obtained by using two lists in which letters of the alphabet were the items to be anticipated. Each list contained 12 letters (*g* and *i* did not occur in either list). They report the mean number of correct anticipations in 15 learning trials (1960, Table 27, p. 165); these data are also listed in Table 7-2.

In order to obtain ratings of complexity and preference, I had the letters of the alphabet rated on these dimensions by 52 subjects. In an effort to give the term *complexity* the broadest kind of meaning, I used the following instruction: "Letters of the alphabet vary somewhat in relative *complexity* along a variety of dimensions. The bases could be such things as structure, sound, meaning, association value, and others." To obtain preference ratings with a broad base, the following instruction was used: "Letters of the alphabet vary somewhat in relative affective value to many people. One end of this affective dimension is represented by the words *boring, unpleasant,* and *avoidance.* The other end is represented by the words *interesting, pleasant,* and *approach."* The latter instruction was adopted on the basis of the findings reported in Chapter 3, where it was shown that experimental subjects see these three dimensions as being highly correlated. By using all three simultaneously, I hoped to define a more nearly universal dimension more likely to be free of idiosyncratic interpretation than might have been the case with any one alone. Since the rating is an empirical one, I have referred to it as the Affective dimension, which should be coordinated to the theoretical Evaluative dimension. Both rating scales ranged from 0 to 100.

The alphabet was arranged in 26 different orders, each letter appearing in each position at least once. These orders were also employed in reverse, yielding 52 different orders. Half of the subjects rated the letters for complexity first and then for affectivity. The other half of the subjects did affectivity ratings first and complexity

TABLE 7-2. Alphabetic Data

| Letter | Frequency[a] | Frequency Rank[a] | Learning Mean Correct[a] | Mean Complexity[b] | Mean Affectivity[b] |
|---|---|---|---|---|---|
| A | 5417 | 3 | 11.4 | 31.3 | 50.6 |
| B | 1049 | 20 | 9.0 | 37.2 | 52.3 |
| C | 1893 | 13 | 9.2 | 30.5 | 44.6 |
| D | 2697 | 11 | 8.1 | 30.9 | 43.7 |
| E | 8532 | 1 | 9.5 | 43.2 | 45.2 |
| F | 1494 | 15 | 6.6 | 39.1 | 45.5 |
| G | 1433 | 16 | | 50.0 | 58.1 |
| H | 3596 | 9 | 6.7 | 50.8 | 51.2 |
| I | 4993 | 4 | | 28.3 | 42.8 |
| J | 119 | 24 | 8.5 | 48.1 | 54.1 |
| K | 493 | 22 | 7.6 | 54.1 | 57.0 |
| L | 2761 | 10 | 7.7 | 33.9 | 54.3 |
| M | 1751 | 14 | 7.8 | 42.3 | 59.1 |
| N | 4820 | 6 | 8.7 | 37.7 | 46.4 |
| O | 4982 | 5 | 11.2 | 26.7 | 47.1 |
| P | 1308 | 19 | 8.6 | 40.8 | 49.4 |
| Q | 61 | 26 | 7.6 | 66.9 | 61.7 |
| R | 4217 | 8 | 8.8 | 50.7 | 55.6 |
| S | 4578 | 7 | 9.2 | 46.0 | 58.8 |
| T | 5983 | 2 | 8.1 | 31.1 | 47.9 |
| U | 2085 | 12 | 7.4 | 43.2 | 43.3 |
| V | 688 | 21 | 6.9 | 42.5 | 48.0 |
| W | 1378 | 17 | 7.4 | 63.9 | 54.3 |
| X | 132 | 23 | 7.4 | 65.2 | 55.4 |
| Y | 1331 | 18 | 6.8 | 56.6 | 51.9 |
| Z | 67 | 25 | 7.6 | 60.3 | 59.7 |

[a]From Underwood and Schulz (1960)
[b]New data

ratings second. Two different orders of the letters were used with each subject, a forward order and a reverse of a different order. Mean complexity and mean affectivity ratings obtained in this manner complete the data in Table 7-2.

Although this and subsequent studies are experimental in design and execution, the primary expression of the various relationships is best indexed by correlation coefficients. The Pierson product moment correlations between the three variables of letter frequency, ease of learning, and subjective complexity are shown in Table 7-3.

*TABLE 7-3.* Alphabetic Data Intercorrelation of Variables

|  | *Learning* | *Complexity* |
|---|---|---|
| Frequency | .57 | .54 |
| Learning |  | .51 |

With an N of 25, a correlation of .32 is significant at the .05 level. The correlations shown, as well as those that follow in this sequence of studies, express the expected relationship as a positive correlation.

With respect to the first question—whether measures of subjective complexity correlate with natural frequency—the evidence is positive. Frequency and complexity in this study show a significant correlation, with a value of .54. Letters that occur with high frequency in English, such as *e, t, a, i,* and *o,* are judged to be less complex than letters such as *k, x, j, z,* and *q,* which occur with a considerably lower frequency. It is obvious that the frequent and infrequent letters differ in a great many other respects that might contribute to complexity judgments; however, my purpose is not to demonstrate that frequency alone is the source of the judgment but only to show that, empirically, the expectation of the Hedgehog is met to a significant degree.

Since there are not multiple measures of psychological complexity in these data, there is no evidence on the second question, the extent to which different estimates of psychological complexity are correlated. The evidence on the third question is positive. The correlation between subjective complexity judgments and ease of learning is significant. When letters judged to be relatively simple are used as response items in a learning experiment, they are learned faster than are letters judged to be complex.

*Bigram Frequency.* Certain letters tend to occur in pairs in English much more often than they would occur adjacent to each other by chance. Underwood and Schulz (1960) present comparative counts of the frequency of such bigrams.

They also present the results of a study in which they obtained learning data on two sets of 12 bigrams each (Underwood and Schulz, 1960, Table 28, p. 168). The bigrams were response items to be anticipated, and the values reported are the mean number of correct anticipations in 15 trials. The bigrams and the frequency and learning values associated with each are shown in Table 7-4 (page 150). To their data, I have added the mean letter-frequency rank calculated from the U Count reported earlier (Table 7-2).

Ratings of complexity and affectivity were obtained from 50 subjects, using the same definition of the terms *complexity* and *affectivity* used in the ratings of the alphabet. Two orders of the bigrams were used. Half the subjects rated each variable first, each subject making the two ratings with a different order of bigrams. The mean ratings for complexity and affectivity are also in Table 7-4. The intercorrelations of four of the five variables are shown in Table 7-5 (page 151).

The answer to the first question is again in the affirmative. The correlations between subjective complexity and the two measures of natural frequency, letters and bigrams, are substantial. Frequent bigrams, such as *er* and *on,* are judged to be simpler than infrequent bigrams, such as *gf* and *kb.*

Again, there are no data relevant to the second question, but the answer to the third question—whether subjective complexity ratings predict ease of learning—is again positive. The correlation is .47, indicating that bigrams judged to be relatively simple are easier to learn as response items than bigrams judged to be relatively complex. It will also be noted that the correlation between subjective complexity and learning, .47, is higher than the correlations between the natural frequencies of either letters or bigrams and learning, .34 and .31.

*Trigram Frequency.* Underwood and Schulz supply data on two sets of 36 trigrams each (1960, Table 29, p. 170; Table 33, p. 187). The two differ slightly in the battery of information that Underwood and Schulz have collected and reported concerning them. What I will refer to as Trigrams-1 is a set of 36 for which they provide trigram frequency data, ratings of pronounceability, and two sets of learning data. Trigrams-2 is a set for which they report trigram frequency data, ratings of frequency, pronounceability ratings, and again two sets of learning data, one for a mixed list and one for an unmixed list. To this information, I have added a calculation of relative letter frequency in terms of the mean ranks of the letters making up the trigrams.

The 72 trigrams from these two lists were rated for complexity and affectivity by 24 subjects in the same experimental procedure used with the bigrams. The results of these experiments, along with

TABLE 7-4. Bigram Data

| Bigrams | Bigram Frequency[a] | Mean Letter Rank[b] | Learning Mean Correct[a] | Mean Complexity[c] | Mean Affectivity[c] |
|---|---|---|---|---|---|
| SU | 598 | 9.5 | 8.11 | 33.6 | 47.5 |
| XP | 237 | 21.0 | 6.83 | 75.4 | 41.9 |
| CA | 1055 | 8.0 | 5.56 | 24.8 | 43.6 |
| LD | 682 | 10.5 | 6.11 | 48.6 | 40.7 |
| OW | 676 | 10.5 | 9.78 | 20.3 | 40.2 |
| BY | 68 | 19.0 | 8.67 | 20.8 | 49.6 |
| UM | 288 | 13.0 | 4.11 | 23.1 | 56.0 |
| DS | 95 | 9.0 | 4.94 | 51.1 | 42.6 |
| NE | 1689 | 3.5 | 5.78 | 32.7 | 43.9 |
| IT | 1334 | 3.5 | 8.94 | 17.4 | 49.9 |
| ER | 4034 | 4.5 | 10.33 | 23.8 | 41.7 |
| GF | 3 | 15.5 | 4.94 | 55.9 | 43.7 |
| QU | 430 | 19.0 | 5.28 | 46.1 | 49.1 |
| KB | 7 | 21.0 | 4.33 | 62.0 | 39.5 |
| UG | 249 | 14.0 | 7.17 | 28.0 | 36.8 |
| TR | 1028 | 5.0 | 7.61 | 40.8 | 45.9 |
| LY | 1100 | 14.0 | 6.56 | 40.5 | 54.1 |
| GS | 64 | 11.5 | 6.00 | 57.4 | 40.7 |
| IM | 441 | 9.5 | 11.17 | 33.8 | 51.4 |
| HA | 1396 | 6.0 | 9.50 | 19.9 | 54.3 |
| EV | 577 | 11.0 | 8.78 | 38.8 | 47.7 |
| NC | 795 | 9.5 | 4.61 | 49.7 | 39.8 |
| DE | 1476 | 6.0 | 5.44 | 25.2 | 46.0 |
| ON | 3107 | 5.0 | 7.22 | 13.3 | 56.2 |

[a]Taken from Underwood and Schulz (1960)
[b]Calculated from Underwood and Schulz (1960)
[c]New data

*TABLE 7-5.* Bigram Data—Intercorrelations of Variables

|  | Letter Frequency | Learning | Complexity |
|---|---|---|---|
| Bigram Frequency | .66 | .34 | .52 |
| Letter Frequency |  | .31 | .58 |
| Learning |  |  | .47 |

These are correlations of 24 mean values for the 24 bigrams. With an N of 24, a correlation of about .33 is significant at the .05 level.

the information provided by Underwood and Schulz, are presented in Tables 7-6 and 7-7. Two tables of intercorrelations were then generated from the basic data of Trigrams-1 and Trigrams-2. These data are in Tables 7-8 and 7-9.

The issue of complexity and frequency is somewhat more ambiguous with trigrams than it is with single letters and bigrams. Here the four correlations are .07, .16, .20, and .40. Only the last of these exceeds the .05 confidence limit. It should also be noted that, in these materials, neither letter frequency nor trigram frequency is highly correlated with any other variable. I will return to this apparent failure to find the predicted relationship between subjective complexity and frequency.

Underwood and Schulz (1960) point to a problem associated with the relative frequencies of bigrams and trigrams. It is possible that some such combinations are not ordinarily perceived in the form in which they appear in the table. Some may be almost the verbal equivalents of a hidden figure in a visual display. For example, the trigram *ing* might be frequently perceived, because it forms a complete and common syllable. On the other hand, the trigram *tio* might be somewhat less familiar, because most of the high frequency of its occurrence is accounted for by the syllable *tion*. This logic led Underwood and Schulz to obtain ratings of the frequencies of trigrams, with the expectation that such ratings were more likely to reflect frequency of perception than frequency of actual occurrence. The ranking of the 36 trigrams in terms of frequency ratings is included in the table of Trigrams-2 (Table 7-7).

These tables do contain primary information on the second of the questions on which I wish to focus. Subjective complexity is only one very good estimate of the theoretical dimension of psychological complexity. Pronounceability is an alternative empirical estimate, and both of the Underwood and Schulz trigram studies provide mean ratings of pronounceability. In addition, the ratings of frequency in Trigrams-2 might be considered to be a third estimate of psychological complexity if we assume the expected relationship between frequency and complexity. This expectation is substantially borne out by the very high intercorrelations between

TABLE 7-6. Trigrams-1

| Trigrams | Letter Frequency Mean Rank[b] | Trigram Frequency[a] | Pronounce-ability[a] | Learning— Study #1[a] | Mean Correct Study #2[b] | Mean Complexity[b] | Mean Affectivity[c] |
|---|---|---|---|---|---|---|---|
| NDE | 6.0 | 253 | 7.63 | 4.28 | 6.62 | 58.8 | 40.3 |
| PLO | 11.0 | 44 | 3.11 | 5.39 | 7.29 | 39.3 | 41.8 |
| OUS | 7.7 | 444 | 3.34 | 5.50 | 9.58 | 40.0 | 45.2 |
| WHA | 9.7 | 61 | 3.23 | 6.50 | 8.12 | 32.1 | 44.7 |
| BOY | 13.7 | 23 | 2.26 | 11.89 | 12.67 | 20.8 | 65.0 |
| VIF | 13.7 | 1 | 3.83 | 5.50 | 5.46 | 50.0 | 48.6 |
| ING | 9.0 | 1673 | 2.46 | 8.89 | 10.04 | 26.1 | 46.2 |
| ATI | 3.3 | 799 | 4.34 | 4.89 | 7.37 | 43.5 | 44.3 |
| URN | 8.7 | 56 | 2.40 | 8.33 | 9.12 | 31.2 | 53.5 |
| HER | 6.0 | 679 | 2.06 | 9.61 | 12.08 | 23.8 | 57.1 |
| CQU | 17.0 | 3 | 8.23 | 2.28 | 7.04 | 77.8 | 37.7 |
| EST | 3.3 | 742 | 2.46 | 8.39 | 9.04 | 34.5 | 52.7 |
| HAT | 4.7 | 333 | 1.77 | 9.17 | 10.79 | 21.1 | 52.9 |
| WHE | 9.0 | 225 | 4.09 | 5.11 | 6.71 | 40.8 | 47.3 |
| DGM | 13.7 | 10 | 8.37 | 7.72 | 6.37 | 67.2 | 38.4 |
| CUB | 15.0 | 2 | 1.80 | 9.44 | 11.29 | 23.5 | 60.2 |
| YIN | 13.0 | 79 | 3.17 | 6.22 | 9.25 | 42.1 | 53.2 |
| ALI | 6.0 | 115 | 3.57 | 6.06 | 9.92 | 36.7 | 55.1 |
| SOU | 7.7 | 184 | 3.40 | 7.00 | 9.08 | 37.7 | 47.2 |
| FRO | 8.7 | 117 | 2.40 | 6.11 | 8.12 | 20.8 | 49.4 |

## TABLE 7-6. (continued)

| Trigrams | Letter Frequency Mean Rank[b] | Trigram Frequency[a] | Pronounce-ability[a] | Learning— Study #1[a] | Mean Correct Study #2[b] | Mean Complexity[b] | Mean Affectivity[c] |
|---|---|---|---|---|---|---|---|
| UND | 9.7 | 384 | 3.83 | 5.39 | 7.75 | 38.9 | 42.4 |
| ITS | 4.7 | 78 | 2.69 | 6.72 | 10.67 | 24.2 | 47.4 |
| OMP | 12.3 | 117 | 4.11 | 5.56 | 6.67 | 26.0 | 49.6 |
| VER | 10.0 | 545 | 2.91 | 6.33 | 9.08 | 23.3 | 53.0 |
| MPA | 12.0 | 58 | 7.34 | 6.17 | 6.83 | 63.1 | 44.5 |
| YLV | 16.3 | 3 | 8.37 | 6.61 | 4.21 | 78.8 | 43.6 |
| PAR | 10.3 | 425 | 1.74 | 8.50 | 11.33 | 29.0 | 50.5 |
| CHI | 9.0 | 200 | 3.29 | 10.61 | 9.21 | 42.5 | 55.9 |
| ENT | 3.0 | 1778 | 3.17 | 7.06 | 8.04 | 37.8 | 50.9 |
| JUM | 16.7 | 3 | 3.11 | 5.67 | 7.71 | 41.7 | 51.5 |
| ABL | 11.0 | 317 | 5.57 | 6.67 | 6.87 | 46.5 | 54.8 |
| NCE | 6.7 | 661 | 7.60 | 4.61 | 6.62 | 54.2 | 45.8 |
| LED | 7.3 | 145 | 1.91 | 8.06 | 9.29 | 23.2 | 46.1 |
| TIO | 3.7 | 1025 | 3.94 | 5.61 | 9.42 | 47.8 | 49.8 |
| ROP | 10.0 | 76 | 3.46 | 5.28 | 7.42 | 40.0 | 44.2 |
| ISH | 7.0 | 258 | 2.23 | 9.67 | 11.37 | 17.8 | 52.2 |

[a]Taken from Underwood and Schulz (1960)
[b]Calculated from Underwood and Schulz (1960)
[c]New data

TABLE 7-7. Trigrams-2

| Trigrams | Letter Frequency Mean Rank[b] | Trigram Frequency[a] | Rated Frequency Rank[a] | Pronounce-ability | Learning—Mixed List[a] | Mean Correct Unmixed[a] | Mean Complexity[c] | Mean Affectivity[c] |
|---|---|---|---|---|---|---|---|---|
| MPR | 13.7 | 101 | 26 | 7.94 | 4.25 | 3.62 | 60.4 | 38.7 |
| KNO | 10.7 | 56 | 3 | 4.40 | 6.50 | 6.58 | 41.9 | 50.4 |
| JUS | 14.3 | 136 | 11 | 3.29 | 8.25 | 9.71 | 21.6 | 49.1 |
| VIL | 12.0 | 46 | 13 | 3.14 | 8.67 | 9.71 | 42.6 | 38.4 |
| FAI | 7.7 | 215 | 16 | 3.83 | 6.42 | 5.54 | 47.3 | 40.3 |
| XPL | 9.0 | 15 | 33 | 8.43 | 6.25 | 3.92 | 79.7 | 39.1 |
| NDE | 6.0 | 253 | 33 | 7.63 | 4.37 | 4.04 | 61.8 | 36.5 |
| GOI | 10.0 | 11 | 19 | 4.60 | 7.50 | 7.42 | 53.5 | 37.6 |
| COM | 10.3 | 301 | 1 | 2.31 | 10.21 | 9.83 | 28.9 | 49.1 |
| LIR | 7.0 | 5 | 20 | 4.03 | 5.79 | 4.33 | 42.6 | 41.4 |
| BLE | 10.3 | 382 | 5 | 4.23 | 7.17 | 7.75 | 39.1 | 38.2 |
| TJU | 7.3 | 1 | 36 | 7.74 | 4.50 | 1.79 | 71.4 | 35.8 |
| COU | 9.7 | 106 | 12 | 3.14 | 8.42 | 6.54 | 38.0 | 46.5 |
| SLO | 7.0 | 63 | 4 | 2.20 | 9.87 | 7.96 | 31.5 | 43.3 |
| NDR | 8.3 | 143 | 32 | 8.14 | 4.50 | 4.50 | 61.5 | 35.2 |
| MPO | 12.3 | 35 | 25 | 7.23 | 5.71 | 5.21 | 55.4 | 38.1 |
| JOR | 11.7 | 214 | 18 | 3.51 | 6.42 | 5.71 | 46.3 | 41.8 |
| LTY | 8.3 | 20 | 14 | 7.03 | 4.00 | 2.50 | 62.6 | 36.0 |
| BLI | 11.7 | 257 | 17 | 3.37 | 6.71 | 5.96 | 47.8 | 35.5 |
| DGM | 5.3 | 10 | 34 | 8.42 | 5.87 | 4.37 | 65.3 | 35.4 |

TABLE 7-7. (continued)

| Trigrams | Letter Frequency Mean Rank[b] | Trigram Frequency[a] | Rated Frequency Rank[a] | Pronounce-ability | Learning— Mixed List[a] | Mean Correct Unmixed[a] | Mean Complexity[c] | Mean Affectivity[c] |
|---|---|---|---|---|---|---|---|---|
| RTI | 5.0 | 280 | 28 | 7.43 | 2.33 | 1.79 | 66.6 | 34.7 |
| WSE | 11.7 | 5 | 29 | 7.06 | 6.54 | 6.33 | 56.8 | 51.3 |
| VEN | 9.3 | 448 | 10 | 2.66 | 9.71 | 9.08 | 43.3 | 46.4 |
| KIV | 11.3 | 1 | 24 | 3.86 | 8.75 | 7.21 | 48.4 | 51.9 |
| FET | 5.3 | 108 | 15 | 2.49 | 7.67 | 10.46 | 39.4 | 43.8 |
| MBE | 11.7 | 68 | 30 | 7.80 | 3.96 | 4.54 | 53.9 | 42.6 |
| SCI | 8.3 | 162 | 2 | 3.60 | 10.54 | 8.54 | 38.3 | 52.6 |
| DYI | 11.3 | 45 | 27 | 6.11 | 4.92 | 4.96 | 66.4 | 36.5 |
| RCE | 7.3 | 197 | 21 | 6.83 | 4.92 | 3.00 | 52.8 | 42.5 |
| JEC | 12.7 | 19 | 23 | 3.66 | 5.79 | 7.17 | 48.1 | 44.2 |
| LAR | 7.0 | 240 | 7 | 2.23 | 9.07 | 6.33 | 32.0 | 49.9 |
| BON | 10.0 | 10 | 8 | 2.11 | 12.04 | 11.87 | 30.4 | 54.2 |
| TLY | 10.0 | 295 | 6 | 5.75 | 4.92 | 5.21 | 59.4 | 38.2 |
| HTF | 8.7 | 4 | 31 | 8.40 | 2.54 | 2.50 | 75.5 | 35.3 |
| GHT | 9.0 | 534 | 9 | 7.63 | 5.29 | 7.04 | 67.5 | 38.8 |
| KBR | 16.7 | 2 | 35 | 8.34 | 4.83 | 1.62 | 71.5 | 41.4 |

[a]Taken from Underwood and Schulz (1960)
[b]Calculated from Underwood and Schulz (1960)
[c]New data

156

TABLE 7-8. Trigrams-1—Intercorrelations of Variables

| | Trigram Frequency | Pronounceability | Learning No. 1 | Learning No. 2 | Complexity |
|---|---|---|---|---|---|
| Letter Frequency | .57 | .32 | .09 | .31 | .40 |
| Trigram Frequency | | .16 | .09 | .16 | .20 |
| Prounceability | | | .55 | .74 | .86 |
| Learning—No. 1 | | | | .70 | .53 |
| Learning—No. 2 | | | | | .71 |

The data are based on means for 36 trigrams. With an N of 36, a correlation of about .27 is significant at the .05 level.

TABLE 7-9. Trigrams-2—Intercorrelations of Variables

| | Trigram Frequency | Rated Frequency | Prounounceability | Learning—Mixed | Learning—Unmixed | Complexity |
|---|---|---|---|---|---|---|
| Letter Frequency | .18 | .02 | .01 | .05 | .11 | .07 |
| Trigram Frequency | | .45 | .17 | .08 | .19 | .16 |
| Rated Frequency | | | .77 | .68 | .69 | .76 |
| Prounounceability | | | | .82 | .80 | .91 |
| Learning—Mixed | | | | | .85 | .81 |
| Learning—Unmixed | | | | | | .77 |

The data are based on means for 36 trigrams. With an N of 36, a correlation of about .27 is significant at the .05 level.

the three variables (complexity, pronounceability, and rated frequency) in the two tables of intercorrelations.

If all three variables can be considered to be estimates of psychological complexity, then each of the three can be examined for its relation to ease of learning, our third focal question. Fortunately, Underwood and Schulz ran two learning studies on each set of trigrams. In Trigrams-1, there was variation between the two studies in terms of the character of the stimulus items; in Trigrams-2, there was variation in terms of whether the lists were relatively homogeneous (unmixed) or heterogeneous (mixed) with respect to trigram frequency. The correlations of the two measures of learning in each study provide an estimate of the upper limit to the correlation between any independent variable and one of the learning measures. It will be noted from the tables of intercorrelations that these two values are .70 in one case and .85 in the other.

All three estimates of psychological complexity show a substantial capacity to predict ease of learning. Subjective complexity correlates with the learning measures .53, .71, .77, and .81. Pronounceability correlates with learning .55, .74, .80, and .82. Rated frequency correlates .68 and .69. All these correlations are, of course, in the predicted directions. Ease of learning goes with ratings of simple, easy pronunciation and ratings of high frequency.

*Nonsense Syllables.* The failure of trigram frequency and the natural frequencies of letters composing them to be related to the other variables poses something of a theoretical problem. The explanation that the trigrams might be hidden figures in words, and that bigrams and letters in turn might be hidden figures as well, suggests an examination of nonsense syllables, which should not be subject to such distortion of true frequency effects. Whatever the rules employed in the construction of nonsense syllables, they should not produce frequencies of adjacency that reflect naturally occurring adjacencies.

A variety of procedures have been used to obtain ratings of meaningfulness for nonsense syllables. Some of the scaling procedures involve whether or not subjects "get" an association, the number of associations given by subjects in a fixed period of time, the number of associations a subject thinks a given item would elicit, ratings of how fast subjects think they could learn a unit relative to other units, ratings of familiarity of the units, ratings of pronounceability of units, and so on. Not only do Underwood and Schulz report that these various measures of meaningfulness are highly intercorrelated, but they report a study by Nobel (1953) in which ratings of scaled familiarity and meaningfulness were correlated .92. They then cite a number of studies demonstrating that meaningfulness and rate of learning covary.

It therefore seemed reasonable to check natural letter frequency against meaningfulness of nonsense syllables. Underwood and Schulz cite a study of meaningfulness of nonsense syllables by Kreuger (1934) as being fairly stable, and they include the product of this study in an appendix of their book. The Kreuger list contains nearly 2000 nonsense syllables in which each of the vowels (including *y* as a vowel) is used as a middle letter, and each of the consonants (including *y* as a consonant) appears as either a first or a last letter but not both (except that *y* does not occur at either end when also in the middle). Subjects were then asked to indicate any associations they had to the syllables during a seven-second period. More than 250 subjects responded to each syllable. In Kreuger's procedure, syllables were then evaluated on a percentage basis in terms of the number of subjects who had any associations. The ratings given range from 14% through 100%.

In order to test for the relationship between letter frequency in English and association value of the nonsense syllables, the following procedure was used. Sets of nonsense syllables corresponding to the nine available class intervals of association value were selected from the Kreuger list (Underwood & Schulz, 1960, Appendix A, pp. 309–317). All the syllables with association values between 14% and 35% were used. Then 25 syllables were selected from each interval of 5 percentage points by a procedure that assured equal distribution throughout the table (essentially choosing every *n*th syllable). The resulting 387 syllables were then evaluated for frequency of letter composition in the following manner. The rank order of each letter was determined from the alphabet U Count, and a mean rank was determined for each syllable. A mean of mean ranks was then determined for each group of syllables for each class interval of ten percentage points.

The result of this analysis is plotted in Figure 7-7, where it can be seen that there is a highly regular relationship between letter frequency and meaningfulness. Nonsense syllables with a low Kreuger association value are composed of letters that have low frequencies of occurrence in English, and nonsense syllables composed of letters with a high frequency of occurrence in English are rated as being more meaningful.

At least one implication of this strong relationship seems clear. If meaningfulness is an excellent predictor of learning, and it is, and if letter frequency is a good predictor of meaningfulness, and it is, then letter frequency should be a good predictor of learning in nonsense syllables.

In view of the discrepancy between this strong inference and the relative failure of natural letter frequency to predict the rate of learning of bigrams and trigrams, it seemed reasonable to obtain ratings of complexity (and affectivity) for nonsense syllables for comparison with the other forms of response items. I therefore

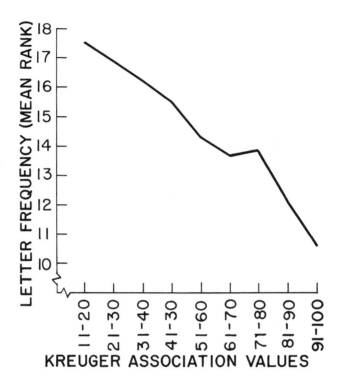

*FIGURE 7-7. Letter Frequency and Meaning in Nonsense Syllables*

chose 27 nonsense syllables, three from each of the nine class intervals of association value. In choosing them, I used a relatively random process within a class interval of meaningfulness, but I generally tried to preserve the correlation between meaningfulness and letter frequency by choosing items for which the mean letter frequency rank was near the regression line in Figure 7-7.

The list of 27 nonsense syllables was then given to 24 subjects, who rated them for complexity and affectivity following what by now appears to be standard procedure. That is, the standard instructions for complexity and affectivity were used, two orders of nonsense syllables were generated, each order was also used in reverse order, each subject had one order for complexity ratings and another order for affective ratings, and half of the subjects rated complexity first, while half rated affectivity first.

All the values thus made available for the 27 nonsense syllables are contained in Table 7-10. The intercorrelations between the variables are shown in Table 7-11.

The intercorrelation between letter frequency rank and association value on the original set of 387 nonsense syllables is .53. Since this set of 27 was selected in such a manner that this correlation was

TABLE 7-10. Nonsense Syllables

| Syllables | Kreuger Association Values | Letter Frequency Mean Rank | Mean Complexity | Mean Affectivity |
|---|---|---|---|---|
| QYJ | 18 | 22.7 | 78.8 | 38.3 |
| XOJ | 14 | 17.3 | 68.1 | 40.8 |
| XUG | 19 | 20.3 | 51.7 | 43.1 |
| VUQ | 25 | 19.7 | 62.7 | 40.2 |
| XUF | 23 | 16.7 | 55.8 | 43.8 |
| YUQ | 29 | 18.7 | 52.1 | 44.0 |
| XYC | 32 | 18.0 | 72.5 | 40.2 |
| ZYH | 33 | 17.3 | 74.8 | 43.5 |
| YIW | 38 | 16.3 | 59.8 | 46.5 |
| ZIY | 42 | 15.7 | 48.3 | 54.0 |
| FUB | 50 | 15.7 | 25.9 | 39.2 |
| XOY | 47 | 15.3 | 55.0 | 52.9 |
| GIJ | 54 | 14.7 | 47.1 | 59.2 |
| SYW | 56 | 14.0 | 68.3 | 43.8 |
| XAY | 59 | 14.7 | 47.5 | 51.9 |
| FEK | 64 | 12.7 | 27.3 | 45.4 |
| LEQ | 64 | 12.3 | 46.5 | 44.4 |
| XEM | 66 | 12.7 | 44.6 | 49.6 |
| HEZ | 71 | 11.7 | 33.1 | 47.5 |
| XEL | 73 | 11.3 | 51.5 | 57.3 |
| SYC | 80 | 12.7 | 50.0 | 46.3 |
| YID | 84 | 11.0 | 25.8 | 55.0 |
| RAX | 90 | 11.3 | 28.3 | 57.3 |
| SUG | 89 | 11.7 | 26.9 | 43.8 |
| BEL | 97 | 10.3 | 10.0 | 62.5 |
| SEN | 97 | 4.5 | 12.9 | 58.3 |
| TAL | 93 | 5.0 | 18.1 | 59.0 |

TABLE 7-11. Nonsense Syllable Data—Intercorrelations of Variables

| | Letter Frequency | Complexity |
|---|---|---|
| Association Value | .92 | .82 |
| Letter Frequency | | .79 |

certain to be maintained or enhanced, it is not surprising that the correlation between association value and letter frequency rank is .92.

Consensual complexity, in the form of mean complexity ratings, proves to be very highly correlated with both letter frequency (.79) and association value (.82). It appears that the combination of the two variables, which was an effect of my selection procedure, proved to have something of an overdetermination effect on subjective complexity; this somewhat overdetermined relationship can be seen in Figure 7-8.

Since I do not have learning data on this particular set of nonsense syllables, the connection to learning must be made by inference rather than by a direct correlational procedure. However, the inference is very strong that the ratings of subjective complexity by my subjects would correlate very highly with learning of these same nonsense syllables as response items by my subjects or any other comparable set of English-speaking subjects.

*Word Frequency.* Underwood and Schulz (1960) generally came to the conclusion that differences in ease of learning of verbal materials could be accounted for without appeal to the concept of meaningfulness. They chose letter frequency and pronounceability as basic determiners of learning (p. 196). Although we generally tend to think of differences between words in terms of meaning, words also vary in frequency and length and should be subject to evaluation in terms of complexity and affectivity. I therefore thought it reasonable to make a study of words to go with the studies of letters, bigrams, trigrams, and nonsense syllables.

Thorndike and Lorge (1944) have provided a classic volume on word counts in the English language. The several counts accumulated in this book must represent frequency counts of something over

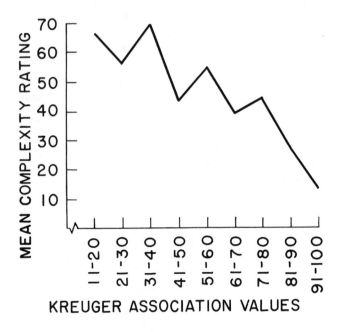

FIGURE 7-8. *Complexity and Meaning of Nonsense Syllables*

20 million words. This volume was used as a basis for selecting 126 words to be rated for complexity and affectivity.

The classification used by Thorndike and Lorge for their most frequently occurring words is "AA," designating words that occur more than 100 times in a million. Another classification, indicated by the digit "1," designates words that occur at least once but not twice in a million. Nearly all the words I have labeled "frequent" in this study were taken from the "AA," list, and nearly all of the words labeled "infrequent" were taken from the "1" list. The minor exceptions were forced by other restrictions placed on the selection process.

Equal numbers of words were selected in each frequency category for each word length, from three letters through nine letters. An effort was made to choose pairs having the same initial letter in the two categories. Since it is clear that letter frequency can have a powerful influence in some circumstances and little influence in others, it was thought expedient to control letter frequency in such a manner that any correlation between word frequency and letter frequency would be eliminated. This was accomplished to a sufficient degree by choosing pairs of words from each frequency category in sets of three, where in one pair the letter frequency of the frequent word of the pair was higher than that of the infrequent member of the pair, in another pair they were essentially equal, and in the third pair the letter frequency of the infrequent word was higher than that of the frequent word. This selection procedure was effective in that, in subsequent statistical tests, letter frequency does not vary significantly between either the word frequency or word length categories, nor are either complexity ratings or affectivity ratings significantly influenced by letter frequency. The obvious inexactness of the selection procedure made it wise to repeat the whole selection process three times.

Thus, the number of words in the study became 126, which is the product of 2 (word frequency) x 7 (word length) x 3 (letter frequency control) x 3 (replications). Again, 24 subjects were asked to rate the 126 words for complexity and affectivity, with all the order control procedures applied in the nonsense syllable study just described.

All the data on these 126 words, along with the particular words used, are in Table 7-12. All the main effects and half the interactions are statistically significant. A more manageable set of marginal means for word frequency and word length is contained in Table 7-13.

Figure 7-9 is a redundant but highly visible representation of the data on complexity. There is a kind of balance between the effects of word frequency on complexity judgments—with the differences

*TABLE 7-12.* Complexity and Affectivity of Words

| | | Frequent Words | | | | | | | | | |
|---|---|---|---|---|---|---|---|---|---|---|---|
| Low-Frequency Letters | | | | Middle-Frequency Letters | | | | High-Frequency Letters | | | |
| | Letter Frequency Mean Rank | Complexity Mean | Affectivity Mean | | Letter Frequency Mean Rank | Complexity Mean | Affectivity Mean | | Letter Frequency Mean Rank | Complexity Mean | Affectivity Mean |
| ask | 10.7 | 12.9 | 39.8 | day | 10.7 | 7.1 | 42.9 | get | 6.3 | 9.0 | 33.5 |
| key | 13.7 | 11.2 | 50.2 | old | 8.7 | 16.9 | 34.4 | use | 6.7 | 13.3 | 36.3 |
| six | 11.3 | 11.0 | 33.5 | two | 8.0 | 17.1 | 37.9 | was | 9.0 | 13.3 | 28.5 |
| back | 14.5 | 15.6 | 31.7 | came | 7.8 | 7.9 | 40.8 | idea | 4.8 | 27.3 | 64.6 |
| type | 10.0 | 29.4 | 39.0 | play | 12.5 | 17.3 | 54.8 | hair | 5.8 | 15.0 | 42.9 |
| jack | 15.5 | 25.2 | 31.9 | stay | 7.5 | 16.9 | 35.8 | year | 7.5 | 20.6 | 34.6 |
| favor | 10.4 | 32.5 | 55.4 | chair | 7.4 | 15.2 | 36.5 | heard | 6.4 | 25.0 | 43.3 |
| judge | 12.8 | 43.8 | 46.5 | spend | 8.8 | 20.4 | 47.1 | ocean | 5.6 | 31.7 | 67.3 |
| never | 7.4 | 23.5 | 31.0 | uncle | 8.5 | 20.8 | 39.6 | raise | 4.6 | 27.3 | 47.5 |
| object | 10.8 | 31.3 | 42.1 | enough | 8.2 | 47.3 | 43.3 | listen | 5.0 | 18.8 | 46.5 |
| public | 13.0 | 33.1 | 45.8 | market | 8.3 | 27.9 | 43.8 | travel | 7.5 | 25.2 | 60.4 |
| square | 9.5 | 25.0 | 38.3 | quarter | 10.0 | 27.7 | 45.4 | unless | 7.2 | 23.3 | 37.9 |
| journal | 9.7 | 38.3 | 56.3 | himself | 8.7 | 22.7 | 44.0 | advance | 8.3 | 35.8 | 49.6 |
| largely | 9.4 | 35.8 | 44.6 | usually | 10.3 | 41.7 | 39.8 | brother | 7.6 | 25.2 | 55.6 |
| perhaps | 9.4 | 36.5 | 46.0 | without | 7.3 | 22.7 | 23.1 | destroy | 7.4 | 37.5 | 31.0 |
| anything | 8.0 | 25.8 | 37.7 | language | 8.4 | 44.0 | 55.8 | children | 7.8 | 28.1 | 56.7 |
| building | 10.4 | 26.5 | 41.7 | remember | 8.4 | 38.1 | 57.7 | exercise | 7.3 | 41.9 | 56.5 |
| shoulder | 8.1 | 36.7 | 46.7 | valuable | 10.0 | 48.3 | 66.3 | increase | 5.4 | 35.6 | 47.3 |
| beautiful | 8.8 | 37.9 | 64.4 | education | 6.3 | 39.2 | 51.3 | forgotten | 6.1 | 30.6 | 35.4 |
| newspaper | 9.0 | 28.3 | 53.3 | machinery | 8.4 | 46.5 | 35.2 | gentlemen | 6.6 | 28.7 | 52.1 |
| wonderful | 9.4 | 37.3 | 60.0 | recognize | 8.2 | 44.2 | 58.5 | ourselves | 8.0 | 36.0 | 45.4 |

TABLE 7-12. (continued)

Infrequent Words

| Low-Frequency Letters | | | | Middle-Frequency Letters | | | | High-Frequency Letters | | | |
|---|---|---|---|---|---|---|---|---|---|---|---|
| Word | Letter Frequency Mean Rank | Complexity Mean | Affectivity Mean | Word | Letter Frequency Mean Rank | Complexity Mean | Affectivity Mean | Word | Letter Frequency Mean Rank | Complexity Mean | Affectivity Mean |
| gym | 16.0 | 26.9 | 42.1 | daw | 10.3 | 42.9 | 43.1 | aft | 6.7 | 34.4 | 37.1 |
| ugh | 12.3 | 29.6 | 31.0 | ope | 8.3 | 57.3 | 41.5 | ken | 9.7 | 31.5 | 36.9 |
| wok | 14.7 | 49.2 | 42.3 | tab | 8.3 | 14.8 | 26.7 | sal | 6.7 | 41.5 | 37.3 |
| inky | 12.5 | 41.5 | 40.8 | cadi | 7.8 | 55.8 | 48.5 | bate | 8.0 | 25.0 | 35.6 |
| hank | 10.0 | 36.0 | 27.1 | perk | 12.5 | 32.4 | 52.5 | tare | 3.5 | 39.4 | 42.7 |
| yogi | 10.8 | 45.8 | 48.3 | shad | 7.5 | 48.3 | 38.1 | jehu | 11.5 | 78.8 | 46.5 |
| harpy | 11.4 | 52.1 | 48.3 | cameo | 7.2 | 44.4 | 67.5 | facet | 6.8 | 49.4 | 52.5 |
| oakum | 11.2 | 65.6 | 46.7 | sahib | 8.6 | 65.6 | 50.4 | jaunt | 9.4 | 49.6 | 64.6 |
| rangy | 10.2 | 44.4 | 40.8 | ulcer | 8.8 | 36.5 | 30.8 | najad | 5.4 | 75.6 | 50.8 |
| lackey | 6.2 | 59.6 | 39.6 | enigma | 7.3 | 70.2 | 60.8 | obtuse | 7.8 | 55.2 | 52.7 |
| tawdry | 9.9 | 64.1 | 50.4 | marcel | 8.2 | 61.6 | 53.1 | python | 9.8 | 54.0 | 42.7 |
| unbind | 9.9 | 39.6 | 35.6 | quince | 10.3 | 45.0 | 46.5 | saline | 5.1 | 55.4 | 41.9 |
| adjudge | 11.1 | 62.1 | 45.2 | halibut | 8.6 | 48.8 | 44.8 | jasmine | 8.4 | 51.0 | 73.1 |
| baleful | 10.1 | 58.8 | 37.5 | unclasp | 10.0 | 31.9 | 44.2 | laconic | 7.7 | 73.8 | 46.0 |
| debauch | 9.9 | 76.0 | 46.7 | winsome | 7.8 | 53.5 | 61.5 | phaeton | 6.4 | 73.5 | 53.3 |
| chambray | 11.0 | 74.2 | 62.7 | landward | 8.6 | 40.2 | 41.7 | adenoids | 6.0 | 58.5 | 43.5 |
| emblazon | 10.5 | 60.4 | 61.0 | runabout | 8.5 | 34.9 | 41.3 | banknote | 8.1 | 32.7 | 38.8 |
| ignominy | 9.1 | 74.8 | 53.1 | vascular | 9.6 | 59.2 | 59.8 | scenario | 5.9 | 66.0 | 75.2 |
| fecundity | 9.1 | 79.8 | 47.5 | elocution | 6.4 | 67.5 | 59.6 | benignant | 7.1 | 77.9 | 54.4 |
| goldfinch | 9.9 | 41.0 | 54.6 | malignity | 8.6 | 67.9 | 38.5 | nefarious | 6.8 | 73.3 | 60.2 |
| obliquity | 11.3 | 71.9 | 52.7 | rapacious | 8.2 | 76.5 | 48.8 | whetstone | 5.6 | 64.2 | 56.9 |

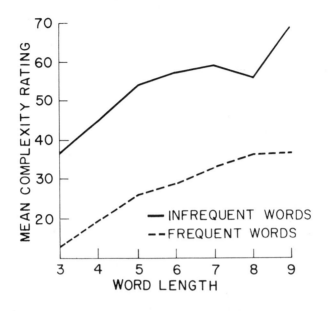

*FIGURE 7-9. Complexity Ratings of Words: Word Length and Frequency*

consistently about 25 scale points—and the effects of word length, which are about 24 and 32 scale points. In spite of the fact that the Thorndike and Lorge count is subject to question in regard to the particular materials that were sampled and also on the basis of age and changes in the language, complexity judgments clearly distinguish both word length, which is not particularly surprising, and word frequency, which perhaps is a little surprising.

No data are presented for the learning of this particular set of words, but there is no doubt that short words are learned more rapidly than long words as response items or that frequent words are learned more rapidly than infrequent words.

It is now possible to look at the whole set of studies in the light of the four focus questions I suggested earlier.

### Question Summaries

*Complexity and Frequency.* The several studies reported in this section provide a number of measures of the extent to which there is the predicted relationship between natural frequencies of occurrence of language elements and subjective complexity. The expected relationship is that, the more frequently an element has occurred naturally, the simpler it will be judged to be.

Most of the relationships established in this series of studies have been expressed in the form of correlation coefficients. The square of the coefficient is a close approximation of the percentage

TABLE 7-13. Mean Complexity and Affectivity Values for Word Length and Frequency

| | Frequent Words | | Infrequent Words | |
|---|---|---|---|---|
| Word Length | Complexity | Affectivity | Complexity | Affectivity |
| 3 | 12.4 | 37.5 | 36.4 | 37.5 |
| 4 | 19.5 | 41.8 | 44.8 | 42.2 |
| 5 | 26.7 | 46.0 | 53.7 | 50.3 |
| 6 | 28.8 | 44.8 | 56.1 | 47.0 |
| 7 | 32.9 | 43.3 | 58.8 | 50.3 |
| 8 | 36.1 | 51.8 | 55.6 | 53.0 |
| 9 | 36.5 | 50.8 | 68.9 | 52.7 |

of the variance the two correlated variables have in common. In the following three summary figures, the common variances are expressed in this fashion.

In Figure 7-10, the relevant comparisons are under the labels "Letter Frequency," "Bigram Frequency," and "Trigram Frequency." The expected relationship is seen to appear in some degree with respect to alphabetic frequency and bigrams but to essentially disappear in trigrams. When frequency of letters is confounded with meaning, as it is in the nonsense syllable study, the relationship is substantial. The data of the very positive results of the study of word frequency are omitted from this figure because the design of that experiment did not lend itself to the correlational form with respect to frequency. Taking all the studies together, one can conclude that there is a strong relationship between natural frequency of occurrence and judgments of complexity, but that the effects of physical frequency can be masked by such factors as the "hidden figure effect" or can be enhanced by partial correlation with other significant variables, such as meaningfulness.

*Estimates of Psychological Complexity.* Subjective complexity obtained by simple scaling procedures is only one possible estimate of the theoretical variable I have called *psychological complexity.* The data in Figure 7-10, which indicate a very high correlation between our scaling of trigrams for complexity and the Underwood and Schulz report of scaled pronounceability, seem to indicate that these two scales are very good but nonetheless imperfect estimates of psychological complexity. Subjective complexity may reflect the stimulus aspects of psychological events more than pronounceability, which may reflect the response aspects. Ratings of frequency of trigrams show much in common with complexity ratings and to that extent may well be regarded as good estimates of psychological complexity. To regard them as such, however, one must assume the

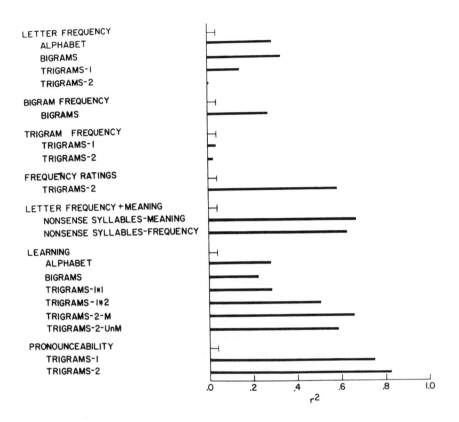

*FIGURE 7-10. Associations with Complexity Rating*

relationship between frequency and complexity that in most in-stances is under test.

The data on the association between complexity and learning are included in Figure 7-10 by the same logic. Assuming that the relationship between complexity and learning can be established, then ease of learning can be used to index complexity. Let us there-fore turn to that relationship.

*Complexity and Learning.* The instances in which actual learning data could be correlated with various other measures are displayed in Figure 7-11. Since Underwood and Schulz provide two learning measures for two different sets of materials, the limit to which any independent measure could be expected to predict learning is set by the $r^2$ values plotted at the bottom of the figure.

The simplest summary generalization one can draw from the figure is that natural frequencies do not predict learning very well, while any set of ratings—whether of frequency, pronounceability, or

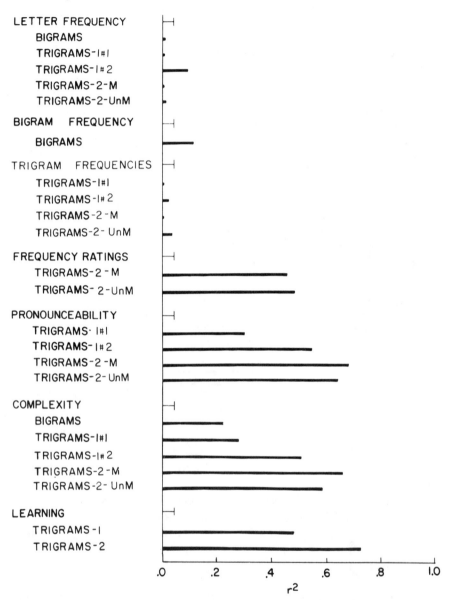

*FIGURE 7-11. Predictions of Learning*

complexity—do almost as well in predicting learning as one can do from a replication of the learning measure itself. Data from the nonsense syllable and the word studies are not displayed in the figure, because a correlational estimate was not available in these studies. However, when all the data are taken together, there is a very strong presumption that these three ratings—frequency, pronounceability, and complexity—would predict the learning of nonsense syllables and words as well.

## Affectivity in Verbal Learning

Very rarely in studies of human verbal learning are subjects asked anything about how they feel about the material they are asked to learn. However, in the Hedgehog, psychological complexity is intimately associated with the preference function. It was therefore only natural to ask subjects in the preceding studies to evaluate the letters, bigrams, trigrams, nonsense syllables, and words on the affective dimension. In order to make the results as general as possible, the instructions given the subjects tied the dimensions of interestingness, pleasantness, and approach/avoidance into a single rating. The mean affective ratings are shown in the various data summary tables given for each of the studies as they were described.

The expected relationship between complexity and affectivity is an inverted-U-shaped function, *if* the full range of complexity values is represented. That is, optimal complexity level should be at some central value of the range, and subjects should find events near this value to be most interesting, most pleasant, and most to be approached. If all the events represented in a study are below optimum, then maximum preference should be expressed for the most complex. If all are above optimum, then maximum preference should be expressed for the least complex.

As elucidated in the previous section, the hypothesis of a progressive decrease in complexity with increased experience has been demonstrated for each of the sets of human verbal learning materials employed in this series of studies. The question now becomes one of the nature of the functional relationship between this battery of measures of psychological complexity and measures of affectivity.

The studies were designed in such a manner that each subject could be regarded as an independent experiment. It is therefore possible to plot scatter diagrams based on the manner in which a single subject made judgments of complexity in relation to that same subject's scaling of affectivity. Since it is theoretically possible (but not likely in adult subjects) for different subjects to generate all three of the theoretically possible curve shapes (monotonically increasing, inverted-U-shaped, and monotonically decreasing), a great many such individual plots were examined. They included all the 52 individual plots of complexity and affectivity for the alphabet (where there was reason to suspect the greatest likelihood of individual differences). They also included a sampling of such individual plots with other stimulus items, and a complete set of plots of the scatter diagrams of mean values on which the correlations in these studies are based. In no case was there justification for any assumption other than the conservative one that the relationship involving affectivity and any other variable is linear. It should be noted, however, that there were individual differences in the sign of the correlation coefficient. A fairly typical pattern would be a range of individual correlations from –.20 to + .60. The correlation of the means for stimuli might then be + .40. I will return to this problem later.

Table 7-14 contains all of the major correlations between affectivity and other variables for all these materials. The signs of the coefficients have been omitted in the table. We can again use the square of the correlation coefficient as a rough index of the degree of association between affectivity and the other variables. This is done graphically in Figure 7-12.

TABLE 7-14. Correlations between Affectivity and Other Miscellaneous Variables

|  | Alphabet | Bigrams | Trigrams-1 | Trigrams-2 | Nonsense Syllables | Words |
|---|---|---|---|---|---|---|
| Letter Frequency | .45 | .17 | .03 | .16 | .71 | |
| Bigram Frequency | | .21 | | | | |
| Trigram Frequency | | | .05 | .04 | | |
| Rated Frequency | | | | .53 | | |
| Pronounceability | | | .54 | .61 | | |
| Association Value | | | | | .70 | |
| Learning | .40 | .21 | .59 | .74 | | |
| | | | .55 | .64 | | |
| Complexity | .69 | .48 | .62 | .69 | .62 | .43 |

In general, the natural frequencies of letters, bigrams, and trigrams do not show significant relationships to affectivity. The only exception is the frequency of letters of the alphabet. It could be argued that the individual letters of the alphabet have been attended to by subjects a sufficient number of times to make natural frequency an effective variable to generate a correlation of .45 with an $r^2$ of about .20, whereas bigrams and trigrams have not been attended to sufficiently often to make their differential frequency a significant variable.

All the other variables exhibit significant and meaningful relationships with affectivity. Since they are highly intercorrelated variables, it is not surprising that, if one shows a relationship, all might be expected to show such covariance. However, a problem arises with this generalization when the signs of these correlation coefficients are taken into account. Furthermore, a detailed examination of the relationships between affectivity and other variables reveals another difficult and theoretically significant problem associated with the degree to which judgments of complexity of one set of materials are coordinate with similar judgments concerning a second set of materials. This problem will be examined first.

Throughout this set of studies of verbal learning materials, and in many other contexts, complexity ratings are made on a scale of 0 to 100. Such ratings are highly reliable and stable within any one set of materials. There is almost an implicit assumption that, if the same scale and same scaling procedures are used with two sets of materials, the results for two disparate sets of stimuli can be plotted in the same figure and that the differences in location of the two curves on the graphic space will say something about the relative complexities of the two sets of stimulus materials. This is a questionable assumption on many grounds, but it is seldom tested. It was tested, however, in the study of word frequency. Here there were two major variables, word length and word frequency. As we saw in Figure 7-9, both variables had a significant effect on complexity judgments.

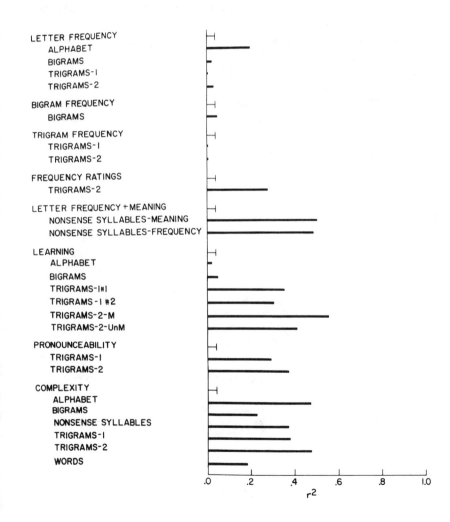

FIGURE 7-12. *Associations with Affectivity*

Figure 7-13 is a plot of the mean affective values for the two levels of word frequency against word length. The upper, heavy line represents the affectivity associated with infrequent words. These words are regarded as more interesting and more pleasant than the frequent words, represented by the broken line. Furthermore, long words are more interesting than short words. The problem is that the differences in affective ratings associated with word length are much greater than the differences associated with word frequency; yet these two variables had about equal effects on complexity judgments. Briefly, there is some discrepancy in these data to the extent to which there is not a simple relationship between complexity and affectivity that rationalizes the two sources of variation, word frequency and word length.

The nature and magnitude of this discrepancy can be made more visually apparent if the mean affectivity ratings are plotted against the mean complexity ratings, as is done in Figure 7-14. The broken line represents the relationship for frequent words, while the solid line represents the relationship for infrequent words. If the complexity scales for all the words were strictly comparable in the sense that subjects could be assumed to have made all their judgments on the same scale, then the data in Figure 7-14 should have

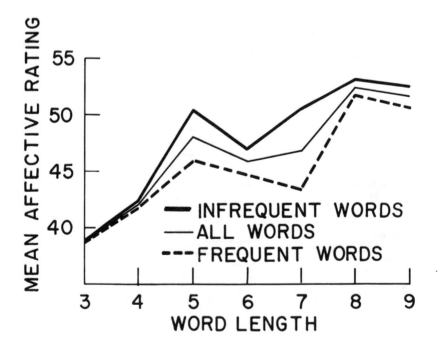

FIGURE 7-13. Affective Value of Words: Word Length and Frequency

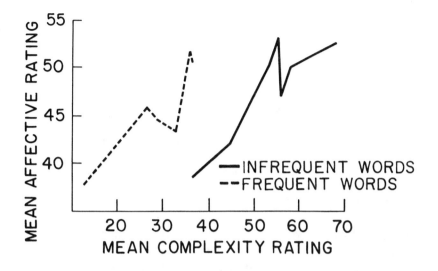

*FIGURE 7-14. Complexity versus Affectivity of Words*

conformed to some regular function that would have permitted the joining of the points to show a relationship between complexity and affectivity regardless of word length or word frequency.

One is forced to make a tentative, post hoc assumption in order to rationalize these results. The assumption is that, when subjects rate the complexity or affectivity of three-letter words, they tend to do so within a frame of reference of three-letter words. When they make judgments concerning four-letter words, they do so with respect to a frame of reference of four-letter words. Furthermore, the frames of reference for three-letter and four-letter words are different from each other. The number of letters thus becomes a major variable that must be taken into account before any attempt at comparative analysis can be regarded as complete.

The overall correlation between complexity and affectivity for words (which was recorded as .43 in Table 7-14 and shown as accounting for a relatively small portion of the variance, about 18.5%, in Figure 7-12) is lower than one might expect because it actually represents a straight line fitted across a series of different but related functions. Table 7-15 presents the correlations between complexity and affectivity for each word length and each frequency independently. The correlations are between mean values, and the N is only 9 (the number of words of each length and frequency in the study), resulting in the variability to be expected with such a small N. However, some suggestion of the results one might expect from an experiment involving a much larger word sample can be taken from the fact that the correlations within word frequencies

TABLE 7-15. Correlations between Complexity and Affectivity

| | Frequent Words | | Infrequent Words |
|---|---|---|---|
| Word Length | | | |
| 3 | -.27 | | .73 |
| 4 | .19 | | .35 |
| 5 | .50 | | .15 |
| 6 | -.09 | | .72 |
| 7 | .19 | | -.09 |
| 8 | .78 | | .74 |
| 9 | -.01 | | -.17 |
| Overall | | | |
| Within | .46 | | .51 |
| Between | | .43 | |

are higher than the correlation for all words. The highest correlations could be expected within word length and frequency.

We can now return to the general problem of the relation of complexity and affectivity when all the studies are taken together and when the signs of the various correlation coefficients are taken into account. The first step in the analysis was to fit curves to the data independently for each set of materials, and for each word length and word frequency. In each instance, the conservative assumption of a straight line fit was made, except for the data on nonsense syllables. The mean values for complexity and affectivity for nonsense syllables show a definite curvilinear relationship and were fit with an exponential function. The results of these operations are shown in Table 7-16 for all materials, including the overall function for words but not the more complicated matrix of functions representing individual word lengths or the two different frequencies. It can be seen that the first four functions involving bigrams, trigrams, and nonsense syllables are negative, indicating that the simpler these materials are the more positive the affective rating, and the more complex these materials are the more negative the affective rating. The other two sets of materials are revealed to have positive correlations, indicating the reverse relationship. With the alphabet and with words, those rated as being more complex are also rated as having a positive affectivity, and those rated as being simple have a more negative affectivity.

It will be recalled that a reversal in sign can be expected in the Hedgehog when a given set of materials is repeated many times, undergoes progressive simplification, and in the process approaches optimal complexity level and then crosses into the region in which it becomes simpler than one would like it to be. If the alphabet and

TABLE 7-16. Affectivity Values Associated with the Complexity of Various Stimulus Materials as Determined by Curve Fitting Procedures

| | Bigrams | Trigrams-1 | Trigrams-2 | Nonsense Syllables | Alphabet | Mean Length Word Frequency |
|---|---|---|---|---|---|---|
| Complexity | | | | | | |
| 10 | 50.8 | 55.8 | 54.0 | 60.0 | | 43.2 |
| 20 | 49.1 | 53.4 | 51.0 | 58.5 | 43.9 | 44.3 |
| 30 | 47.4 | 50.9 | 48.0 | 56.6 | 47.0 | 45.3 |
| 40 | 45.7 | 48.4 | 45.0 | 54.2 | 50.1 | 46.4 |
| 50 | 44.0 | 45.9 | 42.0 | 51.2 | 53.2 | 47.4 |
| 60 | 42.3 | 43.5 | 39.0 | 47.6 | 56.3 | 48.5 |
| 70 | 40.6 | 41.0 | 36.0 | 43.0 | 59.4 | 49.5 |
| r | -.48 | -.62 | -.69 | -.62 | .66 | |
| Slope | .17 | .25 | .30 | | .31 | |
| Asymptote | | | | 66 | | |
| k | | | | | .2 | |

words have been attended to a sufficient number of times in the life histories of our experimental subjects that they have become suboptimal in complexity, and if bigrams, trigrams, and nonsense syllables are strange combinations that have not been simplified in this manner, then the sign of the correlations can be used to "unfold" these plots in the manner shown in Figure 7-15.

In this figure, the horizontal line is the optimal complexity level. Affectivity is assumed to decline in both directions from this point. The values on the ordinate have been arbitrarily anchored at an affective value of 60, for the simple reason that none of the fitted values to these data exceeded this value; theoretically, any value between 60 and 100 would have done as well. Also, the separate functions for words of different lengths and different frequencies, as shown in Table 7-17, have been plotted in place of the single line that would have resulted from plotting the data for words in Table 7-16.

It should be noted that the curves in Figure 7-15 are very close to the actual data. The only steps that have been taken so far include regularizing the data by curve fitting, unfolding the various curves into the Hedgehog conception of the bidirectional affectivity dimension on the basis of the signs of the correlations, and arbitrarily selecting the distances between the upper and lower sets of curves.

An important theoretical issue is at stake in Figure 7-15. The complexity axis in the figure is plotted from high to low (the reverse of normal procedure) in order to make it easy to see it as representing frequency of experience. That is, something experienced infrequently

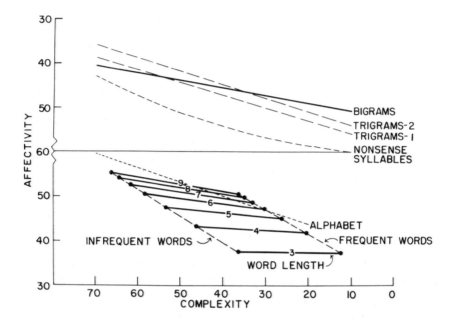

FIGURE 7-15. *Idealized Complexity and Affectivity Curves "Unfolded" on the Basis of Sign of the Correlation Coefficient*

should seem more complex than something experienced with very high frequency. This translation appears to fit the data. Frequent words are substantially farther to the right (simple) end of the complexity scale than are infrequent words. With respect to the alphabet, the frequent letters are on the right end of the line, and the infrequent letters are on the left end. With nonsense syllables, those that most closely resemble words (such as BEL or TEL) are on the right end of the line, while those that least resemble words (such as XOJ or QYJ) are on the left end of the line. The same relationship holds for bigrams and trigrams as well.

Theories that make an effort to relate familiarity with affectivity generally tend to take two forms. In one class of theories, the

*TABLE 7-17.* Affectivity Values Associated with the Complexity Values of Word Lengths, Where Complexity Is Fitted to Exponential Equations and Affectivity Is a Linear Function of Complexity

| Word Length | Frequent Words Complexity | Frequent Words Affectivity | Infrequent Words Complexity | Infrequent Words Affectivity |
|---|---|---|---|---|
| 3 | 12.4 | 37.4 | 36.4 | 37.8 |
| 4 | 20.7 | 42.0 | 46.5 | 43.4 |
| 5 | 26.5 | 45.2 | 53.5 | 47.7 |
| 6 | 30.5 | 47.4 | 58.5 | 50.8 |
| 7 | 33.3 | 48.9 | 61.9 | 52.9 |
| 8 | 35.3 | 50.0 | 64.4 | 54.3 |
| 9 | 36.7 | 50.8 | 66.0 | 55.4 |
| Asymptote | 40 | | 70 | |
| Exponent | .3 | | .3 | |
| Slope | | 5.6 | | 6.1 |

general proposition is that, the more familiar a stimulus is, the better it will be liked. An example is the theory of Zajonc (1968), in which the relation is considered to be a monotonic function represented by the phrase "Familiarity breeds content." The Hedgehog is in the other class, in which affectivity can often be an increasing and then decreasing function of frequency. In the materials plotted in Figure 7-15, the monotonic class of theories are simply refuted in the sense that they cannot simultaneously account for the results of all these experiments, while the unfolded version represents an adequate account derived from the nonmonotonic class of theories, such as the Hedgehog.

When the data are plotted in the manner required by the Hedgehog, it becomes very easy to imagine a solution to the individual differences problem referred to earlier. Within an experiment, it will be recalled, the design was such that a complete experiment was carried out on each individual subject. Individual correlations tended to range in both directions from the mean value, with some positive and some negative, and with a mean value somewhere close to the value and sign of the correlation between the means for those materials. One possible account of this variability between subjects might arise from the assumption of differential frequencies of experience (or other relevant difference) such that, for a given subject, the materials might be above, below, or across optimum level. This interpretation would lead to the expectation that a group of experimental subjects might generate a population of correlations that would vary in sign in quite predictable ways. An individual showing effects of unusual experience with nonsense syllables might be sufficiently transposed down the curve to show a positive (rather than the group negative) correlation. The reverse effect might occur with the alphabet and words, with the inexperienced shifted upward beyond optimum to generate a negative correlation instead of the group positive. Unfortunately, the slopes of the curves also vary, producing an expectation of more negative correlations within individuals the flatter the slope. These effects could jointly account for all the previously noted variation in signs of intra-individual correlations.

The results obtained with words of various lengths forced the consideration of the possibility that complexity (and affectivity) judgments were not all made on the same complexity scale but rather were made within different frames of reference, in this instance determined by the number of letters or characters in the stimulus. Thus, the judgments made concerning one particular three-letter word appear to have been made within the frame of reference of all three-letter words or three-character sequences rather than in a general frame of reference that included words of all lengths. Given this consideration, plotting the means for all sets of materials on the same complexity scale is incorrect to the extent that it implies that all the stimuli were evaluated for complexity and affectivity within the same frame of reference.

The alternative I suggested was to undertake to translate the complexity scale into a scale of frequency of experience. I know of no wholly defensible way of doing that, but an interesting approximation can be achieved if one is willing to make several fairly reasonable assumptions. First, let us assume that each of the curves that I have fit as straight lines is actually a small part of a slowly moving exponential function relating complexity to frequency. Second, let us assume that the frame of reference argument is correct, and that the difference between different frames of reference is largely one of number of characters in the set on the one hand (thus different asymptotes for the exponential) and relative frequency on the other (location along the exponential function). The lines of Figure 7-15 would then be displaced left for infrequent materials and displaced right for frequent materials. What is not known is how far left and how far right to move the data. If one decides, however, to believe the Hedgehog (he is a very honest beast), then the affective values can be used to determine the displacement distances, right and left.

To carry out this hypothetical exercise, a set of values was developed for possible curves relating complexity to frequency. The logic relating asymptotes and exponents to item length discussed at the beginning of this section was used, and the asymptotes were made to correspond to reasonable terminal values of affectivity ratings. Table 7-18 shows the equations chosen to represent items

*TABLE 7-18.* Hypothetical Exponential Equations Relating Complexity to Frequency

| Item Length | Equation |
|:---:|:---:|
| 1 | $C_\psi = k\ 26.80\ (10^{-.020N}) + 26.80$ |
| 2 | $C_\psi = k\ 33.05\ (10^{-.047N}) + 33.05$ |
| 3 | $C_\psi = k\ 37.22\ (10^{-.090N}) + 37.22$ |
| 4 | $C_\psi = k\ 40.00\ (10^{-.158N}) + 40.00$ |
| 5 | $C_\psi = k\ 41.85\ (10^{-.250N}) + 41.85$ |
| 6 | $C_\psi = k\ 43.08\ (10^{-.330N}) + 43.08$ |
| 7 | $C_\psi = k\ 43.90\ (10^{-.400N}) + 43.90$ |
| 8 | $C_\psi = k\ 44.45\ (10^{-.440N}) + 44.45$ |
| 9 | $C_\psi = k\ 44.82\ (10^{-.460N}) + 44.82$ |
| 10 | $C_\psi = k\ 45.60\ (10^{-.480N}) + 45.06$ |
| 11 | $C_\psi = k\ 45.22\ (10^{-.490N}) + 45.22$ |
| 12 | $C_\psi = k\ 45.33\ (10^{-.500N}) + 45.33$ |

of 12 different lengths. The asymptotes were assumed to increase with the lengths of the items; the exponents were also assumed to increase with item length, largely because of generalization. For lack of better values, the apparent asymptotes were chosen in reference to apparent minimum values of affectivity ratings. The result is a set of exponential curves that constitute a possible theoretical relationship.

The next step was to move each of the curve segments of Figure 7-15 either to the right or to the left until it coincided with the exponential curve for the appropriate length of item. Figure 7-16 is the result.

These arbitrary manipulations of the data prove very little, but the solution offered in the figure fits the Hedgehog theory of psychological complexity and preference almost exactly. Some of the assumptions required to make the fit seem plausible. It seems reasonable to me that sets with increasing numbers of characters would become asymptotic in complexity at increasingly higher complexity levels. The "frequency of experience" assumptions required are generally reasonable, although there are some problems. The relation among words—that short words occur more frequently than long words—seems eminently reasonable. The placement of alphabetic frequency far back on the frequency scale requires the assumption that we rarely attend to letters as individual letters. The placement of nonsense syllables with respect to trigrams and three-letter words seems reasonable, but the implied differences in frequency of the alphabet, bigrams, and the three-character elements

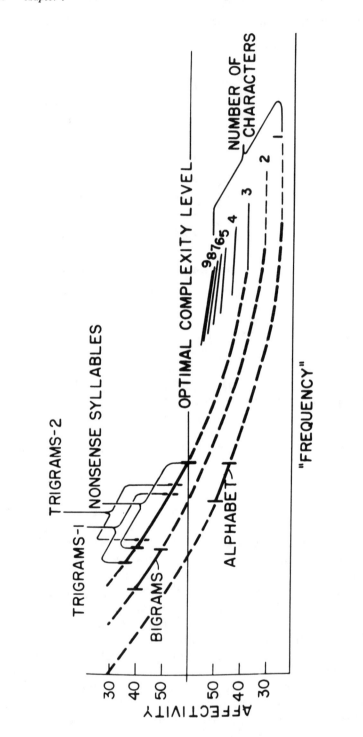

FIGURE 7-16. Idealized and "Unfolded" Complexity and Affectivity Curves Relocated on the Basis of Exponential Complexity/Frequency Formulae

seem somewhat less convincing. Furthermore, there are the problems stemming from the fact that truly independent values of frequency, complexity, and affectivity are not available in these data. In addition, whereas plotting all the results on the complexity scale, as in Figure 7-15, does violence to the frequency notion, plotting them all on a hypothetical frequency scale, as in Figure 7-16, does violence to the similarities in complexity ratings for the various materials.

### Complexity and Preference for Three-Letter Items

In order to solidify certain aspects of Figure 7-16, a final study was developed to provide independent frequency, complexity, and affective data. It was also designed to provide a very large N of words or other three-letter items and a very large N of subjects. This was done in an effort to gain maximum reliability in the results for single individuals as well as in the group results.

Items were chosen for this study using Figure 7-16 as a theory. Seven points were chosen to represent as much of the full range of the three-letter curve as possible, and 50 items were selected to represent each of the seven points. Five sets of words were chosen from the Thorndike-Lorge lists, and sets of nonsense syllables and trigrams were chosen from Underwood and Schulz. Characteristics of the seven groups of words or items are as follows.

1. *100 + per $\bar{M}$ Words.* The most frequent category of words in the Thorndike-Lorge list, labeled "AA," includes words said to occur 100 or more times per million in the English language. There are a great many such words, and a pseudorandom sampling procedure was used to generate a list of 50. The actual frequencies of occurrence of these 50 words are not known. I have assumed that the average frequency would be considerably higher than 100 and have chosen a mean value of 150 per million to represent them. This value does not seem to be unreasonable on logical grounds, and, as will be seen, plotting the means for these words at that point on a log scale yields a reasonably smooth curve.

2. *46-99 per $\bar{M}$ Words.* The next category of words in Thorndike-Lorge, labeled "A," includes words said to occur from 50 to 99 times per million. Because this category is, for some reason, somewhat spare in three-letter words, I extended it down to words that occur 46 times per million and used essentially all the available words. The means for these words are plotted at approximately the midpoint of this interval on a log scale, and thus at a frequency of 70 words per million.

3. *16-30 per $\bar{M}$ Words.* An essentially random sample of words with these values in the Thorndike-Lorge list was selected and subsequently plotted at a point representing 24 per million.

4. *1 per M̄ Words.* A pseudorandom sample of these words was selected; this group is the only one about which there is little ambiguity concerning where to plot it on a frequency scale.

5. *.22-.94 per M̄ Words.* These words were chosen from the list of rare words in the back of the Thorndike-Lorge book, where they are listed as occurring from four to 17 times per 18 million words. These frequencies convert to .22-.94 per million and are plotted at .4 per million on a log scale.

6. *Nonsense Syllables.* The 50 nonsense syllables were selected from the lists in Underwood and Schulz to represent only the highest association values—98%, 99%, and 100%. There are no frequency data available for nonsense syllables. I reasoned that, since they were very high in association value, their mean complexity values might be lower than the rarest Thorndike-Lorge words. In the absence of good data, however, I decided to plot them on the complexity curve wherever they fit and to determine a "frequency" value from that position. They proved to fall between the rarest two categories of words and are plotted at a "frequency" of .65 per million.

7. *Trigrams.* To represent the farthest left position of the three-letter curve in Figure 7-16, I chose 50 of the 72 trigrams used in the previous study on the basis of their complexity ratings, taking the 50 with the highest ratings. In the absence of any information concerning frequency, I have plotted them as if they represented a word frequency of .1 per million.

This list of 350 words was then scrambled into two lists, which were also used in reverse order. Since an analysis of variance based on 118 subjects showed no difference between lists, this variable will not be discussed again.

A set of complexity rating instructions was attached to one list of words and a set of affectivity rating instructions to the other list, and the two lists were combined into one booklet. Half the booklets had complexity instructions first, and half had affectivity instructions first. Subsequent analysis showed that there was a significant difference in complexity ratings depending on whether the words were rated for complexity first or second. Complexity ratings were lower if the complexity rating came first. This effect was not large and appears to be due to the fact that affectivity ratings tended to be higher in absolute terms than complexity ratings, and those who rated affectivity first carried over the set for higher ratings to the complexity phase. However, since this difference did not seem to differentially affect any other variable of interest, it too will be disregarded in most of the following analyses.

A total of 146 individuals completed booklets containing two lists, thus rating a total of 700 words. This task proved to be boring in the extreme, and a number of individuals refused to complete the task or found it impossible to continue to make discriminative judgments throughout the entire list. Thus, a few subjects assigned the same value to all words through the last hundred or so; a few others adopted patterns of ascending and descending values that obviously had nothing to do with the particular items being rated. About 25 such results were discarded. As it became clear that the task was too long and too boring for many subjects, data were obtained in half-booklets in what I will refer to as the Little Study. In this study, 25 individuals filled out complexity booklets, and 27 filled out affectivity booklets. The Little Study had the advantage of being shorter and less boring, but it had the disadvantage that it did not offer the possibility of comparing complexity and affectivity ratings for the same subject.

Taking the two studies together, a total of 171 individuals rated the words for complexity and 173 for affectivity. Table 7-19 displays 350 words alphabetically within each of the seven groups determined by the source or frequency of the items. Each complexity mean involves an N of 171, and each affectivity mean involves an N of 173. Through a variety of mishaps, there were a few items that were either duplicated in two lists or mistyped in one version of the lists. All such items were ignored in subsequent analyses and assigned mean values of 0.00 in Table 7-19. The total number of items that remained for analysis was 330.

Table 7-20 contains the summary values for the data in Table 7-19. The values for complexity and affectivity are thus means of means, the standard deviations are of mean values, and the correlation coefficients are correlations of the 45 to 50 pairs of means.

The overall correlation coefficient of –.51 was explored further in the following manner. The 330 items were ordered from low to high on the basis of the mean complexity ratings shown in Table 7-19. They were then grouped into sets of 11 words, and mean complexity and mean affectivity were determined for each of the 30 groups of words. These means are contained in Table 7-21.

All the mean values of Tables 7-20 and 7-21 are plotted in Figure 7-17, where an attempt has been made to arrange the dimensions of frequency, complexity, and affectivity as they were arranged in Figure 7-1. The meaning and construction of this figure requires considerable discussion.

The frequency values for the seven groups of words (.1, .4, .65, 1, 24, 70, and 150) were positioned on the abscissa with a log spacing for convenience. The mean complexity values for the seven groups of words (taken from Table 7-20) were then plotted against the Complexity scale on the ordinate. The result approximates an exponential function that would become asymptotic at a complexity value of about 25 or slightly below. There is gross general agreement among the mean complexity ratings of the various groups of items in this and the previous experiments. The order of the

TABLE 7-19. Complexity and Affectivity of Three-Letter Verbal Combinations

| | AA Words | | | 46-99 per $\bar{M}$ | |
|---|---|---|---|---|---|
| | Complexity | Affectivity | | Complexity | Affectivity |
| ACT | 32.11 | 54.47 | AID | 30.70 | 61.95 |
| AGE | 31.04 | 48.30 | AIM | 32.76 | 55.49 |
| AIR | 31.02 | 66.87 | ATE | 27.85 | 55.46 |
| AND | 20.16 | 46.99 | BAR | 23.37 | 52.10 |
| ARE | 23.23 | 49.36 | BEE | 21.43 | 45.49 |
| ART | 31.33 | 66.80 | BEG | 25.42 | 34.90 |
| BAD | 19.90 | 36.86 | BID | 24.33 | 44.90 |
| BUT | 22.06 | 41.72 | CAP | 20.84 | 47.90 |
| CAN | 19.68 | 56.03 | CAT | 18.49 | 55.24 |
| CRY | 30.11 | 44.98 | COW | 20.11 | 51.51 |
| CUT | 19.85 | 40.31 | FUN | 23.99 | 70.20 |
| DID | 18.51 | 44.84 | FUR | 31.71 | 57.28 |
| DOG | 18.69 | 60.14 | GAS | 23.98 | 46.76 |
| DUE | 31.98 | 40.13 | GAY | 27.82 | 55.16 |
| EAT | 23.08 | 66.13 | GUN | 26.75 | 33.97 |
| END | 25.22 | 49.09 | HAY | 25.55 | 54.24 |
| FAR | 21.74 | 54.48 | HEN | 21.90 | 48.25 |
| FEW | 28.22 | 41.27 | HIT | 21.85 | 41.12 |
| GET | 22.16 | 50.62 | KEY | 27.27 | 54.89 |
| GOT | 22.38 | 46.51 | KID | 26.45 | 54.82 |
| HAS | 24.80 | 44.69 | LOG | 25.29 | 54.15 |
| HER | 26.91 | 59.71 | MAD | 23.35 | 45.35 |
| HIM | 24.42 | 58.12 | MAP | 25.15 | 54.19 |
| HOT | 22.44 | 51.58 | MIX | 29.51 | 53.56 |
| ICE | 28.75 | 60.38 | MUD | 21.30 | 44.45 |
| ILL | 26.43 | 30.88 | NET | 0.00 | 0.00 |
| ITS | 30.02 | 41.77 | NOD | 26.51 | 49.39 |
| LAY | 28.16 | 61.82 | NUT | 0.00 | 0.00 |
| LEG | 23.12 | 59.11 | OAK | 29.89 | 62.96 |
| LIE | 30.64 | 36.52 | PAN | 22.11 | 52.00 |
| LOT | 22.77 | 48.40 | PEN | 22.25 | 51.36 |
| MAN | 26.76 | 65.82 | PER | 31.40 | 47.37 |
| NEW | 24.98 | 61.16 | PIE | 24.06 | 60.60 |
| NOT | 20.25 | 38.37 | POT | 24.12 | 55.73 |
| ONE | 24.43 | 53.14 | RAW | 27.65 | 44.19 |
| OUT | 28.15 | 43.17 | RAY | 28.64 | 55.95 |
| RAN | 24.23 | 50.84 | ROW | 26.60 | 50.01 |
| RUN | 21.16 | 57.09 | RUB | 25.72 | 53.89 |
| SAW | 24.93 | 47.60 | SAD | 24.83 | 37.69 |
| SEA | 32.74 | 75.10 | SIN | 27.44 | 45.18 |
| SET | 22.11 | 49.97 | SUM | 27.24 | 50.11 |
| SIR | 25.24 | 45.68 | TAX | 31.24 | 32.02 |
| SON | 23.98 | 60.31 | TEA | 24.98 | 61.18 |
| TEN | 16.65 | 44.35 | THY | 40.42 | 53.55 |
| TOO | 22.27 | 48.49 | TIP | 23.54 | 47.87 |
| TRY | 31.40 | 62.12 | TON | 25.58 | 40.24 |
| USE | 30.65 | 52.42 | TOY | 26.24 | 58.25 |
| WAS | 23.69 | 38.17 | WET | 22.08 | 46.16 |
| WIN | 29.17 | 62.96 | WON | 30.72 | 59.42 |
| YET | 28.76 | 44.76 | WIT | 29.66 | 61.73 |

TABLE 7-19. *(continued)*

| | 16–30 per $\overline{M}$ | | | 1 per $\overline{M}$ | |
|---|---|---|---|---|---|
| | Complexity | Affectivity | | Complexity | Affectivity |
| APT | 39.13 | 55.71 | BAA | 27.65 | 39.62 |
| AWE | 39.94 | 49.95 | BAH | 30.75 | 36.65 |
| AYE | 38.92 | 55.17 | BEY | 42.58 | 38.99 |
| BAT | 20.70 | 44.35 | BOO | 18.64 | 40.31 |
| BET | 22.73 | 48.17 | BYE | 31.01 | 46.12 |
| BUD | 24.43 | 58.08 | CAD | 29.27 | 32.94 |
| DAM | 24.64 | 44.39 | CAM | 33.81 | 45.34 |
| DEN | 26.08 | 48.01 | COG | 36.30 | 42.40 |
| DEW | 29.25 | 60.22 | CUD | 31.43 | 34.86 |
| DON | 29.12 | 52.43 | DAW | 40.19 | 35.94 |
| DUG | 25.71 | 45.69 | EFT | 55.60 | 31.79 |
| DYE | 35.11 | 44.41 | ELL | 40.36 | 39.67 |
| ELM | 33.05 | 65.49 | FAY | 34.13 | 45.18 |
| FOE | 35.03 | 36.35 | FIE | 41.08 | 38.62 |
| FOG | 26.66 | 53.87 | HAH | 34.57 | 44.43 |
| FOX | 31.15 | 58.34 | HAW | 0.00 | 0.00 |
| GEM | 31.85 | 63.46 | HOD | 35.66 | 34.06 |
| HAM | 23.57 | 50.22 | HUB | 29.70 | 43.23 |
| HIP | 27.05 | 54.96 | ION | 42.43 | 54.08 |
| HUM | 26.49 | 53.89 | IVE | 42.47 | 41.61 |
| INK | 28.35 | 50.40 | IRK | 39.65 | 37.80 |
| INN | 26.20 | 59.54 | JAG | 36.63 | 49.64 |
| JAM | 25.82 | 53.42 | LEX | 43.09 | 47.46 |
| LEE | 23.33 | 51.24 | LIB | 32.89 | 55.21 |
| LID | 25.48 | 47.96 | LYE | 37.08 | 41.78 |
| LIT | 29.23 | 48.20 | MAW | 39.31 | 39.66 |
| MAT | 23.77 | 51.28 | MIL | 36.46 | 39.84 |
| MOB | 27.05 | 37.63 | MIN | 31.01 | 45.98 |
| OAT | 28.43 | 51.92 | NOB | 29.64 | 41.89 |
| ORE | 36.59 | 51.01 | OPE | 48.51 | 39.36 |
| PAD | 22.50 | 48.21 | PAP | 29.01 | 44.20 |
| PAT | 21.01 | 49.82 | PUN | 29.23 | 52.83 |
| PAW | 26.80 | 48.28 | QUE | 48.81 | 52.93 |
| PEA | 26.37 | 46.51 | SAC | 33.96 | 42.34 |
| PET | 23.93 | 59.59 | SAL | 35.77 | 43.44 |
| PIT | 23.01 | 38.57 | SEN | 35.82 | 41.40 |
| RAG | 21.58 | 40.10 | SEQ | 56.12 | 40.72 |
| RAM | 28.25 | 46.68 | SIS | 27.28 | 53.70 |
| RIP | 23.73 | 41.40 | SOL | 0.00 | 0.00 |
| SAP | 26.57 | 42.37 | SOP | 33.01 | 35.52 |
| SHY | 33.75 | 53.45 | SOU | 0.00 | 0.00 |
| SOW | 30.63 | 44.05 | SUG | 41.30 | 34.57 |
| SPY | 33.99 | 52.80 | SUR | 0.00 | 0.00 |
| TUB | 21.08 | 51.90 | TAB | 23.30 | 47.50 |
| TUG | 26.61 | 43.51 | TEE | 24.92 | 46.23 |
| VAN | 26.75 | 48.21 | TOT | 26.43 | 54.18 |
| WAX | 29.61 | 46.94 | WOW | 25.13 | 63.76 |
| WOE | 36.82 | 38.82 | YAH | 41.45 | 41.36 |
| YEA | 36.04 | 54.60 | YAW | 0.00 | 0.00 |
| YON | 45.96 | 46.60 | YEP | 30.29 | 44.83 |

TABLE 7-19. *(continued)*

| | Nonsense Syllables | | | .22–.94 per M | |
| | Complexity | Affectivity | | Complexity | Affectivity |
|---|---|---|---|---|---|
| BAL | 32.12 | 45.12 | ADZ | 65.01 | 37.88 |
| BOM | 34.39 | 34.83 | ALP | 39.98 | 61.35 |
| COF | 42.02 | 36.85 | ASP | 43.68 | 42.50 |
| DEM | 0.00 | 0.00 | AUK | 55.47 | 32.62 |
| DOM | 39.57 | 41.54 | AWL | 44.94 | 43.13 |
| DUK | 40.92 | 40.23 | BAS | 38.46 | 38.79 |
| DUL | 37.51 | 28.60 | BOA | 39.12 | 48.83 |
| GEN | 37.91 | 41.33 | COS | 39.27 | 37.86 |
| GIV | 32.75 | 56.90 | COZ | 43.68 | 50.72 |
| HIL | 34.95 | 47.77 | DEM | 0.00 | 0.00 |
| HON | 37.71 | 48.24 | EAU | 57.53 | 48.75 |
| HOL | 39.25 | 36.51 | EGO | 41.94 | 60.57 |
| HUR | 42.27 | 40.79 | ELD | 48.74 | 35.83 |
| JEL | 35.67 | 46.57 | FID | 41.33 | 33.44 |
| JIN | 41.41 | 42.62 | FLU | 32.56 | 36.14 |
| KEN | 26.05 | 48.58 | FOB | 39.37 | 36.05 |
| KIS | 38.21 | 67.49 | GAB | 27.74 | 35.71 |
| LAF | 39.61 | 56.06 | GAT | 36.84 | 33.16 |
| LAK | 43.37 | 42.84 | HOB | 31.74 | 41.35 |
| LIF | 44.15 | 42.88 | ILK | 47.51 | 36.75 |
| LIM | 37.36 | 43.86 | ISM | 51.42 | 42.22 |
| LIV | 38.04 | 62.00 | KIP | 37.84 | 46.90 |
| LOC | 40.09 | 37.18 | LAB | 27.44 | 49.58 |
| LOF | 40.38 | 39.71 | MIR | 44.12 | 44.25 |
| LOV | 39.45 | 69.65 | MOT | 38.36 | 40.13 |
| MAC | 31.68 | 45.12 | NIT | 32.03 | 34.79 |
| MAS | 35.90 | 39.14 | NIX | 38.42 | 31.68 |
| MAX | 35.04 | 59.12 | OAF | 40.95 | 37.09 |
| MED | 34.99 | 48.95 | OHM | 52.69 | 47.45 |
| MUS | 41.95 | 40.64 | PIP | 27.20 | 46.66 |
| NEC | 41.98 | 42.09 | QUA | 53.09 | 41.99 |
| PIK | 38.33 | 39.88 | RAH | 0.00 | 0.00 |
| PIL | 34.35 | 40.25 | SIC | 36.71 | 37.29 |
| PUF | 29.78 | 45.20 | SOS | 33.15 | 41.98 |
| PUL | 36.92 | 37.42 | SOY | 35.07 | 50.09 |
| RAH | 0.00 | 0.00 | SPA | 39.70 | 53.38 |
| RAK | 42.87 | 34.38 | TAM | 0.00 | 0.00 |
| REM | 39.26 | 47.98 | TAT | 33.63 | 39.57 |
| RUD | 35.61 | 33.46 | TAW | 40.43 | 37.55 |
| RUF | 37.85 | 43.42 | TOG | 34.13 | 41.07 |
| SAV | 40.66 | 44.20 | TUN | 37.36 | 38.58 |
| SOC | 37.96 | 39.92 | UND | 0.00 | 0.00 |
| SOK | 43.19 | 35.10 | VAS | 42.30 | 44.42 |
| SOL | 0.00 | 0.00 | VIM | 43.04 | 52.62 |
| SUR | 0.00 | 0.00 | VIS | 40.82 | 42.51 |
| TAM | 0.00 | 0.00 | VOX | 42.30 | 49.10 |
| TIC | 29.96 | 38.21 | WEN | 37.36 | 39.06 |
| TOL | 36.88 | 37.64 | WIS | 40.06 | 47.86 |
| VET | 30.65 | 50.74 | YAK | 38.22 | 42.68 |
| YEL | 35.30 | 42.50 | YAW | 0.00 | 0.00 |

TABLE 7-19. *(continued)*

| | Trigrams | |
| | Complexity | Affectivity |
| --- | --- | --- |
| ABL | 55.79 | 41.67 |
| ALI | 40.04 | 47.24 |
| BLE | 52.10 | 31.59 |
| BLI | 55.73 | 36.72 |
| BON | 31.62 | 53.89 |
| CHI | 47.64 | 46.51 |
| COU | 48.05 | 39.72 |
| CQU | 72.43 | 29.87 |
| DGM | 66.61 | 28.11 |
| DYI | 67.16 | 29.46 |
| FAI | 51.01 | 36.94 |
| GHT | 65.47 | 29.18 |
| GOI | 57.37 | 35.19 |
| HTF | 0.00 | 0.00 |
| JEC | 48.02 | 32.52 |
| JOR | 46.74 | 37.56 |
| JUM | 45.13 | 36.64 |
| KBR | 68.35 | 30.39 |
| KIV | 47.09 | 37.61 |
| KNO | 52.98 | 46.29 |
| LAR | 39.04 | 38.64 |
| LED | 26.20 | 43.79 |
| LIR | 44.98 | 34.64 |
| LTY | 65.50 | 33.10 |
| MBE | 62.09 | 32.87 |
| MPA | 61.76 | 32.99 |
| MPO | 62.18 | 30.49 |
| MPR | 63.62 | 29.18 |
| NCE | 56.86 | 38.71 |
| NDR | 66.25 | 26.51 |
| OUS | 52.44 | 31.90 |
| PLO | 43.34 | 33.17 |
| RCE | 59.46 | 33.63 |
| ROP | 38.73 | 34.16 |
| SCI | 49.35 | 49.23 |
| SLO | 35.95 | 37.59 |
| SOU | 0.00 | 0.00 |
| TJU | 69.22 | 31.76 |
| TLY | 62.07 | 34.17 |
| UND | 0.00 | 0.00 |
| URN | 39.19 | 48.80 |
| VEN | 37.16 | 37.84 |
| VIF | 45.95 | 36.47 |
| VIL | 43.89 | 34.25 |
| WHA | 44.02 | 35.75 |
| WHE | 47.80 | 37.84 |
| WSE | 59.95 | 39.73 |
| XPL | 75.46 | 30.96 |
| YIN | 47.01 | 46.80 |
| YLV | 73.25 | 27.16 |

TABLE 7-20. Complexity and Affectivity of Three-Letter Verbal Combinations

| Item Class | N (Items) | Complexity x̄ | Complexity σ | Affectivity x̄ | Affectivity σ | r |
|---|---|---|---|---|---|---|
| Words, 100 or more per M̄ | 50 | 25.3 | 4.2 | 51.2 | 9.65 | .24 |
| Words, 46–99 per M̄ | 48 | 26.0 | 4.0 | 51.1 | 7.9 | .17 |
| Words, 16–30 per M̄ | 50 | 28.6 | 5.7 | 49.8 | 6.6 | .13 |
| Words, 1 per M̄ | 45 | 35.5 | 7.9 | 43.2 | 6.7 | − .30 |
| Nonsense Syllables | 45 | 37.5 | 4.1 | 44.1 | 8.6 | − .18 |
| Words, .22–.94 per M̄ | 45 | 40.8 | 7.8 | 42.5 | 7.0 | .01 |
| Trigrams | 47 | 53.1 | 11.8 | 36.4 | 6.4 | − .67 |
| All Items | 330 | 35.0 | 11.5 | 45.6 | 9.2 | − .51 |

Combinations are ordered in the table in terms of estimated frequency of use. N = 125 subjects for Complexity ratings and 127 subjects for Affectivity ratings.

TABLE 7-21. Three-Letter Items Grouped on the Basis of Rated Complexity Value

| Group | Mean Complexity | Mean Affectivity |
|---|---|---|
| 1 | 19.18 | 46.81 |
| 2 | 21.33 | 47.72 |
| 3 | 22.28 | 48.62 |
| 4 | 23.24 | 50.53 |
| 5 | 23.98 | 52.71 |
| 6 | 24.77 | 52.37 |
| 7 | 25.47 | 48.50 |
| 8 | 26.31 | 49.80 |
| 9 | 26.77 | 48.94 |
| 10 | 27.51 | 48.21 |
| 11 | 28.53 | 50.27 |
| 12 | 29.46 | 49.97 |
| 13 | 30.39 | 48.89 |
| 14 | 31.16 | 49.58 |
| 15 | 32.01 | 49.71 |
| 16 | 33.34 | 49.46 |
| 17 | 34.71 | 44.77 |
| 18 | 35.86 | 41.36 |
| 19 | 36.94 | 40.68 |
| 20 | 37.90 | 45.37 |
| 21 | 38.90 | 43.31 |
| 22 | 39.63 | 48.23 |
| 23 | 40.48 | 41.41 |
| 24 | 41.74 | 41.45 |
| 25 | 42.94 | 42.90 |
| 26 | 44.87 | 40.26 |
| 27 | 48.05 | 41.37 |
| 28 | 53.48 | 38.29 |
| 29 | 59.91 | 36.04 |
| 30 | 68.61 | 30.40 |

The table displays mean affectivity ratings for groups of 11 items, each formed by ordering 330 items in terms of their mean rated complexity values.

seven means is exactly as expected, but there is some reduction in discrimination in the second experiment. This reduction is evident in that the curve in Figure 7-17 covers a slightly reduced range on the complexity scale. This reduced range is most evident on the "frequent" end of the scale. In the previous study, the mean complexity values for "AA" and "1" words are 12.4 and 36.4. In this study of three-letter items only, the means for sets of words in the same categories are 25.3 and 35.5.

There are three likely sources of this reduced discrimination. As was mentioned previously, the task of rating 350 words once for complexity and again for affectivity was beyond the capacities of some experimental subjects. Toward the end of the rating task, all three-letter items began to look alike. The discriminability of the items could also have been affected by the context. In the previous studies, nonsense syllables and trigrams were rated only within a list of other nonsense syllables or other trigrams. The three-letter words were rated in a context of words that varied in length. In the present study, all the items were three letters long. The third possibility is a matter of sampling. In the previous study, there were only nine "frequent" words and nine "infrequent" words. In the present study, there were 50 of each. The issue will be discussed

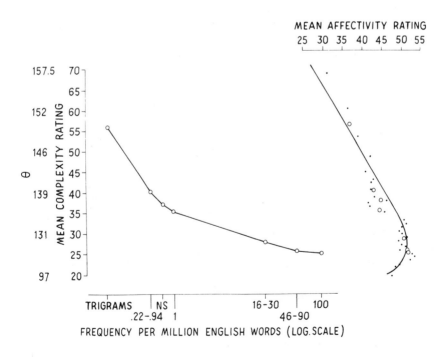

FIGURE 7-17. *The Hedgehog and Verbal Learning*

again subsequently, but it should be pointed out that the ordinate
of Figure 7-17 is an empirical dimension, and data plotted against
it are subject to variation stemming from a large set of experimental
factors. Thus, either subjective complexity or consensual complexity plotted against this ordinate is to some degree fallible as an
estimate of the theoretical dimension of psychological complexity.

On the right side of Figure 7-17, I have plotted mean affectivity
ratings as empirical estimates of preference. The points are positioned with respect to mean complexity on the ordinate and mean
affectivity on the new abscissa (at the top of the figure). The open
circles represent the mean affectivity ratings for the seven groups
of words (taken from Table 7-20). They could be fit easily by a
straight line corresponding to the regression line of the correlation
coefficient of –.51 indicated in Table 7-20. No great violence would
be done by fitting the same line to the solid dots representing the
30 paired means of Table 7-21.

There are several reasons for suggesting that the function between complexity and affectivity is curvilinear, even though the
hypothesis that the relationship is a straight line cannot be rejected
in these data on a statistical basis. In the earlier study of words of
various lengths, the correlation between complexity and affectivity
ratings was positive. It would therefore fall on the inflected (lower)
portion of the curve at the right side of Figure 7-17. The second
justification for plotting the curve as an inverted-U-shaped function
comes from the correlation coefficients describing the relations
between complexity and affectivity ratings within the seven groups
of words, as indicated in Table 7-20. If the overall relation between
complexity and affectivity ratings was a simple negative correlation
(thus a straight line), then the seven correlation coefficients should
simply vary as estimates of the overall correlation of –.51. If the
relationship is, in fact, an inverted-U-shaped function, then the
correlation for trigrams should be large and negative, and the progression should be one in which the correlations become smaller
and then become positive as one moves up toward the top of the
table. This expectation is generally met, with some irregularities.
Despite the irregularities, the correlations for the two most frequent categories of words are both positive and statistically significant.

By this logic, I chose to plot a curve relating complexity to
affectivity in the form seen in Figure 7-17. The equation for the
curve, which was fitted by eye, is:

Affectivity $(E) = .52\ \theta\sin\theta - 4$

The relation between the $\theta$ values of the equation and the mean
complexity values is indicated in Figure 7-17 by scaling the ordinate
with both sets of values. Inspection of the nature of that relationship

reveals that it is not even approximately linear and is probably a very complex function.

The equations relating complexity to frequency and complexity to affectivity are both empirical equations, and it is possible or even likely that other equations could be found to substitute for either, especially the equation relating complexity to affectivity.[1] What Figure 7-17 demonstrates is that it is possible to relate mathematically frequency information to complexity information, which in turn can be related to preference information. Thus, the two equations could be made a part of the theory, and it would be possible to use them in fitting the theory to relevant data.

The data displayed in Figure 7-17 are group data. The Hedgehog theory is a theory of individual processes. Making the two equations a part of the theory would be justified only if it could be shown that the two equations or some substitutes for them could be fit to individual data.

*Intra-Individual Considerations.* The basic study of complexity and preference of three-letter words was designed so that a complete study was carried out on 146 individuals (all but the 52 in the Little Study). Thus, for each individual, I obtained ratings of each of the 350 words on the complexity scale and on the affectivity scale. This procedure permitted the plotting of a scatter diagram for each individual who participated in the study. In addition, at the end of the booklet, each individual was asked to evaluate 11 positions on the complexity scale for affectivity. This procedure was intended to provide information concerning the semantic space of the individual in the absence of experimental stimuli (in this case, three-letter words). In a sense, it was a replication of a part of the semantic distance study reported in the Appendix. The results of this semantic space scaling procedure were also plotted on the scatter diagram in the hope that the degree of agreement between ratings made in the presence and absence of experimental stimuli could be determined. Theoretically, it should then be possible to fit the two equations relating frequency to complexity and complexity to preference to the data of individual subjects, and the latter equation to the semantic distance data as well.

Inspection of this set of 146 scatter diagrams reveals a high level of intra-individual and interindividual variability, both in terms of the rating of the words and in terms of the semantic scale disposition. The variability is high enough that it is clear that the theory cannot be tested adequately for individuals within this set

---

[1]This sine function is not a very satisfactory equation for this purpose, because it generates more than the Wundtian curve and is cyclical in character. The data can be fit with a combination of two exponential equations, but this solution appears to imply a two-factor theory of affect. Adopting two factors when one will do would be very unhedgehoglike.

of data. An alternative procedure was therefore adopted to arrive at some estimate of the extent to which the group results in Figure 7-17 represent all the individuals who participated in the study.

On the basis of an examination of the experimental booklets before they were subject to analysis, I picked out two special groups of protocols for separate analysis. Both were chosen on the basis of the ratings given to the trigrams and the most frequent words. On the basis of this cursory examination, I chose 11 protocols for a special Reverse Group. These were individuals who appeared to be consistent in giving low complexity ratings to trigrams and high complexity ratings to frequent words, the reverse of the more common direction of these ratings. I also picked out 17 protocols, which I have labeled as a Random Group, because they did not seem to be consistent in giving high or low ratings to either set of items. This left 118 protocols, which I have called the Base Group. The selection process was not exhaustive. All 146 protocols have been included in previous analyses, but I felt that separate analyses of these samples might reveal something about the character and range of individual differences.

Table 7-22 gives the distribution of the intra-individual correlations for these subgroups as well as for the total group. The correlations are preponderantly negative, and thus in agreement with the overall correlation of −.51 indicated in Table 7-20. The Reverse Group is clearly sampled from the positive end of the distribution, the Random Group somewhat less so. The high positive correlation in the individual protocols of the Reverse Group means that they were rating frequent words high on both the complexity and affectivity

*TABLE 7-22.* Distribution of Intra-Individual Correlations between Complexity and Affectivity

| r | Reverse | Random | Base | Total |
|---|---|---|---|---|
| +70–79 | 1 | | 2 | 3 |
| +60–69 | 3 | | 3 | 6 |
| +50–59 | 1 | 1 | 1 | 3 |
| +40–49 | 2 | | 2 | 4 |
| +30–39 | 2 | 2 | 6 | 10 |
| +20–29 | | 4 | 8 | 12 |
| +10–19 | 1 | 4 | 5 | 10 |
| + 0– 9 | | 3 | 11 | 14 |
| – 0– 9 | 1 | 2 | 11 | 14 |
| –10–19 | | 1 | 15 | 16 |
| –20–29 | | | 16 | 16 |
| –30–39 | | | 14 | 14 |
| –40–49 | | | 7 | 7 |
| –50–59 | | | 10 | 10 |
| –60–69 | | | 4 | 4 |
| –70–79 | | | 3 | 3 |
| Totals | 11 | 17 | 118 | 146 |

scales, while the high negative correlations of many of the individuals typical of the Base Group indicate that they were rating frequent words low on complexity and high on affectivity.

For those who find it easier to think in terms of mean values rather than in terms of correlation coefficients, the mean complexity values and mean affectivity values of four groups have been calculated in Table 7-23. To the Reverse, Random, and Base Groups, I have added the results for the 52 individuals in the Little Study, who filled out only one set of ratings.

The results for the Base Group do not differ in any significant way from the results for all subjects in Table 7-20 and can therefore be used as a ready reference. The Random Group does show a fairly random set of mean complexity values. However, the affectivity values are remarkably similar to those of the Base Group. Thus, the complexity and affectivity ratings in this group appear disassociated.

The complexity ratings of the Reverse Group are clearly reversed from those of the Base Group, yet the affectivity ratings correspond well with those of the Base Group. It will be recalled that the instruction for the rating of complexity read as follows: "Words vary somewhat in relative *complexity* along a variety of dimensions. The bases could be such things as structure, sound, meaning, association value, and others." This instruction was used in order to cover as much of the meaning of the word *complexity* as possible; however, it obviously allowed the individual to rate words on a single dimension rather than on all of them at once. Members of the Reverse Group appear to have rated the words on the basis of association value, giving high ratings to frequent words with high association value and low ratings to trigrams with low association value. Yet their affectivity ratings were not equally reversed.

The similarities of the affectivity ratings across the three groups in spite of the differences in complexity ratings raise many questions. It is the nature of the Hedgehog to do his one thing tenaciously. This dictates the conclusion that, for the majority of the individuals who participated in this study, subjective complexity is a good and valid estimate of psychological complexity, while for some subjects (at least the Reverse and Random Groups), it is not.

*The Little Study.* As shown in Table 7-23, there are some differences between the results of the Little Study and the Base Group. In the first place, the mean complexity ratings are almost universally lower in the Little Study. It will be recalled that order of rating (complexity or affectivity first in the original analysis) had a demonstrably significant effect on complexity ratings. This effect was explained as a set effect. If complexity was rated first, the ratings

TABLE 7-23. Mean Complexity and Affectivity Ratings for Various Subgroups

| | Base Group | | Random Group | | Reverse Group | | Little Study | |
|---|---|---|---|---|---|---|---|---|
| | Complexity | Affectivity | Complexity | Affectivity | Complexity | Affectivity | Complexity | Affectivity |
| N | 118 | 118 | 17 | 17 | 11 | 11 | 25 | 27 |
| 100 or more per $\bar{M}$ | 21.8 | 51.5 | 45.0 | 51.7 | 53.0 | 53.8 | 16.7 | 52.4 |
| 46–99 per $\bar{M}$ | 24.1 | 50.5 | 44.8 | 52.0 | 50.6 | 51.74 | 17.4 | 52.5 |
| 16–30 per $\bar{M}$ | 27.3 | 49.0 | 44.4 | 52.2 | 48.9 | 52.1 | 20.8 | 50.4 |
| 1 per $\bar{M}$ | 35.7 | 43.7 | 40.8 | 41.9 | 38.1 | 40.1 | 30.3 | 47.0 |
| Nonsense Syllables | 41.0 | 42.9 | 41.7 | 45.3 | 38.1 | 40.5 | 34.1 | 48.5 |
| .22–.94 per $\bar{M}$ | 36.7 | 42.9 | 44.6 | 42.0 | 34.2 | 37.0 | 37.1 | 46.7 |
| Trigrams | 57.6 | 37.4 | 40.5 | 37.4 | 23.8 | 25.8 | 53.5 | 40.5 |
| All Words | 34.6 | 45.5 | 43.2 | 46.2 | 41.2 | 43.3 | 29.7 | 48.4 |

were lower. Since affectivity ratings were generally higher, rating them first appeared to create a set for higher ratings, which then carried over to subsequent complexity ratings. The complexity ratings of the Little Study were not affected by any such set factor and are therefore lower. The affectivity ratings in the Little Study are higher than those in the larger study. This discrepancy arises from the fact that all ratings tended to drop slightly but consistently throughout the task of rating 350 words twice, or 700 words in all. The Little Study does not show as much of this drop, since the individuals involved rated only 350 words.

### SUMMARY

One of the objectives of this series of studies was to determine the extent to which the basic postulate of the Hedgehog—that the complexity of an event should decrease with repeated occurrence—seems verified. Inferences from the theory were confirmed in a set of studies in which animals were exposed to two-dimensional and three-dimensional stimuli varying in a priori complexity. Studies involving music and visual art materials appear to confirm the postulate as well.

The most precise results were obtained from studies involving language materials. Wherever there was clear frequency information concerning a series of items, it was possible to establish that, the more frequently an item has been experienced in the past, the simpler it is likely to seem. Furthermore, consensual complexity ratings appear to be related to frequency information in a manner that is fit reasonably well by the negative exponential equation specified by the theory.

Complexity ratings, in turn, appear to predict rate of learning of verbal materials as response items with a remarkable degree of precision. Ratings of complexity, pronounceability, and frequency appear to predict learning about as well as one measure of learning predicts another learning performance in an approximate replication. All three ratings, each of which can be considered to be an estimate of psychological complexity, predict learning better than most of the available information on natural frequencies. Therefore the Hedgehog would have to be regarded as pretty smart, because he learns so well.

The most innovative aspect of the application of the Hedgehog to human verbal learning is the provision of a theory of motivation for verbal behavior. Taken as a whole, this series of studies demonstrates that verbal materials can be arrayed along a complexity dimension and that preferences among verbal items are related to complexity in the expected inverted-U pattern. Words at or near optimal complexity level are preferred over those either more or less complex.

Motivational principles have not been seen as necessary in most of the traditional areas devoted to aspects of human language structure and acquisition. In any form of grammatical analysis, the emphasis is on the character of the constraint—that is, grammatical structure. The ungrammatical expression is looked upon as error, and the choice of words within grammatical constraints has been of little interest as long as the words chosen have the proper form. The Hedgehog could prove useful in dealing with both ungrammatical structures and choices of words within such structures.

Studies of human verbal learning are generally constructed to minimize motivational aspects as a variable. When a subject is instructed to give a correct answer, the motivation for the production of a word is shifted from the autarkic motivational properties of the word (reflecting of the subject's own evaluation of the word) to the external motivation of optimizing one's performance by fulfilling the experimenter's instructions.

There are many problems of verbal behavior in which motivational principles might well prove to be valuable. The Hedgehog should prove productive in any class of problems in which there is sufficient freedom from constraint to allow choices made in reference to the intrinsic properties of the words that are available.

This series of studies thus fulfilled the basic purpose. Psychological complexity is a variable that is characteristic of the Hedgehog. It was derived from studies of visual material, primarily visual forms. It is applicable to a very wide range of psychological phenomena. It has been demonstrated that it is both precise and powerful in the area of human verbal learning. Thus, the advantage of psychological complexity as a manipulable and predictive variable in human verbal learning stems from the fact that, almost alone among such variables, it can be usefully transferred across psychological problems and areas. Its virtue is in part its role as a unifier in psychology. If this pattern continues as successfully in other areas, the Hedgehog may eventually be knighted and become Sir Hedgehog, the Ubiquitous.

# chapter eight

# Voluntary and involuntary psychological events and their enduring effects

A Hedgehog makes choices, some of them freely. It attends, sometimes selectively; it perceives, it learns, it remembers, it solves problems, and it thinks. The Hedgehog model can thus be seen as part of a general trend in psychology toward integration of disparate concepts. During years of successful analytical pursuit, there has been a tendency for psychological concepts to become relatively isolated from one another and from the context of the functioning of the whole organism. The development of the computer analogy between human functioning and the computer's processing of information, accompanied by the return to respectability of cognitive language in psychology, have produced a movement in the direction of resynthesis. For example, Melton and Martin (1972) say "There is a clear and definite commitment toward coordinating the theoretical concepts of perception, memory and learning," and they add that the same may be predicted for attention, problem solving, and thinking. The Hedgehog model is intended to provide some degree of synthesis, at least to the extent that it can be shown to be productively applicable in each of these areas. In this chapter, I examine the Hedgehog within the system in which it operates. To do so, it will be convenient to discuss the Central Processor, automatic processes, and processes in which the voluntary activity of the Central Processor can be involved.

## THE CENTRAL PROCESSOR

*General Properties.* The Central Processor is, in essence, where we live. It is the center of being, of thought, of action, of will, of manipulation of cognitive material, and of consciousness. However, it should not be reified into a homunculus, a little man in the head, having mythical powers or properties. Rather, the Central Processor should be regarded as a theoretical construct that is firmly grounded in empirical data. Whatever is said about it should be empirically based or should be subject to empirical verification. It has no properties that are not subject to change and modification in the light of relevant data.

*Volition.* In order to achieve reasonable integration of such disparate concepts as those just assigned to the Central Processor, it is convenient, if not necessary, to deal with the long-dormant concept of voluntary action. It is my thesis in this chapter that it is profitable to discuss a Central Process. In analyzing its role in behavior, it is necessary to make a distinction between voluntary and involuntary processes. Although it would be possible to discuss choice behavior and decision processes without directly addressing the issue of volition, it seems fruitful to face the problem openly. William James was almost the last psychologist to discuss the problem, and the rubric "free will" is not likely to appear in the index of scientifically oriented psychology books written in this century. I would like to argue that it is possible to deal with the concept of free will on the same scientific grounds as one deals with concepts such as perception, habit, or motivation.

All psychological constructs are based on data—what people say and what people do. We all are privately convinced that we can and do make many decisions freely. As William James says in his chapter on Attention (1890), "the whole sting and excitement of our voluntary life depends on our sense that in it things are really being decided. It makes no difference whether we actually do have free choice in some absolute philosophical sense, it is a fact that we are all willing to say that we do, and such statements are objective data and an adequate basis for a scientific concept of free will."

The concept of free will is avoided in scientific psychology because it appears to imply mysticism. The appearance of mysticism arises from a pair of mystical beliefs held implicitly by most scientists, although neither is a necessary constituent of science itself. One is belief in a fundamental distinction between mind and body, and the other is belief in a deterministic universe. These propositions are matters of faith because neither can be examined empirically.

The intellectual enterprises we call "science" appear to be based on a deterministic universe. At the heart of these enterprises are the "exact" sciences. If all events in the universe are determined exactly by physical laws, and if the mind is a part of the physical universe, then mental events and behavior must be exactly determined. This conclusion is so intuitively unpalatable and patently untrue that many people who wish to hold to the idea of a deterministic universe have been compelled to suppose that mental events must be of a different kind or order than physical events. They have thus found it necessary to develop a mind/body dualism and to become concerned about the nature of the relationship between mind and body.

Within philosophy there can be an alternative solution. It is possible to conceive of the universe as probabilistic rather than as deterministic and to deny that there is such a thing as an "exact" science. Such an implication can be drawn from the Heisenberg uncertainty principle in physics. Still within the realm of philosophical debate, if the universe is other than deterministic, then there is no absolute necessity for drawing a distinction between mind and body. If no such distinction is drawn, then one may take a metaphysical position of "no difference," a position not ordinarily considered by metaphysicians.

I mention these philosophical considerations to indicate why there is resistance among psychologists to utilizing the concept of free choice and also to indicate that on philosophical grounds there can be a position in which free choice is palatable. However, the justification for the use of the concept within the Hedgehog is not based on faith in a probabilistic universe and the philosophical dismissal of the mind/body dichotomy. It rests instead on the fact that all scientific constructs are based on objective data. Statements concerning free choice are objective data, and the scientific value of the concept rests with its merit as an element of scientific theory.

*Consciousness.* All that is conscious involves the Central Processor, but not all of the material in the Central Processor is conscious material. Some material is constitutionally unavailable to consciousness, while other material may be in the Central Processor, available to consciousness, but unprocessed to the conscious level.

If all action involves the Central Processor, then we must take physical action into account. The execution of a physical movement, even when the organism is not consciously aware of its willful initiation or occurrence, has all the characteristics of psychological events that I have previously described, except that some aspects are not available to consciousness. We are not and cannot be aware of all the afferent input required to initiate a physical activity or of all the afferent feedback involved in the control of the character of the movement.

In some highly organized material, we may be consciously

aware of the code without being consciously aware of the material that is coded. For example, a person may decide on a menu for a meal. The decision is to have onion soup, tossed salad with roquefort dressing, chicken *cordon bleu*, strawberry *granit*, and rosé wine. The menu appears in conscious awareness, but the recipes and production procedures are not brought to consciousness until it is time to procure or prepare some element of the meal.

Some material has become so familiar and simple through experience that it can participate in a process without our being aware of it. Such an element escapes awareness until some conscious effort is made to retrieve it. It is probably true that a part of the retrieval process consists of complicating the simple item enough by context or association to permit its examination. It is possible that relative processing speed is involved. Simple items may not appear in conscious awareness because their simplicity permits such rapid processing that awareness is not possible. Complication in the retrieval process may function to make processing time sufficient in length to permit awareness of the item.

*Thinking.* It seems quite possible that thinking, at least in some of its forms, is an abstract, nonverbal, imageless process, the true nature of which is not easily discernible from the contents of conscious processes. Anderson and Bower (1974) cite Neisser (1967) as arguing that we construct mental representations out of elementary sensory or cognitive data. Objects are recalled only after an elaborate process of reconstruction. Miller suggests that we often speak before we fully understand what we are saying and that we often understand what people mean even though they express it imperfectly ( G. A. Miller, 1972). Shepard (1974) suggests that thinking is not verbal and that verbal accompaniment is merely habitual and epiphenomenal. He says that many tasks involving memory are highly spatial and thus analog in character and that translation into digital, verbal representation often proves impossible.

*Thought and Action.* The connection between thought and thought on the one hand and thought and action on the other is a simple Central Processor operation. Some potential psychological events have the necessary actions integrated within them, and others do not. Thus "think of starting the car engine" and "start the car engine" are closely related but clearly distinguishable psychological events, and the person may choose either to think or to think and act if all the necessary physical elements for the action are present in the environment.

*Central Processing Capacity.* The Central Processor has a normal, optimal capacity, which is to be described in terms of the psychological complexity of the material being processed. It has an upper limit, beyond which it cannot operate effectively, and a lower limit that will induce complexity-seeking activity. The psychological complexity of the material being processed is a function of the complexities of the items and the number of items. New, unfamiliar, and therefore complex items will occupy more of the limited capacity than older, familiar, simplified items. Therefore, the Central Processor can deal with a large number of simple items and a smaller number of complex items. The actual limit of capacity, however, depends on the nature of the material and the method used to assess the amount of the material.

Let us contrast the Hedgehog approach to the problem of capacity with that of writers in the "information processing" tradition, such as Craik and Lockhart (1972) and Restle (1974). These writers distinguish sensory stores, short-term memory stores, and long-term memory stores. These stores are presumed to differ in the amounts of information that can be stored in each and in their durations. Thus, Craik and Lockhart review the literature on the duration of the sensory store for visual material. They cite a range of durations: one second or less (Neisser, 1967), up to 1.5 seconds (Posner, 1969), six seconds (Murdoch, 1971), ten seconds (Phillips & Baddeley, 1971), 25 seconds (Kroll et al., 1970), and longer recognition time for pictures (Shepard, 1967; Haber, 1970a). It seems obvious that duration is a function of the material and the method of assessing the state of the trace.

In the Hedgehog, the basic distinction is between the individual psychological event, with a duration of something of the order of one-half second, and a stream of psychological events, the trace properties of which can be assessed in almost any length or duration. Individual psychological events probably have spatial characteristics not possessed by strings of psychological events, while the latter have temporal properties not primary with respect to individual psychological events. The limited capacity of short-term memory is, in the Hedgehog, a matter of operational criteria of capacity to recirculate items without loss.

This conception of the Central Processor differs somewhat from conceptions in which the Central Processor is identified exclusively with conscious awareness. For example, Posner and Warren (1972) contrast conscious processing and automatic processing. For them, the limited capacity of the Central Processor refers to conscious processing, and only conscious processing occupies the system's capacity. In the Hedgehog, psychological events become automatic when they are simplified below some critical complexity level. Thus, it is not because an event is automatic and unconscious that it does not seem to interfere with conscious processing but because it is simple and thus occupies a portion of the processing mechanism that is small and therefore difficult to detect.

*Structure of the System.* There is some degree of arbitrariness about the structure one chooses to impose on the functioning organism. If one diagrams the system as equivalent to a computer flow diagram, considerable analytical power is achieved. However, there can be some loss as well. For example, distinguishing between a Sensory Store, a Short-Term Memory Store, and a Long-Term Memory Store, each enclosed in a box with arrows indicating transactions between them, leads to a useful analysis of the *differences* among these three elements. The boxes, however, suggest strongly that there is a degree of discontinuity involved in the transition from one to the other. One thus tends to lose the possibility of seeing continuity in the flow of information through the system.

Figure 8-1 shows a set of elements ordered from left to right to indicate a rough temporal sequence: Environment–Sensory Register-Central Processor-Memory-Overt Action. The elements are not enclosed in boxes in order to emphasize that there are a number of processes that appear to change in a continuous fashion as activity moves through the system. Thus, as an event proceeds through the system, there are progressive decreases in the amount of information and in discriminability, while there are increases in degree of organization, resistance to interference, degree of learning, and degree of persistence. Capacity decreases and then increases.

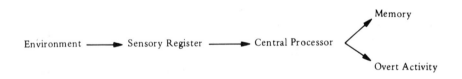

*FIGURE 8-1. Structure of the System (emphasis on continuous changes)*

Although the simple structure of the system portrayed in Figure 8-1 serves to emphasize the systematic changes indicated, it also does violence to a number of functional relationships among the five elements. For example, if the role of memory is to be emphasized, then a very different structure, such as that portrayed in Figure 8-2, is required. Here memory is seen to be involved in the functioning of every other element, including the environment.

One could also choose to emphasize the role of the Central Processor. Since all voluntary activity is associated with activity of the Central Processor (although not all Central Processor activity is voluntary), such a diagram would emphasize voluntary processes, as shown in Figure 8-3.

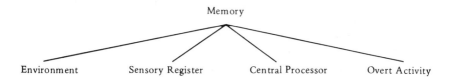

*FIGURE 8-2. Structure of the System (emphasis on the role of memory)*

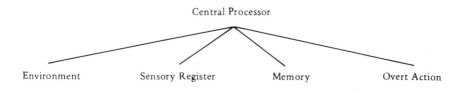

*FIGURE 8-3. Structure of the System (emphasis on volition)*

Thus, diagrams of the system can be useful devices for organizing discussions, but they must not be mistaken for the structure of the system itself, lest the process be distorted. I will make use of all three diagrams but will be bound by none. In what follows, I emphasize the distinction between voluntary and involuntary processes.

## AUTOMATIC FUNCTIONS

### A Continuous Model of the Memory Storage Process

Despite the obvious usefulness of a multi-storage model of memory (such as a division into sensory store, short-term memory store, and long-term memory store), there is virtue in thinking of the process of storage of information in memory as a continuous one. The point of origin for the material to be stored in memory can be a sense organ or the Central Processor. In either case one can generally distinguish processes that are automatic and continuous and two sources of variation, the intervention of the Central Processor and problems associated with consolidation. Processes can be classifed as being either voluntary or automatic. All voluntary activities can be associated with the Central Processor, although not all activities of the Central Processor are voluntary. The problems associated with consolidation constitute a special case. For the moment let us set aside both sources of possible variation and consider the automatic and systematic aspects of memory storage.

*Automatic Complexity Reduction and Loss of Information.* I once heard Dr. John Platt, in a public lecture, describe the human organism as a device for throwing away information. He wrote numbers on the blackboard to represent the enormous amount of information in the environment in any brief time span, progressively smaller numbers to represent the amount of information the sensory receptors were capable of processing and the smaller amount actually processed, and progressively smaller numbers as the resulting activity passed through the elements of the organism as diagrammed in Figure 8-1. Actually, information is lost through a passive filtering process combined with an active process of selection, and at some stages and under some circumstances, information that is not inherent in the stimulus is actually added to the activity by the organism.

Filtering can be described as passive in the sense that it does not ordinarily involve intervention of the Central Processor. Thus, the receptors act as a filter in the sense that they are sensitive only to a limited range of the great variety of energy changes that occur in the environment. The demand characteristics of certain stimuli, such as loud sounds or bright lights, may give these stimuli processing priorities that automatically exclude the processing of other available stimuli. The idea that there are specialized cells in the central nervous system (the so-called feature detectors) that respond in a very selective manner only to certain aspects of the stimulus implies that the selective detection of certain features operates as a filter sorting out unsuitable features of the stimulus complex. Everyone agrees that the central processing mechanism has limited capacity and must thus serve as a filter to reject super-capacity input. The Central Processor can also be regarded as a filter for information to the extent that it involves certain automatic functions and characteristics such as simplification, habituation, the optimal complexity level function, and, possibly, a phase of the consolidation process. Since the effector system has a smaller capacity than the Central Processor, it too serves as an automatic filter to some degree.

The most salient characteristic of the storage process is a very rapid decline in the complexity of the event. In Chapter 6, I discussed the development of a sensory event that usually takes approximately $250\sigma$ from the onset of a stimulus to the point of maximum realization. A visual image, for example, is maximally differentiated and contains a maximum of information at this point. Beyond this point, the amount of information in the event undergoes a rapid decline. Under ordinary circumstances, there is no reason to expect that this decline of information in the trace will follow anything but an exponential course. The decline in quantity of information is truly enormous, even though there is no very good way to measure that quantity systematically. There can be no doubt, however, that a very large number is required to represent the amount of information in the visual environment at any given moment. Although there is a severe reduction in information between the environment and the amount involved in the reaction of the retinae, the amount of information being processed at the receptor level is still very large. What data we have about the amount of information in the trace at other points in the system appear to attest to very rapid simplification. The concept of feature extractor cells in the visual system, involving as it does the idea of cells that respond selectively to limited aspects of the visual stimulus, implies selection and extraction and therefore reduction in the amount of information. Even though studies of memory and the characteristics of various imputed storage mechanisms are confounded by the intervention of the Central Processor and also by a confusion between what has been stored and what can be retrieved, they also tend to show the postulated continuous information loss. Thus, in the Sperling paradigm, subjects can be shown three rows of four letters very briefly. If asked to report them all, they might be able to report 40%, or between four and five items. If, with the same time intervals, they are asked after exposure to report the items in one line only, they might be able to report three, or 75%. The implication is that, in the time it takes to report the items in the sensory store, half of those items are lost. Whether it is the time involved or the act of reporting that produces the loss, there is evidence that subjects might have had nine items in storage when asked to report but have lost half of them in the brief reporting period. In studies of running memory in which subjects are required to respond "old" or "new" to each of a long series of stimuli, accuracy declines the greater the number of intervening items. The implication is that there is a progressive loss in the quality of the trace following its initiation.

*Coding.* Information loss is also implied by the concept of coding. The transduction of energy from one physical form to another, such as the transduction of physical sound vibrations into neurophysiological activity, involves a very large loss in information. Further transformations within the central nervous system also involve loss of complexity and progressive simplification. Each change in form, intensity, and quality consists of an encoding of material into a new form. Such encoding is automatic, instantaneous, and selective of the aspects of the prior form that are preserved in the code.

*Attention.* The concept of attention also implies a reduction in complexity in the sense that what is attended to is less than the total stimulus that could have been attended to. There are many features of stimulus situations that command physical orientation or selective attention. To the extent that the demand values of stimuli control attention, they contribute to the automatic reduction of the complexity of the stimulus field.

*Contribution of Memory to Icon and Echo.* It seems probable that the past experience of the organism is brought to bear on the development of an icon or echo automatically and in a selective manner. One of the debates in the literature of information processing concerns the stage in the processing of information at which the effects of past experience come into play. Some authors, such as Neisser (1967), emphasize the extent to which the initial effects of a stimulus are determined by the character of the stimulus alone. This emphasis leads to a conception of the pre-attentive "icon," which is assumed to be free of the effects of past experience. Earlier, in considering the nature and role of habituation, I concluded that the effect of habituation is present at the moment of inception of a psychological event even though the event is stimulus-initiated. If the effects of immediate past experience (habituation) can influence the nature of the psychological event at its inception, then the effects of experience in the more remote past may influence it as well. Such an effect of learning on the inception and developing character of a psychological event is automatic, pre-attentive, and free of the machinations of the Central Processor. Therefore, it is a good bet that the "icon" of a familiar visual object is not identical with the "icon" of that object the first time it was seen. Finally, even though there is insufficient time to bring the Central Processor into play after the initiation of the event and the full development of its character, there is no compelling logical reason why a prior set, whether the unconscious result of a motive state such as hunger or the conscious result of the operation of the Central Processor, could not influence the course of development of a psychological event. All physical stimuli are essentially chaotic. What is stored in permanent memory is an organized extraction based on past experience.

Not only is the storage of material in memory automatic, but the process of retrieving material from memory is also in some sense automatic. I will assert that the effects of past experience influence the character of the sensory reaction to an external stimulus; in this sense, material in memory is automatically retrieved. Retrieval in the sense of a Central Processor search for the content of memory is a nonautomatic process; however, once the Central Processor has retrieved the appropriate cue, the retrieval of the content associated with that cue is automatic. The automatic character of the storage and retrieval processes is generally occulted by voluntary activity through the Central Processor as it is engaged in manipulating material to make it more accessible in the future as well as in elaborating what has been retrieved from memory into meaningful form.

*Continuous Loss of Discriminability and Concept Formation.* The progressive and continuous simplification of the memory trace is correlated with progressive and continuous change in other characteristics. As information is lost, discriminability from other traces is lost as well. Loss of discriminability is an inevitable product of loss of information. The less the information, the fewer the bases for distinction between particular events. In fact, it is this feature of trace simplification that accounts for the development of concepts. Although concept formation may be enhanced by the intervention of Central Processor activity, it seems likely that concept formation, at least of a primitive sort, could very well occur without such intervention. Concept formation could result if in some sense the trace became progressively better organized as it was simplified, if past experience had a bearing on how it was organized, if, in the process of simplification, the unique properties of the event were lost, and if the product was integrated into an existing cognitive structure.

*Increasing Persistence.* Stimulus input undergoes a number of transductions, and there is a tendency for the effect of stimulation to increase in its persistence. Persistence is extremely short at the receptor level, where parallel processing is not possible and erasure of the effect of one stimulus by the effect of a succeeding stimulus is possible. Early levels must have short persistence so that new inputs can be registered without loss. Increasing organization and loss of discriminability are accompanied by increasing persistence and the possibility of parallel processing. Parallel processing requires lack of interference. There is no stage of processing at which the possibility of interference ceases and the possibility of parallel processing begins. Whether two inputs will interfere depends on their similarities. Inputs that are nearly identical tend to undergo interference, even into long-term memory, until their unique properties are lost through concept formation. Distinctly different inputs acquire integrity, autonomy, freedom from interference, and the capacity for parallel processing within as little as one-half second after initiation.

*Forgetting.* The two automatic processes, simplification through loss of information and a progressive decrease in discriminability, constitute an account of the process of forgetting. Underwood (1972) concludes that the rate of forgetting is independent of learning parameters, that all materials are forgotten at the same rate, and that individual differences in rate of forgetting are minimal. He asks whether there is one powerful, common constituent that is responsible for the observed constant rate of forgetting, which remains uninfluenced by the particular manipulations suggested by current theories of verbal learning. I suggest that the automatic processes I have outlined are that powerful common constituent.

*Recognition versus Recall.* A number of authors have pointed out differences in the variables that influence recognition and recall performances. Underwood (in Melton & Martin, 1972) cites evidence that the correlation between recognition and recall scores is low. Both Underwood and Kintsch (1970, cited in Anderson & Bower, 1974) explain the difference by saying that retrieval tags must be used in recall, whereas the process of recognition is independent of associative retrieval processes. Underwood (1969) distinguishes between discrimination attributes and retrieval attributes, and he says that the process of recognition involves only discrimination attributes, while recall involves both.

The difference between recognition and recall is dramatically apparent in the differential effects of frequency or familiarity of words. It was demonstrated repeatedly in Chapter 7 that, the more frequently a verbal item occurred in the language, the easier it was to learn as a response item in tasks demanding recall. Frequent occurrence of a psychological event has two primary effects: the event becomes progressively simpler, and it becomes less discriminable from other events. Simpler events are easier to recall than complex ones primarily because of the limited capacity of the Central Processor. The simpler the event to be recalled, the greater the number of retrieval tags that can be held in the Central Processor simultaneously. General discriminability is less of a factor in recall, because particular discriminability is provided by the retrieval mechanisms unique to the learning situation in which recall is demanded. In recognition memory, on the other hand, discriminability is paramount. A judgment of whether one has seen a word before is easier to make when the word is rare and complex. Thus, high frequency words are recalled better than low frequency words, and low frequency words are recognized better than high frequency words. This difference has led to a phenomenon referred to as the recognition/recall frequency paradox.

A clear example of this effect has been reported by Glanzer and Bowles (1974) in a recognition memory experiment. They had subjects study booklets containing 200 words. Later, in a test phase, 120 of these study words were paired with 120 new words, and the subjects were asked which of the pair had been seen in the study phase. Half of the words were high frequency words (H), and half were low frequency words (L). The half that had been seen before were referred to as old words (O), and the half that had not been seen before were referred to as new words (N). In the test condition, choices were forced for six kinds of pairs. Four of the pairs, HO-HN, LO-HN, HO-LN, and LO-LN, offered choices involving pairs in which one actually had been seen and one had not. Two pairs, HN-LN and LO-HO, forced choices among pairs for which there was no correct choice. The results are shown in Table 8-1, with the most frequently chosen member of each pair on the left and the frequency with which it was chosen given as a proportion of the total choices made for that pair.

*TABLE 8-1.* Recognition-Recall Frequency Paradox Data

| Word Pair | Choice of Word on Left (Proportion of Total Choices) | Number of Factors |
|---|---|---|
| HN > LN | .67 | 1 |
| LO > HO | .68 | 1 |
| HO > HN | .75 | 1 |
| LO > HN | .80 | 2 |
| HO > LN | .83 | 2 |
| LO > LN | .89 | 3 |

The data are taken from a study by Glanzer and Bowles (1975) of forced-choice recognition of word pairs. A word could be old (O) or new (N), high frequency (H) or low frequency (L). The table is arranged with the most frequently chosen member of each pair on the left. The "Number of Factors" column is explained in the text.

One way to understand the role of discriminability in recognition learning is to separate three factors involved in the decisions the subjects made in this experiment. One factor is whether the item had in fact been in the study set and was therefore an old (O) item. If so, then this factor should have weighed in favor of a positive choice of this item. Therefore, where O is opposite N in the table, O should appear on the left. Discriminability could contribute to the judgment in two ways. If the word was a rare, low frequency word (L), its rareness should have made it more evident to the subject that it had been seen before. Thus, wherever the combination LO appears in the table, it should be on the left, and this should constitute a second factor contributing to the decision of the subject. Discriminability could also contribute to the decision when a new word (N) was involved. If a word is rare, it is easier to decide that it has *not* been seen before than if it is a common word. Therefore, the combination LN is a third factor contributing to the subject's decision. Since it facilitates the judgment that the word has not been seen before, it should appear on the right in the table. The number of such factors operating in each decision is listed in the table, where it can be seen that frequency of choice appears to increase as the number of factors contributing to the choice increases.

This analysis suggests that the distinction between factors that contribute differentially to recognition and recall is to be found on the simplicity/complexity dimension. Recall is facilitated by any factor that contributes to the simplicity of the psychological event. Such factors include repetition, organization by grouping and other forms of chunking, and integration into a preexisting concept. Recognition is facilitated by factors that serve to complicate the event. They include such factors as adding an image to a word, adding a word to an image, or establishing a natural language mediator.

*Organization of the Trace.* Simplification of the trace is not random. Organization can arise from the effects of past experience and from the nature of the stimulus itself. Much of the study of perception is devoted to the analysis of the characteristics of the stimulus situation that will produce a particular perceptual quality. These perceptual principles can be seen as specifying the stimulus characteristics that influence the direction of simplification of the trace.

Gestalt psychologists made a major contribution to the psychology of perception in the development of principles of Gestalt organization. One of the shibboleths of Gestalt psychology was "The whole is greater than the sum of the parts." This saying emphasized the idea that something was added when, for example, 20 scattered stars were rearranged to form a circle or a square. The circle of stars formed a better gestalt than the same stars scattered at random. Psychological complexity and preference theory offers a possible interpretation of the nature and role of gestalt organization. If complexity judgments were obtained of the two stimuli (20 scattered stars and 20 stars arranged in a circle), it seems certain that the circle of stars would be judged to be simpler. It would also be easier to recognize or to use in a more complicated learning task. In terms of judged complexity and ease of learning, the good gestalt could be characterized by the phrase "The whole is less than the sum of the parts." As we shall see subsequently, psychological complexity and preference theory offers a potential means of measuring the quality of gestalt organization with the expectation that, the better the gestalt, the simpler the stimulus.

A minimum of gestalt organization can be achieved by simple physical grouping. For example, Asch demonstrated that, if subjects were instructed to pronounce two nonsense syllables as a single word, *datnik,* they remembered the syllables better than if they were instructed to pronounce them individually, *dat-nik* (Asch, 1969, cited in Anderson & Bower, 1974). Asch describes the quality distinguishing the six-letter word from the two three-letter words as "unity" or "coherence." The quality of "coherence" might be measured directly by obtaining ratings of complexity of *datnik* and *dat-nik.* A general inference can be made that a very familiar six-letter word would possess more coherence than two very familiar three-letter words. The magnitude of this difference might be estimated from the asymptotes of the learning curves calculated and displayed in Table 7-18 (p. 179). There, the asymptote for three-letter words was estimated to be a complexity value of 37.22. Two three-letter words could therefore be expected to have a complexity value of 74.44. The asymptote for six-letter words in the table was calculated to be 43.08. A quantitative estimate of the "coherence" value of a very familiar six-letter word compared to the value for two very familiar three-letter words would be the difference, 31.36.

Physical grouping can also simplify a complex stimulus composed of numbers. Telephone numbers are a familiar example. The set of numbers

3 1 3 7 6 1 4 6 5 3

is beyond the immediate memory span of most individuals in that form. Improvement can be achieved by forming three groups of numbers rather than one:

313   761   4653

Three groups of three, three, and four letters form a better gestalt than one group of ten letters. Although the degree of gestalt organization achieved by this grouping pattern is trivial compared to the amount of simplification potential of a good gestalt of a very complex stimulus, it is critical in the use of the telephone system. Since a single group of ten digits is beyond the memory span of most individuals, making it virtually impossible for them to read a ten-digit number from a telephone book and remember it long enough to dial it correctly, grouping into the three-three-four pattern brings ten digits within the immediate memory span of a large number of telephone users and thus reduces the probable number of dialing errors. This is simplification through the good offices of physical arrangement. If the ten-digit telephone number becomes very familiar through frequent use, not only can it be recalled from permanent memory, but it can be held in short-term memory storage long enough after being recalled to permit dialing with perfect accuracy nearly every time.

When a person is faced with the same task without the helpful assistance of the telephone company, a number of cognitive strategies may be employed. One of them might be identical in pattern to that used by the telephone company. Thus, a mental grouping might be imposed on the string of digits by the insertion of pauses after the third and sixth digits, producing the same result as that achieved by the telephone company.

Simplification can also be achieved in musical stimuli through the insertion of pauses. One can then vary the number of chunks and the number of tones in a chunk independently. Arkes (1971) measured the complexity of such stimuli in the context of a large set of studies. He began with seven square-wave tones ranging over two octaves from 511.8 to 2049.2 Hz. Each tone was given a duration of .167 seconds, with a normal interval between tones also of .167 seconds. A sequence of tones was organized or chunked in two ways. Chunks of three, four, five, or six tones were formed by increasing the duration of the interval between tones to 1.167 seconds at appropriate positions in the sequence. In addition, each chunk consisted of a run (*abcd*), a trill (*abab*), or a repetition (*aaaa*). Arkes then formed sequences of five, eight, ten, 12, or 15 chunks, with the size of the chunks constant within any given sequence. The initial note of each sequence was randomly determined, and the sequence composition in terms of runs, trills, and repetitions was generally random, except that some constraint was imposed to achieve balance. Each combination of chunk length and chunk number was rated twice by 14 subjects.

The relations between judged complexity and chunk size and chunk number are shown in Figure 8-4. The relations are plotted in terms of average number of tones produced by the various combinations of numbers of tones within chunks (3, 4, 5, or 6) x 10 (the average number of sequences) or the number of sequences (5, 8, 10, 12, or 15) x 4.5 (the average number of tones in a sequence). The effect of the number of chunks is statistically significant, but the effect of number of tones within a chunk is not. It is remarkable that doubling the number of notes in a chunk from three to six did not lead to a substantial increase in rated complexity. I will return later

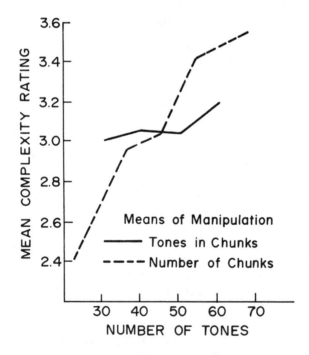

FIGURE 8-4. *Psychological Complexity and Preference for Tones Varying in Chunk Size and Number of Chunks. (From* The Relationship between Repetition and Organization and the Role of Organization in Psychological Complexity, *by H. R. Arkes. Unpublished doctoral dissertation, University of Michigan, 1971. Reprinted by permission.)*

to the problem of the psychological complexity of individual chunks and its effect on the number of chunks that can be held in the Central Processor.

The Gestalt psychologists insist on distinguishing between organization of stimulus elements that represents gestalt quality and organization that arises from experience. In psychological complexity theory, simplification can be achieved either through re-arrangement of the items into a better gestalt organization, in which case simplification is instantaneous, or through repeated experience, in which case simplification is gradual. The effect of either form of simplification can be quantified in terms of its effects on psychological complexity. A pseudo-quantification can be achieved by use of the values of complexity developed in the previous chapter. A word can be regarded as a number of letters organized into a chunk. In ordinary usage, these chunks are separated by spaces (on the printed page) or by pauses (in speech). Thus, there is little ambiguity about where a chunk begins and ends. Furthermore, there can be differences in the degrees of organization of words for a given person. A rare word with uncertain pronunciation and spelling is not as well organized as a frequently written and spoken word. In fact, the equations in Table 7-18 reflect the degree to which a given word is well organized into a chunk. The asymptotes of the 12 equations in Table 7-18 represent a theoretical estimate of the psychological complexities of words used with sufficient frequency that no further simplification, and thus no greater organization, is likely to occur. If one accepts this conception, then a line can be plotted relating the complexities of words of various lengths, as has been done in Figure 8-5. This line represents a limit to the simplification that can occur as a function of frequency of experience.

Within the same space, a hypothetical line can be drawn to represent the complexities of sets of letters possessing no degree of organization. To construct such a line, it is necessary to assume that the individual letters have become asymptotically simplified through experience and that it is possible to present them to a subject in such a fashion that there is no grouping or other connection between letters. Given such assumptions, the line can be constructed by multiplying the asymptotic value for single letters by the number of letters, as has been done for the upper line in Figure 8-5.

In some sense, the space between the two lines in Figure 8-5 represents the potential simplification that can be achieved by organizing an unrelated set of letters into an organized set, whether through frequency of experience, chunking into smaller sets by the insertion of pauses, forming subgroupings through physical arrangement, or in some other manner.

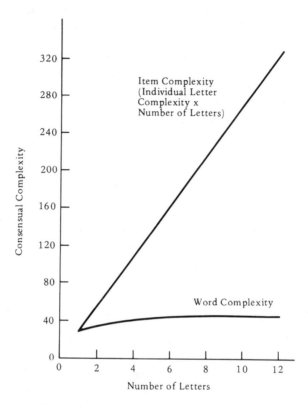

FIGURE 8-5. Comparison of the Complexities of Unrelated Letters and Asymptotically Organized Words

Anderson and Bower (1974) cite a series of studies (Bower & Winzenz, 1969; Bower & Springston, 1970; and Bower, 1972) that illustrate the effects of physical grouping and familiarity on the psychological complexity of verbal material, as indexed by ease of recognition or recall.

In Bower and Winzenz, subjects were given a long series of five-digit items. Their task was to report whether a given set of five digits was one they had heard before ("Old") or one they had not heard before ("New"). The digits were presented as auditory stimuli and grouped in various possible patterns, such as 2-3, 2-1-2, or 1-2-2. For half of the five-digit items, the grouping pattern was the same on successive presentations; for the other half, the grouping varied between the two presentations. Bower and Winzenz report that recognition memory was "very much worse when the string repetition occurred with changed groupings than with unaltered groupings. . . . The difference in correct 'old' responses between the two conditions was about 20%" (Anderson & Bower, 1974, p. 438).

The effect of some degree of familiarity is demonstrated in the Bower and Springston and the Bower studies, in which acronyms were employed. Strings of 12 letters were constructed and grouped into 2-3-3-4 or 4-3-3-2 patterns. They were arranged so that the acronyms either did or did not coincide with the physical groupings, thusly:

| TV | IBM | TWO | USSR | TVIB | MTW | AUS | SR |
|----|-----|-----|------|------|-----|-----|-----|
| ICBM | FBI | USC | BO | IC | BMF | BIU | SCBO |

Bower and Springston report an immediate memory span of 6.7 letters when the physical grouping did not coincide with the acronyms and 9.6 letters when they did coincide. The improvement in recall that can be attributed to the degree of familiarity of the acronyms amounts to 24% of the 12 letters.

The estimates of 20% improvement in recall attributable to grouping and 24% improvement attributable to familiarity of acronyms can be translated into consensual complexity values by assuming that consensual complexity and ease of recall are perfectly correlated. For 12-letter strings, grouping could be estimated to simplify the total complexity of the set 20% of the distance from 12 unrelated letters to zero complexity, and grouping plus familiarity could be estimated to simplify the total complexity by 44% of that distance. These reductions are represented in Figure 8-6 by the two broken lines. This logic makes it an algebraic necessity that the complexity values for memory span for grouped letters and for grouped familiar letters must be the same (approximately 144 units of the consensual complexity scale). By these calculations, the immediate memory span for ungrouped letters of this population of subjects should be 5.38 letters.

The value of 5.38 letters for the immediate memory span of Stanford undergraduates seems too low. The factor that has not been taken into account in Figure 8-6 is task complexity. Since the task required of these subjects was one of perfect serial recall, the consensual complexity value of 12 letters is an underestimate of the total complexity of the task by some unknown amount. However, the curves in Figure 8-6 could be adjusted by obtaining an estimate of task complexity and taking it into account. For example, if the true immediate memory span for letters proved to be 8 for this population, this would amount to an increase of approximately 50 units in consensual complexity values.

*What Is Stored in Memory and in What Form?* The literature on human memory contains a number of strong and opposed opinions concerning precisely what is stored in memory and in what form. There are authors who argue cogently that all memory consists of linguistic propositions (see Anderson & Bower, 1974; Norman &

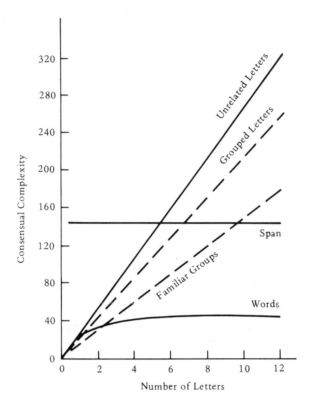

*FIGURE 8-6. Complexity Reduction through Grouping and Familiarity*

Rumelhart, 1975). Storage is in the form of items and nodes in a grammatical structure. There are others who would allow for the storage of images. Pribram (1971) has gone so far as to try to account for the storage of images in a form analogous to holographic photography. Fixation on one form of storage to the exclusion of all others can arise from concentration on a limited set of learning paradigms and materials, from the reification of the computer flow diagram as a model for human memory, or from a confusion of the memory itself and the form in which the memory is reported. Neisser (1967) has pointed out that material retrieved from memory is highly processed, elaborated, and reconstructed. Shepard (1974) indicates that internal representations are much more readily externalized when they are letters, numbers, or words than when they are images, schemata, or spatial transformations.

What is actually stored in memory is probably better conceived as a processed representation of whatever has occurred in the Central Processor, possibly including elements of which we are not consciously aware. Craik and Lockhart (1972) cite considerable evidence that there is little or no memory for information that, although registered in some sense at the receptor, is not attended to or otherwise processed. They cite Moray (1957) as finding no memory for auditory information (words) presented on the unattended channel, a conclusion confirmed by Norman (1969). They cite Neisser (1964) as showing that non-target items in a visual search task left no trace, and they cite a similar conclusion in the work of Turvey (1967). Norman and Rumelhart (1975) argue that visual images are stored in highly processed form, a conclusion drawn in part from the work of Pylyshyn (1973). Wickens (1972) concludes from his very extensive work on relief from proactive inhibition that the item and all of its attributes are stored automatically and simultaneously. Posner and Warren (1972) discuss the great variety of aspects of a situation that can be retrieved from memory. Not only can subjects report an item, but they can report such things as the modality involved, position on the list, and spacing, frequency, and number of items between repetitions of a given item. Subjects are undoubtedly able to recall a great many other aspects, including some that might be difficult to articulate and thus make a part of the record.

The distinction between the single psychological event, which endures for approximately $500\sigma$, and the stream of psychological events, which is endless, offers some basis for distinctions in the matter of what is stored in memory and in what form. Within the single psychological event there can be an item, all of its attributes, a relevant sensory image, and many aspects of the context in which the item occurred. It might be argued that, the richer and more complex the individual psychological event, the better the event as a stimulus item for the recall of an associated subsequent event. Paivio (1969) shows that, either as stimulus items in paired associate learning or as items in a study of recognition memory, objects or pictures are best, followed by concrete nouns, while abstract nouns are least effective. It is argued that concrete nouns are superior to abstract nouns because it is relatively easy to associate an image with a concrete noun and difficult to do so with an abstract noun. Objects and images are best of all, because an actual object is more complex than an imagined object, and a verbal label for an object is likely to be retrieved automatically and instantaneously. It is worthy of note that visual images are almost exclusively confined to single psychological events. Sequential inspection of a visual scene results in an integrated image of the scene in recall.

Memory for sequences of psychological events involves a quite different set of problems. Individual psychological events are highly organized, and many aspects of their organization are related to frequent past experience. In fact, the individual psychological event seems specialized for the utilization of past experience. Sequential information is often (but not always) new and idiosyncratic information. This is certainly true of the usual verbal learning experiment, for the items are old and well learned material, while the order of the items is new. There is thus little reason for Melton and Martin (1972) to emphasize the fact that, in verbal learning studies, order information is forgotten much more rapidly than items. Human behavior is highly flexible. That flexibility is minimal with respect to the character of individual events, but the essence of flexibility lies in the infinite order of such events.

It should also be noted that, although the examination of visual imagery places the emphasis on individual psychological events, examination of auditory imagery places the emphasis on the *sequence* of psychological events. After a lifetime of listening, most of us lack so-called "perfect pitch" and are thus unable to recall accurately a single note, but most of us are able to reproduce a large number of sequential patterns (melodies). Thus, auditory memory seems especially adapted for retaining the sequential pattern of psychological events, just as visual memory seems especially adapted for dealing with the complexities of individual psychological events.

*Automatic Changes in Trace Vulnerability and Accessibility?* If a fixed amount and condition of practice is followed by a test for retention, variation of the time between training and test tends to yield a simple curve indicating that, the greater the time between training and test, the less accessible the material is. The issue of whether material is actually lost from memory or simply becomes less accessible has not been and cannot easily be solved. In either case, the forgetting curve is simple and regular and appears to reflect a simple process. However, several classes of experimental results at least raise a question concerning the simplicity and regularity of the process.

One of these phenomena is the negative bias against repetition reviewed in Chapter 6. The time course of this bias strongly suggests two phases. There appears to be an initial phase during which the tendency not to repeat an event remains unchanged in value. This phase is followed by a gradual disappearance of the negative effect, which can be followed by a positive bias toward repetition. Elsewhere, I have suggested three related hypotheses (see, for example, Walker, 1956, 1958, 1967). The first suggestion was that this temporally correlated phenomenon was intimately related to temporal properties of the memory trace. The second suggestion was that the period during which the negative bias against repetition endured corresponded to a period during which the memory trace was represented by a continuing active neural process that had as its function the laying down of permanent memory. The third suggestion was that the function of the negative bias against repetition was the protection of the active trace from disruption by the same or similar events. In the 1959 article, I made an attempt to lay out a reasonable neural model for a system that would produce all these effects.

A second set of studies that raise a question concerning the simple passive decay of the memory trace involve the production of amnesia through the use of traumatic stimuli shortly after learning has occurred. The most common traumatic stimuli are electro-convulsive shock (ECS) and the intracerebral injection of puromycin. There is a general finding that, with relatively short time intervals, amnesia for the learned material is almost complete. The longer the interval between training and the application of the traumatic stimulus, the less the amnesic effect. This pattern is what one would expect if the memory trace were going through a period of active consolidation, and if the traumatic stimulus put an end to the organized activity before the storage process had been completed. Unfortunately, this simple relation between the time interval and the amount of amnesia is not always found. Moreover, it can often be shown that at least some of the amnesia is more apparent than real, and even when the amnesia seems to be genuine, there are alternative explanations for its appearance that do not involve the destruction of the trace by the effects of the traumatic stimulus. Prominent alternatives to the trace destruction hypothesis generally attribute poor performance to failure to retrieve the memory because of an additional trace added to or overlaying the original trace. The additional trace is produced by the traumatic stimulus and its effects. (See R. R. Miller & Springer, 1973, for a review of these issues.)

A third class of studies that might challenge the simplicity and the regularity of the decline of the memory trace involve unexpected effects of two practice trials, depending on their separation, either in terms of time or in terms of the number of intervening items. They have in common the inference that, since a second training trial is not always as beneficial as it should be, there may have been interference between the traces of the two training trials. Walker and Tarte (1963) varied the temporal spacing between two trials of a paired associates task and maintained a fixed interval between training and test. When the interval between the two training tasks was very short, the effect of the second trial was small. As the interval was increased, the second trial had a progressively more positive effect on memory and finally a decreased effect. We interpreted this result to mean that, when the training trials were closely spaced in time, the habituation-based protective mechanism of the first trace prevented full formation of a trace of the second trial.

Similar effects have been shown for visual and verbal materials in a variety of learning paradigms such as continuous paired associates, in short-term memory studies, and in studies of free recall (Melton, 1970). A typical result is that reported by Peterson, Wampler,

Kirkpatrick, and Saltzman (1963). In a continuous paired associates task, two repetitions of an item were separated by 0, 2, 4, 8, 16, or 32 intervening items. Recall percentages based on the two presentations were 39, 43, 47, 50, 51, and 45. Thus, the effect of the second trial had very different effects on the test for memory depending on how soon after the first trial it occurred.

Hintzman (1974) and Melton (1970) have each reviewed possible explanations for this anomalous effect of distributed practice. Explanations in terms of five different concepts are given: voluntary attention, differential rehearsal, habituation, consolidation, and coding variability. Both authors reject explanations in terms of differential voluntary deployment of attention, largely, as Hintzman points out, because the effect seems not to be affected by experimental efforts to manipulate the attention variable. Both authors also reject the possibility that the effect is attributable to differential effort or rehearsal, because the prevention of rehearsal does not appear to affect the phenomenon and because the effect is present when the material to be learned is pictorial and thus not easily rehearsed. Thus, the distributed practice effect appears not to be attributable to voluntary effort. There is less agreement between Hintzman and Melton with respect to possible roles of the automatic and involuntary variables.

The explanation in terms of habituation appeals to the simple fact that, under many circumstances, repeated stimulation leads to reduced responses. The amount of reduction is empirically related to the time between stimuli, maximum reduction occurring with close spacing. Applied to the distributed practice effect, the argument is that the habituation produced by the first occurrence of an item prevents the complete registration of the second occurrence of the item; the amount of this defect in registration of the second practice trial is proportional to the amount of habituation. The consolidation hypothesis offers two possibilities, one identical to the habituation explanation. The second trial can be seen as disrupting the trace of the first trial and thus preventing complete consolidation, or the inhibitory processes protecting the consolidation of the effects of the first trial can prevent the complete formation of the trace of the second. The encoding variability hypothesis attributed to Martin (Melton & Martin, 1972) is based on three assumptions: (1) there are many ways to encode a stimulus, (2) the more ways a stimulus is actually encoded, the more likely it is to be recalled, and (3) the longer the interval between two practice trials, the more likely the stimulus is to be encoded differently on the two occasions.

Melton (1970) does not discuss the habituation hypothesis, but he rejects the consolidation hypothesis out of hand. He feels that there are as yet insufficient independently defined parametric guidelines for consolidation theory for it to be useful in accounting for the distributed practice effect. He favors Martin's encoding variability hypothesis, probably because, even though it is thought of as an automatic process, it appears more amenable to experimental manipulation than does consolidation. Hintzman (1974), on the other hand, finds some degree of merit in each of the three. With respect to coding variability, he finds variability of the context a more likely source of the difference than variability of the stimulus. In reference to consolidation, he argues that it is more likely that it is the formation of the trace of the second practice trial that is affected than a disruption of the trace of the first. If it is the formation of the trace of the second trial that is affected, then there is little difference between consolidation and habituation as explanatory devices.

In this context, there appears to be empirical evidence that at least the visual trace is maximally vulnerable to interference in the first quarter-second of its development. ECS data can be interpreted as indicating progressive resistance to disturbance from traumatic stimulation with the passage of time. There is general agreement that permanent memory is permanent precisely because of the high resistance to interference of material in long-term storage. Thus, resistance to interference appears also to increase continuously and automatically with the passage of time after the occurrence of an event.

These considerations leave us with two models for the memory storage process, a continuous one and one in which there can be discontinuities. In the continuous model, the occurrence of a psychological event—whether initiated externally by a stimulus in the environment or internally through action of the Central Processor—sets up a trace that automatically and continuously declines in the amount of information within it and in its discriminability from other traces, while it increases in the extent to which it is organized. Discontinuous models of the storage process may involve universal discontinuities, such as those involved in the multi-storage models. They may also involve occasional or accidental discontinuities. For example, discontinuities can occur as the products of traumatic stimuli that may destroy the trace, or there may be trace interference from repeated events that may modify the quality of either or both traces involved.

I have argued that, despite the intellectual convenience and heuristic fruitfulness of the multi-storage models, there is no basis for adopting a multi-store model of the storage process as long as the possible intervention of the Central Processor is excluded from consideration. As for the possibility that discontinuities can be produced by traumatic stimuli or by closely paired activations of the same or similar events, no definitive conclusion can be drawn.

No one would argue with the empirical fact that the accessibility of an item declines (or that the item is forgotten) as a function of time or intervening activity. Three other regular functions correlated in time after the occurrence of a psychological event can be demonstrated empirically. First, there is a habituation effect, which produces a negative bias against the repetition of the event. The habituation effect declines with time. Second, traumatic stimuli applied after the occurrence of an event can produce reduced accessibility of the event. The greater the interval between the event and the application of the traumatic stimulus, the less effective is that stimulus in reducing accessibility. Third, the longer a second training trial is delayed, up to a point, the more effective it is in increasing the capacity of the organism to perform that event. Interpretative choice with respect to these three empirical patterns can be arbitrary in view of the lack of data that are absolutely critical.

My own choices are these. The storage process seems to me to be essentially continuous and regular. The presence of habituation after the event seems to suggest a mechanism of trace protection. The distributed practice effect appears to be the result of the imperfect formation of the trace of the second occurrence of the event. Traumatic stimuli may damage the trace, make retrieval more difficult, or both; the last possibility seems the most likely one.

*Summary of Automatic Processes.* In this section I have emphasized a number of aspects of the occurrence of psychological events that happen automatically and without the intervention of the Central Processor. To the extent that attention is responsive to the demand characteristics of the stimulus, it is automatic. The trace of an event undergoes progressive and continuous loss of information and discriminability, processes that together make up the forgetting process. Automatic concept formation is the product of the selective loss of particular information concerning an event and the preservation of the repeated constant information. The organization of the trace can be influenced by characteristics of the stimulus, but in any case it becomes progressively more organized with the passage of time after the occurrence of an event. Resistance to interference from other events also appears to increase with the passage of time. I have argued that all aspects of an event are stored instantly and automatically, and that some of the effects of past experience influence an event automatically at the moment of its inception; to this extent, retrieval from memory is also automatic and instantaneous.

## VOLUNTARY FUNCTIONING

The Central Processor is the source of all voluntary activity, whether cognitive or physical. Much Central Processor activity is automatic. In what follows I will be concerned with the interaction of voluntary and nonvoluntary activities.

Let us consider a few aspects of Central Processor activity and the possible contributions of psychological complexity and preference theory to the understanding of these functions. I will first consider decision processes and then the ways in which the Central Processor manipulates cognitive material to overcome the apparent limitation on the amount of material that can be processed in a brief period of time.

### Choice Behavior

All choice behavior is Central Processor activity. Most choices are automatic and occur without the intervention of voluntary activity. Some choices are made automatically but only after deliberate cogitation. Figure 8-7 can be used to illustrate both kinds of choices. $E_0$ in the figure represents an event occurring at moment zero, $M_0$. The hedgehog in the figure can choose among five alternatives. The arrows indicate a possible series of choices among successive sets of five, which may or may not be the same set at the successive moments labeled $M_{+1}$, $M_{+2}$, and so on.

Automatic choices are assumed to be made exclusively on the basis of the principle of preference for optimal complexity. The total time involved in Figure 8-7 is therefore approximately 2.5 seconds. If the five columns represent the same set of alternatives

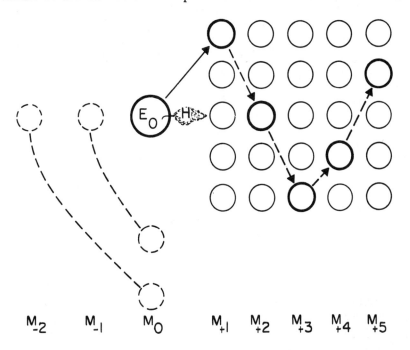

$$M_{-2} \quad M_{-1} \quad M_0 \quad M_{+1} \quad M_{+2} \quad M_{+3} \quad M_{+4} \quad M_{+5}$$

FIGURE 8-7. Choices among Potential Psychological Events

at each of the five moments, then it is implied that they were originally ordered (numbering from the top) 1, 3, 5, 4, and 2. That all five were chosen implies that a single occurrence of each produced sufficient habituation and sufficient reduced preference to inhibit repetition of any one of them before all five had occurred.

Given the hypothesis that decisions are made on the basis of psychological complexity and optimal complexity level, the applicability of the hypothesis can be examined by showing the manner in which the Hedgehog might deal with problems of classical economic decision theory and psychological subjective decision theory.

### Economic Decision Theory

The classical formula for determining the best among certain classes of economic decisions involves probability ($P$), value ($V$), and utility ($U$). The utility of an alternative is the product of the probability of a favorable outcome and the value of that outcome. Since the classical formula assumes that the probability and value can be determined objectively, the terms of the classical formula should bear the subscript $o$. Thus, the classical formula is:

$$P_O \times V_O = U_O.$$

Table 8-2 is a simple exercise of the classical economic decision model. In the left-hand column is a demonstration of what happens when the value is constant across a set of alternatives while the probability varies. Under these conditions, there are wide variations in the utilities of the various alternatives, and the last alternative is clearly the most profitable decision and thus the best. In the right-hand column is an illustration of the results of variation in the value

*TABLE 8-2.* Exercise of the Classical Economic Decision Model

| $P_O$ Varies | | | $P_O$ and $V_O$ Covary | | | $V_O$ Varies | | |
|---|---|---|---|---|---|---|---|---|
| $P_O$ | $\times$  $V_O$ | $=$  $U_O$ | $P_O$ | $\times$  $V_O$ | $=$  $U_O$ | $P_O$ | $\times$  $V_O$ | $=$  $U_O$ |
| .01 | 100 | 1 | .01 | 5000 | 50 | .5 | 2 | 1 |
| .10 | 100 | 10 | .10 | 500 | 50 | .5 | 20 | 10 |
| .20 | 100 | 20 | .20 | 250 | 50 | .5 | 40 | 20 |
| .50 | 100 | 50 | .50 | 100 | 50 | .5 | 100 | 50 |
| .80 | 100 | 80 | .80 | 62.5 | 50 | .5 | 160 | 80 |
| .90 | 100 | 90 | .90 | 55.56 | 50 | .5 | 180 | 90 |
| .99 | 100 | 99 | .99 | 50.51 | 50 | .5 | 198 | 99 |

with the probability held constant. Again, the best decision is the one in which the utility is the largest. The middle column illustrates a class of possible decision alternatives in which probability and value covary in such a way that each of the possible choices has an identical utility. Classical economic decision theory asserts that there are no differences among these alternatives because the utilities are the same for all seven choices.

This economic decision model has great power under many circumstances, but it has severe limitations as a model to predict human choice behavior. Many human economic decisions must be made in circumstances in which the objective value, the objective probability, or both are not known. Even when they are known, human choices will deviate from the ideal in systematic and predictable ways. The classical economic decision model, of course, makes no allowance for individual differences; yet human subjects do differ in their choices in individually characteristic ways. Finally, although classical economic decision theory has nothing to say about choices in the middle column, those alternatives have properties that make them psychologically unequal.

A significant improvement in prediction can be achieved by shifting from an objective economic decision model to a subjective psychological decision model. The improvement in prediction arises in part from systematic differences between objective and subjective value and systematic differences between objective and subjective probability. Additional improvement can arise potentially from the possibility of assessing stable individual or personality differences from characteristic individual differences in subjective value, probability, and utility.

Objective value is an equal-unit linear scale; that is, the difference between $1.00 and $101.00 is exactly the same as the difference between $1,000,000.00 and $1,000,100.00. Subjective .value is probably a curvilinear function of objective value in which each unit that is added to a total has a smaller subjective value than the previous unit that was added. Thus, an artist might care a great deal whether she was offered $1.00 or $101.00 for a painting while caring very little whether she was offered $1,000,000.00 or $1,000,100.00 for the same painting.

There is also a discrepancy between objective probability and human perception of chancy situations. Low probability events are generally seen as much *more* likely to happen than is actually the case, and high probability events are generally seen as much *less* likely to happen than is actually the case. It may be that the discrepancies at the two ends of the objective probability distribution reflect a general human failure to make adequate discriminations at the extremes. Furthermore, to say that one of the two possible events has a probability is equivalent to saying that the alternative has a low probability. For example, consider the likelihood that a house will burn down. The objective probability may be exceedingly low, perhaps as low as one in 10,000 over a ten-year period. Yet, if one asked a sufficient number of individuals what they thought the probability was of their houses burning down in the next ten years, the mean estimate might be of the order of one in 1,000. Whatever the actual values, there would likely be a group tendency to see this low probability event as more of a threat than it actually is. It is partly for this reason that selling insurance is a profitable business even though the calculations of the utilities involved in buying or not buying fire insurance on one's house make the purchase of insurance clearly uneconomical. If the probability of one's house burning down in a ten-year period is one in 10,000, the probability of its not burning down is 9,999 in 10,000. Thus, this very high probability event is systematically seen as less likely than it actually is; in our hypothetical example, it is seen as something of the order of 999 in 1000.

The disparities between objective values and probabilities and subjective values and probabilities justify a rewriting of the decision process formula in subjective terms. Thus:

$$P_S \times V_S = U_S.$$

For illustrative purposes, Table 8-2 can be modified in the light of these considerations in the following manner. Let us assume that we are dealing only with a narrow range of objective values. If so, then it would be reasonable to assume that $V_O$ and $V_S$ did not differ in any significant manner through the range of values seen in Table 8-3. $P_S$, on the other hand, can be expected to vary significantly from $P_O$, with $P_S$ being less extreme than $P_O$ at all values removed from $P_O = .50$. Table 8-3 makes a not improbable comparison.

The top part of Table 8-3 was constructed to illustrate the effect of the human tendency to underestimate extreme probabilities. The effect of this variation in subjective probability is to influence subjective utilities in such a manner that small objective utilities are overestimated and large objective utilities are underestimated.

The lower portion of Table 8-3 represents an effort to show how much difference in objective value would be required to produce the same set of objective utilities, and thus how much distortion of subjective value would be required to produce the same set of subjective utilities as that produced in the top part of the table by the distortion in subjective probability.

The middle portion of the table indicates that, in terms of either the objective or the subjective values, there are many possible sets of alternatives that have equal utility. Neither objective economic decision theory nor subjective psychological decision theory offers a basis for choosing among the available alternatives.

Psychological complexity and preference theory should be useful in predicting which of the alternatives a given subject would prefer. Alternatives such as those in the middle of the table could be rated for complexity and for various affective properties such as interestingness or preference, and the choice should be predictable from a determination of optimal complexity level.

*TABLE 8-3.* Comparison of Possible Objective and Subjective Differences in the Determinants of Utility

| | | *P Varies* | | | |
|---|---|---|---|---|---|
| $P_O$ x | $V_O$ = | $U_O$ | $P_S$ x | $V_S$ = | $U_S$ |
| .01 | 100 | 1 | .10 | 100 | 10 |
| .10 | 100 | 10 | .20 | 100 | 20 |
| .20 | 100 | 20 | .35 | 100 | 35 |
| .50 | 100 | 50 | .50 | 100 | 50 |
| .80 | 100 | 80 | .65 | 100 | 65 |
| .90 | 100 | 90 | .80 | 100 | 80 |
| .99 | 100 | 99 | .90 | 100 | 90 |
| | | *P and V Covary* | | | |
| $P_O$ x | $V_O$ = | $U_O$ | $P_S$ x | $V_S$ = | $U_S$ |
| .01 | 5000 | 50 | .10 | 500 | 50 |
| .10 | 500 | 50 | .20 | 250 | 50 |
| .20 | 250 | 50 | .35 | 142.9 | 50 |
| .50 | 100 | 50 | .50 | 100 | 50 |
| .80 | 62.5 | 50 | .65 | 76.9 | 50 |
| .90 | 55.6 | 50 | .80 | 62.5 | 50 |
| .99 | 50.5 | 50 | .90 | 55.6 | 50 |
| | | *V Varies* | | | |
| $P_O$ x | $V_O$ = | $U_O$ | $P_S$ x | $V_S$ = | $U_S$ |
| .50 | 2 | 1 | .50 | 20 | 10 |
| .50 | 20 | 10 | .50 | 40 | 20 |
| .50 | 40 | 20 | .50 | 70 | 35 |
| .50 | 100 | 50 | .50 | 100 | 50 |
| .50 | 160 | 80 | .50 | 130 | 65 |
| .50 | 180 | 90 | .50 | 160 | 80 |
| .50 | 198 | 99 | .50 | 180 | 90 |

Although this contention seems valid on theoretical grounds, it is not easy to operationalize. In one study, nine bets were constructed, all of which had the same objective utility. They ranged from a situation in which there was one chance in 1000 of winning $50,000 to a situation in which there were 999 chances in 1000 of winning $50.05. Each of the nine bets had a utility value of $50.00. After rating the bets for complexity and interestingness, subjects ordered them in terms of preference. Half of the subjects expressed their preferential choices in terms of the $P_O$, choosing the high probability bet first and the others in order of decreasing probability, thus ignoring the wide range of values involved. One subject ignored the probabilities and ordered the choices in terms of the amount of money. One chose bets in accordance with optimum complexity, and one chose in terms of rated interestingness. The choices of the other four were unrelated to any of the dimensions of the experiment. Adequate operationalization of the match between psychological complexity and preference theory and this formulation of the decision process is still to be developed.

### How to Stuff a Central Processor
### and Get the Stuffing Back

The limited capacity of short-term memory poses an apparent paradox when contrasted with some of the monumental feats of memory all of us are capable of. Actors memorize whole plays. Conductors memorize large numbers of lengthy and complex musical scores. Between the apparently small amount of information in immediate memory span and the large amount of information in a feat of memory there lie a number of interesting psychological problems and issues. This section is devoted to some of them.

The Central Processor appears to operate most comfortably and efficiently when the flow of action is at or near some optimal level. It has a variety of techniques for complicating a situation in which the stimuli are significantly below optimal level. It may direct the organism to seek a more complex environment. It may seek previously unexplored aspects of the same environment. It may turn inward and seek to retrieve material from memory that it can add to the paucity of external input. It may abandon the external environment altogether and fall to daydreaming. In extreme cases, it we can believe some of the reports of stimulus deprivation experiments, the Central Processor can lose voluntary control, with the result that hallucinations are experienced.

More often, the environment provides more stimuli than the Central Processor can handle. In this situation, it can exercise a variety of voluntary behaviors that serve to reduce the amount of information when automatic filtering processes are insufficient. The most obvious is physical locomotion to a less complex environment. If that is not possible or desirable, then attention can be focused on a limited portion of the available stimuli. The oft-repeated example of the operation of this mechanism is selective attention to only one of many conversations at a cocktail party.

One of the most common reactions to information overload is to decide to store only the relatively small amount of information needed to permit the recovery of the super-capacity information from an external storage facility. One could probably generate a very extensive list of such mechanisms, but a few examples should suffice. Most of us forego attempting to memorize more than two or three telephone numbers, depending instead on external storage facilities such as the telephone book or a small register of frequently used numbers. Literate cooks tend to rely on small libraries of cookbooks or on collected recipe files instead of attempting to memorize large numbers of recipes. Dictionaries and reference volumes of all kinds, especially mathematical and engineering handbooks, are external memories. In preliterate societies, the histories and legends of the group are preserved and passed from generation to generation by the mechanism of having a few members of each generation commit the whole opus to memory, and thus to an internal storage facility; in literate societies, the same function is accomplished by depositing such voluminous information in books.

The decision whether to store information internally or externally appears to be based on the relative economy of the two mechanisms. If the information to be stored is either large (history of the society) or very difficult to discriminate (telephone numbers, mathematical tables, or recipes), the decision is usually in favor of storage in an external facility. Information is committed to internal storage, on the other hand, if it is a relatively small set, if it is used in contexts in which external storage might not be immediately available, if no handy external storage mechanism has been invented, and so forth. James G. Miller (1964) overloaded the internal storage capacity of experimental subjects while they were performing a simple task and categorized their reactions as queueing, omission, error, filtering, using multiple channels, decentralizing, and escaping. These behaviors might have been avoided if external storage had been possible.

The problem faced by the Central Processor after a decision to "commit to memory" more material than it can handle at any one time is one of future retrieval of that information. I have argued that the storage of material in memory is automatic. It is equally true that the process of retrieval from memory is in some sense automatic. The problem is to find means of bringing into the Central Processor adequate retrieval cues to make it probable that the material recovered from memory is the desired material.

In this way of looking at the storage and retrieval processes, most of the variables that are ordinarily said to influence learning are really variables that influence the ease and form of retrieval. Under ordinary circumstances, the individual is continuously active, which is to say that there is a constant flow of information, all of which is stored in memory, and all of which subsequently influences the automatic retrieval process. However, whatever is unique about a particular event or sequence of events tends to be forgotten rapidly, with the result that subsequent retrieval is difficult.

The Central Processor appears to screen the flow of information continuously. There are at least two possible models of this process. In one model the Central Processor makes a running decision about whether the material in the stream should be allowed to recede into memory unmodified or whether action should be taken to add retrieval cues that will make subsequent recall easier. In the other model, a decision is made either to remember the material or to forget whatever is passing through the Central Processor. There seems to be little doubt that some individuals are capable of making a positive decision to forget material, although this phenomenon, if it exists, remains almost totally neglected by experimentalists studying memory. For example, there are anecdotal stories indicating that Albert Einstein made use of such a decision to forget material. While working on the theory of relativity, he was seen by his friends as procrastinating in his preparations for the tripos examination at the university. On the urging of his friends he submitted to weeks of boning-up sessions with them, after which he took the examinations successfully. He then observed that it was weeks after the examination before he was again able to think constructively about the theory. When asked how he could manage to integrate the mass of material in a physics handbook that he was known to have read, he replied that he didn't integrate it. Instead, he chose the very few facts that were useful to him in his thinking and actively forgot the rest.

This anecdote and others like it are not evidence. They only leave open the possibility that there is a deliberate, voluntary, active forgetting process that might have functional value in some kinds of intellectual activity. In both models, there is a possible decision that material in the stream of events might be needed on a subsequent occasion. Such a decision is then followed by a number of voluntary actions on the part of the Central Processor.

### Central Processor Conflict between Processing Capacity and Retrieval Demands

There is a fundamental conflict between the limited processing capacity of the Central Processor and the requirement that it develop a capacity to retrieve items on demand from long-term memory. Many Central Processor activities function to simplify material in order to increase the number of items that can be handled simultaneously. On the other hand, the capacity to retrieve items from long-term storage is often improved by adding material to the item that then functions as a tag or handle to make future recall easier.

The Central Processor can focus on only one psychological event at a time, and it can circulate without loss only a limited number of psychological events. There are many circumstances in which it is desirable to manipulate more information or cognitive material than can be immediately handled within the capacity of the Central Processor. There are a variety of mechanisms available for reorganizing or condensing information to bring super-capacity material within the processing capacity of the Central Processor. It may be useful to distinguish several of these mechanisms, such as simplifying through repetition, putting some information in "empty container" codes, reorganizing material into simpler form (as in problem solving), chaining events into lengthy sequences in order to permit use of long-term memory, and condensing sequential events into a single event.

*Simplification.* The effect of repeated experience on the complexity of individual events has been dealt with in Chapter 7. If other properties associated with the complexity of an item are equal, a very familiar item will be simpler than a very unfamiliar item. Repeated experience in the form of immediate rehearsal of an item has a large temporary and a smaller permanent effect on the complexity of an event. Simple events occupy less of the limited capacity of the Central Processor than complex events; therefore, a larger number of simpler events can be recirculated without loss than of more complex events.

*Classification into Groups.* For most individuals, a list of 20 words exceeds the recirculating capacity of the Central Processor. One way to handle such a list is to classify the words into a smaller number of groups. For example, if the 20 words can be grouped into five categories, such as animals, fruits, vegetables, trees, and furniture, the five code items are well within processing capacity. If each code has four items attached, sets of four can be brought into central processing successively without exceeding the limit of five to nine items.

Grouping or classifying bears some relation to inductive reasoning. Much of the experience of education can be described as a process of encoding large amounts of information. On the other hand, a great deal of learning consists of the reverse process, deduction and decoding. Consider the problem of the physics teacher in presenting the code represented by $E = MC^2$. One could easily devote a multi-year instructional program to the task of differentiating this ultimate in informational codes.

In this respect it is worth noting Johnson's (1972) concept of codes as "opaque containers." He points out that, if the code is not recalled, none of the items for which the code stands are recalled. In complexity terms, a code can be an opaque container when its complexity is independent of the number and character of the items with which it is associated.

*Organization into Simpler Form (Chunking).* There are many ways in which the Central Processor reorganizes material so that it has a simpler pattern than the components of the pattern had before reorganization. The telephone number problem is an illustration. Ten items can be organized into a 3-3-4 pattern to make them easier to recirculate without loss. Other examples might be rearranging random items spatially into something organized and familiar, imposing a pattern on a cloud and thus seeing a single form, and performing the cognitive reorganization of material involved in problem solving.

*Serialization.* There are many circumstances in which material can or even must be used in serial form. If firm, reliable connections are established between successive items in a chain, then, if time allows, enormous amounts of information can be handled by the Central Processor by pulling material out of long-term memory. Only a small portion of such a long sequence is in the Central Processor at any one time.

*Serial Condensation.* Under some circumstances, several separate psychological events will become integrated into a single psychological event. Liberman, Mattingly, and Turvey (1972) discuss the word *bæg*. The *b* lasts about two-thirds of the spoken word, the *æ* sound through almost all of the word, and the *g* sound through the last two-thirds. All three sounds are modified in the presence of the others. All three, when enunciated within the context of a single word, sound different than they would if they were enunciated sequentially.

The difference between serialization and serial condensation may provide a solution to a problem of sequential behavior discussed at length by Lashley (1951). In the context of a strict S-R approach to sequential behavior, it follows naturally that a sequence of behavior would be conceived as a pattern of s-r-s-r-s-r in an associative chain. This implies that individual responses in serially ordered behavior are under the control of proprioceptive feedback from the immediately preceding response. Lashley offered two serious objections to this conception. He pointed out that some serial tasks occur too rapidly to allow for the transmission time required for a feedback mechanism. Furthermore, most well ordered sequences exhibit variety in the elements that make them up.

Lashley's first problem, that of too rapid occurrence of elements of the sequence, might be solved by serial condensation. The integration of three otherwise distinct sounds into a single sound *bæg* affects the execution time by making it significantly shorter. Integration could be equivalent to dispensing with the need for proprioceptive feedback to initiate successive elements in the sequence. Indeed, when integrated, the sequential property of the sequence is substantially modified. The flexibility in such sequences would, in this conception, be confined to connections between successive psychological events. It is tempting to suggest that proprioceptive feedback cannot organize patterns within individual psychological events but may be involved in the sequential organization of successive psychological events. This statement must be limited, however, in two ways. Many sequences of psychological events are cognitive in nature, with the result that there is no proprioceptive feedback to play an organizing role. Even when overt action is involved, it seems likely there are intermediate stages during which a particular sequence of actions is not purely a string of discrete events nor a completely integrated unit. In such a condition, one would not expect to find the rigid alternation of the s-r-s-r-s-r sequence, as would seem required in the strict S-R approach to the problem.

It should be obvious that it is rare for one of the five mechanisms I have discussed to be employed individually and exclusively of the others. It should also be obvious that the complex processes with which the Central Processor simplifies material for easy processing while complicating material for easy retrieval are by no means exhausted by this list.

### Organizing or "Chunking"

*Processing Capacity and Short-Term Memory.* In a very fundamental way, the Central Processor is capable of dealing with only one psychological event at a time. It can, however, undertake to organize two or more events into a single event. The number of events it can attempt to integrate by simultaneous processing depends on the complexity of the events and the processing capacity of the organism. The latter is primary and is assumed to be a relatively fixed value.

The phenomenon referred to as short-term memory is a joint function of the processing capacity of the organism and the rate of decline in accessibility or retrievability of the items the organism is undertaking to integrate. Short-term memory studies reveal a "buffer" phenomenon manifest in the apparent "bumping" of the earliest item in a list by the first item that exceeds the processing capacity of the Central Processor. The earliest item will be the first item lost as long as retrievability is perfectly correlated with the order of presentation of the items. However, if the items presented vary greatly in retrievability, independently of the order of presentation, then items that are difficult to retrieve will be lost before earlier items that are inherently easier to retrieve.

The justification for distinguishing between short-term and long-term memory rests on a number of characteristics; however, the major distinction is the amount of information each can, in some sense, "hold." The amount of information that can be held in short-term memory is quite limited, whereas the amount of information that can be held in long-term memory seems to be, for all practical purposes, unlimited.

One of the major hypotheses concerning the information carrying capacity of short-term memory is that of George Miller (see, for example, Miller & Selfridge, 1950, or Miller, 1956). Miller presents data and arguments that seem to justify the conclusion that the number of "chunks" that can be held in immediate memory is relatively fixed at a value of 7 plus or minus 2. Further, he argues that the constancy of the number of chunks is maintained even when the amount of information within the chunks varies.

This hypothesis proves to be relatively viable as long as the amount of information within chunks does not exceed some unknown amount but tends to break down when large quantities of information are condensed within the chunks. For example, Simon (1974) has reported that his own memory span for one-syllable words is seven, while his immediate memory span for very familar eight-word phrases is only three.

In his report, Simon expresses concern for the problem of defining the concept of "chunk." If the concept is defined only in terms of the number of chunks that can be retained in immediate memory, the definition is circular, and there is no possibility of providing an adequate test of the original hypothesis that the number of chunks in immediate memory is constant.

The concept of psychological complexity offers some possibility of advance with this problem. The complexity of chunks can be assessed, as well as the complexity of any number of chunks, and these assessments can be made independently of the short-term memory paradigm. What follows is an effort to explicate a procedure that offers the potential of establishing the relationships between the intra-chunk complexity of the material and the number of chunks that can be held in short-term memory.

Let us define a *chunk* as any complex event that is apprehended by the individual as having unitary character. A chunk is a gestalt. A chunk is a stimulus complex that appears to be organized in some fashion; because it is a chunk, it is apprehended as being simpler than it would have been if the organism had not imposed some sort of organization upon it. Organization can be the product of learning, or it can be the product of either spatial or temporal patterning.

The assertion is that all chunks are not identical in complexity. While retaining their character as chunks, they can vary from rather simple chunks to rather complex ones. Short-term memory can process a larger number of simple chunks than of complex chunks. The magic number seven refers to chunks of a relatively uniform complexity, such as letters of the alphabet and single digits. Theoretically, the magic number could be larger, say 10 plus or minus 3 for simpler chunks, or smaller, say 2 plus or minus 1 for very complex chunks. The general theortetical assertion is that the magic numbers 10 and 2 would be judged to be equally complex by the individual to whom they referred. The next problem is whether the individual judgments of the complexities of the chunks involved would add to a constant (the fixed complexity of short-term memory) or whether there is some number of chunks that maximizes the amount of information that can be processed in short-term memory.

Means of measuring chunks independently of the number in short-term memory are not exhausted by various efforts to measure relative complexity. Chunks can sometimes be identified by short latencies between items assumed to be within a chunk and long latencies between chunks. Marked differences in transitional probabilities between successive items might also be used in a similar manner. The grouping of response items by content class in the recall protocols of free recall experiments might also be used as quantitative evidence of chunking.

*Problem Solving.* In Chapter 7 I undertook to show that the primary effect of learning was a negatively accelerated decrease in the complexity of the psychological event. Many learning curves display a pronounced perturbation rather than a smooth exponential change. Both sudden increases and sudden decreases occur. To illustrate, suppose I asked you to participate in a rote learning experiment in which you are to learn to reproduce a sequence of numbers such as the following:

8 4 0 2 4 2 0 1 2 1 5 6 5 2 8 2 1 4 6 2 3 6 1 8 4

This sequence is obviously beyond your immediate memory span, and mine. Your learning of the list might be represented by the curve for $C_u$ = 20 in Figure 8-8. In the figure, a set of curves has been calculated with arbitrary asymptotic values ranging from 1 to 20. It probably would require many trials for you to master such a list, especially if you obeyed the instructions to learn it by rote.

Suppose, however, that you inadvertently disobeyed instructions. After a number of trials, you noticed that the sequence had a regularity about it, especially when examined in reverse order. You would soon become aware that the very complicated-looking and very difficult 25-digit sequence you have been learning by rote is in fact a very simple, very easy ten-number sequence when seen in reverse. Thus, when it is reversed, the sequence becomes:

4 8 16 32 64 128 256 512 1024 2048

This sudden shift in complexity level of the task, as seen by you, the subject, would be represented by a sudden change in the $C_u$ value from 20 to perhaps 1. This sudden shift is portrayed in Figure 8-9, where the changes in complexity with further occurrences of the

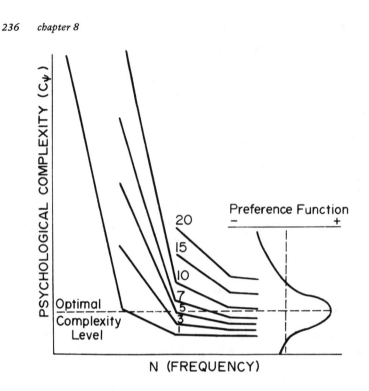

FIGURE 8-8. *Effect of Learning on Preference*

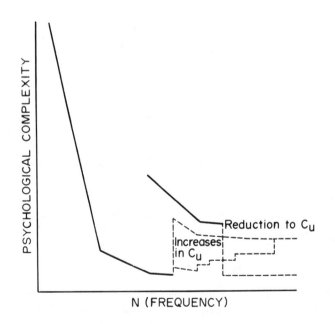

FIGURE 8-9. *Changes in Ultimate Complexity Level with Experience*

event are represented as a broken line after the point at which insight had occurred.

The figure also portrays an example of the reverse kind of perturbation. Some psychological events have the potential of undergoing elaboration or complication—an increase in the ultimate complexity level—with repeated experience. Two patterns of complication are drawn in the figure. In one, the curve for $C_u$ = 1 suddenly rises to match the curve for $C_u$ = 15. I have been unable to think of a realistic example of such a sudden rise without external input to accomplish the change in complexity level. Such a change might occur in the study of a simple organism when a microscope suddenly became available. Through the microscope, the seemingly simple organism might become a very complex one. A much more realistic picture is that portrayed by the curve that rises in a number of smaller steps. Such a curve might represent changes that occur in one's reactions to a game such as bridge or chess, which might at first appear relatively simple but which undergoes successive increases in complexity level as more and more of the game's complexities come into the awareness of the player.

Sudden changes in complexity ratings that can occur in a problem solving situation can be seen in a simple demonstration experiment. The task is the classic water jug problem. For readers who are unfamiliar with this problem, the following simple example will serve to demonstrate the nature of the task.

*The Problem*

> You have two vessels. One holds three pints of water, and the other holds five pints. You have an unlimited supply of water, and you wish to measure precisely two pints. Can this be done? How?

| *Vessels* | *To Obtain* |
|-----------|-------------|
| 5 and 3   | 2           |

The solution to this problem is, of course, very simple. One fills the five-pint vessel to the brim and then fills the three-pint vessel to the brim from the five-pint vessel. This leaves precisely two pints in the five-pint vessel.

I constructed several problems involving either two or five vessels. The problems were displayed on cards containing drawings of the vessels so that differences in size and number were immediately apparent. I asked seven people to acquaint themselves thoroughly with the demonstration problem above and then to rate the new problems for complexity on a 100-point scale after only a quick glance that was insufficient for them to attempt a solution. The problems involving only two vessels were given a mean rating of 24.6, and the problems involving five vessels were given a mean complexity rating of 37.1. The seven subjects then undertook to solve each of the problems; following their efforts, they were again asked to rate the complexity of the problems.

Two problems involving only two vessels were actually much more difficult than the sample problem. They were:

| Vessels | To Obtain |
|---|---|
| 10 and 16 | 4 |
| 7 and 15 | 13 |

Complexity ratings could be expected to undergo a reduction because the problem had already been solved at this point, but they could also be expected to undergo an increase to a new $C_u$ value based on the perception that even a two-vessel problem could be very difficult. For these seven subjects, the net effect of these two processes was an increase in the complexity rating from 24.6 to 30.0.

Two of the problems involving five vessels were actually very easy. They were:

| Vessels | To Obtain |
|---|---|
| 8, 19, 2, 16, and 4 | 31 |
| 6, 36, 9, 3, and 18 | 15 |

After these problems were solved by these subjects, there was a sharp drop in the complexity rating, as expected, from 37.1 to 11.4.

One of the problems involving five vessels presented a situation in which there was no solution. It was:

| Vessels | To Obtain |
|---|---|
| 18, 3, 6, 36, and 9 | 13 |

The complexity ratings for this problem rose from the average of 37.1 to a value of 57.86, reflecting a new and much higher $C_u$ value. It should be pointed out that, even though this problem set forth an impossible task, it did offer the potential of an easy "solution." It could occur to a subject that each of the vessel capacities was divisible by 3, while the quantity to be obtained was not. It would therefore be possible for the subject to become certain that the problem had no solution. There could be large individual differences in how subjects would see the complexity of the task presented when they became certain that there was no solution. In this instance, the subjects were not allowed to work long enough to arrive at that decision but only long enough to determine that it was a difficult problem.

That psychological complexity can be measured in terms of the difficulty of a problem involving temporal processing has been demonstrated much more reliably by Boykin (1972). Boykin studied the relations between problem difficulty and rated complexity, interestingness, and pleasantness. He chose an anagram task in which the primary problem for the subject was to solve the problem by unscrambling scrambled words. Figure 8-10 contains some illustrative

| Number of Letters | Scrambled Version | Unscrambled |
|---|---|---|
| 3 | IGP | PIG |
| 3 | BRI | RIB |
| 4 | GTAO | GOAT |
| 4 | MGAR | GRAM |
| 5 | SRAKH | SHARK |
| 5 | CUHGO | COUGH |
| 7 | RLUEVTU | VULTURE |
| 7 | OVRTYCI | VICTORY |
| 10/11 | ODKGBICMRIN | MOCKINGBIRD |
| 10/11 | AERAOLIZITN | REALIZATION |

*FIGURE 8-10. Sample Anagrams. Examples of anagram task employed by Boykin (1972) in a study of preference and problem difficulty.*

examples of the material presented to Boykin's subjects. Problem difficulty was manipulated by varying the lengths of the words to be unscrambled. Boykin used words of lengths 3, 4, 5, 7, and a set of longer words either 10 or 11 letters in length.

The words were presented in sets of four, of equal length within each set, and subjects were required to first choose the one word of the four that was the name of an animal and then indicate how confident they were of their choices. This procedure was employed in order to control the time variables precisely. Each set was exposed for 25 seconds, and five seconds were allowed for the indication of choice and confidence. A response was regarded as correct only when it was actually correct *and* the subject indicated the highest level of confidence in the correctness of the choice. This procedure virtually eliminated the counting of responses as correct that were correct by chance.

Each subject attempted to solve ten blocks of problems, each block containing one set of each word length. In addition to recording their choices and confidence levels on each trial, subjects were asked to rate either the complexity of the task for each word length, its interestingness, or its pleasantness. Each scale ranged from 1 to 13. Three groups of subjects were used, and each group rated the tasks for only one of the scale dimensions—complexity (N = 20), interestingness (N = 40), or pleasantness (N = 40).

The length of the word in an anagram task represents an a priori scale of problem difficulty. Short words represent easy tasks, and long words represent difficult tasks. The subjects who evaluated the five word lengths for psychological complexity provide an estimate of the extent to which problem difficulty and psychological complexity are related. Figure 8-11 is a plot of that relationship. The relationship is a monotonically increasing function and appears to be approximately exponential. Thus, each addition of a letter to the length of

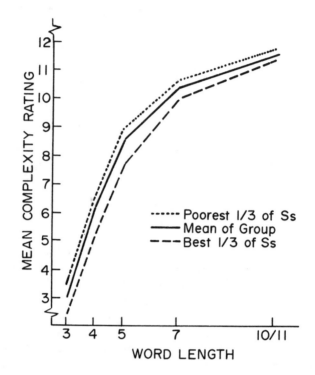

FIGURE 8-11. *Psychological Complexity and Anagram Length*

the word makes a smaller addition to the psychological complexity of the problem. Additional evidence for the correspondence of problem difficulty and psychological complexity comes from the comparison of the ratings of the most and least successful problem solvers in this group. Those who solved the fewest number of problems rated the task as more complex than the average, and those who solved the greatest number of problems rated it as less complex than the average for the group.

The curvilinear relationship in Figure 8-11 justifies plotting subsequent graphs against mean psychological complexity ratings, a psychological scale as opposed to a physical scale. Figure 8-12 lends additional support to this decision. The relationship between percent correct and mean complexity rating is approximately linear until the lower asymptote is reached. The mean complexity ratings derived from Experiment I, in which the subjects rated the tasks for complexity, are used on the abscissa, and the percent correct for each of the three groups is plotted against this scale. It is probably an accident of sampling that the 80 subjects in Experiment II (the pleasantness and interestingness groups) were slightly better problem solvers than the subjects in Experiment I (the complexity group).

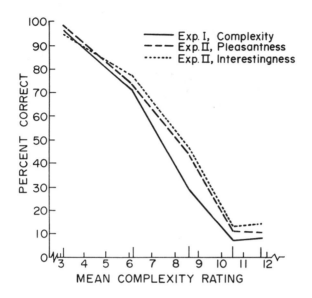

FIGURE 8-12. *Effect of Problem Difficulty on Ratings*

Boykin's experiment provides an opportunity to speculate on the contribution of the task to the complexity of the central process. In Figure 8-5, a comparison was made between the complexities of individual letters and those of well integrated words. The difference between the two curves was assumed to represent the effect of integration of letters into unitary words. This same approach can be used to try to deal with the complexity of the task, as distinguished from the complexities of the items used in the task. The subjects in this experiment gave complexity ratings of the total activity. It would be reasonable to assume that the ratings given were composed of the complexities of the sets of unrelated letters plus the complexity of the task of identifying which of the four sets was the name of an animal. To accomplish this task, it was necessary for subjects to unscramble one or more of the words and to reduce their complexities to the complexity level of a common word.

In Figure 8-13, several of the items of Boykin's anagrams task are positioned to show both the asymptotic complexities of the animal names involved and the item complexities of sets of unorganized letters of each word. The figure also shows a plot of the complexity ratings assigned to tasks involving word lengths of 3, 4, 5, 7, and 10.5 (the largest sets were combinations of words of 10 or 11 letters). The actual position of this plot is somewhat indeterminate. It was constructed by extrapolating the ratings obtained by Boykin down to the value of a single letter, since the anagrams task theoretically disappears at this point. The proportional relations of Boykin's actual data were then used to translate his obtained values into equivalent consensual complexity values. Although the positioning of the curve is reasonable, it is far from precise. For a precise plot, it would be necessary to have the words, the scrambled letters, and the task each rated for complexity within the same context and on the same scale. However, it would be surprising if the results should differ in any gross manner from the proportions seen in the figure.

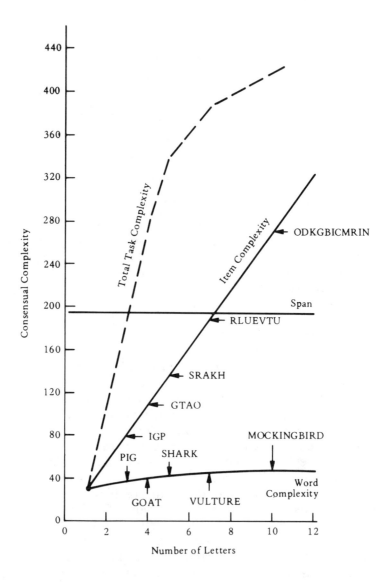

FIGURE 8-13. Combination of Item and Task Complexities

Two features of the set of relations shown in the figure are worthy of additional discussion. In the Hedgehog, it is the psychological complexity of the material that determines optimal complexity level and immediate memory span. If the nature of the task also contributes to the complexity of the material, task complexity should reduce processing capacity. I have drawn a horizontal line in the figure to represent the consensual complexity value of a memory span of seven letters. Boykin's subjects were nearly perfect in handling the anagrams task with three-letter words, with only 4% error at this level. With the addition of one more letter, to four-letter words, the error rate increased by a factor of 7, to 28%. For five-letter anagrams the error rate was 72%, and for words of lengths 7 and 10.5 the error rate climbed to approximately 92%.

The second point worth noting is that the plotted curve is not a linear function but rather appears to be approaching an asymptotic complexity value. There are many possible explanations for this shape of the complexity curve. One possibility is that it is an artifact of the rating scale and procedures used. A second possibility is that, as one increases the length of the words to be unscrambled, the contribution of task complexity undergoes diminishing increments. A third possibility is that the item complexity curve for unrelated letters should itself undergo diminishing contributions as single letters are added to the set.

The task Boykin gave his subjects is a complicated and difficult one. Other tasks given subjects in psychological experiments tend to be less difficult. An effort has been made in Figure 8-14 to approximate the complexities several experimental tasks might contribute to central processing. If recognition is the easiest task, then this form of task should add very little to the sum of the complexities of the individual items. Free recall is a more complex task requirement and should add more to the complexity of the processing requirement of the subject. Serial recall is probably still more difficult, and it should add still more complexity to the information processing task. On the other hand, it is unlikely that a given number of items can be presented in a form that is totally unorganized. Auditory presentation requires serial order, a form of organization that simplifies the task perceptually. Visual presentation would be very difficult to accomplish with the elements in the stimulus totally devoid of pattern. Any patterning involved in the presentation of the items should reduce the complexity of the task.

Although the quantitative values of such factors are not currently known in the context of the complexity values of items, the direction and order of such effects can be indicated as shown in Figure 8-14. The more complex the task imposed on the subject, the greater the total complexity of the task; the more organized the presentation of the stimuli, the less the complexity of the total task. However, it should be noted that, if the organization of the materials in presentation is not the same as that required of the subject's response, presentation organization could add to the complexity of the task.

For most subjects used in verbal learning experiments, most words have approached but not reached asymptote. In Figure 8-14

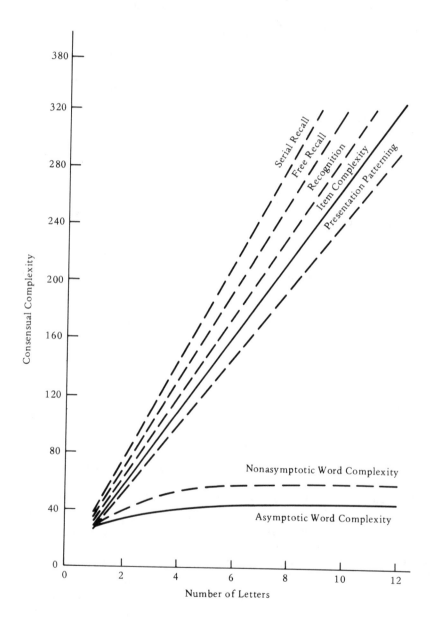

FIGURE 8-14. *Task Complexity Factors*

this factor has been taken into account and represented by a curve for nonasymptotic word complexity, raised by an arbitrary amount in the figure from the asymptotic complexity value. The quantitative values for the broken lines in Figure 8-14 are not known, but the means of assessing those values to estimate psychological complexity of items and task characteristics is available.

*Simplification through Chunking during Learning.* When one has a need to deal with a task that is too complex for immediate processing and thus considerably above the human channel capacity, perhaps the most common response is to organize subsets of the task into chunks. Thus, a ten-digit telephone number is usually chunked into three subsets consisting of a three-digit area code, a three-digit exchange code, and a four-digit address within the exchange. In a great many of the serial learning tasks employed by psychologists since the time of Ebbinghaus, tasks are made learning tasks by being deliberately constructed above human channel capacity; if they were at or below capacity, the material could be reproduced in a single trial, and no learning process would be apparent in the data. Since, according to Miller (1956), channel capacity is approximately 7 plus or minus 2, the typical list to be learned contains ten to 20 items. Such lists are sufficiently long to require more than one trial for mastery and sufficiently short that the patience of neither the subject nor the experimenter is strained unduly by the length of the learning process.

If a list contains 14 digits, and if a subject can repeat approximately seven digits accurately with a single exposure, ideally, a 14-digit list can be organized by the subject into two chunks of seven digits each. However, with chunks of this ideal maximum size, human channel capacity appears to be 1 plus or minus 0 chunks. If it were not, subjects in learning experiments could simply adopt a strategy of organizing a 14-digit list into two chunks of seven digits each and repeat these two organized chunks in a single presentation. Actually, relatively bright undergraduates require from three to 18 repetitions to master a 14-digit list.

Most learning curves in such tasks appear to represent a smooth and gradual accretion of correctly reproduced material. It seems likely, however, that within the individual subject the learning process consists of the formation of one or more (usually more) chunks and the coalescence of these chunks into larger chunks until the whole set of 14 digits can be repeated without error. A plot of individual learning might therefore tend to consist of fits and starts, of large jumps and regressions as the subject struggles to organize the material into a simpler pattern than that presented by the experimenter.

Arkes (1971) has made an initial effort to examine the learning process in the light of psychological complexity theory by looking at the chunking process within individual learning protocols. He presented ten undergraduates with a number of 14-digit strings to be learned. The strings were constructed from random number tables with the constraint that there should be no successive repetitions and no more than three digits in serial order. Subjects learned to a criterion of two successive correct repetitions of five different strings. Each string was presented on a memory drum, with the entire string visible to the subject on each trial for 6 seconds, and with 14 seconds for recall. Arkes thus obtained 50 instances (ten subjects, five lists each) of the mastery of a 14-digit list that was approximately twice the optimal complexity level of his subjects.

During the first two presentations of each of the five strings, Arkes divided the 14-digit string into seven chunks of two digits each by separating such pairs by fine red lines on the tape. I shall not attempt to analyze the extent to which this hint aided the subjects in the chunking process.

The identification of a cognitive chunk within a subject can only be approximated. Arkes employed a number of identification procedures, including analyses of interresponse times. However, I shall discuss the results using only a crude but defensible measure. A chunk can be defined as any two or more consecutive items that are correctly repeated in the correct position and separated from other correct items by at least one incorrect item.

By this criterion, it is obvious that when a subject reached criterion, he or she had organized all 14 items into a single chunk. But what about the first trial? In 49 of the 50 instances, there were one or more chunks present in the output of the subjects. In 38 instances, there was one chunk present, and in 11 instances there were two chunks. Was there any advantage to the two-chunk organization over the one-chunk organization in terms of the number of items reproduced on the first trial? In these protocols, the answer is in the negative. Instances in which there was only one chunk contained a mean of 6.26 correct items. When there were two chunks, there were 6.27 correct items, or 3.13 per chunk. Thus, on the first trial the magic number 7 plus or minus 2 holds whether there is one chunk or two. Yet, at criterion, every subject on every list has 14 items in a single chunk. What happens to the numbers of chunks and to the average chunk size during the acquisition process?

Figure 8-15 is a plot of two manifestations of the chunking process. In each case, the value plotted is mean chunk size, calculated by dividing the number of items within the chunks by the number of chunks. There are two manifestations because of the well known dilemma of how to deal with the fact that trials to criterion is a variable, in this case ranging from three to 18. One alternative is to

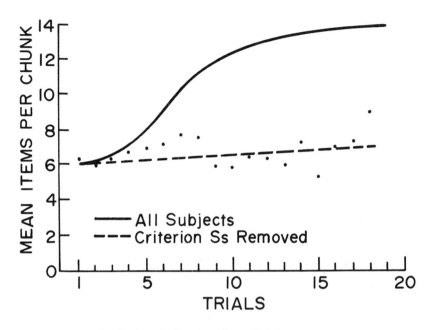

FIGURE 8-15. *Chunk Sizes during Learning of Digits*

retain all criterion performances until all subjects have learned each task to criterion. Using this procedure, the mean number of chunks rises from about 1.2 to about 1.35 by the fifth trial and then quickly subsides to a small fraction over 1.0. In this instance, mean chunk size is a very smooth function that does not look too different from the standard learning curve representing total items correct. However, there is another procedure. One can drop any instance from further consideration after the last trial before criterion. Such a plot represents a decreasing N ranging from 50 on the first trial to 1 on the 18th. This procedure creates a sampling problem, of course, but the results are interesting. I have drawn the curve to rise from about six items to approximately seven as the most conservative curve I could draw by eye through the data. I resisted the temptation to draw it as a horizontal line representing a mean chunk size of about 6.25 items. The dots in the figure represent means of all instances remaining below criterion. It is also true that the mean chunk size on the trial before criterion in all 50 instances varies quite closely around six to seven items.

What are we to make of all this? From the standpoint of psychological complexity theory, subjects have been presented with a task that is nearly double optimal complexity level. Instead of the smooth process of acquisition that is usually plotted as a learning curve, acquisition of a 14-digit list is seen as a process of simultaneous organization of items into more than one chunk and a gradual coalescence of smaller chunks into larger chunks. This process is much more discontinuous than the one we are ordinarily led to think of as the learning process. Nowhere, perhaps, is this discontinuity more apparent than in the fact that the mean gain in number of correct items from the last error trial to the first criterion trial is 3.84 items, while the mean gain on a single trial in the group curve where it is rising fastest is about one item. Another pair of meaningful numbers are the average of all *changes* in number correct prior to criterion, .627 items, and the average of all *gains* (mean items gained only on trials on which there was a gain) prior to achieving the criterion, 3.13 items. Thus, achieving criterion represents a giant leap forward—the biggest leap of all, save for the initial response. The process of chunking to reduce superoptimal complexity is all but hidden in the traditional learning curve.

There is one more way we can look at items and chunks. The fact that the number of items was the same on the first trial, whether in one chunk or two, means that there was at that point no gain in simplification deriving from the incorporation of items into chunks. When the criterion was reached, if the items are now regarded as belonging to one cognitive chunk, then the complexity of a single item had been reduced to about 44.6% (6.25/14) of its complexity at the outset of the learning process. This is probably an overestimation of the amount of reduction in psychological complexity, since some subjects may still have been using two or more chunks that were not revealed by this crude criterion. Interresponse times or some other index of organization may have revealed more than one chunk. Both Melton (1963) and Miller (1956) argue in effect that, if practice were to be continued felicitously and indefinitely, the ultimate result would be a chunk containing 14 items that was essentially no more complex than a single unincorporated digit. In the Hedgehog analysis, indefinite practice would still leave small differences in complexity between digit strings of different lengths.

*The "Daxes" Problem, or How Can More Be Less?* In research on human memory, there is a class of behavior of human subjects that is puzzling because of a seeming paradox. In many memory tasks subjects add something to what they are to remember, and, instead of making the task more difficult, this device appears to make the task easier. For example, given the task of associating the words *cow* and *boots*, a subject may very well add a verb and an article and store *a cow wearing boots.* Such an example suggests that the easier recall is attributable to the subject's translation of the words into an integrated visual image of a cow wearing boots, and the simplification of the task is attributable to its having become a visual image. Whatever the explanation, *a cow wearing boots* is more than *cow/boots*, yet it is easier to remember. Thus, more is actually less.

This example is cited by Anderson and Bower (1974), as is the *daxes* problem, which is not as easy to explain in terms of translation into a visual image, even though that is a possible strategy. The "more becomes less" problem here is that, if subjects are given the nonsense syllable *daxes* to remember, many of them will use the strategy of storing something like *axes* with an initial *d,* which is more than *daxes* because of the addition of "with an initial" as an instruction. Subjects who use the strategy of storing *axes* with an initial *d* do very much better than subjects who attempt to store the unmodified nonsense syllable *daxes.*

Anderson and Bower (1974) provide an elegant solution to this problem in terms of the storage of propositional structures in their HAM program. Instead of translating the material into a visual image, Anderson and Bower analyze the task given to the subject in terms of the propositional structure required to store *d-a-x-e-s* as a nonsense syllable and the structure required to store *d + axes.* Figure 8-16 illustrates the Anderson and Bower propositional structure. According to their count, the first task requires 32 separate associative links, while the second task requires only ten (I count 11). Thus, *d + axes* is easier to store and to retrieve from memory because fewer associative links are required in the process. In HAM, what is learned is the associative links between elements; the items to be associated are assumed to be equally easy or difficult to associate regardless of their character. It is the links that are important, not what is linked.

In the Hedgehog, the *daxes* problem is handled by taking into account both the differences in psychological complexity involved in the associative structure (as in Anderson and Bower) and the differences in the psychological complexities of the items to be associated (not taken into account in Anderson and Bower). In the Hedgehog, differences in associative structure would fall under the general rubric of *task* complexity, while differences in the complexities of the items to be associated would fall under *item* complexity. Individual differences can be taken into account in the Hedgehog in terms of differences in the strategies employed by individual subjects, as well as in differential experience with the items to be associated.

For illustrative purposes, let us ignore the problem of individual differences in language experience and associative strategies and compare the relative psychological complexities of two standard storage strategies. I will use the symbol "+" to indicate a standard self-instruction, "is followed by." Then the two storage strategies could be symbolized as $d + a + x + e + s$ or as $d + axes.$ When these

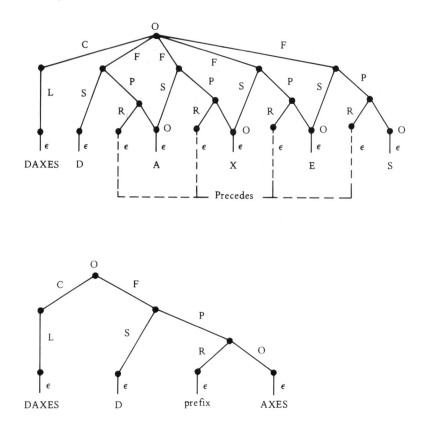

FIGURE 8-16. Propositional Structures Involved in the Memorial Storage of Nonsense Syllable D-A-X-E-S and the Alternate Strategy D-AXES. The circles represent concept nodes; connecting lines represent necessary associations. The symbols have the following meanings: C = Concept, F = Fact, S = Subject, P = Predicate, R = Relation, O = Object, L = Location, and the symbol ∈ indicates set membership. (Adapted from Human Associative Memory, by J. H. Anderson and G. H. Bower. Copyright 1974 by Hemisphere Publishing Corporation. Reprinted by permission.)

elements are translated into symbols of their complexity values, we have

$$C\psi_{(d)} + C\psi_{(+)} + C\psi_{(a)} + C\psi_{(+)} + C\psi_{(x)} + C\psi_{(+)} + C\psi_{(e)} + C\psi_{(+)} + C\psi_{(s)}$$
$$> C\psi_{(d)} + C\psi_{(+)} C\psi_{(axes)}.$$

The item complexities of these two tasks can be estimated from the asymptotes of the consensual complexities for letters and words shown in Table 7-18 (p. 179). The sum of the asymptotes for five individual letters would have a value of 134.00 (5 × 26.8), while the item complexity for the second strategy would be 66.8 (26.8 for the *d* and 40.0 for the four-letter word *axes*). Although we do not have estimates of the consensual complexity values for the task represented by "if followed by," it occurs four times in the separate associations of the five letters and only once in the association of a single letter and a single word. If we let $T$ stand for the complexity value of the task, then it is obvious that

$$(66.8 + T) < (134.00 + 4T).$$

Thus, within the Hedgehog, that it would be easier to learn $d$ + *axes* is predictable from either the complexity of the associative structure or from the nature of the items to be associated.

The Anderson and Bower theory, as represented by HAM, is a powerful special theory. The Hedgehog is a general theory. The *daxes* problem can be used to illustrate the difference. The additional power of the Hedgehog arises from the fact that it can handle problems the Anderson and Bower theory was not designed to handle. Let us take two hypothetical examples.

Suppose we construct two sentence memory tasks that differ markedly in the relative frequencies with which the words used in the sentence appear in the English language. Two sample sentences might be *The dog barked happily* and *The kinkajou levitated precariously.* There is little doubt that the first sentence would be learned much more easily than the second sentence. In Anderson and Bower, the two sentences have the same propositional structure and would therefore be equally easy to learn. In the Hedgehog, the first sentence would be less complex, and thus easier to learn, than the second, because it is composed of shorter, more frequently employed words.

Because the Hedgehog is a general theory, it has the potential of dealing with what might be referred to as condensed or simplified propositional structures. The propositional structure illustrated in Figure 8-16 is a reasonable representation of what a subject might do with "new" sentences, such as *The hippie touched the debutante in the park.* However, it is not at all certain that a familiar phrase such as *four score and seven years ago* would require support from such a propositional structure. It is probably so condense, simplified, and "chunked" from memorization that it is almost a single unit. If so, then the retrieval of such a phrase would not be predictable from an analysis of its propositional structure, whereas it would be predictable from measurement of its relative subjective complexity within the Hedgehog.

*Within-Chunk and Between-Chunk Complexities.* It is a fundamental thesis of the Hedgehog that organizing material into chunks reduces the complexity of the material. Chunked material should therefore be easier to learn than unchunked material, and more material should be fit within the limited processing capacity of the Central Processor when it is chunked than when it is unchunked. One can then raise the question of how to maximize efficiency in learning or short-term memory by varying the number of chunks and the number of items within chunks.

Johnson (1972) cites a number of studies indicating that, when the number of chunks is manipulated, the optimum number of chunks is three. He also cites other studies indicating that subjects who are free to determine the number of chunks tend to group items into three chunks. However, three chunks does not necessarily constitute a magic number. McLean and Gregg (1967) had subjects learn lists of 24 letters. The lists were organized into one, three, four, six, or eight groups; there were thus 24, eight, six, four, or three items in a group. Subjects were self-paced and went through the groups enunciating the letters aloud until the list was learned. Learning time averaged 752 seconds when the letters were ungrouped. When they were grouped into three, four, six, or eight chunks, learning times were 414, 421, 424, and 410 seconds. Thus, there were no real differences between three and eight chunks, but the mean gain over ungrouped letters was about 45%.

It is probably a coincidence, but a study by Crawford, Hunt, and Peak (1966) also showed a 45% gain from grouping in a short-term memory procedure. They composed eight-word sentences made up of three-letter words—for example, *asktheoldmanforthewayout*. In a second condition, the words were rearranged so that they did not form a sentence; in a third, the letters were rearranged so that they did not form words. These stimuli were exposed for .7 seconds. Subjects then wrote down as much as they could of what they had seen, beginning at the left. They were able to report slightly fewer than four letters in the scrambled condition and averaged about seven letters in the words and sentence conditions. Thus, 24 items grouped in three to eight chunks produced in these instances, about a 45% gain in learning efficiency compared to 24 unassociated items.

Mandler (1974) has reported a quite different result in a large series of free recall studies. They generally followed a pattern of study of 52 words followed by free recall of as many words as possible. Study consisted of sorting the items into a specified number of categories (or chunks). Mandler found that, the greater the number of categories (up to seven), the greater the total number of items recalled. Rather than an optimum number or range of categories, Mandler fit a straight line to his data indicating a gain of about 2.5 items for each addition to the number of categories imposed by the experimenter. When subjects were free to choose any number of categories, those who chose the largest number of categories also remembered the largest number of items. Mandler's free recall procedure may comprise a mixture of recall and recognition processes and therefore may not be an unambiguous estimate of the optimal number of chunks for efficient learning and recall. Subjects may recall categories, free associate items that might belong in each category, and then recognize whether or not a given item actually appeared in the list.

*Chunks in Immediate Memory Span.* In a previously mentioned article, Simon (1974) cites a number of sets of data that generally confirm the proposition that the greater the amount of information in the chunk, the smaller the number of chunks in immediate memory span. For example, he cites a study by Brenner (1940) on mean span of immediate recall for various test items. These data are in Table 8-4. Beginning at the top of the table and reading downward, it seems reasonable that each successive type of item contains more information than the one above it. This condition suggests that, the more complex the item, the smaller the number of items that can be processed within the immediate capacity of the Central Processor. The mixture of kinds of materials in the Brenner study prevents any effort to analyze the results in terms of the consensual complexity values in Table 7-18.

*TABLE 8-4.* Mean Span of Immediate Recall (from Brenner, 1940)

| Test | Span |
| --- | --- |
| Digits | 7.98 |
| Constants (visual) | 7.30 |
| Colors | 7.06 |
| Concrete words (visual) | 5.76 |
| Abstract words (visual) | 5.24 |
| Geometrical designs | 5.31 |
| Paired associates (pairs) | 2.50 |
| Nonsense syllables | 2.49 |
| Commands (relating two objects) | 2.42 |
| Sentences (six words) | 1.75 |

However, in the same article, Simon reports some data that come somewhat closer to the conditions and materials calculated from the consensual complexity values of verbal learning material. Simon used himself as the only subject and tested his own short-term memory capacity for a number of kinds of material. These included "familiar" words of one, two, or three syllables and "familiar" two-word and eight-word phrases. Examples of familiar two-word phrases given in the article are *Milky Way, criminal lawyer,* and *differential calculus.* None of his examples of longer phrases was actually eight words, as reported in Table 8-5, but a few examples of longer phrases he cites are *Four score and seven years ago; To be or not to be, that is the question; In the beginning was the word;* and *All's fair in love and war.*

*TABLE 8-5.* Span of Simon's Immediate Recall for Words and Phrases (from Simon, 1974)

| Words and Phrases | Span | | | |
|---|---|---|---|---|
| | Syllables | Words | Imputed Chunks | Syllables (Chunks) |
| 1-syllable | 7 | 7 | 7 | 1.0 |
| 2-syllable | 14 | 7 | 7 | 2.0 |
| 3-syllable | 18 | 6 | 6 | 3.0 |
| 2-word | 22 | 9 | 4 | 5.5 |
| 8-word | 26 | 22 | 3 | 8.7 |

In the table shown here as Table 8-5, Simon used the number of syllables as the basic unit. If one assumes that there are three letters per syllable, then the first and fourth columns in the table can be translated into the number of letters. If one assumes that Simon would have reproduced eight single letters in short-term memory, then a rough graph can be drawn showing the number of letters in Simon's immediate memory span and the number of letters per chunk. These values are plotted in Figure 8-17. Despite the inaccuracies I have introduced in converting Simon's syllables to letters, two rough relationships are apparent. As the number of letters per chunk increases, the number of chunks decreases. On the other hand, as the number of letters per chunk increases, the total number

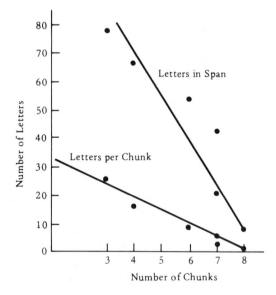

*FIGURE 8-17. Number of Letters, Number of Chunks, and Letters per Chunk in Immediate Memory Span (Simon, 1974)*

of letters in the immediate memory span increases dramatically, from the estimate of eight letters in the immediate memory span for single letters to 78 letters in the 26-syllable, eight-word phrases.

The problem is to determine whether data on the reduction in the complexity of groups of letters as they are formed into words can provide any kind of reasonable account of Simon's immediate memory span data such that the constancy involved is neither the complexity of chunks, nor the number of chunks, but the psychological complexity of the various combinations of intra- and extra-chunk complexities.

Simon does not provide data on the number of individual letters he is able to repeat back accurately in immediate memory span. Let us assume that, if he can report correctly on seven words of two syllables each, he can probably report nine, ten, or 11 single letters. Since the asymptote for a single letter has a complexity value of 26.8, we might set reasonable limits on Simon's immediate memory span, thusly:

9 x 26.8 = 241.2

11 x 26.8 = 294.8

The problem now is to determine whether reasonable calculations can be made, translating the data provided in Table 8-5 into consensual complexity values, such that the complexity values fall within these limits.

In Table 8-5, Simon reports the same memory span (seven) for one-syllable and two-syllable words. If syllables are assumed to average three letters in length, then the asymptotic complexities of three-letter and six-letter words can be used to estimate the consensual complexities of these items. Thus:

7 x 37.21 = 260.47

7 x 43.09 = 301.63

Simon reports a memory span of six for three-syllable words. If we use the complexity value for nine-letter words, the complexity of this task becomes

6 x 44.82 = 268.92.

Simon reports a memory span of four for "familiar" two-word phrases. We have no data on the complexity of phrases, so the best we can do is to set limits on the complexity values that his phrases could have. He reports that his two-word phrases averaged 5.5 syllables per phrase. Thus, on the average, each word had 2.75 syllables; at three letters per syllable, this would be equivalent to two words averaging 8.25 letters each. If each word has an asymptotic complexity value of 44.45, and if the two words were "unrelated," the complexity value of the phrase would be 88.90, and the immediate memory span would be

    4 x 88.90 = 355.60.

This is clearly an overestimate of the psychological complexity value of the phrases, because they were familiar two-word phrases and thus well learned as a pair and on their way to becoming a single entity or chunk. The limit in simplification of such a phrase would be an asymptotic value for a single word of 16.5 letters. This value can be extrapolated as 45.00, yielding a lower limit:

    4 x 45.00 = 180.00.

Thus, the true value of the complexities of Simon's two-word "familiar" phrases should lie between 180.00 and 355.60. How far they depart from 355.60, and how close they come to 180.00, depends on how familiar they had become for Simon through frequent usage as two-word phrases. The best estimate we can make is the mean of the two values:

    (180.00 + 355.60) ÷ 2 = 267.80.

Simon's data on eight-word phrases pose a very difficult problem of complexity estimation, and it is not certain that a reasonable estimate can be obtained. He reports an immediate memory span of three for eight-word phrases. However, he reports a span of 22 words (rather than 24), which are reported to contain 27 syllables. Thus, there was an average of 1.18 syllables or 3.54 letters per word. By interpolation, we can arrive at an estimate of 38.61 for the consensual complexity of a hypothetical word of length 3.54 letters. We can then perform the same set of calculations to determine the lower and upper limits of complexity of his longer phrases containing 7.33 (22/3) words of this length. If the words were totally unrelated, the value would be

    7.33  x  38.61  =  283.01.

If the 7.33-word phrases are regarded as single words, the value would be the asymptotic value for a word of this length, or a complexity value of about 45.00. Since the phrases are highly familiar, 283.01 is a gross overestimate, and 45.00 is a gross underestimate. The average of the two is

    (283.01 + 45.00) ÷ 2 = 164.0.

Three such chunks would sum to

    164.0 x 3 = 492.0.

This estimate of the consensual complexity is clearly out of the range of Simon's immediate memory span. To bring it within the span, one has to assume that something of the order of 80% of the possible simplification had occurred with these very familiar phrases. The calculations would be

$$((( 283.01 - 45.00) \div 5) + 45.00) \times 3 = 277.81.$$

Since he used such phrases as *To be or not to be, that is the question,* a simplification to 20% of the complexity of ten unrelated words seems possible and possibly even reasonable.

These calculations are plotted in Figure 8-18 with the calculated consensual complexity values arrayed against the number of letters involved in the various materials in Simon's studies of his own immediate memory span. The horizontal lines represent the consensual complexities of sets of nine and 11 single letters, assuming Simon's immediate memory span to be 10 plus or minus 1. Proceeding from the left, the first three points represent words of one, two, and three syllables. Only the point for the two-syllable words is outside the range, and that one only by a small amount. Since Simon reported memory spans only in round numbers (7, 7, 6, 4, and 3), the discrepant point would have been within the range if he had rounded this figure to 7 from a very slightly lower figure. It would also have fallen within the range if his one-syllable words averaged very slightly less than three letters in length.

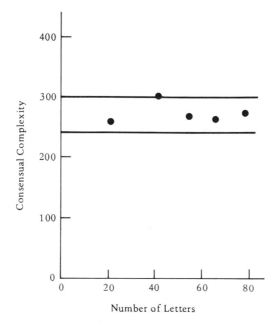

FIGURE 8-18. Calculated Estimates of Simon's Memory Span

The proposition is that what is constant in immediate memory span is some aspect of psychological complexity, not the number of chunks. The psychological complexity of the material to be repeated in immediate memory span is a combination of the psychological complexity of the material within chunks and the number of chunks. Thus, the greater the complexity of the chunks, the smaller the number of chunks that can be repeated back with perfect accuracy in short-term memory. The material in Figure 8-18 certainly does not prove the point, because special assumptions were required in its construction—Simon's memory span for single letters, the 50% simplification as an estimate of the familiarity of two-word phrases, and the 80% simplification estimated for familiar eight-word phrases. The figure does demonstrate, however, the highly likely outcome of a direct test of the proposition that it is the psychological complexity of the material that is constant in short-term memory.

*Complexity and Prodigious Feats of Memory.* Let us examine the intellectual problem of a hypothetical stage performer who has an immediate memory span of eight for unrelated letters. This particular performer composes a one-man show based on the life and writings of some prominent literary figure, such as William Shakespeare. When he has memorized his material, he takes to the platform and recites, without notes or other aids, for a period of possibly three hours during an evening. There may be 100,000 or more letters in the recital material. How is this feat accomplished when his immediate memory has a maximum capacity of eight letters?

The most straightforward and simple answer is that he has a life history of condensing letters into familiar English words, and a familiar word is psychologically much simpler than an equal number of unrelated letters. Furthermore, through the process of memorization, he has condensed sets of words into familiar phrases that are much less psychologically complex than an identical number of unrelated words. In constructing a three-hour program, he has, through memorization and storage in long-term memory, condensed larger chunks containing poems, long prose passages, and other chunking units. The question then becomes, can the process of condensation through familiarity (learning) be used to provide an account of how this man can simultaneously have an immediate memory span of eight letters when the letters are unrelated and a span of 100,000 or more when they are related? Does the concept of psychological complexity provide a potential means for accomplishing this feat? Is it possible to state the immediate memory equivalent of unrelated letters, unrelated words, unrelated phrases, unrelated sets of phrases, and unrelated sets of sets of phrases all in the same terms? The following is a tour de force by the Hedgehog to show precisely how this might be accomplished.

Our previous calculations have related the complexity of unrelated letters to words that have reached asymptote through experience. The range is a consensual complexity value of about 26.8 for a single unrelated letter to a value of slightly over 45.00 for a word of ten or more letters. Calculations based on these values are shown in the graph in the upper left portion of Figure 8-19. The line labeled "Familiar" shows the asymptotic consensual complexity values of words of various lengths, while the line labeled "Unrelated" is the sum of the complexity values of the various numbers of unrelated letters. Our hypothetical stage performer has a span of eight unrelated letters, and the consensual complexity of this span is indicated by the horizontal line labeled "Span." The space between the two lines labeled "Unrelated" and "Familiar" represents the

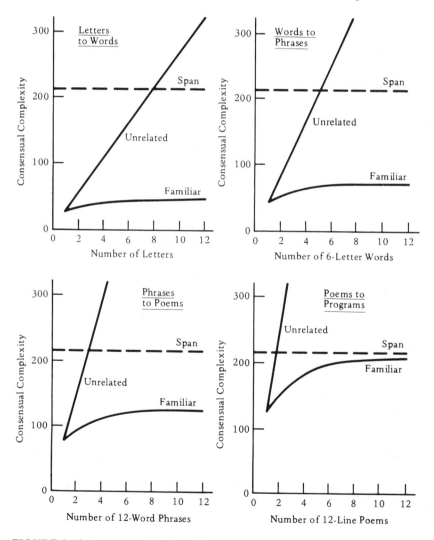

FIGURE 8-19. *Letters to Words to Phrases to Poems to Programs*

potential for simplification of any given number of unrelated letters into a familiar word.

There are a large number of hypothetical characteristics involved in the figure that should be kept in mind. All the values for letters and words of various lengths are hypothetical asymptotes of learning curves, and it is highly unlikely that our performer has condensed all such units to asymptotic value. The "unrelated" curve is the sum of the asymptotic values for each number of letters. This summation supposes that there is no amelioration due to physical or cognitive organization, both of which would reduce the complexity value. In addition, no account is taken of task complexity, which might add to the estimate of complexity depending on whether the performer was asked only to recognize the set of letters or to recall them in order. The latter task certainly would add to the estimate of complexity. Furthermore, what one would like on the ordinate would be a measure of psychological complexity. What is actually plotted is consensual complexity, since all the values involved were estimated from averages of individual subjective complexity values that were then averaged into consensul complexity values for a large group of subjects. These consensual complexity values at least have the virtue of having been obtained with identical operational instructions to the subjects and in very similar contexts.

Although we have no actual data on the complexities of phrases, something approximating an estimate can be calculated by the following logic. If the phrases are composed of words with asymptotic familiarity, then estimates of the consensual complexities of sets of unrelated words of any given length (or mixed lengths, for that matter) can be calculated from the complexities of words of that length. For example, if our phrases are composed of six-letter words, then the asymptotic value for words of that length, 43.09, can be used to calculate the "Unrelated" curve in the graph in the upper right portion of the figure. The "Familiar" curve is calculated by making the assumption that the asymptote of condensation of words into phrases increases with the number of words, as does the asymptote for the curve describing the condensation of letters into phrases. This is a questionable assumption, since it is intuitively reasonable that it might rise to a slightly higher level; in the absense of data, however, the extrapolation from the letter/word relationship to the word/phrase relationship will have to do. Again, the space between the "Familiar" and the "Unfamiliar" lines represents the amount of simplification that can be achieved by condensing unrelated words into familiar phrases.

It should be noted in passing that the habitual use of surface or deep grammar in ordinary speech has precisely the same effect as rote experience in simplifying sets of words from the high complexity value they would have if they were unrelated to the relatively low complexity value achieved through grammatical organization.

If the reader can tolerate another large chunk of unrealistic assumptions, we can proceed from asymptotically familiar phrases to something like a sonnet. The graph in the lower left portion of the figure was made using the asymptote for completely familiar 12-word phrases, 73.44, as the consensual complexity value of a single line of a sonnet. The "Unrelated" curve is this value times the number of such lines, and the "familiar" curve was constructed by making the same assumptions about the effect of familiarity for phrases to poems that was made with respect to the condensation of words into phrases. The abscissa stops at 12 (rather than the 14 lines of a sonnet) for reasons of aesthetic balance in the figure.

Readers who have followed me this far will be able to see how 12 poems can be translated into a program. The asymptote of the "Poem" curve, 123.90, was used to make the calculations for the program, and the asymptotic value for the "Familiar" curve in the lower right-hand graph of the figure comes to a value of 208.15. Since our performer has an immediate memory span of 214.4 in consensual complexity units, it is reasonably clear that he can give a virtuoso performance several hours in length of well memorized material without consulting a written program or making use of any external cues.

Although the values used in these calculations are highly suspect for a variety of reasons, the concept of the simplification of sets of elements in psychological complexity values through repeated experience is valid. Even though the quantities used to make the calculations for the graphs are highly suspect, some further use can be made of them.

It was earlier asserted that it is neither the number of chunks nor the amount of information in the chunks that is constant in immediate memory span. Rather, the constancy resides in the psychological complexity value of the individual chunks in interaction with the number of chunks.

The four graphs in the figure not only show how our performer can use his eight-letter immediate memory span to produce a three-hour recitation program, but they suggest the nature of the equivalences that should hold between the number of letters, the number of six-letter words, the number of 12-word phrases, and the number of 12-line poems that can be held in immediate memory span when all these chunks are at asymptotic value through repeated experience.

In the graphs, the "Unrelated" line crosses the memory span for individual letters at a value of 8 because the assumption was that our performer had precisely that memory span for letters. The intersection of the "Unrelated" line with the span line is at 4.98 words for unrelated words, 2.92 phrases for unrelated 12-word phrases, and 1.73 poems for unrelated 12-line poems. These figures are presented in Table 8-6, along with the equivalent values for individuals with memory spans of nine, ten, 11, and 12 letters. These

TABLE 8-6. Calculated Spans for Words, Phrases, and Poems

| Immediate Memory Span in Consensual Complexity Units | Letters | Immediate Memory Span | | |
| | | 6-Letter Words | 12-Word Phrases | 12-Line Poems |
|---|---|---|---|---|
| 214.4 | 8 | 4.98 | 2.92 | 1.73 |
| 241.2 | 9 | 5.60 | 3.28 | 3.65 |
| 268.0 | 10 | 6.22 | 3.65 | 2.17 |
| 294.8 | 11 | 6.84 | 4.01 | 2.38 |
| 321.6 | 12 | 7.47 | 4.38 | 2.60 |

values are based, of course, on all the unrealistic assumptions made in the process of calculating them. No data were involved other than the consensual complexity values of individual letters and words of various lengths. They stand, therefore, as a theory, the test of which must await a suitable means of assessing the psychological complexity values of these materials empirically.

This exercise was carried to absurd lengths to illustrate the process and method. If a performer did condense a 100,000-word program to a single chunk, it would obviously have a simple form and not the form in which it would be presented from the platform. This tour de force has employed only simplification and chunking as mechanisms. In performance there would be evidence of classification and, above all, serialization. Actual study of such a performance would probably yield evidence of other mechanisms as well.

*Short-Term versus Long-Term Memory.* The account of the performance by an actor reciting continuously for a period of three hours without notes in terms of the psychological complexity of the material is a serious theory that presumably could be tested with profit from a theoretical point of view. On the other hand, it will be viewed as an absurd development by some who think in terms of the traditional conception of short-term versus long-term memory. If it does seem absurd, the absurdity lies in the traditional conception of short-term memory and the magic number 7 plus or minus 2 as constituting a functional entity to be presented as a box in a computer flow diagram.

I would argue that the fundamental distinction is between the characteristics of a single psychological event and those of a stream or sequence of psychological events. It seems obvious that long-term memory is involved automatically in the development and character of the individual psychological event. The character of the psychological event may or may not be affected by Central Processor manipulations, such as search and retrieval of cognitive material from the past. If long-term memory is involved in a single psychological event, then it is clearly involved in all aspects of a series of psychological events.

The phenomenon referred to as short-term memory is hardly a memory process at all. Instead, it is the number of items that can be recirculated or rotated through the Central Processor without loss, the length of a chain of psychological events. I have tried to demonstrate that the length of the chain is dependent on the character of the operations for assessing it and the psychological complexity of the material. The length can range from one event to a very large number, depending on the method of counting the links in the chain and the strength of the connections between them.

## STRUCTURE AND STRUCTURAL CHANGE IN PSYCHOLOGICAL EVENTS

I have devoted the last five chapters to structural characteristics of psychological events. In Chapter 4 I described the stream of psychological events as a sequence of discrete elements that have a practical minimum duration of $500\sigma$ and a maximum that is not much greater. In Chapter 5 I discussed the course of development of a psychological event and its prompt, automatic, and inevitable termination, and replacement by a subsequent event. In Chapter 6 I discussed the temporary aftereffects of the occurrence of an event, which consist primarily of a negative bias against repetition of that event. The primary manifestations of this negative bias against repetition are habituation effects and alternation phenomena. Temporary aftereffects serve to produce variability and flexibility in the stream of psychological events and form the necessary base for adaptive learning.

Enduring changes in psychological events have been the focus of Chapters 7 and 8. Frequency of occurrence is a nearly universal variable of research on learning, and Chapter 7 was devoted to the effect of frequency of occurrence on the complexity of psychological events and consequently on differential preference for the relevant events. In Chapter 8 I have attempted to develop the concept of the Central Processor and to integrate into the Hedgehog model the concepts of consciousness, free will, and the connection between thought and action. I have tried to show that higher mental processes such as problem solving and decision making can be treated in terms of changes in psychological complexity occurring as a function of various forms of organization, including classification, chunking, concept formation, and serial condensation.

In emphasizing the structural aspects of psychological events in this sequence of chapters, I have attempted to achieve some degree of integration of a number of aspects of experimental psychology that have been developed in relative autonomy in recent decades.

These sub-areas of the discipline include sensation, perception, animal learning, human verbal learning, memory and forgetting, information processing, problem solving, decision processes, and thinking. In the five chapters, I focus on the preferential and energetic aspects of psychological events and the interactions of these aspects with the structural characteristics already discussed.

# chapter nine

# Motivation, preference, and all of that

Psychological events are autogenously motivated. The stream of psychological events is continuous from conception to death. There is no way to stop the stream; one can only modify some aspects of its character, direction, and temporal sequence. Single events occur, endure, and cease. Moments of habituation followed by compelled choice of the next available event nearest optimum are the necessary and sufficient causes of behavior.

The preference postulate of the Hedgehog says that there should be an inverted-U-shaped relation between the structural variable—psychological complexity—and any affective variable related to preference. Preference for the event nearest to the optimum is a complete basis of choice among available events. No other motivational principle is needed. Biological and social motives are both to be accounted for by derivation from the basic cycle of habituation and compelled choice.

## TRADITIONAL MOTIVATIONAL CONCEPTS

The preference function of the Hedgehog is asserted to be sufficient to account for all motivational and incentive functions. It should therefore be useful to examine the manner in which the Hedgehog reinterprets the traditional motivational concepts.

### Biological Motives

In the Hedgehog biological motives are biologically imposed programs. Appetitive biological motives such as hunger and thirst involve growing afferent input with increasing deprivation. The afferent input arising from a hunger state, for example, is massive and highly complex. It induces persistent (repeated) psychological events that we refer to as hunger. These events can be reduced in complexity by food ingestion. Thus, the easiest way for an organism to escape from the superoptimal complexity of the hunger state is to eat.

In the hunger state, the psychological events induced by hunger stimuli have long since reached an asymptote in psychological complexity, and that asymptote is far above optimal level. Although the quickest and easiest way to bring superoptimal hunger to optimal level is to eat, afferent input associated with hunger is subject to habituation. If food is not immediately available, habituation will produce periods during which the feeling of hunger will disappear, only to be reinstated periodically through dishabituation. Of course, if fasting is continued, repeated habituation of the input from the hunger state will result in an effectively permanent habituation of feelings of hunger. Thus, many people who have fasted for long periods of time report that, after a sufficient number of days without food, they no longer experienced the distress associated with the superoptimal input of the hunger state.

Pain is a product of superoptimal complexity. Intense lights can be painful without inducing tissue damage. Tissue damage probably disorganizes afferent input, and the disorganization alone is probably an adequate input for pain. Rubbing a minor injury probably simplifies the sensory input through inhibitory effects of the rubbing of adjacent tissue. Rubbing remote tissue usually doesn't alleviate the pain.

### Social Motives

Social motives, such as need for achievement, are often described as being based on the association of a variety of cues with relevant situations. Thus, when a person with a history that has produced the appropriate associations steps into a classroom, the achievement cues induce a series of psychological events that are more complex than optimal. The individual can leave the room and escape the superoptimal complexity or remain uncomfortably in place until some degree of adaptation has occurred. The latter procedure won't be wholly satisfactory, because the preference function is such that adaptation may produce only an increase in unpleasantness. Growing more and more uncomfortable all the time, the person who is high in need for achievement has little choice but to perform a task that leads to the appearance of success cues. Since the achievement-inducing cues are still there, the occurrence of success must inhibit or suppress achievement cues much in the manner in which rubbing a minor hurt suppresses and inhibits the complexity of the pain.

### Needs and Goals

The Hedgehog reverses the usual strategy of motivational analysis. Motivational theory, at least in the broad sense, has the task of categorizing all behavior in terms of need/goal relationships. A representative set might include such biological motives as hunger, thirst, sex, and fear, and such psychological motives as need for affiliation, achievement, and power. Suppose we extend the two sets until we have 15 or 20 discriminable motives. Now let us collect a substantial tabulation of overt behaviors such as that collected by Barker and Wright (1951) in *One Boy's Day* (as discussed in Chapter 4). Now let us categorize each bit of behavior in this day-long record under one or another of our 15 to 20 biological and social motives. It becomes apparent very quickly that a very small number can be placed with confidence under any of them. The largest number, perhaps 90% or more, seem essentially pointless in terms of their role in achieving any of the goals in our list. One is reduced to using such terms as curiosity, exploration, or recreation, and none of these can be fit comfortably into a system in which there must first be a need state and then an instrumental act that reduces the need state. Where is the need that produces curiosity behavior or exploratory behavior or play behavior? Thus, the differentiation of need/goal relationships to account for specifiable categories of behavior, though productive, does not permit an account of a psychologically significant proportion of all the behavior that occurs.

The Hedgehog, on the other hand, offers the potential of accounting for *all* behavior. Play, or what Berlyne (1960) calls ludic behavior, is the most fundamental reflection of human (and animal) motivation. Curiosity, exploration, recreation, and others are loose descriptive terms that categorize the stream of behavior. Biological and social motives provide terms to describe subclasses of the cycle of habituation and compelled choice.

The terms *habituation* and *compelled choice* are technically accurate descriptive terms, but they do not have an appealing literary ring. At the risk of implying more than is intended, one could use other descriptive terms. The organism could be described as undergoing oscillations of boredom and excitement, although both of these terms imply greater intensity or greater swings in intensity than is necessary. *Tedium* and *titillation* could also substitute for *habituation* and *compelled choice*, but again there is surplus meaning.

### Incentives

All psychological events have incentive properties, because all incentive properties are derived from nearness to optimal complexity level. Incentive properties may be regarded as either absolute or relative. The inverted-U-shaped function of the preference dimension of the Hedgehog refers to the absolute incentive properties of psychological events. Events nearest to optimum have the highest positive incentive value. Events have lesser absolute incentive value as they recede from optimal in both directions to the point at which the incentive value is neutral in an absolute sense. Events either less complex or more complex than the corresponding neutral events have negative incentive value. Extremely painful events are on the extreme complex end of the complexity scale.

Much behavior is motivated by relative incentive value. If an extremely painful event can be followed by a less painful (but still painful) event, the less painful event will operate as a positive incentive in the relative sense. An organism undergoing extremely boring events will move to a neutral psychological event (in the absolute sense) as if it were a positive incentive.

### Acquired Incentives

An event that would be neutral on the low side of complexity if it were not associated with arousal may have a positive incentive value if its complexity can be increased by the addition of arousal. Thus, the event induced by the ingestion of a bit of sawdust by a hungry rat may be inherently below optimal complexity level, while the ingestion of a bit of dry food with similar stimulus properties may be a positive incentive primarily because the food has the added capacity to induce an increase in arousal.

Acquired incentives occur when a previously neutral stimulus (a stimulus with little absolute incentive value) is repeatedly associated with an event with greater absolute incentive value (an event closer to optimum). Under these conditions, the neutral stimulus acquires the capacity to induce a more complex (and thus nearer optimum) event than before the association. In the process, the neutral stimulus can come to induce a more complex event in either or both of two ways. The stimulus may acquire the capacity to induce some partial representation of the event, and it may acquire some additional capacity to induce arousal. Both acquired properties would made it a more complex event and thus nearer to optimum.

Previously attractive events (in the absolute sense) can acquire negative incentive properties by being associated with very painful (very complex) events by the same mechanism. The additional structural and arousal properties acquired simply move the event up the complexity dimension to a position that has absolute negative incentive value.

### Needs

Within the Hedgehog, *need* is defined as any condition that produces a nonoptimal state. An incentive is any potential event that will reduce the need, while a reward is any event that actually does reduce the need. Need reduction is a reduction in the discrepancy between the current state and the optimal and may thus involve either an increase or a decrease in complexity. Thus, the mechanism of optimal complexity level should be able to handle all the empirical evidence associated with the operations of biological need states and consummatory rewards, as well as social need states and their resolutions. It is additionally able to deal with other areas, such as verbal learning, play behavior, and thought processes, in which the role of biological and social needs and their reduction has not been apparent.

Psychological events, I have asserted, are autogeneously motivated. The force, energy, and direction of a psychological event are autarkic and intrinsic to the event itself. Extrinsic motivation—motivation extrinsic to the event itself—serves to organize a sequence of events and may influence the character of the event itself if extrinsic factors also involve arousal (a topic to be considered at length later). Thus, motivation in the Hedgehog is intrinsic motivation, although the meaning of the term *intrinsic* is somewhat different from its usual meaning in current psychological literature. There it generally refers to a special kind of motivation involving interaction with some leisure activity or game in which there appears to be no motivation operating other than the interest in the activity for its own sake. In the Hedgehog, all acts, not just a special sub group, are intrinsically motivated. (See Chapter 14.)

### VARIETIES OF
### PREFERENCE FUNCTIONS

A dominant theory in the field of preference is Wundt's classical formulation relating stimulus intensity to hedonic tone. The theoretical formulation relates these two approximately as drawn in Figure 9-1. As stimulus intensity is increased from a very low value, the experience is assumed to increase in pleasantness to a maximum and then to decrease in pleasantness until it ceases to be pleasant and becomes increasingly unpleasant. Wundt's theory was speculative in character and was not based on empirical data. Yet the theory has sufficient intuitive appeal that it has become a standard point of departure in terms of application in such fields as aesthetics, in terms of a theoretical base for experimental investigations, and as a phenomenon to be explained in other terms. The Hedgehog is an alternative to Wundt's theory.

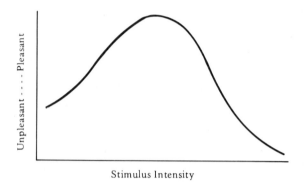

FIGURE 9-1. *Wundt's Hedonic Theory of Preference*

## Preference in the Hedgehog

Preference is a theoretical variable in the Hedgehog. Given a dimension of psychological complexity, it is assumed that for any individual there is a point on the complexity scale that represents optimal complexity. If there are no constraints on the organism's choice, the optimal event will be the one that occurs. If an optimal event is not available, the available event that is nearest to optimum, whether more or less complex than the optimum, will be chosen.

These statements imply that psychological complexity is a metric scale and thus must be expressed in equal units. The preference scale, on the other hand, represents an ideal ordered scale that may be unfolded from a J-scale of expressed preference. That is, if a series of events can be ordered from most to least preferred, and if the psychological complexities of the events are known, it is then possible to unfold the preference order so that those that are less complex than the optimal event can be arrayed on the left and those that are more complex than the optimum can be arrayed on the right. The result will be an inverted-U-shaped function. Other than this expectation that the plotted curve will decrease monotonically in both directions from the optimal point, the theory provides no specifications concerning the shape of the preference function. All the many shapes that fulfill the requirement of being monotonically decreasing from optimum serve to confirm the theory. Disconfirmation would arise only from a nonmonotonicity that could not be accounted for within the terms of the theory.

*One-Factor versus Two-Factor Preference Functions.* The Hedgehog is a one-factor theory of preference. All choices are made in terms of the psychological complexity of the event and its distance from optimum. This is in contrast with two-factor theories such as those of Schneirla (1959, 1965) and Berlyne (see, for example, Berlyne, (1969). Schneirla formulated two systems, an A-system (approach), activated by stimuli of low intensity, and a W-system (withdrawal), activated by intense stimuli. Berlyne argued for a pleasure function that would be monotonically increasing and an unpleasantness function that had a higher threshold but that also increased monotonically. The combination of the two resulted in a classical Wundtian curve of hedonic tone.

In the Hedgehog, the shape of the function relating psychological complexity to some expression of preference is an empirical matter as long as the curve decreases monotonically in each direction from the optimum. However, it was largely to avoid the implication of two factors that a sin function was fitted to the data in Figure 6-17. That equation was

$E = \theta \sin \theta - a$, where

$E$ = some measure of the evaluative or preference function,

$\theta = f$(Complexity), and

$a$ = constant.

If we assume that $a = 3.5$, then the simplest possible psychological event has a complexity value of zero, and this value of $C\psi$ is associated with a $\theta$ value of $0^0$. These values represent a maximum of boredom, are mildly unpleasant, and represent a value of $E$ that is small and negative $(-3.5)$. Optimal complexity level $(C\psi_0)$ occurs when the value of $C\psi$ is such that $\theta = 115.5^0$, in which case the value of $E$ would be maximal at just over 100 arbitrary units of $E$. Neutral complexity values would occur when $C\psi$ was such that $\theta$ = about $14^0$ and again when $\theta = 178^0$. Thus, values of $C\psi$ associated with $\theta$ values increasing from about $14^0$ up to $115.5^0$ would be increasingly pleasant, while values of $C\psi$ associated with $\theta$ values increasing from $115.5^0$ to $178^0$ would be decreasingly pleasant. At values of $C\psi$ related to $\theta$ values significantly above $180^0$, the value of $E$ becomes rapidly negative and thus unpleasant and eventually painful.

The most important of several problems with this equation is the fact that it is cyclical and begins to rise again, a characteristic that makes no psychological sense. Alternatively, the data could have been fitted by a complex function involving two exponential equations:

$$E = \left[ k\,E_0 \left(10^{-aC\psi}\right) + E_0 \right] - \left[ k\,E_0 \left(10^{-aC\psi}\right) + E_0 \right]$$

To have used such a procedure would have been to imply a two-factor process such as that involved in Berlyne's theory. The Hedgehog has no such implication.

*Problems with Empirical*
*Measures of Complexity and Preference*

There are a number of circumstances in which something other than an inverted-U-shaped function relating a measure of complexity to a measure of preference can occur without disturbing the validity of the theory itself. Most such problems are associated with the operations of measurement of either or both complexity and preference. Let us review a few examples of such problems.

Without extensive consideration of the evaluative function, it is a fair assumption that the organism has a variety of mechanisms for controlling the complexity of the central process. It is a postulate of the theory that there is an optimal complexity level of central process operation and that the organism will use whatever means at its disposal to maintain optimal level. The fact that an organism is exposed to a very complex stimulus does not mean that the processing occurring in response to that stimulus is also very complex. The psychological complexity of the central process can differ depending on the modality and on the nature of the constraints under which the organism is operating. Thus, the organism probably has more control over the complexity of visual input than over auditory input.

Constraints on central processing may be peripheral or central, and they may be voluntary or automatic (and thus involuntary). Peripheral control mechanisms include such things as escaping the environment altogether and shutting one's eyes to reduce complex stimuli. Light adaptation to reduce the impact of intense visual stimuli would be an example of central control.

*Processing Rate.* Psychological complexity and preference theory is most unambiguously applicable to an individual psychological event and to comparisons between individual psychological events. In many experimental situations, however, strings of psychological events are assessed as units. A complex picture is examined in a series of visual fixations that permit the integration of many aspects of the picture into a single percept. Auditory stimuli, such as speech or music, require the integration of a sequence of items into single units that are then assessed for complexity and preference. This fact requires that consideration be given to the rate of processing of stimulus material and thus the effect of time on complexity and preference.

We can imagine a condition in which processing time is a direct index of the psychological complexity of sequential material. This might be true, for example, in serial learning in which the experimenter controls the rate of presentation of material and complexity is an increasing function of the amount and cumulative time of exposure. A similar circumstance might be induced if the stimuli are pictures and the subjects are instructed to study the pictures until they think they can reproduce them in exact detail. In each case, processing rate might be regarded as fixed, and processing time would index complexity. If so, then preference could be plotted against processing time, and an inverted-U-shaped function could be expected.

There are other circumstances in which we might expect to find the processing rate to index the psychological complexity of the stimulus. If we hold the exposure time constant and vary the complexity of the material, then the organism might be expected to work harder and faster on complex material than on simple material. Different amounts of material processed under such circumstances would reflect different rates of processing. In such a case, the rate of processing would reflect psychological complexity, and preference should be related to the rate variable.

There could be an optimal rate of processing material that would be preferable to either faster or slower rates. Judgments of complexity could be made with reference to the rate of processing or the total amount processed. If the procedures permit processing at optimal rate, and if judgment is made in terms of rate, then the preference function will be unrelated to the measure of complexity. If rate varies with the complexity of the material, or if the judgment is made in reference to the material processed rather than in reference to the rate, then the complexity scale can range from partial to full correlation with preference.

The relation between stimulus complexity and psychological complexity is certainly influenced by the instructions (constraints) imposed on the organism by the experimenter. Let us explore some of the possibilities of the application of instructional constraints.

1. *One to one correspondence.* Some experimental operations are designed to produce something very close to a one to one correspondence between stimulus and psychological complexity. Thus, if the stimuli are patterns of black and white squares that vary in number of squares and proportions of black and white squares, we might ask subjects to count the number of each or point to every square and thus ensure that the entire stimulus is processed in some fashion. Or we could use a general instruction, such as an indication that the subject will be required to reproduce the pattern, in order to induce something close to complete processing. If our operation is successful, then we might expect something like the pair of figures in Panel A of Figure 9-2. Psychological complexity would be a linear increasing function of stimulus complexity, and the evaluative function would be a Wundtian curve in relation to stimulus complexity. An empirical example from Olson (1977) is in Panel A of Figure 9-3. Scribble patterns differing in a priori complexity produce a linear increase in information processing time.

2. *Negative exponential correspondence.* Many of the experimental operations that have been employed in the field do not enforce processing of stimuli to the limit of their potential complexity. Panel B of Figure 9-2 illustrates this relation between stimulus complexity and psychological complexity. Panel B of Figure 9-3 is an empirical result that appears to be of this type. It was obtained by Olson (1977), who measured processing time while subjects rated a set of black-and-white graphic prints for complexity.

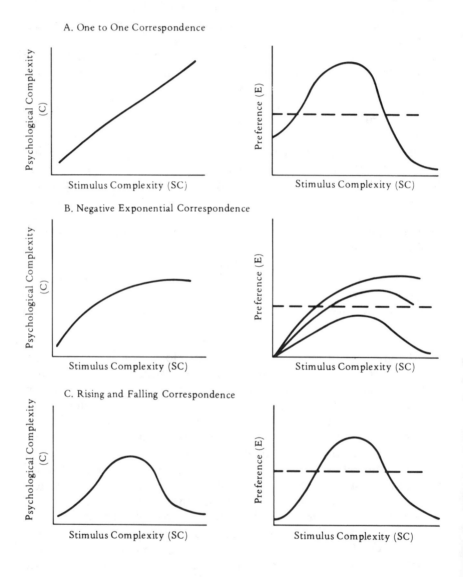

A. One to One Correspondence

B. Negative Exponential Correspondence

C. Rising and Falling Correspondence

FIGURE 9-2. *Defects in the Measurement of Psychological Complexity*

A. One to One Correspondence. Information processing rates for five scribble patterns taken from Vitz (1966) by Olson (1977). Rate calculated by dividing subjective complexity ratings by recognition learning time.

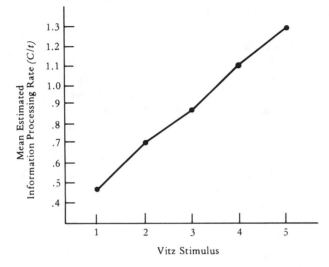

B. Negative Exponential Correspondence. Information processing rates for 12 black-and-white graphics taken from Walker (1969b) by Olson (1977).

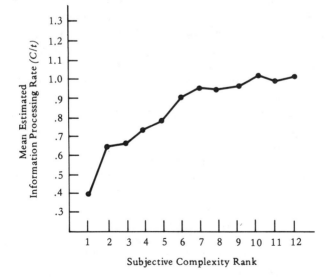

*FIGURE 9-3. Empirical Information Processing Rates. (From* Complexity, Preference, and Information Processing Rate, *by M. H. Olson. Unpublished doctoral dissertation, University of Michigan, 1977. Reprinted by permission.)*

An informative study was done by Wohlwill (1971), who gave three-dimensional objects to children to be explored haptically while the objects were out of sight under a table. He was able to measure the amount of time spent in exploration and was able to count the number of corners and edges actually touched by his subjects. He found that younger children performed a less complete exploration of the more complex stimuli than did older children.

In a special case, it might be assumed that the completeness of exploration is a negative exponential function of the complexity of the stimulus. Under ideal free-choice conditions, the curve might be expected to rise to asymptote precisely at optimal level. However, experimenter instructions or even self-instruction might produce exploration somewhat beyond optimum but still coming to asymptote well below the full potential of the stimulus.

There is a difficult problem here with respect to how much of this "complexity damping" process is under the control of the experimenter or even of the subject. After we have presumably controlled all voluntary mechanisms, there still may be involuntary mechanisms operating to produce a negative exponential relation or even more complex functions. One can think in terms of the capacity limitations of the mechanisms, or automatic mechanisms such as grouping and pattern formation, that would operate to reduce the psychological complexity of the psychological event induced by a complex stimulus.

Whether the negative exponential decrease in rate of increase of psychological complexity is voluntary or automatic, the relation of an evaluative function to stimulus complexity can be varied. It can range between two limits. If psychological complexity rises to optimum only, then the evaluative function will be an identical curve. The higher the curve rises above optimum (C f(SC) in Panel B of Figure 9-2) the greater the tendency for the evaluative curve to show a decline at high stimulus complexity levels. The other limit is the one to one correspondence case, where the evaluative curve would be Wundtian.

3. *Rising and falling correspondence.* It is conceivable that the organism chould choose not to interact with highly complex stimuli. The tendency to escape could increase as stimuli rose above optimum in such a manner that the complexity of the induced process could decrease progressively with increasing stimulus complexity above optimum. This analysis leads to an expectation that the evaluative function could be an inverted U with a quite different origin from that of the inverted U in the Wundtian function. In this case, the falling curve on the right side would be a mirror image of the rising part of the curve on the left side, both of its lowest points could be attributed to boredom, and none of it would be a function of overstimulation. This situation is illustrated in Panel C of Figure 9-2.

*Complexity Scale Range.* Rather than an inverted-U-shaped function relating complexity to preference, it should be possible to obtain either a monotonically increasing or a monotonically decreasing function, depending on the range of the complexity scale. This could occur if something less than the full range of complexity was presented. If all the stimuli are below optimum complexity, a monotonically increasing curve relating complexity to preference should be obtained. The reverse is to be expected if all the stimuli are above optimum.

*Evaluation of Something Other Than the Complexity of the Stimulus.* There are circumstances in which subjects who are asked to evaluate the complexity of a set of stimuli and then to express their preference for these same stimuli produce a chaotic relationship between the two ratings, because the preference rating was made with reference to some aspect of the stimuli other than their intrinsic psychological complexities. For example, such ratings might be carried out on a set of paintings. If the complexity ratings are made with reference to intrinsic properties of the paintings, and if the preference ratings are made in terms of monetary values of the paintings known in some way to the raters, complexity and preference ratings will not be related.

*Habituation Effects.* Something other than an inverted-U-shaped relation between psychological complexity and preference can be obtained by extensive habituation of one or more of the items in a stimulus array. Let us suppose that we have a set of stimuli ordered with respect to psychological complexity and can demonstrate a clear and simple inverted-U-shaped preference function for them. Then let us suppose that we expose the optimal stimulus repeatedly. The effect of such exposure should be to produce large habituation effects, with a consequent temporary loss of both complexity and preference for that stimulus. If we then measure preference for the stimuli, we should obtain a double inverted-U-shaped function, our original preference curve being severely depressed in the middle. The double inverted-U-shaped function characterizes adaptation level theory, such as that of Helson (1959, 1973), and discrepancy theories of affect, such as that of McClelland and Clark (1953). This form of preference curve should be obtainable in any situation in which adaptation level theory applies. It will usually be a temporary phenomenon, with the single inverted-U-shaped function reappearing after a period of time sufficient for the dissipation of the habituation. If some of the effects are permanent, rather than temporary, then the changes in complexity that occurred as a function of the exposure will require rearrangement of the items on the complexity scale with a resultant restoration of the preference function.

*The Measure of Preference.* The shape of the preference function can depend, in part, on the particular language used in scaling the evaluative function. In Chapter 3 a number of dimensions, such as pleasantness/unpleasantness, boring/interesting, and approach/avoidance, were found to be highly correlated when scaled against each other. However, it is possible that the most interesting stimulus of an array might be considerably more complex than the most pleasant stimulus in the same display.

### Hedonism and the Hedgehog

The organism described by the Hedgehog is not a hedonist. Its choices are made in terms of the relative psychological complexities of the available psychological events and their relative distances from optimal complexity level. Predictions are to be made from assessment of psychological complexity and optimal complexity level. Assessment of evaluative characteristics of potential psychological events can be expected to yield correlated dimensions but to predict imperfectly, depending on the degree of the correlation. Since the Hedgehog predicts choice behavior, and since evaluative dimensions are always verbal expressions of experience, the imperfect correlation between experience and behavior is a discrepancy between conscious thought and action. Figure 9-4 diagrams one possible version of this distinction. A stimulus situation is seen to affect the choice response directly and simultaneously and in this instance, to produce a conscious experience that is in reasonable accord with the preferential function. Let us examine two issues in reference to the diagram: reasons for partial dissociation of hedonic quality from preference, and the role of stimulus intensity.

*Pleasure/Pain.* Pleasure and pain are sometimes related to biological needs. Increased need is associated with increased pain or displeasure, while need reduction is associated with pleasure and satisfaction. There is a large body of literature on stimulus seeking that appears to show that some stimulation, such as the sweetness of artificial sweeteners, is also pleasant even though no identifiable biological need is reduced. Pleasure and pain must be dissociated from biological needs for two reasons. The reduction of some biological need states is not necessarily accompanied by pleasure, and feelings of pleasure are not necessarily confined to the reduction of biological need states.

For most of us, our days are filled with situations in which the most satisfying thing we could do at any given moment might be to eat a big dessert, to punch someone in the nose, or to engage in some other grossly pleasant activity that we nevertheless do not engage in. On the other hand, our days are also filled with acts that

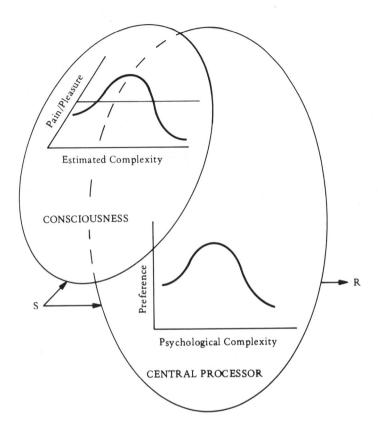

*FIGURE 9-4. Consciousness and the Central Processor*

are inherently unpleasant in a hedonistic sense. Getting up to an alarm when one still wants to sleep or putting shoes on sore and swollen feet are everyday examples. Clinical psychologists and psychiatrists see so many behaviors that defy attribution of hedonistic motives that they have a large bag, labeled "masochism," to put them in.

An enormous amount of human behavior is carried out without being available to consciousness, and another large portion is available to consciousness but is not attended to. Much of what we do attend to—language behavior, for example—has little or no affective properties.

Thus, hedonism seems a poor basis for predicting the course of the stream of psychological events. Although it is true that there is a general tendency to choose pleasurable events and eschew unpleasant ones, this relation does not always hold. Most events have no affective properties, and some choices defy a hedonistic interpretation.

*Stimulus Intensity*

A problem arises when changes in stimulus intensity are equated with changes in stimulus complexity, with more intensity interpreted as greater complexity. There seems little doubt that there is a general kind of relation in which stimuli of relatively weak intensity can be experienced as unpleasant, stronger stimuli as pleasant, and extremely intense stimuli as unpleasant. For example, coffee is unpleasant to most coffee drinkers when either too weak or too strong, and it is pleasant when the brew is of optimal strength. On the other hand, it is doubtful that very weak auditory stimuli are unpleasant, while intense auditory stimuli are distinctly unpleasant. Finally, it is questionable whether pain is pleasant in any intensity. These three examples appear to generate very different preference functions through the manipulation of stimulus intensity.

In psychophysical measurement two different kinds of continua are found. Metathetic continua, which yield equal, just noticeable differences, are usually found when the judgment concerns what kind of stimulus and where. Protothetic continua are found in scaling the effects of stimulus intensity; the size of the just noticeable difference increases systematically with increases in the magnitude of the stimulus.

The relevant quantitative data on stimulus intensity and hedonic tone have been collected by Engle (1928) and are reported in Boring, Langfeld, and Weld (1939). Engle measured the hedonic tone of a number of substances dissolved in water and recorded the number of judgments of pleasant, unpleasant, indifferent, and doubtful for each. The results are reported for from seven to ten subjects who participated in either six or seven sessions; subjects and sessions are not distinguished in the data. The substances were common salt, sulphate of quinine, tartaric acid, and cane sugar. Woodworth (1938) transformed Engle's data in two ways to achieve the picture of the results shown in Figure 9-5. He apparently ignored judgments of indifferent and doubtful and then subtracted the percentage of unpleasant judgments from the percentage of pleasant ones. Secondly, he equated quite different concentrations of the four substances. The length of the abscissa represents a 40% concentration of cane sugar, 10% for salt, 1.12% for tartaric acid, and .004% for quinine sulphate (all by weight).

Given these rather arbitrary adjustments of both scales, generalizations must be made with caution and very tentatively. However, it seems certain that, at very low concentrations of all four substances, judgments of unpleasant were made by some subjects on some trials. Three of the four curves are inverted-U-shaped patterns and conform to some degree with the Wundtian curve. The results for sugar, however, show no significant tendency to decline even at a 40% concentration.

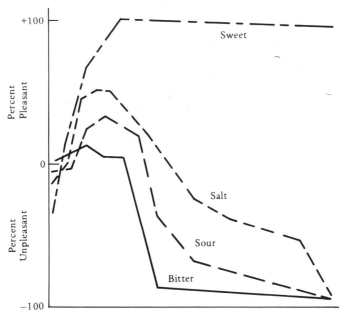

*FIGURE 9-5. Hedonic Tone for Taste. The data are from Engle (1928) as transformed by Woodworth (1938). Ordinate is percent of pleasant/unpleasant judgments, with judgments of "indifferent" or "doubtful" omitted. The abscissa is proportional to the maximum concentrations, which were 40% for cane sugar, 10% for salt, 1.12% for tartaric acid, and .004% for quinine sulphate (all by weight). (Adapted from* Experimental Psychology, *by R. S. Woodworth. Copyright 1938 by Holt, Rinehart & Winston, Inc. Reprinted by permission.)*

One possible explanation for different results with different substances is that the four substances had very different capacities to produce intensity of neural firing. This would suggest that, if one could monitor the intensity of neural activity produced by these substances, and if the abscissa was scaled in terms of intensity of neural activity, then the particular substance employed to produce a given level of neural activity would not be important.

Pfaffman (1969) has reported the results of two experiments that can be roughly combined to provide some evidence on the issue. He tested squirrel monkeys in a two-bottle preference test with various concentrations of sucrose, salt, hydrochloric acid, and quinine. He then plotted the percentage of choices of the various substances when they were offered as alternatives to plain water. In another experiment, he measured the increase in intensity of neural response to various concentrations of the four substances in the chorda tympani nerve in the monkey. Pfaffman used somewhat different values of the concentrations in the two experiments, but, by a process of interpolation and extrapolation, values not common to the two experiments can be estimated. Preference in terms of percent deviation from a 50/50 choice can then be plotted against neural intensity, as shown in Figure 9-6.

The similarities between the two sets of curves in Figures 9-5 and 9-6 seem to me to be remarkable in view of the methodological issues involved in the production of the two graphs and the differences in species, in concentrations, and possibly in substances em-

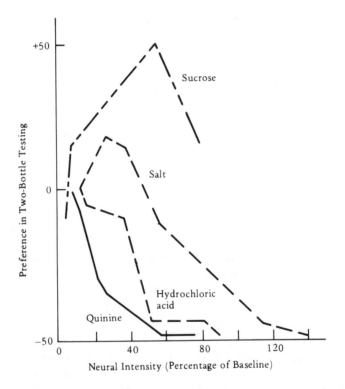

*FIGURE 9-6. Preference and Neural Intensity. The data are replotted from two experiments by Pfaffman (1969). In one experiment, squirrel monkeys were given choices between a bottle containing water and another containing some concentration of the substances used. Ordinate is percent above or below neutral value. In the second experiment, neural intensity recordings were made from the chorda tympani of monkeys while they were tasting the substances. The points in the graph are in several instances interpolations or extrapolations, since Pfaffman did not use the same concentrations in all cases in the two studies. (Constructed from data in "Taste Preference and Reinforcement," by C. Pfaffman. In J. T. Tapp (Ed.),* Reinforcement and Behavior. *Copyright 1969 by Academic Press. Reprinted by permission.)*

ployed. There are also differences. For the monkeys, there were no concentrations of either quinine or hydrochloric acid that they preferred to water. The preference curve for sucrose, on the other hand, shows a clear drop at high concentrations, unlike the comparable curve for human subjects.

An important characteristic of the results in Figure 9-6 is the apparent fact that the differences in preferential choices with the four substances are not to be explained in terms of differences in neural intensity, at least as measured in the chorda tympani in the squirrel monkey. Even when plotted against neural intensity, a variety of preference functions, rather than a single Wundtian function, emerge.

Several interpretations of these results seem possible. One possibility is that recording from the chorda tympani amounts to looking in the wrong place. This interpretation would suggest that, somewhere down the afferent-central-efferent chain, one might find a point where intensity of neural activity would make the four curves coincide. This possibility would require that there be very low and untested concentrations of hydrochloric acid and quinine that squirrel monkeys would prefer to plain water. Although this possibility exists, it appears unlikely.

A second class of interpretation involves accepting the varieties of preference function seen in Figures 9-5 and 9-6 as representing results that are specific to intensity variation but unrepresentative of qualitative variation. Thus, when intensity is varied, one could expect the optimal complexity level to be at the weak end, the strong end, or in the middle, whereas, with qualitative variation of the stimulus, one would always expect the inverted-U-shaped preference function.

A third interpretation is that it is difficult to distinguish at the neural level between quantitative and qualitative differences. Qualitatively more complex stimuli produce quantitatively more intense neural activity. Such an interpretation would suggest that the inverted-U-shaped preference function, while possibly the most frequent result, would not be a universal form. Given this interpretation, one could make only the very weak prediction that there would be a single optimum and that, therefore, there would not be a universal U-shaped preference function. Whether the single optimum was at the simple end, the complex end, or in the middle would be an empirical question.

None of these interpretations is entirely satisfactory. The first two seem unlikely, and the third appears to leave preference unpredictable, since it does not suggest an alternative means of determining which dimensions will have which optimum independent of the assessment of the preference function itself.

## SUMMARY

When the preference postulate is applied to qualitative or structural differences between stimuli, there is no convincing contrary evidence. Within any one class of materials, one might argue for a contrary interpretation, but no alternative interpretation exists that will handle all the preference data from such diverse materials. We do show preference for an optimal complexity in art and music as well as in other areas and to show less preference for stimuli or events either above or below optimum.

Somewhere in the thicket of the intensity variable, the Hedgehog may have sustained a grievous wound. Sugar that can't be too sweet, odors that are pleasant in any concentration, substances that taste bad in any concentration—these may require the Hedgehog to accept a family of related functions, of which the Wundtian hedonic curve is one, in order to handle intensity. It remains to be seen whether the wound will heal by itself or whether the Hedgehog will have to learn some variations on his one trick.

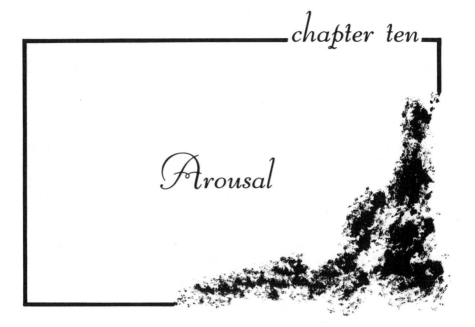

_chapter ten_

$\mathcal{A}$rousal

### THE CONCEPT OF AROUSAL IN THE HEDGEHOG

In the preceding chapter, I asserted that the living organism is autogenous. It behaves continuously, and, while responsive to stimuli, it is not dependent on stimulation to generate the stream of psychological events. On the other hand, there are periods when the stream runs very slowly (for instance, when the organism is sleeping) and periods when the stream runs very rapidly (as in times of great excitement). The concepts of psychological complexity and preference do not appear sufficient to account for this variation in the operating level of the living organism. It therefore seems necessary to add a third, and final, concept to the Hedgehog—the concept of arousal.

In the theory, arousal or arousal level is an energetic variable, in contrast to psychological complexity, which is a structural variable, and preference, which is an evaluative variable. Arousal represents the state of the organism. It is a theoretical variable that can be reflected in the intensity aspects of overt behavior, in the speed and complexity of thought, and in aspects of psychological functioning. It is responsive to, but not dependent on, external stimulation. Thus, the sensitization effect of stimulation discussed in Chapter 6 amounts to an increase in arousal level as a function of certain kinds of stimulation, but not all arousal is a product of stimulation.

### Arousal as a Theoretical Variable

It seems clear that arousal level is lower when a person is asleep than when he or she is awake. The word *arousal* was probably chosen by psychologists because of its meaning in the phrase "arousing a person from sleep." However, it is doubtful if the organism functions at many values of the arousal dimension with any consistency. Rather, one can think of two states—asleep and awake—that usually represent two narrow ranges of the arousal dimension, and the organism is typically in one state or the other. Drowsiness states and states of high excitement occur, of course, but tend to have relatively short durations.

On the level of theory, there are two ways in which arousal interacts with psychological complexity and preference. Both optimal complexity level and the complexities of particular events are affected by the prevailing state of arousal. The interaction of arousal with optimal complexity level can be illustrated as follows. Imagine four states representing four levels of arousal—sleep, drowsiness, normal alertness, and a highly excited state. Preference functions for these four states would require four different inverted-U-shaped curves with optimal points at different positions on the psychological complexity scale. The optimal point for the sleep state would occur at the simple end of the scale. Next would come the optimal point during drowsiness, followed by the one for normal alertness. Finally, the optimal point for the excited state would be farthest toward the complex end of the scale. It is also likely that the associated preference functions would differ in dispersion, with the sleep function being narrow and the one for the excited state relatively broad.

Arousal level also makes contributions to the complexities of particular psychological events. A stimulus without arousal-producing properties of its own will produce a less complex event during sleep than it will during a normal waking state. The Central Processor integrates specific and nonspecific material. Variation in arousal level amounts to variation in the amount of sensitization and thus of nonspecific material available to the Central Processor. Stimuli with arousal-producing properties simply add to the background arousal level of nonspecific material. The effect of arousal on complexity amounts to a shifting of the psychological complexity of the event toward the complex end of the scale. Although the amount of this shift must be determined empirically, one could speculate that it should be small compared to the amount of shift in optimal complexity level.

As a general state of the organism, arousal level can be influenced by external stimuli. Calm, relatively unvarying environments tend to induce low arousal levels, whereas rapidly changing, complex environments tend to produce higher levels of arousal. Yet arousal level is not bound to external stimuli. Individuals can be intensely active in quiet environments and can sleep in complex ones. Furthermore, arousal level is subject to a substantial degree of conscious control. We can adjust our arousal level to anticipated demands of future situations. If very intense effort is going to be required, we can try to pump ourselves up for it. If something much less will be required, we can try to get ourselves down for it. Performing these feats is possible for all of us; however, it is a skill that must be learned. Some of us learn easily, while others require amplification of normal biological feedback to recognize what it is they are trying to control.

### Arousal as an Empirical Variable

A major issue with respect to the measurement of arousal is one of generality versus specificity. Theories involving the concept of arousal tend to be stated in general terms. Hebb's conceptual nervous system (1955), Berlyne's optimal arousal theory (1960 and subsequently), and Malmo's activation theory (1959), among others, share with the Hedgehog a generalized role for an energetic, nonspecific arousal dimension. Empirically, the low end of the arousal dimension is represented by a sleep state. At the high end, the expectation is well described by Mackworth (1969):

> Under certain circumstances, an animal reacts to a stimulus with a widespread pattern of bodily changes. These include activation of the automatic system, mainly sympathetic, increase in muscle tension, orienting behavior toward the stimulus, and damping down of spontaneous synchronous rhythms of the brain. A hypothetical state of arousal has been postulated to explain this generalized response to stimuli which are novel, unexpected, complex, or significant [p.88].

This simple, unidimensional conception of arousal received support from the neurophysiological distinction between specific and nonspecific neural pathways as documented by Moruzzi and Magoun (1949). The reticular system appeared to have a general function that was relatively independent of the character of the stimulus input or the locus of specific activity in the brain. The distinction between specific and nonspecific neural activity is complemented by the concept of direct and indirect neural pathways (Groves & Thompson, 1970), as well as by a concept of general state, used by the same authors to refer to the general level of excitation, arousal, activation, and tendency to respond.

A necessary elaboration of the arousal concept involves conceptualizing inhibition as an active process, rather than as a passive process like fatigue (Mackworth, 1969, p. 90). Habituation is rapid to weak stimuli and slow to strong stimuli (Mackworth, 1969), occurs to regular light flashes but not to irregular ones (Fox, 1964), and is delayed when a decision of whether to respond is involved or when the events in question are complex rather than simple (Sokolov, 1963). The same response may be sensitized or habituated, depending on the procedure. For example, Pinsker, Hening, Carew, and Kandel (1973) sensitized the defensive withdrawal of gill and siphon in Aplysia by giving the animal four brief noxious stimuli each day for four days. The sensitization could last for up to three weeks. On the other hand, the same response was habituated by four ten-trial training sessions occurring 1½ hours apart, and the habituation lasted more than a week (Carew & Mandel, 1973).

Two different patterns of arousal to repetitive stimulation have been noted where the difference is indexed by temporal shifts in the amount or character of the arousal response. Mackworth (1969) notes two kinds of alpha blocking or EEG response. The generalized response is prolonged but disappears rapidly with repetition of the stimulus. The specific response in the part of the cortex specific to the stimulus mode is brief, but it occurs after many more repetitions of the stimulus than does the generalized response. Eventually, in a monotonous situation, the background alpha will itself disappear, and then the response to the stimulus may be the reappearance of the alpha waves. Mackworth cites Sharpless and Jasper (1956) as distinguishing two kinds of arousal response. One is a brief, phasic reaction that shows slow habituation (mediated through the diencephalon); this reaction is quickly restored by the lapse of a few minutes without stimulation. The second is a sustained tonic reaction that shows rapid habituation and that requires 15 minutes or more for restoration (mediated by the reticular formation).

Routtenberg (1968) has postulated two arousal systems that mutually inhibit each other. One is associated with the reticular activating system; it functions in response to high intensities of stimulation and serves to energize reactions. The second responds to low or moderate stimulus intensities, prolongs the effects of stimulation, and thereby serves to facilitate memory and the learning process.

Sokolov (1960, 1963, in Graham, 1973) sees arousal as a function of qualitative aspects of the stimulus rather than of the intensive aspects. A stimulus is interpreted in terms of a model that the central nervous system (CNS) has constructed. A match serves to dampen activities in nonspecific pathways, and a mismatch serves to amplify them. Signals of mismatch lead to elicitation of the orienting reflex. For Sokolov, the orienting reflex involves a generalized system of responses that include central, motor, and autonomic nervous system components that enhance stimulus reception.

The assumption of a simple linear dimension of arousal can be confounded by the properties of the physiological index used to measure or estimate it. For example, Mackworth (1969) points out that, although the evoked potential can be used to index the arousal properties of a stimulus, the enormously complex early components behave quite differently than do the later components of the same electrical response.

The complexity of the problem of measuring arousal can be illustrated by the use of the EEG as an index to distinguish the sleep state from the awake state and to distinguish depth of sleep. The awake or aroused state is characterized by a desynchronized EEG pattern showing highly variable fluctuations of low voltage. The sleep state is characterized by a high voltage, synchronous, slow wave pattern. Depth of sleep should therefore be represented by orderly variation in voltage, wave frequency, or both.

This simple scale of depth of sleep in terms of EEG is complicated by the discovery of rapid eye movement (REM) sleep. In the course of normal sleep, people undergo periods of very rapid eye movement. During these periods, the musculature, except for eye muscles, tends to go into an extremely relaxed condition, sensory thresholds in all modalities tend to rise to high values, frequency of dream reports on awakening tends to be very high, and the EEG pattern tends to show desynchronization and thus resemble the waking pattern. Thus, during REM sleep, the brain gives evidence of being awake, while the body gives evidence of being in the most relaxed state of all.

If EEG is to be used as the index of depth of sleep, then one might follow Dement and Wolpert (1958). Because the EEG pattern in the REM state most resembles the awake state, they placed it next to the awake state and used several EEG patterns of progressively slower wave form to distinguish four deeper states of sleep. In this system, there are thus six distinguishable levels of arousal—awake, REM sleep, and Levels 1, 2, 3, and 4 of non-REM sleep.

A behavioral index of sleep depth is the probability that a person will awaken in response to a controlled stimulus. Williams (1967) instructed subjects to awaken whenever a fixed tone came on and to ignore a neutral stimulus. He found that using probability of awakening as an index made REM the deepest of the sleep states. However, when he punished failure to awaken at the signal by applying shock, REM was intermediate between EEG Levels 1 and 2. These three orders are shown in Figure 10-1.

Williams and Williams (1966) have devised another test of EEG orderings of depth of sleep. This analysis is based on the logic that, if any particular order of EEG states represents a scale of depth of sleep, then a subject during normal sleep should change from any one state only to a state adjacent to it on the scale. They found it useful

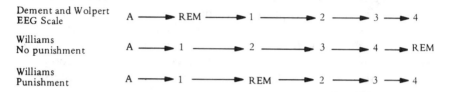

FIGURE 10-1. *Three Measures of Depth of Sleep. The order of depths of sleep taken from Dement and Wolpert (1958) are strictly in terms of the EEG pattern. The two scales from Williams and Williams (1966) are in terms of probability of being awakened by a standard stimulus. In the first, failure to awaken was not punished; in the second, failure to awaken was punished by shock.*

to use only four states, rather than the six previously described. They eliminated Level 1 because its frequency was too small to deal with, and they combined Levels 3 and 4. With the resulting four states, they generated a table of transitional probabilities of passing from one state to the other. The basic data for the first-order transitional probabilities for one subject during three nights of normal sleep are arranged in a diagram in Figure 10-2.

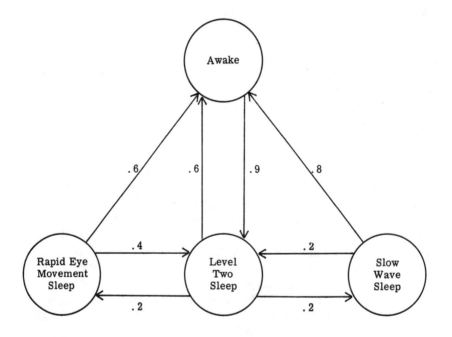

FIGURE 10-2. *Sleep State Transitional Probability Diagram. The diagram shows transitional probabilities of shifting from the awake state into three distinguishable sleep states and the probabilities of shifting from one sleep state to another. Data represent the sleep patterns of one subject for three nights. The data are taken from Williams and Williams, 1966.*

The two most obvious characteristics of transitions from one sleep state to another are that even these four states do not order themselves in a line from the awake state to a deep level of sleep and that the probabilities of going into a state and out of it tend to be different. The most probable sequence is from the awake state to Level 2 sleep and then back to the awake state. Both REM and slow wave sleep are entered only from Level 2. The most likely state to follow either is the awake state. It is most notable that there never appears to be a transition from REM to slow wave sleep or the reverse. Although other subjects show slightly different patterns, with some individuals showing some probability of going directly from the awake state to REM, the total lack of interchange between REM and slow wave sleep appears to be universal.

These facts must lead one to question either the concept of depth of sleep or the adequacy of the EEG measure. One, the other, or both must represent conditions that are more complex than can be represented by a simple linear scale.

Lacey (1967) has been particularly insistent that arousal and its indices constitute a complex problem. He points out that there are at least three different kinds of arousal—autonomic, electrocortical, and behavioral—that are functionally and anatomically separable by appropriate experimental means. Further, he says that there is strong neurophysiological and psychophysiological evidence that different fractions of autonomic, electroencephalographic, and motor responses are mediated separately, by perhaps intimately related but clearly dissociable mechanisms. Lacey also points out that various measures of autonomic state, such as blood pressure, heart rate, blood flow, sweat gland activity, and pupillary activity, are rarely correlated and that the patterns of reactions differ with different tasks. Elsewhere, the Laceys have noted that some autonomic indices are effectors (thus reflecting the state of the organism), and some operate to influence cortical activity. They argue that even the temporary hypertension and tachycardia observed in acute emotional states and in aroused behavior states may not be the direct indices of so-called "arousal" or "activation" that they are so often considered to be. Instead, they may be a sign of the attempt of the organism instrumentally to constrain, to limit, and to terminate the turmoil produced inside the body by appropriate stimulating circumstances.

Any summary of these considerations must be regarded as tentative, but some generalization seems justified and perhaps required. Where it is appropriate to consider arousal as a generalized state of the organism, the level of arousal is in all probability a balance between excitatory and inhibitory factors. Arousal can be varied by quantitative variation of stimulation (intensity) or by discrepancy between the present stimulus and the immediate past history of stimulation. Repeated stimulation can result in sensitization or habituation, and the rate of decline of sensitization or the appearance and persistence of habituation can vary over a wide range. It seems doubtful that any particular cognitive, behavioral, or physiological index of arousal will prove to have a completely general relation to the theoretical concept of arousal level. The extent to which a particular measure or index of arousal can be used to predict aspects of motivational state and learning is an empirical matter.

## EMPIRICAL STUDIES OF AROUSAL

Some questions concerning the generality of the concept of arousal can only be settled empirically. What follows is an account of a fairly large number of studies, many of which have not been previously published. They involve measures of skin resistance in humans, rats, and monkeys, heart rate in the rat, and electrical discharge frequency in the weak electric fish. Each measure was chosen with the expectation that it might be an adequate measure of the arousal level of the organism involved.

These studies were addressed to three questions. The first concerned the extent to which skin resistance in the rat and discharge frequency in the weak electric fish could be measured reliably and correlated with basic variables. The second question was the extent to which these measures could be meaningfully related to traditional manipulations of motivation and emotion and thus might reflect general arousal states in the organism. The third question concerned the correlation of such measures with aspects of learning and performance in more or less standard laboratory problems and therefore how arousal level is related to such problems.

### Skin Resistance in the Rat

Techniques for measuring skin resistance in the rat were developed by Kaplan and Kaplan (1962) and Kaplan and Hobart (1964), based on Lykken (1959). The rat constitutes an excellent choice as subject because of the vast quantity of data available on its behavior in fairly standard laboratory situations in which there is the possibility of monitoring skin resistance on a continuous basis in the freely moving animal.

It was not entirely certain at the outset that variation in skin resistance in the rat would reflect the emotional state of the animal. It is generally assumed that skin resistance changes in human subjects reflect, at least in part, activity in sweat glands in the skin. Rats are not believed to have thermoregulatory sweat glands, and there appears to be no histological evidence of their existence. However, there is equivocal evidence of some related activity.

Marzulli and Callahan (1957) report positive results in tests of capacity to sweat. With rats, they employed a starch-iodine test. The skin of the footpad was painted with a 2% solution of iodine in alcohol and then brushed with a 1:1 mixture of soluble starch and castor oil. When the animals were placed in a compartment heated to 100°F. with 70% humidity, small brown spots developed in the starch—the usual evidence of perspiration. Marzulli and Callahan report 35 to 52 active glands per square centimeter under these conditions. These positive results are encouraging even in the absence of histological evidence of sweat glands in the rat. It should be noted, however, that being placed in an oven is likely to be a frightening experience. It is therefore unclear whether the observed glandular activity was thermoregulatory in nature or the product of an emotional response.

There is some reason to believe that change in skin resistance in the rat might be a direct reflection of the state of the midbrain reticular activating system. For example, Bloch and Bonvallet (1959, 1960) have used skin resistance changes in the cat as a means of mapping the excitatory and inhibitory portions of the midbrain reticular. Their procedure is to implant a fixed electrode in the excitatory area. When stimulation is provided through this electrode, there is an immediate and marked drop in skin resistance in the cat's paw. A second, traveling electrode is then introduced and lowered step by step through the reticular. At each step, stimulation is applied through both electrodes. When the result of stimulating both was a drop in skin resistance, Bloch and Bonvallet assumed that both were in an excitatory portion. When stimulating both resulted in no change in skin resistance, they assumed that the traveling electrode was in an inhibitory portion. Such strong evidence of a direct connection between the excitatory portion of the reticular activating system and skin resistance changes in the cat creates a strong presumption of such a connection in the rat.

The basic procedure in measuring the skin resistance of a freely moving rat is to induce the animal to stand on two pieces of metal in such a manner that its body closes a circuit. The circuit involves a constant current of 10 to 50 microamperes ($\mu$A), with the value in any one arrangement fixed at one level, usually 10 $\mu$A. Variations in the amount of resistance the animal offers to the passage of current produce variations in the voltage.

Two platforms or floor arrangements were used in most of the studies I will report. One is the standard "shock grid floor" found in most commercial apparatus that provides for shocking the animal through the feet. The second could be used in a narrow alley or compartment. It consisted of two pieces of stainless-steel sheet metal arranged to form the floor of a maze alley except for a narrow separation in the middle of the alley. In this arrangement the animal must stand on two electrodes and provide contact when standing still.

There are a number of sources of possible artifact in a skin resistance record, where any variable that is not related to arousal would be considered an artifact. Various means were adopted to deal with them.

An obvious artifact could be produced by the accumulation of dirt on the grid floor or on the parallel strips. This problem was generally handled by frequent cleaning, a procedure that is effective in dealing with the slow accumulation of dirt. In other instances (for example, when shock was employed), there was the possibility of the instant appearance of urine or feces and thus the rapid accumulation of foreign matter on the electrode surfaces. This problem was dealt with in some instances by cleaning the surfaces and in others by a matter of logic. Urine and feces generally tend to reduce the area of contact and produce a higher resistance reading. If shock is employed, the fear induced produces a sharp drop in resistance. Thus, the effects of the artifact and the effects of the variable are of opposite sign. The effects of shock cannot be accounted for by the artifact of foreign matter on the grid floor.

Polarization of the grid or the strips is a persistent possible artifact. In the case of the parallel strips, the record would show a drop in resistance that tended to reach an asymptote some three to five seconds after the animal was placed in the apparatus. This was generally handled by retaining the animal in a starting box for a period and then ignoring the first 30 seconds or so of the record. When the problem was carried out on the grid floor, the animal was rarely still long enough to permit polarization, tending to shift back and forth from one pair of grids to another. Polarization obviously did occur and was uncontrolled. However, it is very doubtful that any of the results reported in these studies can be accounted for in this manner. In general, the recording period for a single measurement was two or more minutes long, and the changes involved were several orders of magnitude larger than that produced by polarization.

The two pieces of apparatus had different properties. The apparatus with the grid floor allowed the animal to roam freely but had the disadvantage of producing a very noisy record of skin resistance. Panel A of Figure 10-3 is such a record taken when an animal was subjected to shock. The highest points on the record, and therefore the lowest readings, represent moments when the animal is still. When contact with the grid is broken as the animal moves about, the resistance value goes to infinity, returning to a readable value when the animal again pauses. Generally, such records were read by taking the lowest value in a fixed period, usually two minutes. In this record, shocking the animal produced a sharp decrease in resistance that persisted over some period of time.

Panel B in the figure is a record of an animal running down a short length of runway to a water bottle, where it spent some time drinking. This record is running much faster than the record in Panel A. Whereas the upper record represents more than 80 minutes, the lower record represents approximately 40 seconds that the animal was in the apparatus. Although the second record is much cleaner

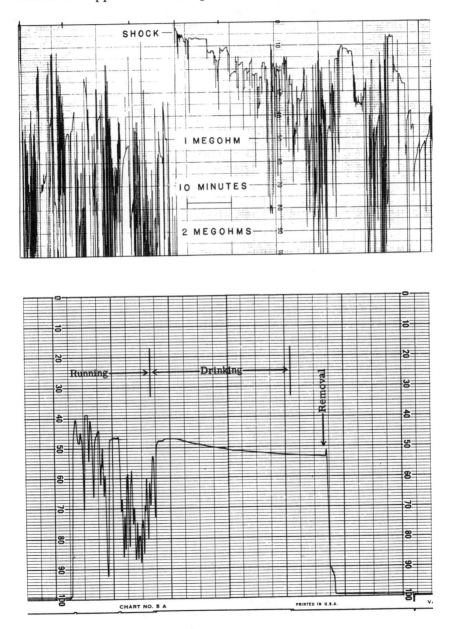

*FIGURE 10-3. Records of Skin Resistance in the Rat*

and apparently easier to interpret, it is obtainable only where the animal is confined in a narrow runway.

### Electrical Discharge Frequency
### in the Weak Electric Fish

The desirability of a continuous measure of arousal that might be obtained without interfering with the organism in such a way as to produce occultation of the phenomena being measured induced a developing interest in the work on the weak electric fish. Some species of fish transmit electrical pulses at very low voltages. They also bear receptors that are sensitive to some aspect of the resulting electrical field. A few of the species appear to vary the frequency of their electrical pulses under conditions that suggest that the frequency might reflect the arousal level of the animal. If so, it might be possible to monitor arousal level by the fairly simple expedient of placing electrodes in the fish tank and amplifying the output of the fish into some sort of recording device. The record might then be a continuous record of the arousal level of the animal. If the behavior of the animal could be observed accurately, then a correlation could be established between arousal level and the behavior.

Dewsbury (1965) gives a brief account of the place of electric fish among other species:

> It appears that on at least six different occasions, fishes have evolved organs which are capable of generating appreciable currents outside their bodies (Keynes, 1957). Today fish with electric organs are known to exist around the world, in salt water and in fresh, and in quite unrelated taxonomic groups. The two salt-water, elasmobranch families, the electric rays (*Torpedo* and *Narcine*) and skates (*Raia*), are found in most temperate oceans and seas. The lone marine teleost, the electric stargazer (*Astroscopus*), is found off the Atlantic and Pacific coast of southern North America. The electric catfish (*Malapterurus*), which was known to the ancient Egyptians, is found in the Nile and other African rivers. The maximum recorded discharges from the above-mentioned electric fishes range from four to 350 or more volts according to Keynes. In those fishes with the more powerful discharges it is clear that the electric organs serve as a potent offensive and/or defensive weapon. For those above-mentioned species which emit discharges of somewhat lesser intensity, the functions of the electrical systems are not understood. In all of these species the electric organs discharge during only a rather small portion of the animal's life.
>
> Two groups of electric fishes, the Mormyridae of Africa and the Gymnotidae of South America, possess electric organs which are almost continuously active. With the exception of the electric eel (*Electrophorus electricus*), which is a member of the gymnotid family, the maximum intensity of the discharge of these fishes as recorded in water is less than one volt. Both groups of fishes are found in turbid tropical rivers, and

both have evolved means of swimming which enable them to move while keeping a straight backbone.

Mortenson (1969) reviewed work on the possible significance of electrogenesis and electroreception in fish. He gives the following account:

... the volume of research on the behavioral significance of the weakly electric systems has been meager. Nonetheless, three hypotheses about the behavioral meaning of the electric systems may be readily discerned in the modest literature.

One hypothesis holds that the knifefishes and mormyroids can discriminate the conductivity of objects in water. Lissmann has developed this view. Briefly:

The electric current generated by the fish may be pictured as spreading out into the surrounding water in the pattern of lines that describes a dipole field. In a large volume of water containing no objects the field is symmetrical. When objects are present the lines of current will converge on those that have better conductivity and diverge from the poor conductors. Such objects alter the electric potential over the surface of the fish. If the fish could register these changes, it would have a means of detecting the objects [Lissmann, 1963, p. 52].

Consistent with this view is the observation by Lissmann and Machin that *Gymnarchus niloticus* can learn to discriminate objects immersed in water on the basis of their conductivity.

Presumably such a system could be used in navigation. There is an apparent limitation to such a function for knifefishes at least: some evidence exists that conductors or nonconductors can only influence the electrosensory system if they are very near to the fish. For example, Hagiwara and his colleagues (Hagiwara, Kusano, & Negishi, 1962; Hagiwara, Szabo, & Enger, 1965) found that conductors and nonconductors could enhance or depress lateral line activity in knifefishes only if the stimulus objects are fairly close to the animals. Perhaps then the knifefishes can only use their electrosensory system to navigate, discriminate, explore, and so forth when objects are close.

A second hypothesis is that the discharge may have a function in social behavior (Marler & Hamilton, 1966). Recently, an abstract (Cleworth, 1967) reporting a relationship between discharge rate and aggressive behavior has provided the first concrete evidence for this view. In one threat display, a dominant fish may cease discharging briefly and then resume firing. If the threatened fish does not retreat, it will then be attacked. Another threat display involves the production of an increase in rate. The attack of a larger or resident fish may be avoided if there is a cessation of discharge. Further research in this area of social behavior may be benefited by the popularization of certain species of weakly electric fish among the tropical fish enthusiasts. If the hobbyists succeed in breeding the animals, then it will be possible to relate discharge to sexual and possibly parental behavior.

A third hypothesis concerns those species of weakly electric fishes with a variable discharge rate. It has been stated that the rate of discharge changes with the "state of excitement" (Lissmann, 1963). All kinds of casual observations consonant with this view have been reported.

Figure 10-4 is a tracing of an oscillographic record of a single pulse of the knife fish, *Gymnotus carapo.* It is a diphasic pulse, and the direction of the initial deflection from zero is a function of the orientation of the fish relative to the electrodes. The recorded voltage varies as a function of the size of the tank and the distance and orientation of the electrodes. For this reason, the recorded voltage is relatively meaningless. The recorded voltage in the figure is approximately 1 millivolt, and the maximum recorded by us is about 10 millivolts. The frequency of output is subject to considerable variation in this species and tends to average around 35 to 55 cycles per second (cps).

Recording of the discharge frequency of the weak electric fish is relatively easy. Electrodes were placed in an electrically shielded tank. The amplified output was typically converted to audio for immediate monitoring, displayed on an oscilloscope, and fed into a frequency-to-voltage converter to produce a permanent record.

Visual observation of the fish was a very difficult problem that required several years for solution. *Gymnotus carapo* is apparently nocturnal. Whenever there is light in the room, the fish tends to sink to the bottom of the tank and rest without movement. In the dark, the fish is quite active most of the time. Numerous efforts were made to provide illumination that would permit a human observer to see while the fish remained active. After many failures, a solution was reached through the use of infrared illumination and remote TV observation. The aquarium was backlighted with a filter that trans-

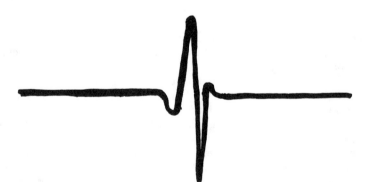

*FIGURE 10-4. Single Electric Organ Discharge Pulse of Gymnotus Carapo. (Redrawn from* Some Correlates of Electric Organ Discharge Frequency in Three Species of Electric Fishes, *by D. A. Dewsbury. Unpublished doctoral dissertation, University of Michigan, 1965. Reprinted by permission.)*

mitted a narrow band of infrared illumination to which the fish gave no signs of being sensitive. A TV camera sensitive to this band permitted monitoring of the behavior of the fish while simultaneously recording the frequency of its electrical emissions. The work done by Dewsbury did not have the benefit of this capacity for behavioral observation, but the later work of Mortenson, who developed the system, did have this facility.

### BASIC STUDIES

The primary interest in skin resistance in the rat and discharge frequency in the weak electric fish lies in the question of the relation of arousal to aspects of motivation, incentive, learning, and performance. However, it was necessary to carry out a number of studies to establish the basic properties of these indices, particularly the skin resistance measure. Although some of these studies are of little intrinsic interest, they represent information that is necessary for the interpretation of the more interesting studies.

### *Typical Values of Skin Resistance*

Skin resistance is measured in ohms. In standard usage, the most common value reported in the literature is the GSR (galvanic skin response). This value is typically the percent deflection or percent change in resistance produced by some stimulus or other relevant manipulation. The values of skin resistance (usually in ohms) that are needed to calculate a GSR value will be referred to as BRL (basic resistance level). In the studies reported here, the long time sample needed to obtain a useful value precludes (except in rare instances) the demonstration of a momentary effect of a stimulus. As a consequence, nearly all these studies involve comparisons of the resistance level over one relatively long period with the resistance level over another long period. Therefore, throughout this document, the basic measure of skin resistance to be reported is the BRL.

To give the reader a feeling for the kind of data obtained in skin resistance studies, data from three studies are shown in Table 10-1. The first study is one by Kaplan (1962, 1963) in which 56 animals were placed in Skinner Boxes for ten-minute periods. Kaplan averaged the three lowest values for the period. For various reasons, four records could not be used. The other two sets of data were obtained in two conditions of a study by B. E. Walker (Walker, 1969b). In that study, to be related later, 18 agouti hooded rats[1]

[1] The agouti hooded rat is a strain developed by Bruce E. Walker from successive crossbreeding of the original Lashley albino strain—a strain of brown laboratory rats imported from Germany by Professor Norman R. F. Maier—and the Long-Evans black hooded rat. The agouti rat is white, with a beige-colored hood and paritally pigmented eyes. It is generally less emotional than other strains, makes an excellent pet, tends to achieve better scores on most learning and performance problems, and is subject to Van Willerbrandt's disease.

TABLE 10-1. Typical Distributions of BRL Values. The table shows distributions of skin resistance values in ohms obtained in three conditions with different time samples in studies by Kaplan (1962, 1963) and by B. E. Walker (Walker, 1969b).

| Ohms | Kaplan | Walker Unweighted | Walker Weighted |
|---|---|---|---|
| 1,910,000–2,000,000 | | 1 | |
| 1,810,000–1,900,000 | | | |
| 1,710,000–1,800,000 | | | |
| 1,610,000–1,700,000 | | | |
| 1,510,000–1,600,000 | | 1 | |
| 1,410,000–1,500,000 | | 2 | |
| 1,310,000–1,400,000 | | 1 | |
| 1,210,000–1,300,000 | | | |
| 1,110,000–1,200,000 | | | |
| 1,010,000–1,100,000 | | | |
| 910,000–1,000,000 | | 1 | |
| 810,000– 900,000 | | | |
| 710,000– 800,000 | 1 | | |
| 610,000– 700,000 | | 2 | 1 |
| 510,000– 600,000 | 2 | 1 | |
| 410,000– 500,000 | 5 | 4 | 2 |
| 310,000– 400,000 | 10 | 8 | 5 |
| 210,000– 300,000 | 19 | 48 | 61 |
| 110,000– 200,000 | 11 | 3 | 3 |
| 0– 100,000 | 4 | | |
| N | 52 | 4 x 18 = 72 | 72 |

ran a short maze once a day for four days. The lowest value obtained during a one-minute period in the starting box was recorded. In the first condition, five or six of the 72 measurements appear to represent instances in which no valid measure was obtained. In the second condition, the animals were wearing saddles carrying lead weights. The effect of the weights was to lower the values and virtually eliminate artifacts. These and other data make clear that a fairly long time sample is required to obtain stable measures with this procedure.

### Diurnal Cycle

The diurnal cycle is the sine qua non of arousal. Unfortunately, it has not been possible to measure skin resistance in a sleeping rat under conditions in which there was any assurance of reasonable contact between the feet of the rat and the measuring grid. However, the diurnal cycle can be easily studied in the weak electric fish. A series of such studies was done. The first study (Dewsbury, 1965) involved three fish. These animals had been on a schedule of eight hours of light and 16 hours of dark for six months. Pulse frequency was then monitored continuously for 72 hours. It was quantified by taking the momentary pulse frequency 25 times per hour, averaging over the hours, and averaging again over the three animals for the three days. The result was the pattern shown in Figure 10-5. Pulse frequency was clearly higher during the dark period than during the period when there was light. Even though the diurnal cycle is apparent in the figure, the demonstration was not wholly satisfactory. Pulse frequency tended to fluctuate during both light and dark cycles, and, since at the time of the study the animal could not be observed, it was not known whether or not these fluctuations were correlated with fluctuations in the level of behavioral acitivity.

Later, Mortenson (1969), with the advantage of improved pulse frequency recording and the capacity for remote observation of the behavior of the animal, was able to improve on the analysis. Figure 10-6 is a tracing of the record of a shift from light to dark for one fish. Several characteristics are apparent in the record. When the light was turned off, the fish immediately became more active, and the frequency of discharge became more variable. Furthermore, there appear to be shifts from the resting frequency of about 40 cps to a higher frequency of about 45–50 cps in the last 30 minutes or so of the record shown. If a frequency of 40 cps represents an inactive state, and if frequencies of 45–50 cps represent an active state, then the fish appears to have been oscillating between active and inactive states. If so, then Dewsbury's measurement technique

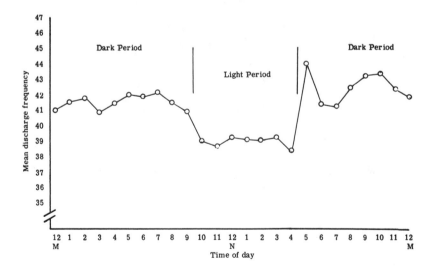

FIGURE 10-5. *Light/Dark Cycle in Weak Electric Fish. The figure shows mean values for three fish for three days, 25 measures per hour. (Adapted from* Some Correlates of Electric Organ Discharge Frequency in Three Species of Electric Fishes, *by D. A. Dewsbury. Unpublished doctoral dissertation, University of Michigan, 1965. Reprinted by permission.)*

would compare an inactive state in the light with an oscillating condition between active and inactive states in the dark. Mortenson was able to verify the fact that the oscillations seen on the left side of the record in Figure 10-6 actually did represent shifts between active and inactive states. While the fish was almost totally inactive in the light,

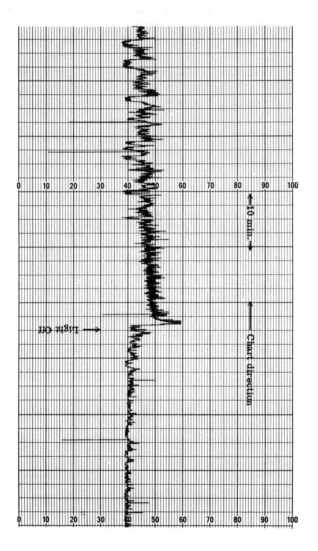

FIGURE 10-6. *Discharge Frequency Chart. Chart of frequency record for 90 minutes beginning in a light period and ending in a dark period for one* Gymnotus carapo. *(Adapted from* Determinants of Electrical Discharge Rate in Gymnotus Carapo, the Banded Knife Fish, *by F. J. Mortenson. Unpublished doctoral dissertation, University of Michigan, 1969. Reprinted by permission.)*

the oscillations in the dark periods represent a mixture of pulse frequency characteristic of active and inactive states.

To obtain a more precise correlation of periods of activity and inactivity, regardless of light condition, Mortenson (1969) studied six fish with a fine-grain analysis. Each fish was observed for three ten-minute periods during the middle of the light cycle and similarly during the dark cycle. The behavior of the fish could be classified as active or inactive with high reliability, and the behavioral state was continuously recorded during the observation periods.

This behavioral observation revealed that there were large individual differences between fish in the frequency of activity and inactivity. These differences are apparent in Table 10-2. There are

*TABLE 10-2.* Percent of Time Behaviorally Active in Darkness and Light

| Fish | Dark | Light |
|------|------|-------|
| C17 | 100.00 | 0.00 |
| C18 | 15.85 | 0.06 |
| C19 | 95.46 | 11.90 |
| C20 | 99.80 | 28.43 |
| C21 | 48.22 | 1.87 |
| C22 | 28.96 | 1.50 |

From *Determinants of Electrical Discharge Rate in Gymnotus Carapo, the Banded Knife Fish,* by F. J. Mortenson. Unpublished doctoral dissertation, University of Michigan, 1969. Reprinted by permission.

differences in activity between the light and dark periods, but the experimental operations did not produce pure examples of actual activity and inactivity in these animals.

In order to obtain a "pure" match between behavioral measures and pulse frequency measures, pulse frequencies can be sorted on the basis of the behavioral criterion. This has been done in Table 10-3. Despite the individual differences, there is clearly a difference

*TABLE 10-3.* Mean Rate of Discharge and Moment-to-Moment Variation in Active and Inactive Periods

| Fish | Dark | | | | Light | | | |
|------|------|--------|------|--------|------|--------|------|--------|
| | Active | | Inactive | | Active | | Inactive | |
| | Mean | Lambda | Mean | Lambda | Mean | Lambda | Mean | Lambda |
| C17 | 40.87 | 1.56 | | | | | | |
| C18 | 36.43 | 1.74 | 30.33 | 1.05 | | | 30.39 | 0.82 |
| C19 | 43.09 | 1.21 | 38.87 | 0.36 | 43.53 | 1.10 | 35.50 | 0.20 |
| C20 | 41.90 | 1.12 | | | 40.75 | 0.90 | 34.43 | 0.50 |
| C21 | 46.27 | 1.55 | 39.44 | 0.56 | 47.29 | 1.41 | 35.96 | 0.42 |
| C22 | 48.64 | 1.64 | 41.97 | 0.71 | 55.09 | 1.88 | 39.33 | 0.47 |

From *Determinants of Electrical Discharge Rate in Gymnotus Carapo, the Banded Knife Fish,* by F. J. Mortenson. Unpublished doctoral dissertation, University of Michigan, 1969. Reprinted by permission.

in frequency of electrical pulse between the active and inactive states. On the average, the difference is about 8 cps, with the more aroused state characterized by a frequency of about 44 cps and the less aroused state by a frequency of about 36 cps.

### Boredom

Most standard psychological experiments with rats require that the animal remain in a standardized environment for some period of time. Frequently they require the animal to have a number of trials and thus to be reintroduced to the same environment a number of times. In relating skin resistance to most psychological variables of interest, it is important to know whether skin resistance change is a simple function of the passage of time in an unvarying environment or whether it changes systematically when an animal is repeatedly placed in the same environment. The term *boredom* is a handy label for the conditions under consideration, and the use of that label here does not imply a real anthropomorphism.

Kaplan investigated this problem in one of the very early studies that has already been cited. She placed 56 animals one at a time in a picnic-type Skinner Box. Such boxes contain an inner plastic box that is about one cubic foot in size. The inner box has a variety of visible lights and levers, is lighted, and is provided with a ventilation fan that is relatively noisy but unvarying. Thus, random noises from outside are generally masked. Such an environment induces a certain amount of exploration on the part of the animals that will subside within a few minutes. With repeated experience, the period of exploration is likely to grow shorter each day.

The animals in the Kaplan study were left in the boxes for 30 minutes per day for three days. During this period, there was no other manipulation of the animal or the environment. The mean resistance levels are shown in Figure 10-7. A single measurement was taken during the first ten minutes and another during the last ten minutes of each of the three days by the method previously described (averaging the three lowest points in the ten-minute record). As can be seen in the figure, there is a significant rise in skin resistance over days; the difference between the two plotted curves reveals the rise within days. Kaplan reports significant *t* tests between Days 1 and 3 in both curves, and between each of the three pairs of points within days.

Again, estimates of the relation between time units and BRL are quite variable. Within days, the differences between the points are approximately 55,000, 64,000, and 83,000 ohms. Since the two measures average 20 minutes in separation, a best guess of 60,000 per 20 minutes would indicate a conservative estimate of a rise in BRL of 3000 ohms per minute in this environment. The changes between days are also variable, being approximately 47,000 and 26,000 ohms

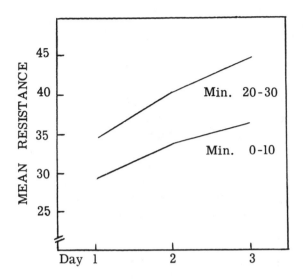

*FIGURE 10-7. BRL and Boredom in the Rat. The figure displays mean resistance (BRL) in 10,000-ohm units. Animals were confined to a Skinner Box for 30 minutes per day for three days. Plotted values are for the first ten minutes and the last ten minutes for each day. (From "Rat Basal Resistance Level under Stress and Nonstress Conditions," by R. Kaplan,* Journal of Comparative and Physiological Psychology, *1963, 56(4), 775-777. Based on* A New Measure of Motivation in Rats, *by R. Kaplan. Unpublished doctoral dissertation, University of Michigan, 1962. Reprinted by permission.)*

in the first measurement period and 56,000 and 45,000 ohms in the second measurement period. A crude and conservative estimate might therefore be an expected rise of about 45,000 ohms per 30-minute day. Thus, the effect of a boring environment on skin resistance in the rat is in the direction to be expected if BRL is a measure of arousal level in the animal.

### Handling

When a rat is picked up by an experimenter for any reason, it seems likely that a change will be produced in the arousal level of the animal. The amount of change might vary considerably with the state of the animal before it is picked up and the manner in which the animal is handled by the experimenter. Since animals are handled routinely in nearly every experiment, it is important to know whether this routine handling produces a change in the skin resistance or BRL.

In a study designed to measure BRL during the course of learning, extinction, and relearning of a straight alley maze (B. E. Walker & Walker, 1964), handling was made an independent variable in the following manner. On each of the 22 trials for 25 animals, a five-minute waiting period was instituted in the starting compartment of a straight alley maze. Half of the animals were removed by the experimenter during the second minute, and the other half were removed during the fourth minute. It was then possible to measure the amount of drop in BRL between the first and third minutes in one group and between the third and fifth in the other.

The effects of handling are apparent in Figure 10-8. Translated into ohms, the drops in value are approximately 32,000 ohms in the first group and about 52,000 ohms in the other. The only meaning that these values can have is that they are relatively large. The particular experimenter in this instance has a very gentle hand with rats and probably produces a minimum of arousal. Other experimenters have been known to produce much greater effects even while attempting to be as gentle as possible.

Very little can be said concerning the recovery rate. Under normal circumstances one could expect BRL to increase over the five-minute period, because the environment of the starting box is unvarying and probably boring. Thus, the decreases in BRL seen in the figure probably replace increases that would have occurred otherwise. For this reason, an estimate of a 50,000-ohm decrease

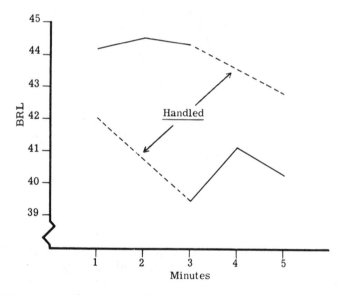

FIGURE 10-8. Effect of Handling by the Experimenter on BRL. The figure displays mean BRL values (in 20,000-ohm units) of two groups of rats handled either during the second minute or the fourth minute of a five-minute delay period in the starting box. (Redrawn from "Learning Extinction, and Relearning of Running and BRL in a Segmented Straight Alley," by B. E. Walker and E. L. Walker, Psychological Record, 1964, 14, 507-513. Reprinted by permission.)

in BRL as a function of handling (and an unknown recovery rate) is about the best estimate that is available.

### Stimulus Change

It is of interest whether simple stimulus change also produces a drop in skin resistance. In studying handling, the amount of change is gross, and it could possibly involve threat not involved in a simpler environmental change. Furthermore, in studying handling, the measurement is of necessity taken some time after manipulation.

Our efforts to determine the effects of stimulus change have met with mixed results. The first study yielded effects of stimulus change that were profound and reliable. A substantial second effort produced results that were entirely negative.

Positive results were obtained in a study of stimulus change and estrus in rats. In this study, which will be reported in detail in the section on biological drives, six male and 14 female rats were tested. They were placed in Skinner Boxes for 25 minutes per day for two days before testing began. On the next five days, they were also placed individually in the boxes for 25 minutes. To produce stimulus change, the outer doors of the picnic-like boxes were opened during the 11th and 12th minutes. They were then closed for 11 minutes and opened again for the final two minutes of the 25-minute period.

The result of the stimulus change operation is clear in the upper portion of Figure 10-9. The upper curve, for the female animals, shows decreases of 180,000 ohms and 45,000 ohms for the two openings of the door. The lower curve, for the male animals, shows decreases in BRL of 190,000 and 125,000 ohms for the two manipulations. Furthermore, in data not shown in the figure, the amount of change in the female animals varied with the stage of estrus, with little or no change occurring during metestrus and the largest stimulus change effect occurring during diestrus.

Negative results were obtained by Dewsbury (Walker, 1969b) in a series of unpublished studies, to be discussed later, of the effects of time of food and water deprivation. A sample of Dewsbury's results is in the lower portion of Figure 10-9. In these studies, Dewsbury was following the general procedure of depriving animals of food or water and testing for differences in BRL by placing the animals in the Skinner Boxes for periods of 20 minutes. In some studies he introduced white noise during the 11th and the 16th minutes and observed no effect of the stimulus change. In one instance, he also used the same stimulus change procedure employed in the earlier study—opening the outer door of the box. Again, no effect of stimulus change was observed.

No satisfactory resolution of the discrepancy between the two sets of results has been achieved. Dewsbury's animals were

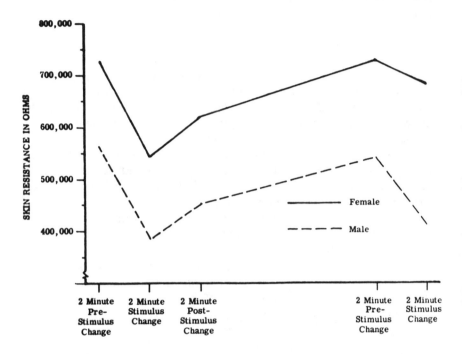

BRL AS A FUNCTION OF TIME AND THE INTRODUCTION OF WHITE NOISE

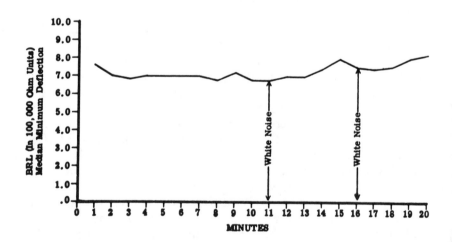

FIGURE 10-9. BRL Response to Stimulus Change. The upper panel is adapted from "Skin Resistance in Relation to Stimulus Change and Estrus in Rats," by E. L. Walker, A. H. Cohen, and C. L. Doyle, Psychological Record, 1964, 14, 25-29. The lower panel showing no effect is from the work of Dewsbury (Walker, 1969b).

generally in the boxes for suitable lengths of time and for a number of days. The number of animals and the number of observations were suitably large. The levels of BRL when the stimulus changes were introduced were high enough to suggest boredom—in the figure, 700,000 to 800,000 ohms on the average. Experimenter differences seem an unlikely explanation, since the measurements in both sets of studies were taken some minutes after the last contact between the animal and the experimenter. This unresolved discrepancy was a major factor in a decision to suspend journal publication until a substantial number of studies could be completed and subjected to comparative analysis.

No such ambiguity appeared in a series of studies of the effect of a variety of stimulus change operations on the pulse frequency of *Gymnotus carapo.* Dewsbury (1965) tested the response to auditory stimuli, which consisted of the sound of a buzzer just outside the tank, the sound of the aerator in the tank, or the two stimuli in combination. He tested each of his three subjects on two days between 10:30 A.M. and noon in the light. Within each day, the stimuli were presented nine times alone and nine times in combination for a total of 27 stimulations. Each stimulus was on for ten seconds. Within each block of nine trials, each stimulus pattern was presented three times in an order determined by a table of random numbers for each block for each animal. Intertrial intervals of 60, 75, 90, 105, and 120 seconds were randomly assigned to adjacent blocks of five trials. The records were read by taking the maximum frequency in successive ten-second periods from 30 seconds before stimulus onset to 50 seconds after.

As shown in Figure 10-10, the stimuli produced a large increase in the discharge frequency. Either stimulus alone produced an increase of about 12 or 13 cps, while both together produced an increase of 17 or more cps. Somewhat surprisingly, there was little or no adaptation to the stimuli either within a day's 27 trials of testing or between the two days. An analysis of variance showed that the effect of the two stimuli together was significantly different from the effect of either alone, but no effect of repeated experience was significant.

Mortenson conducted a number of preliminary studies using various tones for stimuli. With a single animal as subject, he found habituation. He used 300- or 400-cps tones and presented a series of 20-second stimuli. The series contained 30 stimuli with an average intertrial interval of 82.5 seconds. On the basis of this pilot work, a formal experiment to demonstrate habituation to auditory stimuli seemed appropriate.

Mortenson used a 300-cps tone through a speaker located seven inches from the center of the back of the aquarium. The duration of each tone was 20 seconds. A test session consisted of a block of 30

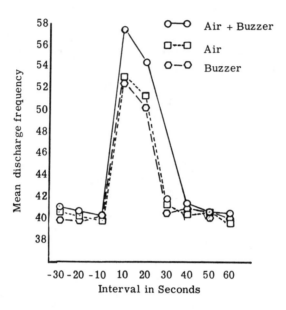

FIGURE 10-10. *Response to Auditory Stimuli in the Fish. The figure displays mean maximum electric organ discharge frequency as a function of stimulus change and successive ten-second intervals surrounding stimulus onset. (From Some Correlates of Electric Organ Discharge Frequency in Three Species of Electric Fishes, by D. A. Dewsbury. Unpublished doctoral dissertation, University of Michigan, 1965. Reprinted by permission.)*

tones, with interstimulus intervals of five, ten, 20, 40, 80, and 160 seconds presented in random order within a block of six intervals. Each of the six subjects was given six testing sessions, which occurred midway in the light and dark periods for three successive days. The data for one subject were lost because of apparatus failure, and only five fish are represented in the results. The results were measured by comparing the discharge rate in the two-second period before the stimulus onset with the discharge rate during the first two seconds of the stimulus.

The primary result is shown in Figure 10-11. The tone produced a significant increase in discharge rate in both the active and inactive states. The increases are not as great as those observed by Dewsbury, but the stimuli were very different in the two studies. In addition, the data in Figure 10-11 display some interesting secondary characteristics. If the tone was presented while the fish was in an inactive state, the response was large, but the animal never became active in response to the presentation of the tone. If the inactive state is analogous to sleep, then the animal never woke up in response to the alarm clock of the tone. The tone was greeted by a rise of 3 or

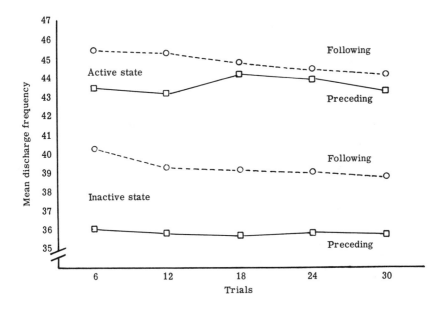

*FIGURE 10-11. Discharge Frequency Changes in Response to Tones. The figure displays the highest rate during two seconds preceding and following stimulus onset during active state (upper pair of curves) and inactive state (lower pair of curves). (From* Determinants of Electrical Discharge Rate in Gymnotus Carapo, the Banded Knife Fish, *by F. J. Mortenson. Unpublished doctoral dissertation, University of Michigan, 1969. Reprinted by permission.)*

4 cps in the discharge frequency, followed by an immediate return to the resting frequency of the inactive state. When the tone was presented while the fish was in an active state, the response was an increase of from 1 to 2 cps.

It was also observed that the size of the response to the stimulus was in part a function of the frequency at the time of onset of the stimulus. Table 10-4 contains the correlations run on the data for each fish for the two states independently.

The simplest conclusion possible from these data appears to be that there is a controlling mechanism governing the upper level of response to stimulation. Thus, the active state is represented by a narrow range of response frequencies, the inactive state is represented by another relatively narrow band, and the two ranges do not overlap. In an analogy with sleep and waking, the two states appear to represent a two-state system, with control mechanisms holding the arousal level within upper and lower limits within each state.

In contrast to Dewsbury's results, Figure 10-11 shows some evidence of adaptation to the repeated presentation of the tone. One possible explanation for this discrepancy is in terms of stimulus

*TABLE 10-4.* Correlations between Initial Discharge Rate and Magnitude of Increase in Response to the Tone for Active and Inactive States

| Fish | Inactive | Active |
|------|----------|--------|
| C17 | - .56 | - .46 |
| C18 | - .54 | - .69 |
| C19 | - .53 | - .37 |
| C21 | - .65 | - .63 |
| C22 | - .69 | - .66 |

Adapted from *Determinants of Electrical Discharge Rate in Gymnotus Carapo, the Banded Knife Fish,* by F. J. Mortenson. Unpublished doctoral dissertation, University of Michigan, 1969. Reprinted by permission.

intensity. There is little profit in attempting to compare the physical intensities of a buzzer, a tone, and an aerator, but the magnitudes of response in the two studies tend to indicate that the stimuli in the Dewsbury study were more intense. If so, adaptation might have occurred with a more extended series of stimuli.

In the Mortenson study, there was experimental control of the intertrial interval with separations within a day ranging from five seconds to 160 seconds. Between days there was a separation of about 40,000 seconds. Figure 10-12 shows the differential effects of variation in the intertrial interval. Very little effect is evident, and what little there appears to be in the figure is not supported by statistical test. Intertrial intervals in this range seemed to have no demonstrable effect on the magnitude of the response to the tone.

One hypothesis concerning the function of the electrical discharge in the weak electric fish is that solid objects distort the electrical field produced by the discharges and that the fish can detect such disturbances. The fish might therefore be able to use this sensory system to detect the presence and character of objects in the immediate environment.

Dewsbury devised a test of the response to the presence of a solid object, in this case a metal spoon, and made a special effort to determine whether adaptation in the response to this object might occur. The spoon was attached to a piece of string and suspended over the tank so that it could be lowered gently into the water from outside the room.

A trial consisted of lowering the spoon into the tank and withdrawing it ten seconds later. Six trials were given each day for the first 30 days of the study. The trials occurred in the light phase of the cycle between noon and 5:00 P.M. This phase of the study was designated Part I. The six trials were separated by four, five, six, seven, or eight minutes, with the interval randomly assigned. In Part II, 20 trials per day were given for six days, with the same intertrial intervals again randomly assigned. In Part III, 20 trials per day for six days were again given, but the intertrial intervals

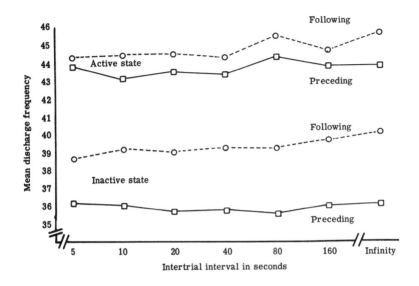

FIGURE 10-12. *Effect of Intertrial Interval on Response to Tones. The figure displays the highest rate in two seconds preceding and following stimulus onset as it varies with the length of the intertrial interval. (From* Determinants of Electrical Discharge Rate in Gymnotus Carapo, the Banded Knife Fish, *by F. J. Mortenson. Unpublished doctoral dissertation, University of Michigan, 1969. Reprinted by permission.)*

were shortened to 60, 75, 90, 105, and 120 seconds. These intervals were again randomly assigned within five-trial blocks. The records were read by taking the maximum discharge frequency in each of ten intervals of ten seconds each beginning 30 seconds before the spoon was lowered into the tank.

The responses of the fish to the introduction of the spoon in the tank in the three parts of the study are shown in Figure 10-13. In each part of the study there was a marked increase in discharge frequency when the spoon was inserted in the tank. Analysis of the effects of repeated introduction of the spoon into the tank did not reveal a statistically significant adaptation to the stimulus even in the third part of the study, in which the 20 trials per day for six days were given with an average intertrial interval of 90 seconds.

Mortenson carried out a series of experiments involving the introduction of aluminum or plexiglass objects in the tank in an effort to establish a correlation between exploratory behavior, which he could observe even in the dark, and discharge frequency. By introducing the object at a fixed point in the center of the tank and then observing the physical position of the fish, he could determine

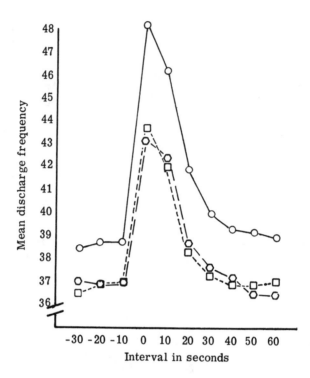

*FIGURE 10-13. Response of the Weak Electric Fish to a Metallic Object. The figure displays the mean maximum electric organ discharge frequency in successive ten-second intervals surrounding stimulus onset as a function of successive parts of the study, with parts differing in number and spacing of stimuli. (From* Some Correlates of Electric Organ Discharge Frequency in Three Species of Electric Fishes, *by D. A. Dewsbury. Unpublished doctoral dissertation, University of Michigan, 1965. Reprinted by permission.)*

the orientation of the fish to the object and the distance between the object and the fish. In the preliminary studies there was some difficulty in determining the first sensory contact between the fish and the object, because the silhouette character of the observation situation did not yield information on the relative depth (distance from the camera) of the fish and object. Nonetheless, there were consistent findings for all subjects.

The fish spent more time in the vicinity of the stimulus in the first ten minutes after it was observed to make its first contact with (discover?) the object than it had spent in the same environment prior to contact. The time spent in that vicinity during the first five minutes after contact was greater than the time spent in the second five minutes. Thus, in all cases, the introduction of a novel aluminum or plexiglas object produced investigative behavior that declined over a ten-minute period. These behavioral relations were exactly paralleled in discharge rate. The rate went up on first contact with the objects and slowly declined during the ten minutes after contact while the fish was exhibiting rapid oscillations in approach and avoidance behavior.

On the basis of these preliminary findings, a formal experiment was designed. A frame was built to fit the top of the tank that would permit a plexiglas plate to be dropped into a fixed position in the center of the tank from left to right and extending from the front to the back of the tank in the line of sight of the TV camera. Before dropping, the plate was suspended three inches above the water. After it was dropped, it rested 1½ inches below the surface with its lower edge 4½ inches from the bottom. The grid that was on the paper covering the lights divided the tank into 14 squares, each 3 x 3 inches. These were in two rows of seven squares each, and the plexiglas plate, when dropped, came to rest with its lower edge in the center of the middle square in the upper row. The fish was said to be in contact with the stimulus when it appeared in the same square as the stimulus.

Each of the six fish was observed three times in the light and three times in the dark on three successive days. Observation periods were for 30 minutes per session, each period being divided into a ten-minute prestimulus period, a ten-minute stimulus period, and a ten-minute poststimulus period. The only deviations from this pattern were minor ones arising from the rule that the stimulus was neither introduced nor withdrawn while the fish was in the stimulus square. The plate was introduced by releasing it from outside the room. It could then drop the 3 inches to the water and 1½ inches below the surface, making a total drop of 4½ inches. Apparently, these characteristics of stimulus presentation were important, for the results of the formal study were quite different from the results of the preliminary observations.

In the dark, only one of the six fish showed the expected pattern of exploring the stimulus in the ten-minute period following its introduction with the exploration accompanied by an elevated discharge frequency. Four of the fish showed a reverse pattern at least once. The reverse pattern was to become inactive within 15 seconds of the presentation of the stimulus. The fish would sink to the bottom of the tank in the characteristic position, with the anal fin in the sand. Assumption of this position was accompanied by a reduction in discharge frequency to the rate characteristic of the inactive state. One fish became inactive once, one became inactive twice, and the other two became inactive three times. The average duration of the inactive state was 281.33 seconds. The sixth fish showed still a different pattern. It remained active, but it avoided the stimulus square. It spent an average of 83 seconds in the stimulus square before the introduction of the stimulus, but, while the stimulus was present, it spent an average of only 28 seconds there.

When the stimulus was introduced during the light period, and thus when the fish were nearly universally inactive, an interesting effect was observed. Introduction of the stimulus produced a reduction in the variability of the discharge. Mean lambda before the introduction of the plate was about .65; in the ten minutes of stimulus presentation and in the ten minutes after its withdrawal, the mean lambda was about .35. If those few occasions when the fish was in an active state before stimulus presentation are eliminated, then the mean lambda before stimulus presentation was about .55 lambda and again about .35 in the other two periods. These differences are all statistically significant.

Thus, introducing the plexiglas plate by dropping it into the tank with a splash tended to make active fish inactive and inactive fish less variable in the discharge frequency. In other words, the stimulus tended to produce a hushed, freezing behavior. This behavior might be similar to the freezing behavior observed in many animals in response to sudden stimuli, or it might be similar to the death-feigning behavior of some marsupials. Freezing behavior is generally rigid and alert, whereas death-feigning behavior appears abnormally relaxed. There is no obvious basis for choosing between the two in this case.

In summary, the introduction of foreign objects into the tank produced two patterns of behavior. One was an exploratory investigation of the object that was accompanied by an increase in the discharge frequency. The other was an immediate change to an inactive behavioral state, accompanied by a reduction of discharge frequency and a reduction in its variability—a hushed state resembling either the freezing behavior of startled animals or the feigned death of marsupials.

### Effect of Weight
### of the Animal on Skin Resistance

Although it is not intrinsically interesting, it is necessary to know the effect of the weight of an animal on skin resistance, since weight covaries with variables of interest, such as sex differences. It is obvious that the amount of resistance that will be recorded will vary as a function of the weight of the animal. A human observer can make contact on the grids or on the parallel strip bars and induce the resistance reading to fluctuate by varying the amount of pressure exerted at the points of contact. There are two general ways of determining the magnitude of this effect in experiments with animals. One is to weigh a group of animals and take skin resistance measures under a set of standard conditions. The two values can then be correlated, and a regression equation can be used to evaluate the quantitative relationship between weight and

BRL. The other class of procedure is to induce weight differences—for instance, by attaching standard weights to the animal. The effect of weight on skin resistance can then be seen in differences in value between readings with and without the weights attached to the same animal. Both of these techniques can be employed in a single study (B. E. Walker, in Walker, 1969b).

In the studies to be reported, weighting was accomplished in the same way in which horses are handicapped in handicap races. Small "saddles" were made for the animals to wear on all trials. On some trials, fish weights were inserted in small pockets in the saddles to increase the weight of the animal and thus the pressure exerted against the grid floor. The results can be seen in Figure 10-14.

Skin resistance was significantly lower during trials in which the animals carried small lead weights in the pockets of the saddles than it was during trials without the weights. The mean weight difference was approximately 35 grams. There is one obvious anomaly in the BRL curves on the left in the figure: the curve for the weighted condition drops unexpectedly during the last four trials. The post hoc explanation is that the 40 grams of weight that the animals

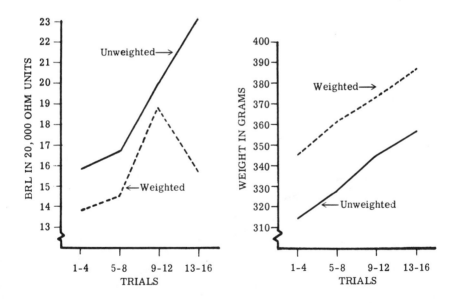

FIGURE 10-14. *Skin Resistance and Weight. The figure on the left shows the skin resistance of animals while carrying weights (35 grams) compared to the skin resistance of the same animals when they were not carrying weights. The figure on the right shows the mean weights throughout the experiment, again divided on the basis of being with or without weights added to the saddles. (From B. E. Walker, reported in Walker, 1969b.)*

gained during the experiment made the saddling and weighting process stressful. Whatever its source, the unexpected drop vitiated the hope of establishing a quantitative relation between weight and resistance. The four estimates obtained from the figure—1100, 1300, 700, and 4000 ohms per gram—are too variable to be used for this purpose.

The second approach to the problem of the relationship between weight and skin resistance is to examine the relationship between individual differences in weight and individual differences in skin resistance. It is apparent in Figure 10-14 that major changes in both weight and skin resistance were occurring during the course of the experiment. Therefore, correlations were run on data samples at selected points in the course of the study that did not involve great changes in either BRL or weight. Three correlations were run on three sets of data, all involving trials when weights were not employed. The results can be seen in Figure 10-15.

On the first two trials (both run on the same day), the correlation was -.67. The slope of regression line yields an estimate of approximately 720 ohms per gram. Measures taken on trials 11-14 (trials 3-6 in Figure 10-14) yield a correlation of -.47 and an estimate of about 650 ohms per gram. The correlation on trials 23-24 (trials

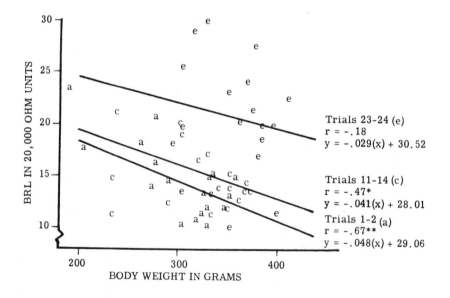

*FIGURE 10-15. Individual Differences in Skin Resistance and Weight. The figure displays correlations between individual differences in weight and skin resistance on selected trials with no artificial weights involved. (From B. E. Walker, reported in Walker, 1969b.)*

15–16 in Figure 10-14) is only –.18, and the slope of regression line yields an estimate of approximately 500 ohms per gram.

Thus, the manipulation of weights by means of weighted saddles yielded estimates of 700, 1100, 1300, and 4000 ohms per gram, and the individual difference analysis yielded estimates of 500, 650, and 720 ohms per gram. Since the one estimate from the manipulation of weights is probably in part a function of the inadvertent stress on the animal, it can probably be rejected. Since the other three estimates were also obtained immediately after the insertion of weights, any mild stress this operation might have caused would have tended to lower the resistance level compared to trials on which there were no weights. Therefore, all the estimates taken from the weight manipulation are probably high. The variation in the estimates makes it clear that no simple translation of ohms into grams is reasonable.

One can conclude, however, that skin resistance does vary significantly as a function of the weight of the animal. It will therefore be necessary to take possible variation of weight into account in all studies in which it could be a factor. If one had to make an estimate of the quantitative relationship between weight and BRL, about the best guess that one could achieve from this study would be that 1 gram in weight is equal to from 500 to 1000 ohms.

### Individual Differences

It is a common observation that there are observable differences in "emotionality" among rats that are of the same sex and strain and that have a common heritage and similar histories. Some are calm and stoic when handled; others are likely to be skittish. Some are quite safe to handle, and some are likely to bite the experimenter. It is therefore of interest to know whether there are individual differences in skin resistance that might reflect these differences in emotional disposition.

A fairly exhaustive analysis (Walker, 1969b) failed to establish such differences unequivocally. Individual differences in BRL show positive correlations when the measurements are taken under similar conditions, but they are of a magnitude that one might expect from weight differences. On the other hand, measures taken under quiet conditions and measures taken immediately after the animals have been shocked appear to be essentially uncorrelated. Therefore, no clear individual differences in BRL based on emotionality were found.

### Sex Differences

There are probably sex differences in skin resistance, with male animals showing lower resistance. In the upper portion of Figure 10-9, clear differences can be seen between BRL measures for male rats and those for female rats. The average difference in the figure is approximately 186,000 ohms. The average weight difference between males and females is 40–60 grams. At 50 grams, weight would have to produce a difference of 3720 ohms per gram to account for the difference. This is far in excess of the average of 625 ohms per gram found in the study of individual differences in weight and BRL.

### Developmental Differences in Skin Resistance

There are a number of reasons one might expect to find differences in skin resistance with age differences. First, there are data from Richter (1950) showing that activity level varies with the age of the animal, increasing up to a point and decreasing later in life. Data from Candland and Campbell (1962) show a similar pattern for general activity and measures of emotionality in the rat in an open field situation. If skin resistance is a measure of arousal, one might expect to see skin resistance fall and then rise with age in the rat. Further, there have been a number of studies, reviewed by Duffy (1962), showing that skin resistance does vary with age in humans.

Dewsbury (Walker, 1969b) made substantial efforts to measure developmental changes in skin resistance over the first few months of life, actually 27 to 125 days. During this period, skin resistance could be expected to fall, on the basis of the expected increase in activity level. We know from previous studies that the increasing weight of the animal should also produce a decrease in skin resistance. The results shown in Figure 10-16 generally show the expected drop. By use of a regression equation, Dewsbury was able to show that the drop could not be attributed exclusively to weight differences. A prediction of skin resistance from weight alone would lead one to expect a drop to occur much earlier than it actually did. The figure also shows sex differences, as well as differences attributable to the amount of handling the animal received. Handling produces an increase in arousal and thus a decrease in skin resistance. With repeated handling, less and less arousal results. In the figure, 41 males and 27 females are represented. Of these, 25 were tested at 27 days of age and retested twice more, 21 were tested for the first time at 76 days of age and were retested once, and 22 were tested for the first time at 125 days of age. The magnitudes of the various effects in combination are apparent in the figure. Especially clear are the effects of repeated experience, which produced increases in skin resistance that were more than enough to overcome the effects of increased maturity and increased weight.

Although the magnitude of the developmental effect cannot be estimated from these data in the face of the confounding of weight changes, sex differences, and the effects of handling, there is little doubt that there is a developmental decrease in resistance.

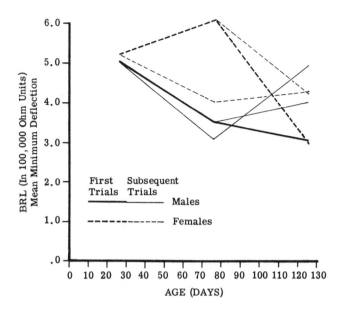

*FIGURE 10-16. Developmental Changes in Skin Resistance. The data are plotted separately by sex of the animal and according to whether the measurement was a first test or subsequent test in the apparatus. (From Dewsbury, reported in Walker, 1969b.)*

The presumption is at least strong enough to make it imperative that the age of the organism be carefully controlled in experiments in which it might otherwise covary with the variables of interest.

### Early Experience and BRL

It is fairly well established that variation in the amount of early stimulation of rats can produce differences in emotionality in adulthood. In one of the most commonly used forms of experimental manipulation, rats are removed from the home cage once a day during the first few days after birth and placed for brief periods in individual containers. Although this class of manipulation has been shown to have many physiological effects (Levine, 1962), the major effect is generally taken to be a decrease in emotionality as indicated by amount of activity in an open field and the number of fecal boluses left in the field. For example, Denenberg and colleagues (1967) found that rats handled during the first ten days of life defecated significantly less in the open field than did rats handled during the first 20 days of life or rats that had not been handled at all.

If skin resistance as measured by the Kaplan technique reflects relative emotionality, and if the Denenberg early-experience manipulation affects emotionality, then rats handled in this manner should show higher skin resistance later in their development than animals that have not been handled. Dewsbury (Walker, 1969b) carried out a study in which he handled some animals once a day for the first ten days after birth. They were placed individually in a large glass jar that had a layer of sawdust at the bottom; after three minutes they were returned to the mother. Skin resistance of both the handled and the control animals was measured on the 43rd day after birth. The animals were placed individually in a Skinner Box for 20 minutes each. The results in Table 10-5 show no statistically significant differences between the two groups.

*TABLE 10-5.* Effects of Early Handling Experience on Skin Resistance

| Variable | Handled | Not Handled |
|---|---|---|
| Number of litters | 3 | 4 |
| Number of animals | 28 | 33 |
| Mean litter size | 9.33 | 8.25 |
| Number of males | 14 | 13 |
| Number of females | 14 | 20 |
| Mean weight in grams, Day 43 | 81.6 | 83.7 |
| Mean weight, males | 82.6 | 89.4 |
| Mean weight, females | 80.6 | 80.1 |
| BRL measures (in 20,000-ohm units) | | |
| First 5 minutes | 30.2 | 31.9 |
| Second 5 minutes | 30.1 | 32.9 |
| Third 5 minutes | 30.0 | 31.9 |
| Fourth 5 minutes | 32.0 | 34.7 |
| 20-minute period | 27.3 | 27.2 |
| Males | 27.1 | 27.0 |
| Females | 27.5 | 27.3 |
| Mean boluses | 0.82 | 0.39 |
| Correlations — weight and BRL | | |
| All subjects | −.17 | |
| Males | −.23 | |
| Females | −.10 | |

From a study by Dewsbury, reported in Walker, 1969b.

### Selective Breeding for High and Low BRL

Rats have been bred for a variety of behavioral characteristics. Hull once developed a strain of emotional rats, and Tryon's maze-bright and maze-dull rats have been employed in a number of psychological experiments. It seemed to be possibly worth the effort to develop strains of rats showing high skin resistance or low skin resistance, which presumably would reflect differences in emotionality.

The first two of the four generations involved in this study were the animals employed in the experiments designed to study the development of BRL discussed earlier. The parental group consisted of two litters from parents that had been selected for high and low BRL. Matings from this generation, also selected on the basis of high or low BRL, produced seven litters, three from high BRL parents and four from low BRL parents. Pairings from this generation produced five litters, two high BRL litters and three low BRL litters. Animals in this generation were the subjects of this study. They were divided into six groups—three groups each from the high BRL and the low BRL parents tested for the first time at 27, 75, or 125 days of age. Animals tested at the younger age were retested at the later ages.

Figure 10-17 shows the mean values for a pair of groups tested for the first time at 125 days of age. The test consisted of a 20-minute period in the Skinner Box, during which time the lowest BRL value for each minute was recorded. In 17 of the 20 one-minute periods, the offspring of the high BRL parents showed the higher mean BRL values.

Figure 10-18 shows the mean BRL values obtained at each of the three testing periods. If one looks only at the results of the first test for each group, one can see a dramatic difference that emerges in the two strains at 75 days. The animals bred of low BRL parents show a large drop at this age that is not seen in the other group until 125 days. The weights, sexual composition, and handling

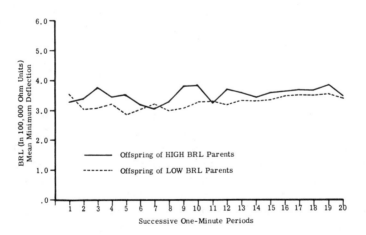

*FIGURE 10-17. Selective Breeding for BRL. The figure displays mean BRL values for successive one-minute recording periods over 20 minutes in the Skinner Box for the animals bred of high BRL parents and animals bred of low BRL parents in the fourth generation. (From Dewsbury, reported in Walker, 1969b.)*

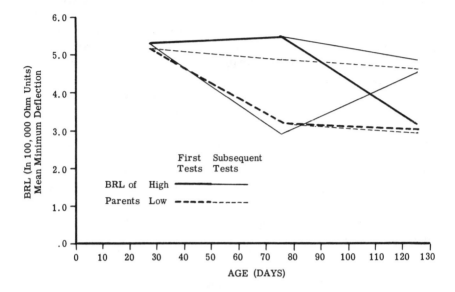

FIGURE 10-18. *Interaction of Selective Breeding, Age, and the Effects of Repeated Experience. The figure displays mean BRL values of two strains of animals bred through four generations for high and low BRL. (From a study by Dewsbury, reported in Walker, 1969b.)*

history are the same for these two groups. These results suggest that the effort to breed rats selectively for skin resistance, and thus presumably for arousal, was effective. The complex effects of repeated experience shown in the figure, while subject to complex compatible interpretation, should serve as cautionary evidence.

### Summary Conclusions
### from Basic Studies of BRL

Three variables stand out as producing highly predictable and significant changes in BRL in this set of studies. First, if animals are left in an unchanging environment and repeatedly introduced into the same unchanging evironment, the skin resistance measures rise significantly within each day and between days. Second, even the normal gentle handling of an animal during the course of the carrying out of an experiment produces a sharp drop in skin resistance during the period of handling. Both of these results are consistent with the possibility that variations in skin resistance generally tend to reflect differences in the emotional state of the animal. Continued and repeated experience in an unchanging environment generally produces boredom in human subjects. Handling could be expected to produce arousal in the animal. Third, weight is also highly significant in its relation to BRL, but it is a variable to be dealt with in experiments rather than a variable that is of interest with respect to arousal.

Six other variables reported in this section may possibly reflect differences in BRL and thus in arousal and emotionality, but they yield data that cannot be interpreted unambiguously. First, stimulus change in a context of a previously unvarying environment sometimes produces large differences in BRL and at other times appears to produce no change. The question of the difference between conditions in which BRL changes do occur and those in which they do not was not resolved in this series of studies.

Second, there are sex differences in BRL, with male animals showing much lower skin resistance than female animals. Although differences in the average weights of male and female rats account for some of the sex difference in BRL, it seems likely that there is a residual sex difference reflecting differences in arousal under standard testing conditions. However, means of factoring out the effect of weight are insufficiently precise to permit a strong conclusion.

Third, there are individual differences in BRL that are correlated with individual differences in the weight of the animal. It seems likely that there is residual variance reflecting individual differences in emotionality, but there is insufficient evidence in these data to permit a firm conclusion on which further studies could be based.

Fourth, BRL decreases with age in the developing rat, but the variable of the animal's weight is so overpowering that the likely development of low resistance at a critical stage in the development of emotionality in the rat could not be demonstrated unambiguously. From the data, an increase in emotionality with increasing age seems probable but by no means certain.

Fifth, an effort to produce differences in skin resistance at a later age as a product of handling during the first ten days after birth was entirely unsuccessful. Although positive results have previously been reported showing that rats subjected to this handling procedure are less emotional than unhandled rats, neither skin resistance nor number of boluses left during an open field test showed the predicted results. Since the number of boluses is a measure that had previously been shown to be significant, it is not clear from these results whether skin resistance simply doesn't reflect the effects of handling or whether the handling procedure employed in this study doesn't produce differences in emotionality.

Sixth, the effort to produce a generation of "emotional" rats by the criterion of low skin resistance and a generation of "unemotional" rats by the criterion of high skin resistance was only modestly successful. It seemed likely that it could be done, but there was sufficient ambiguity in the results with the fourth generation that the effort was abandoned.

## AROUSAL AND BIOLOGICAL DRIVES

The concepts of *arousal* and *drive* are in some sense alternative energetic concepts, although there are considerable differences between them. Arousal is a reflection of the general state of the organism; typically, it has a value somewhere in the middle of the possible range of values. The conditions that produce variation in arousal are to be determined empirically. Drive, on the other hand, is usually closely tied to the operations that produce it, such as time of food privation. It has a cue stimulus component as well as an energizing component, and it has an ideal value of zero, representing the absence of drive. The biological drives that have been studied most extensively are hunger, thirst, sex, and fear. Since the operations that vary drive strength are well known and easy to manipulate, they offer an unambiguous set of operations for exploring the relation between arousal and drive. Accordingly, a series of studies was done involving sex drive in the female rat, hunger, thirst, and fear in the rat, and hunger and fear in the weak electric fish.

### Estrus in the Female Rat

The female rat typically has a four-day estrus cycle. The various stages of the cycle can be determined rather simply by injecting a small amount of distilled water into the vagina, withdrawing the water, and observing the nature of the suspended vaginal material under a low-power microscope. The four categories and the differences in vaginal material to be seen at each stage are the following:

> *Proestrus:* Numerous cells, mostly round with large single nuclei
> *Estrus:* Numerous cells, mostly cornified and without nuclei
> *Metestrus:* Numerous cells, some cornified, some nucleated
> *Diestrus:* Few cells of any kind, some polynucleated

Two colleagues and I studied the relation of arousal to estrus by tracking estrus while measuring skin resistance under standard conditions over a five-day period (Walker, Cohen, & Doyle, 1964). We placed the animals in Skinner Boxes with the light and fan on and the operant lever inactivated. The rats were left there for 25-minute periods on five consecutive days. During the first ten minutes of each period, the environment was unchanging. Stimulus change was produced by opening the outer door (the inner door is clear plastic) and thus exposing the animal to the sights and sounds outside the picnic-like apparatus box. The outer door was opened at the end of ten minutes, closed at the end of the 12th minute, and opened again at the end of the 23rd minute. The animals were removed at the end of the 25th minute. Among the BRL measures taken were the lowest readings in the two-minute periods just prior to the opening of the door and the lowest readings during the two-minute periods while the door was open; thus, there were two measures for each animal on each of the five days.

Figure 10-19 indicates that there was some variation in skin resistance; the stage of estrus with the highest reading occurred during diestrus, and the lowest readings were obtained in estrus and metestrus. However, these differences were not statistically significant. They represent mean values for the two-minute periods just prior to stimulus change. The lines terminating in arrows indicate the amount of change in BRL (thus GSR) that occurred in response to stimulus change. The largest change, on the average, occurred in diestrus and the smallest during metestrus. This difference is statistically significant (p = < .05).

In the same figure, I have incorporated results taken from Richter (1950). Richter plotted the number of wheel revolutions per day made by an animal in an activity wheel. He also tracked the stage of estrus and plotted his results in the same manner as the BRL results were plotted. The mean number of wheel revolutions is scaled on the right-hand ordinate in the figure.

Inspection of the three sets of values in the figure (BRL, GSR, and Wheel Turning) indicate little or no correspondence between

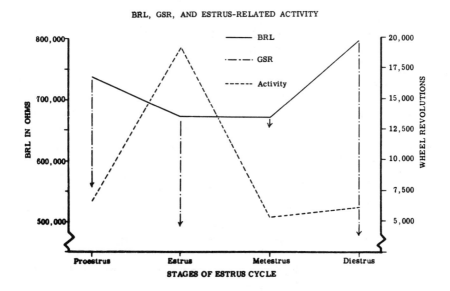

*FIGURE 10-19. BRL, GSR, and Estrus-Related Activity. The solid line shows the mean BRL of female rats at four points in the estrus cycle. The descending lines with arrows indicate the mean responses to stimulus change at each of the four stages of estrus. The dashed curve that is superimposed are data taken from Richter (1950) on wheel turning as it is related to the four stages of estrus (see ordinate on the right). (From Walker, Cohen, & Doyle, 1964.)*

them. The high point and the low point in wheel turning both occur at the lowest values of BRL. The largest and smallest responses to stimulus change both occur at the lowest values of wheel turning. Thus, one must conclude that neither BRL nor GSR could be used to predict the wheel turning data, and the latter have been taken as the classical index of variation in drive level with estrus in the female rat.

### Hunger and Thirst

It is generally assumed that increases in time of deprivation of food or water increase the level of drive. If skin resistance (either BRL or GSR) is an index of arousal, and if arousal and drive are correlated, then there should be a relationship between time of deprivation of food or water and skin resistance. Since an increase in arousal should be indexed by a decrease in skin resistance, the expected relation between time of food or water deprivation and BRL is that BRL should decrease as time of deprivation increases.

Campbell and Sheffield (1953) have suggested that animals in an unvarying environment will not necessarily show a relationship between time of deprivation and activity. However, they suggest that a hungry animal may show more activity in the presence of stimulus change than a satiated animal. If this idea is carried over to the relation between skin resistance and time of deprivation, it might be expected that BRL would not vary with time of deprivation but that changes in skin resistance in response to stimulus change (GSR) might so vary.

Dewsbury (Walker, 1969b) studied the effect of time of food and water deprivation on BRL and GSR in rats in a series of well controlled studies. The results shown in Figure 10-20 are typical. The procedure involved placing animals in the standard Skinner Box for a period of perhaps 20 minutes. White noise was then introduced during the 11th and 12th minutes. As can be seen in the figure, time of deprivation, whether of food or water, appears to have had no significant influence on either the BRL or the response to stimulus change (GSR). It is, of course, impossible to assert the null case. Nevertheless, the persistent failure to obtain differences or changes in skin resistance levels through a series of experiments makes it seem likely that hunger, thirst, and skin resistance are unrelated in the rat.

The next experiments concern the weak electric fish. If the discharge frequency of *Gymnotus carapo* is related to the level of arousal, and if the level of arousal is related to the intensity of the biological drive of hunger, then discharge frequency should vary with the classic manipulation of hunger—time of deprivation of food.

Dewsbury conducted two separate experiments with *Gymnotus carapo* to test this possibility. In the first of these studies, the

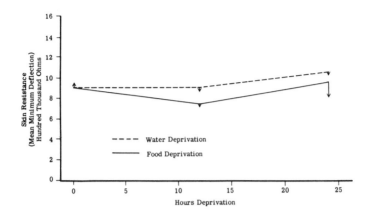

FIGURE 10-20. *BRL and GSR as a Function of Food or Water Deprivation. The plotted values that are connected by lines are the mean minimum values for the two minutes before the introduction of white noise. The arrows indicate the amount and direction of (GSR) change induced by white noise in the 11th and 12th minutes. (From a study by Dewsbury, reported in Walker, 1969b.)*

procedure consisted of feeding three fish liberally, removing food from the tank, and then observing the discharge frequency four times a day for four days, two observation periods during the light and two during the dark. The procedure was then repeated four times for each fish (Dewsbury, 1965).

As can be seen in Figure 10-21, time of deprivation did not seem to affect the discharge frequency in any significant manner either in the light or in the dark. There was a slight rise on the fourth day in the dark, but it was not statistically significant, and it was in part compensated for by a slight drop in frequency in the light.

In order to be sure that the slight upturn in the dark curve did not represent the beginning of a deprivation effect, a second experiment was devised to extend the period of deprivation and to increase the stability of the mean values by taking 120 readings at each test point rather than the 24 used in the first study. The procedure in the second experiment was identical to that of the first, except that time of deprivation was extended to six days, readings were taken only at 8:00 A.M. (just before the end of the dark period), and readings were taken from the record every 7.5 seconds for 15 minutes.

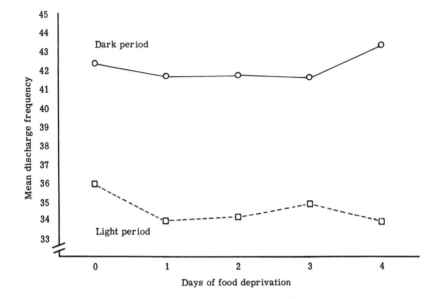

FIGURE 10-21. *Discharge Frequency and Time of Food Privation. The figure displays mean electric discharge frequency as a function of food privation over a four-day period. (From* Some Correlates of Electric Organ Discharge Frequency in Three Species of Electric Fishes, *by D. A. Dewsbury. Unpublished doctoral dissertation, University of Michigan, 1965. Reprinted by permission.)*

No effect of time of deprivation was apparent in the results of this study. The mean discharge frequency at zero, two, and four days of food deprivation was approximately 43.5 cps. At six days, it was 41.5 cps. Therefore, there was no increase in frequency with time of food deprivation.

Thus, the results obtained with the weak electrical fish agree with those obtained in the series of studies of skin resistance in the rat. If skin resistance in the rat and output frequency in the fish are indices of arousal, then arousal does not appear to vary with hunger or thirst.

### Shock-Induced Fear

The most effective manipulation of motivation employed by psychologists to induce prompt and effective behavior in rats is the application of shock. Rats will learn some tasks in a single trial to avoid or escape even mild shock. Strong shock can produce rapid learning that is very highly resistant to experimental extinction. If any biological drive or motive should be reflected in skin resistance changes in the rat or changes in output frequency in the fish, it should be the fear induced by electric shock.

The first study of the effects of shock on BRL in the rat was done by Rachel Kaplan (1962, 1963). Her general procedure was to place animals in Skinner Boxes for 90 minutes a day for four days. Shock was introduced at the end of the 30th minute on the third and fourth days. Four groups received either 0, 4, 5, or 6 milliamperes of shock for a period of five seconds.

Kaplan reported her results by plotting the mean BRL value in the ten-minute period before shock and the mean BRL value in the five-minute period after shock. A five-minute period after shock was chosen because it appeared that rather rapid changes were occurring in BRL during the first ten minutes after shock.

Figure 10-22 shows the effects of shock as Kaplan reported them. Shock obviously produced a dramatic drop in skin resistance. The decreases shown for Day 3 are approximately 500,000 ohms, and those for Day 4 are almost as great.

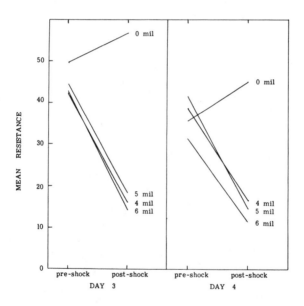

FIGURE 10-22. *Effect of Shock on Skin Resistance in the Rat. The values plotted are the mean BRL values (in 20,000 ohm units) for four groups shocked at different intensities at the end of the first 30 minutes of the 90 minute periods in the Skinner Boxes on the third and fourth days. The pre-shock means are of the lowest values in the ten-minute period preceding the shock, and the post-shock means are of the lowest values recorded in the five-minute period immediately after shock. (From "Rat Basal Resistance Level under Stress and Nonstress Conditions," by R. Kaplan,* Journal of Comparative and Physiological Psychology, *1963, 56(4), 775–777. Copyright 1963 by the American Psychological Association. Based on* A New Measure of Motivation in Rats, *by R. Kaplan. Unpublished doctoral dissertation, University of Michigan, 1962. Reprinted by permission.)*

Several other features of the data are of interest. The differences shown between the effects of the three intensities of shock are not statistically significant, and, in the data for the first experience of shock, they are not in the expected order. It seems highly likely, therefore, that the shock is producing fright rather than pain. One might expect pain to vary with intensity, but, if the shock only frightens the animal, the intensity might not be expected to make much difference.

Since shock produced such a robust effect on skin resistance, a number of additional studies were carried out by Dewsbury, B. E. Walker, and Williams (Walker, 1969b). In one of these, an effort was made to determine whether the form of shock and the kind of apparatus made any difference. One group of 15 animals was run in the Skinner Boxes using a 4-mA shock to replicate one of Kaplan's groups. The procedure differed from Kaplan's in two respects: the animals were not subjected to lengthy prior experience in the boxes, and the measurements were taken by dividing the record into five-minute segments both before and after shock. I will refer to this replication as Experiment 2.

Another 15 animals were shocked in the starting box of a linear maze with the parallel stainless-steel strip floors. Since a prolonged shock would permit the animal to find a way to escape or avoid the shock in this apparatus, a condenser discharge type of shock was applied. The current was approximately 1 mA and was delivered in something less than .01 second. I will refer to this study as Experiment 1. In this study, with the more regular record of the parallel strips, the records were read in two-minute segments.

Figure 10-23 shows the results in these two pieces of apparatus. It is apparent that they are highly comparable. The recovery from being handled is characteristically apparent in Experiment 1. The dramatic drop in BRL in response to the shock is present in both curves. As Kaplan reported, recovery appears to require at least 35 to 40 minutes. The rapid changes in BRL during the first few minutes after shock, which led Kaplan to use a five-minute sample period rather than a ten-minute one, is quite apparent in the curve for Experiment 1. The lowest value was recorded in the first two-minute period after the shock. There is an immediate recovery. It is obvious that the results of shock are not dependent on a particular piece of apparatus or on a very special form or intensity of shock.

A second experiment was carried out with 30 animals shocked in the starting box with the same condenser discharge type of shock employed in Experiment 1. These animals were subjected to the same experience on two successive days. The results are plotted in Figure 10-24. The two days yield results that are essentially indistinguishable. They both show the same pattern of a large drop in

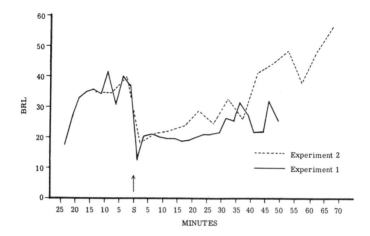

*FIGURE 10-23. BRL Recovery after Shock. Experiment 1 shows the effect of a 1 milliampere condenser discharge type of shock applied to the rat in the starting box with parallel stainless-steel strip floors. Experiment 2 shows the effects of a five-second square wave dc shock at 120 per second applied through the shock grid of a Skinner Box. (From Dewsbury, Walker, and Williams, in Walker, 1969b.)*

BRL following shock, and they both show incomplete recovery after 50 minutes.

Taken together, the experiments concerning the effects of shock on skin resistance yield a highly consistent picture. A wide range of shock intensities, from a 1-mA condenser discharge type lasting less than .01 second to a five-second shock of dc square waves of 6 mA at 120 per second, delivered in two quite different pieces of apparatus, all yield a very similar pattern of BRL changes. There is an abrupt drop in skin resistance of as much as 500,000 ohms, followed by a recovery of 15–25% of that value within the first few minutes, which is in turn followed by a slower recovery phase lasting 30 minutes or more.

In sharp contrast to the data previously reported on the appetitive drives, for which the results were quite negative, these results appear to be a convincing demonstration that BRL does reflect something about the emotional state of the animal. However, the suspicion still had to be entertained that the results, while shock correlated, might not be simple reflections of the arousal level of the animal. Accordingly, a final study of the effects of shock on BRL was designed. The study was based on an effort to manipulate the time of recovery from the shock. We reasoned that, if shock was

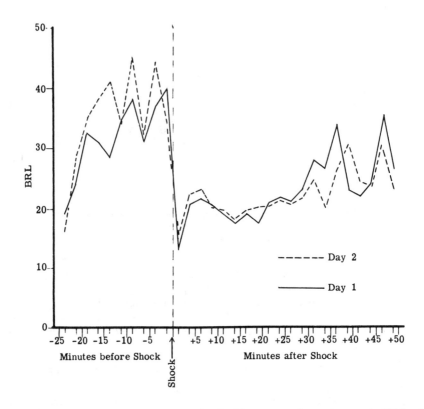

*FIGURE 10-24. BRL Response to Shock. The curves show changes in BRL of 30 animals in response to shock on two successive days. The animals were shocked with a condenser discharge type of shock in the starting alley of a linear maze equipped with two stainless-steel strips in the floor. Measurement is the lowest value recorded in each successive 150-second period. (Study by Dewsbury, B. E. Walker, and Williams, reported in Walker, 1969b.)*

inducing fear, and if it was fear that was reflected in the pattern of BRL values, then a manipulation designed to vary the duration of the fear should produce a correlated manipulation in the BRL.

The experimental apparatus consisted of a long maze that was divided into visually distinctive sections by transparent doors. Rats could be shocked in one end of the maze and then allowed to run varying distances from the place of shock. It was expected that, the farther a rat was allowed to run, the quicker would be its recovery from the fear induced by the shock.

As can be seen in Figure 10-25, this expectation was met. The animals retained in the shock compartment were slowest to recover, and the two groups allowed to escape either three or six sections

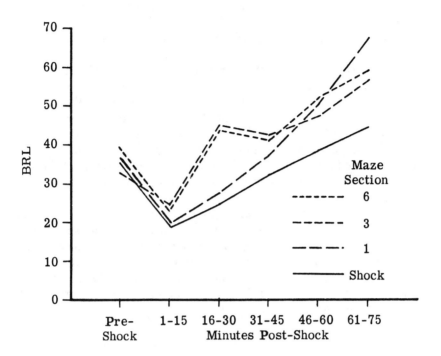

*FIGURE 10-25. BRL as a Function of Time after Shock and Distance from Shock Place. The curves show the recovery pattern by time for each of four groups of animals, divided on the basis of how far they were permitted to run after being shocked. Each point is a mean of four days. (Study by Dewsbury, B. E. Walker, and Williams, reported in Walker, 1969b.)*

away recovered more rapidly. The largest difference occurred in the second 15-minute period after the shock.

These results are particularly meaningful because neither time-correlated nor place-correlated artifacts can account for the results. This is apparent from the fact that the animals that were allowed to escape only to the adjacent compartment show a recovery pattern much like that of the animals retained in the place where they had been shocked. The real difference in recovery time occurred between two groups that were permitted to move but that moved different distances—one or three sections of the maze. The results are also important because they suggest a means of manipulating BRL value, and thus presumably arousal level, in studies of the effect of arousal level on learning and performance.

These experiments with the rat were supplemented by Dewsbury (1965), who examined the extent to which shock could produce significant pulse frequency changes in the weak electric fish.

In the rat, an electric shock is a strange stimulus. Since *Gymnotus carapo* is an electric fish, it was by no means certain that the results would be similar.

Dewsbury placed stainless-steel plates in the tanks to serve as shock electrodes. Shock was a 60 cps constant-current shock set to deliver 1 mA and was of momentary duration. Each of three fish was subjected to six shocks per day for three days with intervals of four, five, six, seven, and eight minutes separating the shocks. The intervals were randomly distributed within a block of shocks for each animal on each day. The record was read by taking the maximum discharge frequency in each of the three ten-second intervals preceding shock and each of the six ten-second intervals following shock. This experiment was carried out during the light portion of the light/dark cycle.

Figure 10-26 shows a clear increase in frequency of output following the shock and a rather quick return to the pre-shock baseline. The three fish showed large individual differences in the response to shock. One increased output by about 13 pulses per second (pps) on the average, a second fish increased output by about 7 pps on the average, and the third fish, C3, increased its output by only 2.6 pps on the average.

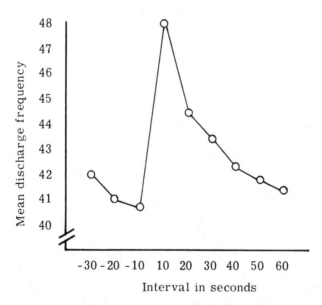

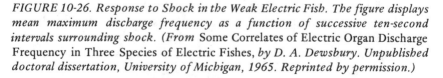

*FIGURE 10-26. Response to Shock in the Weak Electric Fish. The figure displays mean maximum discharge frequency as a function of successive ten-second intervals surrounding shock. (From* Some Correlates of Electric Organ Discharge Frequency in Three Species of Electric Fishes, *by D. A. Dewsbury. Unpublished doctoral dissertation, University of Michigan, 1965. Reprinted by permission.)*

C3 was therefore subjected to a fourth test day in which the shock intensity was increased to 10 mA, a tenfold increase. On this day, increase in frequency was 4.2 pps. It therefore seems unlikely that increase in frequency is closely related to the intensity of the stimulus. In any case, electric shock produces a significant increase in the discharge frequency of *Gymnotus carapo.*

### Summary of Arousal and Biological Drives

If one classes hunger, thirst, and sex as appetitive drives, then the results of these studies are essentially negative with respect to BRL and GSR in the rat and pulse frequency in fish as indices of arousal. Arousal level, as measured by skin resistance or pulse frequency, and drive level, as tracked in estrus or manipulated by time of deprivation of food and water, are unrelated. If fear is classified as an aversive drive, and if electric shocks produce fear in rats and in electric fish, then there is a relation between fear and skin resistance in the rat and fear and pulse frequency in the weak electric fish. Thus, the conclusion to be drawn is that arousal does not vary with strength of appetitive drives but does vary with the intensity of aversive drives.

## AROUSAL AND INCENTIVES

Behavior can be manipulated effectively through the control of rewards. The question of what mechanism accounts for the operation of rewards is open to debate. Moreover, it is difficult to formulate definitions of what is rewarding that are not in terms of the postulated effect of rewards on learning. The term *incentive* is usually defined in terms of approach or avoidance behavior—a positive incentive being one that is approached and a negative incentive being one that is avoided. Some psychologists associate incentives with the reduction of biological drives; for them, positive incentives are stimuli that reduce biological drives, whereas negative incentives are stimuli that induce or increase biological drives.

If skin resistance varied with the application of incentives, it might be possible to acquire information of critical value with respect to the reward/incentive mechanism. For example, if variation in drive did not produce correlated variation in BRL, but if an incentive did produce such variation, then the postulated relation between incentives and drive reduction would be called into serious question.

The pursuit of this problem with the techniques for measuring skin resistance developed by the Kaplans is technically very difficult. In order to obtain a useful measure of skin resistance using the standard shock grid floor, a two-minute time sample is usually required. Occasionally one-minute samples have yielded data of some value. However, most events associated with the application of an incentive could be expected to occupy time intervals on the order of one or two seconds rather than one or two minutes. For this reason, any work on incentives must be done with the parallel stainless-steel strips.

Even with the parallel stainless-steel strips, movement artifacts are quite critical. For example, we made a large number of efforts to determine the effects on skin resistance of electrical stimulation of some portion of the limbic system. Animals were obtained from Dr. James Olds that had chronically implanted electrodes and that would eventually undergo histological verification of the location. The animals were selected on the basis that the placement was in an area that produced self-stimulation. In every instance, the application of current appeared to produce slight movements. In the record, it was not possible to distinguish between those changes produced by the stimulation that could be attributed to the incentive properties and those that could be attributed to the movement-produced properties. Radical procedures such as the use of curare were not undertaken.

A rat's manner of eating also precludes a close temporal correlation between the ingestion of food and the observation of possible correlated changes in BRL. Typically, the rat will grasp food with the forepaws and assume a sitting position, but very slight movements, even so slight as the wiggling of the vibrissa, may produce variation in the pressure of the footpads on the floor and thus produce movement artifact.

Only two situations appear to yield information that has any usefulness or validity. The application of shock produces such large differences in skin resistance that the gross changes in skin resistance could not be artifactual. The second situation is one in which an animal is drinking from a standard watering tube. While drinking from a tube placed close to the floor, the animal tends to stand on all four feet very quietly and lap at the tube at a very rapid rate. Under such conditions, movement artifact is virtually absent from the record.

### Fear Reduction

As noted earlier, shock produces a dramatic drop in skin resistance, frequently of the order of 500,000 ohms. The amount of drop depends, of course, on the pre-shock skin resistance level. Typically, the drop is immediate and terminates in the vicinity of 75,000 ohms, which appears to be a minimum value. It will also be recalled that individual difference data show high positive correlations between measures taken on the same animals at different times unless one of those measures was taken immediately after shock. Shock, and presumably the fear induced by shock, tend to eliminate individual differences.

The reduction or dissipation of fear is evident in the two phases of recovery from shock. There is a rapid recovery of about 25% of the pre-shock BRL within the first few minutes, followed by a more gradual return to normal levels over 30 minutes or more.

### Thirst Reduction in the Rat

The basic procedure was to allow animals to run down a short runway and to drink from a water tube projecting from the goal box wall. BRL was measured through the floor of the maze, and an additional circuit permitted recording of periods when the animal was actually drinking. (A typical record of BRL and drinking behavior was shown in the lower panel of Figure 10-3.)

Dewsbury (Walker, 1969b) obtained 240 records from 24 animals run once a day for 12 days. Drinking occurred on 199 of those trials; on 41 trials no contact was made with the drinking tube. A comparison of BRL on drinking trials compared to non-drinking trials is shown in Figure 10-27. On trials when some drinking occurred, resistance increased on 160 trials, showed no change on 14 trials, and decreased on 25 trials. The mean change was an increase of 108,200 ohms.

In an experiment by Dewsbury and Barbara Stoddard (Walker, 1969b), a comparison was made between the effects on BRL of drinking milk or water. Figure 10-28 shows means of 148 trials of

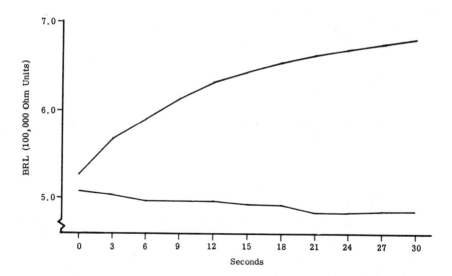

FIGURE 10-27. *Effect of Drinking Behavior on BRL in the Rat. The figure displays mean BRL values on trials during which rats drank continuously for 30 seconds (upper curve) compared to BRL values on those trials during which the animals did not drink and stood still in the goal box. (From Dewsbury, reported in Walker, 1969b.)*

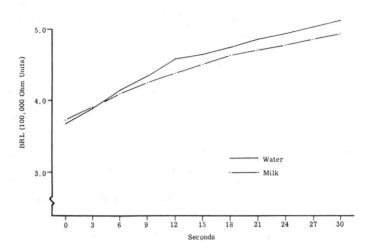

*FIGURE 10-28. BRL Response while Drinking Milk or Water. The figure is a comparison of mean BRL changes for animals drinking water for 30 seconds continuously in the goal box with similar data for animals drinking milk (Dewsbury & Barbara Stoddard, in Walker, 1969b).*

water drinking and 148 of milk drinking. As can be seen, adding a nutritive substance to the water did not have a significant effect on the amount of change in BRL.

In still another experiment, a comparison was made between the effects of drinking three types of liquid: plain water, a 7.5% solution of sucrose, and a 15% solution. These results appear in Figure 10-29.

Finally, comparisons were made of the effects of water, two concentrations of sucrose, and two concentrations of saccharine. In all conditions, the animals showed increases in skin resistance while drinking, but in no instance were there reliably more increases in resistance from substances added to the water. These results are shown in Figure 10-30.

### BRL and Food Reward in the Monkey

One effort was made to track BRL changes in a single rhesus monkey. This animal was being tested in a discrimination learning situation by Dr. Charles M. Butter. The animal was learning a standard three-stimulus discrimination problem while seated in a permanent experimental chair. In this type of experiment, the monkey faces a screen that can be raised to expose the stimuli. One stimulus contains a reward; the other two do not.

BRL was measured by use of the electrodes used in human research. These are zinc electrodes placed on top of corn pads into

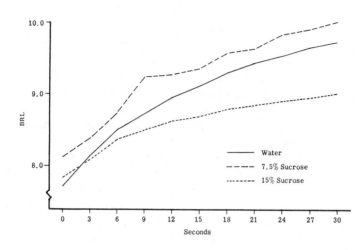

FIGURE 10-29. *BRL Response while Drinking Sucrose or Water. The figure displays mean values of BRL (in 100,000-ohm units) for animals drinking for 30 seconds consecutively in the goal box. The comparison is between animals drinking water with animals drinking two concentrations of sucrose. (From a study by Dewsbury & Stoddard, reported in Walker, 1969b.)*

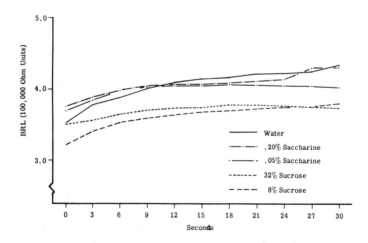

FIGURE 10-30. *BRL Response while Drinking Sucrose, Saccharine, or Water. The figure displays mean BRL values of animals consuming water or two different concentrations of sucrose and two of saccharine for 30 consecutive seconds in the goal box. (Study by Dewsbury & Stoddard, reported in Walker, 1969b.)*

which zinc sulphate electrode paste has been placed. They work effectively with human subjects, who can be instructed to keep the hand that has electrodes attached to it immobile. The monkey tends to move both hands, and the result is a large amount of movement artifact. Nevertheless, as can be seen in Figure 10-31, suggestive records were obtained.

In this figure, the "stimulus change" trials consist of a series of 58 adaptation trials during which no rewards were provided when the screen was lifted. There was a rise of about 120,000 ohms in the 30-second period immediately after the raising of the screen. For those trials in which the animal chose the correct stimulus and received a reward of one grape, there was an initial drop of about 80,000 ohms while the animal was removing the stimulus and retrieving the grape. This drop was followed by a rise of about 110,000 ohms by the end of the 30-second period. The line for the "grape reward" trials in the figure represents 132 such trials out of a larger number, many of which contained movement artifacts. The third curve is for extinction trials (33 trials), which showed an initial drop of about 190,000 ohms followed by virtually no change (at most a rise of 10,000 to 20,000 ohms). Thus, the data on Charlie Butter's monkey, Watson, seem to show a drop in resistance attributable to the exertion involved in making the choice and a rise of about 100,000 ohms associated with the consumption of the food reward.

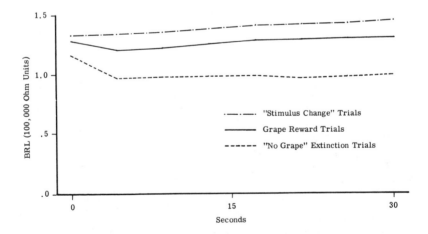

FIGURE 10-31. *Monkey Response to Grape Reward. The figure displays mean BRL values for Charlie Butter's monkey, Watson, on three kinds of trials in a discrimination learning problem. Two of the curves compare trials on which a grape reward was received with trials on which the exposure door was opened but no reward received. The third curve is for a series of extinction trials. (From Walker, 1969b.)*

Such a rise occurs from the stimulus change of the raised screen, but no such rise occurs on an extinction trial.

### Discharge Rate Changes
### at Feeding in the Weak Electric Fish

One of the most reliable changes in discharge rate in *Gymnotus carapo* is that associated with the feeding response. If a meal worm is dropped in the tank, there is soon a very marked rise in frequency of discharge, and for a period of several seconds there is marked variation in frequency.

Before it became possible to observe the feeding response, it was not possible to determine whether the increase was associated with the search phase, with the consumption phase, or with a post-consumption phase. The interpretation of the frequency change might differ depending on which phase was associated with the increased output. If the increase in frequency were associated with the search phase, one might infer that the variation in frequency represented a kind of echo-ranging use of the electrical discharge similar to the echo-ranging of bats and porpoises. If it were associated with the consumption or post-consumption phase of feeding, then it would more likely be related to the emotional condition of the animal.

There are several technical problems associated with research on the correlation between the phases of feeding and the discharge frequency of these fish. The most common food consists of small worms. If an experimenter enters the room and drops a worm into the tank, the fish is disturbed by the presence of the experimenter. It is therefore difficult or impossible to separate the effects of the presence of the experimenter from the activity induced by the presence of the worm. The obvious answer is to construct an automatic worm ejector than can drop a worm into the water without producing any other effect on the behavior of the fish. Unfortunately, even though several such devices were designed and built, none worked well enough to permit use in a formal study. The operation of some disturbed the fish, while some failed to deliver worms on cue.

Figure 10-32 (Walker, 1969b) is a photographic record of the response of one of Mortenson's fish while feeding. In this record, the chart is moving at a rapid speed, and the fish is in a continuously active state throughout. When the experimenters walk down the hall and one of them enters the room, frequency rises from 49 pps to 68 pps, drops immediately to about 59 pps, and then slowly descends to the baseline of 49–50 pps. The fish can be observed to search the bottom for the worm with a slightly elevated frequency of output. Typically, when the fish finds the worm, it sucks the worm into its mouth, forces it out, sucks it in, and may repeat the process two or three times before swallowing it. In this instance,

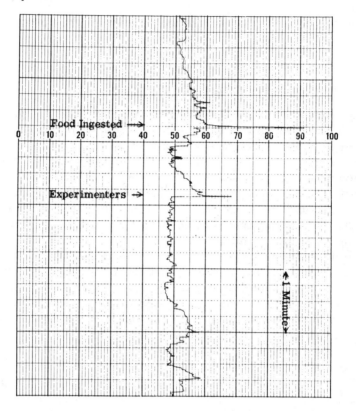

*FIGURE 10-32. Chart Record of Response of the Weak Electric Fish to Experimenter and to Food. The figure is a photograph of the chart record of response of one Gymnotus carapo to the entrance of an experimenter into the room and the dropping of a worm into the tank. The chart speed is 4 inches per minute, thus 15 seconds for each vertical division line. The record reads from right to left. (From Determinants of Electrical Discharge Rate in Gymnotus Carapo, the Banded Knife Fish, by F. J. Mortenson. Unpublished doctoral dissertation, University of Michigan, 1969. Reprinted by permission.)*

the fish swallowed the worm immediately, and the peak frequency of about 91 pps is associated with the swallowing of the accepted worm. I would therefore guess that *Gymnotus carapo* does not use its electrical discharges as a prey-locating device but rather that the increased frequency represents some aspect of the excitement of the chase. This conclusion, however, is highly speculative. The nature of the necessary experiment is clear, and the means of carrying it out almost at hand, but the experiment has not been done for lack of time, energy, and money.

One experiment on feeding was carried out by Dewsbury (1965) without benefit of a capacity to observe the fish while it was feeding. He was able to compare average discharge frequency during fairly long feeding periods with comparable non-feeding periods.

To obtain the results shown in Figure 10-33, Dewsbury fed his fish at either 7:30 or 9:30 during the dark cycle. When they were not fed at 7:30, he entered the room and carried out all the operations of feeding except for the actual placing of worms in the tank. He carried out the same control at 9:30 when they were not fed at that hour.

The figure shows the discharge frequencies by half-hour periods on each of three days. When food is delivered at 7:30, the mean frequency rises and remains elevated during the following two hours, which presumably represents continuous feeding. When the experimenter entered at 7:30 on the second day, or at 9:30 on the first and third, no effect was apparent. On the second day, there was a marked elevation in discharge frequency associated with feeding at this unusual hour.

Figure 10-34 is a somewhat finer-grained analysis. Readings were taken from the original record every 75 seconds during the five-hour feeding period. These readings were averaged in pairs, so that each value represented a 2½-minute interval. The mean values for each of the three fish across each of the three test days were then combined to record the 30 minutes before feeding and the 30

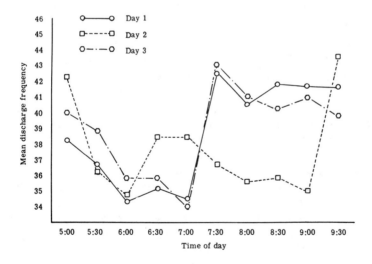

FIGURE 10-33. *Discharge Frequency Changes at Feeding. The figure shows mean electric organ discharge frequency changes in response to feeding on three days with feeding at 7:30 p.m. on two days and at 9:30 p.m. on the other. The experimenter entered the room at both times on all days to control for experimenter disturbance. (From* Some Correlates of Electric Organ Discharge Frequency in Three Species of Electric Fishes, *by D. A. Dewsbury. Unpublished doctoral dissertation, University of Michigan, 1965. Reprinted by permission.)*

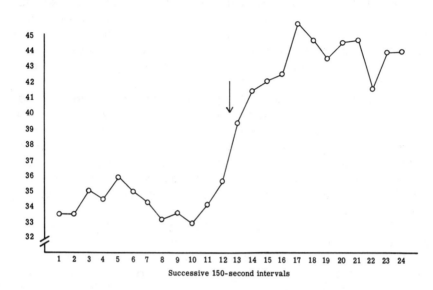

FIGURE 10-34. Discharge Frequency before and after Feeding. The figure displays mean electric organ discharge frequency within the half-hour before and the half-hour after feeding. (From Some Correlates of Electric Organ Discharge Frequency in Three Species of Electric Fishes, by D. A. Dewsbury. Unpublished doctoral dissertation, Univeristy of Michigan, 1965. Reprinted by permission.)

minutes after feeding regardless of whether the animals were fed at 7:30 or 9:30. The gradual rise after the introduction of food probably represents differential latency in the beginning of feeding. In other words, some fish, on some days, found food immediately and began to feed immediately; others began feeding with latencies of several minutes. The apparent rise in the curve is probably accounted for by the combining of the records of those animals that were feeding and those that were not feeding in the early part of the period during which food was available.

These data establish highly significant increases in discharge frequency in Gymnotus carapo during feeding periods. The increased output is probably associated with increased arousal and probably is not associated with the search for food itself, but good, unambiguous, experimental data are not available on the point.

### Summary of Arousal and Incentives

Both measures—skin resistance in the rat and monkey and electrical discharge frequency in Gymnotus carapo—show marked changes when measured at the time a traditional incentive condition occurs. Skin resistance rises when a thirsty rat drinks water, milk, a sugar solution, or a saccharine solution. The monkey shows a rise in skin resistance when it receives a food reward. Skin resistance rises in the rat during a period in which it is recovering from the effects of shock. All these effects are consistent with an interpretation that the effect of an incentive is to reduce arousal level.

On the other hand, changes in the output frequency in the weak electric fish in the presence of food were clearly increases in frequency that accompanied increases in physical activity and therefore probably reflected increases in arousal level. There was a decrease in frequency immediately after the ingestion of the food. The difference in results with rats and fish is probably a function of differences in the measuring situation. The fish was observed before it could anticipate the incentive, when it was consumed, and afterwards. The rat and monkey, on the other hand, were observed only after the anticipation of reward was well established.

## THE CONCEPT OF AROUSAL
## AND DATA ON SKIN RESISTANCE IN THE RAT
## AND ON DISCHARGE FREQUENCY IN FISHES

The concept of arousal, as it has been defined within the Hedgehog, is not coordinated to any particular physiological measure. However, the studies I have described were designed to determine the extent to which there was covariation between critical situations and behaviors that are expected to be related to arousal and values of skin resistance in the rat and pulse frequency in the weak electric fish. Since covariation appeared systematically in some situations that might be related to arousal and did not appear in others, a caveat is in order. Each of the summary generalizations these data permit should be prefaced with the caution that the statement is true if and only if the measure in question is accepted as a true measure of arousal.

Although a variety of studies were recounted in this chapter, for the purposes of summary we can formulate three pertinent questions. (1) What is the relation between measured arousal and variation in appetitive drive states? (2) Are arousal measures reflective of excitement and of gross aspects of the diurnal cycle of sleep and awake states? (3) How are measures of arousal related to rewards and the role of rewards in learning?

1. No systematic relation was found between these measures of arousal and variation in appetitive biological drive states. Variation in the classical manipulations of appetitive drives—time of food and water deprivation and the estrus cycle in the female rat—are not accompanied by variations in skin resistance in the rat. Deprivation of food did not produce a change in the discharge frequency in the fish. One can therefore conclude that arousal is unrelated to variation in appetitive biological drives.

2. The results tend to show a positive relationship between the measures used and manipulations that should produce variations in levels of excitement or in emotional state. If a rat is kept in an unvarying environment, arousal level goes down. If it is placed in the same environment a number of times, arousal level is lower each time the animal is placed in the boring environment. If the rat is shocked, arousal rises to extremely high levels. There is an immediate partial recovery, followed by a slow "calming down" that can last for an hour or more. Handling the animal increases arousal level, and simple stimulus change sometimes does and sometimes doesn't increase arousal. No evidence could be obtained concerning the diurnal cycle in the rat.

It is tempting to try to relate the active and inactive states in *Gymnotus carapo* to the awake and sleeping states. The mutually exclusive categories of the behavior and the non-overlapping discharge frequencies clearly establish a two-state system, analogous to the near dichotomy between the sleeping and waking states. If one accepts the analogy, then there is clear evidence of a general tendency for the fish to be in either one of two arousal states, with the arousal, as indexed by discharge frequency, held within relatively narrow variation around the mean state. These data, given the analogy, would verify the hypothesis that sleeping and waking represent two arousal states that characterize the organism most of the time. Transitional or in-between states are rarely seen. Such an interpretation must be made with caution, since other correlates of sleeping and waking, such as EEG and arousal probability under stimulation, are not available in the fish.

The fish responds to auditory stimuli with an increase in frequency that would fit the arousal interpretation, but the comparison of the response in the active and inactive states gives some pause. Generally, when a sleeping organism is stimulated, it tends to awaken fully. The fish tends to respond with an increase in discharge frequency that is large but that does not bring the fish into the active-state range. The fish adapts to repeated presentations of a tone but does not seem to adapt readily to stimuli that might be interpreted as being strong.

The introduction of objects into the tank also yields somewhat conflicting results in regard to arousal. Active exploration of a novel stimulus is accompanied by an increase in discharge rate, as if the novel stimulus has produced an increase in arousal. The interpretation of "novelty" in this case makes sense simply because of the obvious unfamiliarity, for these fish, of metal spoons, aluminum strips, and plexiglass plates. However, since the discharge frequency undergoes little, if any, adaptation to repeated presentation of these stimuli, the term *novelty* seems inappropriate. Perhaps the word *foreign* would be better.

There is a difficult problem of interpretation when these fish respond to the introduction of a foreign stimulus by becoming inactive and assuming what has been referred to as a state analogous to the sleep state. If the behavior is interpreted as being akin to fright behavior, then this organism appears to be frightened into a state distinguishable from its regular sleep state only by a subtle but genuine reduction in variability of its discharge rate—thus a super-sleep state. Foreign objects, then, appear to elicit either excited exploration or a super-sleep state unique to this organism.

In other manipulations related to excitement, the fish showed results parallel to those obtained from the rat. Introduction of food into the tank led to an elevation in discharge frequency that appears to be related to an elevation in the general level of excitement rather than to any specific function of the food-seeking process. The application of shock also produced an elevation in discharge frequency that dissipated with time.

Thus, the answer to the second question is universally positive. Both measures—skin resistance in the rat and pulse frequency in the fish—vary as one might expect them to if they were true measures of arousal as related to the diurnal cycle or to variations in states of excitement.

3. The variation in these measures associated with reward suggest an alternative to classical need-reduction interpretations of the role of reward in learning. In the rat, consumption of water, ingestion of food, and removal of shock all produce gross decreases in arousal level. In the fish, the introduction of food or shock is accompanied by an increase in pulse frequency, and the consumption of food or the removal of shock is followed by a sharp decrease in frequency.

One can therefore probably assume that most consummatory acts are followed by a decrease in arousal. If so, then most of the situations that have been interpreted as involving need reduction do involve arousal reduction. However, since arousal does not vary with the need or drive level as manipulated through time of deprivation, the observed arousal reduction reflects a change in the emotional state rather than in the need state. One would have to conclude from these data that reward consumption and escape from noxious stimulation are emotionally satisfying but are not demonstrably related to the immediate reduction of a need. The findings suggest, but do not establish, that the efficacy of reward in learning is related to the emotional aspects rather than to the motivational aspects as far as the immediate effects of reward are concerned.

# chapter eleven

# _Arousal and learning_

In the Hedgehog, learning is identified with structural change, and the major structural dimension is psychological complexity. Arousal, in contrast, is an energetic variable. Strict adherence to this distinction will result in the classification of many studies, especially animals studies, as studies of arousal rather than studies of learning. In common language, what the organism has learned is what the organism knows, and, when something is learned, it is something new to the organism. Arousal, on the other hand, goes with the performance of what has already been learned; it expresses what the organism wants, and it consists of the performance of acts already acquired. The difference between the Hedgehog treatment of learning and a traditional treatment can be illustrated by examining the traditional concepts of reward and reinforcement as seen by the Hedgehog.

Reward has two functions: it induces arousal, and it can serve as an information function to indicate that the prior sequence of events was a successful one. Reward focuses attention. When it appears to "reinforce" a chain of responses, it does so by stimulating retrieval of the immediately prior sequence of events in order that the chain may be reviewed and rehearsed and attention focused on the details. Multiple-trial learning is required only when short-term memory is insufficient to permit immediate retrieval of all the relevant steps in the sequence. Thus, reward does not function directly as a factor in learning, and the effects of reward are not on the learning process. Instead, reward is a programming process, an incentive for performance.

The term *reinforcement* is not employed within the Hedgehog. The term *reinforcement* implies an incentive function and a role in strengthening an association or bond between two items in the stream of psychological events. As Kenneth Spence used to say, "The unconditioned stimulus both forces and reinforces the response." In another context (Walker, 1969a), I examined the literature in an effort to find reinforcement effects on behavior, as distinct from incentive effects. The outcome was negative. There are whole sets of experimental studies addressed to the issue of whether learning occurs without reinforcement. Some of the labels for these studies are latent learning, stimulus seeking, latent extinction, extinction of overlearned responses, extinction considered as new learning, sensory preconditioning, and others. There is no evidence that reinforcement is necessary for learning to occur, nor is there evidence that learning is better with reinforcement than without it. This is, of course, a null argument and therefore difficult to establish.

However, if reinforcement theory is put in a positive form, such as "The greater the number of reinforcements, the greater the habit strength or associative bond," then the theory can be positively disproved. The typical learning curve under continued reinforcement is one that rises and falls. Figure 7-5 is only one of many examples; I have cited others elsewhere (Walker, 1969a). In the sense of influencing learning as opposed to performance—what the organism knows as opposed to what the organism wants, something new in the stream of behavior as opposed to a change in the frequency or rate of some behavior already in the stream—a reinforcement effect cannot be demonstrated. If a reinforcement effect cannot be demonstrated, and it cannot, then it has no scientific merit. If it has no scientific merit, and it does not, then its continued use as a variable in the control of behavior has the status of a magic incantation and the practical value of snake oil.

## EMPIRICAL STUDIES OF AROUSAL, LEARNING, AND PERFORMANCE

### Operant Performance and Arousal

One of the most fundamental phenomena in learning is the greater resistance to extinction exhibited by animals that have been rewarded only intermittently as compared to that of animals that have been rewarded continuously. If habit strength is associated with the number of rewards, then animals with the greater number of rewards should take longest to extinguish. In fact, animals that have been rewarded only a few times on a partial reward schedule will often press longer after reward has been discontinued than animals that have been rewarded many times, but on a schedule that yielded a reward for each performance of the response.

One type of explanation for this phenomenon involves a redefinition of the response. Thus, Mowrer and Jones (1945) suggested that a response was whatever the animal was rewarded for doing. If an animal was rewarded only 50% of the time, then it took two presses to elicit the reward, and therefore a "response" was two presses. If the animal was rewarded only 25% of the time, then a response was four presses. Mowrer and Jones performed an experiment in which the results were analyzed using this logic and found that the number of response units was directly rather than inversely proportional to the number of rewards.

A number of other investigators have suggested that a part of the difference in performance between animals on a 100% reward schedule and animals on a partial reward schedule might be due to the motivational and emotional aspects of the situation. Partial reward is frequently described as a relatively frustrating condition. It is possible that frustration motivates the response to increase the output during extinction. Among investigators who have argued in this manner are Adelman and Maatsch (1956), Amsel and Roussel (1952), and Holder, Marx, Holder, and Collier (1957).

If frustration or any other emotion produced by non-reward is related to arousal, and if arousal is inversely related to skin resistance, then animals in a partial reward situation should show lower skin resistance than animals receiving 100% reward. It might also be possible to relate the level of arousal during a partial reward schedule and the level of arousal during extinction to the number of responses produced.

*Arousal in a Discriminated Operant Situation.* Warner, under the tutorial direction of Kaplan (Walker, 1969b), trained several groups of animals to press a lever to obtain food. Figure 11-1 shows the development of discrimination between periods when food was available and periods when it was not. Such periods were signalled by either light or sound, and all combinations of signal and food availability were used in subgroups of animals to control for any direct effect of such stimuli.

Examination of the figures suggests that there are correlated changes in BRL with reward and non-reward conditions from the first day of training. Skin resistance is relatively high during periods when the animal is being rewarded and relatively low when the reward is withdrawn. In general, discrimination is apparent in the BRL records before evidence of discrimination develops in the lever-pressing records. As the lever-pressing discrimination develops, the fluctuations in the curves for lever pressing and skin resistance tend to come into coordinated oscillation. When the animal is pressing the lever and receiving food, the BRL values are high. When the negative stimulus is present and lever pressing is reduced, BRL values are low, indicating high arousal.

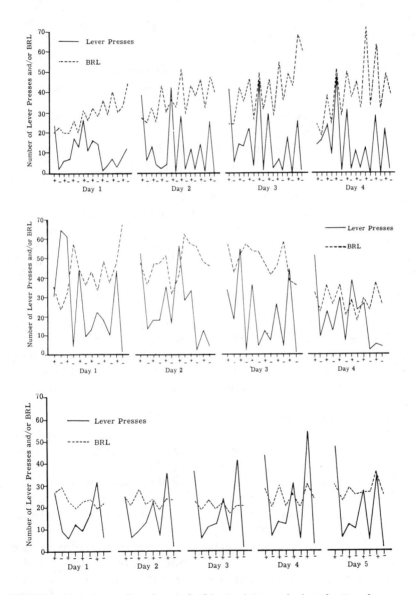

*FIGURE 11-1. Lever Pressing and Skin Resistance during the Development of a Discriminated Operant Response. The figure displays the development of a discriminated operant response to light and sound stimuli between periods of availability (+) and nonavailability (-) of food rewards. The panels are replications. (Study by Warner & Kaplan, reported in Walker, 1969b.)*

*Fixed Ratio Reward and BRL.* Williams (Walker, 1969b) measured skin resistance during performance and extinction of several fixed ratio reward conditions. After a period of 100% reward, seven groups of animals were formed, with two animals in each group. One group continued on 100% reward; the remaining six groups were gradually trained to fixed ratios of 5, 10, and 20 to 1, with two groups at each ratio. One group at each ratio was given the same number of rewards as the 100% reward group, the other was given the same number of responses and thus a smaller absolute number of rewards. After ten days of fixed ratio performance, all subjects were tested for resistance to extinction.

Figure 11-2 shows BRL as a function of the various reinforcement conditions on the last day of training. With the number of rewards constant, and thus with the number of responses varying between groups in ratios up to 20 to 1, BRL rises to the .20 ratio and falls through the .10 ratio to the .05 ratio. Thus, the animals seem most aroused under the 20 to 1 condition, next under 10 to 1, and unexpectedly more under the 1 to 1 condition than under the 5 to 1 condition. With the number of responses constant, and thus with the absolute number of rewards decreasing to 1 in 5, 1 in 10, and 1 in 20, arousal increases to 1 in 10 and then rises at 1 in 20. One can conclude either that the results are randomly related to the reward schedule or that the relationship is more complex than one would have thought.

The lower panel of Figure 11-2 shows the results during extinction. The number of lever pressings is shown on the left, and the BRL is shown in the middle. On the right is a plot of "response units" as defined by Mowrer; that is five, ten, or 20 responses are calculated as a unit in the ratio groups, and the number of units is plotted.

The number of lever presses to extinction rises and then falls in both groups in the left-hand figure. This is not an unexpected finding, since it has been reported a number of times before (see, for example, Grant & Hake, 1951; Grant, Hake, & Hornseth, 1951; Grant & Schippler, 1952). Such results obviously require at least two opposed processes. In this case, the number of rewards appears to be a factor and could be used to account for the difference between the two curves. However, the number of rewards is constant in the upper (solid line) curve. A second factor is therefore needed to account for the rise in output of lever pressings and a third factor to account for the drop in the curve at the 20:1 ratio. The curve for skin resistance is roughly similar to the curve for the number of presses. High skin resistance (low arousal) goes with high output of responses, and low skin resistance (high arousal) goes with the lower output.

As an aid to trying to develop an explanation of these results, the number of lever pressings was converted to response units. These data are shown on the right. Several facts are apparent from this figure. The upper curve does not fit the response unit hypothesis of Mowrer, since it is not horizontal. Even when plotted in this fashion, the output at a ratio of 5:1 is nearly twice the output

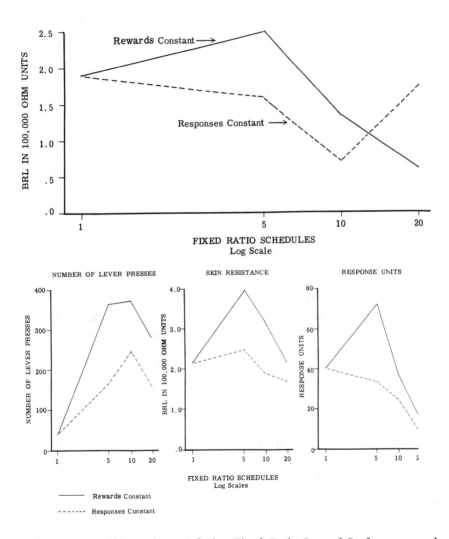

FIGURE 11-2. *Skin Resistance during Fixed Ratio Reward Performance and Extinction. The upper panel shows performance during reward at ratios of 1, 5, 10, or 20 to 1, with either the number of rewards or the number of responses held constant. The lower panel shows analyses of results during extinction. (Study by Williams, reported in Walker, 1969b.)*

under continuous reward. Furthermore, there appears to be a better match between plots of lever pressing and skin resistance when lever pressing is plotted in response units.

The results plotted in Figure 11-2 are all statistically significant even though there were only two animals in each of the seven groups. However, the results are so unusual that a replication seemed desirable. It also seemed desirable to reduce the variability in the results as much as possible through experimental arrangements. Accordingly, small boxes were constructed that held the animals in a lever oriented position. The construction was such that the hind paws of the animal rested on parallel stainless-steel strips, while the front paws could not reach the strips. Using this apparatus, the experiment was repeated with 28 animals, permitting the assignment of four animals to each group. Otherwise the experiment was identical to the previous one.

Figure 11-3 is a plot of skin resistance during the last day of the acquisition phase. This figure looks remarkably like the corresponding figure from the first experiment (upper panel, Figure 11-2), except that the downward turn of the curve for a fixed number of rewards occurs at a ratio of 5:1 in the first study and at a ratio of 10:1 in the second. Also, the two curves in the figure do not quite cross in the second study as they do in the first. Otherwise, the patterns are so similar that the possibility of a random relationship seems unacceptable.

In Figure 11-3 the curve for the condition involving the larger number of rewards is higher, indicating less arousal, than the curve for a constant number of responses (and thus fewer rewards). Within the constant reward condition, there was higher resistance at ratios of 5:1 and 10:1 than at 1:1 or 20:1 in both studies. For the condition in which the number of responses was held constant, the patterns are also very similar in the two studies, with the highest arousal (lowest BRL) occurring at a ratio of 10:1.

Figure 11-3 also shows the results of extinction in the second study, and here the results are somewhat different from those of the first study. In the narrow confines of the box, the number of responses to extinction increases monotonically with progressively smaller ratios when the number of rewards is held constant. With the number of responses constant (and thus with the number of rewards decreasing progressively), the number of presses to extinction remains relatively constant. The trends in skin resistance do not show the inverted-U form of the earlier study. The curve for the constant number of rewards and thus the greater number of lever presses is consistently higher than the dashed line representing the progressively smaller number of rewards. There is no simple relationship between the number of lever presses and BRL across the various ratio schedules. Table 11-1 is a conversion of the number of lever presses to response units. These values show two regular decreasing functions of the number of response units with the smaller ratios. Again, these data do not show a simple relationship to the BRL values of Figure 11-3.

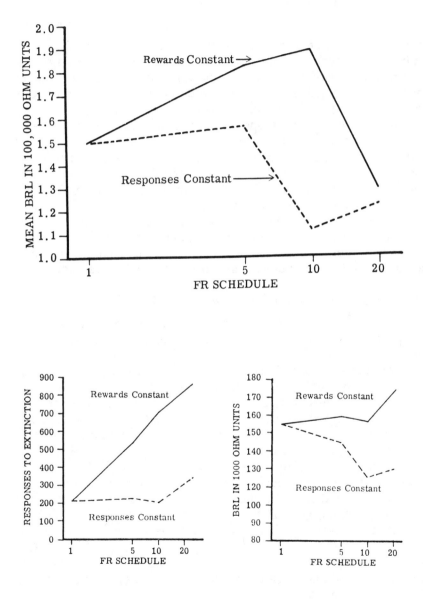

FIGURE 11-3. *Skin Resistance during Fixed Ratio Reward Performance and Extinction (Replication). (Study by Williams, reported in Walker, 1969b.)*

*TABLE 11-1.* Response Units to Extinction

| Reward Ratio | Responses Constant | Rewards Constant |
|:---:|:---:|:---:|
| 1:1 | 214.3 | |
| 1:5 | 47.9 | 108.6 |
| 1:10 | 20.6 | 71.3 |
| 1:20 | 17.4 | 44.4 |

*Summary of Operant Performance and Arousal.* The preceding studies on operant performance and arousal were addressed to the possibility that partial reward affected the emotional state of the animal and that the emotional state, in turn, affected the number of lever presses obtained in extinction.

In the discriminated operant situation, periods of non-reward produced high arousal from the beginning of training, so that alternating periods of the presence and absence of reward were perfectly correlated with high and low BRL records, respectively. Partial reward of the fixed ratio variety produced low arousal with the higher absolute number of rewards during acquisition, but there was a suggestion that this generalization would not hold if reward ratios were much beyond 20:1. During extinction, both the number of lever presses and the skin resistance measures showed complex rather than simple relations to each other and to skin resistance.

### Arousal and the Goal Gradient

The *goal gradient* is the name given to the tendency of animals to increase speed while running a maze and then decrease speed as they approach the goal. This phenomenon has been given two major interpretations. Hull (1932) proposed motivational and associative interpretations but never made a clear choice between the two. Spence (1956), however, has given a clear motivational interpretation. Stimuli closer to the goal are assumed to be more strongly conditioned to the fractional anticipatory goal response and thus result in stronger incentive motivation ($K$).

DiLollo and Walker (1964) reported the first of a series of studies of the relation between arousal as measured by skin resistance and the goal gradient phenomenon. A linear maze was divided into six segments, and, as the animal moved from one segment to another toward the goal, it was held for a period of one minute in each segment in order to permit measurement of BRL. One group of animals received food reward in both the fifth and sixth segments of the maze, while another group received reward only in the sixth segment.

The goal gradient phenomenon is pictured in Figure 11-4. Starting latency at the successive gates rises to the fourth gate and drops at the fifth as the animals enter the final compartment. Skin

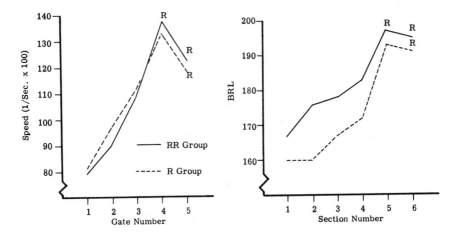

FIGURE 11-4. *The Goal Gradient in Terms of Speed and BRL. The figures display mean starting speed (left) and mean BRL (right) as functions of position in a six-section segmented alley. R indicates the position of reward in both the fifth and sixth sections for one group (RR) and in the sixth section only for the other (R). (Redrawn from "Speed and Basal Resistance Level in a Segmented Straight Alley," by V. DiLollo and E. L. Walker,* Psychological Record, *1964, 14, 499-505. Reprinted by permission.)*

resistance appears to follow a similar pattern, rising through successive sections of the maze to the fifth section and then showing a slight drop in the goal section. The changes with position in the maze are statistically significant in both cases, but the difference between the two groups of animals is not significant in either case.

The rise and fall in the figure appears to be the classical goal gradient. Both Spence's interpretation of the increase in speed along the runway and Hull's interpretation of the downturn approaching the goal involved the position of the reward. Spence's interpretation was in terms of increasing vigor of $r_g$ (fractional anticipatory goal response) as the stimuli in the maze approach those of the goal box as a function of generalization. Hull's motivational interpretation of the decrease near the end of the maze was in terms of the interference between the fractional anticipatory goal response and the instrumental acts necessary to reach the reward. Thus, both interpretations are oriented to the position of the reward and the physical location of the consummatory response.

The data in Figure 11-4 contradict these interpretations. The goal gradient in the RR group, which had rewards in both the fifth and sixth sections of the maze, is essentially identical to that of the R group, which had a reward only in the sixth section. The goal gradient in these data is anchored to the beginning and the end of the run rather than to the placement of the reward. This finding suggests that an explanation of the goal gradient, when one is found, must be sought elsewhere in the experimental situation.

Further analyses of the data were undertaken to determine the course of development of the goal gradient. Figure 11-5 shows the course of learning to run the maze in terms of both speed and BRL. The left-hand figure shows that the speed rose to a maximum during the fourth block of four trials and then showed a drop. BRL showed a similar pattern. The drop during the final block of trials is not unusual. There are many situations in which performance increases and then decreases under continued reward.

The correlation between speed and BRL is of genuine interest. The most common treatment of the roles of drive and incentive during the course of learning invokes some kind of association of the drive to the stimuli of the situation and/or an association of the stimuli of the situation with the incentive substance. Thus, the drive level associated with time of deprivation would not change, but any changes that would occur during learning would be an increase in the expression of the drive in the learning situation and an increase in the energizing function of the incentive. By this reasoning, if BRL is an expression of the arousal level, one would expect an increase in arousal over the 20 learning trials and thus a decrease

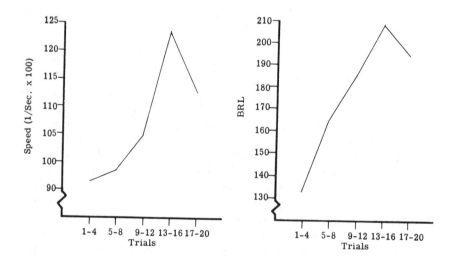

FIGURE 11-5. *The Development of Speed and BRL. The figures show mean starting speed (left) and mean BRL (right) as functions of successive blocks of four trials for both the RR and the R groups combined. (Redrawn from "Speed and Basal Resistance Level in a Segmented Straight Alley," by V. DiLollo and E. L. Walker,* Psychological Record, *1964, 14, 499–505. Reprinted by permission.)*

in BRL—exactly the opposite of the picture seen in Figure 11-5. In that figure, it is clear that skin resistance rises as learning progresses. It thus appears that the animal is most aroused on the first trial and undergoes a gradual decrease in arousal as its performance in the task becomes more and more efficient.

Figure 11-6 is an effort to combine the data of the two earlier figures into a single picture so that the development of the goal gradient in terms of both speed and BRL can be seen. In this figure, the speed curves show no goal gradient during the first block of four trials, but the gradient is apparent in the other four blocks. In the BRL curves, the rising skin resistance is apparent from the first, but the downturn at the end, indicating an increase in arousal, is not apparent until the last two blocks of trials.

A casual observation made during the course of running this experiment suggested an alternative interpretation to the Hull-Spence approach. The animals in this experiment were being run in squads of six in six identical mazes, and they were being run as nearly simultaneously as possible. Since this was a difficult task for a single experimenter, two experimenters worked at the same time, with each handling three mazes and the animals being run in them.

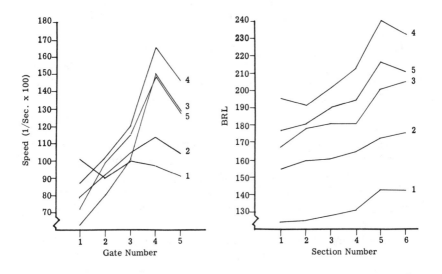

FIGURE 11-6. Development of the Goal Gradient. The figures are plots of interaction between position in the maze and successive blocks of four trials (labeled 1 to 5 in the figure) for speed (left) and BRL (right). (Redrawn from "Speed and Basal Resistance Level in a Segmented Straight Alley," by V. DiLollo and E. L. Walker, Psychological Record, 1964, 14, 499–505. Reprinted by permission.)

The recording instruments were outside the experimental room. It was noted that three of the instruments recording BRL were giving substantially lower values than were the other three. The effect was marked enough that any casual observer could separate one set of three from the other. To be sure of the source, a number of minor tests were attempted, including shifting the channels back and forth so that the recording instruments were matched with different mazes. The net effect was to determine that the three consistently lower readings were being taken from the animals handled by one of the experimenters and that the higher readings were being taken from the animals handled by the other experimenter. The effect was independent of the particular animals, the particular mazes, and the particular recording instruments. A third experimenter was substituted for the one whose animals gave the abnormally high readings of BRL. This experimenter produced BRL values (in his animals) that were lower than the readings obtained by the experimenter he replaced but still higher than those obtained by the remaining experimenter.

Even though the observation was a casual one, it was clear that different experimenters produced different levels of BRL. The hypothesis that seemed worth entertaining was that different experimenters produced different amounts of fear while handling the animals and that the different levels of fear yielded different skin resistance values.

Our observation also suggested that the classical "goal gradient" might be an experimenter variable. It is well known among experimenters who have worked with the goal gradient that it is an elusive phenomenon. Sometimes it is clearly apparent in a set of data, and sometimes it seems to be absent. It is conceivable that the goal gradient is a product of an animal that has been frightened by the experimenter. The animal increases speed in getting away from the starting box as an escape reaction from the handling. After it has run enough trials to know that it will again be picked up by the experimenter from the goal box, a slight avoidance tendency begins to develop as the goal box is approached. This hypothesis appears to account for all of the data.

Three more experiments were devised to contribute information to the two major questions raised by the results of the goal gradient experiment. The first question concerned the replicability of the rise in BRL (thus decrease in arousal) that seems associated with learning. The second question concerned the possibility that the goal gradient might be an experimenter variable.

*The Dissociation of BRL and Running Speed through Stimulus Change.* The primary objective of the next experiment in the series was to find a manipulation that would change BRL during the course of a learning experiment without a major effect on running speed. It seemed possible that the rise in skin resistance was a simple adaptation phenomenon or else that it was closely tied with running speed, however the running speed was produced. To determine whether the latter was the case, it was decided to carry out training in a maze with one set of stimuli, then shift the animals to a similar maze with another set of stimuli, and then return them to the first maze. If the stimulus change did not seriously affect running speed but did affect BRL, then it would appear that the correlation between running speed and BRL was not an artifactual product of the rapid running.

It was decided at the same time to investigate two other associated variables. Since handling technique appeared to have made a difference in the previous study, handling was made a variable in this one. Half of the animals were handled extensively for a number of days prior to the experiment, while the other half were not. At the same time, individual or group housing seemed worth investigating for its effect on performance. The study was thus devised to investigate stimulus change, handling, and housing (Weems & Walker, 1964).

The major findings in terms of mean latency and mean BRL as a function of training are shown in Figure 11-7. The plotted mean latencies involve 96 values per point. They represent values for 16 animals at each of the six gates of the maze. Mean BRLs are also of 96 values per point. As in previous studies, as latency dropped during the first stages of training, the mean BRL value tended to

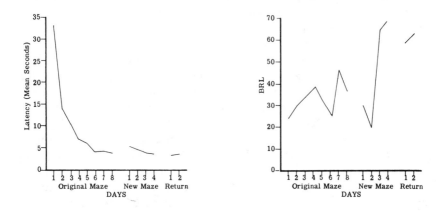

FIGURE 11-7. *BRL and Latency Changes in Response to Change in Maze Stimuli. The figures are plots of mean latency (left) and BRL (right) as functions of eight days of training in one segmented straight runway, four days of continued training in an adjacent runway with a different striped pattern, and a final two days of training in the original maze. (Redrawn from "Speed and Basal Resistance Level (BRL) in a Segmented Straight Alley as a Function of Alteration of Stimuli, Gentling, and Isolation," by L. B. Weens, Jr. and E. L. Walker,* Psychological Record, *1964, 14, 515–519. Reprinted by permission.)*

rise. Both trends were statistically significant in spite of the irregularity in the curve of mean BRL as a function of training. The two mazes differed only in the striped patterns on the walls, one having broad stripes and the other having narrow stripes. The shift from the original maze to the other for four days produced very little change in the mean latencies but appears to have produced a drop in BRL for the first two days after the shift. The return to the original maze had no effect on starting latency and produced a slight but statistically insignificant drop in BRL. Thus, the procedure of changing an animal from one maze to the other appears to have produced a shift in BRL while having little effect on running speed. In view of the objective of this operation, the irregularities in the BRL curve are worthy of special comment.

Because animal storage facilities were not adequate to handle all of the animals being used at one time, it was necessary to store some animals in a hallway within the storage facilities. When laboratory classes must use the facilities, there is no way to keep experimental animals from being exposed to the shouting and noise of undergraduate students. The low values of BRL on days 4, 5, and 8 of original training and on day 2 in the other maze unfortunately coincide with those days on which there was heavy use of the facilities by the students in the elementary laboratory. Thus, Figure 11-7 confirms, to a degree, the correlation between running speed and learning seen in the previous study by DiLollo and Walker. It also shows, however, that BRL can be modified, whether by an adventitious and wholly unwanted set of disturbances in the laboratory environment or by the change in wall pattern of the maze, without a major change in running speed.

There were several essentially negative but meaningful findings. No differences in latency or BRL were obtained that could be attributed to handling, pattern of housing, or whether training was initiated in the maze with the broad or narrow stripes. Furthermore, no clear goal gradient curves emerged in any phase of training in either latency or BRL.

In separate analyses of variance on the three phases of training, two BRL differences approached the 5% level of significance. They are the social variable during original training and the handling variable during the four days of shift to the other maze. Both differences, however, were opposite the expected direction, in that the nonhandled animals and the animals caged singly showed higher BRL values and thus lower levels of arousal. Since these were only two of a fairly large number of possible tests, it must be assumed that they arose by chance, and it must be concluded that none of these variables had a significant effect on BRL or latency.

Goal gradient effects are minimal in these data. There was a tendency for the latency to be high and the BRL low in the starting box in relation to the values of these measures taken in other sections of the maze, but values beyond this point do not show a gradient pattern.

*BRL in Learning, Extinction, and Relearning.* The next study was designed to determine whether the rise in BRL during learning was related to the stage of learning or whether it was attributable to habituation. In the first case, BRL should rise during learning and fall during extinction; in the second, it should continue to rise during the extinction phase (B.E. Walker & Walker, 1964). Animals were given two trials a day in the linear maze. They had five days of learning, four days of extinction, and two days of relearning.

Figure 11-8 shows the effects of learning, extinction, and relearning on mean starting latency and on BRL measured in the delay chamber before each run and in the various sections of the maze during the run. The original acquisition curve appears to have reached an asymptote in ten trials. Latency in extinction reached the starting latency in eight trials. Four trials were sufficient to reestablish the short latency response. The low latency on the first day of the retraining occurred as a function of very short latencies at the last two gates. The animals were apparently able to see the reinserted water bottles through the clear plastic doors.

The figure also shows BRL scores as a function of days in the maze proper and in the delay chamber. The BRL scores in both instances are inversely related to latency and would therefore be positively correlated with speed as plotted in the Di Lollo and Walker study described earlier. It is clear, therefore, that skin resistance in this maze situation varies with the learned performance and is not a simple expression of adaptation to the situation.

If these skin resistance scores are reinterpreted in terms of arousal, Figure 11-8 seems to show that at the beginning of training the animals are highly aroused. As training proceeds, the animals are starting from each compartment with greater and greater alacrity, while the skin resistance measure is reflecting a progressively lower state of arousal. Furthermore, during extinction, skin resistance falls as latency increases, indicating progressive increases in arousal as extinction proceeds. The relearning data indicate that the process is reversible.

It will also be noted that the skin resistance measures taken in the delay chamber prior to the run appear to be a close reflection of the measures taken in the maze itself. It seems possible, then, to interpret these results as indicating that the arousal level reflected in BRL measures characterizes the state of the animal in the total situation rather than in a specific position in the maze. This interpretation receives additional support in this study from plots of the latencies and BRL measures as a function of minutes in the delay chamber and sections and gates of the maze itself. These values are shown in Figure 11-9 in terms of means across the three periods

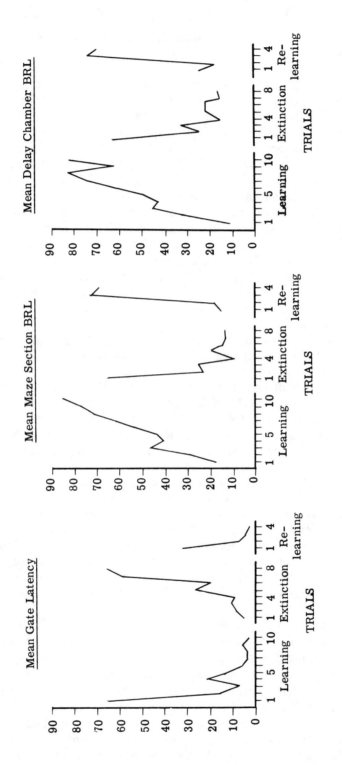

FIGURE 11-8. *Learning, Extinction, and Relearning.* *The figures display mean gate latency (left), skin resistance in maze sections (center), and skin resistance in the starting box (right) during acquisition, extinction, and reacquisition in a segmented straight runway. BRL is in 20,000-obm units; Latency is in seconds.* *(Redrawn from "Learning, Extinction, and Relearning of Running and BRL in a Segmented Straight Alley," by. B. E. Walker and E. L. Walker, Psychological Record, 1964, 14, 507–513. Reprinted by permission.)*

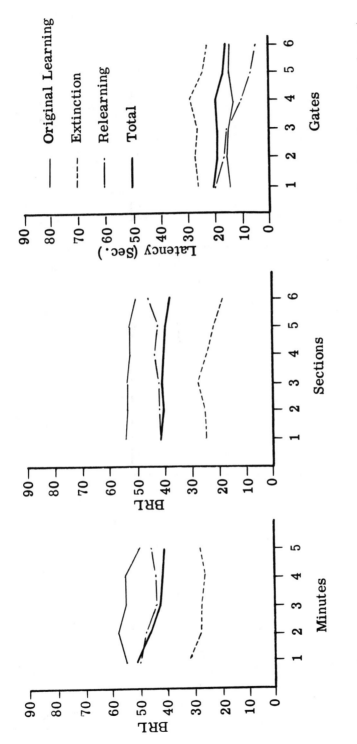

*FIGURE 11-9. The Goal Gradient (Overall Means). The figures are plots of skin resistance as a function of successive minutes in the starting chamber (left), skin resistance as a function of maze section (center), and starting latency as a function of gate position in a segmented straight runway. Values are means across all trials of original learning, all trials of extinction, all trials of relearning, and total trials. (Redrawn from "Learning, Extinction, and Relearning of Running and BRL in a Segmented Straight Alley," by B. E. Walker and E. L. Walker, Psychological Record, 1964, 14, 507–513. Reprinted by permission.)*

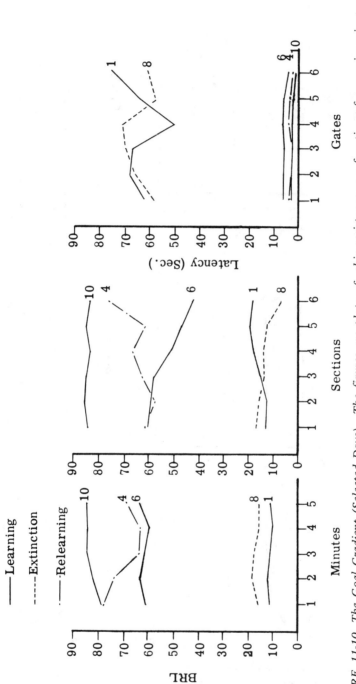

FIGURE 11-10. *The Goal Gradient (Selected Days). The figures are plots of skin resistance as a function of successive minutes in the starting chamber (left), skin resistance as a function of maze section (center), and starting latency as a function of gate position (right) in a segmented straight runway. Values are for selected days of learning (the first, sixth, and tenth trials), extinction (eighth trial), and relearning (fourth trial). (Redrawn from "Learning, Extinction, and Relearning of Running and BRL in a Segmented Straight Alley," by B. E. Walker and E. L. Walker, Psychological Record, 1964, 14, 507–513. Reprinted by permission.)*

(learning, extinction, and relearning) and in terms of overall means. No systematic goal gradient appears in any of the curves in this figure. A plot of a selection of individual days is shown in Figure 11-10, and once again there is no apparent goal gradient. The days selected are representative of all days with respect to the lack of a goal gradient phenomenon.

There are a number of differences in procedure between the Di Lollo and Walker study and the present one. It is tempting to try to account for the presence of a goal gradient in both running speed and BRL in the Di Lollo and Walker study and the absence of a goal gradient in this one in terms of the experimenter variable. It is a casual, and therefore untrustworthy, observation that the experimenter in this study had an unusual ability to handle rats without disturbing them; however, no objective measures of experimenter differences are available. It is a fact that the range of BRL values obtained in the two studies was different. In the Di Lollo and Walker study, the mean BRL values ranged from approximately 300,000 to 600,000 ohms. In the present study, they ranged from roughly 250,000 to 1,750,000 ohms. The smaller values in the Di Lollo and Walker study indicate that, throughout the study, the animals were more aroused than they were at the lowest arousal points in the present one. However, other differences in procedure might just as well account for the difference in BRL level. Some important differences are the drive used (hunger versus thirst), the amount of reward, or even the method of handling the data (latency versus speed). Therefore, the issue cannot be regarded as determined. On the other hand, this study appears to establish a correlation between skin resistance and running speed that is a function of expressed habit strength. Both results can be offered in support of an interpretation of the goal gradient phenomenon in the Di Lollo and Walker study in terms of reaction of handling rather than to variation in the intensity of $r_g$. The absence of a goal gradient in either running speed or in BRL in the present study can also be given such an interpretation.

*The Manipulation of the Goal Gradient through Shock Placement.* The last study in this series was an attempt to use shock to exaggerate the effects of handling. The idea was that, if handling aroused the animal and produced a greater tendency to run away from the spot where the animal had been placed, and if anticipation of being handled again produced slowing near the goal box from which the animal was picked up, a frightening shock added to handling should exaggerate the effect. In order to make all of the effects of shock apparent, four groups of animals were run. One group with normal handling served as a standard. The second group was shocked each trial before being placed in the maze, the third group was shocked each day after being removed from the maze, and the fourth group was shocked both before and after the maze experience (Williams, in Walker, 1969). The four groups were given the following designations:

NS—no shock given at any time.
SB—shock given before maze running.
SA—shock given after maze running.
SBA—shock given before and after maze running.

Figure 11-11 shows that one trial a day for six days was sufficient for significant learning to occur. The NS and SB groups showed decreases in latency characteristic of a typical learning curve. Groups SA and SBA did not show latency decreases. Thus, the animals that were not shocked learned to run fast in the maze. The animals shocked before being placed in the maze ran even faster. However, those animals shocked afterward did not show improvement, and those shocked before and after actually decreased their running speed.

The BRL measures plotted on the right side of Figure 11-11 show that the animals that were not shocked showed the typical increase in BRL that accompanies learning. However, none of the groups that were shocked showed any real change.

Figure 11-12 should reveal goal gradient effects. The left-hand graph shows mean starting latencies for the last two days at each of the six starting gates, and the right-hand graph shows mean BRL values for the two delay chambers and the seven sections of the maze. The latency curve for the NS group shows a general trend toward faster starting as the goal is approached, and the BRL curve

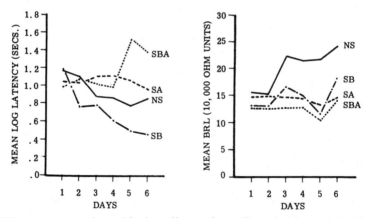

FIGURE 11-11. Learning with the Effects of Handling Exaggerated by Shock. The figures show mean running latency and mean BRL during six days of training in the linear maze. The NS group did not receive shock in the delay boxes, the SB group received shock before running the maze, the SA group received shock after running, and the SBA group received shock before and after running. (Study by Williams, reported in Walker, 1969b.)

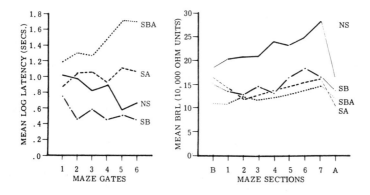

FIGURE 11-12. *The Goal Gradient under Shock Manipulation. The figures show mean latencies and mean BRL values for the different maze gates and maze sections. BRL was measured during the last 30 seconds the animal was in the delay box chamber in the "Before" condition (B) and in the first 30 seconds in the delay chamber in the "After" condition (A). Data are for the fifth and sixth days. (Study by Williams, reported in Walker, 1969b.)*

for this group rises over the same span. The effect of handling is evident in the drop in BRL for this group between the last section of the maze and the period in the delay box. The curves for the SB group are similar to those for the NS group, except that these animals are running faster and have lower BRL values.

It should be noted that within each of the groups higher BRL accompanies faster running speeds. However, the reverse is true between groups. The SB group, running significantly faster than the NS group, shows the lower BRL.

No simple interpretation of the results for the SA or the SBA groups is immediately apparent. The SA group shows little change in running speed, while the SBA group slows up significantly as it approaches the end of the maze. BRL for the three shocked groups remains low throughout training and throughout the maze. As a final problem of the relation between BRL and running speed, the three shocked groups all have approximately the same skin resistance levels and are running the maze at very different speeds.

*Summary of Goal Gradient Studies.* The results of this set of goal gradient studies do not lend themselves to a simple summary. The goal gradient appears to be an experimenter variable produced by rapid running to escape the handling that occurs just before entry into the maze and anticipatory slowing up as the animal approaches the goal box where it will again be picked up and handled by the experimenter.

The evidence for this conclusion is substantial but not over-powering. The primary piece of evidence is the fact that, in one study in which a marked gradient was found, it was oriented to the end of the maze rather than to the position of reward. Further, some experimenters obtain a goal gradient and others do not in similar situations. It seems likely but not certain that the difference is attributable to the difference in experimenters. Handling does produce a drop in BRL and thus a probable increase in arousal. Therefore, the hypothesis that the goal gradient is a variable related to the experimenter rather than to the experimental subject or situation seems viable.

The relation of skin resistance and thus arousal to learning and performance is ambiguous. As performance improves in a straight runway, skin resistance rises, indicating decreased arousal. Extinction seems to produce an increase in arousal, and relearning seems to produce a decrease. In the goal gradient situation, the correlation between speed of running and arousal appears to be the same. When speed is high, arousal is low. When arousal is high, speed is low. However, a change in the stimuli of the maze can produce a drop in skin resistance, indicating increased arousal, without an accompanying decrease in speed of running. In the last study, when shock was used, there were large speed changes that were unaccompanied by arousal changes. A tentative conclusion is that the arousal measured by BRL relates to the state of certainty of the animal in the learning situation. If the animal is uncertain, then it will be relatively highly aroused. As learning proceeds and the animal becomes certain of the reward, arousal tends to drop. However, this relationship can be masked by other emotion-related aspects of the situation. When shock is used, the animals all become aroused and fearful. This condition is reflected in a uniformly low BRL and thus high state of arousal. Between the three groups, running speed could be manipulated by the position of the shock in the sequence.

The relationship between skin resistance and arousal on the one hand, and learning and performance variables on the other, is thus sufficiently complex to justify further exploration.

### Conditioning of Skin Resistance

Few psychologists would doubt that the application of shock to the rat produces a state of fear. It also seems certain that conditioned fear can be established by presenting a neutral stimulus that is followed within a few seconds by shock. The neutral stimulus will take on fear-inducing properties through a process of conditioning in a very few trials. It should therefore be possible to condition the BRL response through the pairing of a neutral CS with shock. As indicated earlier, a major difficulty associated with the demonstration of BRL conditioning involves the unreliability of short-term samples of BRL records where there is likely to be movement artifact. Shock produces considerable movement in most cases and "freezing" behavior in the others. A mixture of records showing extensive movement and freezing behavior could be expected to give highly variable estimates of skin resistance.

Dewsbury (Walker, 1969b) used a Skinner Box in an effort to condition BRL. The CS consisted of turning the lights off; ten seconds later the animal was shocked for a period of one minute. Animals had one trial a day, and shock was introduced on the fifth day. The BRL values for all 16 days of the study are shown in Figure 11-13. Classical conditioning almost certainly occurred, but the results of this experiment are complicated by the fact that the animals tended to adapt to the shock.

The dashed line shows the course of BRL in the ten-second period immediately preceding the shock. It shows an erratic course, for about four days rising after the introduction of shock and then falling. The solid curve shows the course of the mean BRL measurements taken during the CS. It shows a somewhat erratic course over days as well, but on all days except the 14th, it shows a decrease

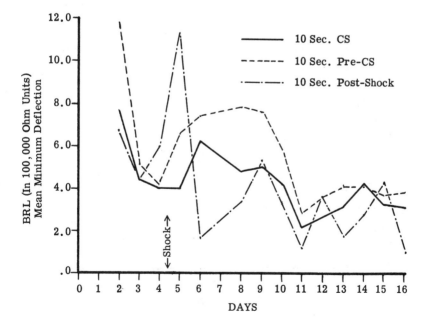

FIGURE 11-13. *BRL Conditioning. The figure shows mean BRL pre-CS, during CS, and in the period immediately after shock (on days when shock occurred) in a classical conditioning situation. (Study by Dewsbury, reported in Walker, 1969b.)*

in value upon introduction of the CS. In general, the decrease seems largest for the first four or five days after the introduction of shock. The third curve shows the post-shock BRL, which is generally, but not always, lower than the values obtained during the CS.

The effect of the classical conditioning procedure can best be seen in Figure 11-14. Here the difference between BRL in the pre-CS period and the CS period is plotted. The difference was large on day 2, when the CS was first introduced. By the fourth day the animals were fairly well adapted to the CS. Introduction of shock produced an increase in the difference (the expected effect of conditioning) that persisted until the 14th day before disappearing. Since the animals were being shocked repeatedly, and for as much as a full minute at a time, it is clear that they underwent adaptation to the shock and eventually ceased to fear it.

Although there seems little doubt that the procedure produced classical conditioning of BRL, there are several reasons why the results appear to be less than satisfactory. Considerable variability is evident in the two figures. Some of this variability stems from the very short measurement period (ten seconds in each case). The shock was of such long duration that adaptation apparently occurred.

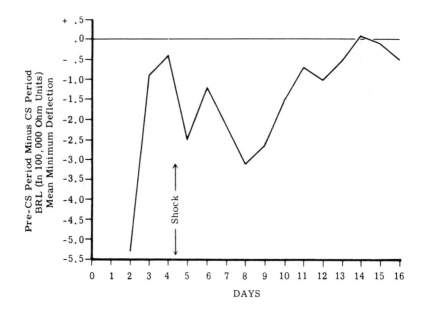

FIGURE 11-14. *Change in BRL from Pre-CS to CS Period. (Study by Dewsbury, reported in Walker, 1969b.)*

It therefore seemed worthwhile to undertake a further demonstration of the conditioning of BRL.

In the study of BRL and partial reward reported earlier (see Figure 11-3), Williams (Walker, 1969b) had constructed a small plastic box that was just large enough to hold a rat and that could be fastened to the wall of the Skinner Box, allowing the animal access to the lever. The box was constructed so that the animal's hind paws were firmly in contact with two stainless-steel strips. This apparatus was now used to shape four rats with food reinforcement to a stable VR 10 schedule. Conditioning was carried out with a 2000-cps tone of 60 seconds duration followed by a condenser discharge type of shock of 1 milliampere intensity and with a duration of less than .01 second.

One trial was given with the CS alone, and then six trials were given with the CS followed by the shock. Figure 11-15 shows the results. The left-hand figure shows mean BRL on the single trial with the CS alone. The CS produced a drop in skin resistance. This figure also shows the mean course of BRL during the six conditioning trials. There was a clear drop in skin resistance during the CS followed by a further drop when the shock was introduced. The figure on the right converts these figures to percentage drop. Here it is quite

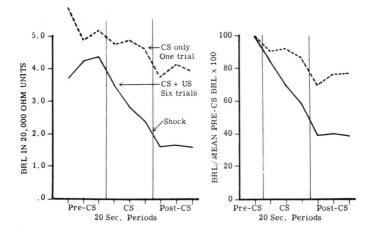

FIGURE 11-15. Conditioned BRL in Conditioned Suppression Setting. The figure on the left shows mean BRL for CS before conditioning and after conditioning for four animals in a conditioned suppression setting. The figure on the right converts these data to percentage change in BRL in the two situations. (Study by Williams, reported in Walker, 1969b.)

apparent that the conditioning of BRL occurred in this situation. One can conclude, therefore, that the conditioning of skin resistance occurs as one would expect if BRL measured arousal level or fear induced by shock.

*BRL and Heart Rate as Indices of Arousal in Conditioned Suppression.* The phenomenon of conditioned suppression offers an excellent opportunity to establish the correlation between a physiological index of arousal and learned performance. In the conditioned suppression paradigm, the usual pattern is to set up an operant response for an appetitive reward, such as food, and then introduce punishment, usually shock, and observe the effect of the punishment on the operant rate of the instrumental response.

If the shock is introduced in an avoidance conditioning paradigm, the simultaneous effects of the introduction of the CS on the operant response and on the index of arousal can be observed. If a differential stimulus (DS) is presented as well, then the development of discrimination between the CS and DS can be observed in both the instrumental response and the index of arousal. If the delivery of the shock is made contingent on responding in one animal and made independent of responding in another, then the effect of the contingency can also be observed in both classes of measures.

The only physiological index of arousal reported so far in this sequence of studies is variation in skin resistance. Heart rate is also frequently employed for this purpose. If both skin resistance and heart rate are measured in the same situation, then one can potentially correlate the two indices of arousal with each other and with the instrumental response performance.

A study to accomplish all of these objectives was designed and executed by Williams (J. L. Williams, 1968, 1969). Skin resistance was measured using the usual procedure. Heart rate was measured with a modification of the body strap electrode technique developed by Ferraro, Silver, and Snapper (1965).

For this experiment, Williams used the small plastic boxes that could be fastened to the wall of the Skinner Box to keep the rear feet of the animal on stainless-steel recording strips and to keep the animal oriented toward the lever and the food tray. Animals were shaped to press the lever for food and then carried through a series of steps, beginning with one-hour exposures to various fixed ratio schedules of reward (FR 2, FR 5, FR 10, and FR 15). Finally, the animals received daily sessions of one hour with variable interval schedules: VI 10 seconds, VI 20 seconds, and VI 30 seconds. The terminal VI 30-second schedule was in operation for the remainder of the experiment.

After the subjects had received VI 30-second training for ten days, they were given three daily habituation sessions during which tones of 2000 and 6000 cps at 70 decibels were presented. Three one-minute presentations of each of the two frequencies of tone were given each session, and the order of their presentation was randomized. The intertrial interval between tones varied between ten and 15 minutes. The animals were not removed from the boxes until five minutes had elapsed following the last tone presentation. Between the running of each pair of animals, the EKG electrodes and the strip electrodes on the floor of the boxes were thoroughly cleaned.

Upon completion of the habituation phase, discrimination training was begun with six tone presentations per session, three of the high frequency and three of the low frequency. As during the habituation sessions, intervals of ten to 15 minutes separated each of these presentations. For half of the animals, the high-pitched tone served as a CS for shock (US) and the low tone as a neutral or differential stimulus (DS). The stimulus conditions were reversed for the other subjects. The animals were run in pairs, with the presentations of tone and shock occurring in each of the chambers at the same time. The partners were matched on the basis of the number of responses they had made during the final habituation session. One member of the pair was assigned to a response-contingent condition and the other to a yoked condition, and assignments were made randomly.

At the beginning of each discrimination session, each animal had the cardiac electrodes fastened about it and was placed into a box with the VI 30 schedule in effect. After ten minutes had elapsed from the start of the session, the first tone presentation was given. For animals in the contingent group after the tone had been on for one minute, a "contingency period" was in effect for an additional minute, with the tone still being heard. During this contingency period, both response-contingent and yoked subjects received a 1-milliampere shock for .5 second after the contingent subject pressed the lever. The offset of shock was accompanied by the termination of the CS; thus no subject received more than one shock per CS presentation. If the contingent subject did not press the lever during the contingency period, the CS remained on for a total of two minutes, and neither animal received shock.

Discrimination sessions were given every other day to each pair of animals until all the contingent subjects had learned to "passively avoid" the shock by not responding during the three CS contingency periods of a given session. Then the animals received extinction sessions on alternate days. The presentations of tone and food were scheduled exactly as they had been during the discrimination sessions, except that the animals were never shocked. These sessions were continued until all animals failed to show a significant ($p < .10$) difference between the reduction in their response rates during the CS and DS presentations.

The number of lever responses, heartbeats per minute, and the lowest deflections in basal skin resistance were determined for the one-minute period prior to the stimulus (prestimulus), for the initial minute of the stimulus preceding the "contingency period" (stimulus), and for a 20-second period following the offset of the stimulus and/or shock (poststimulus). The response scores for each of these periods were means of the readings obtained during successive ten-second intervals. Since heart rate was recorded by means of a tachograph, a continuous measure was obtained in terms of the number of heartbeats per minute, based on the size of the interbeat interval. The skin resistance score consisted of the mean of the lowest resistance readings recorded during each of the intervals. It was assumed that relatively firm contact was made with electrode strips at least once every ten seconds.

In order to determine the magnitude of each of the CRs, the mean response value for the prestimulus period was subtracted from the mean for the stimulus period. The peak of the URs for the different response measures was found to occur within 20 seconds following the termination of the CS and shock. Thus, the magnitude of the URs was obtained by subtracting the mean prestimulus value from the mean reading for the two ten-second intervals following the offset of shock.

Although the procedure and apparatus produced a maximum in reliability, they also produced a degree of stress in the animals. The very small compartment, coupled with the procedures necessary each day to attach electrodes, tended to produce a general state of arousal. When shock was instituted as an additional source of stress, the arousal level became very high.

Figure 11-16 shows the general course of the three measures throughout the period of the experiment. The basic data of the figure are the values of each measure during the 60-second periods prior to presentation of the CS and DS stimuli. The adaptation period data are used as a reference, and other values are plotted in terms of their relation (in percent) to the values obtained during the adaptation period. In absolute terms, the mean lever pressing rate at the end of the adaptation period was about 58 presses per minute, the mean heart rate was about 490 beats per minute, and the mean BRL was approximately 220,000 ohms. It would be difficult to estimate what the lever pressing rate might have been under less confined circumstances. Heart rate may reflect arousal, but no comparative data are available. The skin resistance value, however, is quite low. Had the animals been less confined, one

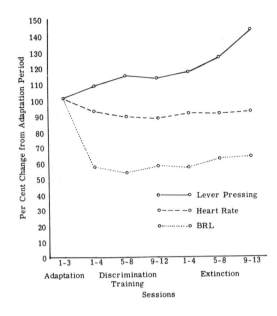

*FIGURE 11-16. Relative General Change in Lever Pressing, Heart Rate, and BRL from Adaptation to Discrimination Training and Extinction. The curves show the relative effect of the introduction of shock on the three measures of performance during the course of the experiment. The measurements were taken during the 60-second period prior to the onset of the CS and DS and therefore represent the general effect of the avoidance training involving shock. (From "Response Contingency and Effects of Punishment: Changes in Autonomic and Skeletal Responses," by J. L. Williams,* Journal of Comparative and Physiological Psychology, *1969, 68, 118-125. Based on* The Role of Response Contingency on the Effects of Punishment: I. A Review of Relevant Theories and Empirical Findings. II. An Experimental Investigation of the Changes in Skeletal and Autonomic Responses, *by J. L. Williams. Unpublished doctoral dissertation, University of Michigan, 1968. Reprinted by permission.)*

might have expected values between 400,000 and 500,000 ohms. Therefore, even though such cross comparisons between different situations are hazardous, it seems probable that the animals were showing an arousal state somewhat higher than normal.

With the introduction of shock at the beginning of the training period, BRL dropped to about half of its former value, down to about 100,000 ohms. Since this value is very close to the minimum value of about 70,000 ohms observed immediately after shock, it is obvious that, once shock was introduced into this confining situation, the arousal level, as indexed by skin resistance, attained a high and chronic level that endured throughout the experimental period. Heart rate dropped only slightly during the course of the experiment, and lever pressing rate actually increased during the periods of stimulus absence. If one regards the data of Figure 11-16 as indicating the effect of conditioning to the stimuli of the general situation, then the situation is conditioned to increased lever pressing, a slightly decreased heart rate, and a markedly decreased BRL. The levels of each of the measures in Figure 11-16 represent baselines for conditioning to the specific CS and levels that must show differential response to show discrimination learning.

Figure 11-17 shows the course of discrimination learning and the course of conditioning in the three measures. In the case of discrimination learning, the difference between the response to the CS and the DS was taken as the measure of learning. The maximum difference found during the course of the experiment was taken as 100%, and all other differences were expressed as a percentage of the maximum. Since the response to the DS could be greater than the response to the CS, negative values were possible and did occur. It is clear in the figure that discrimination in terms of lever pressing was at a maximum at the end of the training phase, whereas discrimination in terms of heart rate was at a maximum only near the end of the extinction period. Furthermore, when the lever pressing response no longer showed discrimination at the end of the extinction period, there was a very clear discrimination between the CS and the DS in heart rate. The onset of the CS produced a marked slowing of the heart rate, while the onset of the DS did not produce such a slowing. BRL, on the other hand, appears quite variable, because the maximum absolute effect that was observed in extinction is quite small. Real evidence of discrimination in BRL did not appear until the last eight sessions of extinction and is quite apparent in the records of BRL when there is no longer evidence of discrimination in the lever pressing response.

The lower curve represents conditioning and is a comparison of the responses in the 60 seconds before the CS with the responses in the first 60 seconds of the CS. Here, skin resistance changes appeared to occur first, with heart rate changes and lever pressing somewhat behind. During extinction, the conditioned suppression of lever pressing disappeared completely in the 11th and 12th days, whereas both heart rate and skin resistance continued to show substantial conditioning.

The absolute differences involved in conditioning are larger in all three measures than they are in discrimination learning. Conditioning produced a suppression of virtually all of the lever pressing, from 57 to .5 presses per minute. It produced a maximum decrease of 75.5 beats per minute in heart rate and a drop of 12,000 ohms in BRL. Discrimination learning produced a maximum differential of

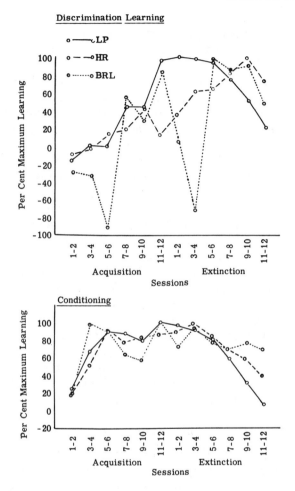

FIGURE 11-17. *Relative Courses of Learning in Three Measures. The upper curve shows the development and extinction of discrimination learning. The measures were taken during the second ten-second period after onset of the CS. The difference in response to the CS and DS was taken as the index of discrimination. With each measure, the maximum difference is taken as 100%. The data are for the contingent group only.*

*The lower curve shows conditioning data for the same group. The difference in response between the 60-second pre-CS and the 60-second CS period is taken as the index of conditioning. The maximum difference found with each measure is taken as 100%. (From "Response Contingency and Effects of Punishment: Changes in Autonomic and Skeletal Responses," by J. L. Williams,* Journal of Comparative and Physiological Psychology, *1969, 68, 118-125. Based on* The Role of Response Contingency on The Effects of Punishment: I. A Review of Relevant Theories and Empirical Findings. II. An Experimental Investigation of the Changes in Skeletal and Autonomic Responses, *by J. L. Williams. Unpublished doctoral dissertation, University of Michigan, 1968. Reprinted by permission.)*

6.6 lever presses, 45 beats per minute in heart rate, and 7000 ohms in skin resistance. This large difference in magnitude of effect accounts for the fact that the discrimination learning curves are more variable than the conditioning curves.

The differential rates of conditioning and extinction of the three measures, along with the differential development of discrimination between the CS and DS and its extinction, all argue that the skeletal and autonomic responses are at least partially dissociated. If either heart rate or skin resistance is taken as an index of arousal or fear, then one must conclude from these results that fear is essentially independent of the instrumental responses and that fear reduction cannot be the basis for acquisition of the response.

Williams reported in detail on the comparison between the contingent and yoked animals. Essentially, in terms of heart rate and skin resistance changes, the yoked animals showed fear that was equal to or greater than that of the contingent animals, yet they did not show as much conditioned suppression and did not show as complete discrimination. In his conclusions, Williams says that his results do not support the so-called "noncontingent" theories of punishment, such as that of Estes (1944), which claim that the relationship between the CS and the punishment, rather than the relationship between the response and the punishment, is critical in suppressing behavior. Williams also says that the fact that the two groups did not differ in autonomic response to the CS is contrary to two-factor theories such as that of Mowrer (1947).

### Discrimination Learning under Manipulated Arousal

The most direct way of approaching the problem of the role of arousal in learning and performance is to manipulate the level of arousal during the course of the learning of a simple task. Since animals appear to show recovery from the effects of shock on a predictable time course, it should be possible to present a simple learning problem to groups of animals that differ in how long it has been since they experienced shock. If the training of one group is carried out under the relatively high arousal induced by recent shock and the training of another group is carried out under lower levels of arousal, the effect of arousal on learning and performance should be revealed.

In the study of the effects of shock on BRL, there was a rapid recovery of about 25% of the total BRL change in the first three or four minutes. In the study of the effect on recovery rate of removal from the place of shock, it was found that animals permitted to run some distance from the place of shock recovered most of the BRL change in about 15 minutes. Based on these data, Williams (Walker, 1969b) devised a study of discrimination learning under manipulated arousal that took the following general form. A distinctive delay box was added to a simple Y-maze. Animals that were to learn under high arousal were retained in the delay box for 15 minutes, shocked, and then permitted access to the starting box of the Y-maze. They were permitted to make a choice between the two alternatives two minutes after being shocked. Animals in the low-arousal group were placed in the delay box and shocked at the end of a two-minute period. They were then admitted to the starting box and retained for 15 minutes before being permitted to choose. The expectation was that the difference in time since shock would have the effect of making the arousal levels at the time of choice very different for the two groups of animals.

The effort to manipulate skin resistance, and thus arousal level, was effective. Table 11-2 shows mean BRL readings in the starting box and at the choice point. The BRL values for the high-arousal group are consistently lower (thus indicating higher arousal) in both compartments than are the values for the low-arousal group. In the starting box the difference between groups is approximately 48,000 ohms. At the choice point the difference is approximately 100,000 ohms.

*TABLE 11-2.* Effect of Arousal Manipulation during Training (BRL in 100,000-ohm units)

| | Trials | | | | |
|---|---|---|---|---|---|
| Starting Box | 1–2 | 3–4 | 5–6 | 7–8 | Mean |
| High-Arousal Group | 2.38 | 2.35 | 2.90 | 2.43 | 2.50 |
| Low-Arousal Group | 2.83 | 2.72 | 3.11 | 3.26 | 2.98 |
| Choice Point | | | | | |
| High-Arousal Group | 2.40 | 2.60 | 3.17 | 2.30 | 2.62 |
| Low-Arousal Group | 3.63 | 3.45 | 3.87 | 3.54 | 3.62 |

The effect of the manipulation of arousal on learning and performance is shown in Figure 11-18. The curves showing percent correct do not appear to be significantly different for the two groups. However, the curves showing the mean latency of choice are different. Through the first four days of training, the low-arousal group took a much longer time to make its choices. In the last four days, there was no difference between the two groups.

Taken at face value, the results appear to indicate that high arousal affected performance by producing faster running in this discrimination situation but that it did not affect the rate of learning. The two conclusions should probably be weighted differently. The two groups did not differ in rate of learning, but this was an extremely simple problem, and extensive preliminary training was provided. It is not certain what would have happened if a much

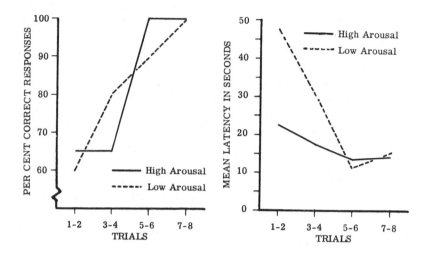

*FIGURE 11-18. Discrimination and Manipulated Arousal. The figures show mean percent correct choices and mean latency of choice for eight trials of a simple discrimination learning task. Arousal level at the time of choice had been manipulated through variation in time since shock.*

more difficult, and therefore much more discriminative, problem had been used. The effect of arousal on running speed, however, seems well established. Highly aroused animals run faster. Although this finding is clear, the range of conditions over which one might expect to find this result is not. In this study, animals were running away from shock and toward a liquid reward. The faster running of the high-arousal group could be interpreted as shock-escape behavior. The relatively short latency choices of the last four days of training in both groups seem to reflect rapid approach behavior. In summary, high arousal appears to produce a faster, more vigorous performance of the learned response, but it does not appear to affect the rate of learning.

*Approach-Approach and Avoidance-Avoidance Conflict.* Conflicting action tendencies should produce arousal. According to Lewin's classic analysis of conflict, conflicting tendencies to approach two different situations should produce mild conflict and a mild increase in arousal. Conflicting tendencies to avoid two different situations should produce a maximum of conflict and thus a maximum of arousal. If BRL reflects the arousal state, BRL should be significantly lower in an avoidance-avoidance conflict situation than in an approach-approach conflict situation.

J. Susan Frohman (Walker, 1969b) established approach tendencies toward a set of stimuli and avoidance tendencies toward another set. Animals were then faced with a pair of stimuli to which they had acquired approach tendencies and a pair to which they had acquired avoidance tendencies in a situation in which they could be held in the presence of these stimulus sets long enough to measure their skin resistance. For comparison purposes, some animals were trained with food reward for a correct choice and non-reward for an incorrect choice, while other animals were trained with food reward for the correct choice and shock for the incorrect choice. The difference in the arousal levels produced by the conflict situations could thus be compared with differences produced by the presence or absence of shock.

The maze had a 10-inch starting alley with an opaque door. The animal could be released into an 8-inch delay chamber with a transparent door through which the animal could see the choice alleys and their associated stimuli. It was thus possible to detain the animal in the presence of conflict-inducing stimuli long enough to obtain a measure of BRL. When the animal was released from the delay chamber, latency of response could be measured.

The stimuli to be discriminated were black-and-white horizontal or vertical bars painted on clear plastic and attached to the goal box doors and walls. A water bottle could be attached to the end of the goal box to provide water reward, and shock (a condenser discharge type with a maximum current of about .7 milliamperes and a duration of about 8 milliseconds) could be delivered when appropriate through the floor. Animals were trained to a criterion of 12 correct choices in succession in the discrimination situation. Since shock was delivered only for an error, animals receiving shock for error had gone a number of days without shock by the time the learning criterion was met.

Testing for the effect of conflict was accomplished by presenting trials on which both alleys had the same stimulus in place, either positive (approach-approach) or negative (avoidance-avoidance). Each animal was given two trials per day, one of each variety, with the order of trials reversed on successive days. There were ten days of such testing, but the results are reported only from the first two, since later test trials were affected by the fact that reward was given on both sides on the approach-approach trials and on neither side on the avoidance-avoidance trials.

Table 11-3 shows that the response speeds were considerably faster in the approach-approach situation. Speeds were also faster when shock had not been used as punishment for the wrong choice, even though the animals that were shocked had not experienced shock for several days before the test trials. The type of conflict produced bigger differences than the presence or absence of shock.

Table 11-4 reveals that mean BRL also followed the expected pattern. Animals in the approach-approach situation showed higher

*TABLE 11-3.* Response Speeds in Conflict Situations (1/latency in seconds)

| Conflict Type | No Shock | Shock | Difference Due to Shock |
|---|---|---|---|
| Approach-Approach | .295 | .120 | .175 |
| Avoidance-Avoidance | .095 | .035 | .060 |
| Difference Due to Conflict Type | .200 | .085 | |

Study by Frohman, reported in Walker, 1969b.

*TABLE 11-4.* BRL in Conflict Situations (100,000-ohm units)

| Conflict Type | No Shock | Shock | Difference Due to Shock |
|---|---|---|---|
| Approach-Approach | 3.03 | 2.95 | .08 |
| Avoidance-Avoidance | 2.82 | 2.75 | .07 |
| Difference Due to Conflict Type | .21 | .20 | |

Study by Frohman, reported in Walker, 1969b.

skin resistance and thus less arousal than animals in the avoidance-avoidance situation. The differences are statistically significant for the type of conflict in both tables and for the shock variable with respect to speed, but the effect of shock on BRL is not significant.

Thus, the expected effect of the two types of conflict on arousal did occur. The approach-approach conflict situation, which should not create much stress, yielded faster response speeds and higher BRL (thus lower arousal) than the avoidance-avoidance conflict with its slower response speeds and lower skin resistance (thus higher arousal).

### Summary of Arousal and Learning in Animals

Arousal can certainly be conditioned. It also varies with the state of learning, but the relationship is exactly the reverse of the traditional treatment of drive and learning. Arousal is high before learning and in extinction and is low when the act has been learned. However, arousal can be manipulated during the process without major effect on the learned performance. It therefore seems that arousal is the product of the state of learning rather than the driving force. This conclusion is supported by a number of other findings. Arousal is lower in an approach-approach conflict situation than it is in an avoidance-avoidance conflict situation. When the arousal level during choice in a discrimination learning situation is manipulated, it appears to affect the speed of the performance and not the accuracy. There is sometimes a goal gradient in runway data and sometimes not. If there is a goal gradient in running speed, there appears to be one in the arousal measurement. If there is no goal gradient in speed, there appears to be none in arousal. This phenomenon seems to be related to the effects of the experimenter's handling of the animal. Partial reinforcement schedules are accompanied by different arousal levels, as one might expect if the different schedules were differentially frustrating; however, the relationships are complex.

Finally, the rate of acquisition and extinction of conditioned arousal and conditioned suppression appear to be dissociated. Arousal (in terms of skin resistance) is conditioned more rapidly and extinguished more slowly than the skeletal response. Discrimination is quite apparent in the skeletal response, while the indices of arousal show an indiscriminately high level.

In the one study in which both skin resistance and heart rate were measured, heart rate showed discriminations when skin resistance showed indiscriminately high arousal. In terms of rate of acquisition and extinction, heart rate and skin resistance showed about the same level of dissociation as skin resistance and the skeletal response. One can conclude that the three measures probably reflect a common state but that the relationship between the three measures is not causal. If they are not causal, then it is unlikely that theories of learning involving such dynamics as the conditioning of arousal, the motivation of the skeletal response by the arousal, and the learning of the response through arousal reduction can be supported.

One can then ask whether variation in skin resistance is a good measure of arousal. There are at least two senses in which it is a good measure. First, the variety of results make any explanation in terms of artifact of measurement untenable. Skin resistance does reflect some aspect of the state of the organism. Second, it is consistently manipulable with varying degrees of face validity through a variety of means, such as manipulations of emotion, activation, or arousal conceived as a dimension from sleeping to waking.

However, there are several reasons why skin resistance is a poor measure of arousal. It is relatively labile and varies with situations one would like to ignore. Animals can be upset by minor incidents associated with their handling, or they can be aroused by something so simple as people moving around in the environment. It is a poor measure because it has a ceiling. With skin resistance at a low level, other measures show discriminations when skin resistance does not. It is a poor measure because, since it does not vary with differences in appetitive drive, it doesn't relate directly to drive theory and learning theory based on drives and drive reduction. Furthermore, since it shows low arousal when a response is well learned and high arousal when it is not, it contradicts the assumed relation between effective drive and stage of learning.

The status of arousal and skin resistance at this point is something like the following. Skin resistance does measure some meaningful aspect of the state of the organism, and it does so sufficiently well to justify its use as a measure of arousal. The assumption of a logical coordination between skin resistance as a measure and arousal as a theoretical concept yields statements that are sufficiently meaningful that the coordination seems justified. Therefore, it is reasonable to interpret the empirical results of these studies as relating arousal to aspects of behavior.

## AROUSAL AND VERBAL LEARNING

So far in this chapter we have dealt with arousal and animal learning. Although it has been traditional to ignore such factors as motivation and arousal in human verbal learning and memory research, common experience provides evidence suggesting that research on arousal and human verbal behavior might be worthwhile. It is common experience to be able to remember in vivid detail events that are highly emotional in character. Such events stand out in our memory so distinctly that they must have been easier to learn or easier to remember than similar events that aroused less emotion. To the extent that this common experience can be verified in a laboratory setting, the Hedgehog offers two possible explanations for it: enhanced learning or recall could be related either to the affective variable and thus the preference function or to the arousal dimension.

Words have affective properties based on the frequency with which they are used. We saw in Chapter 7 that the ease with which words are learned as response items is predictable from familiarity or frequency of use. Familiar words are easy to learn in the paired associates paradigm, whereas rare words are more difficult to learn and recall. Since preference bears an inverted-U-shaped relation to frequency of use, the relation between preference and learning is a complex one. Preferred words of optimal psychological complexity are moderately easy to learn; however, they are more difficult to learn than less preferred familiar words and easier to learn than less preferred rare and difficult words. It should be noted that it is the familiarity of the response item that contributes to ease of learning in the paired associates situation. According to Underwood and Schulz (1960), ease of learning and recall are unaffected by the relative familiarity of the stimulus word. Thus, the data reviewed in Chapter 7 offer no evidence to support the idea that the evaluative or affective properties of a situation are the source of the ready recall of emotional events.

The alternative possibility within the Hedgehog is that it is the arousal properties of an event that account for differential capacity to recall it. It might be that those events that occur when the organism is in a highly aroused state are easier to recall than similar events that occur when the organism is in a state of low arousal. Let us examine some studies in which an effort was made to determine the extent to which the level of arousal during acquisition determined the ease of later recall.

### Arousal, Incentive, and Short-Term Memory

Incentives have arousal properties. As we saw in Chapter 10, anticipation of an incentive can produce an elevation of arousal level, and consumption of an incentive can produce a rapid decline in arousal. Weiner and Walker (1966) manipulated the arousal properties of items to be learned in a short-term memory experiment. Subjects were asked to pronounce trigrams of low association value and to recall them either 4.67 or 15 seconds later. The interval was filled with a reading of digits that was paced by a metronome.

There were four incentive conditions. A control group had no incentive. One group received one cent and another five cents for each correctly recalled trigram. A fourth group received a mild shock for each incorrect response. To insure that the incentive conditions were correctly anticipated, the slides on which the trigrams were printed had different colored backgrounds—red, green, yellow, or white. The subjects were pretrained so that they were clearly aware of the nature of the incentive condition while pronouncing the trigram and while attempting to recall it. In all, 20 subjects attempted to recall 80 trigrams, 20 in each incentive condition and half of each group at each delay condition (either 4.67 or 15 seconds).

As can be seen in Figure 11-19, the incentive condition did affect recall performance. Recall was better with shock for incorrect recall and for the larger (five cent) reward than for the one cent reward or the no-incentive control condition. The main effects of incentive, the interaction between incentive and delay, and the difference seen in the figure at 15 seconds delay are all statistically significant. Stronger and larger incentives produced better recall performance than smaller and weaker incentives.

There are at least two problems with the interpretation of this result in terms of the effects of arousal. First, although it seems likely that the incentive conditions did produce differences in arousal level, it also seems possible that there could have been differences in attention and effort associated with the incentives. Thus the differences seen in Figure 11-19 might have occurred without there having been differences in arousal.

Second, there is some question concerning what to expect in recall as a function of differences in arousal. It was demonstrated in Chapter 6 that large rewards lead to a greater tendency to alternate

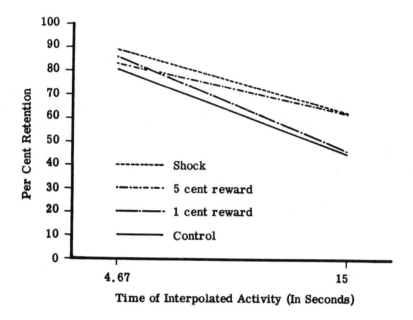

FIGURE 11-19. *Short-Term Memory and Incentive. (Redrawn from "Motivational Factors in Short-Term Retention," by B. Weiner and E. L. Walker,* Journal of Experimental Psychology, *1966, 71, 190–193. Copyright 1966 by the American Psychological Association. Reprinted by permission.)*

than small rewards. I attributed this effect to the greater arousal produced by the large reward, the greater habituation effect of the greater arousal, and the greater eventual tendency to repeat a rewarded response after recovery from habituation. I further suggested that the greater habituation might have the function of protecting the memory trace from interference during an active phase. The expected effect of the application of a reward after the occurrence of an event is diagrammed in Figure 11-20 (Walker, 1967). In the figure, the reward or incentive is applied after the 15–30 seconds assumed to be the duration of the short-term memory period. In the Weiner and Walker study, the effects of the incentive are presumed to be present during the event itself and during the short-term memory period. It is therefore a reasonable question whether increased arousal should produce greater or lesser availability of the item during this period. Greater arousal during the event should produce a more intense event, and the line expressing the probability of retrieval of the item should start at a level higher than the one drawn in the figure. The result should be that a high-arousal item will be more available during the short-term memory period,

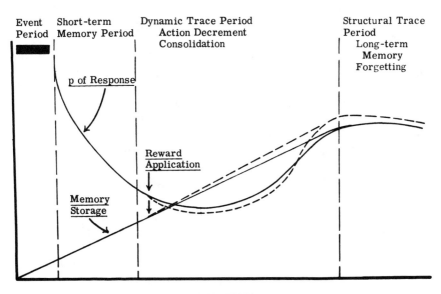

**LOG TIME**

*FIGURE 11-20. Model of the Memory Trace. A model of the memory storage process that distinguishes three functionally different memory trace periods. (Redrawn from "Arousal and the Memory Trace," by E. L. Walker. In D. P. Kimble (Ed.),* The Organization of Recall. *Copyright 1967 by the New York Academy of Sciences. Reprinted by permission.)*

less available during the dynamic trace period, and more available in the structural trace period of the diagram. The Weiner and Walker results testing for recall at 4.67 and 15 seconds confirm this expectation.

### Arousal and Long-Term Memory

The memory trace model in Figure 11-20 has two implications for recall in long-term memory. First, after the short-term memory period has come to an end, items learned under high arousal should be less available than items learned under low arousal. Second, at some later time, the availability of the two classes of items should be reversed, and items learned under high arousal should be easier to recall.

This rather unlikely sounding result was obtained by Klein-smith and Kaplan (1963, 1964). They used words as stimulus items and single digit numbers as response items. By measuring the GSR of subjects to the stimulus items, they were able to classify the level of arousal produced by each item as High, Medium, or Low. Then they observed whether the probability of recall of an item varied with the level of arousal produced by the stimulus word. Recall was tested at a variety of intervals, such as two minutes, 20 minutes, 45 minutes, 1440 minutes (one day), and 10,080 minutes (one week). Recall was poor for high-arousal items and very good for low-arousal items when the interval was short (two minutes), but at the three longer intervals (beginning with 45 minutes) the reverse was true: at the long intervals, high-arousal items were recalled much better than low-arousal items. Some of the words in this study, such as *kiss* and *vomit,* were chosen to elicit an emotional reaction. However, in a second study in which nonsense syllables were used, the same relationships were found with recall at two minutes and one week.

Walker and Tarte (1963) did a partial replication of the Kleinsmith and Kaplan studies and obtained similar results. In the replication, three lists of words were used, one composed of emotional words such as *kiss* and *vomit,* one composed of relatively neutral words such as *glass* and *walk,* and one that was mixed. Whether the data are analyzed by comparing the three lists or by looking at the responses within individuals, the results are very much the same and in general agreement with Kleinsmith and Kaplan. The upper panel of Figure 11-21 shows that, when low-arousal words were used as stimulus items, there was relatively high recall at two minutes but considerable forgetting after one week. When high-arousal words were used as stimulus items, recall at two minutes was slightly less than that for low-arousal words, but there was no forgetting even over a week of delay.

For the purpose of analysis within individuals, the three words that produced the largest GSR for a given subject were designated High arousal words, the three with the smallest GSR were designated Low arousal words, and the remaining two words were designated Mid arousal words. Panel B of the figure shows the results of this analysis. High arousal items show increased recall with the passage of time, while Mid and Low arousal items show forgetting. These results agree with Kleinsmith and Kaplan, although the separation between the High and Low arousal recall scores at a delay of two minutes is not as dramatic in these data as it is in the Kleinsmith and Kaplan papers.

*Serial Position*

The serial position of items was rigidly controlled in the Walker and Tarte study. It was therefore possible to plot the serial position curves for recall after a two-minute delay for comparison with the serial position curve after a delay of one week with everything identical for the two except the delay interval.

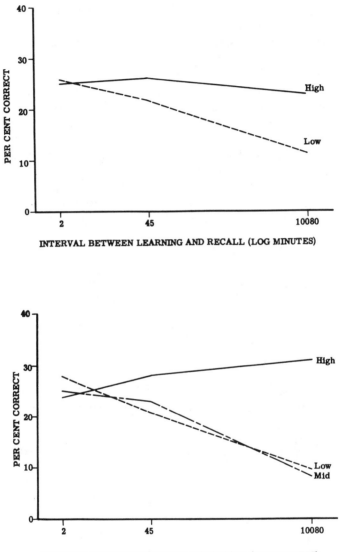

*FIGURE 11-21. Recall as a Function of Arousal and Time. (Redrawn from "Memory Storage as a Function of Arousal and Time with Homogeneous and Heterogeneous Lists," by E. L. Walker and R. D. Tarte,* Journal of Verbal Learning and Verbal Behavior, *1963, 2, 113–119. Copyright 1963 by Academic Press. Reprinted by permission.)*

As shown in the upper two panels of Figure 11-22, the results were dramatically different for the two delay periods. At two minutes, there is a small primacy effect (better recall of the first words on the list) and a large recency effect (better recall of the last items in the list). At one week the recency effect has disappeared and there is a very pronounced primacy effect. The lower right-hand panel of the figure shows the relative GSR values obtained during training as a function of serial position. The near match between the GSR curve and the recall curve for the one-week interval is impressive. It appears that the capacity to retrieve material from long-term memory is determined by the level of arousal during the learning of the individual items. The lower left-hand panel is a hypothetical serial position curve based on Melton's (1963) suggestion that the capacity to recall a learned item drops sharply during the first few seconds or minutes after learning. The serial position curve at two minutes seems accounted for by a combination of the two factors—rapid forgetting

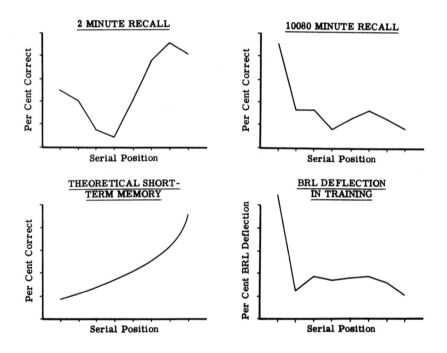

FIGURE 11-22. *Serial Position Effects.* (*Redrawn from "Memory Storage as a Function of Arousal and Time with Homogeneous and Heterogeneous Lists," by E. L. Walker and R. D. Tarte,* Journal of Verbal Learning and Verbal Behavior, *1963, 2, 113-119. Copyright 1963 by Academic Press. Reprinted by permission.*)

and arousal level during learning—whereas the recall curve at one week appears to be associated only with arousal level.

### Trace Interference

In a study that has not been reported elsewhere, Janice Erskine and I attempted to determine whether recall of high- and low-arousal paired associates would be differentially interfered with by an interfering task before recall. If paired associate items in which the stimulus is a high-arousal word show poor immediate recall because the trace is temporarily protected, then interference should be relatively ineffective immediately after learning. On the other hand, interference might be maximal for pairs in which the stimulus word produced low arousal and high immediate availability.

Learning consisted of a single presentation of the words employed by Kleinsmith and Kaplan. The response items were single digits ranging from 2 to 9, and the interfering learning was a presentation of the same list of words to be associated with two-digit numbers. The interference task was presented to four different groups of eight subjects each at varying intervals after original learning. The intervals were two minutes, 20 minutes, 45 minutes, and 24 hours. The test for retention of original learning was done 48 hours after original learning.

Figure 11-23 shows that there was much more interference with the low-arousal items than with the high-arousal items when

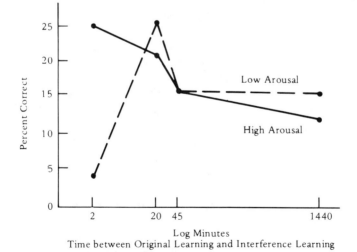

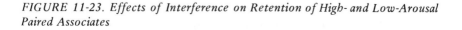

FIGURE 11-23. *Effects of Interference on Retention of High- and Low-Arousal Paired Associates*

the interfering task occurred immediately after original learning. The results at the other intervals are not as clear, with the high-arousal items appearing to show the effects of greater interference at two of the intervals.

Although the results of the Erskine study appeared to support the relative invulnerability of the trace from a high-arousal paired associate, the irregularity of the curves suggested replication and extension. If memory traces are differentially subject to interference depending on the arousal level at acquisition and on the time at which the interference is introduced, then a second training trial might also be differentially effective depending on these two variables.

Tarte carried out two rather large and elaborate studies to compare arousal and intertrial interval effects on interference and on the effects of a second training trial. The results of these studies have been reported in part in Walker (1967). In the first study, involving 192 subjects, the Erskine study was replicated with intervals of two, six, 20, and 45 minutes between the training trial and the interference trial. Recall trials were run one week later. A second group of subjects was treated precisely the same way, except that a second training trial was carried out two, six, 20, or 45 minutes after the original training trial.

The interaction of arousal level and intertrial interval can be seen in Figure 11-24. In Panel A it appears that pairs learned under high arousal benefited more from a second trial than did pairs learned under low arousal at the three short intervals but not at the 45-minute interval. The results for the interference trial in Panel B are quite different from Erskine's. Subjects were better able to recall high-arousal items and thus showed greater resistance to interference at all intervals except the two-minute interval, where the greatest differential effect was seen in the Erskine study. No general conclusion seems warranted by these two studies, other than that arousal during learning appears to produce better recall.

A cursory comparison of the two panels will show that there was no dramatic difference in this study between the effects of a second training trial and those of an interference trial. Because of this result, a second study involving a second learning trial and an interference trial was carried out with 160 subjects. The intervals between the two training trials were 2, 4.5, 10, 22, and 45 minutes; recall was tested at one week.

Figure 11-25 combines the results of these two studies, which involved a total of 352 subjects. For reference, Control performance is shown. This group had a single training trial and recall at one week. They recalled 20% of the response digits. Also for reference, the reader might remember that, since the response items were the digits 2 through 9, a subject could achieve an average of approximately 12.5% correct by simply guessing.

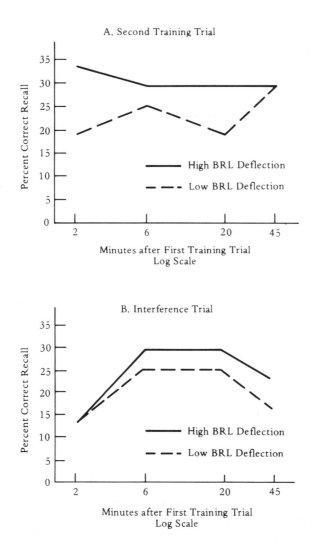

FIGURE 11-24. *Interaction between Arousal and the Effects of a Second Train-ing Trial or an Interference Trial on Long-Term Recall. (Redrawn from "Arousal and the Memory Trace," by E. L. Walker. In D. P. Kimble (Ed.),* The Organiza-tion of Recall. *Copyright 1967 by the New York Academy of Sciences. Re-printed by permission.)*

No simple pattern of trace augmentation from a second trial or trace interference from an interference trial is evident in the figure. It is remarkable that a second training trial makes no con-tribution at intertrial intervals of two, 20, or 22 minutes, and it is astonishing that an interference trial appears to have a positive rather than a negative effect at intervals of 4.5, 6, 10, 20, and 22 minutes. I know of no simple model of the memory trace for human

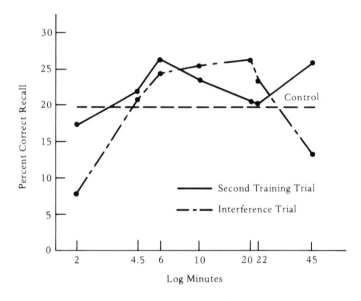

*FIGURE 11-25. Effects of a Second Training Trial or an Interference Trial on Long-Term Recall*

verbal memory, including the one shown in Figure 11-20, that will provide a simple account of the results in Figure 11-25. It is clear, however, that the phenomena are highly time dependent in complex ways, and this fact is usually overlooked in research on human memory.

### Summary of Arousal and Verbal Learning

Learning and retrieval of verbal materials involve structural changes. It is a clear implication of the material in Chapter 7 that ease of learning and recall is monotonically related to frequency and familiarity and thus related to the affective dimension by the familiar inverted-U function of the preference variable.

The data on arousal and learning of verbal materials reported in this chapter make it clear that material learned under relatively high arousal is generally easier to recall than material acquired under relatively low arousal. There is some evidence in these data that high arousal during learning sets up a trace that is more resistant to interference than material learned under low arousal. However, no simple model of the memory trace for verbal materials seems capable of accounting for the complex pattern of recall capacity tested at various times after learning.

The conclusions drawn from our studies of arousal in human learning and memory can be tempered to some degree on the basis of earlier studies of arousal and animal learning. In the animal work, arousal appeared to be one of the products of the learning process rather than a producer of learning. Arousal also appeared to be associated more closely with performance than with learning. Thus, if we can generalize from the animal to the human work, the relation between high arousal and better recall should be indirect rather than direct. One possible indirect path could be through attention. Very intense attention could be associated with high arousal and better recall, while more relaxed attention could be associated with low arousal and poorer recall. There is, however, no direct evidence for this role of attention.

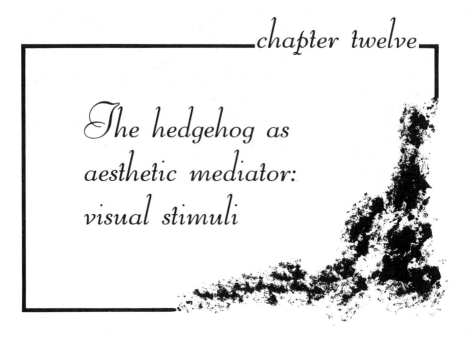

_chapter twelve_

𝒯he hedgehog as
aesthetic mediator:
visual stimuli

### THE HEDGEHOG AND ISSUES IN AESTHETICS

One of the potential applications of psychological complexity and preference theory is to aspects of classic problems and issues in the field of aesthetics. If the theory is successful, its major intellectual virtue will arise from its simplicity and its nearly universal applicability. Whether it is successful will be determined by the extent to which it can deal with the multiplicity of controversies in aesthetics through empirical test. This chapter and the next outline the first steps of a potential program of research and theory.

The Hedgehog is a psychological theory rooted in experimental psychology. This fact alone has significant implications with respect to a number of issues in aesthetics. Let us consider a few of them.

#### Analysis versus Synthesis

Daniel Berlyne (1971) has made a very useful distinction between classical and experimental aesthetics. In classical aesthetics, it is traditional to begin with aesthetic products such as paintings, poetry, or music and undertake an analysis of the characteristics and qualities that determine their relative aesthetic desirability. The key word is *analysis.* Experimental aesthetics proceeds in the opposite direction. It begins with general psychological principles and attempts to create a synthesis of the aesthetic experience while remaining on relatively firm empirical and theoretical grounds. The key word is *synthesis*. Whatever the Hedgehog has to say is in the mode of experimental aesthetics.

## Aesthetic Experience or Aesthetic Product?

A certain amount of confusion arises in the field of aesthetics from a very natural tendency to attribute aesthetic properties to objects. A painting, a natural scene, and a musical composition may be described in natural language as being a beautiful painting, an ugly natural scene, and a harsh and unpleasant musical composition. However, if aesthetic qualities are the properties of objects, then a beautiful object should be beautiful to everyone who views it, and it is obvious that this is not the case. One might therefore decide that aesthetic qualities are aspects of the human experience of the object. Given this view, it is more reasonable to expect individuals to differ in their reactions to the same or similar objects. Since the metaphysical position of the Hedgehog is one in which there are only data, and there is thus no fundamental distinction between the perceiver and the perceived, there is no reason to expect all individuals to report the same reaction and no reason to expect a physical object to remain constant. Rather, it is to be expected from the theory that the data obtained from individuals concerning their reactions to the object will change with repeated experiences. Consequently, the question of whether beauty resides in the object or in the eye of the viewer takes on the very different form of whether a particular viewer's judgment agrees with some reference group (or mean) value judgment. The distinction between the viewer and the object viewed is so deep seated in the common language that it is awkward to undertake to exclude the distinction from written and spoken material. It is for this reason that I will continue, just as you will, to speak of the aesthetic properties of objects even though we all know that aesthetic properties are characteristics revealed in our behavior, including our verbal behavior.

## Aesthetics and Usefulness

A work of art is often defined as a product or an activity that has aesthetic properties but that does not have any other use. Whatever usefulness this definition has, and I cannot think of any pragmatic value I wish to defend, it can also be counterproductive. I would argue that useful objects can have aesthetic properties and can share those properties with "useless" works of art. I would also assert that I know of no set of principles that are applicable to useless works of art that are not equally applicable to useful objects.

There is another sense in which the terms *useful* and *useless* have objectionable implications. The judgment of useful or useless stems from a very narrow conception of human needs. This conception leads to short lists of biological needs, often followed by lists of varying length of social needs. The implication is that all human needs are exhausted by these lists. It seems much more reasonable to me to identify a human need, if one thinks in these terms, by defining a predominant class of human activity that is clearly identifiable and distinguishable from other classes of human activity in terms of the object or goal that seems to be the end result of the activity. Aesthetic behavior is clearly identifiable with the goal of aesthetic experience. Therefore, by this system of classification, aesthetic needs are as real as the need for food. In this sense, an aesthetic object is as useful as a handy-dandy screw driver. Anyone who has read this far in this volume will not find it surprising that the Hedgehog, if required to classify and order human needs, might very well select aesthetic needs as the primary need of which all others are special cases.

### Multi-Level Structure in Aesthetic Products

A major problem in many areas of the fine arts is the near impossibility of matching the level of complexity preferred by the artist with that preferred by any significant population. Since artists are intensely involved in their media many hours a day, the effect of experience is to produce preference for products that are far above the preferred complexity levels of their audience. The same principle seems to argue that even if they find an audience, their continued experience with whatever they have produced will soon lead to boredom and dislike.

Interest in a visual product can be sustained either by not allowing it to be seen frequently, as with classical pictures in museums, or by designing the piece so that it can be seen or experienced at different levels of complexity by people with differing relevant experiences. Such a multi-level product can also grow on an individual who experiences it repeatedly. Otherwise it will simply grow out of fashion and disappear. Architectural works have the worst time with this problem because of their very permanence and because very few buildings are designed as multi-level visual experiences.

What happens when circumstances induce an individual to experience the same visual aspect repeatedly, such as the facade of the building where I had my office and which I had therefore been exposed to literally thousands of times? The individual simply ceases to attend to such a stimulus because it has fallen far below his or her optimal complexity level.

To illustrate with an anecdote, I have worn a moustache for nearly 40 years. I damaged it in shaving one time and had to cut it off and start over. I was amused that it took my family nearly a week to notice that it was gone. When they finally did notice, I grew it back. The faces of our loved ones become so familiar that we might be surprised to realize that it has been a long time since we really looked at the face of a wife or husband. It is easier for a wife to move the furniture than to rearrange her husband's face.

I might add that much of what I said about visual arts applies as well to literature. If a written work is to attain popularity, endure over the years, and justify being read more than once, it must offer the reader several levels of potential complexity.

### Aesthetic Products and the "Reality/Irreality" Dimension

Drama is less psychologically complex than life because it can be identified as not being real. The dramatic scene is held at some degree of psychological distance. The greater the psychological distance, the simpler the event. There are probably individual differences in the distance adjustment that individuals make in watching drama.

Unfortunately, the simplicity of this analysis is confounded by two developmental factors. As one grows older, these two factors influence the complexity level of the dramatic stimulus that will match one's optimal complexity level. (1) The normal developmental progression requires dramatic structure to become more and more complex in order to come nearer the optimal complexity level of the individual and thus to engage his or her attention and involvement. (2) On the other hand, very young children do not have the personal history of tragedy that operates to complicate the reaction to dramatic scenes. This complication has the effect, through association or elaboration, of making the use of adjustments of psychological distance more difficult.

Let us imagine a play in which a son destroys his father—for example, *Oedipus Rex.* Let us imagine two male members of the audience who are the same age of Oedipus. Both have been in considerable conflict with their fathers as they have struggled to establish their independence. The father of one is living, and the father of the other has just died of a heart attack attributed to strain and overwork. The first member of the audience can hold the murder of Oedipus' father at a greater psychological distance than can the member of the audience whose father has just died. The first may enjoy the play because it is near his optimal complexity level, but the second might find it too close to home and therefore too complex an event to be pleasurable.

Great drama might be defined as drama that retains its viability over many generations, drama that wears well enough on an individual that it can be experienced repeatedly and enjoyed on each occasion, or drama that appeals to individuals who represent a very broad spectrum of age or experience. All three of these criteria demand internal structure that permits the drama to be processed at a variety of levels.

### Diversity and Unity

Analytic theories of aesthetics vary widely in the character and number of terms employed to deal with the dimensions of the aesthetic experience. Most theories employ two principles, although there are a few with a single principle and some with more than two. (For a more definitive treatment of a great many such theories, see Berlyne, 1971.) Two-factor theories share the tendency to have one principle that is reasonably well represented by the concept of *diversity*, and a second principle that might be represented by the concept of *unity*. I have listed many of the concepts mentioned by Berlyne plus a few more and have attempted a classification of them in Table 12-1.

True to its nature, the Hedgehog becomes a potential aesthetic mediator by substituting a single factor, psychological complexity, for the two factors of classical aesthetics. Unmodulated, unpatterned, ununified diversity can be conceived as a very close correlate of great psychological complexity. Whenever the application of any form of organization—whether that organization is called form, pattern, unity, or whatever—serves to constrain untrammelled diversity, it can be seen as functioning to reduce the complexity the event would otherwise have. Thus, diversity and unity are reduced to the single variable of psychological complexity. The maximum aesthetic experience will accompany the occurrence of a psychological event of optimal complexity level.

### Modality and Time

A significant problem in experimental aesthetics arises when one examines the language of aesthetics and psychological concepts for bases on which to build. Much of the language used to describe visual aesthetics, especially that related to color, is not comfortably adequate to describe auditory aesthetics, except by strained analogy. Similarly, the musical notion of consonance seems inapplicable to visual experience. Psychological concepts arising from studies of audition and vision seem equally specific to the sense modalities of their origin.

Furthermore, it tends to make a difference whether time is conspicuously involved. I have attempted to classify a few of the relevant psychological concepts into *static* aspects, which are essentially simultaneous, and *dynamic* aspects, which are essentially se-

*TABLE 12-1.* Concepts from Aesthetics

| Diversity | | Unity | |
|---|---|---|---|
| complexity | ambiguity | abstract | banal |
| cacophony | concrete | biguity[a] | brilliant |
| conflict | differentiation | clarity | coherence |
| diffuse | discrete | combining | consonance |
| disharmony | disorientation | order | expected |
| disparity | dissonance | harmony | integrated |
| numerosity | multiplicity | intelligent | lawful |
| obscure | original | oriented | pattern |
| rapid | strong | redundancy | regularity |
| uncertain | unexpected | resolution | slow |
| unintelligent | unlawful | stable | stringency |
| unstable | variation | symmetry | synthesis |
| antithesis | | unification | uniformity |

[a]The term *biguity* is a non-word that expresses the opposite of ambiguity. I first heard it used by John W. Atkinson.

*TABLE 12-2.* Psychological Concepts for Use in Experimental Aesthetics

| | Static (Simultaneous) | Dynamic (Successive) |
|---|---|---|
| *Visual* | 1. span of apprehension<br>2. good figure<br>3. ------------<br>4. ------------<br>5. ------------ | 1. visual memory span<br>2. ---------------<br>3. ---------------<br>4. chunk<br>5. phi phenomenon |
| *Auditory* | 1. ------------<br>2. harmony<br>3. consonance/dissonance<br>4. ------------<br>5. ------------ | 1. auditory memory span<br>2. melody<br>3. ---------------<br>4. chunk<br>5. auditory phi phenomenon |

quential. In Table 12-2, I have set up a two-by-two table to illustrate the differences I have in mind. It is very difficult to find concepts that are applicable in all four quadrants, and I have tried to indicate that problem by numbering the concepts and leaving blanks where no equivalent concept comes easily to mind. Span of apprehension, visual memory span, and auditory memory span seem to belong together, but even if they do, they have no obvious counterpart in the auditory-simultaneous category. In some cases, items that seem to belong together, such as harmony and melody, are differentiated precisely to point out differences between them, even if both might be associated with the Gestalt concept of good figure. Roger Shepard, as I will discuss later, appears to have demonstrated an auditory equivalent of visual phi phenomena, but finding a static analog for phi does not appear possible.

### Integrative Function of the Hedgehog

Just as the Hedgehog offers the potential for dealing with all aspects of diversity and unity by means of the single variable of psychological complexity, the simple theory of psychological complexity and preference can potentially be applied equally to all four quadrants of Table 12-2. Figure 12-1 is an attempt to illustrate that diversity—whether visual or auditory, static or dynamic—is to be assessed in terms of psychological complexity. Furthermore, when any form of unity is imposed on diverse stimuli, regardless of quadrant, the effect is a reduction in psychological complexity. The theory is assumed to be operable, as has been demonstrated in earlier chapters, in many areas of psychological functioning not ordinarily considered to belong to the aesthetic realm. It is also assumed to function in all areas of the traditional fine arts—in literature, drama, poetry, music, and the visual and performing arts.

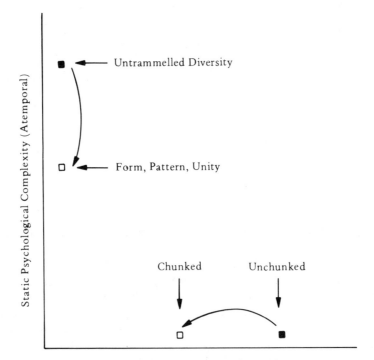

FIGURE 12-1. *Integrative Function of the Hedgehog. The integrative function of the Hedgehog is illustrated through the assertion that all aspects of diversity and unity in aesthetics, as well as psychological concepts (whether visual or auditory), are conceived as being reducible to a single variable, psychological complexity.*

## Optimal Complexity Level
### and the Aesthetic Experience

Among classical aestheticians, the essence of aesthetics consists of the aesthetic experience and the materials that induce such an experience in the viewer or listener. Among experimental aestheticians, the essence is the statement of the theoretical conditions that lead to or induce the aesthetic experience. It may be worthwhile to recapitulate here some of the features of the Hedgehog theory, especially as its approach to this problem differs from the specifications of prior conditions made by experimental aestheticians. For all such, maximum aesthetic experience is associated with some sort of optimal state.

In Chapter 3, all theoretical concepts in psychology were said to be classifiable into one of three classes—structural, energetic, or evaluative. As a logical possibility, aesthetic experience could result from optimization of variables in any one of the three realms. However, an aesthetic experience is a feature of the evaluative realm. Therefore, for a theory to explain the aesthetic experience in evaluative terms is circular. On the other hand, a specification of the conditions leading to the aesthetic experience in terms of either an energetic concept or a structural concept would be noncircular.

The Hedgehog chooses to optimize psychological complexity, a structural variable. Berlyne (1971) and Kreitler and Kreitler (1972) choose energetic variables, Berlyne choosing arousal and the Kreitlers choosing tension. It cannot be strongly argued that one choice, structural or energetic, is right and the other wrong. However, the Hedgehog, being true to its nature, chooses the simpler of the two concepts. Stimuli have only structural properties, and it is thus the structural aspects of psychological events that have logical and temporal priority. If some aspect of the energetic variable is to be optimized in order to result in an evaluative experience, then all three concept realms are involved in a logical chain with a particular order—first the structural effect, which in turn induces an energetic effect (arousal or tension), which then results in an evaluative effect (the aesthetic experience). This logical order also implies a three-step temporal order in reaction. It is also implied that all three steps must occur and be congruent on all occasions. The arousal condition cannot occur without appropriate prior structural conditions, and it must always occur when those structural conditions occur. The evaluative effect can occur only when arousal conditions are those specified by the theory and must occur when arousal conditions are appropriate.

Because it chooses psychological complexity as the dimension to be optimized, the Hedgehog is a simpler theory. Since the theory is a theory of choice behavior, the only inflexibility resides in the postulate that the event nearest optimum will be chosen. If there is then to be an aesthetic experience, it can be the direct product of the structural aspects of the event, which may or may not be accompanied by a change in arousal. In terms of temporal sequence, the occurrence of an event can be followed directly in time by an aesthetic experience, by an arousal change, by both simultaneously, or by neither. Let me expand two implications of this statement.

First is the implication that the aesthetic experience has no special association with psychological events induced by a product of the fine arts. Optimal psychological complexity is the determiner of attentional focus and of choice of acts. Whatever principle governs the occurrence of evaluative properties is equally applicable to activities such as viewing paintings, playing games, listening to music, reading this page for the reader, and writing it for the author.

Second, if the aesthetic experience is a hedonic one, a good feeling of pleasure, then it is subject to the vagaries of the hedonic experience in general. The Hedgehog, however, regards hedonic qualities to be vagarious and epiphenomenal and has respectfully declined to specify the conditions under which hedonic experience must inevitably occur, treating the problem as an empirical one. Let me indicate two bases for the reserved position of this simple animal. The first is a general argument concerning the status of hedonism as a determiner of behavior, and the second is an indication of the difficulties that have been self-induced by Berlyne and the Kreitlers in attempting a theoretical specification of the conditions under which the hedonic experience must occur.

There are at least two generalizations about everyday experience that seem to refute the principle that hedonism is a controlling factor in behavior. The great majority of the items in the stream of psychological events have no obvious hedonic properties associated with them. Most of the events that occur in our individual streams are neither pleasant nor unpleasant. Hedonic quality is not an intrinsic property of most of what we do. Since within the theory all that we do is determined by optimal complexity level, and since most of what we do has no hedonic value, there is little reason to establish a close association between the determinants of behavior and the determinants of hedonic experience. If we are asked, after the fact, why we did such-and-such a thing, we will sometimes use a hedonistic attribution, such as "Well, I liked doing it better than the other things I could have done." But this statement expresses *attributed* rather than *experienced* hedonic quality and is an analogous statement. In other words, we tend to draw an analogy with a subclass of psychological event that does have hedonic properties.

The second reason for rejecting hedonic quality as a determiner of most behavior is the frequently observed fact that people do things quite voluntarily, on occasion, that cause them to experience pain. If behavior were directed by hedonic principles, or principles of arousal change inflexibly associated with hedonic properties, then people would not do such things.

What is the place of hedonism, then, in the dynamics of behavior? I would argue that most psychological events have no hedonic properties at all. Those classes of psychological events that do have hedonic properties are limited to a special few, nearly all of which do have or once had profound biological significance in terms of individual or group survival. Many of these are now vestigial in precisely the sense in which the appendix in all of us and the mamillary nipples on the male chest are vestigial. In the absence of extended illustration and argument, perhaps a single example might do. The unpleasantness of extremely bitter substances may have served to produce selection for the capacity to find poisonous plants bitter and unpleasant and to reject them before swallowing. But the unpleasantness of the bitter taste is vestigial for someone with malaria who can be helped with quinine.

Hedonic qualities are therefore unsuitable as basic determiners of behavioral choice, even though there are subclasses of behavior in which the pleasure-pain principle appears to work. Hedonic qualities are unsuitable because most behavior has no hedonic value, much attributed hedonic value is in fact analogous, and much voluntary human behavior violates the pleasure-pain principle.

In attempting to specify the theoretical conditions under which the hedonic experience should occur, Berlyne suggests that pleasure should accompany a return from a superoptimal state of arousal to an optimal level. The Kreitlers specify a release of tension. Both have difficulty accounting for how the organism volunteers to experience an arousal jag, in the case of Berlyne, or to induce a state of tension, in the Kreitlers' version. If the organism is motivated to seek optimal arousal or seek reduced tension, then the organism should not choose to experience a superoptimal level of arousal, or seek to induce increased tension, just to get back to where it wished to be in the first place. The seeking of an arousal jag and the seeking of increased tension appear to be wholly ad hoc and contradictory motivational principles. In addition, both appear to postulate an invariable relation between the experience of pleasure and the return to the optimal or desired state.

### The Determiners of the Aesthetic Response

The Hedgehog has no power in the process of analyzing the nature of the aesthetic response—in the attempt to reduce the ineffable to the effable. However, the conditions under which aesthetic responses might be expected to occur can be specified without the invocation of any special principles.

An event that is at or near one's optimal complexity level should produce a positive aesthetic experience. The quality of this basic experience depends on its nearness to optimal complexity level. Such experiences are so common as possibly to go unrecognized. They are simply momentary pleasures. They are the least intense of all aesthetic experiences, but they share their momentary character with aesthetic experiences from all other sources. Habituation inevitably produces simplification, with the result that no aesthetic experience can be sustained for very long. No matter how pleasurable an activity, its optimal character cannot be prolonged.

More intense and interesting aesthetic responses occur when there is a sharp and sudden contrast in complexity. Music is an ideal medium for the temporal manipulation of aesthetic experiences. It is much more difficult to avoid hearing sounds than to avoid seeing pictorial material. In music, the composer or performer has control of the temporal sequence of events, whereas the painter must leave that sequence to the whims of the viewer. A sequence of psychological events that is below optimal complexity level followed by an event that suddenly increases in complexity to an appropriate level produces an intense aesthetic experience. Likewise, an aesthetic reaction is produced when a sequence of psychological events that is significantly too complex for the listener is suddenly resolved into an event at or near optimal complexity.

Habituation can also be used as a mechanism in the manipulation of aesthetic responses. If an event that is initially optimal is prolonged or repeated, the effect is to induce a state of boredom. Boredom is the product of a suboptimal state that can serve as the platform from which one can then restore optimality with a consequent pleasurable reaction. The degree of pleasure can be controlled by the amount of habituation produced before optimality is restored. Since an aesthetic response is, of necessity, brief, an aesthetically pleasing musical composition or performance is one in which the composer or performer has arranged a significant number of momentary aesthetic responses.

Although the Hedgehog provides intellectual handles that can be used in the manipulation of aesthetic responses, these handles do not provide a panacea. Individual differences are so great that it is truly remarkable when the same set of stimuli induce positive aesthetic responses in any significant portion of a group of people.

## EXPERIMENTAL STUDIES OF STIMULUS COMPLEXITY AND PREFERENCE

Most of the work that has been done by others in efforts to investigate stimulus complexity and preference has involved one of two approaches to the selection of stimulus materials. One approach is to select stimulus materials of differing complexity on the basis of a simple kind of face validity. This approach is handicapped because one cannot plot preference against such nonmetricized stimuli. The second common approach is to generate a set of stimuli with a known physical or quantitative dimensionality. An example is the use of differing numbers of dots where the number of dots forms a physical dimension with at least an expectation of a monotonically increasing relation to complexity. There are also a number of stimuli that have been generated by some simple rule. For example, a square might be laid out on a fine grid of regular points. The rule might then be to choose a point at random and move it one step in any of the eight possible directions. The sequence of figures generated in this way would be presumed to increase in complexity as more and more dots are moved repeatedly. This approach yields a meaningful physical dimension but profoundly uninteresting stimuli.

An alternative approach is to select sets of psychologically interesting stimuli and to determine their relative complexities through use of one or more psychological scaling techniques. The result might be a set of materials of much more interest than any previously available, and for which there might be meaningful quantitative dimensions.

In the studies to be discussed in this section, there were generally three aims:

1. to develop sets of visual stimuli with established complexity values based on psychological scaling techniques,
2. to develop a methodology for employing these stimuli with human subjects, and
3. to investigate the relation of complexity and preference.

These objectives have generally been accomplished. Research still needs to be done on relating arousal to these stimuli and verifying changes with experience in optimum complexity and arousal.

The stimuli employed in these studies were derived from four sources.

1. *Tartan patterns.* A number of tartan patterns were photographed in black and white to serve as stimuli. These had several virtues as stimuli, but one of the most important was that the number of squares in each pattern gave a physical measure of complexity. It was thus possible to check psychological scaling techniques against a physical scale with this set of stimuli.

2. *Stage set designs.* A number of drawings of stage set designs were photographed for use as stimuli. They had the virtue of representing well established styles in set design that differ in apparent complexity.

3. *Black-and-white graphics.* A large set of black-and-white graphics, all highly representational and symbolic and all done by well-known artists, were also selected. These had the advantage of

being well known to individuals who had studied art but not to most other individuals.

4. *Modern art.* A large set of colored prints of modern paintings was selected. They were chosen because they contained no symbolic material and were generally not identifiable in origin.

All stimulus materials were either in their original forms or photographed and reduced to 4 inch by 6 inch pictures. Each was then given a randomly selected code number, which was placed on the back. Finally, each was encased with plastic contact acetate to preserve the original quality during handling.

### Tartan Patterns

The tartan patterns used in these studies were taken from Innes (1938). From a larger list, the 21 patterns listed in Table 12-3 were selected and tested. As can be seen in the table, the number of squares in the sample varied from 91 to 2680.

*TABLE 12-3.* Tartan Patterns by Name and Physical Characteristics

| Code No. | Tartan | Number of Rectangles | Number of Rectangles in a Set |
|---|---|---|---|
| 1 | Royal Stewart | 1350 | 625 |
| 2 | Forbes | 759 | 841 |
| 3 | MacArthur | 187 | 81 |
| 4 | Skene | 945 | 169 |
| 5 | Brodie | 117 | 121 |
| 6 | Anderson | 2680 | 1369 |
| 7 | MacDonell of Glengarry | 2109 | 625 |
| 8 | MacKay | 247 | 121 |
| 9 | MacAulay | 195 | 121 |
| 10 | Kerr | 1815 | 361 |
| 11 | Carnegie | 1036 | 625 |
| 12 | Ramsey | 345 | 121 |
| 13 | Keith | 285 | 81 |
| 14 | Sutherland | 1025 | 529 |
| 15 | MacDonald of Sleat | 273 | 49 |
| 16 | Wallace | 165 | 49 |
| 17 | MacDonald of Clanranald | 1519 | 441 |
| 18 | Frazer | 247 | 121 |
| 19 | Urquart | 1891 | 529 |
| 20 | Montgomerie | 91 | 49 |
| 21 | Maclachlan | 405 | 121 |

In the first study, subjects were asked to rate each of the 21 tartan patterns from simple to complex. They were to use a scale of 1 to 100, with 1 representing the lowest degree of complexity and 100 the highest. They were then asked to rate each pattern with respect to how much they liked it. Again they were to use a scale ranging from 1 to 100, with 1 representing the lowest degree of liking and 100 the greatest degree of liking.

The ratings of complexity are compared to the physical properties of the tartan patterns in Figure 12-2. The number of squares is plotted on a log scale as an approximation of the psychophysical function that is probably involved in judging differences in number of squares. The physical scale and the psychological scale are in fairly good agreement in the figure. Since there are other possible physical dimensions in the stimuli, such as gray-scale and relative proportions, this level of agreement seems satisfactory. In fact, it seems possible that the psychological scale might come closer to representing complexity than does the physical scale.

The relation of the psychological scale of complexity and a similar psychological scale of liking is shown in Figure 12-3. There is an obvious relation between the two measures, with the subjects expressing a greater liking for the less complex tartan patterns. There is no evidence of an optimum in the middle range of values of complexity.

As a part of the same study, the subjects were asked to make a second evaluation of the extent to which they liked the tartan patterns. This time the patterns were offered in pairs, and the subjects were asked to assign a value to the difference in their liking for the two members of each pair. If the difference in liking was maximum, a value of 10 was to be assigned. If it was minimum, a value of

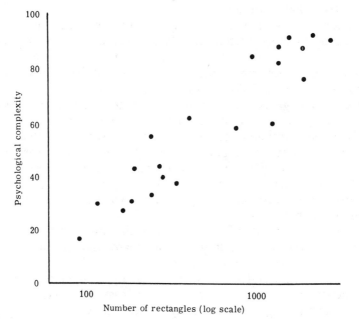

FIGURE 12-2. *Physical and Psychological Scales of Complexity in Tartan Patterns*

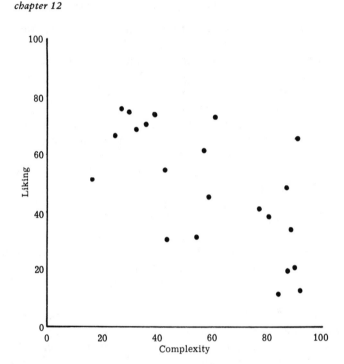

FIGURE 12-3. *Complexity and Liking for Tartan Patterns*

1 was to be assigned. Such data can be computer analyzed using the Shepard-Kruskal technique.

There are two major advantages to the Shepard-Kruskal scaling and scaling analysis technique. Data collected in this way can be analyzed for any number of dimensions. If a variable such as complexity, liking, or preference is actually multidimensional, the Shepard-Kruskal technique potentially can reveal that fact. The second advantage is that the data collected from a single subject can be subjected to multidimensional analysis. A disadvantage is that a one-dimensional solution is not necessarily the "best" solution. The computer program simply projects a line through the multidimensional space from an arbitrary starting point. It is the best line from that point but not necessarily the best starting point. It is often therefore necessary to ask the computer for an *n*-dimensional solution and try to match each dimension to some criterion. A second disadvantage of the analysis technique is that there are no internal criteria for determining how many dimensions are meaningful. For these reasons, we adopted the arbitrary practice of asking the computer for ten different analyses, specifying numbers of dimensions from one to ten in each case. The data from each individual and the group were analyzed separately.

After the subjects had finished their ratings of how well they liked the patterns, they were asked for extensive explanations of the reasons for their liking a given pattern. Many hours were spent in an effort to match individual Shepard-Kruskal dimensions with the verbal protocols, but the effort was fruitless. Liking seemed to be a single dimension, and elaboration of the basis for liking did not improve understanding of the dimensions.

Figure 12-4 is a sample of the Shepard-Kruskal analysis. In that figure, a two-dimensional solution for liking is plotted against the complexity ratings. The first dimension shows little or no relationship between the two variables. The second dimension shows a clear relationship very similar to that shown in Figure 12-3.

Figure 12-5 is an effort to determine the relationship between the liking scale derived from the simple rating on a 100-point scale and the Shepard-Kruskal analysis of preference. The one-dimensional Shepard-Kruskal solution yields no relationship. When the two dimensions of a two-dimensional solution are plotted, the first dimension shows little or no relationship, while the second dimension shows a rather high correlation.

One further study was carried out with the tartan patterns that was methodological in character. We wished to know what effect the range of stimuli had on ratings of complexity. Arrangements

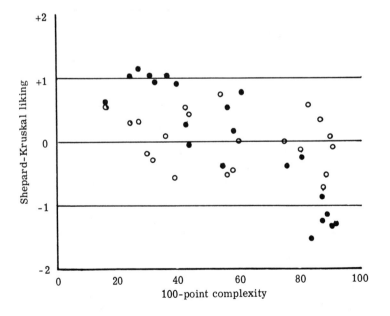

FIGURE 12-4. *Shepard-Kruskal Liking Dimensions and Complexity*

were therefore made to have subjects rate ten tartan patterns representing the simpler designs, ten representing the more complex designs, and ten representing the whole range.

The subjects were 15 males and 15 females of college age. They were divided into three groups of ten subjects each. Three sets of

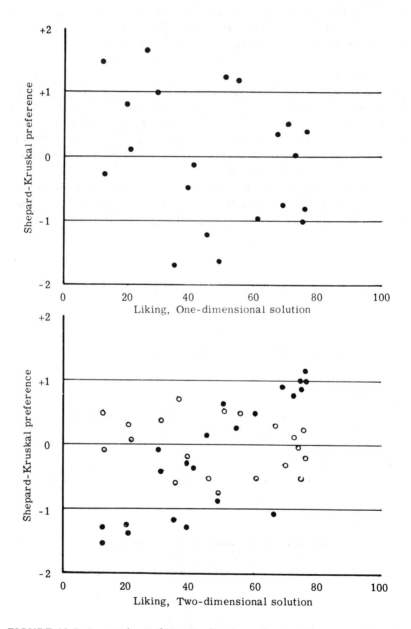

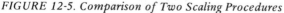

FIGURE 12-5. *Comparison of Two Scaling Procedures*

stimuli were made up from the tartan patterns that had been rated for complexity in earlier studies. The high-complexity set included those rated 1, 2, 3, 4, 6, 7, 8, 9, 10, and 12. The low-complexity set included those rated 11, 13, 14, 15, 16, 17, 18, 19, 20, and 21. The full-range set included those rated 1, 3, 6, 8, 11, 12, 15, 17, 19, and 21.

Each group rated all three sets. One group rated the low set, then the high, and then the full-range set. Another group rated the high, then the low, and then the full-range set. The third group rated the full-range set first and was then split, with half of the subjects rating the low-complexity set first and the other half the high-complexity set first. This arrangement comes pretty close to counter-balancing order of presentation. Tests for order effect revealed that there was no systematic order effect, and order was therefore ignored in subsequent analysis.

Figure 12-6 is a plot of the results of the three sets of ratings. It is apparent that, when subjects rate a restricted range of stimuli, they tend to use more of the range than they do when rating a wider range. Thus, the middle-range stimuli were rated more complex when in a set of low complexity and less complex when in a set of higher complexity.

Figure 12-7 is a plot of the second result of this study. In addition to the complexity ratings, the subjects were asked to rate each

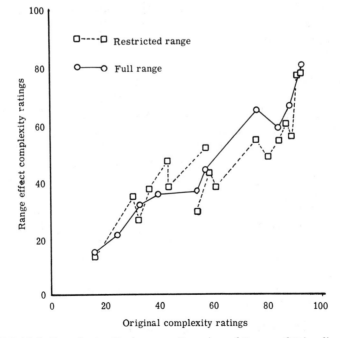

*FIGURE 12-6. Complexity Ratings as a Function of Range of Stimuli*

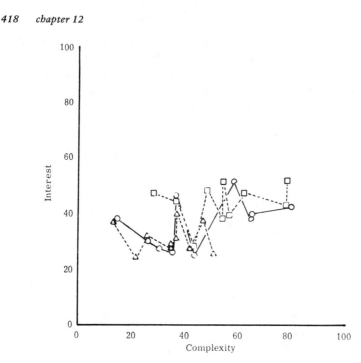

*FIGURE 12-7. Complexity and Interestingness*

pattern for "interestingness." There was very little consistency in the ratings of this variable. What little there is shows the more complex patterns being rated more interesting. Since earlier subjects had expressed a liking for the simpler patterns, liking and interestingness do not appear to be closely related, and what relationship there is appears to be inverse.

*Summary of Tartan Studies.* This set of materials was selected because it offered a physical dimension (number of squares) that had a degree of face validity as a complexity dimension. The physical scale and a simple psychological rating scale showed good agreement.

The relation of complexity and liking was a simple monotonic one, with subjects expressing greater liking for the simpler patterns. Ratings of interestingness and ratings of liking were essentially unrelated.

Comparison of a simple scaling of liking with results from a more complex Shepard-Kruskal scaling technique yielded no advantage of the more complex technique, either in terms of the establishment of more than one dimension of liking or in terms of individual difference analysis.

### Stage Set Designs

The design of stage settings is subject to classification with respect to style, and the various styles differ in complexity as one of the descriptive dimensions. In conjunction with a doctoral dissertation on differences in audience reaction to styles of stage setting (Pickett, 1970), a group of 30 photographs of drawings of stage sets became available.

The 30 photographs were subjected to two kinds of preliminary appraisal. They were submitted to a panel of scholars in drama for quantitative evaluation of the extent to which each represented any of several styles. They were also rated for complexity and preference by a small group of subjects using a simple rating procedure. On the basis of these two preliminary procedures, 12 drawings were selected for use in the dissertation. The criterion of choice was primarily that the panel of scholars be in agreement on the style designations and that a wide range of complexity values be represented (Walker, 1969b).

The settings selected represented three styles—romantic, classical or formal, and baroque. The romantic settings were: one by Chaperon for *Faust,* one by Adolph Appia for *Little Eyolf,* one by Karl Fichot for *Parsifal,* and one by P. L. Ciceri for *Ali Baba.* The formal or classical settings were: one from Karl Czeschka for *King Lear,* one from Norman Bel Gedes for *Hamlet,* one from T. C. Pillart for *Oedipus,* and one from Adolph Appia for *Orpheus.* The baroque settings included one from Fabrizio Galliari, one from Ferdinando Bibiena, and two from Carlo Bibiena; the plays for which they were designed were not designated in the source.

The 12 stage set drawings were then rated four different times by a group of subjects consisting of nine undergraduates and seven graduate students. They were rated for complexity and preference on a simple seven-point scale and rated for both again using the Shepard-Kruskal technique of rating the difference between pairs on a scale of 1 to 10.

The results are in the upper portion of Figure 12-8. The three styles are distinguished in terms of complexity almost without overlap. The four baroque settings were rated as much more complex than the others. The four classical/formal settings were rated on the simple end of the scale. The romantic are in the middle except for one setting that was classed with the formal in terms of complexity.

These subjects expressed a preference for the baroque settings. The classical/formal sets were least preferred, but the styles are not differentiated in terms of preference to nearly the extent they are in terms of complexity. The relationship between complexity and preference is thus a monotonically increasing preference for settings of increasing complexity. It might be noted that this is the reverse of the relationship between complexity and liking noted in the studies of tartan patterns, but it agrees with the ratings of interestingness.

The Shepard-Kruskal ratings were extensively analyzed using six dimensions in both the analyses of individual data and in the analysis of the group data. Again, the efforts to rationalize the individual data proved utterly fruitless. The analysis of group data was equally frustrating. When the Shepard-Kruskal analyses of complexity were compared with the results of the seven-point scale, the only systematic relationship that emerged was a U-shaped functional

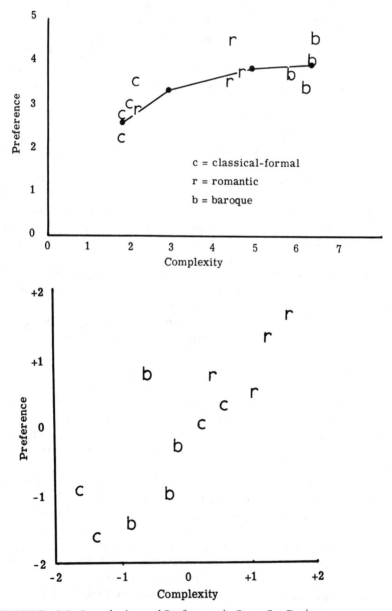

FIGURE 12-8. *Complexity and Preference in Stage Set Designs*

relationship with one of the Shepard-Kruskal dimensions. Sets rated both high and low in complexity on the seven-point scale were at one end of the Shepard-Kruskal dimension, and those in the middle were on the other end.

With six dimensions of complexity and six of preference available, 30 pairs can be matched. The lower part of Figure 12-8 is a plot of the one pairing that showed a systematic relationship. This plot is so linear that one would think the two dimensions were measurements of the same variable. The other possibility is that this relationship is a chance one drawn from a set of 30.

The methodological conclusion to be drawn from these efforts is that the simple rating scale functions as well as or better than, the more complex multidimensional one, since the latter added no information concerning either variable or the relation between the two.

### Complexity, Preference, and Experience with Graphics

Theories that relate preference to stimulus complexity generally agree in predicting that a subject will prefer a stimulus of moderate complexity to one that is extremely simple or extremely complex. The Hedgehog predicts that, with increased experience with a class of stimuli, the preferred stimulus should tend to be chosen from a point closer to the more complex end of the scale.

Kathleen Sinclair (1967) made an attempt to verify the existence of an optimal complexity level in the middle range of a scale of complexity and to determine whether the optimal point is higher for subjects with more experience with the range of stimuli. The basic design was to choose a set of graphics that were highly representational and that were produced by well-known artists. These stimuli were then rated for complexity and preference by a group of law students who were naive with respect to graphic prints, by a group of art history students, and by a group of graduate students in art. The latter two groups could be expected to recognize many, if not all, the graphics and to be able to identify the artist in each case.

The first step in the process was to choose 30 prints of graphic art by seven recognized artists. All of the prints were black and white, were the same size (4.5 inches by 5 inches), and were mounted on slightly larger white cardboards and covered with clear acetate for protection.

In the first phase of the study, this set of 30 prints was given to 40 subjects individually. The group of subjects was equally divided between students in law school and students in either art or art history. The subjects were asked to look through the entire set and then to assign ratings of complexity using whole numbers between 1 and 7.

Mean ratings for the 30 prints were then used as a basis for choosing a set of 15 prints for the second phase of the study. Five prints each were chosen from the high, mid, and low portions of the range of ratings with the additional prescription that the standard deviations of the ratings should be minimal.

In the second phase of the study, 60 subjects were divided into three groups of 20 each. A "Naive" group consisted of 20 law students who had had little experience with the kind of graphic materials used in the study. Few of these subjects were able to recognize any of the prints or identify any of the artists. An "Art" group was composed of 20 senior or graduate students in art. An "Art History" group was composed of 20 graduate students majoring in art history. That the "Art" and "Art History" groups had had considerable more experience with the stimulus materials is demonstrated by the fact that all of the members of these two groups recognized all of the artists and most of the prints used in the study. The list of 15 prints ordered from most to least complex in terms of the mean complexity scores obtained in the first phase of the study is contained in Table 12-4.

Table 12-5 gives the results of the second phase of the study along with the complexity ratings from the first phase. The stability of the complexity ratings is quite apparent. The correlation (rho) between the ratings in the two phases is .94. The correlations between the ratings given by the three groups are .93, .94, and .94.

*TABLE 12-4.* List of Graphic Prints

| Mean Complexity Rating | Artist and Title of Print |
|---|---|
| 6.4 | Durer, *The Men's Bath* |
| 6.2 | Durer, *The Sea-Monster*, 1500 |
| 5.9 | Breughel, *The Donkey at School*, 1556 |
| 5.6 | Durer, *Les Trois Graces*, 1491 |
| 4.3 | Durer, *Portrait of the Artist's Mother*, 1514 |
| 4.0 | Chagall, *David Gives Vent to His Grief*, 1931 |
| 3.95 | Toulouse-Lautrec, *La Goulue au Moulin Rouge*, 1891 |
| 3.9 | Goya, *Self Destruction*, 1800 |
| 3.7 | Toulouse-Lautrec, *La Goulue avec une Tanseur*, 1891 |
| 3.6 | Picasso, *The Ball*, 1904 |
| 2.7 | Matisse, *Portrait of Prof. T. Whitmore*, 1937 |
| 2.6 | Chagall, *The Musician*, 1919 |
| 2.4 | Chagall, *My Mother*, 1919 |
| 1.5 | Matisse, *The Princess N.* |
| 1.4 | Matisse, *Henri de Montherlant*, 1937 |

The table displays ratings given by subjects for complexity and preference in the second phase of the study, arranged in order of the mean complexity values obtained in the first phase.

*TABLE 12-5.* Complexity and Preference Scores

| Mean Complexity Phase 1 | Naive | | Art | | Art History | | Mean Complexity Phase 2 |
| --- | --- | --- | --- | --- | --- | --- | --- |
| | Pref. | Comp. | Pref. | Comp. | Pref. | Comp. | |
| 6.4 | 4.8 | 6.5 | 3.4 | 5.6 | 3.3 | 6.4 | 6.2 |
| 6.2 | 4.2 | 6.2 | 3.2 | 5.6 | 3.5 | 5.2 | 5.7 |
| 5.9 | 3.7 | 5.8 | 4.0 | 5.4 | 4.0 | 5.2 | 5.5 |
| 5.6 | 4.3 | 5.0 | 3.4 | 4.7 | 3.6 | 4.3 | 4.7 |
| 4.3 | 4.8 | 4.4 | 5.7 | 4.3 | 4.7 | 4.1 | 4.3 |
| 4.0 | 3.7 | 3.3 | 3.9 | 3.8 | 3.9 | 3.1 | 3.4 |
| 3.95 | 4.3 | 3.4 | 6.2 | 4.5 | 5.8 | 4.3 | 4.1 |
| 3.9 | 4.8 | 3.8 | 5.4 | 3.9 | 4.8 | 3.9 | 3.9 |
| 3.7 | 4.3 | 3.4 | 6.2 | 4.7 | 4.8 | 3.9 | 4.0 |
| 3.6 | 4.3 | 3.9 | 4.8 | 4.6 | 5.3 | 3.8 | 4.1 |
| 2.7 | 3.5 | 3.1 | 3.7 | 3.4 | 4.1 | 3.1 | 3.2 |
| 2.6 | 3.4 | 2.7 | 4.1 | 3.5 | 3.3 | 3.5 | 3.2 |
| 2.4 | 2.8 | 2.3 | 3.8 | 3.0 | 3.5 | 2.9 | 2.6 |
| 1.5 | 3.3 | 2.1 | 3.7 | 2.4 | 4.3 | 2.9 | 2.5 |
| 1.4 | 3.1 | 1.5 | 4.7 | 2.6 | 5.1 | 2.2 | 2.1 |

The table displays mean complexity and preference scores for the 15 prints by each of three groups of subjects. The prints are arranged in the same order as they are in Table 12-4, with the most complex print first.

A plot of complexity against preference in which all 15 points of each curve possible from Table 12-5 were included would be extremely difficult to read. As a simplification, the 15 values for complexity were ordered and grouped in sets of three within each group. A mean was obtained for each set of three, and mean values for preference for each set were also obtained. A plot of complexity versus perference using these values is shown in Figure 12-9.

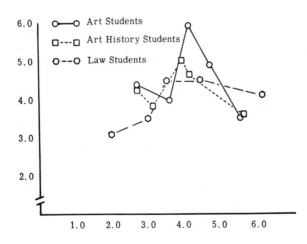

*FIGURE 12-9. Optimal Complexity and Experience*

The curves in Figure 12-9 are obviously different, and the differences are statistically significant. The curve for the naive subjects is relatively flat, and these subjects tended to use most of the range of complexity. However, the flatness of the curve indicates that they did not show very consistent preferences except for a general preference for the more complex end of the scale. The curves for the more sophisticated subjects are constricted in range on the complexity scale. They tended to see the graphics in a context that made them more nearly alike in complexity. Their major preference was for the middle range of complexity values.

With the more sophisticated groups, the location of the optimum as a function of the amount of experience is in the direction predicted by the theory. The art history students have considerably less experience with graphics than the graduate students in art, and their optimum is to the left of that for the art students. However, this apparent difference is not sufficiently great to accept as evidence. A clear demonstration of the movement of the optimum up the complexity scale with increased experience is yet to be demonstrated unequivocally with these materials.

### Modern Art

The most extensive work on measurement techniques and methodology was devoted to the development of a set of materials representing modern abstract art. A large set of stimulus materials was prepared, and from this set 42 abstract paintings were selected. These materials were all in color and were abstract in the sense of being nonrepresentational and generally devoid of symbolic material. Table 12-6 is a list of the paintings used in the preliminary study. The objective was to develop a standardized set of stimulus materials that would then be available for use in studies of complexity and preference, especially studies involving extensive exposure and possible changes in preference with exposure.

Subjects were asked to make four ratings of the paintings. First they were to rate complexity and preference on seven-point scales, and then they were to perform the Shepard-Kruskal scaling task, rating differences in complexity or preference between pairs on a scale of 1 to 10. With 42 stimulus items, the task of rating all possible pairs twice, once for complexity and once for preference, proved to be almost beyond the patience of willing subjects. They complained about the difficulty of the task and the growing unpleasantness. Of the 15 subjects who agreed to perform the scaling task, only seven completed the entire sequence of judgments. These seven subjects were each interviewed at length concerning the bases of their choices. These interviews provided a lengthy protocol against which to compare the scales derived.

TABLE 12-6. Modern Paintings Rated by Subjects for Complexity on a Seven-Point Scale

| Set Number | Seven-Point Complexity Rating | Painter | Painting | Year |
|---|---|---|---|---|
| 1 | 5.6 | Jackson Pollack | #1 | 1949 |
| | 4.5 | Jo Schreiter | *Execution of the Hope* | 1957 |
| | 4.1 | Singier | *Les Amoureux et la Plage* | 1954 |
| G | 3;2 | Sugai' | *Yamato* | 1956 |
| | 3.5 | Tobey | *Tatouage* | 1958 |
| 2 | 6.1 | Singier | *L'Ete* | 1945 |
| 3 | 3.4 | Hofmann | *Pompei* | 1959 |
| 4 | 2.4 | Sugai' | *Yayoi* | 1958 |
| 5 | 5.8 | Willi Baumeister | *Animated Landscape* | 1946 |
| | 2.5 | Stamos | *Avignon II* | 1958 |
| 6 | 1.4 | Piet Mondriaan | *Composition* | 1927 |
| | 4.5 | Max Ackermann | *Jubilation* | 1954 |
| F | 3.4 | Piet Mondriaan | *Composition* | 1913 |
| 7 | 5.5 | Corneille | *Tropical Splendour* | 1958 |
| 8 | 5.3 | Wassily Kandinsky | *Pink Composition* | |
| 9 | 2.3 | Soulages | *Peinture* | 1957 |
| | 4.9 | Corneille | *Landscape of America* | 1958 |
| | 2.4 | Dubuffet | *Table* | 1957 |
| E | 4.7 | Vieira Da Silva | *Red Interior* | 1951 |
| 10 | 5.5 | Marca-Relli | *Summer Noon* | 1956 |
| | 4.4 | Bram Van Velde | *Composition Collection Marie Cuttoli* | 1957 |
| | 4.9 | Bram Van Velde | *Composition* | 1957 |
| | 4.0 | Lyonel Feininger | *Month of R. Rega III* | |
| 11 | 6.4 | Goodnough | *Summer* | 1959–60 |
| 12 | 2.1 | Stamos | *Persian Bride* | 1958 |
| 13 | 4.3 | Le Moal | *Ocean* | 1959 |
| D | 3.3 | Lingier | *Soleil et Sable* | 1956 |
| | 3.3 | Sugai' | *Oni* | 1958 |
| 14 | 5.1 | Prassinos | *Le Clown* | 1960 |
| 15 | 1.5 | Mark Rothko | *Number 10* | 1950 |
| C | 4.5 | Schneider | *Peinture 65 B* | 1954 |
| B | 5.8 | Dubuffet | *Garden Bleche Grignotte* | 1956 |
| 16 | 3.8 | Poliakoff | *Oil* | 1953 |
| 17 | 2.8 | Sugai' | *Sugata* | 1958 |
| 18 | 3.5 | Schneider | *Peinture 95 B* | 1955 |
| 19 | 4.4 | Tobey | *Intersection* | 1954 |
| | 4.1 | Tobey | *Pacific Circle* | 1956 |
| | 3.5 | Soulages | *Peinture* | 1958 |
| 20 | 3.0 | Pierre Soulages | *Composition* | |
| | 4.3 | Tobey | *Summer* | 1957 |
| 21 | 3.9 | Goetz | *Peinture* | 1954 |
| A | 2.8 | Tobey | *Yellow Harvest* | 1956 |

The abstract paintings are rich in complexity. They vary in color, technique, degree of homogeneity of line and shape, number of transitions from one color or brightness to another, suggestiveness of meaningful material, and so on. It was felt that ratings of complexity and preference with such materials might well be multidimensional. If they did prove to be multidimensional, the Shepard-

Kruskal analysis should reveal dimensions that could be matched against the verbal protocol for each subject.

The general procedure in pursuing this objective was to obtain Shepard-Kruskal analyses from the computer in a number of degrees of detail. For each subject the computer generated ten solutions, from one dimension through ten dimensions, thus 55 dimensions for complexity and 55 for preference for each of the seven subjects.

Analyses of the data for individual subjects tended to take the following form. The one-dimensional solutions and the two dimensions of the two-dimensional solutions for complexity and preference were plotted for each individual. The resulting plots varied in the extent of apparent relations, but examination of a large number of such plots revealed nothing that was meaningfully different from the later analysis of the group data. The second step was to use the Shepard-Kruskal dimensions in pairs to arrange the paintings in two-dimensional arrays. A wall of a room was utilized for this purpose. A vertical scale was fastened to the wall from floor to ceiling, and a horizontal scale was fastened to the wall from left to right. Then, for example, the two-dimensional Shepard-Kruskal solution for an individual subject was used to place each of the 42 paintings on the wall in accordance with assigned values from the analysis. If the scales were complexity scales, then the array was examined to see whether there was any way of making sense of the dimensions in terms of complexity. If the array represented preference, then it was examined to see whether the basis of preference along each of the dimensions could be determined. These examinations were aided by the protocols taken from the subjects in an effort to determine why a given painting should occupy a particular position in the array.

Several experimenters spent a great many hours at this task. Many arrays were photographed in color and examined later in an effort to establish meaningfulness. Although it was not done systematically, a number of arrays were examined by the subjects who had provided the original data. The net outcome was the conclusion that multidimensional analyses of these data did not yield more than one dimension of either complexity or preference in the data of individual subjects.

For a variety of reasons, it was decided that working with 42 stimuli was unnecessarily cumbersome. The mean seven-point complexity values for the 15 subjects were then used to reduce the set of 42 paintings to a set of 21 experimental paintings and a practice set of seven. Table 12-6 contains the mean complexity values. It also contains the code number assigned to the 21 paintings of the experimental set and the letters A through G, which were used to identify the paintings in the practice set. This small set was then rated by 15 subjects on both seven-point and Shepard-Kruskal scales. An effort was made to determine the extent of agreement of the two scaling techniques and whether any advantage accrued from the use of the more complicated Shepard-Kruskal procedure.

Figure 12-10 shows a comparison of the seven-point ratings of complexity with the one-dimensional Shepard-Kruskal solution and both dimensions of the two-dimensional solution. In all three cases there is good agreement in these grouped data. If a stimulus is rated

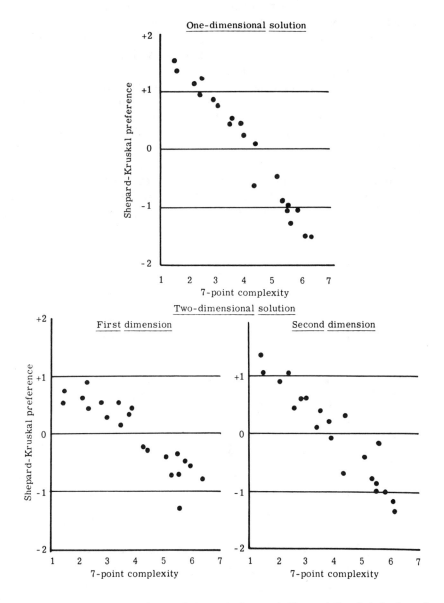

*FIGURE 12-10. Comparison of Seven-Point and Shepard-Kruskal Scales of Complexity*

as complex on one scale, it is likely to be rated as complex by use of the other method. The two dimensions of the two-dimensional Shepard-Kruskal solution both show good agreement with the seven-point ratings, suggesting that they are highly correlated dimensions within the Shepard-Kruskal analysis.

Figure 12-11 is a plot of the seven-point complexity and preference values. Almost no trend is apparent in the data beyond a minor tendency for mean preference for some of the more complex stimuli to be somewhat low. Figure 12-12 shows a comparison of the Shepard-Kruskal one-dimensional solutions for complexity and preference. Again, no reliable trend is apparent. Figure 12-13 contains the plots of seven-point complexity ratings and three Shepard-Kruskal dimensions of preference. None show relationships.

Two conclusions seem justified on the basis of these studies. First, it seems probable that, when subjects are asked to rate a set of abstract paintings for complexity or preference, they do just that. Complexity and preference are a simple pair of dimensions from the standpoint of the subjects and are thus not composed of contributing sets of underlying dimensions. Second, in these data no systematic relationship between complexity and preference could be demonstrated.

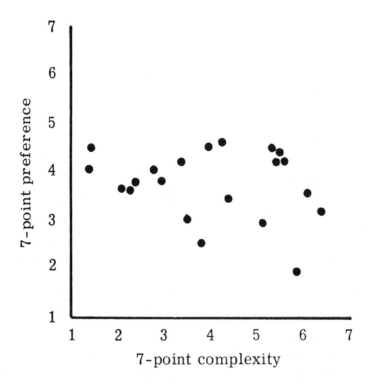

FIGURE 12-11. *Complexity versus Preference for Modern Paintings*

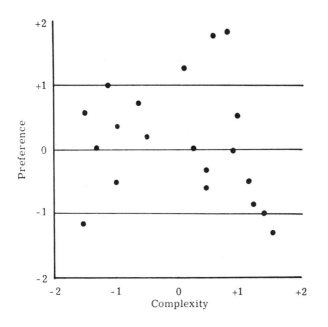

*FIGURE 12-12. Complexity versus Preference for Modern Paintings*

A possible explanation for the lack of relationship between complexity and preference in these data might lie in the experience factor. The theory predicts that there will be changes in complexity and preference with experience. It could be that such changes were occurring rapidly enough that the mean judgments represented valid judgments from different points in time that were not co-ordinate because of the order of presentation and the amount of experience provided in the experimental situation.

Based on this possibility, an effort was made to introduce a simple control of experience within the experimental setting and to collect a new set of data with a larger number of subjects. The simple seven-point scaling procedure was used. The demonstration set of seven paintings was used to explain the procedure. The 40 subjects were then asked to rate each of the 21 pictures in the experimental set for complexity and preference. In an effort to exert some additional control over amount of experience with the stimuli, half of the subjects rated them for complexity first and preference second, and half rated them for preference first and complexity second.

The major results in terms of complexity and preference are plotted in Figure 12-14. There is a definite relation between the two, with preference being expressed for the more complex of the

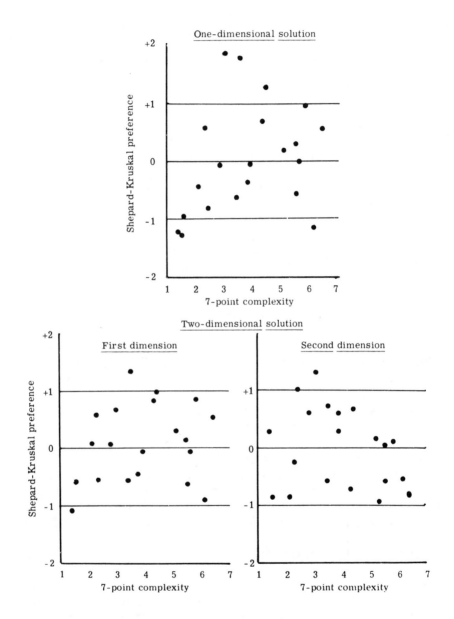

*FIGURE 12-13. Complexity versus Preference for Modern Paintings. (Seven-point scales of complexity versus Shepard-Kruskal preference solutions)*

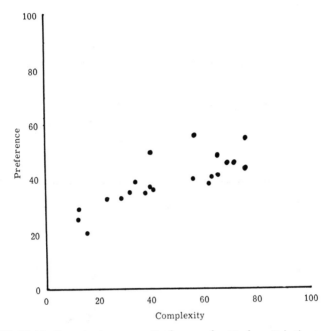

*FIGURE 12-14. Complexity versus Preference for Modern Paintings*

paintings. The data in Figure 12-15 are identical to the data in Figure 12-14, but the means are plotted separately for the two orders in which the ratings were made. If complexity is rated first and preference second, little or no relationship is apparent in the data, as seen in the upper figure. If preference is rated first and complexity second, then a relationship is clearly apparent.

It is not immediately obvious why the two orders should give different results. The probable cause seems to be that the amount of experience for the two groups differs when they are making each of the ratings, but the cause might prove to be more complex when a satisfactory explanation is developed from future research.

### Summary of Results from
### Human Studies of Complexity and Preference

The major effort in the foregoing studies was to develop several sets of visual stimulus materials for use in future research. The research has produced four sets, each of which yields reliable ratings of complexity and preference.

The methodological conclusions are simple and somewhat disappointing. Multidimensional analysis of ratings of complexity and preference does not seem fruitful. The simplest rating tasks, in

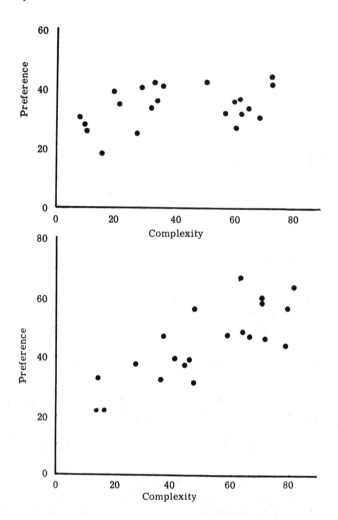

FIGURE 12-15. Complexity and Preference and Order of Rating

which subjects are asked to assign absolute ratings on scales of 1 to 7, 1 to 10, or 1 to 100, seem to yield results that are as functional for future research as the more complex scaling techniques. The Shepard-Kruskal technique imposes a very difficult task on the subjects and requires that they be exposed to the stimuli a number of times and for considerable periods. It seems likely that the complexity value and preference for the stimuli are being occulted by extensive change during the process of rating, with the result that the overall results are relatively useless. The effect of the order of rating for complexity and preference at least suggests extreme care in designing future studies so that even brief experience with the stimuli is adequately controlled.

The search for an optimum complexity value along the complexity dimension yielded rather varied results. Representative results with each of the four sets of stimulus materials are plotted in Figure 12-16. With the tartan patterns, subjects expressed maximum liking for the simplest stimuli, however, they tended to find the more complex patterns more interesting. Maximum preference was expressed for the mid-range of the black-and-white graphics and for the most complex of the stage settings and modern paintings.

The effect of experience on complexity and preference was explored systematically in only one study. In that study, the more experienced art students used a more restricted range of complexity ratings than did the naive subjects. The experienced subjects showed

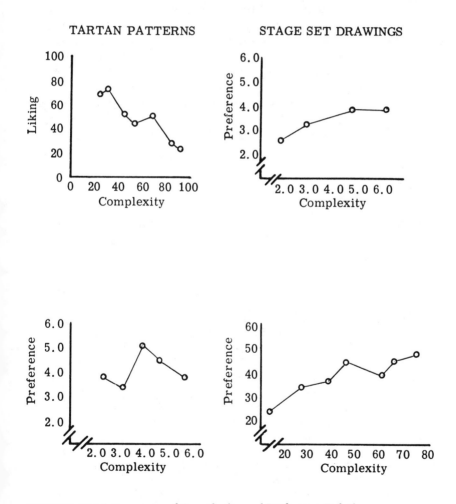

FIGURE 12-16. Summary of Complexity and Preference Relations

optimal preference in the middle of the complexity range and used a greater range of preference judgments than did the naive subjects. In other studies, it seems likely that very short experiences with stimuli affected ratings, so that ratings of complexity and preference appear to be quite labile over short periods of experience.

### AESTHETICS IN COGNITIVE TASKS

If the essence of aesthetics is in the aesthetic experience rather than in the object, then any cognitive experience can have aesthetic properties. In Chapter 7 I recounted a number of studies of the complexity and affective quality of single letters, bigrams, trigrams, nonsense syllables, and words of different lengths and frequencies of occurrence in English. The results there were similar to those found with visual materials. Among familiar items, such as letters and words, preference was expressed for the more complex over the simpler. Among unfamiliar items, such as bigrams, trigrams, and nonsense syllables, preference was expressed for the simpler items.

In Chapter 8 I recounted a study by Boykin involving the solution of anagram problems. In the course of that study, he obtained ratings of pleasantness from one group of subjects and ratings of interestingness from another group carrying out identical tasks. Figure 12-17 is a plot of the mean values for the two sets of ratings

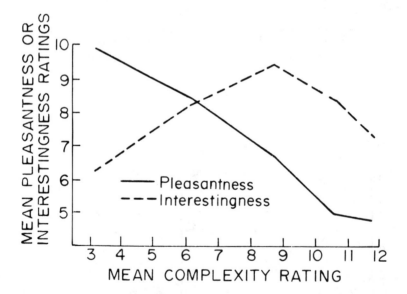

FIGURE 12-17. Problem Difficulty, Pleasantness, and Interestingness. (Redrawn from "Verbally Expressed Preference and Problem-Solving Proficiency," by A. W. Boykin, Jr., Journal of Experimental Psychology: Human Perception and Performance, 1977, 3, 165-174. Based on Verbally Expressed Preference and Complexity Judgments as They Relate to Levels of Performance in a Problem-Solving Situation, by A. W. Boykin, Jr. Unpublished doctoral dissertation, University of Michigan, 1972.)

compared to ratings of complexity of the tasks. His subjects rated the easiest tasks as most pleasant and the most difficult tasks as least pleasant. Ratings of interestingness, however, revealed an inverted-U-shaped relation to complexity.

In Chapter 3, studies were reported in which evaluative variables when analyzed in the absence of stimuli showed high intercorrelations. It was for this reason that a more global evaluative scale was employed in studies of the complexity and affectivity of verbal materials. The results in Figure 12-17 appear similar to those obtained with the tartan patterns, where subjects liked the simpler patterns best but found the more complex patterns more interesting. The results with the tartan patterns and those obtained in the anagrams task can be explained if the optimum complexity level is somewhat lower on the complexity scale for ratings of liking and pleasantness and somewhat higher on the scale for interestingness.

## VISUAL AESTHETICS IN ANIMALS

Preference for complexity can be studied in animals by use of stimuli that differ in a priori complexity value. A series of studies was reported in Chapter 7 to demonstrate the effect of experience on optimal complexity level. In those studies, rats were shown to shift preference from stimuli of lesser complexity to stimuli of greater complexity over an extended period of exposure. The data of those experiments can be analyzed for evidence of an inverted-U-shaped preference function.

Figure 12-18 shows such analyses for three of the studies reported in Chapter 7. The panel on the left shows the percent of time animals spent in the presence of a gray compartment (G), a compartment with one baffle (1B), a compartment with two baffles (2B), and a compartment with more than three baffles (3+B). The animals were tested for 30 minutes per day for five days, and they quickly came to prefer the most complex of the stimuli. In the right-hand panel of the figure are the results when the stimuli were panels of gray, horizontal stripes (H), vertical stripes (V), or a checkered pattern (C). Over five days with 30 minutes exposure per day, the gray compartment was preferred. Thus, animals in one study showed preference for the most complex stimulus and those in another study for the simplest, where complexity is judged on a priori grounds. The middle panel of the figure shows the results obtained when the two manipulations of baffles and wall patterns were combined. An inverted-U-shaped function is obtained whether one assumes that the compartment with one baffle is simpler than the compartment lined with horizontal stripes (as plotted in the figure) or whether the figure is replotted with the compartment lined with horizontal stripes considered to be the simpler of the two. There can be little doubt concerning the relative complexities of the other two

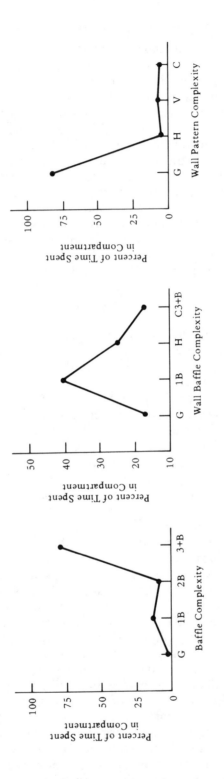

FIGURE 12-18. Preference for Stimulus Complexity in Rats. The panels show the results of three experiments. The left panel shows preference among compartments that were gray (G), contained one baffle (1B), two baffles (2B), or more than three baffles (3+B). The right panel shows preference among compartments with gray walls (G), horizontally striped walls (H), vertically striped walls (V), or checked walls (C). Exposure was 30 minutes per day for five days in both cases. The middle panel shows the results obtained when the stimuli were combined, with the exposure being 100 minutes per day for six days. (Redrawn from "Response to Stimulus Complexity in the Rat," by E. L. Walker and B. E. Walker, Psychological Record, 1964, 14, 489–497. Reprinted by permission.)

stimuli, gray walls and a complex baffle pattern combined with checkered walls.

In a study by Boykin (Walker, 1969b), rats were used to seek the range effect found with human subjects in the study involving the tartan patterns. Boykin devised nine levels of a priori complexity of wall patterns for a five-compartment maze in which there was equal access to the compartments from the center of the maze. The stimuli, in order of complexity, were horizontal stripes, vertical stripes, and checkered patterns with four, nine, 16, 25, 49, 91, or 144 checks in a space 4 inches square. One group of animals was exposed to the five simplest patterns, another group to the five most complex patterns, and a third group to five stimuli representing the whole range. Figure 12-19 shows the results. With exposure for ten minutes per day over a 12-day period, there is some evidence of preference for the more complex stimuli. There was also a complex range effect. The group exposed to the full range showed more pronounced preferences than either of the other groups, and the group exposed to the simplest portion of the scale showed almost no preference at all.

Sales (1968) also obtained preference data for checkered patterns in a manner quite different from that of Boykin. As we discussed in Chapter 5, he permitted rats to stick their heads through a small hole to light up and thus make visible a range of panels differing in complexity. The groups did not differ in the numbers of times they lighted the various panels, but they did differ in how

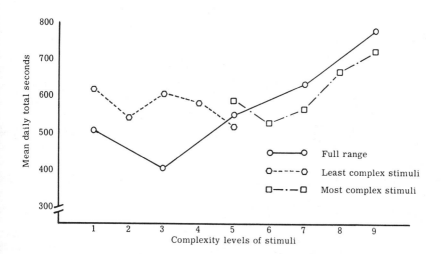

*FIGURE 12-19. The Effect of Stimulus Range on Preference. The figure displays mean time (in seconds) spent in each compartment by the three groups with choices of stimuli in different ranges of complexity.*

long they remained exposed to the various patterns. Figure 5-2 shows an inverted-U relation to complexity with a preference for the panel with 16 squares.

Although the results of studies of preference for complexity in rats are consistent with the theory, they constitute weak evidence. As indicated earlier, animals provide only one piece of information—choice behavior. If one assumes the validity of the complexity scale, then one can interpret choice behavior as an expression of preference for complexity. On the other hand, if one assumes the preference function, then the choice behavior of the animal can be used to scale the complexity of the stimulus. This is a weak position in comparison with the power involved in the possibility of independent assessment of both complexity and preference.

### SUMMARY

In this chapter I have tried to illustrate the applicability of psychological complexity and preference theory to a wide range of stimulus materials, subject tasks, and even organisms. Results compatible with the theory were obtained with visual stimuli ranging from tartan patterns to stage set designs along with more traditional visual art materials. The theory appears applicable to cognitive tasks such as the effort to solve anagram problems. The Hedgehog appears equally applicable to the preferences of rats in the presence of stimuli varying in complexity in either two or three dimensions. This wide range of materials and settings serves to illustrate the integrative character of the theory and the ubiquity of its applicability.

# chapter thirteen

𝒯he hedgehog as
aesthetic mediator:
auditory stimuli

## THE HEDGEHOG AND PROBLEMS IN
## THE EXPERIMENTAL AESTHETICS OF MUSIC

Whereas visual displays place the emphasis on static, spatial aspects of perception, music and speech place the emphasis on temporal patterns. It is the thesis of the Hedgehog that the ubiquity of psychological complexity and preference theory includes the possibility of dealing with the fundamental problems of the experimental aesthetics of music.

In this chapter, I discuss a variety of experimental studies utilizing auditory stimuli. These studies are addressed to such diverse problems as the optimal complexity level for musical compositions, the effect of number and phrasing of notes on judgments of complexity and preference, and the origins of consonance in musical dichords.

### COMPLEXITY AND
### PREFERENCE FOR MELODIES

Determining the presence of an optimal level of preference for musical compositions presents a number of interesting methodological and theoretical problems. Some of these can be examined in data collected by Heyduk (1972, 1975) and discussed at some length in Chapter 6. It may be recalled that Heyduk constructed four brief (30-second) musical compositions for the piano. The four were composed to differ in complexity with Composition A the least complex, followed by B, then by C, and finally by D. Thus the complexity ordering for the four was $D > C > B > A$, and the ratings Heyduk obtained from his subjects agreed with this ordering.

Here I will be concerned only with the initial steps of Heyduk's experimental design. He had each of 120 subjects listen to the four melodies to familiarize themselves with the set. Then each of the four was played a second time, and after each composition was played, the subjects rated it for how much they liked it and how complex it sounded. Both the liking and the complexity ratings were made on a scale of 1–13.

Psychological complexity and preference theory is a theory of process within the individual. It should therefore hold true for the choices of individual subjects. There are a number of ways of testing whether the preference ratings of a given subject agree with the theory. One way is to use a variety of Coombs' (1964) unfolding technique for ordered data.

To apply the technique, the ratings given by the subject are reduced to rankings under the conservative assumption that the rating scale values are not on an equal-interval scale. The preference order supplied by a subject can then be compared to any one of several measures of the relative complexity of the stimuli. One measure of complexity is the *a priori complexity* ordering, which is based on the manipulations employed in constructing the stimuli. In this case, the complexity ordering is $D > C > B > A$, indicating that composition D is the most complex and composition A the least. A second measure of complexity is the one I have called *consensual complexity*. This ordering is based on the mean complexity rating (or ranking) assigned by a reference group. Heyduk had constructed his stimuli well, and in his study a priori complexity and consensual complexity yield the same ordering of the four stimuli. Still another possible basis for ordering the four stimuli for complexity could be the ratings supplied by the subject. The individual subject might or might not agree with the group on the relative complexities of the four stimuli. I will refer to this ordering of the complexity of the stimuli as the *subjective complexity* ordering. We thus have a choice of three ways of ordering the complexity of the stimuli. Since a priori complexity ordering and consensual complexity ordering agree in Heyduk's data, we are left with a choice of two.

The preference order (how much each composition was liked relative to the others) can then be matched with the complexity orderings. To illustrate, let us use the consensual complexity ordering, $D > C > B > A$. Subjects could have ordered their preference (or liking) for these stimuli in 24 different orders. Since a subject's optimal complexity level could be in any position along the complexity scale, eight of the 24 possible orderings would agree with the theory, and 16 would not. The eight that would agree, if complexity and preference are plotted together, would form the one possible monotonically increasing function, the one possible monotonically decreasing function, and the six possible inverted-U-shaped functions. The 16 orderings that would controvert the theory would all form either U-shaped or other nonmonotonic functions.

Using this technique, the preference order provided by each subject on each occasion can be examined to determine whether it agrees with the theory. Then the number of such agreements can be compared with the number expected by chance to determine the extent to which the theory holds in these data. The result of this analysis of individual protocols is presented in Table 13-1. It will be noted that the expected proportions of supporting protocols vary slightly from a $p$ of .333. These variances are due to the fact that the probability of a supporting protocol arising by chance is smaller if either D or A is rated as the most preferred and larger if B or C is so rated. In the table, the actual frequencies of each choice are taken into account. It is apparent from the table that the theory can be used to predict preference order from the complexity of the stimuli much better than chance. Theoretically, subjective complexity should be a better basis for prediction than consensual complexity, but it is not. My guess is that this difference is attributable to the fact that, when subjective complexity is used, both orderings, preference order and complexity order, are subject to

*TABLE 13-1.* Psychological Complexity and Liking

| Alternative Bases for Ordering Liking | Observed Number of Supporting Protocols | Expected Number of Supporting Protocols | Expected Proportion of Supporting Protocols | $X^2$ | $p$ |
|---|---|---|---|---|---|
| *Individual Protocol Analysis* (N = 120) | | | | | |
| *Initial Ratings* | | | | | |
| Consensual Complexity | 85 | 42.7 | .356 | 64.0 | < .001 |
| Subjective Complexity | 73 | 36.4 | .303 | 51.4 | < .001 |
| *Final Ratings* | | | | | |
| Consensual Complexity | 91 | 41.3 | .344 | 89.4 | < .001 |
| Subjective Complexity | 83 | 35.6 | .297 | 87.8 | < .001 |

Redrawn from "Psychological Complexity and Preference: A Hedgehog Theory of Behavior," by E. L. Walker. In D. E. Berlyne and K. B. Madsen (Eds.), *Pleasure, Reward, Preference.* Copyright 1973 by Academic Press. Reprinted by permission.

error. When consensual complexity is used, since it agrees with the a priori ordering, it is the same for all subjects and is not subject to error.

An additional aspect of this anaylsis should be mentioned. Examination of the protocols that do not agree with the theory indicates that they generally depart from the expectations of the theory in minor ways and are not distributed equally among the 16 other possible orderings.

The analysis of individual protocols reveals what might be hidden under the highly regular-looking relationships between complexity and preference in a group analysis. Figure 13-1 is a plot of mean complexity and mean liking ratings for these stimuli for 120 subjects the first time they heard the four selections. Consensual complexity is clearly a simple linear function of a priori complexity. The mean liking rating shows the classical inverted-U-shaped function, with a group optimal complexity level somewhere around the complexity of Composition C.

In an area in which the results of measurement appear to be unusually sensitive to subtleties of the technique of measurement, another study of Heyduk's lends welcome encouragement. In this study he followed the pattern of the study just described except that, instead of forcing subjects to listen to a particular composition 16 times, he permitted the subjects 16 choices of which composition they would like to hear. This design permits two measures

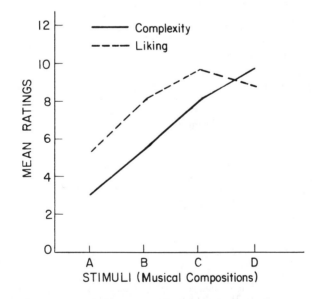

FIGURE 13-1. *Psychological Complexity and Preference for Musical Compositions*

of liking—the rating of liking on the 1–13 scale and the frequency of choice.

A comparison of the two methods of evaluating liking for the stimuli is shown in Figure 13-2. The 24 subjects in this study liked the more complex stimuli somewhat more than the 120 in the main experiment. However, the encouragement comes from the fact that the two scales can be adjusted to make the two curves, representing mean liking rating and mean frequency of choice, nearly coincide. This correspondence is all the more remarkable since there are two factors that would tend to flatten the curve for frequency of choice. First, if the subjects needed to hear each of the four compositions several times in order to be certain of their identification, their choices would tend to be distributed. This is indeed the case. Response to extrinsic aspects of the stimuli, or specific exploration, is evident from the fact that the probability of a subject's choosing each of the four before choosing to hear any one a second time is considerably beyond chance. Second, habituation should depress liking for the most frequently chosen stimuli selectively. Despite these factors, the curves agree quite closely in shape.

Another study at least remotely related to the complexity of melody was recounted in Chapter 8. In that context we were con-

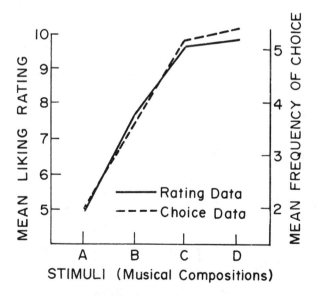

FIGURE 13-2. *Method of Measurement and Preference. (Redrawn from* Static and Dynamic Aspects of Rated and Exploratory Preference for Musical Compositions, *by R. G. Heyduk. Unpublished doctoral dissertation, University of Michigan, 1972. Reprinted by permission.)*

cerned with the organization of sets of tones into chunks by the introduction of pauses in sequences of tones. Arkes (1971) had found that he could vary the number of tones within chunks over a range of three to six chunks without making a substantial change in the complexity ratings given by his subjects. When he varied the number of chunks from five through eight, ten, and 12 to 15, there were very substantial differences in ratings of complexity. These results may be seen in Figure 8-4 (p. 212).

Arkes also had his subjects rate the stimuli for how much they liked them. The results are shown in Figure 13-3. When the number of tones within a chunk is varied, there is a clear preference for the simpler chunks containing only three tones. When the number of chunks is varied, there is a mild preference for melodic sequences in the middle of the complexity range.

These two studies lend general confirmation to the expectations of psychological complexity and preference theory as applied to the aesthetic response to melody-like auditory stimuli. They also raise some cautionary questions. For example, in the Heyduk study a statistically significant number of individual protocols conform to the theory, but a large number do not. No simple explanation is available to account for those protocols that deviate from the theory. In the study by Arkes, both group curves fall within the range of theoretical expectations, but they nevertheless raise significant questions. Although variation in the number of chunks produced a

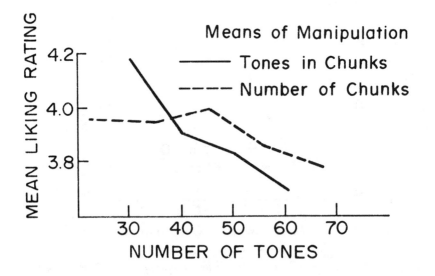

FIGURE 13-3. *Preference for Numbers of Tones with Variation of Chunk Size and Number of Chunks*

wide range of complexity ratings, it also produced a narrow range of preference judgments. There was a general tendency in the Heyduk study for his subjects to like the more complex stimuli the most, whereas in the Arkes study the more complex stimuli were liked the least. This latter result is probably attributable to the melodic character of Heyduk's stimuli; in contrast, the Arkes stimuli were generally artificial and unmusical. Thus, the success of the predictions is encouraging, and the problems that remain provide a stimulus to further development.

## CONSONANCE AND DISSONANCE

In the literature of the aesthetics of music, the terms *consonance* and *dissonance* are used to describe a dimension of aesthetic experience associated with the harmonic properties of two or more tones sounded simultaneously. Some combinations are labeled consonant and are variously described as being "stable," "complete in themselves," and "pleasant." Dissonant combinations are thus "unstable," "incomplete," and "unpleasant."

The psychological phenomena of consonance and dissonance offer a variety of intriguing problems that have commanded the attention of investigators from a number of disciplines, including mathematicians, physicists, physiologists, aestheticians, and psychologists. The primary problems have concerned the manner in which various musical intervals are to be ordered on a scale from most consonant to most dissonant and how the ordering is to be explained once it has been.

Table 13-2 contains the results of a small sample of efforts to order the 13 intervals within an octave of the most commonly employed equal-tempered diatonic scale in Western music. Two systems of notation are given in the table. The row labeled "interval" contains the notation corresponding to the commonly employed names for the intervals. Thus, "unison" refers to the pairing of identical tones, as would occur if two voices sang the same note simultaneously. The symbol "m2" refers to the minor second interval, while "M2" refers to the major second. "P4" and "P5" refer to the so-called "perfect fourth" and "perfect fifth." The minor fifth is usually referred to as the *tritone.* A shorthand notation has been introduced in the table; the notation "2" stands for the major second, "2" stands for the minor second, and so on.

The first two orderings of consonance and dissonance in the table are based on the mathematical and physical properties of the physical stimulus produced by the various intervals. The ordering provided by Pythagoras is based on his well-known observation of the pattern of vibration of taut strings. Two vibrating strings of equal length produce unison, and the ratio of the two frequencies

*TABLE 13-2.* Various Orderings of the Consonance of Musical Intervals

| Notation | Interval | | | | | | | | | | | | |
|---|---|---|---|---|---|---|---|---|---|---|---|---|---|
| | Unison | m2 | M2 | m3 | M3 | P4 | Tritone | P5 | m6 | M6 | m7 | M7 | P8 |
| | 1 | 2 | 2 | 3 | 3 | 4 | 5 | 5 | 6 | 6 | 7 | 7 | 8 |
| *Mathematical* | | | | | | | | | | | | | |
| Pythagoras | 1 | 8 | 5 | 4 | 6 | 3 | 3 | 6 | 7 | 2 | 2 | 7 | 5 |
| Taylor | 1 = | 8 | 5 | 4 | 6 | 3 | 3 = | 6 = | 7 = | 5 | 2 = | 7 | 2 |
| *Various Psycho-logical* | | | | | | | | | | | | | |
| Helmholtz | 1 | 8 | 5 | 4 | 6 | 3 | 3 | 6 | 7 | 2 | 5 | 7 | 2 |
| Stumpf | 1 | 8 | 5 | 4 | 3 = | 3 | 6 = | 6 | 7 = | 7 | 2 = | 2 = | 5 |
| Lipps | | 8 | 5 | 4 | 3 | 6 | 3 | 6 | 5 | 7 | 2 | 7 | 2 |
| Malmberg (Tuning Fork) | 1 | 8 | 5 | 6 | 4 | 3 | 6 | 5 | 3 | 7 | 7 | 2 | 2 |
| Malmberg (Piano) | 1 = | 8 | 5 | 6 | 3 | 4 | 6 | 3 | 5 | 7 | 2 | 7 | 2 |
| Plomp & Levelt | 1 = | 8 | 5 | 6 | 4 | 7 | 3 | 6 | 3 = | 5 | 7 | 2 | 2 |
| Plomp (Loudness correction) | 1 = | 8 | 5 | 6 | 4 | 7 | 3 | 6 | 5 | 3 | 7 | 2 | 2 |
| *Historical Preference* | | | | | | | | | | | | | |
| Moore | 1 | 8 | 5 | 4 | 3 = | 3 = | 6 = | 6 | 7 | 2 = | 2 = | 5 = | 7 |

is 1:1. An interval of an octave is produced by two strings standing in a ratio of 2:1. The perfect fifth has a ratio of 3:2, the perfect fourth a ratio of 4:3, the imperfect third a ratio of 5:4, the imperfect second a ratio of 9:8, and so on. The Pythagorean order displayed in Table 13-2 is determined by the size of the sum of the numerator and the denominator of the ratio of the two frequencies involved. The labels *perfect* and *imperfect* are arbitrary and refer to the aesthetic properties of the mathematical series, which have no necessary connection with the aesthetic properties of the intervals as heard by a human listener.

The second ordering, by Taylor (1965), is also based on the physical properties of the sound stimulus. Where the Pythagorean ordering is based exclusively on the ratios of the fundamental frequencies of the two notes, Taylor takes account of the numbers of summation and differential tones and the beat frequencies produced when any two notes are sounded together. He constructed a diagram in the following fashion. If the abscissa represents an octave span in frequency, then each point on the abscissa can represent an interval, the size of which is a function of the distance from such a point to the frequency on the left of the abscissa. The scale thus ranges from unison to a full octave. On the ordinate, Taylor also scales frequency in octaves and plots each of the summation and differential tones as a straight line across the space represented by the diagram. The result is a complex of lines crossing the diagram at various angles. There are many points at which these lines, representing tonal frequencies in the complex sound of the dichord, intersect and many points at which no lines intersect. One can project a perpendicular line from any point on the interval scale and count the number of lines that cross it. At points of intersection, the number of crossing lines is small, and where there is no intersection of the lines representing the summation and differential tones, the number will be large. The ordering listed for Taylor in Table 13-2 is based on this counting procedure. Where an "=" appears in the table, Taylor's method does not discriminate between the intervals involved. Two other characteristics of Taylor's order should be noted. The procedure does not take into account the relative loudness levels of the fundamental and the various summation and differential tones. Second, Taylor's frequency manipulation is continuous, and there is some uncertainty about where to place a perpendicular because of the frequency compromises involved in tempering the diatonic scale. If no such compromises are allowed, the order of intervals from Taylor's calculations is $\underline{1} = \underline{8} < \underline{5} < \underline{4} = \underline{6} <$ others.

The division in the table between mathematical and psychological orderings is arbitrary and a matter of degree. Helmholtz (1875) was concerned with the "beat" frequencies of all of the partials and felt that there was a maximum of dissonance when such a frequency was 33 cps. Stumpf (1883) had subjects judge whether they were hearing one tone or two and ordered intervals on the basis of the frequency of confusion. Lipps (1885) based his ordering on the supposition that we are able to count acoustic vibrations and that we prefer combinations in which they coincide most often. Malmberg (1918) based orderings on judgments of "smoothness, purity, and blending" and found slightly different orders depending on whether the stimuli were produced by tuning forks or by a piano. Plomp and Levelt (1965) based their orderings on ratings of dissonance gathered to test a "critical bandwidth" theory. Critical bandwidth, according to Zwicker, Flottorp, and Stevens (1957), is the interval over which the perceived loudness of a tone is influenced by the presence of a second. The effect rises to a maximum as one proceeds from unison to an interval representing about 25% of the total effect and then declines. The relative extent of the critical bandwidth varies with frequency. It is reported as extending about 25 Hz around a fundamental of 100 Hz and about 2000 Hz around a fundamental of 15,000 Hz.

Plomp and Levelt suggest that dissonance is at a maximum where the loudness interaction effect is at a maximum, at about 25% of the critical bandwidth. Using this analysis and following the Helmholtz procedure, they proceed to calculate the sum of dissonance values of overtone pairs for each dichord to produce hypothetical dissonance values for each of the semitone intervals of the untempered scale. When these values are adjusted for the tempered scale, their calculations yield the orderings in Table 13-2. These calculations do not take into account differential loudness of the partials involved. When this is done, a slightly different ordering is generated, shown in the table as "Plomp (Loudness Correction)."

The ordering suggested by Moore (1914) is set apart from the others primarily to emphasize the effect of learning. Moore thus represents a number of authors who have demonstrated either logically or experimentally that the judgment of relative consonance may very well shift with experience. Among other things, Moore undertakes to demonstrate that what has been judged as dissonant at one period of history comes to be judged as consonant at a later age. Furthermore, Moore argues that the preferred interval, and thus what is judged as consonant and what is judged as dissonant, shifts in an orderly sequence from left to right through the intervals displayed in Table 13-2. For a more complete and detailed review of the contributions to the history of the problem, the reader is referred to Berlyne (1971), Plomp and Levelt (1965), Wellek (1963), and Lundin (1947). Here I will list a generalized set of problems and issues that appear to account for the general lack of agreement in Table 13-2 and that suggest the need for alternative approaches to the problem.

1. *The definition of consonance and dissonance.* The definitions of consonance and dissonance given in the first paragraph of this section contain elements of both a structural variable, such as complexity, and an evaluative variable, such as pleasantness. Berlyne (1971), for example, cites Francès (1958) as concluding that experienced musicians can separate the concepts of consonance and pleasantness and acquire a taste for dissonance, while less experienced subjects cannot make the distinction and tend to prefer the simpler intervals.

2. *Differences in the physical scale.* The mathematical beauty of the intervals of the Pythagorean scale is quickly lost in the modifications imposed by the irregularities of the Western diatonic scale. The latter represents a series of compromises in frequency between the requirements of scales of different keys to permit modulation from one key to another without retuning the instrument. The black keys on the piano, for example, are notes added to the scales because the demands of these keys are sometimes highly discriminable by the human ear. Smaller differences have been judged to be unimportant and are accommodated by tuning the strings to a compromise frequency. Furthermore, even though most standardized scales imply the assumption that a given interval is the same regardless of the absolute frequencies of its component notes, this assumption is merely convenient for the construction of musical instruments and is not psychologically sound. It can be shown, for

example, that an octave in the middle of the audible frequency range is psychologically larger than an octave from the higher or lower registers (see Woodworth, 1938).

3. *Stimulus and transduction complexity.* Even under conditions of the most elaborate and precise experimental control of the stimulus, there is no assurance that the experimenter can specify what is being processed by the organism. Most sound sources emit complex wave forms in which the fundamental frequency accounts for only a portion of the total energy. Even when physically pure tones are used, the external portions of the ear contribute complexity to the stimulus. It is well known that the cochlea generates its own complex frequencies—cochlear microphonics—in the presence of a pure tone, and it is possible that additional complexities are contributed by the process of transduction of the physical stimulus into a neural representation. Even with heroic controls, there is no assurance that the organism is not contributing complexity to the immediate experience based on its extensive past auditory history.

4. *Pitch scales.* In all of the efforts recorded in Table 13-2, there is an implicit assumption that pitch is a monotonically increasing function of frequency. There is good reason to reject this assumption on psychological grounds. Two notes that are precisely an octave apart are perceived as the *same* note. This quality of sameness of two notes an octave apart denies the reasonableness of the monotonicity of the pitch scale. It seems probable that the circularity of some quality of the pitch scale is the primary source of the peculiar disorder in the sequences of numbers in Table 13-2.

5. *Limitations of stimulus range.* Some of the explanations of consonance and dissonance that seem reasonable when applied to a limited stimulus range can be easily shown to have limited explanatory power when a wider range of stimuli is considered. For example, the critical bandwidth hypothesis may give a reasonable account of the dissonance of a minor second interval (2), but it seems inapplicable as an account of the dissonance of a minor fifth (5).

6. *Dichotic aural phenomena.* Rarely has the availability and function of two aural receivers rather than one been taken into serious consideration. Although there have been instances in which the two tones composing an interval have been presented to the two ears by means of earphones to eliminate physical interaction and interaction on the basilar membrane, there are other binaural effects that have not generally been considered. We employ differences in signal between the two ears to locate the direction from which a sound is emanating. In doing so, we blend two signals that must differ in phase and that may differ in other characteristics. Recent evidence of brain laterality of function might suggest different processing of signals to the two ears.

7. *Individual differences.* Virtually no one has taken account of

the problem posed by very large individual differences. The orderings listed in Table 13-2 are based on a conception of a universal or standard subject. It is well known that many individuals are "tone deaf," and there is reason to believe that there could be wide differences in the manner in which different individuals transduce the same physical stimulus. If so, the orderings in Table 13-2 could be true of a group of subjects without being characteristic of the experiences of any individual subject.

8. *Learning.* If our perception of consonance, complexity, pleasingness, and preference can change with experience, then we can expect even larger individual differences based on the amount of experience an individual has had with music, as well as the differential experience with particular intervals and thus the frequency of their employment in the musical compositions to which the individual has been exposed.

9. *Part versus total process.* Virtually none of the studies aimed at analyzing the basis for consonance has been addressed to the entire process. There is variation in what has been controlled and what has been manipulated, but in each instance one or more significant factors have been ignored, and in virtually all instances the relevance of learning and individual differences have been omitted from serious consideration.

This incomplete list of problems suggests that there is need for further work that should represent a substantial reconception of the concepts of consonance and dissonance. What follows is just such a reconception, together with a report of a series of studies designed to begin the illumination of that position and an effort to integrate the results of those studies.

### Consonance and Dissonance Reconceptualized

The dimension of consonance/dissonance as used in the literature of music contains at least two factors, structural and evaluative, that under many circumstances are not perfectly correlated. The structural dimension can be related to the concept of psychological complexity, and the evaluative factor can be related to preference as manifested in judgments of pleasantness and unpleasantness. There is thus a need to obtain ratings of complexity and preference along with ratings of consonance and dissonance in order to determine the relationships among the multiple dimensions of consonance and dissonance.

The factor of differential experience with musical intervals must be taken into account. It is frequently found, for example, that subjects who are relatively inexperienced in music do not separate the concepts of consonance and pleasantness, whereas experienced musicians do tend to make the distinction and express preferences for intervals that would be judged to be dissonant by the less experienced. Thus, for experienced musicians, the relationship of preference to complexity might tend to follow the inverted-U-shaped function of psychological complexity and preference theory (see Walker, 1973b; Berlyne, 1971). Furthermore, there is a distinct possibility that, in addition to a shift in preference with experience, there might be changes in perceived complexity.

The concept of pitch as a monotonically increasing function of frequency needs to be reexamined. Such a conception violates the apparent psychological identity of two tones an octave apart. Thus middle C and the C above middle C are clearly the *same* note in different octaves. Shepard (1964) distinguishes between two qualities of pitch that he refers to as *tonality* and *height* (which I will call *octavity*). Tonality is the property that distinguishes a tone from other tones within a single octave and is referred to by the letter designations of tone pitch—A, B, C, D, and so forth. Octavity is the quality of pitch that distinguishes two tones of identical tonality that are one or more octaves apart. Tonality is conceivable as a circular dimension with the notes of the scale arranged clockwise in a circular and thus endless sequence. Shepard (1964) documented tonality by producing an auditory illusion of an ever-ascending (or descending) sequence of tones on a closed loop tape that actually contained tones differing in tonality through an octave but not differing in height (octavity). When octavity is taken into account and conceived as a simple linear dimension, pitch is represented by a helix or spring-like figure. Shepard credits this conception of the pitch scale as a helix to Drobisch (1846) as cited by Ruckmick (1929). The representation of the pitch scale as a helix invites the correlation of the complexities of various dichords to the distance between the two tones as positioned on a helical scale. Since the contribution of octavity can be expected to be small and its value relative to tonality differences unknown, I will discuss properties of dichord intervals primarily in terms of tonality differences alone, as represented in Figure 13-4.

In the figure the helix represents the tonality values of the notes of little more than an octave as they would appear on a piano keyboard, except that for convenience they are represented as an equal-tempered scale. The dichord intervals are indicated by the notation inside the helix; thus, 1 indicates unison, 2 indicates a minor second, 2 indicates a major second, and so on up to 8, representing two notes an octave apart. Three intervals larger than an octave—the major ninth, the major tenth, and the major 11th—are also indicated. It should be noted from the figure that a comparison of the relative consonance of four pairs of intervals—for example, 4 and 11—should permit an assessment of the contribution of octavity to consonance. These intervals greater than an octave are employed in the Aeschbach study to be reported later.

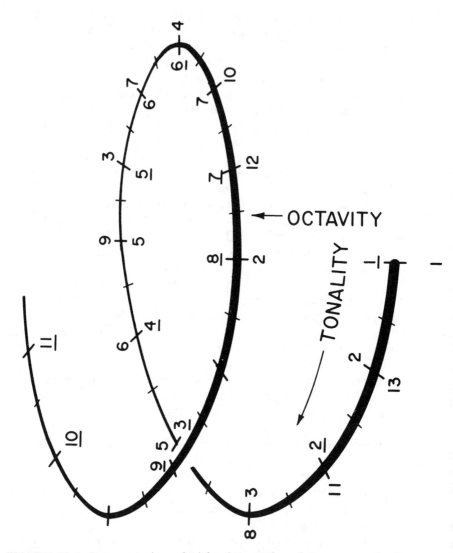

FIGURE 13-4. Representation of Dichord Intervals and Consonance Ranks on a Helical Representation of Pitch. The figure is a diagram representing pitch as a helix with tonality as a circular dimension and octavity as a vertical dimension. The numbers inside the helix represent various dichord intervals of an equal-tempered scale, using the bottom of the helix as the reference fundamental tone. The notation for the intervals is that employed in Table 13-2. Three intervals larger than an octave used in the Aeschbach study to be reported later are indicated as 9, 10, and 11. The unlabeled smaller divisions represent quarter-tone intervals employed in three of the Ayres studies to be reported later. They will be labeled as q1, q2, and so on, with their integers being taken from the immediately preceding semitone interval as one moves in a clockwise direction. The consonance ranks outside the helix are taken from the Malmberg piano results of Table 13-2.

Each of the semitone intervals labeled in the figure can be divided into quartertone intervals, and these are indicated by the smaller divisions of the helix. Employment of quartertone intervals can be used as one means of assessing the influence of experience on judged consonance, since they are intervals rarely heard in Western music. These intervals are employed in three of the four studies by Ayres to be reported later.

The numbers outside the helix represent the rankings of consonance obtained by Malmberg with stimuli generated from dichords played on the piano. The choice of this particular set of results from Malmberg is essentially arbitrary. No two of the orders in Table 13-2 are in complete agreement, and there is no rational means of combining the various orderings into one "standard" order. The Malmberg order chosen has the virtues of having been obtained from a familiar stimulus source (the piano), of having been derived from human judgments of consonance (thus involving the whole range of factors from the complexity of the physical stimulus through the physics and mechanics of the auditory system, as well as neurophysiological and psychological aspects), and of being in some sense typical of consonance orders.

In Table 13-2 the apparent disorder of a series of numbers such as 1, 8, 5, 4, and so on invites a search for a set of variables underlying the series that could produce such an order. Some degree of order can be discerned from the set of consonance rankings from Malmberg as arranged on the circular dimension of tonality in Figure 13-4. The most dissonant intervals, ranks 12 and 13, lie immediately adjacent to unison and the octave, which are the most consonant. There is a general tendency for the rankings to decrease as one proceeds around the tonality circle in either direction. On the other hand, the tritone, 5, which lies opposite the unison and octave, is rated as highly dissonant, and both the major fourth, 4, and the minor sixth, 6, interrupt the declining sequence of ranks from the unison and octave. From the rankings alone it would seem that a minimum of two factors contributing to consonance and dissonance ratings would be required to unfold the circular dimension of tonality. I will refer to one of those factors as *proximity*, because it is at a maximum near unison and the octave and declines in both directions. I will refer to the second factor as *distality*, in recognition of the fact that it is at a maximum somewhere near the point farthest from unison and the octave and declines in some pattern from such a point.

The series of five studies to be recounted were addressed to a series of problems and permit revealing analyses when considered as a group. The major problems and issues are the following: (1) What are the interrelationships of ratings of consonance/dissonance, complexity, pleasantness, and preferential choice? (2) What is the magnitude of individual differences in rating in relation to the magnitude of group orderings of dichord intervals? (3) To what extent can the four factors of proximity, distality, octavity, and differential experience provide an exhaustive reconstruction of the consonance and dissonance of dichord intervals?

### Experimental Problems and Methods

*The Aeschbach Study.* Susan Aeschbach (1974) employed several stimuli involving intervals greater than an octave and obtained ratings of three variables; consonance/dissonance, complexity, and pleasingness. Thus, this study provides primary information on the psychological nature of consonance and dissonance, the extent of individual differences, and the relative contribution of octavity.

The stimuli were ten dichord intervals, including all major intervals from the second through the 11th. The tones were generated by sine wave oscillators and recorded on tape. Each of three tapes contained 180 dichords, 18 of each interval size, with the sequence of intervals randomly chosen. The frequencies used spanned four octaves from 98.0 Hz to 1567.98 Hz. This range permitted the presentation of the same interval 18 times, while the same interval involving the same frequencies might occur no more than three times on the same tape. Minor adjustments in frequency (no more than 1 Hz) were made to eliminate obvious beats, and the intensities of some tones were adjusted to make them equally audible. Both adjustments were made by ear. The intervals were presented in pairs; each was presented twice, with two seconds between the two presentations of the same interval and nine seconds between the presentations of one interval and the presentations of the other interval.

Each of 20 subjects made all three ratings. Half of the subjects rated consonance first, and half rated complexity first. All rated pleasingness in the third session. Ratings were made on a scale of 0–100, and the direction of the scale—that is, whether 0 or 100 represented the more consonant, complex, or pleasing end of the scale—was varied from subject to subject.

*Ayres I.* This study (Ayres, 1974) was designed to obtain ratings of consonance and complexity as well as preferential choices among 13 intervals in a single octave. The stimuli were generated on a VCS3 synthesizer with keyboard. The dichords produced by this instrument consist of pairs of triangle tones. In a triangle tone, the relative loudnesses of partials, beginning with the fundamental, are 1, 1/2, 1/3, 1/4, and so on. A triangle tone is one of the fullest of musical tones in the sense that most musical tones are weaker in some or all of the upper partials. The synthesizer, which generated a modified sine wave, was afflicted with certain anomalies; the unison tended to produce a slight wah-wah, the minor second produced a buzz in the speaker, and there were detectable slight drifts in pitch, both during the sounding of some notes and through the span of the experimental session. The instrument was tuned by ear to ameliorate these characteristics.

The 13 intervals of the standard semitone scale (including unison) with middle C as the fundamental (approximately 262 Hz) were arranged in 13 orders using a Latin Square design. In the rating sessions, the dichords were sounded for two seconds, with seven seconds between dichords. Complexity ratings on a continuous seven-point scale were obtained from 11 subjects. Consonance ratings on a similar scale were obtained from 13 different subjects. Preferential choices were obtained from 11 subjects, ten of whom had provided consonance ratings. Preferential choices were obtained by arranging the keyboard to produce a dichord involving middle C whenever any key was pressed. The dichords sounded for two seconds after the release of the key, and the subjects were instructed to choose freely but not to hold the keys down and to try to avoid the playing of tunes.

*Ayres II.* I pointed out earlier that intervals involving quartertones are rarely heard by those exposed primarily to Western music. Quartertone intervals therefore provide one means of assessing the effects of prior experience on consonance and related dimensions. This (Ayres, 1975) study provided consonance and pleasantness ratings of the 25 intervals within an octave produced by dividing each semitone interval in two.

The stimuli were generated by the synthesizer employed in Ayres I. All intervals involved middle C as a fundamental. Three sets of 25 dichords were recorded on tapes, with arrangement in randomized order within each set. Each dichord endured for four seconds and was followed by a silent interval of five seconds.

Consonance was rated on a nine-point scale (1 = most consonant) by 23 subjects in two groups of 11 and 12. Pleasantness was rated by 25 subjects on a similar scale (1 = most pleasant) in two groups of 12 and 13 subjects. One tape was used for familiarization, and the other two were used in different groups as a partial control of order effects.

*Ayres III.* In an effort to improve the precision and stability of consonance orderings, the 25 quartertone intervals were evaluated for consonance using the paired comparisons scaling procedure (Ayres, 1975). A new set of tape recordings was prepared using the same set of 25 quartertone dichords employed in Ayres II. The dichords were recorded in pairs with members sounding for 1.5

seconds and with a separation of two seconds between members of the pairs. The 300 possible pairs were recorded in four blocks of 75 pairs each. Each dichord appeared in first place 12 times and in second place 12 times in the 24 comparisons in which each appeared.

Each of 24 subjects rated two of the four sets of stimuli (thus half of the total set) by choosing which of the pair of dichords was the more consonant. Half of the subjects were chosen to represent individuals with extensive musical backgrounds, and half were chosen to represent individuals with little musical background.

*Ayres IV.* A major source of experience with tones is human speech. Terhardt (1974) has distinguished between two sources of consonance: *spectral pitch,* resulting from central processing of the actual pitches of the components of the sound, and *virtual pitch,* resulting from the effects of past experience, primarily the hearing of human speech. Since the processing of speech is known to be strongly lateral, it is possible that the perception of consonance in the dominant hemisphere is different from its perception in the nondominant hemisphere. This problem was addressed by obtaining consonance ratings for quartertone dichords heard through only one ear at a time (Ayres, 1975).

Two sets of 25 dichords were recorded, each sounding for 1.5 seconds with five seconds between dichords. Using headphones, eight subjects made separate consonance ratings for each ear on the nine-point scale. Half rated the stimuli with the dominant ear first, and the other half rated the stimuli with the nondominant ear first.

### Some Empirical Results

Comparison of the results of the five studies will be facilitated if the values obtained are expressed in a common and comparable form. To this end, all the data have been reduced to standard scores and converted to the area under the normal curve represented by each point. Furthermore, all scales have been oriented to have low values express simplicity, consonance, and low values of preferential choice or pleasantness. High values therefore reflect ratings of greater complexity, dissonance, and frequency of preferential choice (thus pleasingness).

The primary results of all five studies are presented in Table 13-3. The values shown are means obtained in the individual rating procedures and subsequently converted to a comparable form.

*Individual Differences.* Any consideration of the nature and explanation of consonance and dissonance phenomena must take into account the presence and magnitude of individual differences, even if that consideration is only cautionary. Some estimate of the magnitude of the differences in evaluations given to dichords by different individuals can be seen in the variations in rankings accorded the ten major intervals employed in the Aeschbach study. These evaluations have been tabulated in Table 13-4. The range of individual differences is quite remarkable. Although 18 of 20 subjects rated the octave as the simplest interval, one rated it second and one rated it tenth out of ten. The order in which the intervals are listed in Table 13-4 was determined by mean rank. There is apparent agreement that the octave and the major fifth are the simplest, the most consonant, and the most pleasant of the ten intervals, but otherwise the orders tend to differ rather widely. The large relative magnitude of these individual differences, which are representative of the individual differences in all of the studies to be presented, must be kept in mind as group results are discussed.

*Simplicity/Complexity and Consonance/Dissonance.* Two of the studies, Aeschbach and Ayres I, provide estimates of the relative complexities and consonance of sets of intervals. In the Aeschbach study, the scaling procedures were employed with the same set of subjects. In the Ayres study, the two sets of ratings were obtained from different subjects. In both studies, the two scales are highly correlated; $r = .960$ in the Aeschbach study, and $r = .830$ in the Ayres study. Thus, intervals that are rated as consonant are rated as simple, and intervals rated as complex are rated as dissonant. These correlations are sufficiently high that we can assume that they are reflections of the same underlying process, psychological complexity. Subsequently, I will assume that the two scales of rated complexity and the five scales of rated consonance constitute seven different estimates of what I will refer to as complexity/consonance.

*Complexity/Consonance and Preference.* Three of the studies yielded scale values for some manifestation of the evaluative dimension of preference. The correlations between complexity/consonance and pleasingness ratings or preferential choice data are shown in Table 13-5. All five correlations between the relevant mean values in Table 13-5 are negative in sign and very high. All of these experimental subjects rated as most pleasing, or expressed a preference for, the simplest and most consonant of the intervals to which they were exposed and rated the most dissonant and most complex intervals as unpleasant or nonpreferred. Inspection of the scatter plots for these five correlations (not included here) indicates that the relationships are quite linear.

This finding of a monotonically linear relationship between estimates of preference and complexity/consonance was not expected on the basis of Moore's (1914) argument for a historical progression in preference from $\underline{1}$ to $\underline{8}$ to $\underline{5}$ to $\underline{4}$, and so on, as indicated

TABLE 13-3. Equivalent Scales of Complexity, Consonance, and Preference

| Interval | Complexity | | Consonance/Dissonance | | | | | Preference | | |
|---|---|---|---|---|---|---|---|---|---|---|
| | Aeschbach | Ayres I | Aeschbach | Ayres I | Ayres II | Ayres III | Ayres IV | Aeschbach | Ayres I | Ayres II |
| 1 | | 4.65 | | 10.03 | .35 | 5.16 | 6.30 | | 86.86 | 98.90 |
| q1̲ | | | | | 74.86 | 79.95 | 9.34 | | | 8.38 |
| 2 | | 88.00 | | 96.08 | 91.77 | 91.62 | 84.61 | | 4.65 | 12.30 |
| q2 | | | | | 62.55 | 89.07 | 94.18 | | | 30.50 |
| 2̲ | 92.51 | 46.41 | 89.62 | 83.40 | 75.80 | 46.81 | 86.21 | 6.81 | 41.29 | 53.98 |
| q2̲ | | | | | 64.06 | 56.36 | 89.07 | | | 63.31 |
| 3 | | 53.59 | | 31.21 | 11.70 | 19.49 | 54.78 | | 38.97 | 84.85 |
| q3 | | | | | 34.46 | 34.83 | 46.81 | | | 83.40 |
| 3̲ | 66.28 | 52.39 | 55.17 | 34.83 | 4.27 | 2.81 | 22.06 | 41.68 | 73.24 | 88.30 |
| q3̲ | | | | | 37.83 | 66.64 | 33.36 | | | 55.96 |
| 4 | 41.68 | 45.22 | 47.21 | 34.83 | 14.46 | 9.68 | 13.14 | 58.71 | 52.39 | 90.32 |
| q4̲ | | | | | 62.55 | 70.19 | 57.53 | | | 30.50 |
| 5 | | 78.52 | | 75.80 | 73.24 | 59.87 | 60.26 | | 21.77 | 66.28 |
| q5 | | | | | 70.19 | 65.17 | 41.29 | | | 23.27 |
| 5̲ | 18.94 | 29.81 | 16.85 | 12.30 | 9.18 | 8.69 | 6.30 | 78.23 | 76.73 | 87.29 |
| q5̲ | | | | | 82.38 | 57.53 | 60.26 | | | 21.77 |
| 6 | | 49.60 | | 70.54 | 42.86 | 37.83 | 54.78 | | 36.69 | 75.80 |
| q6 | | | | | 64.06 | 68.79 | 52.39 | | | 63.31 |
| 6̲ | 42.86 | 29.12 | 33.72 | 35.57 | 34.46 | 32.64 | 38.59 | 68.44 | 73.24 | 83.40 |
| q6̲ | | | | | 81.33 | 50.80 | 79.10 | | | 10.20 |
| 7 | | 88.30 | | 62.93 | 58.71 | 73.89 | 81.06 | | 18.41 | 17.11 |
| q7 | | | | | 83.65 | 79.39 | 86.21 | | | 10.38 |
| 7̲ | 84.85 | 92.51 | 93.32 | 88.30 | 80.23 | 87.49 | 90.32 | 6.81 | 17.11 | 9.18 |

| | | | | | | | | | |
|---|---|---|---|---|---|---|---|---|---|
| $q\frac{7}{8}$ | 1.62 | 3.92 | | 83.65 | 93.57 | 22.06 | 95.82 | 97.83 | 10.38 |
| $\frac{8}{q8}$ | | | 7.78 | 20.05 | 3.92 | 2.22 | | | 87.29 |
| $\frac{9}{q9}$ | 66.28 | 75.17 | | | | | 28.77 | | |
| $\frac{9}{q9}$ | | | | | | | | | |
| $\frac{10}{q10}$ | 46.41 | 30.15 | | | | | 70.88 | | |
| $\frac{10}{q10}$ | | | | | | | | | |
| $\frac{q10}{11}$ | 57.53 | 57.93 | | | | | 49.60 | | |

*TABLE 13-4.* Individual Differences in Rankings of Complexity, Consonance, and Pleasantness. Numbers in parentheses represent tied rank (Aeschbach, 1975).

### Complexity

| Interval | 1 | 2 | 3 | 4 | 5 | 6 | 7 | 8 | 9 | 10 |
|---|---|---|---|---|---|---|---|---|---|---|
| 8 | 18 | 1 | | | | | | | | 1 |
| 5 | 10 | 4 | | (1) | 1 | 1 | 2 | 1 | | |
| 6 | 2 | 4 | 3 | 2 (1) | 2 | 4 | 1 | 1 | | |
| 4 | | 1 | 4 | 4 | 1 | 6 | 1 | 3 | | |
| 10 | 1 | 1 | 2 | 4 (1) | 4 (1) | 2 | | 1 | 1 | 2 |
| 11 | | 2 | 1 | 4 | 2 | 1 | 3 | 5 | 1 | 1 |
| 9 | | 1 | 2 | 1 | 1 | 3 | 6 | 4 | 1 | 1 |
| 3 | | 1 | | 2 (1) | 3 | 3 | 1 | 4 | 5 | |
| 7 | 1 | 1 | | 1 (1) | 1 | | 2 | 1 | 6 (1) | 5 |
| 2 | | | 3 | 1 | | 1 | 1 | | 3 (1) | 10 |

### Consonance

| Interval | 1 | 2 | 3 | 4 | 5 | 6 | 7 | 8 | 9 | 10 |
|---|---|---|---|---|---|---|---|---|---|---|
| 8 | 12 | 4 | | 3 | | | 1 | | | |
| 5 | 2 | 7 | 4 | 3 | 2 | 1 | | (1) | | |
| 10 | 3 | 2 | 6 | 1 | 2 | 4 | 2 | | | |
| 6 | 1 | 3 | 2 | 6 | 4 | 1 | 3 | | | |
| 4 | 1 | 1 | 2 | 3 | 3 | 3 | 3 | 4 | | |
| 11 | | | 2 | 4 | 4 | 3 | 3 | 3 | 1 | |
| 3 | | | 6 | 1 | 1 | 5 | | 3 | 3 | 1 |
| 9 | | | | 1 | 1 | 2 | 6 | 5 (1) | 3 | 1 |
| 2 | 1 | | 1 | | 1 | | 2 | 2 | 3 | 10 |
| 7 | | | | | | 1 | | 2 | 9 | 8 |

### Pleasantness

| Interval | 1 | 2 | 3 | 4 | 5 | 6 | 7 | 8 | 9 | 10 |
|---|---|---|---|---|---|---|---|---|---|---|
| 8 | 12 | 1 | 3 | 1 | 3 | | | | | |
| 5 | 1 | 6 (1) | 1 (1) | 2 | 3 | 3 | 1 | 1 | | |
| 6 | | 6 | 2 (1) | 3 | 4 | 3 | 1 | | | |
| 10 | 2 | 2 (1) | 2 (2) | 5 | 1 | 1 (1) | 2 (1) | | | |
| 4 | | 1 | 4 (1) | 3 | 1 | 4 (1) | 2 (1) | 1 | 1 | |
| 11 | 1 | 2 | 1 (1) | 1 | 4 | 3 | 3 | 2 | 2 | |
| 3 | 2 | 1 | | | 2 | 3 | 5 (2) | 1 | 4 | |
| 9 | | | 2 (1) | | 1 | 1 | 2 (2) | 8 | 3 | |
| 7 | | | (1) | 1 | 1 | | | 3 | 4 | 10 |
| 2 | 2 | | | | | 1 | | 1 | 6 | 10 |

Numbers in parentheses represent tied ranks.

TABLE 13-5. Correlations of Preference and Complexity/Consonance

| Preference | Complexity | Consonance |
|---|---|---|
| Aeschbach (Pleasingness ratings) | − .963 | − .991 |
| Ayres I (Frequency of preferential choice) | − .936 | − .896 |
| Ayres II (Pleasingness ratings) | | − .874 |

in Table 13-2. One might have expected an inverted-U-shaped function with maximum preference for some interval more complex or dissonant than the unison or octave. It is possible that the stimuli generated by laboratory equipment may be sufficiently unfamiliar that essentially all of them are more complex than the mean optimal complexity levels of these subjects. However, little confidence can be accorded this speculation in light of a consideration of the effects of experience, which will be discussed later.

*Dominant versus Nondominant Ear.* Differences in the ratings of consonance and dissonance in the dominant and nondominant ear were not statistically significant in the Ayres IV study. There is a possibility, however, that a more extensive study would reveal the expected difference. The direction of the obtained difference (.275 scale points on a nine-point scale) was as expected, with the intervals being rated more consonant when heard in the dominant ear. However, given the fact that there were only eight subjects in this study, and given the magnitude of the individual differences in Table 13-4, the error term used in the calculation of significance level is quite large.

### Complexity/Consonance Reconceptualized

Earlier it was suggested that a reconceptualization of the consonance/dissonance problem based on a circular representation of the tonality dimension of pitch might be revealing. It was also suggested that there might be as many as four factors contributing to the experience of the complexity/consonance of intervals. What follows is an inductive effort to determine whether the four factors of octavity, proximity, distality, and experience can account for the disordered appearance of the sequences of intervals indicated in Table 13-2.

The primary results reported in Table 13-3 include two evaluations of complexity and five of consonance. Since complexity and consonance ratings are so highly correlated, they can be considered to be estimates of the same theoretical variable, psychological complexity. Given this assumption, a "best estimate" of complexity/consonance can be obtained by averaging the various values in Table 13-3 to obtain a single value for each interval tested. Such "best estimate" values would represent the means of two, three, five, or seven estimates. The results of this operation are plotted in Figure 13-5. It might be noted, for reference, that this "best estimate" value for complexity/consonance yields a rank order of intervals (1, 8, 5, 4, 3, 3, 6, 6, 5, 7, 2, 7, 2) that agrees as well with the orderings in Table 13-2 as the various orders within the table agree with one another.

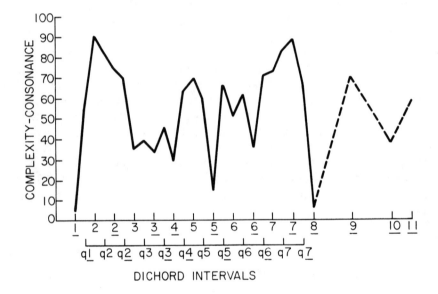

FIGURE 13-5. *Empirical Estimates of the Relative Complexity/Consonance of Musical Intervals. The figure displays "best estimate" values composed of the means of from two to seven means of either complexity or consonance/dissonance scaling procedures.*

*Octavity.* Visual inspection of Figure 13-5 reveals precisely what a variety of statistical analyses reveal: there is no apparent contribution of the octave to complexity/consonance. A variety of potential quantitative analyses of octavity are vitiated by the possible effects of differential experience on complexity/consonance. For example, four comparisons (between 8 and 1, between 9 and 2, between 10 and 3, and between 11 and 4) involve tones that have the "same" tonality values but are an octave apart. They should therefore yield four estimates of the increase in complexity/consonance produced by the addition of an octave to the interval involved. However, the four intervals with the smaller numbers are all heard much more frequently than the four with the larger numbers. If the effect of repeated experience is to make an interval sound more consonant that it would have without the experience, then each of the four comparisons would be affected by an unknown amount. If one assumes that of all the intervals involved in these comparisons, 4 has been heard most frequently and should thus be most simplified through experience, then 11 should be rated as much more complex than 4. It is, 57.73 to 29.27. The 10 should be rated as more complex than 3, and it is, 38.28 to 33.88; but the reverse relation holds between 9 and 2, where 2 is rated as the more complex, 74.39 to 70.73. A variety of least-square linear fits to subsets of the data from one of the studies or from the "best estimate" values yield both positive and negative slopes centering around zero, and all are subject to distortion from the effects of differential experience with some of the intervals. One is therefore forced to conclude either that the octave makes no contribution to complexity/consonance or that the contribution is quite small and well within the error range in these studies. It is worthy of note that in Stumpf's (1883) study, 8, the octave, was the interval most frequently reported as a single tone rather than as a pair. Shepard (1964) notes that individuals in his sample who were regarded as having perfect pitch, in that they could name a tone in terms of its tonality characteristics, were unable to identify the octave from which the tone came. Finally, in trying to account for the values of the "best estimate" curve in Figure 13-5, I could find no value of octavity that improved the post hoc account of the data.

*Proximity.* In discussing the Malmberg data shown in Figure 13-4, I pointed out that some factor making a positive contribution to dissonance was at a maximum on either side of the fundamental note and then decreased as one moved around the circle in either direction from the fundamental. This proximity effect was evident in the large rank values near the fundamental, which decrease thereafter.

In Figure 13-5, the proximity effect is evident in the two peaks (at 2 and 7). Furthermore, the two ends of the octave are nearly mirror images of each other; if the points ranging from 1 to 3 are folded over to coincide with the points from 6 to $\underline{8}$, the corresponding data points nearly coincide.

In an effort to estimate the relative contribution of proximity to scaled complexity/consonance, a trial value was assigned to each quartertone interval. These values are contained in Table 13-6 in the $C_p$ column and in Figure 13-6. Since there was no compelling reason to do otherwise, the values were assigned as mirror images

*TABLE 13-6.* Scale Value Estimates of Proximity ($C_p$), Distality ($C_d$), and Experience Effects ($C_e$), Compared to Best Estimate Effects ($C_{be}$) from Figure 13-5.

| Interval | $C_p$ | $C_d$ | $C_e$ | $\Sigma$ | $C_{be}$ | Error |
|---|---|---|---|---|---|---|
| $\underline{1}$ | .00 | 5.00 | .00 | 5.00 | 5.30 | - .30 |
| q$\underline{1}$ | 51.50 | 9.50 | .00 | 61.00 | 54.72 | 6.28 |
| 2 | 75.50 | 14.00 | .00 | 89.50 | 90.42 | - .92 |
| q2 | 65.00 | 18.00 | .00 | 83.00 | 81.93 | 1.07 |
| $\underline{2}$ | 53.50 | 22.50 | .00 | 76.00 | 74.39 | 1.61 |
| q$\underline{2}$ | 40.00 | 27.00 | .00 | 67.00 | 69.83 | - 2.83 |
| 3 | 21.00 | 31.50 | - 16.81 | 35.69 | 34.15 | 1.54 |
| q3 | 2.00 | 36.50 | .00 | 38.50 | 38.70 | - .20 |
| $\underline{3}$ | .00 | 42.00 | - 6.58 | 35.42 | 33.88 | 1.54 |
| q$\underline{3}$ | .00 | 45.50 | .00 | 45.50 | 45.94 | - .44 |
| 4 | .00 | 57.50 | - 26.50 | 31.00 | 29.46 | 1.54 |
| q$\underline{4}$ | .00 | 63.00 | .00 | 63.00 | 63.42 | - .42 |
| 5 | .00 | 65.50 | .00 | 65.50 | 69.54 | - 4.04 |
| q5 | .00 | 66.00 | .00 | 66.00 | 58.88 | 7.12 |
| $\underline{5}$ | .00 | 66.00 | - 54.42 | 14.58 | 14.58 | .00 |
| q$\underline{5}$ | .00 | 65.50 | .00 | 65.50 | 66.72 | - 1.22 |
| 6 | .00 | 65.00 | - 12.34 | 52.56 | 51.12 | 1.54 |
| q6 | 2.00 | 63.00 | .00 | 65.00 | 61.75 | 3.25 |
| $\underline{6}$ | 21.00 | 36.50 | - 20.68 | 36.82 | 35.28 | 1.54 |
| q$\underline{6}$ | 40.00 | 29.00 | .00 | 69.00 | 70.41 | - 1.41 |
| 7 | 53.50 | 21.00 | .00 | 74.50 | 72.98 | 1.52 |
| q7 | 65.00 | 16.50 | .00 | 81.50 | 83.08 | - 1.58 |
| $\underline{7}$ | 75.50 | 12.00 | .00 | 87.50 | 88.15 | - .65 |
| q$\underline{7}$ | 51.50 | 8.50 | .00 | 60.00 | 66.43 | - 6.43 |
| $\underline{8}$ | .00 | 5.00 | .00 | 5.00 | 6.15 | - 1.15 |
| q$\underline{8}$ | | | | | | |
| 9 | | | | | | |
| q9 | | | | | | |
| $\underline{9}$ | 53.50 | 22.50 | .00 | 76.00 | 70.73 | 5.27 |
| q$\underline{9}$ | | | | | | |
| 10 | | | | | | |
| q10 | | | | | | |
| $\underline{10}$ | .00 | 42.00 | .00 | 42.00 | 38.28 | 3.78 |
| q$\underline{10}$ | | | | | | |
| $\underline{11}$ | .00 | 57.50 | .00 | 57.50 | 57.73 | - .23 |

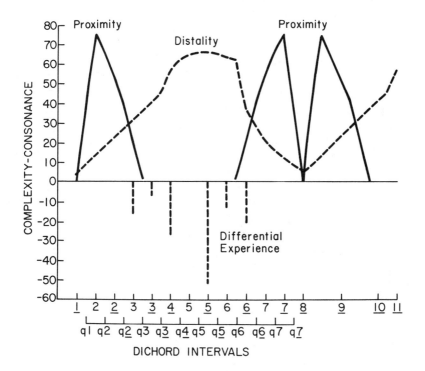

*FIGURE 13-6. Estimated Values of Proximity, Distality, and Differential Experience Effects. The figure is a graph of values for three factors required to account for complexity/consonance. The fourth factor, octavity, appears to have a zero value in these data.*

and were given the same values in the second octave as they were given in the first.

Proximity stands in some degree of correspondence with critical bandwidth (Zwicker, Flottorp, & Stevens, 1957). The frequency range over which two tones appear to interact, as evidenced by their effect on each other's perceived loudness, is estimated to be about .5 of an octave when the center frequency of the dichord is 100 Hz and about .13 of an octave when the center frequency is 15,000 Hz. As drawn in Figure 13-6, the proximity effect extends about .3 of an octave. Since the best estimate figures plotted in Figure 13-5 represent data obtained primarily with the use of a frequency of 262 Hz as a fundamental and include ratings from the Aeschbach data extending over several octaves, this range for proximity corresponds to critical bandwidth as well as could be hoped.

The maximum of the proximity effect in Figure 13-6 is at about 28% of the range, agreeing reasonably closely with the figure of approximately 25% in the Plomp and Levelt (1965) data.

*Distality.* A highly speculative set of values was assigned to distality ($C_d$). They were determined in the following, highly informal manner. The effects of proximity alone were presumed to be removed by subtracting the proximity effect from the best estimate. The residual was then plotted. Since the 3, $\underline{3}$, $\underline{4}$, $\underline{5}$, 6, and $\underline{6}$ intervals were expected to be most simplified by experience, and since each appears to project below any smooth curve, these intervals were essentially ignored in the process of estimating distality. The smoothest possible curve was then fit to the remaining points. The quantities in the $C_p$ column of Table 13-6 and the distality curve in Figure 13-6 are the result. No strong brief can be made for the shape and character of the distality curve. It should be noted, however, that a brief can be made for its asymmetry and for the unlikelihood that its maximum value is in the center of the octave, in the 5 position. Numerous efforts to achieve either of these curve characteristics were made, to no avail.

The original stimulus for the conception of distality is the notorious dissonance of the minor fifth, the tritone, labeled "5" in our notation. That the effect must be distributed for some distance from the position of the tritone is suggested by the tendency for other intervals in the vicinity of the tritone to be rated dissonant, as indicated, for example, in Figure 13-5. The necessity for taking a factor such as distality into account is obvious from the curves in Figure 13-6. The exact shape of the function remains to be determined.

An auditory phenomenon that might possibly be related to the distality effect is the temporary hearing loss observed after exposure to intense stimuli. Davis, Morgan, Hawkins, Galambos, and Smith (1950) found the greatest loss at about one-half an octave above the exposure frequency. The extent of the effect over the frequency range, as well as the rate of recovery from loss, is reported to be related to the intensity and duration of the stimuli and to be subject to great variation both within and among individuals. The authors attribute the loss to "nerve deafness" in these human subjects. Stebbins, Clark, Pearson, and Weiland (1973) observed a similar phenomenon in some monkeys. In both humans and monkeys there is evidence of a half-octave shift with moderately intense exposure sounds and more extensive upward shifts with more intense stimuli. The two phenomena, complexity/consonance effects of distality and temporary residual deafness from exposure to intense stimuli, have in common the maximum effect at about a half octave and large individual differences. A determination of whether the two effects are in fact related must await further experimental efforts. It should be noted, however, that by this reasoning distality not only differs from proximity in locus of maximum effect on the tonality circle but might prove to be neural in origin, in contrast to the probable basis for proximity in the physical properties of the basilar membrane.

*Effects of Differential Experience.* Moore (1914) advanced the hypothesis that repeated exposure to a given musical interval would produce a gradual decrease in dissonance, or increase in consonance. He made a strong case for his hypothesis both by experiment and by analysis of the history of preferences for musical intervals. Psychological complexity and preference theory postulates that repeated occurrences of the same event should lead to progressive simplification of that event toward an asymptotic limit. With music, the effect should be that an interval originally heard to be very complex and dissonant will gradually come to be heard as less complex and less dissonant. These studies offered several opportunities to test these expectations.

As pointed out previously, the data on preferences for musical intervals in three of the studies, Aeschbach, Ayres I, and Ayres II, failed to yield critical evidence. The relationships obtained do not contradict the theory, but neither do they offer any real support. Strong support would be evident if, for example, the subjects as a group had preferred the 4 and 5 to 1 and 8. In this respect, the subjects in all three studies behaved as did the early Greeks who, according to Moore, preferred to sing in unison or its near equivalent with men's and boys' voices an octave apart.

Aeschbach obtained supplementary data from her subjects on the extent of their past experience with music. No statistically significant differences could be shown between subjects' ratings on the basis of their musical experience. In the Ayres III study, half of the 24 subjects chosen had extensive musical backgrounds, and the other half did not. Again, no statistically significant difference could be demonstrated between these two groups.

In three studies, Ayres employed both semitone and quartertone intervals. Since quartertone intervals are rarely heard in Western music, one might expect that the subjects would have had differential exposure to the semitone and quartertone intervals, resulting in the quartertone intervals being rated more complex and more dissonant than the semitone intervals. This hypothesis is not easily tested in any direct fashion. It is true that the 12 quartertone intervals are rated as more than 13 scale points more complex or more dissonant than the 13 semitone intervals employed in the same studies. However, the 13 semitone intervals have the benefit of including both 1 and 8, which may be consonant because they provide no source of dissonance, as well as intervals such as 5, and 4, which are heard very frequently. A direct comparison of all semitone with all quartertone intervals may therefore yield spurious results.

In describing the manner in which the distality effect, $C_d$ was estimated, I indicated that the six most frequent semitone intervals were ignored because they might have undergone different amounts of simplification through differential experience. The amount of that possible effect was estimated in the following manner. When the proximity and distality effects are subtracted from the data in Figure 13-5, the six intervals in question all have negative values. When the mean of the residual means of the other 19 intervals is subtracted from each of the six, a potential "learning" or "experience" effect is obtained. These values are given in Table 13-6 in the $C_e$ column, and they are plotted in Figure 13-6 as vertical lines projected into the negative space of the figure. Examination of the table and figure will show that the largest effect is shown by 5, followed by 4, 6, 3, 6, and 3.

With respect to this set of intervals, the Moore order is 5, followed by 4, followed by the other four, all of them judged to be equal with respect to differential experience. As for the intervals 1 and 8, one could suppose either that there is no dissonance in such intervals to be overcome through experience or that such effects had already been accounted for by the particular functions selected for the proximity and distality functions. To this extent, the results appear to confirm the expectations arising from the Moore theory and from psychological complexity and preference theory.

An alternative to differential experience as an explanation of the negative values labeled $C_e$ in Table 13-6 and "differential experience" in Figure 13-6 can be offered in terms of some of the properties of the physical stimulus as described by Taylor (1965) in his account of the numbers of summation and differential tones and beat frequencies produced by the various musical intervals. On an equal-tempered scale, 5 is the simplest, 4 and 6 appear to be equally complex but more complex than 5, and a third low point that is more complex than the others appears near q3 and 3 on one side and near q6 and 6 on the other. The order in Table 13-2 of 1 = 8 < 5 < 4 < 6 < 3 < others is attained by counting lines above points on the abscissa corresponding to the piano scale. Thus, a moderately reasonable case can be made for an "experiential" explanation of the column labeled $C_e$ based on the agreement with the Moore order in Table 13-2, and a moderately reasonable case can be made for the values in column $C_e$ in terms of the physical properties of the stimulus based on the Taylor analysis.

*Combined Effects.* When the three sets of values in Table 13-6 and Figure 13-6 are summed the result is the $\Sigma$ column of Table 13-6 and the graph in Figure 13-7. Visually, at least, it is very difficult to distinguish between Figure 13-5, which contains the empirical data, and Figure 13-7, which is the theoretical sum of the three factors (actually four, since octavity is assumed to have zero effects at all intervals).

Several comments should be made concerning Figure 13-7 and the comparison with Figure 13-5. There is no apparent quartertone effect remaining in Figure 13-5. Such an effect should show as a systematic tendency for the quartertone intervals to be higher than

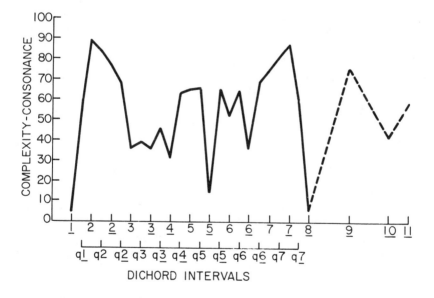

FIGURE 13-7. *Theoretical Reconstruction of Complexity/Consonance. The figure combines the three factors of proximity, distality, and differential experience effects displayed separately in Figure 13-6.*

the adjacent semitone intervals, leading to a sawtoothed appearance. No such effect is apparent, nor is any evident in the "Error" column of Table 13-6.

The "Error" column was obtained by subtracting the "best estimate" value from the sum of the theoretical values. As can be seen in the table, most of the discrepancies are small. The largest discrepancies are in the vicinity of 5 and q5, with mirrored discrepencies at q1 and q7. Examination of the relevant means in Table 13-3 indicates that these discrepancies are likely to be the result of errors of measurement. Of all the studies, Ayres IV had the smallest number of subjects, eight. The q1, q5, and q7 values in Ayres IV reflect large empirical discrepancies from the values obtained in Ayres II and Ayres III.

*Conclusions.* One can argue from the foregoing considerations that the experience of consonance and dissonance for musical dichords is the product of several factors rather than a single factor. Further, the several factors may have quite different origins. There appears to be a *proximity* effect that produces a maximum of dissonance when the second note of the pair is very close to the fundamental or to the octave of the fundamental. This effect may be the product of the physical interaction of the effects of the two tones on the action of the basilar membrane. There also appears to be a strong *distality* effect, with a maximum effect for intervals formed of tones half an octave or slightly farther apart. This effect might be related to the temporary elevation of auditory loudness thresholds about half an octave above the stimulating frequency. If so, it might be neural in origin, since the temporary deafness from the stimulation of the ear with intense tones is attributed to long-lasting habituation phenomena and is referred to as "nerve deafness" by its discoverers.

There are substantial reductions in the dissonance of the intervals labeled 5 and 4, as well as of several others commonly heard in musical compositions. These reductions are precisely what one would expect from *differential experience* with these musical intervals. On the other hand, the same differences might be attributable to the differential physical complexities of the stimuli, as calculated from the presence of beat frequencies and summation and differential tones in the physical stimuli.

No effect of the octave on relative complexity/consonance could be demonstrated in these data.

There seems little doubt that the experience of consonance and dissonance is the product of several factors operating more or less independently, and, in view of the large inter- and intra-individual differences found in these and other studies, the group processes may not hold true within any single individual.

### Summary of Consonance and Dissonance

The sequential orderings of musical dichords on a dimension of consonance and dissonance is related to the tonality aspect of the helical conception of pitch. There is a tendency for the most dissonant intervals to be adjacent to the fundamental and the octave and for dissonance to decline around the helix in either direction. This phenomenon is labeled the *proximity effect.* Several intervals involving tones nearly opposite the fundamental—for example, the minor fifth—interrupt this decline with a sharp rise in dissonance, labeled the *distality effect. Octavity,* the quality that distinguishes the same tones played an octave apart, could be a third source of dissonance. Finally, there is some reason to believe that *differential experience* with an interval might produce a reduction in the perceived dissonance of the interval. If so, then one might expect to find changes in preference in the direction of more dissonant intervals.

### THE HEDGEHOG AND AESTHETICS

In Chapter 1, psychological complexity and preference theory was stated in ten words: *Psychological events nearest optimum complexity are preferred. Occurrence produces simplification.* When applied to the aesthetic response to visual and auditory materials, the theory is restated to indicate that an individual will prefer, and therefore experience the maximum aesthetic experience from, pictures or melodies that are nearest his or her own optimum. Materials that are either more or less complex for that individual will be less preferred. As an individual experiences more and more material of a given class, all such material will undergo progressive simplification, with the result that the optimum complexity level will move to more and more physically complex material.

In Chapters 12 and 13 I have reviewed a number of studies employing materials such as modern paintings and graphics that are clearly materials of the fine arts. We have also used artificial materials with similar results. The findings are generally compatible with the theory and serve to suggest that psychological complexity and preference theory is a suitable tool for use in approaching aesthetics in the synthesis mode of experimental aesthetics. Since earlier chapters in this book were intended to demonstrate the integrative character of the Hedgehog in the various subdisciplines of experimental psychology, these findings also serve to demonstrate the firm grounding of experimental aesthetics in the foundations of experimental psychology.

# chapter fourteen

# The hedgehog and problems of lifelong learning

The Hedgehog is ubiquitously applicable. It provides intellectual tools that permit a grasp of a great many social problems in which issues related to learning and motivation are involved. Among many examples are the decline in Scholastic Aptitude Test (SAT) scores in the 1970s, attempted explanations of this decline in terms of family size and birth order, and a deep feeling among large segments of the population that our schools are somehow failing to meet their educational commitments.

The Hedgehog has implications of a profound character for how we choose to deal with these and related issues. Furthermore, unlike many theories of motivation and learning, psychological complexity and preference theory provides the means of explaining the nature of the difficulty, assessing the magnitude of the problem, and suggesting multiple means of effective remediation.

In this chapter, I undertake to illustrate the manner in which the Hedgehog can be used to explain, assess, and suggest remedial plans in a number of areas in which academic achievement is the core of the problem. The treatment will be illustrative rather than exhaustive. In order to develop these illustrations, it will be necessary to expand on three issues—the nature of responses to the full range of psychological complexity, the nature of academic progress, and the manipulation of motivation.

## HEDGEHOG CONCEPTS
## AND ACADEMIC ACHIEVEMENT

Academic achievement is usually measured in terms of two correlated dimensions. In part, academic learning consists of the acquisition of knowledge about an ever-expanding range of subjects or topics. However, the greatest social concern is expressed about the development of cognitive skills in the core areas of reading, writing, and mathematics. In these areas, progress is indexed by the difficulty level of the material that is mastered. Whereas the achievement of breadth involves material learned at the same level of psychological complexity, the development of depth in cognitive or physical skills amounts to an upward shift in the optimal complexity level of the performance against an external scale of the difficulty of the material. In the remainder of this chapter, I emphasize the development of cognitive skills that can be ordered in terms of level of difficulty and thus matched to differences in psychological complexity.

### The Individual and the Full Range
### of Psychological Complexity/Difficulty

Several aspects of the Hedgehog should be reemphasized in the context of problems of lifelong learning and academic achievement. Psychological complexity is a characteristic of the psychological event as it occurs in the individual. Since difficulty is perfectly correlated with psychological complexity, the term *psychological complexity* refers to the difficulty of a psychological event for a particular individual.

Figure 14-1 represents the full range of complexity/difficulty for an individual along an academically relevant dimension. Several landmarks are indicated on the scale by inverted arrows and the

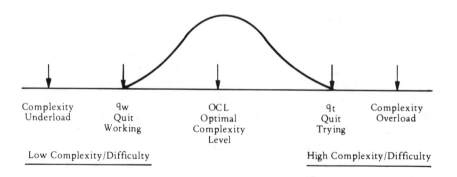

| Complexity Underload | $q_w$ Quit Working | OCL Optimal Complexity Level | $q_t$ Quit Trying | Complexity Overload |
|---|---|---|---|---|

Low Complexity/Difficulty                    High Complexity/Difficulty

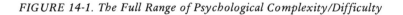

*FIGURE 14-1. The Full Range of Psychological Complexity/Difficulty*

spaces between arrows. The optimal complexity level (OCL) in the middle of the scale represents the level of task difficulty that this individual finds most pleasant or interesting, the level of task difficulty he will choose if allowed to choose freely and the level at which he will work most vigorously without external inducement.

*Quit Working ($q_w$).* As one moves from OCL in the figure toward the left, and thus into tasks that are less complex and less difficult than the optimum task, both the tendency to choose the task and the vigor of execution will decline until a point is reached at which the psychological event involved is so simple and boring that it will not be undertaken at all. This is the $q_w$, or "quit working" point. The inverted-U function does not drop below the line because the individual will not voluntarily execute events that are any simpler than the $q_w$ event without external constraint.

If individuals are induced or forced to engage in events that are below the $q_w$ point on their own scales of psychological complexity/difficulty, they will find these events boring and unpleasant and will engage in behaviors directed toward alleviation of the situation. They may simply leave the physical situation. If that is not possible, they may attempt to complicate the physical or social environment responsible for their displeasure. If that is not possible, they may seek previously unexplored complexity in the familiar stimulus, they may daydream or even hallucinate, or they may simply fall asleep.

*Quit Trying ($q_t$).* As psychological events grow more complex and difficult than optimum, the increase in difficulty is accompanied by a decrease in vigor of execution and a decrease in the pleasure derived from the events. There is a point at which the individual will not voluntarily undertake the task or continue in attempts to execute it because of the complexity/difficulty level. This is the point at which the individual will quit trying ($q_t$).

If, through the imposition of constraints, individuals are forced to try tasks beyond their $q_t$ points, the most likely response is one of escape behavior. If escape is impossible, they will try to find ways of simplifying the task to bring it within the $q_w$-$q_t$ range. They may narrow their attention to a part of the task, undertake to chunk the task into simpler form, abstract a simpler representation of the task, or, if all else fails, endure the full complexity of the task until simplification occurs through the slow process of simplification through repeated experience.

### The Nature of Academic Progress

Academic progress consists of a shift toward more complex psychological events on an academically meaningful dimension, such as reading level. Figure 14-2 illustrates three stages of progress on

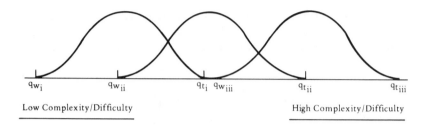

$q_{w_i}$        $q_{w_{ii}}$        $q_{t_i}$  $q_{w_{iii}}$        $q_{t_{ii}}$        $q_{t_{iii}}$

Low Complexity/Difficulty                    High Complexity/Difficulty

*FIGURE 14-2. The Nature of Academic Progress*

such a scale. The three curves might represent three grade levels or any other sequential milestones. The important point is that, as academic progress is made, not only does the peak of the curve shift up the scale, but the associated $q_w$ and $q_t$ points shift up the scale as well. Material that is at the "quit trying" point at one stage of development can be at optimal level at another. Material that is optimal at one stage of development can recede beyond the "quit working" point at another.

### Motivation for Learning and Its Manipulation

Three sources of motivation for learning can profitably be distinguished, because the effectiveness of educational procedures differs among the three. The three classes are as follows.

1. *Autarkic motivation.* The word *autarkic* means self-sufficient. *Autarkic motivation* refers to motivation to perform a task for the sake of the performance alone, unsupported by motivation from any other source. The source of autarkic motivation is the task itself. Behavior that is autarkically motivated will result in what Berlyne (1960, p. 79) called *intrinsic exploration.* Autarkic motivation is automatic, autonomous, and spontaneous. It is intrinsic to the task being performed.

2. *Idiocratic motivation.* Idocratic motivation has its source in the individual. It is motivation that is characteristic of a given person and is a stable aspect of the personality. Idiocratic motivation is not dependent on any external source of support. The performance of a given task can be motivated idiocratically if it is seen by the individual to serve some personal motive. Behavior that is idiocratically motivated can result in what Berlyne (1960, p. 79) called *extrinsic exploration,* in which the individual seeks cues for guidance for some succeeding response with an independent source of biological value. Idiocratic motivation is autogenous and endogenous to the person. It is extrinsic to the task being performed, but its source is intrinsic to the person performing the task.

3. *Extraneous motivation.* This class of motive has its source outside the individual. It is not essential, it is not intrinsic in any sense, and it is foreign to the person. The essential feature of extraneous motivation is that extraneously motivated behavior will occur only when the source of the motivation is present and operating. Extraneously motivated behavior will cease when the source of the motivation is removed.

*Autarkic Motivation.* Many of the things people do they do simply because they feel like doing them. No external or remote purpose is involved. If subsequently they are asked why they did these things, they are likely to say that they did them because they were interesting, because they found them pleasant, because they enjoyed doing them, and, sometimes, because they were bored. As an example, consider the working of crossword puzzles in the daily paper. Under most circumstances, doing crossword puzzles is an expression of autarkic motivation. Let us imagine that we have a cooperative person who likes crossword puzzles and that we have 15 different crossword puzzles ordered on a broad range of difficulty, from extremely simple (1) to extremely complex (15). Suppose we have given this friendly and cooperative person the opportunity to work on as many of the puzzles as he wished and on whichever of them he chose.

If we have matched the set of puzzles properly to the experience and ability of our subject, we might find that he chose to work on puzzles with difficulty levels of 3, 4, 5, 6, and 7. If we ask him which he enjoyed the most, he might well choose puzzle 5 as the most enjoyable, then say that 4 and 6 were almost as much fun, while 3 and 7 were fun but 3 was almost too simple and 7 was almost too difficult. When we ask him about the others, he might say that two of them, 1 and 2, looked too simple, while the others, 8 through 15, looked too difficult.

Our person's behavior in choosing puzzles, his evaluation of how enjoyable they were, and his judgments about those he did not attempt would permit us to place the puzzles along the complexity/ difficulty dimension of Figure 14-3. Puzzles 1 and 2 would be below the $q_w$ point for the curve labeled "Autarkic Motivation." Puzzles 3, 4, 5, 6, and 7 would be ordered between $q_w$ and $q_t$ for the same curve, and puzzles 8 through 15 would be placed in order beyond the $q_t$ point.

*Idiocratic Motivation.* Suppose we now give our friendly, cooperative subject a strong lecture on the value of doing crossword puzzles. We might undertake to convince him that doing crossword puzzles is exceptionally good practice in the use of words as well as an opportunity to learn new ones and that vocabulary size and facility are exceedingly important in the attainment of his educational and

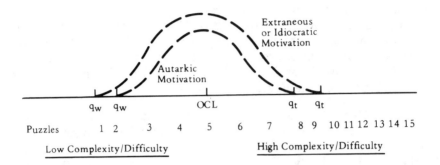

*FIGURE 14-3. Effect of Combining Motives*

career goals. If we are successful in convincing our friend, then we have added an increment to the motivation to do all puzzles. This increment is extrinsic to puzzles but is an internalized value. It can be labeled *idiocratic,* since it would persist if we allowed our friend to take the puzzles home and work on them ad lib.

Within the Hedgehog, adding motivation external to the intrinsic value of the puzzles themselves should lead to an increase in arousal associated with the activity of doing puzzles and should increase the range of difficulty within which our friend would work. He would now probably choose to do a simpler puzzle or two because doing them would be "good practice" with words, and possibly he would choose to do puzzles 8 and 9 because he would "learn new words" as well as get practice. These effects are represented in the second curve of Figure 14-3. Because the added motivation has been internalized, it will persist, with the result that the pleasure associated with doing puzzles that had been too simple or too complex will also persist.

One effect of the strong lecture we have given to our cooperative friend has been omitted from the figure. The increase in level of arousal that our lecture has produced would raise the optimal complexity level to some degree. Thus, $q_w$, OCL, and $q_t$ for the upper curve might shift somewhat to the right. I think this shift is a real and very important effect, but it constitutes only one of a number of complications that might serve only to obscure the simplicity of the general principles involved in conceptualizing the ideal educational situation.

*Extraneous Motivation.* Extraneous motivation is motivation that is externally applied with no effort to induce the individual to internalize it. It is not only extrinsic to the task but external to the individual. Because it is external to the individual, it is wholly dependent on the situation, and, unlike idiocratic motivation, will disappear when the individual is removed from the situation in which the motivational constraint has been applied.

Extraneous means of inducing an individual to work on a task that would otherwise be out of the range of autarkic motivation involve interesting affective consequences. If we have induced our friend to work on puzzles of difficulty levels 1, 2, 8, and 9 only by applying an external constraint, he will find the doing of the puzzles mildly pleasant at the time. However, when the external constraint is removed, the motivational level will return to the lesser curve of autarkic motivation alone, and our friend will find both simple and complex puzzles distinctly unpleasant.

*Complexity of the Task before and after Mastery.* One characteristic of the relations among complexity, motivation, preference, and performance that should be noted is the fate of a task after it is done. The motivational properties of a task are a reflection of its complexity for the individual involved, both in the contemplation of doing it and in the actual performance. For many tasks, of which the crossword puzzle is an example, doing the task reduces its complexity to a very low level and thus puts it out of the range of the prevailing motivation. A person would not undertake to do the same crossword puzzle again, even if an unsullied copy were available. There is thus a second type of $q_w$, or "quit work" point, at the end of such a task. Other tasks that do not undergo such simplification in the process of their execution are terminated either by habituation or by the availability of a task closer to the optimal. Tasks of this sort, such as playing golf, are resumed when habituation is dissipated and the opportunity to perform them is again presented.

*Generalized $q_w$ and $q_t$.* The major difference between idiocratic and extraneous motivation is the fact that the former will become integrated with the type of task, whereas the latter will dissipate immediately when the constraints are removed. There are important long-range consequences if either of these patterns occurs persistently with respect to a particular kind of subject matter, such as mathematics.

To make the point, let us take two fictional instructors with different teaching styles. Both have teaching tasks in which the students are to learn mathematical procedures that are beyond their upper difficulty range, given their present levels of motivation for mathematics.

One instructor undertakes to increase the motive level of her students by making the task relevant to their preexisting goals. If that is not enough, she undertakes to identify herself with the students and get them to identify with her and thus arouse affiliative motives and enlist them in the task. Suppose she succeeds. Suppose she persists in applying these and other techniques that result in the enlisting of internalized motives to learn mathematics and that she does so over a long period of time. The result will be that her students will come to like or even love mathematics and will find distinct pleasure in learning new techniques and higher-level mathematical concepts. They will see difficult mathematical problems as challenging and mathematical accomplishment as rewarding. Suppose that these same students are fortunate enough to have teachers in other subjects who use the same techniques. The result will be that they will see academic work in all aspects as pleasant and experience the doing of academic work as pleasurable. Furthermore, academic work will be internally motivated, with the result that it will not be dependent on the presence of the teacher or associated exclusively with the academic setting. In the extreme case, the result will be an erudite and scholarly person imbued with the love of learning.

Another instructor, in contrast, does not undertake to invest the task with idiocratic motives. He arouses extraneous motivation by offering rewards or by threatening reprisals and punishments for nonperformance. His efforts are successful in that he succeeds in inducing his students to execute the difficult tasks and drill effectively on the dull ones. However, as soon as the external rewards are no longer offered and the possibility of reprisal is past, the added motivation will no longer be functional. When that happens, even though the students performed the tasks and found them moderately enjoyable under externally imposed motivation, both the difficult tasks and the easy ones will fall outside the range of positive affect. Their evaluation of tasks of these types will be negative. A few such instances may not be important. Many such in one academic area, such as mathematics or foreign language, will lead to a generalized $q_t$ or "quit trying" reaction with respect to difficult aspects of the subject matter, as often happens in mathematics, or to a generalized $q_w$ or "quit working" reaction with respect to such dull tasks as practicing scales on a violin. Repeated and persistent experiences of this kind across a broad range of academic subjects add up to hating the teacher, hating all teachers, hating the school, hating all schools, and eventually to a very generalized state of $q_t$ and $q_w$, a generalized tendency to quit trying and quit working. Since this condition predisposes to a rejection of constraints, the former pupils will drop out of school. They will decide that they are erudite enough for their own purposes and will be forced to adopt purposes for which their erudition is enough.

## Individual Differences

The Hedgehog implies a radically different approach to the issue of individual differences in intelligence from the set of conceptions that pervade our society and educational system. To make the nature of these differences clear, let me specify what *is* implied by psychological complexity and preference theory, and then discuss some of the common conceptions that are *not* implied.

*Individual Differences in Hedgehogs.* The curve in Figure 14-1 represented an individual's responses to the full range of psychological complexity. There can be individual differences in the height of this curve. Since the height of the curve represents the level of motivation, interest, and pleasure in the activity, it is an exceedingly important individual difference variable that makes a major contribution to academic progress. In spite of its importance, this variable is almost completely overlooked in standard conceptions of intelligence.

Individuals do differ in their levels of motivation for learning academic material.

First, there can be individual differences in the spread of the curve in Figure 14-1, and thus in the distance along the psychological complexity dimension between the optimal complexity level and either $q_w$, $q_t$, or both. Thus, although the smooth gaussian curve of Figure 14-1 probably represents the average person, as well as many individual persons, some individuals will prefer more difficult tasks, while others will opt for easier tasks. Second, individuals also differ in their willingness to persist in very simple and boring tasks or to persist in the face of extremely difficult and challenging tasks. Although these differences are usually referred to as personality differences, they make a major contribution to overall academic achievement. Third, there can be individual differences in the rate of progress up the psychological complexity dimension. Individuals differ in the rate at which they are able to simplify complex material, whether through cognitive reorganization, simplification through rote practice, or both. If other significant variables are equal, this difference will be expressed as a difference between quick and slow learners.

Thus, the three ways in which individuals can differ with respect to predicted academic achievement are:

1. level of motivation for the material,
2. preferred level of difficulty, and
3. rate of simplification of complex material.

*The Concept of Intelligence.* The concept of intelligence is largely misconceived in our culture, and the results of standardized tests of intelligence are grossly misinterpreted and misused. This is not the place for a complete analysis of the problem of intelligence, but a few major points will serve to contrast the usual approach with the Hedgehog interpretation of academic achievement and individual differences in progress.

The development of standardized intelligence tests by Binet and by Terman was a major intellectual achievement. The task was to predict scholastic progress. The technique employed in developing such tests was almost strictly empirical. Items that could be ordered in terms of difficulty were given to children of various ages. In any age group, those who performed best in the group could be expected to do well on similar material at a later date, and those who performed poorly could be expected to do poorly later on. Verification of this expectation was an empirical matter.

For groups of individuals, standardized tests of intelligence predict very well. For this reason, if they are properly interpreted and lead to appropriate action, they can be very useful. Unfortunately, it is rare that they are appropriately interpreted, and all too often misinterpretation leads to inappropriate action.

One misconception is that intelligence tests measure ability rather than achievement. Actually, they assess the performance of the individual at the time the test is given, and that performance is purely an achievement measure. If ability is to be inferred from the results of an intelligence test, the inference must be made from comparison of that performance with the performance of the same individual at a different time or with the performance of other individuals. Furthermore, it is necessary to assume that the observed differences are attributable to differences in ability rather than to differences in opportunity or differences in appropriateness of the test material itself. Such assumptions are purely arbitrary. The conservative assumption is that intelligence tests are primarily tests of achievement.

It is also assumed that intelligence tests constitute measures of cognitive development. Motivation is assumed to be standardized by the routine of the testing procedure. Such testing procedure is rarely rigorous enough to equate the idiocratic motivation of all the subjects, and no account whatsoever has been taken of individual differences in autarkic motivation. Therefore, standardized tests of intelligence measure how motivated individuals are to perform the task as well as how well they are able to perform it.

Intelligence tests are standardized on groups. The performances of third-grade groups may be compared with the performances of sixth-grade groups, and their differential performance is used to select items that distinguish between them. Such items selected on the basis of group performance may do very well in predicting group performance. However, there is a point of logic that is almost universally overlooked. Standardization on groups permits only the weakest and most tenuous basis for predicting the performance of an individual from individual test performance. Perhaps the easiest way to see the magnitude of the problem is to visualize the actual process of standardizing an intelligence test to predict the future performance of the individual involved.

To standardize an individual test of intelligence that would be useful in predicting the future performance of that individual, it would be necessary to define that future performance precisely, select a large battery of test items, and then actually check performance on those test items by that individual against the criterion performance at some later date. If we ignore all the practical and logical problems associated with this procedure, and if we then imagine that we have been moderately successful, and if we then imagine that we have constructed such tests for a number of individuals, we are then in a position to guess whether we would have the makings of a successful group test. It seems highly unlikely that there would be enough commonality among the individual tests to permit group prediction without going through the procedure of standardization for the group. And there is no more reason to expect a test standardized on groups to predict the performance of an individual than there is to expect a test standardized on an individual to predict the performance of a group.

Standardized intelligence tests predict moderately well for those groups on which they were originally standardized but have limited usefulness for groups that were not included in the standardization. The Stanford-Binet test was standardized on middle- and upper-class White children attending middle- and upper-class schools in California, and it does reasonably well in predicting how well groups of these children will perform in these schools. However, there are two grievous problems associated with this limited basis for standardization. The criterion of performance in this limited class of academic settings is probably inappropriate to many schools in the United States because of differences in ethnic and linguistic background. Furthermore, since other groups that differ in cultural respects were not included in the standardization procedure, the tests can be expected to be poor prognosticators for these groups.

The magnitude of these problems can be seen in the fate of sex differences in intelligence. When the Stanford-Binet test was standardized, sex differences were regarded as a variable to be eliminated. The result was that an item was rejected from the test battery if there was a significant difference between boys and girls in their performances on the item. The test was therefore constructed in such a way that sex differences could not appear. This justified but wholly arbitrary decision illustrates the risk of employing a test on a population for which it was not standardized. It is obvious that tests could be constructed to show the superiority of boys over girls, girls over boys, Indians over Whites, Blacks over Indians, and so on, in any pattern one cared to go. It should be obvious that the use of such tests to document the inferiority or superiority of any one group compared to any other group is arbitrary and in a fundamental sense meaningless or even vicious.

The calculation of an IQ, or intelligence quotient, requires the assumption of a perfect correlation between the rate of intellectual growth and the ultimate level of intellectual achievement. In this conception, an individual who at the age of 6 is able to perform as well as the average 12-year-old will be labeled a genius, and it will be expected that his or her ultimate achievement will be twice that of the 6-year-old who performs like an average 6-year-old. This assumption is probably false, even though major characteristics of our educational system are based on it. Figure 14-4 illustrates this

A. Conception Involved in IQ Calculation

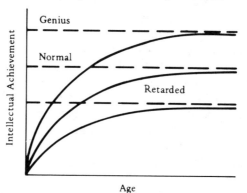

B. Alternate Conception of Intellectual Growth

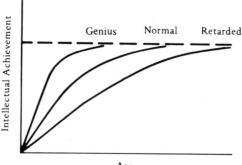

FIGURE 14-4. *Two Conceptions of Progress in Intellectual Growth*

conception in the upper panel. An alternative conception is illustrated in the lower panel. Here it is assumed that the genius and the retarded individual could reach the same level of intellectual achievement and that the difference lies in the rate at which they approach this level. This alternate conception is possibly false theoretically, is certainly false in real life, but is in many ways preferable to the IQ conception.

If one accepts the conception illustrated in Panel A of Figure 14-4, then it is reasonable to keep children in school a fixed number of years, such as 12, and permit them to graduate from the 12th grade on the basis of their ages—even though the class will contain potential geniuses who have been bored beyond belief, individuals who have developed according to the standard expectation, and individuals who are unable to read or make the calculations necessary to shop for groceries. The alternative is to organize the school system in terms of intellectual achievement standards. The genius might graduate from high school at age 12, the normal individual at age 18, and the retarded individual at age 24 or 30, depending on how long the individual took in growing to the required standards of achievement.

Neither conception illustrated in the figure is correct. However, the social consequences of the two conceptions are quite different. Following the false IQ conception leads to very real failure to develop the full potential of the very rapid or the very slow. Following the false conception that individuals differ only in rate, not ultimate achievement level, leads to maximum realization of human potential for intellectual achievement. Because of its radical empiricist philosophy and its belief in pragmatism as a basis for choice, the Hedgehog favors false alternative number two.

A similar argument can be made in the matter of genetic differences in intelligence. It is clear that there are racial differences in intellectual *achievement* within our educational system, but, given the content and standards employed in that system, there is no persuasive evidence that there are racial differences in *intelligence.* If the reader has followed the argument concerning the nature of the concept of intelligence, it will be clear that any differences between races could not be demonstrated reliably with any of the available intelligence tests. Therefore, neither the belief that there are such differences nor the belief that there are not such differences can be based on scientifically acceptable evidence. In such a case, the ultimate criterion must be the social consequences of adopting one faith or the other. If a religious faith in race differences is adopted, then no effort will be made to correct the "deficiencies" of one race; indeed, efforts to ameliorate such deficiencies will be actively prevented in the certain belief that they are genetic and uncorrectable. If a religious faith that there are no differences is adopted, then every effort will be made to remediate whatever is seen as an intellectual deficiency. Since the social consequences of failing to make the effort are unacceptable, this second course follows even if one is an agnostic on the issue. The Hedgehog is an agnostic.

## THE HEDGEHOG IN AN EDUCATIONAL CONTEXT

### The Ideal Educational Institution

Someone once said that the ideal educational institution consisted of a pupil on one end of a log and Mark Hopkins on the other.[1] There is probably a germ of truth in this silly statement, but it is very difficult to find. The statement assumes that calling the object on one end of the log a pupil tells us something useful, and, while possibly it does, it doesn't tell us enough. Neither is it obvious what is implied by the word *ideal.* The author of this *mal mot* left that problem up to Mark Hopkins, and that is a hotel in San Francisco.

The image can be made useful, however, if one undertakes to be somewhat more explicit about what is meant by *pupil, ideal, educational institution,* and a *Mark Hopkins.* Figure 14-5 is one version of the ideal educational institution. A Hedgehog is on one end of the log, and Mark Hopkins has been replaced by an ambiguous

EEEK!
! ! !

*FIGURE 14-5. The Ideal Hedgehog Educational Institution*

[1]Yes, I know that it was Garfield who said it. I also know that it wasn't a log but a bench in a log building. I also know that Garfield was making the point that the ideal educational institution didn't require buildings, equipment, or libraries, and, therefore, that the additional funds the College thought it needed probably wouldn't be forthcoming. Somehow I like the image of Hopkins and the pupil sitting on a log without all of the claptrap of truth attached to the image.

personality that is most often a parent, a second-grade teacher, or a university professor. It was tempting to draw her as a Mother Hedgehog, for in reality the instructor or tutor is a Hedgehog too, a fact that is often overlooked in education by pupils, teachers, and educational administrators. Let us therefore examine some of the implications of the character of the Hedgehog for the behavior of pupils and the behavior of tutors, an interaction that is supervised by the educational establishment.

One of the characteristics of Hedgehogs that is relevant to their role as pupil (or tutor) requires some emphasis even though it is clearly implied in previous discussions. A Hedgehog is fully autonomous, and continuously active; it cannot be stopped, except temporarily, as long as it is alive, and it eats information. The animal is continuously in the process of acquiring information and seeking more information that is compatible with its tastes and processing capacity. Consequently, an educational institution has no need to be concerned about whether its charges are learning or not—they are learning continuously; its only concern should be *what* the pupil is learning. To illustrate the point, during the early history of the United States a number of individuals could be described as having risen to a state of erudition with no contact whatsoever with a formal educational institution. Their numbers were small. The numbers would have been larger, and they might have become even more erudite, if they had had the benefit of guidance and educational resources. Thus the educational institution does not produce learning; a Hedgehog needs no help in this regard—in fact, it can't be stopped. Educational institutions can only determine what is to be learned, struggle to produce erudition in the sense of producing love of learning, provide guidance, and make educational resources available.

### Sources of Intellectual
### Development and Their Relative Effectiveness

Since Hedgehogs learn continuously and in every context in which they find themselves, there is some virtue in discussing a few of the major sources of information. When one thinks of the intellectual development of a child, the tendency is to think exclusively of the schools. Actually, although schools are important for intellectual development, they are only one source of information, and they may not be the most important source. Of the many other sources, parents, peers, television, and printed material are of varying degrees of importance in the developmental process and progress. Let us examine some of the evidence concerning the effectiveness of some of these sources in the light of the principles of motivation and learning specified by the Hedgehog.

*Bases for Effectiveness of Sources of Information.* We can distinguish four variables that contribute to the relative effectiveness of a source of information.

The first variable concerns the intellectual progress of the child with respect to the fundamental aspects of cognitive development. These aspects include such skills as reading, writing, the capacity to deal with numbers, and the ability to solve the problems of everyday life wisely. Information sources with which the individual child interacts vary widely with respect to how much of a contribution they make to this kind of cognitive development.

The second variable concerns the level of complexity/difficulty of the material to be learned. For the material to be effectively learned, it must be at the appropriate level of difficulty for the individual. Figure 14-6 is an effort to illustrate the point. If material is near or beyond either the $q_t$ or $q_w$ point, little or no effective learning will occur in the individual's interaction with that source.

The amount of learning that occurs is a function of the amount of time the individual spends in interaction with a particular source of information. Sources can differ greatly with respect to time of interaction, and this variable can be manipulated effectively in many situations.

The fourth source of difference in effectiveness stems from the motivation variable. Sources differ considerably in their capacities to invest a task with idiocratic motivation either because of the past history of the individual or because of the way in which the material to be learned is presented.

With these four variables in mind, let us examine a few of the nonscholastic sources of intellectual development.

*Television.* There is little doubt that television is a very important factor in the intellectual development of children. As a source of information, it scores very high on two of the four conditions of source effectiveness. There are innumerable studies showing that children spend great amounts of time interacting with television. That they do so voluntarily or even insistently is adequate evidence that the medium is motivationally effective.

*"You tickle me!"*

FIGURE 14-6. *Taste is a Matter of Optimal Complexity Level*

On the other hand, the weakness of television as a resource for promoting intellectual growth of the kind in which we are interested lies in the kind and level of the material it provides. Television is an entertainment medium that offers little experience for the viewer that is relevant to academic skills. In fact, it is so effective from a motivational standpoint that it probably prevents many individuals from spending time at academically relevant tasks such as reading or writing. If so, it actually inhibits intellectual growth. That it does so effectively is suggested by data such as those of Wachs, Uzgirls, and Hunt (1971), who reported correlations as high as -.81 between the amount of time the television was on in the home and performance by toddlers on a set of "learning and foresight" tasks.

*Parents.* The role of parents in stimulating the intellectual development of their children is so obvious that it hardly requires discussion. Parents are or should be the primary source of intellectually relevant interaction in the preschool years and should continue to be a potent and effective force after the child enters school. Parents have the potential for being an effective source of stimulation of intellectual growth in terms of all four of our requirements. They have the potential to choose the right material, provide it at the right level, motivate the child, and control the interaction time. To the extent that they fail to provide such stimulation, the intellectual development of the child will obviously suffer. Zajonc (1976) argues effectively that children in families with only one parent show inferior intellectual development compared to that of children living with two parents. This would be the expected result if in single-parent families the time of interaction between the child and the parent is reduced.

*Peers.* Children learn from one another. Figure 14-7 is a revision of the ideal educational institution and is intended to portray the substantial and important role peers and siblings play in an individual's intellectual development, whatever the setting. Children spend a great deal of time with one another, and they have the capacity to motivate one another. When they are at about the same level of intellectual development, what they have to offer one another is likely to be very close to their optimum levels of complexity. They should therefore be potent educational influences. On the other hand, it may be difficult for peers to provide an individual with relevant information that is higher than optimum level and consequently grist for simplification. It is therefore necessary to examine relevant data to determine the net effect of peer or sibling interaction on the intellectual growth of the individual.

Siblings should spend more time interacting with one another in large families than in small families. An only child, of course, has

*FIGURE 14-7. Revised Ideal Hedgehog Educational Institution*

no siblings with whom to interact. One might guess that, on the average, the only child will spend more time interacting with parents than will children in larger families. It also seems likely that an only child will spend more time alone than will children in larger families. As the number of children increases, one might expect three things to happen in the interaction pattern in the family. Children should spend a greater proportion of their time interacting with one another; they should spend less time alone; and they should spend a smaller and smaller proportion of their time interacting with parents.

Zajonc (1976) has reviewed large amounts of data on the intellectual achievement levels of children in families of various sizes. A consistent finding is that there is a general and substantial trend for the intellectual level of the children to decrease as the size of the family increases. This finding seems to be independent of the country in which the study was done and the instrument used to measure intellectual achievement. Zajonc cites transformed Raven scores of 19-year-olds in the Netherlands (Belmont & Marolla, 1973), National Merit Scholarship scores in the United States (Breland, 1974a, 1974b), and IQ scores from France and Scotland. The various researchers cited all agree with Whiteman and Deutsch (1968) that there is a substantial negative correlation between the number of children in the family and scores on measures of intellectual achievement.

If this effect of family size is to be attributed to the interaction pattern, then one would expect the effect to be exaggerated in families with twins or triplets. Twins might be expected to spend more time interacting with each other than siblings of different ages. Two studies cited by Zajonc are relevant to this point. In an intellectual-achievement study by Tabah and Sutter (1954), single-birth children had average scores of 101.2, while twins who were otherwise comparable had scores of 89.2. In a study by Record, McKoewn, and Edwards (1970), single-birth children had scores averaging 100.1, twins 95.7, and triplets 91.6. Zajonc also cites evidence that, when only one twin survives, his or her intellectual achievement level is higher than that of twin children who both survive. These data suggest rather strongly that intellectual development is slower the greater the proportion of time the developing individual spends with siblings as opposed to adults.

Most of the data cited by Zajonc show a major reversal of the trend for larger families to produce lower intellectual achievement levels. The only child shows a lower level of achievement than children in two-child families. This effect is evident in three of the four major sets of data but does not show in the set of data from Scotland. In two of the data sets, the intellectual achievement of children in three-child families is slightly superior to that of the only child. A possible explanation of this effect is that the only child spends a disproportionate amount of time alone. The presence of a sibling makes a contribution to intellectual development to the extent that it substitutes for time in which there is no social interaction and at the same time does not substantially reduce the amount of time spent interacting with the parent.

There is one more effect that appears in some of the detailed breakdown of the data cited by Zajonc. It might be called the Benjamin Franklin effect, since Ben was the youngest child in a very large family. When there are a large number of children, the intellectual level of the group can begin to rise as new members are born into the group. The explanation for the Benjamin Franklin effect may very well be that the oldest children in very large families are approaching adulthood when the youngest are added to the group. As these older children help in caring for the younger ones, their advanced stage of development may make a positive rather than a negative contribution to the intellectual atmosphere of the family as a whole and to the progress of the youngest children in particular.

Zajonc and Marcus (1975) have developed a confluence model to account for these effects as well as others not considered here. One of the basic ideas in the Zajonc and Marcus account is that an estimate of the intellectual level of the family is lowered substantially with the arrival of a child. A simple calculation of the magnitude of this effect can be made by assuming that each parent has a value of 100 as a contributor to the intellectual atmosphere of the household and that the newborn child has a value of 0. The sum of the contributions of each member is divided by the number of people in the family, yielding an estimate of the intellectual level of the family. Thus, the parents alone have a value of 100: (100 + 100)/2. When a child is born, the mean intellectual value of the household drops to 67: (100 + 100 + 0)/3. When a second child is born, the first child has developed to the point of making a small but positive contribution to the intellectual atmosphere. Let us assume that the first child is 1 year old and has realized 5% of his or her potential. Then the formula would be (100 + 100 + 5 + 0)/4, yielding a value of 51.3.

These simple calculations have been made in Table 14-1 for families with from one to ten children with the assumption that a child is born each year and that each child develops 5% of its potential each year. The results, which are very similar to the Zajonc formula, are shown in the column labeled "Psychological Complexity of the Environment."

TABLE 14-1. Calculation of Effect of Family Size on the Quality of the Learning Environment

| Number of Children | Psychological Complexity of the Environment | Proportion of Interaction Time | Factor of Sibling Interaction | Product of Factors |
|---|---|---|---|---|
| 1 | 67.0 | .60 | 1.00 | 40.0 |
| 2 | 51.3 | .90 | .99 | 45.7 |
| 3 | 43.0 | .95 | .97 | 39.6 |
| 4 | 38.3 | 1.00 | .94 | 36.0 |
| 5 | 35.7 | 1.00 | .90 | 32.1 |
| 6 | 34.4 | 1.00 | .85 | 29.2 |
| 7 | 33.9 | 1.00 | .81 | 27.5 |
| 8 | 34.0 | 1.00 | .78 | 26.5 |
| 9 | 34.5 | 1.00 | .76 | 26.2 |
| 10 | 35.4 | 1.00 | .75 | 26.5 |

In the third column, labeled "Proportion of Interaction Time," I have tried to take into account the amount of time children can be expected to spend alone in families of varying size. I have made the quite arbitrary assumption that in families of four or more children the amount of time a child spends alone is not affected by further additions to the household. In smaller families this "alone time" has been expressed as a proportion of maximum interaction time and is smallest for the only child. The effect of this variable would be to produce the lower intellectual development of the only child as compared to the development of those in families with two or three children.

In the fourth column, I have undertaken to account for the probability that, as families grow larger, the amount of time the children spend in interaction with the parents will decrease, and the proportion of time spent interacting with siblings of lower intellectual development levels will increase. The effect of such increases in proportion of interaction with siblings would be to reduce the effective level of the intellectual atmosphere for that child. This effect is therefore expressed as a loss. When these three factors are multiplied, the result is the "Product of Factors" column, whose values are plotted in Figure 14-8.

The figure shows the rise in the intellectual level of the environment when a second child is added to the family. This rise is due to the reduction in the amount of time the children spend alone, as compared to the only child. The curve also shows the Benjamin Franklin effect as it begins to rise in the transition from a family with nine children to a family with ten. It would obviously continue to rise if the calculations were made for even larger families.

The values in Table 14-1 and in Figure 14-8 constitute one possible elaboration of the Hedgehog theory of learning environments. The values are arbitrary. However, this realization of the theory has the virtue of specifying the variables that can be expected to modify the character of the results. The intellectual development levels of the individual parents could be a factor. In addition, families with only one parent should show a lower level of achievement than families with two parents. If the children are spaced farther apart, then the Benjamin Franklin effect should occur in families smaller than those shown in Figure 14-8. Since the most important variables in this situation are the intellectual level of the interactions involved

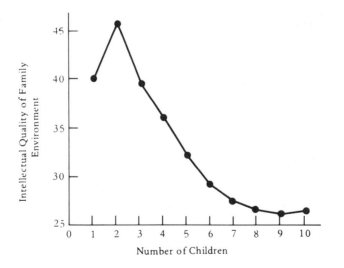

*FIGURE 14-8. Hedgehog Estimate of Effect of Family Size on Quality of Intellectual Environment*

and the proportion and amount of time spent in interactions at appropriate levels, the theory offers an explanation of many possible effects. Furthermore, it offers the possibility of checking the roots of such effects empirically as well as pointing to ways of reducing deleterious effects and creating conditions favorable to maximum intellectual development. The following is an application of the theory to two problems—the decline in SAT scores and the controversy over racial differences in achievement.

1. *The decline in SAT scores.* There is great public concern because of what appears to be a progressive decline in performance on the Scholastic Aptitude Tests (SAT), which are normally taken by high school students at an average age of about 17 years. Zajonc (1976) reviews data showing a steady decline in average SAT scores, from a high of 490 in 1962 to a mean score of 453 in 1974. This amounts to a drop of about one-third of a standard deviation, and it is socially significant in that it reflects the fact that students are graduating from high school without being able to read effectively or handle simple quantitative transactions.

Zajonc (1976) demonstrates a substantial correlation between the mean SAT score and the mean birth order of the individuals making up the class. Since the birth orders of future classes is known, the correlation Zajonc has demonstrated can be used to project the SAT scores of future classes, a feat that Zajonc accomplished visually in his article. A slightly different form of this prediction is shown in Figure 14-9.

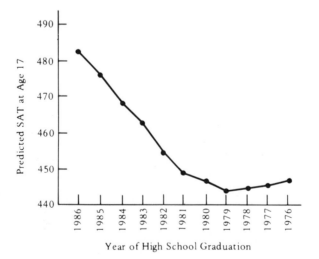

FIGURE 14-9. *Prediction of Future SAT Scores at Age 17 from Data on Family Size*

The predictions shown in the figure were calculated in the following manner. In the most stable part of the curve shown by Zajonc, SAT scores dropped from 485 in 1965 to 453 in 1975. This drop of 32 points is associated with a change in average birth order from 2.38 to 2.87, or an increase of .49 in average birth order. This permits a calculation of a drop of -.653 in SAT for each .01 increase in the average birth order. Since we know the expected average birth order of children now in school, it is possible to use this information to predict the SAT scores they will have when they graduate from high school. This has been done in the figure.

The figure can be read in several ways. As drawn it shows that the high school senior class of 1977 should have been slightly inferior to the class of 1976. The poorest class should be those in the ninth grade in 1976, who should have been seniors in 1979. Beginning in 1980, the SAT scores should begin to rise and continue to rise until the group in the second grade in 1976 become high school seniors in the year 1986. The phenomenon analyzed by Zajonc and shown in a different version in Figure 14-9 is attributable to the trend toward large families after World War II and the reversal of that trend in the mid 1960s and early 1970s.

2. *Race differences.* The major error made by those who would argue that there are genetic differences in intelligence is one of misinterpretation of correlations. For example, it might be found that White children do better in school than Black children. Racists might interpret this difference as evidence of the inferiority of the Black race. In so doing they may overlook the fact that children from lower socioeconomic neighborhoods do less well in school than do children from middle-class neighborhoods and that a high proportion of Blacks live in poor neighborhoods. Thus it is possible that poor school performance has nothing to do with race but does have something to do with socioeconomic status.

Two kinds of arguments can be made against the genetic interpretation of racial differences in intelligence, one offered by Zajonc and another by Boykin. Zajonc's argument is that significant differences between the two races in factors unrelated to genetics are sufficient to account for race differences in school achievement. Boykin's argument is in terms of cultural differences in life-style.

Zajonc (1976) cites data showing that in 1960 Black families had 3.05 children on the average, while White families had only 2.27. This difference in family size could account for most, if not all, of the scholastic achievement differences between the races, since, by our formula, this difference alone could account for 51 points in SAT scores. In addition, according to Zajonc, Black mothers are nearly three years younger than White mothers at the time of the birth of their first child; the spacing of children among Black families is only 22.8 months compared to 29.7 months among White families; and, over the span of 1960 to 1974, 28.6% of Black families contained a single parent, while only about 8% of White families were single-parent families. All these factors would operate to the disadvantage of Black youngsters with respect to academic achievement, and they are sufficiently powerful in their effects that no residual race difference is left to be accounted for on genetic grounds.

Boykin (1977b) argues that lower-class children have a quality he calls *verve* that is relatively absent in middle- and upper-class children and that operates as a negative factor in the quiet, constrained, and controlled atmosphere of the typical classroom. Verve is in part a product of a high activity level and a highly varied, active, and changing environment. Boykin constructed a simple experiment to show the effects of the variable. He gave Black and White children a series of 20 tasks that consisted of five examples each of a ten-digit recall task, a story listening task, a visual scanning task, and a ten-dot reproduction task. These tasks were presented either in blocks in which each block consisted of the same type of task or in a varied condition in which the type of task changed from one task to the next. White children did better on the unvaried task, but Black children did better on the varied task. Boykin also cites a similar study by Marshall (1969) in which the groups were middle- and lower-class White children. The middle-class children did better on the unvaried task, whereas the lower-class children did better on the varied task. These results suggest that verve is a social-class variable and that it operates to the disadvantage of lower-class students, Black or White, in schools that are conducted in a style characteristic of the middle class.

## THE HEDGEHOG AND ISSUES OF EDUCATIONAL POLICY, PRACTICE, AND OUTCOME

Psychological complexity and preference theory is a relatively simple theory that can be applied to a great many problems and situations. Its ubiquity is one of its virtues. Most ubiquitous theories suffer the disadvantage that the terms of the theory cannot easily be measured or estimated from empirical data. A second virtue of the Hedgehog is that the potential for measurement is a part of the essence of the theory.

The ubiquity of the theory means that there is nearly an infinite number of situations in which it could potentially be applied in the educational setting. No substantial number can be covered here, but a few examples might suggest many others to the reader. Let us therefore explore a few educational problems.

## Educational Strategy
## and Technique in the Hedgehog

Educational strategy in the Hedgehog is based on an optimistic point of view. No educational problem is entirely hopeless; it is only teachers who lose hope as individuals. Although individuals do differ in academic achievement, the differences are attributable to some unknown combination of the effects of experience and three variables: individuals' basic levels of motivation for learning the material, the level of difficulty preferred by different individuals, and the different rates of simplification that characterize each individuals' processing of the material. All three are subject to tuitional influence. Thus, techniques of Hedgehog teaching fall into three classes:

1. The teacher can undertake to enlist additional motivation of the idiocratic variety.

2. The teacher can try to achieve the best possible match between the difficulty of the material and the optimal complexity level of the pupil.

3. The teacher can increase the time of interaction between the pupil and the material on which progress is desired or necessary.

### The Teacher in the Role of Tutor

The tutor's task, as specified by the Hedgehog, is simple in conception even if it is almost impossibly difficult in execution. It is to keep the student Hedgehog guided toward some goal through terrains of information that are most frequently either too complex for its present capacity or too simple for its present tastes. I have discussed earlier some effects of the manipulation of complexity motivation. Let me review now the dimensions for the manipulation of complexity.

The tutor can only do two things: simplify material that is too complex at that moment for the particular Hedgehog being tutored or complicate material that is too simple. Let me expand briefly on an oversimplified set of procedure categories by classifying most of a large number of procedures as manifestations of three—*explanation, practice,* and *elaboration.* I mean these three categories to be taken as very broad labels. By *explanation,* I mean all of the procedures that can be used to produce an abrupt drop in the complexity of a task or event for an organism. By *practice*, I mean all varieties of rehearsal—all kinds of repetition of what appears to be the same task or event. By *elaboration,* I mean all manipulations intended to make the Hedgehog see that what the Hedgehog sees as simple and too boring to pursue further is actually more complex than it appears to the Hedgehog to be.

This classification of principles of motivation and learning that operate in an educational setting is diagrammed in Figure 14-10.

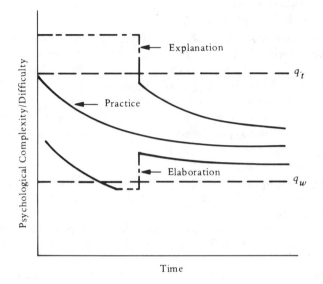

*FIGURE 14-10. Varieties of Complexity Change Procedures*

The two horizontal broken lines labeled $q_t$ and $q_w$ represent the difficulty levels that will induce the Hedgehog to quit trying because the task is too difficult or induce it to quit working because the task is too simple and boring. These two limits define the optimal complexity range within which the Hedgehog will work on the task at hand rather than on something that is irrelevant, perhaps, to the educational goals that have been set for the Hedgehog by the educational institution. Optimal complexity level, which is not shown in the diagram, would be in the middle of this range and would represent the level of difficulty the Hedgehog will like the most and at which it will work hardest.

In the diagram, the three curves labeled *explanation, practice,* and *elaboration* can represent three different students, Joe Dumb, Harry Average, and Mary Bright, who are being taught by a reasonably competent tutor. Joe Dumb isn't really dumb, but some relevant educational experience is missing in his background, and the task at hand is too difficult for him. He has quit trying because the task is above his $q_t$ level. Our tutor notices that Joe is teasing Mary instead of working at the task at hand. Being a competent tutor, he skips all other tempting alternative reactions, such as shaming Joe for teasing Mary, and queries Joe about the task. He soon discovers that Joe misunderstood a part of the problem. When Joe's misunderstanding is removed through explanation, the task falls below his $q_t$ level, and he promptly goes back to work. In the figure, Joe's behavior with respect to the task is represented by the upper curve. The curve initially is shown as dotted and horizontal because

Joe isn't working on the task, and the task is undergoing no change in difficulty for him. It is during this period that Joe is goofing off and the teacher is questioning Joe about the task. When the tutor removes Joe's misunderstanding through explanation, there is a sudden drop in the complexity of the task for Joe, and he goes to work. Meanwhile, Harry Average has been working right along on his own, so the tutor leaves him alone. But then the tutor notices that Mary Bright has quit working (the lower solid curve has become dotted). He quickly determines that Mary Bright is bored because the task is too simple. He therefore seeks, successfully, to enrich the task by connecting the dull, simple task to other aspects in Mary's repertoire. The task is thus brought above Mary's $q_w$ level, and Mary promptly goes back to work on her own. Now all three of our tutor's pupils are working away on their own, practicing. While they are working, the tasks on which they are working become simpler for all of them. Within the Hedgehog, when a task becomes simpler, all of the characteristics of the learned response improve in value. The task can be executed more efficiently (better and faster), it can be recognized or recalled later on much more quickly, and it will be easier to associate with other tasks already learned or to be learned later. Thus, although practice may not make perfect, it does produce learning.

### Learning and Teaching— The Pupil's Role and the Tutor's Role

The pupil's role in the dyad of pupil/tutor is a simple one. The pupil's task is to learn. Furthermore, it is to learn what the tutor wants the pupil to learn. Since Hedgehogs have an insatiable appetite for learning, they will be learning something at all times. Their role as pupils then, is specifically addressed to learning whatever is specified by their tutors.

The tutor's role is somewhat more complicated. It is the tutor's job to specify what is to be learned and then to induce the pupil to learn it. In this fairly abstract discussion of the educational process, I will ignore the knotty problems associated with the determination of what is to be learned. I will simply assume that the educational or task goals of the tutor are clear, unambiguous, and at hand.

Given a set of tutorial objectives, the necessary steps are reasonably clear. The tutor must determine where the optimal complexity level and range for this material are for a particular pupil. Then the tutor must determine whether the task as a whole falls within the pupil's optimal complexity range. If it does, there is no further problem in this respect, but usually it doesn't. When it doesn't, the tutor must plan a sequence of activities that begins with a relevant portion of the task that is within the optimal complexity range of the pupil and continues with other relevant pieces until the total task can be brought within the pupil's optimal complexity range. The tutor must thus plan a sequence of psychological events that will induce the pupil to work continuously on the task until the learning objective has been met. Thus armed, the tutor initiates learning activity in the pupil. If the tutor's efforts have been effective, the pupil will begin learning—the only job the pupil has. If the tutor has been unsuccessful, the pupil either won't begin trying or won't begin working, depending on the nature of the tutor's error.

Once learning has begun, the pupil's progress must be monitored continuously for the most efficient learning to be produced. Close monitoring and quick adjustment designed to keep the difficulty of the task precisely at optimal complexity level require constant attention and great skill on the part of the tutor. When attention is not close or when monitoring is less than completely effective, a reasonably dramatic index of the tutor's relative failure will be provided by instances in which the pupil reaches either the $q_t$ or $q_w$ level and stops working on the task. Then the tutor must determine whether it is $q_t$, as in the case of Joe Dumb, or $q_w$, as in the case of Mary Bright, and institute either explanation or elaboration as appropriate. Alternatively, the tutor may undertake to manipulate the motivational level of the Hedgehog in order to increase the distance between $q_t$ and $q_w$. This involves adding idiocratic motivation so that the pupil will become more erudite and will continue to place a favorable affective evaluation on his or her learning experience. Or the tutor may decide that it is important for this Hedgehog to learn here and now and that it really doesn't matter how the beast will feel about learning in the future. If this is the tutor's attitude, extraneous motivation can be employed to increase the distance between $q_t$ and $q_w$. The tutor therefore calls into play additional constraints and forces that are not seen as relevant to the task at hand by the pupil doing the learning.

### Education is a Three-Hedgehog Game

The slightly inaccurate heading above is intended to emphasize that an understanding of educational institutions is facilitated if one keeps in mind that, although there may be only one teacher, there is usually more than one student. The minimum multiplicity of students is two. Two students provide the possibility of peer relationships and interactions. If peer relationships are thought of as part of education, then a minimum educational institution consists of one teacher and two students. This minimum number provides for at least one student/student relationship to go with the two student/teacher relationships. Thus, education is at a minimum a three-Hedgehog game, even though in most educational settings the place is overrun with Hedgehogs.

The peer relationship is exceedingly important in education, and some aspects of its importance are often overlooked. *Peers learn from one another.* In our little illustration involving Joe, Harry, and Mary, there was a point at which Joe reached his $q_t$ and, for want of anything better to do, started teasing Mary. In this interaction, Joe was learning something from Mary, and Mary was learning something from Joe, and what was being learned was probably not relevant to the educational objectives set by the teacher. The learning taking place may have been, by some standard, good or bad learning, important or unimportant learning, but it was learning.

Not all peer learning is irrelevant to worthwhile educational objectives. Most university professors who hold the Ph.D. will be quick to acknowledge, perhaps with considerable enthusiasm, that when they were graduate students they learned as much or more from their fellow graduate students as they did from their professors. The observation that even the best schools tend to turn out their outstanding students in bunches is at least consistent with the hypothesis that it is the interaction with high quality peers, as much as the interaction of high quality students with high quality teachers, that produces distinguished erudition.

Thus, it is undeniable that peers learn from one another, and what they learn may or may not be relevant to an identifiable objective of the educational institution or setting involved. There is little evidence on the subject, but I have a strong suspicion that the portion of what peers learn that is relevant to easily identifiable educational objectives increases strikingly through the 20 years required to move from the first grade to a Ph.D. degree.

When two peers are educating each other, it is clear that they are alternately shifting back and forth between the roles of pupil and tutor, even though they both are behaving like the theoretical Hedgehog. (You help me move farther away from my $q_t$ point now, and I'll help you move closer to your optimal complexity level later.)

As I mentioned in reference to Figure 14-5, I was tempted to draw the teacher as a Hedgehog as well in order to underscore the point that the behavior of the person who fulfills this role is equally subject to Hedgehog principles of motivation and learning. This point, and the point that peers educate each other, are represented in the revised ideal Hedgehog educational institution pictured in Figure 14-7. What all of this implies is that the concepts of student and teacher have to do with status, whereas the notions of pupil and tutor have to do with roles. Roles are easier to change than statuses.

In addition to emphasizing that the tutorial role includes learning on the part of the tutor, drawing the teacher as a Hedgehog is a reminder that the tutor's motivational structure, no less than the pupil's, must be taken into account. The status of being the teacher simply implies that the individual will spend a larger portion of his or her time in the tutor role and thus a smaller portion in the pupil role. To illustrate the point, let us return to the problem of Joe Dumb, Harry Average, and Mary Bright. The teacher in this case was Edward Moderately Competent. If Alice Master Teacher had been in charge, there would have been a somewhat different looking picture. Alice would have known about Joe Dumb's problem in advance, and she would have used explanation to bring Joe below his $q_t$ level long before Joe got a chance to tease Mary Bright. Furthermore, she would have anticipated Mary's drift toward acute boredom and her $q_w$ level and would have used elaboration to increase the complexity of the task much sooner. Probably she would also have raised it higher, not only nearer Mary's optimal complexity level but somewhat above it so that Mary would be happily occupied for some time to come. She might also have used a little elaborational technique on Harry Average to increase his pleasure and interest even though Harry was working happily just below optimum and would probably have continued to do so, if left alone, for some time. Edward earned his middle name of Moderately because he didn't recognize that he had a problem until Joe started to tease Mary. In short, Edward had not done a very good job of advance planning, and he was insensitive to the subtleties of the monitoring task he should have been performing while his pupils were working. He earned his last name of Competent because, when he did know he had a problem, he was able to determine its nature and respond appropriately with explanation and elaboration.

Things could have been worse—much worse. The institution had been smart enough to choose not to rehire Marjorie Incompetent when the voters turned down the school tax proposal and the budget had to be cut as a result. Not only had Marjorie been unable to plan ahead or to monitor, but she had had a number of unsuccessful experiences when she had tried to use explanation and elaboration. Suppose, however, that the voters had passed the tax proposal and that Marjorie had been in charge of the classroom setting. We can imagine the course of events proceeding somewhat as follows.

Marjorie's diagnosis of Joe Dumb's problem is that he is bored. Her attempts to use elaboration only result in Joe's being in even more trouble and continuing to "refuse" to try. Marjorie therefore sends him to a corner of the room or perhaps to the principal. She doesn't like that dumb, stubborn boy at all. When she catches Mary staring out the window instead of working, she tries explanation. Mary is polite enough to listen, but as soon as Marjorie turns her back, Mary finds something else to occupy her that is irrelevant, such as teasing Harry. Mary is then sent to erase the blackboard and clean erasers. Marjorie doesn't like Mary Bright very well, either. The apple of Marjorie's eye is Harry. With him, all she has to do is give him the material and let him go to work. Having nothing better to do, Marjorie stares out the window and plans the stops she must make on her way home. For her, Joe and Mary offer problems beyond her own $q_t$ level, while Harry, since he is no problem, is below her $q_w$ level. Marjorie won't mind very much being fired; she doesn't like the job very well anyway.

This analysis of the educational setting in terms of psychological complexity and preference theory permits a fresh look at a number of issues of educational policy and practice. It does not, however, provide solutions; it only suggests where to look for them.

### Teaching Effectiveness and Measurement Problems

It is difficult to measure teaching effectiveness using traditional conceptions of educational measurement. One of the major reasons is that the measurement of achievement in an educational subject is a joint product of the efficiency of the teacher and the efficiency of the learner. The educational objective is set in some abstract fashion—abstract in the sense that the match between the goal and the population of learners is only approximate and is made on the basis of group rather than individual requirements. Since learners are automatic information consumers, they will tackle the situations presented to them to the best of their ability, with a standardized amount and kind of help from the teacher, and the amount of progress they make will be determined by their starting positions and their own rates of information processing. Given a group goal, a standard procedure applicable to all students (regardless of what the procedure is), and a heterogeneous population of students, the outcome measured in terms of content mastery by the group is likely to be very nearly the same, regardless of the character of the standard procedure. Any standard procedure works well with some students, but not with others. Thus, different standardized procedures tend to yield almost exactly the same amount of progress in achievement.

Psychological complexity and preference theory suggests some major modifications in educational measurement. For the sake of simplicity, let me indicate three categories of Hedgehog educational measurement: complexity, preference, and persistence at the educational task.

As I have indicated earlier, psychological complexity is a theoretical variable that is intended to be a standard yardstick against which all structural variables can be oriented and ordered. Difficulty of the material is the major manifestation of psychological complexity in the content of information relevant to educational achievement. When the amount of material mastered by the learner is the primary quantity that is measured, usually the measurement also reflects the difficulty dimension insofar as, to learn more, the student has had to master more and more difficult material. Thus, the dimension of psychological complexity is the element within the Hedgehog that bears the burden of the most common forms of educational measurement.

The potential value of the measurement of preference in educational contexts is almost untapped. Since there is an invariant relation between what different individuals like, in some broad sense, and what they will work on, it is obvious that the most efficient learning will occur when the tasks to be performed are also the tasks that the learners prefer to work on. The measurement of difficulty defines the scale, and the measurement of preference defines the student's position on the scale. If individual students are set to work at the positions on the difficulty scale where they prefer to work, then they will work automatically. If the path upward on the difficulty scale is clearly marked, they will progress up the scale at the greatest speed that practice and their individual talents for problem solving (self-explanation) permit. This description is also the definition of learning at maximum efficiency. Inducing a student to work on tasks that are either too difficult or too easy is not only inefficient from a learning standpoint but clearly has the potential of producing a marked distaste for the material. Thus, if one takes preference into account in providing material at the appropriate levels of difficulty, then one can achieve the clear and exceedingly important gain of producing erudition, love of learning. If one consistently fails to take the preferences of the learners into account, the effect will be to build toward the opposite of erudition—a dislike of academic material, a resistance to learning such material, and, if the failure to consider preference is carried to extremes over a long period of time, a basic anti-intellectualism. It is an interesting thought that the failure to take preference into account in the basic educational programs in the lower grades in this country has as its primary systematic product the development of the opposite of erudition. From this point of view, what the school system mostly succeeds in producing is many varieties and degrees of intellectual handicap. This is the only point of view to take when it is clear that in the ideal educational institution, in which preference would be taken into account, the only product would be erudite students.

Emphasizing the complexity variable without taking preference into account leads to inefficient learning. An alternative measure of educational progress that would put the emphasis on preference would be related to the amount of available work time that was spent on tasks relevant to an educational objective in comparison with the amount of time spent on nonrelevant tasks. The ideal tutor is one who is able to monitor the current complexity level of the pupil and control the flow of tasks in such a way that the pupil is always working on educationally relevant tasks and, furthermore, is working on such tasks with maximum zest and pleasure. The measurement of maximum efficiency that is implied here would require constant knowledge of optimal complexity level, distance of the provided material from optimum, some measure of intensity of activity, and a measure of the evaluative aspects—how the student feels about the material. Such an ideal measuring system is theoretically possible but is probably exceedingly difficult from a practical standpoint. Despite the practical difficulties, the nature of such an ideal measurement might be worth specifying for the sake of conceptual clarification.

The most fundamental values are the optimal complexity level and the complexity level at which the pupil is working at any given moment. An ideal measure of learning efficiency would be the size of the discrepancy between the working complexity level and the optimal complexity level. Samples of such discrepancies during a work period could lead to an average complexity discrepancy. Perfect efficiency would be represented by a zero discrepancy level—an ideal not to be attained, because the complexity of the working level undergoes constant change. However, a very efficient work period would be one in which the average discrepancy is very small.

A crude but highly practical index of learning efficiency can be developed if some degree of departure from this ideal measure is permitted. A relatively simple measure might be devised that takes preference into account. We can define the optimal range of complexity, which can be referred to as *orc*. *Orc* is defined as the range between $q_t$, the difficulty level at which the pupil quits trying, and $q_w$, the difficulty (or simplicity) level at which the pupil quits working. In many situations, a classroom observer would find it relatively easy to determine when the students, taken individually, are engrossed in activity relevant to some stated educational objective and when they are not. From the standpoint of educational efficiency, it doesn't matter whether a student's nonrelevant activity results because the student has reached the $q_t$ point or the $q_w$ point. The significant fact is that the student isn't working on any task associated with an educational objective. The student's record would consist of time measurements classified as either $t_{orc}$ or $t_{qt} + t_{qw}$. Since for the purposes of this measure of efficiency, the difference between $t_{qt}$ and $t_{qw}$ is unimportant, the symbol $t_q$ can be used to represent both. The measure of educational efficiency then becomes

$$\text{Educational Efficiency} = \frac{t_{orc}}{t_{orc} + t_q}.$$

In this simple index, if $t_q = 0$, then the index of efficiency is 1.00. As $t_q$ becomes large, $t_{orc}$ must of necessity become small. In the limiting case in which $t_{orc} = 0$, the index of educational efficiency is also 0.

This Hedgehog index of educational efficiency has the great virtue of ignoring the content aspects of education in the evaluation process. It assumes that the objectives are known and that the relevant materials and tasks are readily available. Given the truth of these assumptions, a high value of the index will ensure that the educational process is proceeding at a maximum rate, because learning will be proceeding at the maximum rate for each of the individual students involved. If we give an achievement or content oriented test before and after a learning period of maximum efficiency, the difference in the two scores will reflect the maximum learning that could have occurred for each of the individual students involved. Any difference in progress between students will be the product of fundamental individual differences in rate of information processing. If grades are to be assigned, then all pupils should receive the same grade even though they have achieved different performance levels with respect to the content. If differential grading must be employed, then it is the teacher or the system that should be given grades A through F, depending upon the value of the index achieved by the teacher or the system. The extent to which students have met educational objectives, measured in terms of level of content mastery, can and must be measured; however, it should reflect progress up a complexity scale. It should be used to adjust the kind and level of task provided and should never be used to reflect a value judgment concerning relative student merit.

I realize that the index of educational efficiency that I have proposed is not wholly free of error. The classroom observer will have great difficulty detecting covert $q_t$ and $q_w$, but whatever obfuscating behavior the use of such an index induces on the part of the student or the teacher can also be detected and dealt with. The phenomenon of the comic book folded into the Latin reader has been with us for a long time. Whatever the magnitude and source of error, the index of educational efficiency is a measure of the extent to which human potential has been realized in a given situation, and the difference between a high value that might have occurred and a lesser value that actually does occur will be a quantitative estimate of wasted human potential.

### Class Size

The issue of the upper limit of class size is hotly debated at the university level and is frequently a subject of labor negotiations in the primary and secondary school systems. In most such debates, some number of students per teacher is specified as an ideal number or a number above which class size must not be permitted to rise if dire consequences are not to follow. The double negative of the last sentence symbolizes the contorted thought involved in the setting of any fixed value for class size.

If agreement can be reached concerning educational objectives, then the index of educational efficiency becomes the appropriate measure for determining what the appropriate size of class is in any particular setting, with any particular teacher, and with any particular set of educational resources. One can envision a situation in which the instructor in charge is Alice Master Teacher and in which the available materials are unlimited in quantity, wholly appropriate to the educational objectives specified, and precisely matched in difficulty with the students' abilities and previous progress. The last requirement can be met only if the group of students is homogeneous with respect to their ability and previous progress. Under these conditions the size of the class that could progress with a very high index of efficiency is almost unlimited. Given the appropriate technical resources, such as unlimited TV facilities, the class could be several million in number without loss of efficiency.

The conditions just specified are never met, and unlimited class size has never been seriously proposed by even the least knowledgeable and least responsible citizen. Of the many discrepancies between the conditions under which unlimited class size would work and normal conditions, perhaps the most important is that the ideal situation is one in which there is no need for the teacher to monitor the progress or behavior of the student. The specification of the ideal is such that neither $q_t$ nor $q_w$ would ever occur. If the class is heterogeneous with respect to achievement level and speed of learning, then the teacher has a monitoring role to perform for each of the students individually. Under these conditions, there is no fixed class size that is ideal, but, when we look at the teacher as a Hedgehog, we might choose George Miller's magic number 7 plus or minus 2 as the appropriate class size. With a heterogeneous group of students, even Alice Master Teacher can be expected to be exceedingly busy and to be operating at or near her own optimal complexity level in order to keep each of her seven charges within his or her individual optimal complexity range. Even here, there really is no magic number. If Alice Master Teacher has seven charges, and if the index of educational efficiency drops because of frequent occurrences of $q_t$ and $q_w$ phenomena among her charges, then the group is obviously too large for efficient learning. Even if her charges remain continuously occupied performing relevant tasks and the index of educational efficiency thus remains at 1.00, the question of whether class size can be increased beyond seven will depend on Alice Master Teacher's optimal complexity level. A number smaller than her optimum will produce $q_w$ periods in her own stream of psychological events. A number larger than her optimum will lead to the occurrence of $q_t$ periods with respect to some or all of her students.

It is clear that the index of educational efficiency is applicable to the behavior of the teacher as well as to the behavior of the students. One of the beauties of this index, whether applied to the teacher or the student, is that maximum efficiency corresponds precisely with maximum degree of interestingness and pleasantness that can be achieved in the task, both by the student in interaction with the learning materials and by the teacher in interaction with the students. Thus, optimal class size can be almost any number, depending on the heterogeneity of the class, the nature of the educational objectives, and the skills and talents of the teacher.

### Heterogeneity of Class Composition

One of the elements required to create a very large class that still functions with maximum efficiency is absolute homogeneity in ability and previous progress among the students in the class. This ideal cannot be attained, of course, but there are a number of existing educational procedures that operate to produce some degree of homogeneity among the students in a class. Grade levels themselves tend to perform this function, and the practice of detaining a slower student in the same grade or advancing an able student to a higher one tends to improve on the efficiency of the practice to some degree. Other mechanisms include varieties of tracking within schools and the specialization of schools within districts. Among colleges and universities there is specialization in subject matter and specialization in terms of student abilities and levels of progress. For example, one can expect a considerable difference in average student quality between the leading university in the country and the poorest junior college, even when the subject matter (freshman English, perhaps) is the same. Homogeneity leads to potential efficiency.

Heterogeneity in class composition is sometimes held to be a virtue, usually in the context of providing an equal education for deprived students. Quite apart from the ethical or social issues involved, there are two inevitable consequences of a program in education that requires heterogeneity in class composition. The first consequence is that, as the heterogeneity of the class increases, educational efficiency decreases. There will be more and longer instances of individual students reaching either a $q_t$ or a $q_w$ point, thus reducing their learning efficiency. It follows that heterogeneity in class composition is expensive. It is accomplished at the expense of the students whose learning efficiency is reduced, or it is accomplished at the expense of the educational support mechanism that must support either the smaller class sizes or the greater number of teaching personnel required to maintain some degree of educational efficiency with heterogeneous classes.

The second inevitable consequence stems from the often unrecognized fact that much of the learning that occurs in an educational setting consists of peers learning from one another. Earlier, I suggested that most of such peer tutoring in the lowest grades is not relevant to any recognized goal or objective of the educational system, whereas a large portion of the peer instruction between Ph.D. candidates *is* relevant. Thus, with heterogeneity in class composition at the lower educational levels, much that is considered undesirable tends to be learned as well as much that is considered to be desirable. If we group into a single class children from two subcultures, one in which interpersonal respect and courtesy are highly regarded and one in which drug use and violence are endemic, individuals from the two cultures will certainly learn from one another both during periods of $q_t$ and $q_w$ and during periods set aside by the system for noneducational objectives, such as lunch hour. The presence of two smaller Hedgehogs in the depiction of the ideal educational institution in Figure 14-7 symbolizes this problem. It is clearly ethical to expose children with bad habits to children with good ones, because they may thereby learn better habits or more desirable information. However, since Hedgehog peers alternate in their roles of pupil and tutor, it is not so clearly ethical to expose children with good habits to children with bad habits so that they too can learn bad habits and less desirable information.

### The Dropout Problem

It is clear from the analysis so far that individuals can be induced to continue progress toward an educational objective, and thus stay in the school system, as long as they see the educational objective as being appropriate to their own objectives and as long as the educational tasks they are asked to perform are within their optimal complexity ranges. Yet the portion of the age population that is in school at any given level is smaller than the portion in the next lower level. There is thus a progressive loss in numbers as one moves to higher levels of education. Why?

Perhaps three major reasons are suggested by the Hedgehog. They are related to the $q_t$ point, the $q_w$ point, and the handling of educational objectives and goals.

If students are mismatched in the system, the mismatch can be either of two kinds. If the system consistently places individuals in situations where they are required to work on tasks that are beyond their current capacities, then the work will consistently be above their $q_t$ points. The stages of generalization of this tendency to quit trying were developed previously in this chapter. If the system consistently places individuals in situations where the tasks they are asked to perform are below their $q_w$ points, they will be bored by the particular tasks presented, will become bored by tasks of that class in general, and will become bored with the teacher, the classroom, the school, and perhaps with schooling in general. They also will buck the constraining traces and drop out.

The nature and employment of educational objectives are crucially important in this context. If the educational objectives of the teacher are actually irrelevant to a particular student, or if they are relevant but the student is not made aware of their relevance or nature or both, then the tasks cannot be invested with idiocratic motivation. Whatever learning does occur will therefore be the result of autarkic motivation alone or a combination of autarkic motivation and extraneous motivation. If only autarkic motivation is involved, considerable learning will occur, but little of it will necessarily be directed toward the educational objectives of the school. If extraneous motivation is predominant, then the individual will come to hate school and everything associated with it when outside of the constraints of the school situation.

The solutions, or at least the directions in which solutions are to be sought, are contained within the analysis. (1) Educational objectives should be chosen so that they are suitable for the individual involved, or they should be made relevant to the tasks the individual is expected to engage in, or both. (2) The flow of tasks should be chosen at a level of difficulty that is very close to the individual's optimal complexity level and should keep up with this level throughout the period of his or her educational development.

Since dropouts from the educational system are the product of generalized $q_t$ and $q_w$, and since it is probably true that our index of educational efficiency can be applied to time periods of almost any length, applying the index to dropouts from the system produces an index of the system's educational efficiency. If one takes the ten-year period between the ages of 6 and 16, then the number of student years spent in school becomes the value of *orc*, and the number of student years lost through dropout becomes the value of *q*. A crude index of system efficiency can then be calculated for use in comparing systems. An efficient educational system is one in which there are no dropouts. A system that is unable to adjust to the capacities of some of its students, usually the very fast and the very slow, will lose those students through either overt or covert dropping out of the system. The price of such inefficiency is a profound waste of human potential, whether those who drop out do so because of a generalized $q_t$ or a generalized $q_w$.

## Education without Teachers

There are a great number of educational subsystems that might be grouped under the rubric of educational technology. These systems include programmed learning, computer-assisted instruction, self-paced plans, and many others. There is a persistent need to evaluate such subsystems. It should be obvious that, if any manifestation of educational technology is insightfully conceived, magnificently constructed, and made easily available, students will be able to learn from such a system better than from a poor teacher. However, there are two major differences between almost all technological systems and a live teacher that make it extremely doubtful that even the best technological system can approach the educational efficiency of an Alice Master Teacher.

Alice Master Teacher can monitor the progress of her pupils continuously and can respond appropriately to pupil problems that she has not anticipated. Many good technological systems provide techniques of periodic assessment and monitoring, but even the best of such systems is not likely to be able to anticipate every individual or even idiosyncratic difficulty the learner may develop. Alice Master Teacher can be creative in the process of assessing, monitoring, and adjusting the learning process for the individual student. Technical systems are never creative once completed.

Furthermore, except for the most general and abstract statement of educational objectives, the content of education tends to undergo continuous evolutionary change. Even the slightest change in objectives requires expensive and usually difficult reprogramming of the technological system. Alice Master Teacher is the ideal programmer, often able to adjust to either minor or major changes in educational objectives with little delay and at no additional expense. Thus, Alice Master Teacher is unlikely to be surpassed by any technological development, because she is both intelligent and motivated. She possesses flexibility and creativity. No technological subsystem can boast manifestations of these characteristics in any competitive degree.

### Bootstrapping School Quality through Peer Learning

The recognition that the intellectual quality of a student's peers constitutes a major contribution to the quality of the intellectual atmosphere in which learning occurs leads to a class of possible procedures for improving the quality of peers. There are many ways in which peer quality could serve as a mechanism for improving educational quality. Let us construct a hypothetical instance in order to illustrate the point.

Most teachers would agree that a real benefit would arise if it were possible to take three children from a class, somehow accelerate their intellectual growth, and then return them to the class. If this were to occur, the intellectual quality of the entire class would be improved considerably through the improved quality of the interaction of these three with their peers and with the teacher.

In these days of shrinking student enrollment at the grade school level, let us visualize a situation in which class size can be cut to approximately 24 and in which the school district has nine school buildings but can accommodate its student population in only eight.

We will designate a building nearest the geographical center of the district as a "Star" school. In this one school, there will be enough teachers—perhaps one teacher for every six students—that students can be given very individual and intensive attention. This school will also be provided with the best equipment and material available. The student population of this school will be composed of three students from each grade level from each of the other eight schools in the district. The students will stay in this intensive atmosphere for one year and will then return to their original classes in their home schools, to be replaced by new sets of three. In eight years, every student will have spent a year in the Star school sometime during his or her grade school career.

When students return to their home schools and to their regular classes, their accelerated development can be utilized in a variety of ways to benefit the whole class. As the proportion of students in the class who have benefited from the Star treatment increases, the intellectual achievement of the entire class should be materially elevated. It could also be envisioned that, although a few teachers might comprise a permanent faculty for the Star school, the majority of the faculty would be composed of teachers from the other eight schools who would also serve for a year at a time in the Star school before returning to their regular posts in the other eight schools.

Although this particular pattern undoubtedly could be improved upon, it is delineated here to suggest that the quality of schools can be improved through peer learning once it is recognized how important the intellectual levels of peers are for the progress of the individual student.

### The Parent Package

Just as Hedgehog theory suggests improving the quality of schools by improving the quality of students in the classes, it also suggests that academic progress can be considerably accelerated through judicious use of the students' own parents.

Suppose that the basic academic material were appropriately scaled in terms of difficulty level so that material could be provided at any time that matched the level of achievement of the individual student. A parent package could then be prepared and made available to any parent who wished to assist the child at home. The parent package would provide a review and refresher course for the parent and ensure that parental efforts to help the child would be in accord with the educational objectives set up by the school system. Whenever a parent chose to work with a student at home, there could be a snowball effect. Academically relevant work could be substituted for some small piece of TV viewing time. The intellectual quality of the home would be elevated. Peers in the home would benefit. Any additional progress the individual student made by this procedure would be a positive addition to the academic atmosphere of the student's class.

### PRÉCIS

From the standpoint of psychological complexity and preference theory, an image of the ideal educational institution can be envisioned. It consists of a population of Hedgehogs, including one with the status of teacher and several with the status of student. Each is living and learning in a continuous stream of thought and behavior that is autonomous, active, and inevitable. In the ideal school teachers are in possession of a clear and desirable set of educational objectives that they can modify as the occasion demands and of an abundance of relevant and necessary materials. They monitor the progress of each of their pupils periodically and at intervals that permit them to keep each individual working very close to his or her optimal complexity level. If any circumstance arises that leads to a pupil reaching a $q_t$ or $q_w$ point, the teacher's diagnosis is both prompt and correct, and the appropriate technique of explanation or elaboration is employed. The number of pupils in each class is precisely the number that brings the teacher's task to his or her own optimal complexity level.

As the skills of the teachers increase, the size of their classes can be increased as necessary to bring them back to a position near their optimal complexity levels. Their progress in this respect is clearly a function of their frequent shifts from the role of tutor to the role of pupil as they learn more and more about the character of their students, the particular ways in which their students live their own streams of psychological events, and the skills that permit them to deal with their students efficiently. Within the optimal number of pupils, the ideal class is so composed that whenever two or more of its members have the opportunity to interact with each other as pupils and tutors, much of their interaction will further an educational objective or serve some other useful and desirable purpose. Since in this ideal school everyone is working at a maximum level, progress toward the goals of the institution will be at an absolute maximum, and the rate of development of the human potential represented by this group of student Hedgehogs will also be at a maximum. Moreover, because of the correlation between motivation and the affective aspects of the situation, the teachers will find their job fascinating, will love their pupils, and will have great loyalty to their institution. Likewise, their pupils will be having the time of their lives. They will enjoy their work, love their teachers, and honor their school, and delinquency will be unknown.

Fairy story? No. It is not. It is an ideal and therefore exceedingly difficult to attain, but it is attainable. Whether attained or not, it represents the yardstick against which existing educational institutions can be measured and suggests the directions in which difficulties can be resolved. Not only will Alice Master Teacher be happy in her work, but her pupils will never drop out and will inevitably become erudite Hedgehogs.

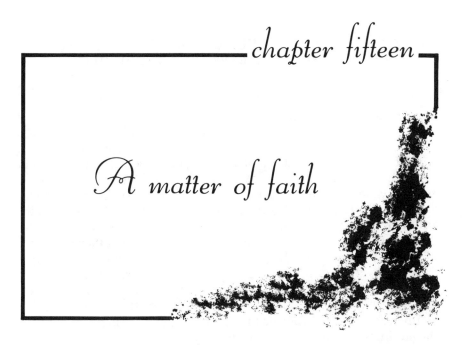

*chapter fifteen*

*A matter of faith*

I have made some rather strong claims for the Hedgehog. I believe they are justified. However, I occasionally entertain an image of this rather stupid little beast as Thomas Hood (1798–1845) pictured him in the poem "Her Dream":

> Here lies a hedgehog rolled up the wrong way
> Tormenting himself with his prickles.

*FIGURE 15-1. Hedgehog Repose*

# APPENDIX: STUDIES IN THE SEMANTIC
# SPACE OF EXPERIMENTAL SUBJECTS

## INTRODUCTION

This section contains an original report of a number of studies of the semantic space of experimental subjects. They were carried out in an effort to aid in my understanding of two persistent problems associated with psychological complexity and preference theory. (1) Different investigators have used different language in their instructions to experimental subjects. One investigator may ask for ratings of *liking* and another for *pleasantness*. It seems equally possible that experimental subjects see these terms as identical and that they see them as quite different. These studies explore the relations seen between some of the relevant words by experimental subjects. (2) Predictions from most theories in this area concern the manner in which, for example, structural and evaluative dimensions of ratings *of stimuli* are related to each other. It seems almost required that we learn something of the ways in which the relevant words are seen to be related to each other *in the absence of experimental stimuli.* These studies may help to clarify these two issues.

## FREE ASSOCIATION DATA

Information concerning the semantic space of experimental subjects can be obtained from free association data. A study was carried out using six of the words and their opposites listed under Subject Language in Table 3-2 (p. 27). A small group of 17 subjects was gathered casually from the people dropping into the outer office to get a cup of coffee. Each was asked to give the first five associations that occurred to him or her in response to each of the 12 stimulus words. Since there were 17 subjects and five responses per subject, 85 responses were tabulated for each word. As an examination of Table A-1 shows, there were 66 possible pairs of stimulus words. Each of these pairs was examined for frequency of common associates. The frequencies for any pair could range from zero to 85. Because it seemed like a good idea at the time, each actual frequency was converted to a percentage of the maximum possible. Also because it seemed like a good idea at the time, I chose to ignore the frequency "one" in order to simplify the matrix. The matrix is shown in Table A-1.

The information concerning positive associative strengths contained in Table A-1 is reorganized into the categories of com-

*TABLE A-1.* Associative Strength Derived from Free Association Data. (Seventeen subjects were asked to give five free associations to each of the 12 theory-related words in the table. The frequencies of common associations were tabulated and then converted to proportions of the maximum possible frequency [85], arbitrarily ignoring frequencies of one. The result is an index in which the higher the number, the stronger the association.)

| | *Active* | *Passive* | *Boring* | *Interesting* | *Like* | *Dislike* | *Prefer* | *Prefer not* | *Complex* | *Simple* | *Go away from* | *Go toward* |
|---|---|---|---|---|---|---|---|---|---|---|---|---|
| Active | | 33 | 0 | 0 | 0 | 0 | 0 | 0 | 0 | 0 | 0 | 0 |
| Passive | | | 0 | 0 | 0 | 0 | 0 | 0 | 0 | 0 | 0 | 0 |
| Boring | | | | 0 | 0 | 16 | 0 | 0 | 0 | 19 | 0 | 0 |
| Interesting | | | | | 23 | 4 | 9 | 0 | 12 | 0 | 0 | 6 |
| Like | | | | | | 8 | 50 | 0 | 0 | 0 | 4 | 19 |
| Dislike | | | | | | | 17 | 44 | 0 | 6 | 21 | 4 |
| Prefer | | | | | | | | 4 | 0 | 0 | 0 | 17 |
| Prefer not | | | | | | | | | 0 | 0 | 10 | 0 |
| Complex | | | | | | | | | | 14 | 0 | 0 |
| Simple | | | | | | | | | | | 0 | 0 |
| Go away from | | | | | | | | | | | | 9 |
| Go toward | | | | | | | | | | | | |

plexity and preference theory and is presented in this form in Table A-2. All nonzero values in Table A-1 appear at least once in Table A-2.

## The Problem of Opposites

A problem in interpreting the pattern of associative strengths into a theoretically meaningful semantic space is immediately apparent from the associative strengths shown by opposites. Five of the six pairs of opposites show positive associative strengths, and one pair, *active/passive*, shows the third highest associative strength in the matrix. The average associative strength of the six pairs of opposites is slightly over 11. Furthermore, there are a number of other pairs of words that derive some small associative strength from relationships with words of opposite meaning. An example is the association between *go toward* and both *like* and *dislike*. *Interesting* is also associated with both *like* and *dislike*. We can conclude that pairs of opposite words occupy positions closer to each other in a semantic space than do unrelated words, but, beyond that conclusion, we are left with little basis for interpreting a particular associative strength. Recognizing this degree of ambiguity, we can proceed with great caution to an effort to determine what we can about the character of the semantic space.

*TABLE A-2.* Categories of Associative Meaning. (Categories of word pairs with associative strengths [numbers] taken from Table A-1. Each category contains all of the positive values in the matrix.)

| *Structure* | *Evaluative: Verbal Behavior* |
|---|---|
| 14 Complex/Simple | 8 Like/Dislike |
| 12 Complex/Interesting | 50 Like/Prefer |
| 19 Simple/Boring | 23 Like/Interesting |
| 6 Simple/Dislike | 19 Like/Go toward |
| | 4 Like/Go away from |
| *Energy* | 44 Dislike/Prefer not |
| | 21 Dislike/Go away from |
| 33 Active/Passive | 17 Dislike/Prefer |
| | 16 Dislike/Boring |
| *Evaluative: Overt Behavior (Verbal)* | 6 Dislike/Simple |
| | 4 Dislike/Interesting |
| 9 Go toward/Go away from | 4 Dislike/Go toward |
| 19 Go toward/Like | 4 Prefer/Prefer not |
| 17 Go toward/Prefer | 50 Prefer/Like |
| 6 Go toward/Interesting | 17 Prefer/Dislike |
| 4 Go toward/Dislike | 17 Prefer/Go toward |
| 21 Go away from/Dislike | 9 Prefer/Interesting |
| 10 Go away from/Prefer not | 44 Prefer not/Dislike |
| 4 Go away from/Like | 10 Prefer not Go away from |

*Structure/Evaluative*

0 Interesting/Boring
23 Interesting/Like
12 Interesting/Complex
9 Interesting/Prefer
6 Interesting/Go toward
4 Interesting/Dislike
19 Boring/Simple
16 Boring Dislike

### Structural Aspects

The only word pair in the set representing the structural aspect of complexity and preference theory is the pair *complex/simple*. The most prominent associations of this pair are with *boring* and *interesting,* with some degree of association with the dimension represented by *like.* However, these associations are weak and represent about the same magnitude of semantic distance represented by *complex* and *simple* as opposites.

### Energetic Aspects

The theoretical term *arousal* was represented in the set of stimulus words by the *active/passive* pair. These opposites are strongly associated with each other but did not generate any other common associates.

### Evaluative Aspects

The direction-of-behavior dimensions, as represented by the *go toward/go away from* pair, is related in some degree to all three of the verbal behavior dimensions—*liking, preference,* and *interest.* Within the latter set, there are numerous associative connections, but the patterns do not appear to lend themselves to any strong theoretical conclusions.

### Summary

Although the free association method yielded results that were mildly interesting, they did not make a major contribution to our conception of the two problems with which we began—the relative equivalence of relevant words for experimental subjects and the extent to which psychological complexity and preference theory might be represented in the semantic space of experimental subjects.

## SIMILARITY ASSOCIATION DATA

Rather than engage in further analysis of the free association data, I decided to carry out a further study. The first step was to add nine more word pairs, with the additions chosen from the large number of free associates elicited by the stimulus words in the free association study. The second step was to make up test booklets containing 15 stimulus words to which subjects were asked to respond by producing five *similar* words. There were two forms of the booklet. One contained 15 words representing one member of each of the 15 pairs of opposites, and the other form contained the opposites of all of the words in the first form. The two forms were given to two sets of 50 subjects, with the coffee urn bunch supplemented by undergraduates being taught by staff members who frequented the coffee urn.

Similarity strengths were determined by tabulating all of the associations for each of the 50 subjects responding to each booklet. Comparisons were made for all possible pairs of words (435). The score for each pair of words was obtained by adding the frequency with which a word was associated to one member of the pair to the frequency with which the same word was associated to the other member and then tabulating the totals for all such common associates. Since each of 50 subjects gave five associates to each stimulus word, there were 250 associates to each stimulus word. Theoretically, scores could range from zero (if none of the associated words were common to the pair) to 500 (if the associates to the two words of a pair were identical). Actually, the frequency scores ranged from zero to 258, as indicated in Table A-3. The mean score was 34.6.

TABLE A-3. Similarity Scores. (The table displays a matrix of similarity scores to 30 words generated by two groups of 50 subjects responding with five similar words to each of 15 stimulus words. One booklet contained the first 15 words in the left-hand colum, and the other booklet contained the second set of 15 words.)

| | Complex | Boring | Like | Prefer not | Go toward | Ugly | Bright | Hate | Easy | Avoidance | Good | Punishment | Pleasant | Undesirable | Active | Simple | Interesting | Dislike | Prefer | Go away | Beautiful | Dull | Love | Difficult | Approach | Bad | Reward | Unpleasant | Desirable |
|---|---|---|---|---|---|---|---|---|---|---|---|---|---|---|---|---|---|---|---|---|---|---|---|---|---|---|---|---|---|
| Passive | 6 | 114 | 7 | 20 | 0 | 9 | 3 | 2 | 80 | 3 | 17 | 2 | 65 | 11 | 11 | 86 | 12 | 9 | 2 | 2 | 23 | 70 | 15 | 8 | 0 | 4 | 0 | 10 | 8 |
| Complex | | 7 | 0 | 6 | 0 | 2 | 2 | 4 | 61 | 4 | 5 | 2 | 16 | 0 | 0 | 100 | 69 | 10 | 2 | 0 | 0 | 28 | 4 | 266 | 0 | 2 | 0 | 49 | 7 |
| Boring | | | 10 | 7 | 0 | 15 | 0 | 2 | 108 | 9 | 5 | 2 | 10 | 35 | 0 | 147 | 70 | 49 | 0 | 2 | 2 | 285 | 0 | 0 | 0 | 11 | 0 | 127 | 0 |
| Like | | | | 42 | 42 | 3 | 28 | 64 | 14 | 15 | 86 | 6 | 82 | 0 | 5 | 7 | 56 | 4 | 252 | 11 | 82 | 3 | 174 | 3 | 72 | 7 | 52 | 12 | 123 |
| Prefer not | | | | | 5 | 32 | 0 | 40 | 0 | 149 | 2 | 59 | 2 | 132 | 0 | 0 | 2 | 136 | 77 | 110 | 0 | 41 | 12 | 46 | 18 | 89 | 2 | 111 | 7 |
| Go toward | | | | | | 0 | 0 | 0 | 6 | 48 | 7 | 5 | 2 | 0 | 7 | 4 | 9 | 3 | 80 | 13 | 0 | 0 | 24 | 0 | 223 | 0 | 36 | 0 | 11 |
| Ugly | | | | | | | 8 | 29 | 0 | 23 | 19 | 5 | 6 | 188 | 4 | 14 | 7 | 71 | 2 | 10 | 8 | 40 | 17 | 11 | 2 | 137 | 0 | 175 | 9 |
| Bright | | | | | | | | 0 | 43 | 15 | 28 | 0 | 42 | 0 | 40 | 13 | 21 | 2 | 5 | 10 | 44 | 10 | 24 | 0 | 2 | 0 | 11 | 3 | 29 |
| Hate | | | | | | | | | 3 | 94 | 4 | 95 | 0 | 81 | 2 | 5 | 3 | 269 | 10 | 50 | 8 | 43 | 19 | 34 | 19 | 75 | 6 | 59 | 14 |
| Easy | | | | | | | | | | 2 | 28 | 0 | 149 | 0 | 34 | 151 | 55 | 5 | 45 | 19 | 16 | 122 | 26 | 96 | 0 | 6 | 16 | 14 | 41 |
| Avoidance | | | | | | | | | | | 2 | 35 | 6 | 71 | 13 | 48 | 4 | 134 | 4 | 122 | 0 | 14 | 0 | 27 | 19 | 44 | 4 | 54 | 0 |
| Good | | | | | | | | | | | | 25 | 184 | 26 | 20 | 24 | 65 | 10 | 85 | 3 | 128 | 5 | 50 | 11 | 16 | 9 | 48 | 49 | 191 |
| Punishment | | | | | | | | | | | | | 8 | 82 | 2 | 0 | 7 | 71 | 2 | 12 | 5 | 12 | 3 | 7 | 9 | 54 | 37 | 79 | 2 |
| Pleasant | | | | | | | | | | | | | | 4 | | 105 | 110 | 5 | 56 | 18 | 171 | 19 | 93 | 20 | 10 | 2 | 66 | 1 | 179 |
| Undesirable | | | | | | | | | | | | | | | | 21 | 15 | 122 | 4 | 41 | 20 | 97 | 3 | 24 | 5 | 182 | 10 | 231 | 1 |
| Active | | | | | | | | | | | | | | | | 21 | 40 | 7 | 7 | 13 | 8 | 6 | 6 | 22 | 13 | 8 | 13 | 7 | 17 |
| Simple | | | | | | | | | | | | | | | | | 84 | 8 | 3 | 13 | 14 | 188 | 11 | 125 | 0 | 4 | 10 | 19 | 21 |
| Interesting | | | | | | | | | | | | | | | | | | 11 | 94 | 4 | 166 | 39 | 55 | 57 | 10 | 11 | 35 | 10 | 113 |
| Dislike | | | | | | | | | | | | | | | | | | | 59 | 33 | 14 | 81 | 61 | 21 | 16 | 153 | 9 | 115 | 13 |
| Prefer | | | | | | | | | | | | | | | | | | | | 9 | 37 | 2 | 162 | 11 | 53 | 31 | 36 | 8 | 119 |

| | | | | | | | | |
|---|---|---|---|---|---|---|---|---|
| Go away | 2 | | | | 19 | 2 | 31 | 7 |
| Beautiful | 7 | 9 | 6 | 12 | 16 | 21 | 15 | 158 |
| Dull | 6 | 65 | 9 | 23 | 30 | 2 | 81 | 0 |
| Love | 0 | 103 | 0 | | 17 | 43 | 5 | 141 |
| Difficult | 18 | 28 | 2 | | 12 | 10 | 135 | 9 |
| | | | | | | | | |
| Approach | | | | | 4 | 27 | 4 | 33 |
| Bad | | | | | 12 | 200 | | 18 |
| Reward | | | | | | 11 | | 64 |
| Unpleasant | | | | | | | 11 | |
| Desirable | | | | | | | | 11 |

### Opposites

This study was constructed to discourage opposites as similarity associates. Each subject had a list of 15 words that, internally, contained no opposites. All subjects were instructed to write down the five *most similar* words they could think of. Each member of a pair of opposites was responded to by an entirely different set of 50 subjects. Yet the 15 pairs of opposites generated similarity strength scores ranging from one to 100, with a mean of 31.8. If this had been a free association study, opposites would undoubtedly have generated much higher associative strengths.

### Theoretical and Arbitrary Bases for Analyzing Similarity Associates

The 15 pairs of words can be classified into the same theory-relevant groups used in the free association study. Arousal is again represented only by the *active/passive* pair. The structural term, *psychological complexity,* is represented only by the *simple/complex* pair. The evaluative direction-of-behavior concept is represented by *go toward/go away from* and by *approach/avoidance.* The other 11 pairs can be loosely interpreted as representing evaluative verbal behavior.

There is a practical problem of reducing to some manageable size the number of comparisons to be considered of the 435 available. This problem was solved in a wholly arbitrary fashion. Since the mean frequency in the matrix is 34.6 and the mean frequency of opposites 31.8, it was arbitrarily decided to consider only frequencies of 32 or greater. It will be seen in what follows that a higher criterion might well have been used without loss of meaningful relationships.

### The Structural Dimension

The associations made to the *complex/simple* pair are contained in Table A-4. It is apparent that there is a strong association between *complexity/simple* on the one hand and *difficult/easy* on the other. This association is of special interest because of the work of Arkes and Boykin, who have related the complexity dimension to verbal learning and problem solving (see Chapter 9). I would assume that, the more complex the task, the greater the difficulty, and that complexity and preference theory should be applicable to these traditional areas of psychological research. The picture is complicated somewhat by the fact that the word *simple* shows a relatively strong similarity association to both *easy* and *difficult.*

There is also a strong association between the *complex/simple* pair and the *interesting/boring* pair. This association is enhanced by the association between *simple* and *dull. Dull* was brought into

TABLE A-4. Similarity Strengths on the Structural Dimension. (The table displays words associated to the words *complex* and *simple,* the numbers in each case representing frequency of common associations. Maximum possible frequency = 500.)

| 100 Complex/Simple | |
|---|---|
| 266 Complex/Difficult | 188 Simple/Dull |
| 69 Complex/Interesting | 151 Simple/Easy |
| 61 Complex/Easy | 147 Simple/Boring |
| 49 Complex/Unpleasant | 125 Simple/Difficult |
| 45 Complex/Active | 105 Simple/Pleasant |
| | 86 Simple/Passive |
| | 84 Simple/Interesting |
| | 48 Simple/Avoidance |

the study as the opposite of the word *bright.* However, as will be seen later, the associations of similarities that *dull* generated make it apparent that the subjects were interpreting it as essentially equivalent to the word *boring.*

The verbal evaluative pair, *pleasant/unpleasant* generates similarity associates to both *simple* and *complex* in a somewhat mixed pattern—as might be expected from the theory, according to which (1) mid-range values of complexity would be most pleasant, and (2) both extremes would be somewhat unpleasant, with the complex end the more unpleasant of the two. However, this specific pattern could not easily be revealed by association data.

### The Energy Dimension

The concept of arousal is represented by the *active/passive* pair. The associations to this pair are shown in Table A-5. The results in terms of similarity associates are not radically different from those in the free association study. No strong associates are given to the word *active.* The only association to the word *passive* that seems interpretable is *boring,* although the other four words in the table are intuitively reasonable. However, one might hazard the guess that, if *inactive* had been used as the opposite of *active,* the associa-

TABLE A-5. Similarity Strengths on the Arousal Dimension. (The table displays words associated to the words *active* and *passive,* with the numbers in each case representing frequency of common associations. Maximum possible frequency = 500.)

| 13 Active/Passive | |
|---|---|
| 45 Active/Complex | 114 Passive/Boring |
| 40 Active/Bright | 86 Passive/Simple |
| 40 Active/Interesting | 80 Passive/Easy |
| 34 Active/Easy | 70 Passive/Dull |
| | 65 Passive/Pleasant |

tions on the right side of the table would have been appreciably lower.

In a general sense, I am tempted to conclude that, in a semantic space generated by free association and similarity association procedures, the arousal dimension is unrelated to the other three.

### The Evaluative Dimension: The Direction of Behavior

The evaluative direction-of-behavior dimension is represented in the similarity association study by two word pairs, *approach/ avoidance* and *go toward/go away from.* The similarity associates of these two pairs are shown in Table A-6. It is gratifying to find that the two pairs are very closely associated with each other. It is also appropriate that the other strong associates are from the evaluative verbal dimension, *like/dislike* and *prefer/prefer not.* There is also a degree of justification from these strong associations for considering the direction of overt behavior (as verbally expressed) and the verbal evaluative dimension (as represented by *preference* and *liking*) to be measures of the same variable. It is also worth noting for theoretical purposes that neither *interesting* nor *boring* appears in association with the direction-of-behavior dimension.

### Verbal Evaluative Dimension

The 11 word pairs representing the verbal evaluative dimension are loosely grouped under this rubric because they were frequent associates of *like, prefer,* and *interesting* in the free association study. The size of the list can be reduced somewhat by discussing a few of the interlopers individually.

*Easy/Difficult.* This pair was included in the list because of the frequency with which it appeared as a free associate in the first study and because of the fact that it can be interpreted as representing the complexity dimension in learning and problem solving tasks. The results of the similarity associates to these two words are shown in Table A-7. The close association with the complexity dimension is apparent. The associations of *easy* with *pleasant* and of *difficult* with *unpleasant* are stronger than the associations between these evaluative words and the *complex/simple* pair. Oddly, enough, however, *easy* is also associated with *dull* and *boring,* as well as with *pleasant.* The confusion is amplified somewhat by the fact that the associations to the word *difficult* remain almost uniformly negative.

*Reward/Punishment.* Although this pair of words might ordinarily be considered to belong more to the theory language than to the language of experimental subjects—and thus be subject to different

*TABLE A-6.* Similarity Strengths on the Dimension of Direction of Behavior. (The table displays words associated to the words *approach, avoidance, go toward,* and *go away from.* The numbers represent frequency of common associations. Maximum possible frequency = 500.)

| 19 Approach/Avoidance | |
|---|---|
| 223 Approach/Go toward | 149 Avoidance/Prefer not |
| 72 Approach/Like | 134 Avoidance/Dislike |
| 53 Approach/Prefer | 122 Avoidance/Go away from |
| 33 Approach/Desirable | 94 Avoidance/Hate |
| | 71 Avoidance/Undesirable |
| | 54 Avoidance/Unpleasant |
| | 48 Avoidance/Go toward |
| | 48 Avoidance/Simple |
| | 44 Avoidance/Bad |
| | 35 Avoidance/Punishment |

| 13 Go toward/Go away from | |
|---|---|
| 223 Go toward/Approach | 122 Go away from/Avoidance |
| 80 Go toward/Prefer | 110 Go away from/Prefer not |
| 48 Go toward/Avoidance | 50 Go away from/Hate |
| 42 Go toward/Like | 41 Go away from/Undesirable |
| 36 Go toward/Reward | 33 Go away from/Dislike |

*TABLE A-7.* Similarity Strengths on the *Easy/Difficult* Dimension. (The table displays words associated to the words *easy* and *difficult.* The numbers represent frequencies of common associations. Maximum possible frequency = 500.)

| 96 Easy/Difficult | |
|---|---|
| 151 Easy/Simple | 266 Difficult/Complex |
| 149 Easy/Pleasant | 135 Difficult/Unpleasant |
| 122 Easy/Dull | 125 Difficult/Simple |
| 108 Easy/Boring | 103 Difficult/Dull |
| 80 Easy/Passive | 67 Difficult/Boring |
| 61 Easy/Complex | 57 Difficult/Interesting |
| 55 Easy/Interesting | 46 Difficult/Prefer not |
| 45 Easy/Prefer | 34 Difficult/Hate |
| 43 Easy/Bright | |
| 41 Easy/Desirable | |
| 34 Easy/Active | |

interpretations by psychologists and subjects—in this case the subjects all were current or past students of psychology. This fact may account for the emergence of the pair in the free association study. It may also account, in part, for the remarkably low set of similarity associates shown in Table A-8. All associations to *reward* are positive but very weak , while associations to the word *punishment* are negative and also very weak.

*Bright/Dull.* This pair yielded a rather atypical result, as can be seen in Table A-9. The word *bright* generated nothing in the way of strong associates. The word *dull,* on the other hand, apparently

TABLE A-8. Similarity Strengths on the *Reward/Punishment* Dimension. (The table displays words associated to the words *reward* and *punishment*. The numbers represent frequency of common associations. Maximum possible frequency = 500.)

| 37 Reward/Punishment | |
|---|---|
| 66  Reward/Pleasant | 95  Punishment/Hate |
| 64  Reward/Desirable | 82  Punishment/Undesirable |
| 52  Reward/Like | 79  Punishment/Unpleasant |
| 48  Reward/Good | 71  Punishment/Dislike |
| 43  Reward/Love | 59  Punishment/Prefer not |
| 36  Reward/Prefer | 54  Punishment/Bad |
| 36  Reward/Go toward | 35  Punishment/Avoidance |
| 35  Reward/Interesting | |

TABLE A-9. Similarity Strengths on the *Bright/Dull* Dimension. (The table displays words associated to the words *bright* and *dull*. The numbers represent frequency of common associations. Maximum possible frequency = 500.)

| 10 Bright/Dull | |
|---|---|
| 44  Bright/Beautiful | 285  Dull/Boring |
| 43  Bright/Easy | 188  Dull/Simple |
| 42  Bright/Pleasant | 122  Dull/Easy |
| 40  Bright/Active | 103  Dull/Difficult |
| | 97  Dull/Undesirable |
| | 81  Dull/Unpleasant |
| | 81  Dull/Dislike |
| | 70  Dull/Passive |
| | 43  Dull/Hate |
| | 41  Dull/Prefer not |
| | 40  Dull/Ugly |
| | 39  Dull/Interesting |

was interpreted not in the sense of the opposite of *bright* but in the sense of boredom. The confusion is further enhanced by the other strong associates to the word *dull—simple, easy,* and *difficult.*

The results with this pair of words pinpoint an experimental problem. If the two members of a pair of opposites have strong associates that are unrelated to the dimension they represent, then it matters greatly which end of the pair one chooses to present to the subject or whether one presents both ends and emphasizes the dimension they represent.

*Interesting/Boring.* Similarity associates to this pair might have been expected to yield results that would have clarified the problems discussed in Chapter 3, where contradictory results were found when subjects were asked to respond to the complexity dimension in terms of *interest* as opposed to responding in terms of *liking* or *pleasantness.* Is *interest* a structural or an evaluative variable? The data in Table A-10 offer little aid in answering this question. If the

*TABLE A-10.* Similarity Strengths on the *Interesting/Boring* Dimension. (The table displays words associated to the words *interesting* and *boring*. The numbers represent frequency of common associations. Maximum possible frequency = 500.)

| 70 Interesting/Boring | | |
|---|---|---|
| 166 Interesting/Beautiful | 285 | Boring/Dull |
| 113 Interesting/Desirable | 147 | Boring/Simple |
| 110 Interesting/Pleasant | 127 | Boring/Unpleasant |
| 94 Interesting/Prefer | 114 | Boring/Passive |
| 84 Interesting/Simple | 108 | Boring/Easy |
| 69 Interesting/Complex | 67 | Boring/Difficult |
| 65 Interesting/Good | 49 | Boring/Dislike |
| 57 Interesting/Difficult | 35 | Boring/Undesirable |
| 56 Interesting/Like | | |
| 55 Interesting/Easy | | |
| 55 Interesting/Love | | |
| 40 Interesting/Active | | |
| 39 Interesting/Dull | | |
| 35 Interesting/Reward | | |

*interesting/boring* pair is appropriate language for eliciting what Berlyne calls "specific exploration," then the strong associations should have been with *simple* and *complex*. If, instead, *interesting* and *boring* function as verbal evaluative terms, then the strong associations should have been with other verbal evaluative terms. Neither result is clearly apparent in Table A-10. *Interesting* is associated with *beautiful, desirable,* and *pleasant* but it is only weakly associated with *complex. Boring,* on the other hand, is associated with *simple* and even more strongly with *dull.* The inconclusiveness of these results lead me to retain the *interesting/boring* pair in the next analysis, shown in Table A-11.

The two submatrices in Table A-11 are composed of the remaining affective words in the original set of 15 pairs with the addition of the *interesting/boring* pair. It is not surprising to find that these matrices contain most of the pairs with high similarity-associative strengths. The mean matrix values in the right-hand column of the table gave a rough measure of the relative similarity strengths within this particular set of words. The overall mean values for the two matrices are 117 for the upper and 102.6 for the lower, in contrast to the mean of 34.6 for the complete original matrix in Table A-3.

The lowest mean value within each of the matrices is generated by the *interesting/boring* pair. This degree of isolation within a similarity space seems to lend support to Berlyne's distinction between specific exploration, which is presumably related to the interestingness of the stimulus display, and diversive exploration, which is presumably related to pleasantness. However, the associative strengths of the specific words *interesting/pleasant* and *boring/*

TABLE A-11. Similarity Strengths of Affective Words. (The table displays submatrices taken from Table A-3 showing relative similarity strengths in terms of frequencies of common associates and mean frequencies of common associates within the submatrix. Maximum possible frequency = 500.)

| | Good | Pleasant | Interesting | Prefer | Beautiful | Love | Desirable | Mean |
|---|---|---|---|---|---|---|---|---|
| | | | | *Positive Words* | | | | |
| Like | 86 | 82 | 56 | 252 | 82 | 174 | 123 | 122.1 |
| Good | | 184 | 65 | 85 | 128 | 50 | 191 | 112.7 |
| Pleasant | | | 110 | 56 | 171 | 93 | 179 | 125.0 |
| Interesting | | | | 94 | 166 | 55 | 113 | 94.1 |
| Prefer | | | | | 37 | 162 | 119 | 115.0 |
| Beautiful | | | | | | 65 | 158 | 115.3 |
| Love | | | | | | | 141 | 105.7 |
| Desirable | | | | | | | | 146.3 |

| | Bad | Unpleasant | Boring | Prefer not | Ugly | Hate | Undesirable | Mean |
|---|---|---|---|---|---|---|---|---|
| | | | | *Negative Words* | | | | |
| Dislike | 153 | 115 | 49 | 136 | 71 | 269 | 122 | 130.7 |
| Bad | | 200 | 11 | 89 | 137 | 75 | 182 | 121.0 |
| Unpleasant | | | 127 | 111 | 175 | 59 | 231 | 145.4 |
| Boring | | | | 7 | 15 | 2 | 35 | 35.1 |
| Prefer not | | | | | 32 | 40 | 132 | 78.1 |
| Ugly | | | | | | 29 | 188 | 92.4 |
| Hate | | | | | | | 81 | 79.3 |
| Undesirable | | | | | | | | 138.7 |

*unpleasant* are both above the mean matrix values of *interesting* and *boring*. Thus, this form of semantic analysis doesn't really provide a satisfactory answer to the problem posed by the difference in results obtained in complexity studies when the question is "Which is the most interesting?" and when the question is "Which is the most pleasant?"

The words *pleasant, like,* and (sometimes) *prefer* are generally used interchangeably in studies of complexity and preference. This practice receives some degree of sanction from the results shown in Table A-11. The pairs represented by *desirable, pleasant,* and *like* generate the three highest mean similarity associates strengths in each matrix. The pair represented by the word *prefer,* however, does not appear to belong to the same set. From these data, then, one could conclude that it is reasonable to use *pleasing* and *like* interchangeably, and that one would be equally well off using *desirable* and *undesirable*. On the other hand, one might run the risk of moving to a new semantic dimension if one chose to use the pairs represented by *prefer, love, beautiful,* or *good.*

### Associative Strength as a
### Measure of Semantic Distance

I should like to summarize the outcome of these studies of associative strength as a measure of semantic distances among this particular set of words typically used or potentially usable in studies of complexity and preference. There are really two sets of conclusions to be drawn. One set is related to the substantive findings and the other set to the methodology. With respect to the substantive findings, five conclusions can be drawn.

1. It seems reasonable to conclude that psychological complexity and preference theory does not reduce simply to a matter of semantics. The clearest evidence for this conclusion is the lack of relationship between *active/passive* and any of the other language used. If a theoretical relationship is established between complexity and arousal, it will not be the result of a simple relationship between *arousal* and *complexity* in the semantic structure of the experimental subjects.

2. The results suggest that there is a degree of justification for equating at least the verbal equivalent of overt approach and avoidance behavior with verbal evaluations such as *pleasant* and *liking.*

3. There is encouraging evidence that *complexity* and *difficulty* are sufficiently similar to permit translation from one to the other when dealing with problems in which difficulty is a reasonable dimension of the task.

4. Several words that are used interchangeably in studies of complexity and preference, such as *pleasant* and *liking,* are strongly enough associated in this method to appear to justify this usage.

5. Unfortunately, these data do not offer a resolution to the question of whether the *interesting/boring* language is related to a structural dimension, an evaluative dimension, or both.

With respect to the methodology of the use of associative strengths as an index of subjects' semantic space, my conclusions are as follows.

1. The major limitation of the method arises from the use of frequencies as an index of distance in the semantic space. The distance between the strongest association among the pairs of words and the zero distance of identity in meaning is indeterminate. Opposites show positive associative strength, indicating that words such as *good* and *bad* are closer together in the semantic space than are unrelated words. However, there is great variation in associative strength among opposites. Pairs of words that generate low but positive associative strengths represent separations that bear an unknown relation to the limit of unrelatedness. Thus, the method

appears to array word pairs on a scale of relative semantic distance, but the scalar properties of the distances derived from frequencies are limited in their suitability for the construction of a semantic space with properties that are in accord with those of complexity and preference theory. The nonmonotonic, inverted-U relationships postulated in complexity and preference theory are best demonstrated using dimensions of complexity and preference that have something approximating the equal-unit metric properties of Euclidean distances. Semantic space generated from frequencies of common associates appears to have scalar properties of a much lower order.

2. One additional methodological note appears to be important enough for repetition and emphasis. Experimenters in complexity and preference tend to be relatively casual in their choice of one or the other of a pair of opposites. Thus, subjects in one experiment may be asked to rank stimuli in terms of how complex they are, while in another they are asked to rank the stimuli in terms of how simple they are. Examination of the associates of such pairs in both the free association and the similarity association studies shows clearly that the associations to words that appear to be opposite in meaning can actually be quite different. This finding suggests that the use of both words simultaneously would minimize possible differences in interpretation and thus minimize experimental error.

## JUDGED SEMANTIC DISTANCE DATA

The problem to which these studies are addressed is the question of whether complexity and preference theory is simply a matter of semantics. If one succeeds in finding stable relationships between variables such as complexity, preference, and arousal, are these relationships primarily within a psychological theory or are they primarily within the semantic space of experimental subjects?

Thus far we have approached the problem of the nature of semantic space within experimental subjects through a free association experiment and then an experiment on the association of similarities. The information obtained was helpful to some degree, but the metric properties of frequencies of association as a measure of semantic distance left us somewhat removed from tests of the postulated relationships within complexity and preference theory.

This result—which might well have been anticipated before the experiments were done in the first place—suggests that a very strong, very direct approach to the problem might be more profitable. Why not assume that there are semantic distances with metric properties and simply ask experimental subjects to produce them? The procedure is risky in the sense that one might, through the nature of the experimental instructions, create semantic structures that don't really exist in the subjects. This risk is countered, however, by another argument. If one forces experimental subjects to yield appropriate semantic structures, and if these structures do not correspond with the structure of the theory, and if the theory can be verified independently through experimental data, then one has a strong argument that complexity and preference theory isn't all a matter of semantics of experimental subjects.

I began this construction with the intention of trying to determine a reference scale that could then be used in further tests. Three points on an ideal scale immediately suggest themselves. Words that are identical in meaning should be regarded as being zero distance apart. Words that are opposite in meaning should be a great distance apart. But how should the distance relationship between opposites compare to that between unrelated words?

It is not difficult to imagine semantic spaces in which any of several distance relationships could hold. I can conceive opposites as being half as far apart in a semantic space as unrelated words. I can also conceive opposites being exactly as far apart or even twice as far apart as unrelated words. The question that one can ask, then, is this: what is the relative semantic distance between opposites and unrelated words in the semantic spaces of experimental subjects? The most direct approach to this problem is to ask the question directly.

The coffee urn mob was approached again and asked the following question: "If the distance between totally unrelated words is 100 units, and the distance between identical words is 0 units, how far apart do the following pairs of words seem to you?"

It is interesting to report that the normally calm and docile habitués of the coffee urn were distinctly agitated by this task. Although the question seems clear and simple on the surface, the subjects insisted on clarification of what I wanted (an insistance I resisted), they generally thought about the problem much longer than usual, and several wanted to come back and change their answers after they thought about the problem a while longer.

Some of the reason for their agitation is apparent in the results, which are given in Table A-12. There is almost no agreement among subjects. If 100 units is taken as the standard distance between unrelated words, then by my informal analysis (you may make your own from the table), the various subjects produced the following results. One subject has a semantic space in which opposites are twice as far apart as unrelated words. Six of the 21 subjects appear to consider opposites the same distance apart as unrelated words. Two subjects tend to place opposites at three-quarters of the distance and two more at two-thirds of the distance of unrelated words. Six more think of opposites as half as far apart, one subject thinks of them as a third as far apart, one as a quarter as far apart, and two as one-fifth as far apart as unrelated words.

*TABLE A-12.* Semantic Distances of Opposites

| Subject Number | Active/Passive | Simple/Complex | Interesting/Boring | Like/Dislike | Prefer/Prefer not | Go toward/Go away | Beautiful/Ugly | Bright/Dull | Love/Hate | Easy/Difficult | Approach/Avoidance | Good/Bad | Reward/Punishment | Pleasant/Unpleasant | Desirable/Undesirable |
|---|---|---|---|---|---|---|---|---|---|---|---|---|---|---|---|
| 1 | 50 | 50 | 50 | 50 | 50 | 50 | 50 | 50 | 50 | 50 | 50 | 50 | 50 | 50 | 50 |
| 2 | 10 | 30 | 10 | 10 | 10 | 10 | 20 | 30 | 30 | 30 | 30 | 30 | 30 | 15 | 15 |
| 3 | 50 | 50 | 40 | 50 | 50 | 50 | 50 | 40 | 50 | 50 | 40 | 50 | 50 | 50 | 50 |
| 4 | 90 | 100 | 70 | 100 | 100 | 100 | 60 | 100 | 100 | 100 | 100 | 100 | 50 | 100 | 100 |
| 5 | 100 | 100 | 100 | 50 | 100 | 100 | 80 | 85 | 40 | 70 | 100 | 70 | 100 | 90 | 100 |
| 6 | 100 | 100 | 100 | 100 | 100 | 100 | 100 | 100 | 100 | 100 | 100 | 100 | 100 | 100 | 100 |
| 7 | 100 | 100 | 100 | 100 | 80 | 100 | 100 | 70 | 70 | 80 | 85 | 100 | 90 | 80 | 80 |
| 8 | 100 | 100 | 90 | 50 | 30 | 20 | 50 | 60 | 80 | 10 | 70 | 5 | 70 | 100 | 100 |
| 9 | 100 | 100 | 100 | 50 | 40 | 30 | 50 | 100 | 100 | 20 | 40 | 50 | 80 | 90 | 50 |
| 10 | 50 | 50 | 50 | 25 | 25 | 25 | 25 | 25 | 10 | 50 | 25 | 25 | 25 | 25 | 25 |
| 11 | 60 | 70 | 70 | 40 | 35 | 50 | 70 | 60 | 70 | 60 | 50 | 45 | 55 | 45 | 50 |
| 12 | 200 | 200 | 200 | 200 | 200 | 200 | 200 | 200 | 200 | 200 | 200 | 200 | 200 | 200 | 200 |
| 13 | 60 | 45 | 80 | 85 | 40 | 95 | 55 | 90 | 75 | 80 | 80 | 85 | 85 | 80 | 55 |
| 14 | 20 | 20 | 20 | 15 | 15 | 19 | 20 | 20 | 20 | 20 | 20 | 20 | 20 | 16 | 16 |
| 15 | 50 | 75 | 50 | 100 | 75 | 90 | 20 | 50 | 30 | 40 | 50 | 100 | 50 | 100 | 100 |
| 16 | 100 | 100 | 100 | 100 | 50 | 100 | 100 | 100 | 50 | 100 | 50 | 100 | 100 | 100 | 100 |
| 17 | 50 | 50 | 50 | 50 | 50 | 50 | 50 | 50 | 50 | 50 | 50 | 50 | 50 | 50 | 50 |
| 18 | 33 | 33 | 30 | 33 | 28 | 28 | 33 | 38 | 33 | 33 | 28 | 33 | 28 | 33 | 28 |
| 19 | 50 | 50 | 70 | 70 | 0 | 75 | 70 | 50 | 70 | 50 | 75 | 70 | 75 | 70 | 70 |
| 20 | 100 | 100 | 100 | 50 | 50 | 100 | 100 | 100 | 100 | 100 | 100 | 100 | 100 | 50 | 50 |
| 21 | 95 | 90 | 65 | 50 | 65 | 95 | 100 | 75 | 100 | 95 | 75 | 100 | 80 | 80 | 80 |

Four of the 21 subjects refused to distinguish between the 15 sets of opposites and assigned the same value to each pair. The remaining 17 subjects did make discriminations. In view of the heterogeneity of the conceptions of opposites, there is very little justification for calculating means for the 15 columns in Table A-12, but I have done so anyway. This operation results in the data displayed in Figure A-1. The mean of the 15 pairs is slightly over 69. The largest mean is nearly 77; the smallest is slightly less than 57. For whatever it is worth, the rank order correlation between the semantic distances displayed in Figure A-1 and the semantic distances indicated by the frequencies of common associates in Table A-3 turns out to be zero.

If we chose to use the distance between opposites as a standard for comparison with other semantic distances, we would be encouraged by the similarity of the mean distances of the 15 pairs in Figure A-1. However, we would be discouraged by the lack of uniformity in subjects' conceptions of the relation between opposites and unrelated words, as evidenced by the data in Table A-12. Yet there is an appeal to the distance between opposites as a unit of measurement in a semantic space. Perhaps something could be learned from an enforced structure in which opposites are required

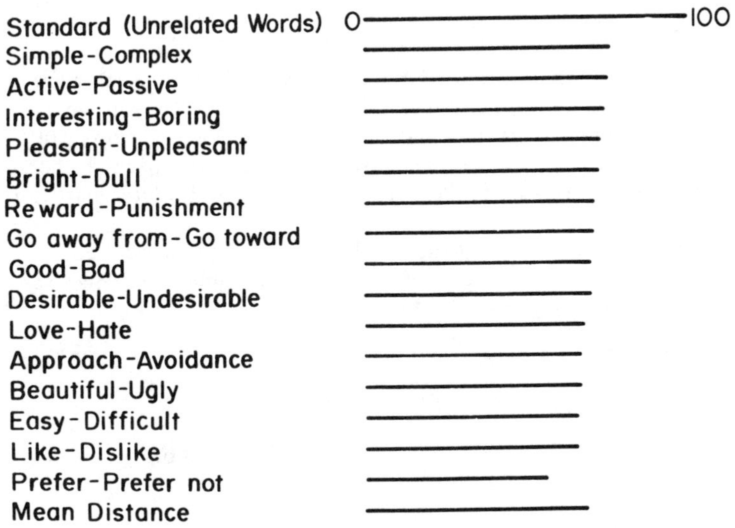

| | |
|---|---|
| Standard (Unrelated Words) | 0 ————————— 100 |
| Simple - Complex | ——————— |
| Active - Passive | ——————— |
| Interesting - Boring | ——————— |
| Pleasant - Unpleasant | ——————— |
| Bright - Dull | ——————— |
| Reward - Punishment | ——————— |
| Go away from - Go toward | ——————— |
| Good - Bad | ——————— |
| Desirable - Undesirable | ——————— |
| Love - Hate | ——————— |
| Approach - Avoidance | ——————— |
| Beautiful - Ugly | ——————— |
| Easy - Difficult | ——————— |
| Like - Dislike | ——————— |
| Prefer - Prefer not | ————— |
| Mean Distance | ————— |

FIGURE A-1. *Mean Semantic Distances of Opposites*

to be 100 units apart and unrelated words 200 units apart. It seemed worth a try.

### Walker Scales of Semantic Distance

None of the standard scaling techniques that I was able to find in the literature seemed appropriate for my purpose. I therefore invented one. It is a very direct (and unsophisticated) scaling procedure in which the instructions to the subject contain a concise statement of a particular conception of semantic space and ask the subject to adopt that conception as a framework for his or her responses. Because the procedure is an invention, and because the instructions are relatively brief, let me quote directly from the document given to 25 members of the coffee urn gang.

#### Semantic Distances

This is a study that is designed to determine the distances between various words in a semantic space. More properly, we would like to know something about the way in which pairs of dimensions defined by words that are opposite in meaning are related to each other in a semantic space.

In previous studies we have found that people do not agree on many aspects of the character of semantic space. For example, there is little agreement on how far words of opposite meaning are apart in such a space in comparison to the distance of unrelated words. I would therefore like you to accept a common but not universal arrangement in which words of opposite meaning are considered to be 100 units apart, while words that are unrelated in meaning are 200 units apart.

For example, if the words *black* and *white* are 100 units apart, the words *bell* and *loam* would be 200 units apart.

In what you are being asked to do, the general pattern will be to present two pairs of words, each of which will be designated as defining 100-unit scales. For example, the words might be *black* and *white* to define one scale and *happy* and *sad* define the other. You will be asked to assign a number of values from one of the scales (e.g., *happy* 100 to 0 *sad*) to a variety of values of the first scale. The next page might be the result of the performance of this task with *black* and *white* and *happy* and *sad*.

Let us assume that the greatest *happiness* you can imagine represents a value of 100, and the greatest *sadness* you can imagine represents a value of 0, thus:

Happy                                                              Sad
100 _____ 0

Now please assign a value from that scale in each of the blanks on the following scale.

| Black | 10 | _____ |
| Very Dark Grey | 20 | _____ |
| Moderately Dark Grey | 40 | _____ |
| Slightly Dark Grey | 50 | _____ |
| Grey | 60 | _____ |
| Slightly Light Grey | 70 | _____ |
| Moderately Light Grey | 80 | _____ |
| Very Light Grey | 100 | _____ |
| White | 70 | _____ |

The second set of blanks is for your use in disagreeing with the values that have been inserted in the first set.

On some of the following pages, you will find more than one set of scales to be related to the major one laid out on the left-hand side of the page (where the black/white scale is above). Please try to make each set of judgments on a page independent of the previous judgments you have made.

On the pages that followed, the subjects were asked to make 15 sets of judgments. Six dimensions were involved. They were:

| Low complexity | to | High complexity |
| Low arousal | to | High arousal |
| Easy | to | Difficult |
| Boring | to | Interesting |
| Unpleasant | to | Pleasant |
| Avoidance | to | Approach |

The left-hand pole was given a value of zero, and the right-hand pole was given a value of 100. Furthermore, each of the first five dimensions were accompanied by 11 descriptive phrases to anchor particular values of the dimension. The list of phrases for the *complexity* dimension were: 100, *chaotic*; 90, *extremely complex*; 80, *very complex*; 70, *moderately complex*; 60, *slightly complex*; 50, *neither complex nor simple*; 40, *slightly simple*; 30, *moderately simple*; 20, *very simple*; 10, *extremely simple*; 0, *undifferentiated*. The subject then assigned values for each of the other five dimensions (ranging from 0 to 100) to each of the values of *complexity*. When the results of this study became available (as will be seen subsequently), it became apparent that the descriptive phrases *chaotic, neither complex nor simple*, and *undifferentiated* were seen by some of the coffee urn mob as not belonging on a linear dimension of complexity. As a consequence, this portion of the study was carried out a second time, several months later, with 25 new subjects, in the same manner, but with a booklet in which the *complexity* dimension was defined with the following descriptive phrases: 100, *extremely complex*; 80, *very complex*; 60, *slightly complex*; 40, *slightly simple*; 20, *very simple*; and 0, *extremely simple*. The values 90, 70, 50, 30, and 10 were not associated with any descriptive phrases. Both sets of results are plotted in the subsequent figures, the first set of data plotted as a solid line and the second set as a broken line.

On the next page of the booklet in the original study, the *arousal* dimension was similarly categorized with the highest value labeled *maximum possible arousal,* the middle value labeled *middle level arousal,* and the lowest value labeled *minimum possible arousal.* The subjects scaled *arousal* against the other four dimensions, with the intervening labels carrying the same adjectives used with the *complexity* scale. On the next page, the *difficulty* dimension was arrayed on the left, and the subjects scaled the remaining three dimensions. The *boring/interesting* dimension was on the left of the next page, and it was then scaled against the remaining two dimensions. On the final page, *unpleasant/pleasant* was arrayed on the left, and the subjects scaled *avoidance/approach.*

The data were analyzed in two ways. Group results were obtained by simply averaging the scale values for the 25 subjects; these results will be presented in graphic form. However, it is also important to know the degree to which the group results represent the semantic spaces of all the subjects. Since each subject produced 15 plottable curves showing his or her conception of the manner in which the pairs of dimensions being evaluated were related to each other, it was possible to categorize each subject's responses into curve type.

Six categories were used in classification: monotonically increasing, monotonically decreasing, inverted-U-shaped, U-shaped, uncorrelated, and unclassifiable. No U-shaped curves appeared in the first study, but examples of each of the other five did.

Two criterion levels were used in classification, strict and liberal. In using the strict criterion, no deviation was permitted. For a curve to be classified as a monotonically increasing curve, each successive value had to be equal to or greater than the preceding value. An inverted-U-shaped curve was required to rise to a maximum and decrease beyond that point without reversal. The more liberal criterion was more intuitive in character but was reliable and reproducible nonetheless. The middle 9 to 11 values were used to determine the general curve shape, and (considering all 11 values) as many as three deviations from the strict criterion were accepted. Most of these deviations occurred at either extreme or in the very middle value and probably resulted from idiosyncratic interpretations of the descriptive terms used in those positions. All but a very few of the curves classified under the liberal criterion had a single deviation from the strict criterion.

The results of this analysis, applied only to the first 25 subjects who had the original *complexity* scale, are shown in Table A-13. The first number in each instance is the classification according to the strict criterion, and the number in brackets is the classification by the liberal criterion. The right-hand side of the table is an Index of Consensus, which, in this case, is the percentage of subjects who responded to that pair in the most popular manner. The values in the curve-type columns represented in the Index of Consensus are italicized.

A cursory examination of Table A-13 will reveal that in some instances there is good agreement among subjects on the nature of the relationship, but in some instances there are critical differences. The information in Table A-13 is needed to interpret the meaning of the 15 graphs of group means now to be considered.

*Complexity and Difficulty.* *Complexity* seems appropriate to a dimension of visual stimulation, whereas *difficulty* seems more appropriate to tasks the subject performs. Yet experimental subjects see the two dimensions as being very closely related. The plot of the group results in Figure A-2 is a monotonically increasing function with a small inflection at each end and an index of consensus of 48 for the first study (solid line). Actually, there is more agreement among subjects than either the shape of the curve or the index of consensus indicates. All six subjects who gave results classified as inverted-U-shaped functions did so by indicating that, for them, *undifferentiated* was not as easy as *very simple.* Four of the unclassified subjects were so labeled because they inflected the upper end or both ends of the scale for the terminal positions only. Thus, if the two end positions are ignored, the index of consensus would be 88 for a monotonically increasing relation between complexity and difficulty. In the second study, with the simplified *complexity* scale, 20 of 25 subjects gave a monotonically increasing

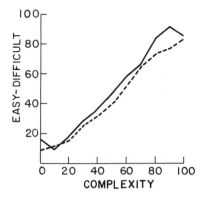

*FIGURE A-2. Structural Dimensions*

function by the strict criterion, and 23 of 25 (92%) by the liberal criterion. The results of this study are shown by the broken line in the figure. Thus, for most purposes, the words *complexity* and *difficulty* represent dimensions that are used interchangeably by subjects.

*Interrelations of Evaluative Terms.* Three evaluative dimensions were explored. *Pleasant* and *unpleasant* were chosen to represent the hedonic dimension, *boring* and *interesting* were added as a second evaluative scale because they are sometimes thought to be different in their connotation, and *approach* and *avoidance* were chosen to be the verbal equivalent of an overt behavior index of evaluation. All three relationships plotted in Figure A-3 are highly similar, monotonically increasing functions. The two that involve *pleasant* and *unpleasant* yield the highest indices of consensus obtained in this study, 84, while the relationship between *boring* and *interesting* and *approach* and *avoidance* yields an index of consensus of 72, which was the fourth highest of the 15 comparisons. Examination of the individual protocols reveals that all deviations from the simple monotonically increasing function were minor, in all but one instance involving a single value in the sequence of 11. Most of these resulted from an interpretation of the middle position on the scale, *neither pleasant nor unpleasant* or *neither boring nor interesting,* as not lying on the scale at all. With a less rigid criterion for consensus, all three indices of consensus would be 100. Thus, one can conclude, for most purposes, that *boring, unpleasant,* and *avoidance,* on the one hand, and *interesting, pleasant,* and *approach,* on the other, are essentially equivalent and do not justify differential theoretical treatment.

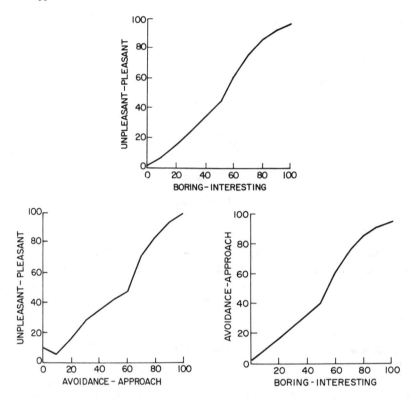

FIGURE A-3. *Evaluative Dimensions*

*Structural Variables versus Evaluative Variables.* Most theories of complexity and preference contain an expectation that complexity will be related to preference by an inverted-U-shaped function. This study of subject semantics permits an examination of whether experimental subjects also postulate such a relationship between structural and evaluative variables. The structural dimensions in this study were those involving *complexity* and *difficulty*, while the evaluative dimensions involve *pleasantness, interest,* and *approach/avoidance.*

The six relationships that are related to this problem are shown in Figure A-4. The solid lines show the results of the first study; the broken lines show the results of the second. All six appear to be inverted-U-shaped functions to some degree. However, there is very little agreement among experimental subjects. The data in Table A-13 indicate that more subjects see the relationship between each structural variable and the *boring/interesting* dimension as a monotonically increasing function than see it as an inverted-U-shaped function. The reverse is true with the other two evaluative functions,

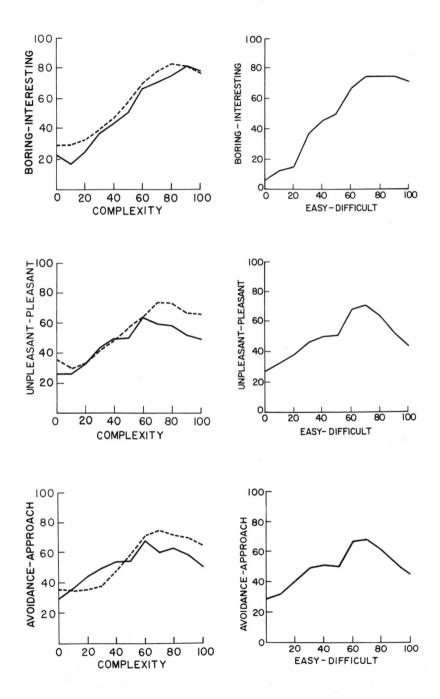

*FIGURE A-4. Structural versus Evaluative Dimensions*

*TABLE A-13.* Curve Types in Sematic Space

| Variable | Monotonic Increasing | Inverted-U-shaped | Monotonic Decreasing | Uncorrelated | Unclassified | Index of Consensus |
|---|---|---|---|---|---|---|
| Complexity Arousal | 13 (24) | 3 (0) | | | 9 (1) | 52 (96) |
| Complexity Easy/Difficult | 12 (22) | 6 (0) | | | 7 (3) | 48 (88) |
| Complexity Boring/Interesting | 8 (16) | 3 (6) | | 1 (1) | 11 (2) | 32 (64) |
| Complexity Pleasant/Unpleasant | 4 (5) | 8 (15) | | 2 (2) | 11 (3) | 32 (60) |
| Complexity Approach/Avoidance | 3 (7) | 5 (11) | 2 (3) | | 15 (4) | 20 (44) |
| Arousal Easy/Difficult | 16 (19) | 4 (4) | | | 5 (2) | 64 (76) |
| Arousal Boring/Interesting | 20 (25) | 1 (0) | | | 4 (0) | 80 (100) |
| Arousal Pleasant/Unpleasant | 14 (19) | 3 (4) | | 1 (1) | 7 (1) | 56 (76) |
| Arousal Approach/Avoidance | 15 (20) | 1 (2) | | | 9 (3) | 60 (80) |
| Easy/Difficult Boring/Interesting | 10 (13) | 9 (12) | | | 6 (0) | 40 (52) |
| Easy/Difficult Pleasant/Unpleasant | 5 (7) | 7 (12) | 2 (3) | 0 (1) | 11 (2) | 28 (48) |

| | | | | | |
|---|---|---|---|---|---|
| Easy/Difficult Approach/Avoidance | 4 (7) | 8 *(12)* | 4 (5) | 9 (1) | 32 (48) |
| Boring/Interesting Pleasant/Unpleasant | 21 (25) | 1 (0) | | 3 (0) | 84 (100) |
| Boring/Interesting Approach/Avoidance | 18 (25) | 2 (0) | | 5 (0) | 72 (100) |
| Pleasant/Unpleasant Approach/Avoidance | 21 (25) | | | 4 (0) | 84 (100) |

*pleasantness* and *approach/avoidance*, with more subjects seeing the relationships as inverted-U-shaped functions than monotonically increasing. It is also true that there are, within this set of six functions, a scattering of monotonically decreasing functions—subjects who see the *easy* end of the *difficulty* scale going with *approach* behavior and the *difficult* end going with *avoidance* behavior, for example. There are even a few who see one or more of the relationships as being uncorrelated and express the relationship with a horizontal line. In all six cases, the indices of consensus are quite low—32, 32, 20, 40, 28, and 32 in the cases of the strict criterion and 64, 60, 44, 52, 48, and 48 in the case of the more liberal criterion of classification. The second study yielded similar results. Thus, while the curves representing the group results appear to be inverted-U-shaped functions, the group curves are composed of individual curves that display considerable variety and a very low level of consensus.

*Arousal.* The theoretical concept of arousal has a degree of correspondence to the same word used in common speech. In fact, there may be less ambiguity concerning its meaning in common speech than there is in its theoretical meaning. For this reason, the dimension of *arousal* was included in this investigation of semantic relations in the language of experimental subjects. Figure A-5 portrays the relation of *arousal* to each of the other five dimensions. It seems somewhat remarkable that subjects tend strongly to see *arousal* as a monotonically increasing function of each of the other five. Examination of the information in Table A-13 indicates that there is very good agreement among subjects on the nature of the relationship. Low *arousal* goes with low *complexity, easy* problems, *unpleasantness, boredom,* and *avoidance.* High *arousal* is associated with high *complexity, difficulty, pleasantness, interestingness,* and *approach* behavior.

The similarity of the five relationships between the *arousal* dimension and the others constitutes something of an anomaly. If arousal level is highly correlated with the complexity level, as it is. in complexity and preference theory, then one would expect the monotonically increasing relationship between *arousal* and both the *complexity* and the *difficulty* dimensions, but one would also expect an inverted-U-shaped relation between *arousal* and the three evaluative dimensions. The latter expectation is not met. If, on the other hand, *arousal,* as used by experimental subjects, is essentially equivalent to the evaluative dimensions, one would expect monotonically increasing functions between arousal and each of the evaluative dimensions. This expectation *is* met in the relevant graphs. However, one would also expect inverted-U-shaped functions between *arousal* and the structural dimensions of *complexity* and

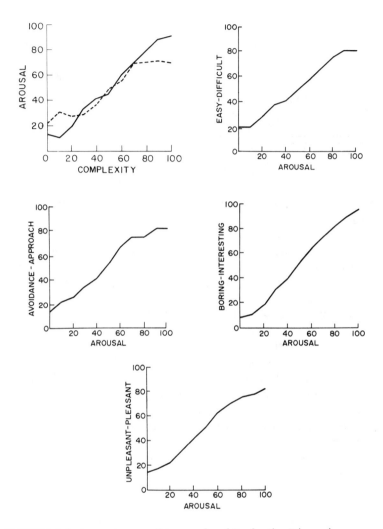

*FIGURE A-5. Arousal versus Structural and Evaluative Dimensions*

*difficulty.* This expectation is not met, thus, *arousal* appears to be an independent or orthogonal dimension.

### SUMMARY

The most general statements that can be used to summarize the results of this investigation of complexity and preference theory as seen by typical experimental subjects are portrayed in Figure A-6. In spite of some differences among them, there is sufficient commonness to the three evaluative dimensions, *pleasantness, interestingness,* and *approach/avoidance,* that they can be treated as a single evaluative dimension. There is sufficient similarity in the

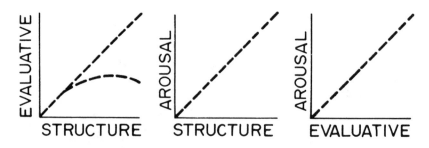

*FIGURE A-6. Summary Generalizations*

*complexity* and *difficulty* dimensions that they can be treated as a single structural dimension.

As illustrated in the figure, a significant number of subjects see the evaluative dimension as a monotonically increasing function of the structural dimension, while another significant portion of the subjects see the two related by an inverted-U-shaped function. In the language of experimental subjects, the energy variable, as represented by the word *arousal*, is a monotonically increasing function of both the structural and evaluative dimensions, and there is a high degree of consensus with respect to these relationships.

The results of these studies of the semantic space of experimental subjects were obtained in terms of the meanings of the words themselves and in the absence of experimental stimuli. Although they are possibly of intrinsic interest, the major purpose of these studies was to provide a basis for interpreting studies of complexity and preference that have already been carried out and reported, and for determining the language to be used in future studies.

*references*

Adelman, H. M., & Maatsch, J. L. Learning and extinction based upon frustration, food reward, and exploratory tendency. *Journal of Experimental Psychology,* 1956, *52,* 311–315.

Aeschbach, S. *Ratings of dichords along the continua of complexity-simplicity, consonance-dissonance, and pleasing-displeasing.* Honors dissertation, University of Michigan, 1975.

Amsel, A., & Roussel, J. Motivational properties of frustration: I. Effect on a running response of the addition of frustration to the motivational complex. *Journal of Experimental Psychology,* 1952, *43,* 363–368.

Anderson, J. H., & Bower, G. H. *Human associative memory.* Washington, D.C.: Hemisphere, 1974.

Applezweig (Appley), M. H. *The role of effort in learning and extinction.* Doctoral dissertation, University of Michigan, 1949.

Arkes, H. R. *The relationship between repetition and organization and the role of organization in psychological complexity.* Doctoral dissertation, University of Michigan, 1971.

Asch, G. E. A reformulation of the problem of associations. *American Psychologist,* 1969, *24,* 92–102.

Askew, H. R. *Effects of intertrial interval and stimulus intensity on habituation of the headshake response in rats.* Doctoral dissertation, Michigan State University, 1969.

Atkinson, J. W., & Birch, D. *The dynamics of action.* New York: Wiley, 1970.

Averbach, E., & Coriell, A. S. Short-term memory in vision. *Bell System Technical Journal,* 1961, *40,* 309–328.

Ayres, T. *Exploratory behavior with musical intervals as related to measures of consonance and dissonance.* Research paper, Amherst College, 1974.

Ayres, T. *Psychological and physiological factors in the consonance of musical intervals.* Honors dissertation, Amherst College, 1975.

Barker, R. G. *The stream of behavior.* New York: Appleton-Century-Crofts, 1963.

Barker, R. G., & Wright, H. F. *One boy's day.* New York: Harper, 1951.

Belmont, L., & Marolla, F. A. Birth order, family size, and intelligence. *Science,* 1973, *182,* 1096–1101.

Berlin, I. *The hedgehog and the fox: An essay on Tolstoy's view of history.* New York: Simon and Schuster, 1966.

Berlyne, D. E. *Conflict, arousal and curiosity.* New York: McGraw-Hill, 1960.

Berlyne, D. E. Curiosity and exploration. *Science,* 1966, *153,* 25–33.

Berlyne, D. E. The reward value of indifferent stimulation. In J. T. Tapp (Ed.), *Reinforcement and behavior.* New York: Academic Press, 1969.

Berlyne, D. E. *Psychobiology and aesthetics.* New York: Appleton-Century-Crofts, 1971.

Berlyne, D. E., & Madsen, K. B. (Eds.), *Pleasure, reward, preference.* New York: Academic Press, 1973.

Berlyne, D. E., & Peckham, S. The semantic differential and other measures of reaction to visual complexity. *Canadian Journal of Psychology,* 1966, *20,* 125–135.

Bloch, V., & Bonvallet, M. *Journal of Physiology, Paris,* 1959, *51,* 405.

Bloch, V., & Bonvallet, M. *Journal de Physiologie,* 1960, *52,* 25–26.

Boothe, B. E., Rosenfeld, A. H., & Walker, E. L. *Toward a science of psychiatry.* Monterey, Calif.: Brooks/Cole, 1974.

Boring, E. G., Langfeld, H. S., & Weld, H. P. *Psychology.* New York: Wiley, 1939.

Bower, G. H. Perceptual groups as coding units in immediate memory. *Psychonomic Science,* 1972, *27,* 217–219.

Bower, G. H., & Springston, F. Pauses as recoding points in letter series. *Journal of Experimental Psychology,* 1970, *83,* 421–430.

Bower, G. H., & Winzenz, D. Group structure, coding, and memory for digit series. *Journal of Experimental Psychology Monographs,* 1969, *80,* 1–17.

Boykin, A. W., Jr. *Verbally expressed preference and complexity judgments as they relate to levels of performance in a problem-solving situation.* Doctoral dissertation, University of Michigan, 1972.

Boykin, A. W. Verbally expressed preference and problem-solving proficiency. *Journal of Experimental Psychology: Human Perception and Performance,* 1977, *3,* 165–174. (a)

Boykin, A. W. Experimental psychology from a Black perspective. *Journal of Black Psychology,* 1977, *3,* 29–49. (b)

Breland, H. M. Data on effect of birth order and family size in National Merit Scholarship scores. *Child Development,* 1974, *45,* 1011. (a)

Breland, H. M. Birth order, family size, and intelligence. *Science,* 1974, *184,* 114. (b)

Brenner, R. Span of immediate recall. *Journal of Experimental Psychology,* 1940, *183,* 482–488.

Campbell, B. A., & Sheffield, F. D. Relation of random activity to food deprivation. *Journal of Comparative and Physiological Psychology,* 1953, *46,* 320–322.

Candland, D. K., & Campbell, B. A. Development of fear in the rat as measured by behavior in the open field. *Journal of Comparative and Physiological Psychology,* 1962, *55,* 593–596.

Carew, T. J., & Kandel, E. R. Acquisition and retention of long-term habituation in Aplysia: Correlation of behavioral and cellular processes. *Science,* 1973, *182,* 1158–1160.

Caron, R. F., & Caron, A. J. Degree of stimulus complexity and habituation of visual fixation in infants. *Psychonomic Science,* 1969, *14,* 78–79.

Chaitin, G. J. Randomness and mathematical proof. *Science,* 1975, *232,* 47–52.

Cleworth, P. A. *The role of electrical discharges in social behavior of Gymnotus carapo.* Paper presented at meetings of the American Society of Ichthyologists and Herpetologists, 1967.

Collins, W. E., & Updegraff, B. P. A comparison of nystagmus habituation in the cat and dog. *Acta Oto-laryngologica,* 1966, *62,* 19–26.

Coombs, C. H. *Theory of data.* New York: Wiley, 1964.

Coombs, C. H., Dawes, R. M., & Tversky, A. *Mathematical psychology.* Englewood, N.J.: Prentice-Hall, 1970.

Craik, F. I. M., & Lockhart, R. S. Levels of processing: A framework for memory research. *Journal of Verbal Learning and Verbal Behavior,* 1972, *11,* 671-684.

Crawford, J., Hunt, E., & Peak, G. Inverse forgetting in short-term memory. *Journal of Experimental Psychology,* 1966, *72,* 415-422.

Davis, H., Morgan, C. T., Hawkins, J. E., Jr., Galambos, R., & Smith, F. W. Temporary deafness following exposure to loud tones and noises. (Final report, 9-30-43.) *Acta Oto-laryngologica,* 1950, Supplement LXXXVIII.

Davis, M., & Wagner, A. R. Startle responsiveness after habituation to different intensities of tone. *Psychonomic Science,* 1968, *12,* 337-338.

Day, H. I. *Exploratory behavior as a function of individual differences and level of arousal.* Doctoral dissertation, University of Toronto, 1965.

Day, H. I., & Crawford, G. C. *Developmental changes in attitudes toward complexity.* Paper presented at meetings of the Society for Research in Child Development, Minneapolis, Minn.: 1971.

Dember, W. N., & Earl, R. W. Analysis of exploratory, manipulatory, and curiosity behavior. *Psychological Review,* 1957, *64,* 91-96.

Dement, W., & Wolpert, E. The relation of eye movement, body motility, and external stimuli to dream content. *Journal of Experimental Psychology,* 1958, *55,* 543-553.

Denenberg, V. H., Morton, J. R. C., Kline, N. J., & Grota, L. J. Effects of duration of infantile stimulation upon emotionality. *Canadian Journal of Psychology,* 1962, *16,* 72-76.

Denny, M. R., & Leckart, B. T. Alternation behavior: Learning and extinction one trial per day. *Journal of Comparative and Physiological Psychology,* 1965, *60,* 229-232.

DeValois, R. L. The relation of different levels and kinds of motivation to variability in behavior. *Journal of Experimental Psychology,* 1954, *47,* 392-398.

Dewsbury, D. A. *Some correlates of electric organ discharge frequency in three species of electric fishes.* Doctoral dissertation, University of Michigan, 1965.

Dewsbury, D. A. Stimulus-produced changes in discharge rate of an electric fish and their relation to arousal. *Psychological Record,* 1966, *16,* 495-504.

DiLollo, V., & Walker, E. L. Speed and basal resistance level in a segmented straight alley. *Psychological Record,* 1964, *14,* 499-505.

Drobisch, M. W. Über die mathematische Bestimmung der Musikalischen Intervale. In Fürstlich, *Jablonowskischen Gesellschaft der Wissenschaften.* Leipzig: Weidmann'sche Buchhandlung, 1846.

Duffy, E. *Activation and behavior.* New York: Wiley, 1962.

Eisenstein, E. M., & Peretz, B. Comparative analysis of habituation in invertebrates. In H. V. S. Peeke & M. J. Herz (Eds.), *Habituation* (Vol. II). New York: Academic Press, 1973.

Engle, R. Experimentelle Untersuchungen über die Abhängigkeit der Lust and Unlust von der Reizstärke beim Geschmackssinn. *Archiv gesamte Psychologie,* 1928, *64,* 1-36.

Estes, W. K. An experimental study of punishment. *Psychological Monographs,* 1944, *57,* Whole No. 263.

Farel, P. B. Post-transectional hyperexcitability and centrally mediated response decrements in the chronic spinal frog. Cited in Thompson, Groves, Teyler, & Roemer (1973).

Farel, P. B., & Thompson, R. F. Habituation and dishabituation to dorsal root stimulation in the isolated frog spinal cord. Cited in Thompson, Groves, Teyler, & Roemer (1973).

Ferraro, D. P., Silver, M. P., & Snapper, A. G. A method of cardiac recording from surface electrodes in rats during free-operant procedures. *Journal of the Experimental Analysis of Behavior,* 1965, *8,* 17–18.

Fox, S. Evoked potential habituation and sensory pattern preference as determined by stimulus information. *Journal of Comparative and Physiological Psychology,* 1964, *58,* 257–272.

Francès, R. *Le perception de la musique.* Paris: Vrin, 1958.

Frank, K., & Fuortes, M. G. F. Unitary activity of spinal interneurons of cats. *Journal of Physiology (London),* 1956, *131,* 424–436.

Franzisket, L. Characteristics of instinctive behavior and learning in reflex activity of the frog. *Animal Behavior,* 1963, *11,* 318–324.

Gardner, L. E. *Habituation in the earthworm: Retention and overhabituation.* Doctoral dissertation, Michigan State University, 1966.

Glanzer, M. The role of stimulus satiation in spontaneous alternation. *Journal of Experimental Psychology,* 1953, *45,* 387–393.

Glanzer, M., & Bowles, N. *Analysis of the word frequency effect in recognition memory.* Paper presented at meetings of the Psychonomic Society, Denver, Colo., 1974.

Graham, F. K. Habituation and dishabituation of responses innervated by the central nervous system. In H. V. S. Peeke & M. J. Herz (Eds.), *Habituation* (Vol. I). New York: Academic Press, 1973.

Grant, D. A., & Hake, H. W. Dark adaptation and the Humphreys' random reinforcement phenomenon in human eyelid conditioning. *Journal of Experimental Psychology,* 1952, *42,* 417–423.

Grant, D. A., Hake, H. W., & Hornseth, J. P. Acquisition and extinction of a verbal conditioned response with differing percentages of reinforcement. *Journal of Experimental Psychology,* 1951, *42,* 1–5.

Grant, D. A., & Schippler, L. M. The acquisition and extinction of conditioned eyelid responses as a function of percentage of fixed ratio random reinforcement. *Journal of Experimental Psychology,* 1952, *43,* 313–320.

Groves, P. M., Lee, D., & Thompson, R. F. Effects of stimulus frequency and intensity on habituation and sensitization in acute spinal cat. *Physiology and Behavior,* 1969, *4,* 383–388.

Groves, P. M., & Thompson, R. F. Habituation: A dual process theory. *Psychological Review,* 1970, *77,* 419–450.

Groves, P. M., & Thompson, R. F. A dual process theory of habituation: Neural mechanisms. In H. V. S. Peeke & M. J. Herz (Eds.), *Habituation* (Vol. II). New York: Academic Press, 1973.

Haber, R. N. How we remember what we see. *Scientific American,* 1970, *222* (5), 104–112. (a)

Haber, R. N. *Representation and processing of information from brief visual displays.* Paper presented at meeting of the Committee on Vision of the National Academy of Sciences—National Research Council, 1970. (b)

Haber, R. N. Where are the visions in visual imagery? In *Imagery, current cognitive approaches.* New York: Academic Press, 1971.

Haber, R. N., & Standing, L. Direct estimates of apparent duration of flash followed by visual noise. *Canadian Journal of Psychology,* 1970, *24,* 216–229.

Hagiwara, S., Kusano, K., & Negishi, K. Physiological properties of electro-receptors of some gymnotids. *Journal of Neurophysiology,* 1962, *25,* 430–449.

Hagiwara, S., Szabo, T., & Enger, P. S. Electroreceptor mechanisms in a high-frequency weakly electric fish, *Sternarchus albifrons. Journal of Neuro-physiology,* 1965, *28,* 784–795.

Hebb, D. O. *The organization of behavior.* New York: Wiley, 1949.

Hebb, D. O. Drives and the C. N. S. (conceptual nervous system). *Psychological Review,* 1955, *62,* 243–254.

Helmholtz, H. *On the sensation of tone as a physiological basis for a theory of music.* (Trans. Alexander Ellis.) London: Longmans, Green, 1875.

Helson, H. Adaptation-level theory. In S. Koch (Ed.), *Psychology: A study of a science.* New York: McGraw-Hill, 1959.

Helson, H. A common model for affectivity and perception: An adaptation-level approach. In D. E. Berlyne & K. B. Madsen (Eds.), *Pleasure, reward, preference.* New York: Academic Press, 1973.

Heyduk, R. G. *Static and dynamic aspects of rated and exploratory preference for musical compositions.* Doctoral dissertation, University of Michigan, 1972.

Heyduk, R. G. Rated preference of musical compositions as it relates to com-plexity and exposure frequency. *Perception and Psychophysics,* 1975, *17,* 84–91.

Hinde, R. A. Factors governing the changes in the strength of a partially inborn response, as shown by mobbing behavior in the chaffinch (III). *Proceed-ings of the Royal Society of Biology,* 1960, *153,* 398–420.

Hintzman, D. L. Theoretical implications of the spacing effect. In R. L. Solso (Ed.), *Theories of cognitive psychology.* New York: Wiley, 1974.

Hochberg, J. In the mind's eye. In R. N. Haber (Ed.), *Contemporary theory and research in visual perception.* New York: Holt, 1968.

Holder, W. B., Marx, M. H., Holder, E. E., & Collier, G. Response strength as a function of delay of reward in runway. *Journal of Experimental Psychol-ogy,* 1957, *53,* 316–323.

Hull, C. L. The goal gradient hypothesis and maze learning. *Psychological Re-view,* 1932, *39,* 25–43.

Hull, C. L. *A behavior system.* New Haven: Yale University Press, 1952.

Innes, T. *The tartan of the clans and families of Scotland.* Edinburgh and Lon-don: Johnson, 1938.

James, J. P., & Hughes, G. R. Generalization of habituation of the GSR to white noise of varying intensities. *Psychonomic Science,* 1969, *14,* 463–464.

James, W. *Principles of psychology* (Vol. 1). New York: Holt, 1890.

James, W. *Psychology (Briefer Course).* New York: Holt, 1893.

Johnson, N. F. Organization and the concept of the memory code. In A. W. Melton & E. Martin (Eds.), *Coding processes in human memory.* Wash-ington, D.C.: V. H. Winston & Sons, 1972.

Joyce, J. *Ulysses.* New York: Random House, 1961 (Originally published in 1914.)

Kaplan, R. *A new measure of motivation in rats.* Doctoral dissertation, Uni-versity of Michigan, 1962.

Kaplan, R. Rat basal resistance level under stress and nonstress conditions. *Journal of Comparative and Physiological Psychology,* 1963, *56,* 775–777.

Kaplan, S., & Hobart, J. L. A versatile device for the measurement of skin resistance in the rat and humans. *American Journal of Psychology*, 1964, 77, 309–310.

Kaplan, S., & Kaplan, R. Skin resistance recording in the unrestrained rat. *Science*, 1962, *138*, 1403–1404.

Keynes, R. D. Electric organs. In M. E. Brown (Ed.), *The physiology of fishes* (Vol. 2). New York: Academic Press, 1957.

Kimble, D. P., & Ray, R. S. Reflex habituation and potentiation in *Rana pipiens*. *Animal Behavior*, 1965, *13*, 530–533.

Kimble, G. A. Conditioning as a function of the time between conditioned and unconditioned stimuli. *Journal of Experimental Psychology*, 1947, *37*, 1–15.

Kintsch, W. *Learning, memory, and conceptual processes.* New York: Wiley, 1970.

Kleinsmith, L. J., & Kaplan, S. Paired associates learning as a function of arousal and interpolated interval. *Journal of Experimental Psychology*, 1963, *65*, 190–193.

Kleinsmith, L. J., & Kaplan, S. The interaction of arousal and recall interval in nonsense syllable paired associates learning. *Journal of Experimental Psychology*, 1964, *67*, 124–126.

Koepke, J. E., & Pribram, K. H. Habituation of GSR as a function of stimulus duration and spontaneous activity. *Journal of Comparative and Physiological Psychology*, 1966, *61*, 442–448.

Kreitler, H., & Kreitler, S. *Psychology of the arts.* Durham: Duke University Press, 1972.

Kristofferson, A. B. Successive discrimination as a two-state, quantal process. *Science*, 1967, *158*, 1337–1339.

Kroll, N. E. A., Parks, T., Parkinson, S. R., Bieber, S. L., & Johnson, A. L. Short-term memory while shadowing. Recall of visually and aurally presented letters. *Journal of Experimental Psychology*, 1970, *85*, 220–224.

Krueger, W. C. F. The relative difficulty of nonsense syllables. *Journal of Experimental Psychology*, 1934, *17*, 145–153.

Lacey, J. I. Somatic response patterning and stress: Some revisions of activation theory. In M. H. Appley & R. Turnbull (Eds.), *Psychological stress: Some issues in research.* New York: Appleton-Century-Crofts, 1967.

Lashley, K. S. The problem of serial order in behavior. In L. A. Jeffress (Ed.), *Cerebral mechanisms in behavior, The Hixon Symposium.* New York: Wiley, 1951.

Levine, S. Psychophysiological effects of infantile stimulation. In E. L. Bliss (Ed.), *Roots of behavior.* New York: Harper, 1962.

Liberman, A. M., Mattingly, I. G., & Turvey, M. T. Language codes and memory codes. In A. W. Melton & E. Martin (Eds.), *Coding processes in human memory.* Washington, D.C.: V. H. Winston & Sons, 1972.

Lipps, T. *Psychologische Studien.* Heidelberg: Weiss, 1885.

Lissmann, H. W. Electric location in fishes. *Scientific American*, 1963, *208-3*, 50–59.

Lissmann, H. W., & Machin, K. E. Mechanism of object location in *Gymnarchus niloticus* and similar fish. *Journal of Experimental Biology*, 1958, *35*, 451–486.

Lundin, R. W. Toward a cultural theory of consonance. *Journal of Psychology*, 1947, *23*, 45–49.

Lykken, D. T. Properties of electrodes used in electrodermal measurements. *Journal of Comparative and Physiological Psychology*, 1959, *52*, 629–634.

Mackworth, J. F. *Vigilance and habituation: A neurophysiological approach.* Baltimore: Penguin, 1969.

Mackworth, N. H., & Morandi, A. J. The gaze selects informative details within pictures. *Perception and Psychophysics*, 1967, *2*, 547–552.

Mackworth, N. H., & Otto, D. A. Habituation of the visual orienting response in young children. *Perception and Psychophysics*, 1970, *7*, 173–178.

Malmberg, C. F. The perception of consonance and dissonance. *Psychological Monographs*, 1918, *25*, No. 2, 93–133.

Malmo, R. B. Activation: A neurophysiological dimension. *Psychological Review*, 1959, *66*, 367–386.

Mandler, G. Organization and memory. In R. L. Solso (Ed.), *Theories of cognitive psychology.* New York: Wiley, 1974.

Marler, P. & Hamilton, J. H., III. *Mechanisms of animal behavior.* New York: Wiley, 1966.

Marshall, H. Learning as a function of task interest, reinforcement and social class variables. *Journal of Educational Psychology*, 1969, *60*, 133–137.

Marzulli, F. N., & Callahan, J. F. The capacity of certain laboratory animals to sweat. *Journal of the American Veterinary Medical Association*, 1957, *131*, 80–81.

McClelland, D. C., Atkinson, J. W., Clark, R. A., & Lowell, E. L. (Eds.), *The achievement motive.* New York: Appleton-Century-Crofts, 1953.

McClelland, D. C., & Clark, R. A. Antecedent conditions for affective arousal. In D. C. McClelland, J. W. Atkinson, R. A. Clark, & E. L. Lowell (Eds.), *The achievement motive.* New York: Appleton-Century-Crofts, 1953.

McLean, R. S., & Gregg, L. W. Effects of induced chunking on temporal aspects of serial recitation. *Journal of Experimental Psychology*, 1967, *74*, 455–459.

Melton, A. W. Implications of short-term memory for a general theory of memory. *Journal of Verbal Learning and Verbal Behavior*, 1963, *2*, 1–21.

Melton, A. W. The situation with respect to the spacing of repetitions in memory. *Journal of Verbal Learning and Verbal Behavior*, 1970, *9*, 596–606.

Melton, A. W., & Martin, E. *Coding processes in human memory.* Washington, D.C.: V. H. Winston & Sons, 1972.

Miller, G. A. The magic number seven, plus or minus two: some limits on our capacity to process information. *Psychological Review*, 1956, *63*, 81–97.

Miller, G. A. English verbs of motion: A case study in semantics and lexical memory. In A. W. Melton & E. Martin (Eds.), *Coding processes in human memory.* Washington, D.C.: V. H. Winston & Sons, 1972.

Miller, G. A., & Selfridge, J. Verbal context and recall of meaningful material. *American Journal of Psychology*, 1950, *63*, 176–185.

Miller, J. G. Adjusting to overloads of information. In D. Rioch & E. Weinstein (Eds.), *Disorders of communication.* Baltimore: Williams and Wilkins, 1964.

Miller, R. R., & Springer, A. D. Amnesia, consolidation and retrieval. *Psychological Review*, 1973, *80*, 69–79.

Montgomery, K. C. Exploratory behavior and its relation to spontaneous alternation in a series of maze exposures. *Journal of Comparative and Physiological Psychology*, 1952, *45*, 50–57.

Moore, H. T. The genetic aspects of consonance and dissonance. *Psychological Monographs*, 1914, *17*, No. 2, 1–68.

Moray, N. Attention in dichotic listening: Affective cues and the influence of instructions. *Quarterly Journal of Experimental Psychology*, 1957, *9*, 56–60.

Mortenson, F. J. *Determinants of electrical discharge rate in Gymnotus carapo, the banded knife fish.* Doctoral dissertation, University of Michigan, 1969.

Moruzzi, G., & Magoun, H. W. Brain stem reticular formation and activation of the EEG. *Electroencephalography and Clinical Neurophysiology*, 1949, *1*, 455–473.

Mowrer, O. H. On the dual nature of learning—a reinterpretation of "conditioning" and "problem-solving." *Harvard Educational Review*, 1947, *17*, 102–148.

Mowrer, O. H., & Jones, H. Habit strength as a function of pattern of reinforcement. *Journal of Experimental Psychology*, 1945, *35*, 293–311.

Murdock, B. B., Jr. Four channel effects in short-term memory. *Psychonomic Science*, 1971, *24*, 197–198.

Neisser, U. Visual search. *Scientific American*, 1964, *210-2*, 94–102.

Neisser, U. *Cognitive psychology.* New York: Appleton, 1967.

Newell, A., & Simon, H. A. *Human problem solving.* New York: Prentice-Hall, 1972.

Nice, M. M., & Pelkwyk, J. J. ter. Enemy recognition by song sparrows. *Auk*, 1941, *58*, 195–214.

Nobel, C. E. The meaning-familiarity relationship. *Psychological Review*, 1953, *60*, 89–98.

Norman, D. A. Memory while shadowing. *Quarterly Journal of Experimental Psychology*, 1969, *21*, 85–93.

Norman, D. A., & Rumelhart, D. E. *Explorations in cognition.* San Francisco: Freeman, 1975.

Norton, S. On the discontinuous nature of behavior. *Journal of Theoretical Biology*, 1968, *21*, 229–243.

Olson, M. H. *Complexity, preference and information processing rate.* Doctoral dissertation, University of Michigan, 1977.

Osgood, C. E. The nature and measurement of meaning. *Psychological Bulletin*, 1952, *49*, 197–237.

Osgood, C. E., Suci, G. J., & Tannenbaum, P. H. *The measurement of meaning.* Urbana: University of Illinois Press, 1957.

Paivio, A. Mental imagery in associative learning and memory. *Psychological Review*, 1969, *76*, 241–263.

Peeke, H. V. S. Habituation of conspecific aggression in the three-spined stickleback (*Gasterosteus aculeatus L.*). *Behavior*, 1969, *36*, 137–156.

Peeke, H. V. S., & Herz, M. J. *Habituation. Vol. I., Behavioral studies; Vol. II, Physiological substrates.* New York: Academic Press, 1973.

Peirce, C. S. The treatise of Petrus Peregrinus on the lodestone. In A. W. Burks (Ed.), *Collected papers of Charles Peirce* (Vol. VII). Cambridge: Harvard University Press, 1932.

Peterson, L. R., Wampler, R., Kirkpatrick, M., & Saltzman, D. Effects of spacing presentations on retention of a paired associate over short intervals. *Journal of Experimental Psychology*, 1963, *66*, 206–209.

Petrinovich, L. A species-meaningful analysis of habituation. In H. V. S. Peeke &

M. J. Herz (Eds.), *Habituation* (Vol. I). New York: Academic Press, 1973.

Pfaffman, C. Taste preference and reinforcement. In J. T. Tapp (Ed.), *Reinforcement and behavior*. New York: Academic Press, 1969.

Phillips, W. A., & Baddeley, A. D. Reaction time and short-term visual memory. *Psychonomic Science*, 1971, *22*, 73–74.

Pickett, W. An experiment in response by different temperament types to different styles of stage set design. Doctoral dissertation, University of Michigan, 1970.

Pillsbury, W. B. *Journal of Philosophy*, 1913, *10*, 181–185.

Pinsker, H. M., Hening, W. A., Carew, T. J., & Kandel, E. R. Long term sensitization of a defensive withdrawal reflex in Aplysia. *Science*, 1973, *182*, 1039–1042.

Plomp, R., & Levelt, W. J. M. Tonal consonance and critical bandwidth. *Journal of the Acoustical Society of America*, 1965, *38*, 548–560.

Posner, M. I. Abstraction and the process of recognition. In G. H. Bower & J. T. Spence (Eds.), *The psychology of learning and motivation: Advances in research and theory* (Vol. III). New York: McGraw-Hill, 1969.

Posner, M. I., & Boies, S. J. Components of attention. *Psychological Review*, 1971, *78*, 391–408.

Posner, M. I., & Warren, R. E. Traces, concepts, and conscious constructions. In A. W. Melton & E. Martin, *Coding processes in human memory*. Washington, D.C.: V. H. Winston & Sons, 1972.

Pribram, K. H. *Languages of the brain*. Englewood Cliffs, N. J.: Prentice-Hall, 1971.

Pritchard, R. M., Heron, W., & Hebb, D. O. Visual perception approached by the method of stabilized images. *Canadian Journal of Psychology*, 1960, *14*, 67–77.

Pylyshyn, Z. W. What the mind's eye tells the mind's brain: A critique of mental imagery. *Psychological Bulletin*, 1973, *80*, 1–24.

Raskin, D. C., Kotses, H., & Bever, J. Autonomic indicators of orienting and defensive reflexes. *Journal of Experimental Psychology*, 1969, *80*, 423–433.

Ratner, S. C. Habituation: Research and theory. In J. H. Reynierse (Ed.), *Current issues in animal learning*. Lincoln: University of Nebraska Press, 1970.

Record, R. G., McKeown, T., & Edwards, J. H. An investigation of the difference in measured intelligence between twins and single births. *Annals of the Human Genetic Society*, 1970, *34*, 11–20.

Restle, F. Critique of pure memory. In R. L. Solso (Ed.), *Theories of cognitive psychology*. New York: Wiley, 1974.

Reynolds, B. The magnitude of the trace conditioned response as a function of the magnitude of the stimulus trace. *Journal of Experimental Psychology*, 1945, *35*, 15–30.

Richter, C. P. Symposium: Contributions of psychology to the understanding of problems of personality and behavior. IV. Biological foundations of personality differences. In N. L. Munn, *Handbook of psychological research in the rat*. Cambridge, Mass.: Houghton Mifflin, 1950.

Routtenberg, A. The two-arousal hypothesis: Reticular formation and limbic system. *Psychological Review*, 1968, *75*, 51–80.

Ruckmick, C. A. A new classification of tonal qualities. *Psychological Review,* 1929, *36,* 172–180.

Sales, S. M. Stimulus complexity as a determinant of approach behavior and inspection time in the hooded rat. *Canadian Journal of Psychology/ Review of Canadian Psychology,* 1968, *22,* 11–17.

Schneirla, T. C. An evolutionary and developmental theory of biphasic processes underlying approach and withdrawal. In M. R. Jones (Ed.), *Nebraska symposium on motivation.* Lincoln: University of Nebraska Press, 1959.

Schneirla, T. C. Aspects of stimulation and organization in approach-with-drawal processes underlying vertebrate behavior development. In D. L. Lehrman, R. Hinde, & E. Shaw (Eds.), *Advances in the study of behavior.* New York: Academic Press, 1965.

Scott, J. P., Jr. *Complex spontaneous behavior in the rat.* Doctoral dissertation, University of Michigan, 1972.

Sharpless, S., & Jasper, H. Habituation and the arousal reaction. *Brain,* 1956, *LXXIX,* Part IV, 655–681.

Shepard, R. N. Circularity in judgments of relative pitch. *Journal of the Acoustical Society of America,* 1964, *36,* 2346–2353.

Shepard, R. N. Recognition memory for words, sentences and pictures. *Journal of Verbal Learning and Verbal Behavior,* 1967, *6,* 156–163.

Shepard, R. N. In discussion. In R. L. Solso (Ed.), *Theories of cognitive psychology.* New York: Wiley, 1974.

Simon, H. A. How big is a chunk? *Science,* 1974, *183,* 482–488.

Sinclair, K. *Optimal complexity and aesthetic preference.* Honors dissertation, University of Michigan, 1967. (Also cited in Walker, 1969b.)

Snyder, R. E., & Papsdorf, J. D. The interaction of ITI interpolated stimuli and ISI on classical conditioning of the nictitating membrane response of the rabbit. *Psychonomic Science,* 1968, *12,* 191–192.

Sokolov, E. N. In M. A. Mrazier (Ed.), *The central nervous system and behavior, transactions of the third conference.* Josiah Macy, Jr. Foundation, 1960.

Sokolov, E. N. *Perception and the conditioned reflex.* New York: Macmillan, 1963.

Spence, K. W. *Behavior theory and conditioning.* New Haven: Yale University Press, 1956.

Sperling, G. The information available in brief visual presentations. *Psychological Monographs,* 1960, *74,* No. 11.

Stebbins, W. C., Clark, W. W., Pearson, R. D., & Weiland, N. G. Noise-and-drug-induced hearing loss in monkeys. *Advances in Oto-Rhino-Larynogology,* 1973, *20,* 42–63.

Stumpf, C. *Tonepsychologie.* Leipzig: Hirzel, 1883.

Szalai, A. (Ed.), in collaboration with Converse, P. E., Feldheim, P., Scheuch, E. K., & Stone, P. J. *The use of time. Daily activities of urban and suburban populations in twelve countries.* The Hague, Paris: Mouton, 1972.

Tabah, L., & Sutter, J. IQ scores of twins. *Annals of Human Genetics,* 1954, *19,* 120.

Taylor, C. A. *The physics of musical sounds.* New York: American Elsevier, 1965.

Terhardt, E. Pitch, consonance, and harmony. *Journal of the Acoustical Society of America,* 1974, *55,* 1061–1068.

Thomas, H. Preferences for random shapes: Ages six through nineteen years. *Child Development*, 1966, *37*, 843-859.

Thomas, H. Spatial models and multidimensional scaling of random shapes. *American Journal of Psychology*, 1968, *81*, 551-558.

Thomas, H. Pattern variability and numerosity as determinants of individual preference in children and adults. *Child Development*, 1969, *40*, 1155-1166.

Thomas, H. Discrepancy hypothesis: Methodological and theoretical considerations. *Psychological Review*, 1971, *78*, 249-259.

Thompson, R. F., Groves, P. M., Teyler, T. J., & Roemer, R. A. A dual-process theory of habituation: Theory and behavior. In H. V. S. Peeke & M. J. Herz (Eds.), *Habituation*, Vol. I. New York: Academic Press, 1973.

Thompson, R. F., & Spencer, W. A. Habituation: A model phenomenon for the study of neuronal substrates of behavior. *Psychological Review*, 1966, *73*, 16-43.

Thorndike, E. L., & Lorge, I. *The teacher's word book of 30,000 words.* New York: Teacher's College, 1944.

Timberlake, W. D. *An analysis of exploration, grooming, and pausing in the rat.* Doctoral dissertation, University of Michigan, 1969.

Turvey, M. T. Repetition and preperceptual information store. *Journal of Experimental Psychology*, 1967, *74*, 289-293.

Underwood, B. J. Some correlates of item repetition in free recall learning. *Journal of Verbal Learning and Verbal Behavior*, 1969, *8*, 83-94.

Underwood, B. J. Are we overloading memory? In A. W. Melton & E. Martin (Eds.), *Coding processes in human memory.* Washington, D.C.: V. H. Winston & Sons, 1972.

Underwood, B. J., & Schulz, R. W. *Meaningfulness and verbal learning.* New York: Lippincott, 1960.

VanDeventer, J. M. *Responses to repeated tactile stimulation in the planarian, Dugesia tigrina.* Doctoral dissertation, Michigan State University, 1967.

Verveer, E. M., Barry, H., Jr., & Bousfield, W. A. Change in affectivity with repetition. *American Journal of Psychology*, 1933, *45*, 130-134.

Vitz, P. C. Preference for different amounts of visual complexity. *Behavioral Sciences*, 1966, *11*, 105-114.

Wachs, T., Uzgirls, I., & Hunt, J. McV. Cognitive development in infants of different age levels and from different environmental backgrounds: An exploratory investigation. *Merrill-Palmer Quarterly*, 1971, *17*, 283-316.

Walker, B. E., & Walker, E. L. Learning, extinction and relearning of running and BRL in a segmented straight alley. *Psychological Record*, 1964, *14*, 507-513.

Walker, E. L. The duration and course of the reaction decrement and the influence of reward. *Journal of Comparative and Physiological Psychology*, 1956, *49*, 167-176.

Walker, E. L. Action decrement and its relation to learning. *Psychological Review*, 1958, *65*, 129-142.

Walker, E. L. Psychological complexity as a basis for a theory of motivation and choice. In D. Levine (Ed.), *Nebraska symposium on motivation.* Lincoln: University of Nebraska Press, 1964.

Walker, E. L. Arousal and the memory trace. In D. P. Kimble (Ed.), *The organization of recall.* New York: New York Academy of Science, 1967.

Walker, E. L. Reinforcement—"The one ring." In J. T. Tapp (Ed.), *Reinforcement and behavior.* New York: Academic Press, 1969. (a)

Walker, E. L. *Stimulus-produced arousal patterns and learning.* Final Report, HD 00904 1-8. Ann Arbor: Department of Psychology, University of Michigan, 1969. (b)

Walker, E. L. Complexity and preference in animals and men. *Annals of the New York Academy of Sciences,* 1970, *169,* 619–652.

Walker, E. L. Psychological complexity and preference: A hedgehog theory of behavior. In D. E. Berlyne & K. B. Madsen (Eds.), *Pleasure, reward and preference.* New York: Academic Press, 1973. (a)

Walker, E. L. Arousal potential and Beethoven's fifth symphony. Review of D. E. Berlyne, Aesthetics and psychobiology. *Contemporary Psychology,* 1973, *18,* 363–364. (b)

Walker, E. L., Cohen, Avis H., & Doyle, C. L. Skin resistance in relation to stimulus change and estrus in rats. *Psychological Record,* 1964, *14,* 25–29.

Walker, E. L., Dember, W. N., Earl, R. W., Fawl, C. L., & Karoly, A. J. Choice alternation: III. Response intensity versus response discriminability. *Journal of Comparative and Physiological Psychology,* 1955, *48,* 80–85.

Walker, E. L., Dember, W. N., Earl, R. W., & Karoly, A. J. Choice alternation I. Stimulus versus place versus response. *Journal of Comparative and Physiological Psychology,* 1955, *48,* 19–23.

Walker, E. L., Knotter, M. C., & DeValois, R. L. Drive specificity and learning: The acquisition of a spatial response to food under conditions of water deprivation and food satiation. *Journal of Experimental Psychology,* 1950, *40,* 161–168.

Walker, E. L., & Motoyoshi, R. The effects of amount of reward and distribution of practice on active and inactive memory traces. *Journal of Comparative and Physiological Psychology,* 1962, *55,* 32–36.

Walker, E. L., & Paradise, N. E. A positive correlation between action decrement and learning. *Journal of Experimental Psychology,* 1958, *56,* 45–47.

Walker, E. L., & Tarte, R. D. Memory storage as a function of arousal and time with homogeneous and heterogeneous lists. *Journal of Verbal Learning and Verbal Behavior,* 1963, *2,* 113–119.

Walker, E. L., & Walker, B. E. Response to stimulus complexity in the rat. *Psychological Record,* 1964, *14,* 489–497.

Wall, P. D. Repetitive discharge of neurons. *Journal of Neurophysiology,* 1959, *22,* 305–320.

Weems, L. B., Jr., & Walker, E. L. Speed and basal resistance level (BRL) in a segmented straight alley as a function of alteration of stimuli, gentling, and isolation. *Psychological Record,* 1964, *14,* 515–519.

Weiner, B., & Walker, E. L. Motivational factors in short-term retention. *Journal of Experimental Psychology,* 1966, *71,* 190–193.

Wellek, A. *Musikpsychologie and Musikästhetik.* Frankfort: Akademische Verlagsgesellschaft, 1963.

Wester, K. Habituation to electrical stimulation of the thalamus in unanesthesized cats. *Electroencephalography and Clinical Neurophysiology,* 1971, *30,* 52–61.

Whiteman, M., & Deutsch, M. Social disadvantage as related to intellective and language development. In M. Deutsch, A. Jenson, & I. Katz (Eds.), *Social class, race and psychological development.* New York: Holt, Rinehart & Winston, 1968.

Wickens, D. D. Characteristics of word encoding. In A. W. Melton & E. Martin (Eds.), *Coding processes in human memory*. Washington, D.C.: V. H. Winston & Sons, 1972.

Williams, H. L. The problem of defining depth of sleep. In *Sleep and altered states of consciousness*, Association for Research in Nervous and Mental Diseases, Vol. XLV. Baltimore: Williams & Wilkins, 1967.

Williams, H. L., & Williams, C. L. Nocturnal EEG profiles and performance. *Psychophysiology*, 1966, *3*, 164–175.

Williams, J. L. *The role of response contingency on the effects of punishment: I. A review of relevant theories and empirical findings. II. An experimental investigation of the changes in skeletal and autonomic responses*. Doctoral dissertation, University of Michigan, 1968.

Williams, J. L. Response contingency and effects of punishment: Changes in autonomic and skeletal responses. *Journal of Comparative and Physiological Psychology*, 1969, *68*, 118–125.

Wohlwill, J. F. *Developmental evidence of differences between specific and diversive exploration*. Paper presented at meetings of the Society for Research in Child Development, Minneapolis, Minn.: 1971.

Woodworth, R. S. *Experimental psychology*, New York: Holt, 1938.

Wundt, W. *Grundzüge der physiologischen Psychologie*. Leipzig: Engleman, 1874.

Zajonc, R. B. Attitudinal effects of mere exposure. *Journal of Personality and Social Psychology, Monograph Supplements*, 1968, *9*, No. 2, Part 2.

Zajonc, R. B. Family configuration and intelligence. *Science*, 1976, *192*, 227–236.

Zajonc, R. B., & Marcus, G. G. Birth order and intellectual development. *Psychological Review*, 1975, *82*, 74–88.

Zwicker, E., Flottorp, G., & Stevens, S. S. Critical bandwidth in loudness summation. *Journal of the Acoustical Society of America*, 1957, *29*, No. 5.

# index

Academic achievement, 474–486
Academic progress, nature of, 475–476
Action decrement, 121–122
Activation theory, 287
Adaptation level, 277
Adaptation theory, 27
Adelman, H. M., 352
Aeschbach, S., 452, 454, 457–461, 467
Aesthetics, 400–438
  analysis versus synthesis, 400–401
  animals (visual), 435–438
  cognitive tasks, 434–435
  diversity and unity, 404
  experience, 407–409
  Hedgehog integration, 406
  melodies, 439–445
  modality and time, 404–405
  multi-level structure, 402–403
  music, 439–472
  products, 401
  reality/irreality, 403–404
  response, determiners of, 409–410
  usefulness, 401–402
Agouti hooded rats, 299
Alphabetic (letter) frequency, 146–148, 151–156, 158–166, 169–170, 175–176
Alternation phenomena, 70, 108, 110, 123–124
  restart, 119
Amsel, A., 352
Anagram task, 238–245
Anderson, J. H., 200, 208, 210, 214–215, 249, 251
Appley, M. H., 123–124
Approach-approach conflict, arousal, 384–386
A priori complexity, 6, 17, 440–441
Archilocus, 2
Arkes, H. R., 211–212, 245–248, 444–445, 522

Arousal:
  approach-approach conflict, 384–386
  autonomic, 291
  avoidance-avoidance conflict, 384–386
  behavioral, 291
  biological drives, 326–337
  boredom, 304–305
  coordination of empirical and theoretical, 21–24
  definition, 8, 285
  developmental differences, 320–321
  discriminated operant, 352–353
  diurnal cycle, 300–303
  early experience effects, 321–322
  electric fish, 269–299
  electrocortical, 291
  empirical studies of, 292–299
    variable, 287–292
  estrus, 326–328
  fear reduction, 338–339
  fixed ratio reward, 354–358
  goal gradient, 358–372
  handling, 305–307
  Hedgehog conception, 285–349
  hunger, 328–330
  individual differences, 9, 319
  incentive, 337–347
    short-term memory, 389–391
  interaction with complexity/preference, 8, 286
  jag, 409
  learning, 350–399
  levels of sleep, 289–291
  long-term memory, 391–392
  manipulated, and learning, 382–384
  operant performance, 351–358
  optimal theory, vii, 287
  performance, 350–399
  selective breeding, 322–324

Arousal (*continued*)
  sex, 319–320
  shock-induced fear, 330–337
  stimulus change, 307–316
  theoretical variable, 286–287
  thirst, 328–330
    reduction, 339–340
  verbal learning, 388–399
  weight, 316–319
Asch, G. E., 210
Askew, H. R., 89
A-system (approach), 271
Atkinson, J. W., 46–49, 119
Attention, 205
  span of, 62
Autarkic motivation, 196, 476–477,
  510
Automatic functions, 203–222
  complexity reduction, 203–205
  processing, 201
  trace vulnerability and accessibility,
    218–222
Autonomic arousal, 291
Averbach, E., 58
Avoidance-avoidance conflict, and
  arousal, 384–386
Avoidance conditioning, 139–140
Ayres, T., 452–461, 467

Baddeley, A. D., 201
*bæg*, 232
Barker, R. G., 5, 35, 40–42, 44,
  50, 267
Barry, H., 106–107, 140
Behavioral arousal, 291
Behavioral indices of complexity, 20
Belmont, L., 490
Ben Franklin effect, 491
Bergez, J., x
Berlin, I., 2
Berlyne, D. E., vii, ix, 30–32, 267,
  271, 287, 400, 404, 407, 441,
  448, 451, 476, 527
Bever, J., 73, 88
Bigram frequency, 148–151, 170,
  175
Binet, A., 482
Biological drives, arousal, 326–337
Biological motives, 266
  and complexity, 130–131

Birch, D., 46–49, 119
Bloch, V., 293
Boies, S. J., 61
Bonvallet, M., 293
Boothe, B. E., ix
Bootstrapping school quality, 511–
  512
Boredom, 12
  in rats, 304–305, 309
Boring, E. G., 280
Bousfield, W. A., 106–107, 140
Bower, G. H., 200, 208, 210, 214–
  215, 249, 251
Bowles, N., 208–209
Boykin, A. W., x, 113–114, 238–
  245, 434, 437, 495–496, 522
Breland, H. M., 490
Brenner, R., 253
BRL (Basal Resistance Level)
  boredom, in rats, 304–305, 309
  conditioning of, 372–382
  definition, 299
  developmental differences, 320–
    321
  dissociation from speed, 362–365
  early experience, 321–322
  estrus in rats, 307–308, 326–328
  food reward, monkey, 340–342
  handling, 305–307
  individual differences, 319
  learning, extinction, relearning,
    365–368
  selective breeding, 322–324
  sex differences, 319–320
  stimulus change, 307–316, 362–
    365
  typical values, 299
  weight, 316–319
Buda, C., ix
Butter, C. M., 340–342

Caldwell, J., 113–114
Callahan, J. F., 293
Campbell, B. A., 320, 328
Candland, D. K., 320
Carew, T. J., 288
Caron, A. J., 90, 95
Caron, R. F., 90, 95
Center for Advanced Study in the
  Behavioral Sciences, ix

Central Processor, 129, 197–203
  capacity, 200–202
  capacity-retrieval demands, 230–233
  consciousness, 279
  how to stuff, 228–230
  role of, 198–203
  structure of system, 202–203
Chaitin, G. J., 16
Choice:
  free, 53–54, 62, 108
  limits of, 51–54
Choice behavior, 129, 197–198, 223–224
Chunking, 231–263
  definition, 234
  during learning, 245–248
  immediate memory span, 253–258
  within and between complexities, 251–253
Clark, R. A., 27, 277
Clark, W. W., 466
Class:
  heterogeneity, 508–509
  size, 506–508
Classification, memory, 231
Cleworth, P. A., 297
Coding, 205
  empty container, 230
  variability, 220–222
Cohen, A. H., 308, 326–327
Collier, G., 352
Collins, W. E., 80
Complexity:
  affectivity, 174
  frequency, 166
  intensity, 56
  reduction, automatic, 203–205
Complexity/consonance
  reconceptualized, 461–462
Complexity scales:
  a priori, 17, 441
  behavioral, 20
  consensual, 17, 441
  neurophysiological, 20–21
  physical, 16–17
  psychological, 15
  stimulus, 15
  subjective, 17, 441
Complication, 71, 80, 82–108, 237

Concept formation, 206–207
Conceptual nervous system, 287
Conditioning, 61–62
  heart rate and BRL, 376–382
  skin resistance, 372–382
*Conflict, Arousal and Curiosity*, vii
Consciousness, 199–200
  central processor, 279
  processing, 201
Consensual complexity, 17, 441
  definition, 6
Consolidation, 220–222
Consonance/dissonance, 445–471
  definition, 445
  ear dominance, 461
  preference, 457–461
  reconceptualized, 450–454
  simplicity/complexity, 457
Constraints:
  environmental, 8, 50–51
  programmatic, 8, 50–51
Coombs, C. H., 26–27, 440
Coriell, A. S., 58
Craik, F. I. M., 201, 216
Crawford, G. C., 31
Crawford, J., 252
Critical band width, 447

Data analysis, problems of, 24–33
Data realms (behavioral, neurophysiological, verbal), 18–21
Davis, H., 466
Davis, M., 93
Dawes, R. M., 26–27
DAXES problem, 248–251
Day, H. I., 31
Decision theory:
  classical economic, 224–225
  psychological, 224–228
Defensive reaction, 87
Dember, W. N., vii, 125
Dement, W., 289–290
Denenberg, V. H., 321
Denny, M. R., 81
Depth of sleep, 289–291
Determinism, 198–199
Deutsch, M., 490
DeValois, R. L., 117–121
Development:
  effectiveness of information

Development (*continued*)
  sources, 487–488
  intellectual, 482, 487–496
  parents, 489
  peers, 489
  television, 488–489
Developmental differences, 9
  arousal, 320–321
Dewey, R., x
Dewsbury, D. A., x, 72, 90, 296–
  301, 307–309, 312–313, 320–
  324, 328–330, 332, 334–336,
  339–341, 344–346, 373–374
Differential experience (factor in
  consonance), 454, 461, 464–465,
  467–471
DiLollo, V., 358–361, 364–365, 369
Discrepancy theory, 27, 277
Discriminated operant, arousal,
  352–353
Discrimination learning, manipulated
  arousal, 382–384
Dishabituation, 94–95
Dissonance: *see* Consonance/
  dissonance
Distality, 453–454, 461, 464–467,
  469–471
Diurnal cycle, arousal, 300–303
Diversive exploration, 31–32
Doyle, C. L., x, 308, 326–327
Drobisch, M. W., 451
Drop-out problem, 509–510
Duffy, E., 320
*Dynamics of Action, The*, 46–49

Earl, R. W., vii, 125, 139
Early experience effect on BRL,
  321–322
Ebbinghaus, H., 245
Echo, 206
ECS, 218
Education:
  efficiency, 505–506
  Hedgehog strategy, 497
  ideal institution, 486–487
  policy, 496–513
  as a three-Hedgehog game, 500–
    503
  without teachers, 510–511
Edwards, J. H., 491
Effort, effect on latency, 123–124

Ehrlich, N., ix
Einstein, A., 1, 230
Eisenstein, E. M., 74
Elaboration, 237, 497–500
Electric fish, 296–299
Electrocortical arousal, 291
Empirical language, 15–17, 21–24
Empty container codes, 230
Energetic variables, 21–24
Enger, P. S., 297
Engle, R., 280–281
Environmental constraints, 8, 50–51
Equations:
  complexity and affectivity, 190–
    191
  educational efficiency, 505–506
  learning, 131–132, 143–144
  stimulus trace decay, 67
Erasmus, 2
Erskine, J., 395, 397
Estes, W. K., 382
Estrus in the rat, 307–308, 326–
  328
Evaluative variables, 21–24
Experience, effect on animals, 133–
  140
Experimental extinction:
  arousal, 365–368
  as learning, 96
Experimental stimuli, number of,
  26–27
Experimentation, problems of,
  24–33
Explanation, 497–500
Exploration:
  diversive, 31–32, 527
  extrinsic, 476
  haptic, 276
  intrinsic, 476
  specific, 31–32, 527
External motivation, 196
Extraneous motivation, 477–480,
  510
Eye movement, 20
Eysenck, H., 37–39, 44, 95

Familiarity breeds content, 132–133
Farel, P. B., 85–86
Fawl, C. L., 125
Fear:
  reduction, arousal, 338–339

Fear: (*continued*)
  shock-induced, arousal, 330-337
Feature detection, 58
Ferraro, D. P., 376
Fine, R., ix
Fixed ratio reward, 354-358
Flottorp, G., 447, 465
Forgetting, 207
Fox, S., 288
Fox theories, 2-3
Frances, R., 448
Frank, K., 82
Franzisket, L., 73, 86
Free association, 35-36
  data, 516-519
Free will, 12, 51-54, 62, 129, 197-263
Frequency and psychological complexity, 144-145
Freud, S., 3
Frohman, J. S., 384, 386
Fuortes, M. G. F., 82

Gadlin, H., ix
Galambos, R., 466
Gambler's fallacy, 70
Gardner, L. E., 87
Garfield, 486
Gestalt:
  psychologists, 210, 213
  status of whole, 210
Glanzer, M., 125, 208-209
Goal gradient:
  arousal, 358-372
  manipulation with shock, 369-371
Graham, F. K., 74, 288
Grant, D. A., 354
Graphics, 411-412, 421-424, 433
Gregg, L. W., 252
Group mean, fallacy of, 32-33
Groves, P. M., 64-65, 68, 71-72, 74-77, 79-80, 82-83, 85, 87-90, 92-93, 102, 287

Haber, R. N., 58-60, 67, 201
Habituation:
  compelled choice, 267
  definition, 70-71
  differences (age, individual, sex), 95-96
  distinguished from learning, 70-71

Habituation: (*continued*)
  learning, 96-97, 124-125
  other correlates, 124-125
  performance variables, 74-77
  preference, 97-108, 277
  psychological event, 78
  simplification, 77-80
Hagiwara, S., 297
Hake, H. W., 354
HAM, 249, 251
Hamilton, J. H., 297
Handling, effect on BRL, 305-307
Haptic exploration, 276
Hart, D., ix
Hawkins, J. E., 466
Hebb, D. O., 27, 60, 287
Hedgehog, identity and metaphor, 1-3, 9-13
Hedonic tone, 269-270, 280-281
Hedonism:
  curve, Wundtian, 7
  Hedgehog, 278-279
  refutation of, 408-409
Height, 451
Heisenberg, W., 199
Helix (pitch), 451-452
Helmholtz, H., 446-447
Helson, H., 273, 277
Hening, W. A., 288
*Her Dream*, 515
Heron, W., 60
Herz, M. J., 71, 74, 88
Heyduk, R. G., 98-108, 140, 439-445
Hilgard, E. R., 15
Hinde, R. A., 81
Hintzman, D. L., 220-221
Hobart, J. L., 292
Hochberg, J., 58-59
Holder, E. E., 352
Holder, W. B., 352
Holographic memory storage, 216
Hood, T., 515
Hopkins, M., 486
Hornseth, J. P., 354
Hughes, G. R., 91
Hull, C. L., 61, 65-67, 322, 358
Hunger, arousal, 328-330
Hunt, E., 252
Hunt, J. McV., 489

Icon, 58, 206
  persistence of, 67
Idiocratic motivation, 476–478, 510
Image:
  icon, 58, 206
  stabilized, 60
  stimulus-induced, 57–61
  visual, 57–61
Incentives:
  acquired, 268
  arousal, 337–347
Individual differences:
  arousal, BRL, 9, 319
  information processing rate, 9
Innes, T., 412
Intelligence:
  ability and achievement, 482–486
  concept of, 481–486
  IQ, 484–485
  race differences, 483–484
  sex differences, 483
Intensity and complexity, 56
Interstimulus interval, 82–86
I-scale, 26–27

James, J. P., 91
James, W., 4–5, 35–36, 198
Jasper, H., 288
Johnson, N. F., 231, 252
Jones, H., 352
Joyce, J., 36, 44
J-scale, 26–27

Kandel, E. R., 288
Kaplan, R., 292, 299–300, 304–
  305, 321, 331–332, 337
Kaplan, S., 321, 337, 352–353,
  391–392, 395
Karoly, A. J., 125
Keynes, R. D., 296
Kimbel, D. P., 391, 396
Kimble, G. A., 61, 65, 73, 86
Kintsch, W., 208
Kirkpatrick, M., 220
Kleinsmith, L. J., 391–392, 395
Knotter, M. C., 120–121
Koepke, J. E., 95
Korsør symposium, 36
Kotses, H., 73, 88
Kreitler, H., 407–409
Kreiter, S., 407–409

Kristofferson, A. B., 57
Kroll, N. E. A., 201
Krueger, W. C. F., 158–160
Kruskal scaling procedure, 29
Kusano, K., 297

Lacey, J. I., 291
Langfeld, H. S., 280
Language:
  behavioral, 18–21
  complexity and preference, 146–
    168
  empirical, 15–17, 21–24
  experimental subjects, 21–24, 516–
    544
  neurophysiological, 18–21
  problems, 14–24
  theoretical, 14–17, 21–24
  verbal, 18–21
Learning:
  arousal, 365–368
  asymptotic level, 132
  definition, 130
  equation, 131–132, 143–144, 179
  Hedgehog account, 131
  individual differences, 481
  insight, 130
  lifelong, 473–514
  operant paradigm, 110
  paired associates, 130
  problem solving, 130
  psychological complexity, 130–133
  rising and falling curves, 131
  serial, 130
  teaching, 499–500
  verbal, 143–195
    affectivity, 169–181
    arousal, 388–399
    empirical questions, 144–146
Leckart, B. T., 81
Lee, D., 64–65, 83, 85
Levelt, W. J. M., 446–448, 466
Levine, D., 140
Levine, S., 321
Liberman, A. M., 232
Lipps, T., 446–447
Lissman, H. W., 297–298
Lockhart, R. S., 201, 216
Long-term memory stores, 201
  versus short-term, 262–263

Lorge, I., 144, 161–165, 181–182
Ludic behavior, 267
Lundin, R. W., 448
Lykken, D. T., 292

Maatsch, J. L., 352
Machin, K. E., 297
Mackworth, J. F., 71, 74, 94–96, 287–289
Mackworth, N. H., 20, 28, 95
Madsen, K. B., ix, 441
Magic number 500σ, 57–68
Magoun, H. W., 287
Maier, N. R. F., 299
Malmberg, C. F., 446–447, 452–453, 463
Malmo, R. B., 287
Mandler, G., 252
Marcus, G. G., 491
Marler, P., 297
Marolla, F. A., 490
Marshall, H., 496
Martin, E., 197, 208, 218, 220–221
Marx, M. H., 352
Marzulli, F. N., 293
Mattingly, I. G., 232
McClelland, D. C., 27, 277
McKoewn, T., 491
McLean, R. S., 252
Measurement problems, teaching effectiveness, 503–506
Melton, A. W., 197, 208, 218–220, 248, 394
Memory:
  arousal, 389–392
  prodigious feats, 259–262
  short-term versus long-term, 262–263
Memory storage:
  continuous model, 203–222
  form of, 215–218
  holographic, 216
Memory trace:
  interference, 395–398
  model of, 391
Mere exposure theory, 106
Metathetic continua, 280
Miller, G. A., 234, 245, 248, 507
Miller, J. G., 229
Miller, R. R., 219

Mind-body problem, 198–199
Modern art, 412, 424–431, 433
Molly Bloom, 36, 44
Moment, psychological, 5
Montgomery, K. C., 125
Moore, H. T., 446, 448, 457, 467–468
Morandi, A. J., 20
Moray, N., 217
Morgan, C. T., 466
Mortenson, F. J., 297–299, 301–303, 310–313, 343–344
Moruzzi, G., 287
Motion perception, 59
Motivation, 265–284
  autarkic, definition, 476–477
  biological, 266
  extraneous, definition, 477–479
  idiocratic, definition, 476–479
  needs, 269
  needs and goals, 267
  social, 266–267
  traditional concepts, 265–269
Motoyoshi, R., 116–117
Mowrer, O. H., 352, 354–355
Multidimensionality, problem of, 29–32
Multiple psychological events, 27
Murdock, B. B., 201
Musical compositions, 98–108
  effect of experience, 140–143

Nagy, K., ix
National Institute of Mental Health, ix
Needs and goals, 267, 269
Negishi, K., 297
Neisser, U., 58–59, 200–201, 206, 216–217
Nerve deafness, 466, 470
Neuron types (N, S, H, H-S), 73–77, 79
Neurophysiological indices of complexity, 20–21
Neurophysiological time factors, 64–65
Newell, A., 46–47
Nice, M. M., 72
Nobel, C. E., 157

Nonrandomness:
  animal, 113–115
  human, 110–115
Nonsense syllables, 157–161, 175,
  182, 194
Norman, D. A., 215–217
Norton, S., 42–46

Occultation, 24–25, 35, 43
  definition, 100–102
Octavity, 451, 454, 461, 463, 465,
  469, 471
Olds, J., 338
Olson, M. H., x, 273–275
*One Boy's Day,* 267
Opaque containers, 231
Operant performance, arousal, 351–358
Optimal arousal theory, 287
Optimal complexity level (OCL),
  478, 481
  definition, 7
*orc,* definition, 505
Organizing, 233–263
Orientation reaction, 87
Orienting reflex, 288
Osgood, C. E., 30
Otto, D. A., 95

Paivio, A., 217
Papsdorf, J. D., 62
Paradise, N. E., 125–126
Parallel processing, 207
Parent package, 512–513
Peak, G., 252
Pearson, R. D., 466
Peckham, S., 30–31
Peeke, H. V. S., 71, 73–74, 88
Peer learning, 501, 512–513
Peirce, C. S., 100
Pelkwyk, J. J. ter, 72
Peretz, B., 74
Peterson, L. R., 219
Petrinovich, L., 96
Pfaffman, C., 281–282
Phillips, W. A., 201
Pickett, W., 419
Picture recognition, 60
Pillsbury, W. B., 62
Pinsker, H. M., 288

Platt, J., 203–204
Pleasurable event, automatic
  termination, 12
Plomp, R., 446–448, 466
Posner, M. I., 61, 201, 217
Practice, 497–500
Preference:
  empirical coordinates, 21–24
  equation, 271
  function, 7
  habituation effects, 277
  Hedgehog definition, 7, 270
  measurement problems, 272–278
  neural intensity, 281–283
  one- versus two-factor, 270–271
  stimulus intensity, 280–284
  varieties of function, 269–283
Pribram, K. H., 95, 216
Pritchard, R. M., 60
Probabilistic universe, 199
Problem solving, 47, 235–245
Processing capacity, 233–235
Programmatic constraints, 8, 50–51
Pronounceability, 149–157
Prototethic continuua, 280
Proximity, 453–454, 461, 463–466,
  469–471
Psychoanalytic therapy, 35–36
Psychological complexity:
  definition, 6
  empirical coordinates, 21–24
Psychological Complexity and
  Preference Theory:
  ten-chapter statement, 1–349
  ten-page statement, 4–13
  ten-word statement, 1
Psychological distance, 403
Psychological event:
  basic unit of activity, 5
  direction of repetition effects,
    71–75
  discontinuous character, 55–56
  duration, 119–122
  *effects of occurrence:*
    antirepetition bias, 8
    complication, 56
    enduring, 129–196
    habituation, 55–56
    increases in complexity, 9

Psychological event: (*continued*)
  learning, 55–56
  learning as simplification, 8
  semipermanent, 56
  simplification, 8, 56
  sudden complexity decrease, 9
  temporary, 56, 70–128
  variability of choice, 8
elicitation of, 57
$500\sigma$, 5
involuntary, 197–264
model time/intensity function,
  65–68
neurophysiological data,
  time, 64–65
stream of: *see* Stream of psychological events
structure and change, 263–264
voluntary, 197–264
Pylyshyn, Z. W., 217
Pythagoras, 445–446, 448

Quit trying ($q_t$), 475–478, 481,
  498–500, 505–507, 509–510
  generalized, 479–480
Quit working ($q_w$), 475–478, 481,
  498–500, 505–507, 509–510
  generalized, 479–480

Race differences, intelligence, 483–
  484, 495–496
Randomness, measurement of, 16
Raskin, D. C., 73, 88
Ratner, S. C., 80–81, 87, 89
Ray, R. S., 73, 86
Reaction time, 61–62
Reading behavior, 59
Recall versus recognition, 207–209
Record, R. G., 491
Reinforcement, 351
Response units, 352, 355–358
Restle, F., 201
Reticular system, 287
  activating, 288
Reward:
  effect on learning, 130
  fixed ratio, 354–358
  functions of, 350–351
  temporary effects, 115–119
Reynierse, J. H., 81

Reynolds, B., 61, 65
$r_g$, fractional anticipatory goal
  response, 359, 369
Richter, C. P., 327
Roemer, R. A., 68, 71–72, 85,
  87–90, 92–93
Rosenfeld, A., ix
Roussel, J., 352
Routtenberg, A., 288
Ruckmick, C. A., 451
Rumelhart, D. E., 216–217

Sales, S. M., ix, 62–64, 437
SAT (Scholastic Aptitude Test), 473
  decline in scores, 494–495
Satiation theory, 105–106
Sawyer, T., 110
Schippler, L. M., 354
Schneirla, T. C., 271
Schulz, R. W., 144–161, 166–167,
  181–182, 388
Scott, J. P., ix, 117–119
Selective breeding, arousal, 322–324
Selfridge, J., 234
Semantic distance, 529–543
  judged distance data, 530–543
  measures of associative strength,
    529–530
  Walker scale, 533–543
Semantic problems, 22–24
Semantic space of experimental
  subjects, 21–24, 516–644
Sensitization, 70–71, 75–77, 80
Sensory stores, 201
Serial condensation, 232–233
Serialization, 232
Serial position, 392–395
Sex differences, arousal in rats,
  319–320
Sharpless, S., 288
Sheffield, F. D., 328
Shepard, R. N., 200–201, 216,
  405, 451, 463
Shepard-Kruskal, 414–415, 418–421,
  424–430, 432
  multidimensional analysis, 29
Short-term memory, 233–235
  store, 201
  versus long-term, 262–263

Silver, M. P., 376
Similarities association data, 519–530
Simon, H. A., 46–47, 235, 253–258
Simplification, 71, 82–108, 231
  equation, 78
  habituation, 77–80
Sinclair, K., 141–142, 421
Skinner, B. F., 2
Skin resistance: see BRL
Sleep levels, arousal, 289–291
Smith, F. W., 466
Snapper, A. G., 376
Snyder, R. E., 62
Social motives, 266–267
Sokolov, E. N., 87, 288
Span of attention, 62
Specific exploration, 31–32, 527
Spence, K. W., 351, 358
Spencer, W. A., 85, 96
Sperling, G., 58
  paradigm, 205
Spontaneous counting, 119
Spontaneous recovery, 80–82
Springer, A. D. 219
Springston, F., 214–215
S-R pathways, 68, 75, 77, 79
Stabilized images, 60
Stage set designs, 411, 418–421, 433
Standing, L., 60
Stanford Binet, 483
State pathways system, 68, 75, 77
Stebbins, W. C., 466
Stevens, S. S., 447, 465
Stimulus change, arousal, 307–316
  dissociation from speed, 362–365
Stimulus complexity:
  definition, 6
  frequency of response, 63–64
Stimulus-induced visual images, 57–61
Stimulus intensity, 87–94
  generalization, 90–94
  habituation, 88
  preference, 280–284
Stimulus number, 82–86
Stimulus trace decay equation, 67
Stoddard, B., ix, 339–341
Stream of Behavior, The, 5

Stream of consciousness, 4–5
Stream of psychological events, 4–5, 11–13, 34–54
  arbitrary time units, 42–46
  dynamic accounts, 46–54
  Hedgehog, 50–54
  need/goal accounts, 40–42
  objective descriptions, 36–46
    casual observations, 36–39
  statistical accounts of groups, 39
  varieties of, 35
Stream of thought, 35–36
Structural variables, 21–24
Stumpf, C., 446–447, 463
Subjective complexity, 6, 17, 441
Suci, G. J., 30
Sutter, J., 491
Szabo, T., 297
Szalai, A., 39

Tabah, L., 491
Tannenbaum, P. H., 30
Tapp, J. T., 282
Tartan patterns, 411–418, 433
Tarte, R. D., 219, 392–394, 397
Taylor, C. A., 446–447, 468
Teacher as tutor, 497–499
Teacher's role, 499–500
Tedium, 267
Terman, L. M., 482
Tesserae, 40–42
Teyler, T. J., 68, 71–72, 85, 87–90, 92–93
Theoretical language, 14–17, 21–24
Theoretical terms, 5–6
Theoretical variables, Hedgehog, 15
Theory, simplicity of, 1
Thinking, 200
Thirst, arousal, 328–330
  reduction, arousal, 339–340
Thomas, H., 25, 27, 29
Thompson, R. F., 64–65, 68, 71–72, 74–77, 79–80, 82–83, 85, 87–90, 92–93, 96, 102, 287
Thorndike, E. L., 144, 161–165, 181–182
Thought, stream of, 35–36
  and action, 200
Timberlake, W. D., 42–46
Titillation, 267

Tolman, E., 14
Tolstoy, L., 2
Tonality, 451
Trace:
  automatic changes in, 218-222
  interference, 395-398
  organization of, 209-215
Trigram frequency, 150-157, 170, 175, 182, 194
Tryon, R. C., 322
Turvey, M. T., 217, 232
Tutor's role, 499-500
Tversky, A., 26-27

*Ulysses,* 36
Uncertainty principle, 199
Underwood, B. J., 144-161, 166-167, 181-182, 207-208, 388
Unfolding technique, 440
  I-scale, 26-27
Updegraff, B. P., 80
Uzgirls, I., 489

Van Deventer, J. M., 81
Variables, classes of, 21-24
Verve, 496
Verveer, E. M., 106-107, 140
Visual art, effects of experience, 140-143
Visual images, 57-61
  effect of experience, 79
  four-phase conception, 57
Volition, 198-199
  psychological events, 197-264
  voluntary functioning, 222-263

Wachs, T., 489
Wagner, A. R., 93
Walker, B. E., ix, 31, 134-138, 299-300, 305-306, 317-318, 332-335, 365-368, 436

Walker, E. L., 4, 29, 31, 72, 116, 119-123, 125, 131, 134, 139-142, 218-219, 299-300, 305-308, 317-318, 320-324, 326-329, 332-335, 339-343, 351, 353-355, 357-361, 363-371, 373-375, 384-386, 389-394, 396-397, 419, 436-437, 441, 451
Wall, P. D., 82
Wampler, R., 219
Warner, M., 352-353
Warren, R. E., 201, 217
Weems, L. B., 363
Weiland, N. G., 466
Weiner, B., 389-391
Weld, H. P., 280
Wellek, A., 448
Wester, K., 72-73
Whiteman, M., 490
Wickens, D. D., 217
Williams, C. L., 289
Williams, H. L., 289-290
Williams, J. L., 332-334, 354-355, 357, 369-371, 375-382
Winzenz, D., 214
Wohlwill, J. F., 19-20, 28, 276
Wolpert, E., 289-290
Woodworth, R. S., 280-281, 449
Word frequency, 161-168, 172-195
Wright, H. F., 40-42, 44, 267
W-system (withdrawal), 271
Wundt, W., 269-270
  hedonic curve, 7, 191

Zajonc, R. B., 105, 132, 177, 489-492, 494-495
Zwicker, E., 447, 465